Eccentric Cubicle

Kaden Harris

O'REILLY®

BEIJING • CAMBRIDGE • FARNHAM • KÖLN • PARIS • SEBASTOPOL • TAIPEI • TOKYO

Eccentric Cubicle

by Kaden Harris

Published by Make:Books, an imprint of Maker Media, a division of O'Reilly Media, Inc., 1005 Gravenstein Highway North, Sebastopol, CA 95472.

O'Reilly books may be purchased for educational, business, or sales promotional use. For more information, contact our corporate/institutional sales department: 800-998-9938 or corporate@oreilly.com.

Print History
October 2007
First Edition

Publisher: Dale Dougherty
Associate Publisher and Executive Editor: Dan Woods
Editor: Tom Sgouros
Copy Editor: Nancy Kotary
Creative Director: Daniel Carter
Designer: Anne Mellinger
Production Manager: Terry Bronson
Indexer: Patti Schiendelman
Cover Photograph: Kaden Harris
Author Photograph: Kaia "The Sourceress" Howe

ISBN-10: 0-596-51054-3
ISBN-13: 978-0-596-51054-1

Contents

Author's Note: Meet Your Maker

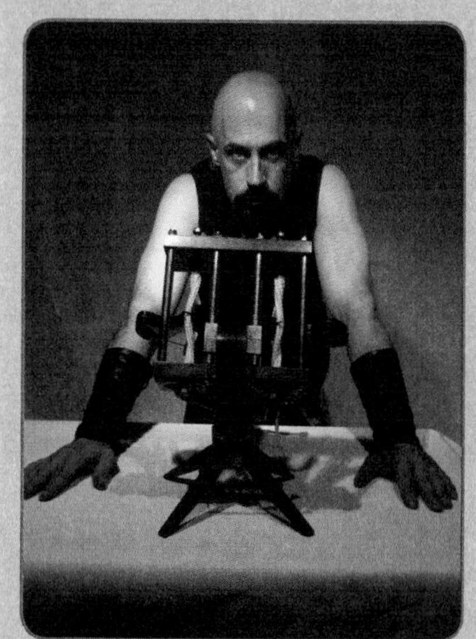

It is quite possible that I have the coolest job in the world. I make my living fabricating what have come to be known as "antiques from a parallel universe." (You can get a better grasp of what I do from my website: www.eccentricgenius.ca.) I sell these things to discerning clients worldwide, some of whom consider them to be "art."

This still kinda wigs me out a bit.

A typical workday involves (among other things) woodworking, metalworking, chemistry, drafting, mechanical engineering, and cheese tossing. I have no formal training in any of these subjects.

I cannot remember a time when I didn't build stuff. Lincoln Logs? Mechano? Technik? I cut my teeth on 'em. With "the Maker way" ingrained from an early age, I've built an unholy amount of stuff over the years, usually due to poverty, often because it was the only way to get *just the right thing*. I grew my skill set from trial and error, libraries, the Net, and from relentlessly picking the brains of *anyone* with useful knowledge to share.

I do not hesitate to RTFM.

My philosophy of life in three lines:

Learn *when* you can, teach *what* you can.
Pay attention.
Practice, practice, practice.

I'm Kaden.

I am *not* used to being referred to as an artist. Or even a craftsman. Any artistic or craftsmanlike characteristics of the stuff I build are purely coincidental.

Well, mostly. I'll never admit to it in a court of law though.

Actually, when you look my pieces, there's not a whole lot of ornamentation present (aside from the occasional hot-rod flame). They're just basic, well-fabricated mechanisms, performing unexpected functions, wrapped up in odd industrial design.

Industrial design (ID)[1] is *not* an arcane ritual best left to the Porsche Group: it's an essential skill for Makers, which encompasses material selection, ergonomics, visual aesthetics, and ease of construction. Finessing form and function into a graceful, efficient mechanism on a shoestring budget is not rocket science, but you have to keep an open mind. Extending your repertoire of fabrication techniques beyond duct tape and Krazy Glue helps too, as does imaginative material sourcing.

I have bodged together some atrocious things in my time. My seven-minute mechanical log-rolling machine[2] build still

1 And not to be confused with "inside diameter." You'll see "ID" and "OD" all over these projects, but mostly these acronymes refer to the interior and exterior measurements of tubes and pipes.

2 FWIW, I'm still convinced that lumberjack bars could be the next big thing, even though replacing the dartboard with an axe-tossing arena may cause insurers a bit of concern. The thought of slick hipsters dropping thick coin on custom chainsaws to impress the chicks with never fails to brighten my day.

evokes belly laughs from those unfortunate enough to have witnessed the madness. After the first few catastrophic device failures, building to last becomes increasingly important. This is something MacGyver never had to worry about: his kludges had to last only 15 minutes or until the bomb was defused.

Lucky bastard.

As useful as duct tape, hot-melt glue, and cyanoacrylate are, at the end of the day, they don't make for a strong, reliable mechanism. Quick 'n' dirty emergency patch jobs are one thing; building a mechanism intended for daily use over an extended period of time is entirely another.[3] There are better, stronger, time-tested fabrication techniques available that will make your builds solid, durable, and efficient. Learn these skills once, and you'll use them for a lifetime, in applications you've likely not yet considered.

Building to last raises another issue: you (and your current and future loved ones) will be living with the fruits of your labours for years, not days, which makes the industrial design and aesthetics of the project significantly more important at a number of levels.

Let me put it bluntly, for the fellas, who may need it blunt. A mechanism, regardless of utility, held together by a table-sized amorphous blob of hot-melt glue *is not a chick magnet*.

Are we clear on that? Good.

Carry on.

"You've got to know the rules before you can break 'em," is one of those time-honored axioms you regularly hear being tossed around in conversations pertaining to creativity. A less frequently encountered, but equally thought-provoking truism is, "You've got to know your tools, or you're gonna break 'em."

Cute, huh?

Yeah, both are generally generally true. Here's the real rub: knowing the rules is gonna do you absolutely no good whatsoever if you can't use the freakin' tools involved *properly*.

Although this is especially true when confronted with the space-age technological wonderment of modern power tools, it's easy to forget that basic skills like "measure length," "hammer nail," and "drill hole" are also filed under "Tools, Proper Use Of." This involves more than just reading the manual. Common sense plays a big role, and there's always a set of motor skills and ergonomic considerations that need to be developed in order to get the most out of the tool in question without causing damage to either the tool or the workpiece. You need to understand the basic principles that make a tool or technique *work*: the "why," as well as the "what." A solid grasp of this stuff will let you assimilate the practical lore you'll be encountering, which will in turn let you take a basic skill like "Saw, Cutting a Straight Line With" and use it in woodworking to master the mythical isometric waffle-tail joint.

But wait — there's more:

If you know your tools well enough, you'll have *significantly* increased your chances that "breaking the rules" will result in a successful outcome. You'll also start finding yourself making and defining your own rules and your own lore, which you will inevitably pass on to others, enriching both yourself and your "community."

You will feel immense pride at this.

Some skills file under "Apply as Needed." I've learned that there are others that need to be always on, kinda like an inline spellchecker.

Safety is one. Industrial design is another. So are ergonomics and material science. Simple physics is *definitely* one. Stuff you're always aware of, in the design stage, while fabricating, and during field testing. After a while, you'll notice that your collection of inline skills and reference points has kinda accreted itself into a personalized Swiss Army Knowledge Base on a . . . er . . . need-to-know basis. You'll find yourself using it in previously unconsidered ways.

Unorthodox application of primary skills and knowledge is *important*. Understanding the basic principles that make specific skills and techniques *work* allows you to make them both scalable and transferable. The first time you realize, "Duh . . . I can use that in a _______ , too!!" will be a completely epiphanous experience.

This approach to building a skill set gives you the chops to be able to look at basic mechanisms and subassemblies in *exactly* the same way. Know the "what" and the "why" of them, and implement them via oblique strategies.[4]

Material and component sourcing? Same deal. Understand the basic "whats and whys," and you'll start

3 Yes, I know your cousin Bruno built a breeder reactor in his basement constructed entirely from duct tape. No, I am not impressed. Nor will his neighbors be when his throbbing mass of adhesive begins delaminating and everyone in the immediate vicinity starts glowing in the dark.

4 The whole "think outside the box" meme that world + dog was on about a few years ago?

Not a new thing.

In the 70s, "lateral thinking" was a semirevolutionary pop-cult approach to problem solving. Then, as now, there were actually some people who truly understood the process.

Brian Eno and Peter Schmidt first assembled and published the Oblique Strategies in 1975 as a deck of reference cards for use during creative dilemmas. Although optimized for use during music composition, they can be an invaluable source of alternative approaches for your consideration during problematic endeavours.

noticing that there are limitless resources in unexpected places. You'll experience a paradigm shift in your relationship with "Makin' Stuff."

Your friends will eventually get used to accompanying you while you rummage around in thrift shops, scrap yards, and dumpsters.

Call it "The Philosophy of Improvisational Fabrication."

It's the Maker Way.

The Stuff We're Gonna Build

. . . which brings us to this book, and the projects contained herein.

First off, I'd like to point out that we need another DIY Ambient Orb project like we need a new hole drilled in our skulls (which is not to say that there isn't a time and place for recreational trepanning, but that, of course, is another book altogether). Ditto for Lego X-Y Plotters, and I think I speak for all of us when I passionately plead for a five-year moratorium on cheap digital camera mods.

Do not get me started on iPod accessories.

The intent is to infuse the new-school Maker community with a therapeutic dose of slightly non-Euclidean engineering, classic shop techniques, and surreally interpreted physics — projects intended to make people say "It does ***WHAT***?"

What's not to love?

These are projects with balls, albeit an uneven number of them. In a parallel universe, three doors down and across the street, these devices are de facto standard office cube accessories, available at your local big-box business supply outlet. As we're not fortunate enough to exist in such an enlightened timeline, we're gonna have to build 'em ourselves.

Remember, they laughed at Philo T. Farnsworth too.

Active Deskchop
Sharp blade. Gravity. Unsuspecting cigars. Carrots. Bratwurst. The occasional pepperoni stick. Over-engineered and cunningly executed, this postmillennial version of the classic French revolutionary femme fatale is the last word in cigar accessories. Or desktop snack choppers.

BallistaMail
Hail the Ballista! The Greco-Roman Cruise missile: a big-ass torsion-powered crossbow, good for launching spears, javelins and the occasional boulder, the ballista scales down to an intimidatingly powerful interoffice mail delivery system. Your memos will never be ignored again.

Maple Mike
A desktop simulation of the perfect golf swing *and* targetable projectile acceleration in one easy to use/easy to build project.

Because golf is a rung on the ladder to boardroom success. So are targetable projectiles.

DeskBeam Bass
Four strings of butt-shakin' bottom-end, harnessing the acoustic resonance of your desk as a speaker system. The first half of the "Desktop D 'n' B Audience Participation Muzak" series.

The Gysin Device
Harness your subconscious for enhanced creativity: Brion Gysin's lucid dreaming induction device, as popularised by William Burroughs (and notoriously implicated in Kurt Cobain's unfortunate demise). Not a whole lot to add, other than "does what it says on the packet." Now you can have the same experience in the comfort of your own cubicle. Sitar not included.

iBlow USB Bubble Machine
Convince IT that it has something to do with your PC's liquid cooling system.

Liquid Light Meets the Disco Skull
These popular catalog items from a slightly trippier parallel universe version of ThinkGeek add necessary ambience to casual Fridays. Throwback 60s psychedelic liquid lighting, with a postmillennial tech upgrade and hot-*damn*-that's-cool rotating mirror-tiled disco skull dispersion mechanism. Name one other project that seamlessly incorporates high-intensity L.E.D.s, glass cutters, the much-maligned glue gun, and barbeque rotisseries. G'wan . . . try.

Haze-o-Matic 3000
Bring "the fog of war" to your contract negotiations. Befuddle your supervisor. Intimidate the interns. A mechanism that's as inherently cool as a fog machine *needs* to be Goldbergianly complex. It's subassemblies gone wild, like you've never seen them before.

Hammerhead Live Mechanical Percussion Sequencer
Programmable acoustic drum sequencer. It's Jules Verne's TR-808. With hammers. No, really.

The second half of the "Desktop D 'n' B Audience Participation Muzak" series.

And some bonus content:

Finishes

Brewing up your own custom wood finishes is the closest woodworking equivalent of coding in assembly language, short of plantin' an acorn, waiting 70 years, then cutting the now proud oak and milling it into 1" x 8"s. It's the quintessential display of a craftsman's personal commitment to his artistic mission statement. A homebrew hand-blended finish lovingly applied to a piece, then hand rubbed to a soft warm glow fairly shrieks "*This* is hand freakin' crafted, suckahs."

Instant street cred, ya know whut I'm sayin? Mixing up finishes in the comfort of your own kitchen is also easy, economical, relatively environmentally friendly, and surprisingly fun. Of course it also has the potential to be shockingly messy if you're prone to sudden outbreaks of clumsy.

We just won't think about that, okay? Rein in your inner klutz and show the world that you can mix more than just cocktails.

ZOMG EASTER EGGS!!

Well, sorta. Scattered throughout the book are a bunch of quick 'n' easy DIYs that'll augment your workshop and/or your knowledge base. I call 'em the *nano* projects. Consider it time well spent to do a casual cover-to-cover browse to excavate and take advantage of these lagniappes before embarking on any specific major projects.

These are all things I personally consider to be essential during the course of day-to-day makin': underappreciated tools, needful accessories, cunning bodges and worthy lore . . . stuff that makes for a better Maker.

They're on the house. Help yourself.

Contacting Us

We have a web page for this book, where we list errata, examples, bonus additional information and comprehensive 1:1 scale cutting diagrams for the projects. You can access this page at: www.oreilly.com/catalog/EccentricCubicle

To comment or ask technical questions about this book, send email to: bookquestions@oreilly.com

Please address comments and questions concerning this book to the publisher:

O'Reilly & Associates, Inc.
1005 Gravenstein Highway North
Sebastopol, CA 95472
(800) 998-9938 (in the United States or Canada)
(707) 829-0515 (international or local)
(707) 829-0104 (fax)

For more information about our books, conferences, Resource Centers, and the O'Reilly Network, see our website at: www.oreilly.com

To engage the author of this book in a ribald and (quite likely) surreally non-Euclidean exchange regarding the philosophy of improvisational fabrication, advanced scrap-fu technique, or any other topic covered in this or any other book, send email to kaden@eccentricgenius.ca.

Acknowledgements

Thanks to:

- My wife, Kaia "the Sourceress" Howe, Rebuilder of lives, and my infinite muse
- Augustus Fernando Harris, Gerald Robert Harris, and Terran Michael Harris
- Phil Watson and the crew & clients of NorthStar Recycling, 1170 Powell St., Vancouver
- John Young and Doug "The Tall Guy" Hawes, YMCA New Ventures
- Joe Turato: Technology, material and motivational resource Übermensch
- Tom Sgouros, editor guy and surrealist banjo phenom
- Cory Doctorow
- Paul Spinrad
- Villy and Jim, H.A.M.C. White Rock
- Pierre Moerlen and Pip Pyle
- ...and Mark Fraunfelder, to whom I owe several internal organs.

Active Deskchop, BallistaMail, and Maple Mike

1 Introduction: The Philosophy of Improvisational Fabrication

A Maker's life is rarely fully funded, with an unlimited budget, a state-of-the-art shop facility, and a team of brilliant young assistants poised to spring into action and help bring a creative vision into reality. In terms of toolage, raw materials, and skillset/knowledge base, "work with what ya got" is pretty much standard-issue methodology for [insert really high percentage here] of us. Whether this situation ultimately proves to be limiting or liberating depends entirely on your attitude towards "comfort zones, working outside of."

Now, I've never met an out-of-the blue creative impulse that didn't warrant at least two sketches, a few Google inquiries and a cursory rummage through the parts bins. Before I know it, it's 6:00 the next morning, and I'm waist-deep in technology I know almost nothing about, watching the coffee distill, wondering "what the Hell was I thinking?" and counting down the minutes until the scrap yards open their gates.

Comfort zone? What comfort zone?

Over time, this seat-of-the-pants approach to Making coalesced into something that's almost definable, and definitely learnable: The Philosophy of Improvisational Fabrication. Common sense from a Maker perspective, it's based on the following pillars.

The 5 "F"s:

Cliché alert: it's one of those cutesy, alliterative lists self-help books are so fond of.

Live with it.

Figure out what you're building

What's it supposed to do, and how's it supposed to do it? Parse your project down to the basic mechanisms required to make it work. Pay attention to how these subassemblies act and interact. Get a comfortable understanding of the factors at play, the physics involved, and the Aristotelian "total is greater than the sum of the parts" factor. There'll be a number of different approaches available for each component mechanism: never be afraid to consider a Plan B . . . or C.

Critical components become apparent as you go, which helps when you're sourcing parts, and you'll suss out the control points you'll need to consider when doing your U.I.

My experience has been that breaking *anything* down to its contextual basic components is the single most valuable technique for getting a tangible understanding of what you're dealing with. Of course, once you've gained that understanding, feel free to improvise with wild abandon. Not much different from playing jazz or writing code, when you think about it.

Forage for parts

Improvisational fabrication works best with a rich and varied array of raw material. Repurpose components from scrap yards, thrift shops and dumpsters. eBay is your friend. The design (both industrial and visual) of your project will coalesce around the aesthetic of one or two of the components you source, which makes a "big picture" view of the mechanism essential. When this occurs, hit the drawing board/CAD app and start dealing with specifics. Your parts list will shuffle itself into three categories: parts you've found and repurposed, parts you have to buy, and parts you have to fabricate from scratch.

You now have a firm grasp of the task ahead.

Cool.

If you have any blanks in the skill set required to deal realistically with the job at hand, now would be the time to learn stuff. This learning may lead to the discovery of blanks in your tool set, at which point the financial realities of pursuing Plan A may spur heightened enthusiasm for Plan B — so be prepared.

Fabricate the damned thing

Projects define themselves as a series of subassemblies. Consider the sequence of these events carefully, both from an efficiency standpoint and from an assembly standpoint. Wherever possible, make disassembly as easy as assembly. It is a foregone conclusion that you'll be taking the project apart repeatedly.

There *is* a logical order to do things in, which may or may not be the most apparent build path. Take your time, and ponder where needed.

Despite your best intentions, there's a strong possibility that some particularly clever aspect of your design is *not* gonna work, and you'll be troubleshooting/redesigning on the fly. This is a character-building experience which will expand your vocabulary of colourful pejoratives and have you rummaging through your parts bins at 3:30 a.m. looking for a 10-32 lefthand thread brass thumbwheel.

Think while building, pay attention, and be patient.

Fine-tune the mechanisms and aesthetics

A well-thought-out design, accurately built to realistic tolerances, will work, plain and simple. How *well* it works usually depends for the most part on a few crucial measurements lying well to the right of the decimal point. Identifying these tuning points, and implementing workable methods of adjusting these factors, are part of the industrial design "big picture" you should always be cognizant of. Successful improvisation deals with these issues at every stage of the build.

Finishing and detailing a smoothly functioning mechanism is always fun. The personality of the project should be pretty tangible by that point, which makes customizing and accessorizing less of an ordeal, and more of an obsession. Once again, having the will to adapt is essential. The Great Cosmic Random presents unexpected options much more frequently than most people care to acknowledge. When they become apparent to you, embrace them with confidence and enthusiasm.

Field test the finished device

Use what you build. A lot. Pay attention to how it functions, how it handles the strains of operation, and how easy it is to use. If you're lucky, you'll be able to patch any problem areas before long-term damage occurs; at the very least, you'll learn what *not* to do on Rev 2.0.

Get *someone else* to use it, and pay attention to how they interact with what you've built. If they have issues, deal with them. You're gonna be hearing, "Whoooaa . . . is that ever cool! Can I try it?" more often than you ever imagined. Don't disappoint the masses!

You might want to keep Plans B and C handy, in case a radical rework or two are needed. And when you're well and truly satisfied with your work, a celebratory cocktail is appropriate.

What a Bunch of Tools

About ten years ago, I built a *very* formidable four-poster bed using only a Swiss Army knife and a rock.

I am not making this up.

Fortunately, the décor style I was building for was a wiggy "H.P. Lovecraft meets the Addams Family" kinda theme. (Like it could be anything else with this honkin' big chain-draped monstrosity of a bed sitting dead center.) It looked better than it sounds.

Events such as that make a fella *truly* appreciate tools. Lots and lots of tools.

Tool collections start small and grow as needed. Depending on the fabrication techniques you choose to explore, they can grow at a disconcerting rate. I'm a meat 'n' spuds classic tool guy for the most part, and I'll bodge a tool together rather than buy something if it's feasible . . . but that's me.

I assume you have basic handyman/car maintenance tools: screwdrivers, locking pliers, hammers, tape measure, soldering iron, adjustable wrench, and maybe a set of sockets and box wrenches. That sort of stuff.

A well-equipped home workshop? Well, it'd help a lot, but it's not essential to start out with.

Here's what I personally view as essential tools. Your definition of "essential" will vary; your disposable income will *still* disappear like blinis in Gdansk.

Saws

Let's talk about saws first. There are about 8 billion different kinds of them, and at some point in your Maker career, you're going to wish you owned each and every one of them.

I've built my toolset by buying to need: I needed to mill stock out of bigger chunks of wood. If you personally feel motivated enough to do that with a handsaw, I salute you, and when you're in town, the walnut martinis are on me. Me, I bought a *table saw*. Or "rescued" a table saw, actually, having come across the legendary Rockwell Beaver alone, unloved and abandoned in the laneway behind a soon-to-be demolished Italian restaurant of dubious repute. Table saws are the undisputed king of the shop: loud, dangerous, and effective: everything a power tool should be.

That lets me mill stock, do compound miter cuts with pretty good accuracy, and make sawdust with alarming efficiency. They're very hackable tools, and can be jigged and modded for countless other tasks. There exists a thriving aftermarket accessories sector, with countless manufacturers offering miraculous-sounding bolt-on geegaws, gizmos, and all-important doodads in exchange for the contents of your bank account. I recently retired the Rockwell and got a new table saw of Asian origin that has a sliding miter table built in instead of the traditional slot-and-insert thingie most similar toolage has. This innovation has apparently caused quite the hullabaloo in the traditional woodworking community, with many Grandpa Simpson types loudly predicting the end of the world as we know it.

Get over it . . . it's a saw.

I bought one near the bottom of the manufacturers' line, just to see what all the fuss was about. It's okay, actually. The build quality of the saw is horrendous in general, but it's accurate, and the sliding table is really quite versatile. Out of the box it's more useful than a regular table saw, but nothing you can't jig together in half an hour on a standard machine.

I needed precise miter cuts: I snagged a German-made frame-maker's *mitering saw* at a thrift shop for $12.99. Not a whole lot of frills: stock clamping, end stop, front and rear depth stops, and preset stops in the mitering gauge at the usual angles. It does what it says on the packet — no muss, no fuss. Highly recommended, even if you have a good table saw, just for the finesse factor inherent in doing it by hand.

I needed to cut finicky curves in all kindsa stuff: I bought a *scroll saw*. A *coping saw* would do exactly the same thing, at 1/20th the speed and no small expenditure of elbow grease. You likely don't need one.

Band saws I'm undecided on: I traded for one about three months ago, and have yet to experience one of those "Damn, I need a band saw" moments. When it finally happens, I'll be prepared. Thanks again, Joey.

I needed to cut doweling off flush with surfaces; I bought a *Kugihiki*, which is a Japanese *flush-cutting handsaw*. The teeth on the flexible blade are kerfed in one direction only, which protects the surface you're flush-cutting from damage. The saw cuts on both the push and the pull strokes so it practically melts through wood. Nothing short of miraculous, actually. You need one, if only to impress visitors

I needed to cut metal; I bought large and small hacksaw frames, and keep 'em filled with the best blades I can afford. That's the thing about *hacksaws*: the frame just holds the blade in place. Love the blade, not the frame, as it were. Now, I know a lot of you are thinking: "What's he on about with hacksaws? I possess the mystical Dremel, king of all of tools! Materials of all ilk bow before my mighty cutting power."

Uh huh . . . well, knock yourself out, Mr. Weensy Abrasive Disk. Send us a postcard when you finish cutting up that 1" x 1" copper bus bar.

I've had the same handsaws for years, and frankly, none of them are any good. A traditional *22" carpenter's handsaw* can do a lot of things reasonably well, but nothing exceptionally well — except make sawdust. They do that with impressive coverage. Your standard *miter box* is good for 45-, 60-, and 90-degree cuts, and a 45-degree bevel if you're lucky — none of which will be particularly precise. You need to have both, but don't break the bank on them. Better to invest your tool-buyin' dollar on more specifically purposed equipment.

Saw wise, buy what you need.

Here's the rest of the Daily Tools. Some are run-of the mill, some specialty, some homemade.

All invaluable.

Cutting Holes

Drills You're gonna need an *electric drill*. A drill press would be nice, but isn't really essential. I've never been satisfied with any of those clamp-yer-drill-into-this-gizmo-and-voilà-instant-drill-press thingies on the market, although your results may vary. Given a choice between cordless convenience and the consistent torque and speed provided by a corded tool, I'd opt for something with a cord.

The *drill press* is absolutely the unsung hero of the workshop. I seriously overuse mine. I've bodged together jigs to turn it into a lathe, router, and thickness sander: a bunch of stuff nature never intended for the poor thing. I'm drawing up a poor-man's CNC (computer numeric control) sliding vise for it, even though there's no real chance that I'll ever have the time to build it. Commercially available drill presses range from dirt cheap to OMFG expensive. You can

Figure 01.01: **The Drill Doctor**

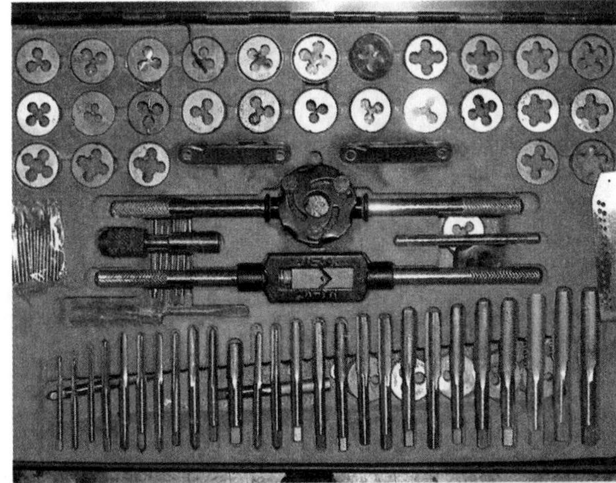

Figure 01.02: **Taps and dies: magic toolage**

shop according to your own budget, but I strongly suggest actually getting your hands on any model that you're considering buying. You need to feel for yourself exactly how solid the mechanism is (or isn't). On Planet Drill Press, "solid" beats "bells 'n' whistles" every single time.

Bits If you haven't invested in a reasonably good-quality set of bits, from at least 3/8" to 1/32", now is the time to do so. You're a Maker. Makers make holes. Get a set of *Forstner bits*, too; they'll let you drill smooth-walled, flat-bottomed, large-diameter holes in wood. Yes, this is important. *Hole saws* in various diameters are good to have around, in that they make both large-diameter holes and large-diameter circular plugs, which can easily turn into wheels, pulleys, or cogs. This is a marked improvement over *spade bits*, which make large-diameter holes and prodigious amounts of wood shavings. Spade bits win on depth of hole however. Buy what you need, and buy reasonable quality, bearing in mind that they're gonna go dull eventually.

There's a strong tendency to treat drill bits as disposable toolage, as sharp drills are essential, and putting a fresh edge on a bit by hand is an entirely arcane skill, well beyond the ken of we mortals. If you find yourself drilling a lot of holes in a lot of materials, then take a close look at the Drill Doctor, a semi-automated bit-sharpening machine that does what it says on the package. You will toast the inventor of this machine with high-quality hooch each and every time it saves you a run to the hardware store on a snowy afternoon because your 5/16" bit is too dull to bore cheese. Not an essential tool, but an exceptionally useful one to the busy, forward-thinking, and frugal drillfella. It may take a while, but it *will* save you money eventually, and really, it's a pleasure to know you're *always* working with a sharp bit. **[Figure 01.01]**

Cutting fluid The juice that facilitates working with metal. Lubricant, coolant, general-purpose metalworking mojo in a bottle. Hardcore alloy artists can get unrealistically passionate about this stuff, for some reason. A friend of mine has different formulas on hand for a bewildering variety of metal/tool/tool speed combinations. Me, I keep a can of WD-40 parked by the drill press and apply as needed. (I'm gonna hear about this, I can just tell.)

Tap and die set Sounds like a punk version of Riverdance, no?

We're talking *thread cutting* here. "Turn a piece of brass rod into a bolt" thread cutting. "Drill a hole and cut threads into it" thread cutting. Makin' nuts and bolts, dammit. Very useful tools indeed.

The basic set pictured covers metric and most SAE sizes up to 3/8" and set me back about a hundred bucks. I've added a set of jewelers' sizes to it, and a few nonstandard types (left-hand threads, mostly), as well as stocking up on the smaller-diameter taps that see the most use and are most prone to dulling and breakage. **[Figure 01.02]**

Cutting Other Stuff

Model-maker's chisel set Buy the best quality set you can afford, and guard it jealously.

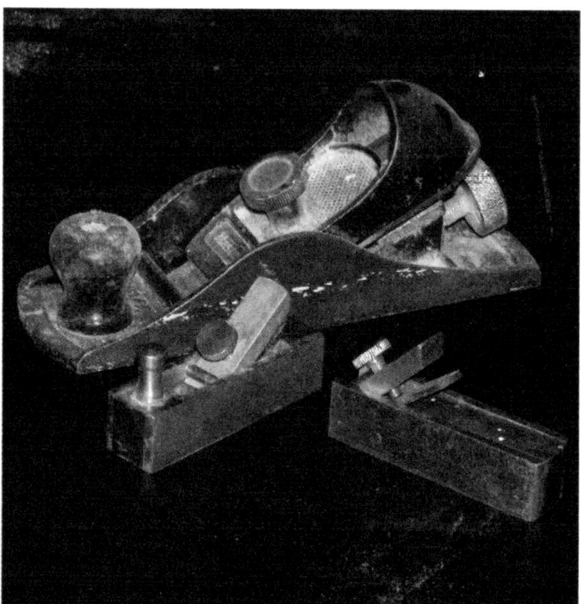

Figure 01.03: **Planes, jack and otherwise**

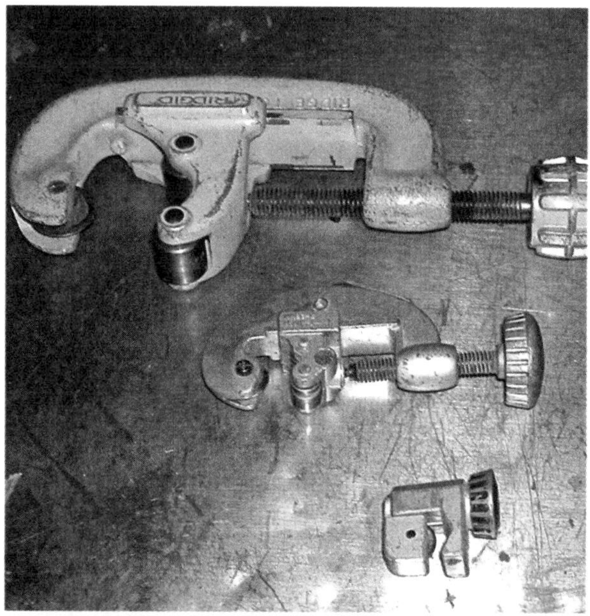

Figure 01.04: **Pipe cutters: utterly indispensable. Buy several immediately.**

Razor knife Spend the extra money to get a high-quality one with a solid blade-locking mechanism and an ergonomic handle, and don't be afraid to refresh your cutting edge. Use in conjunction with the following item.

Self-healing cutting mat Don't argue — just buy a nice big one and use it. Improves cut accuracy, and saves your blades. Really impresses visitors too, for some reason.

Jack plane, and planes in general Man, do tools have the coolest names, or what?

Smoothes out wood surfaces, and reduces dimension subtly. Get a modest-sized one to start out, and plan on messing up a lot of wood until you become one with the tool. It's a worthwhile investment over time. Also worth getting is a pair of miniatures: I actually use mine more than any full-sized plane in the house. You can find them on the 'Bay dirt-cheap: cutesy little block and chisel planes, about ⅛th regular size. If you keep the blades sharp, they're invaluable. **[Figure 01.03]**

Pipe cutter Damn straight, Bunkie. We're cuttin' pipe! Well, tubing actually. Either way, the thing about pipe is that it doesn't stretch. It doesn't take kindly to compression either: any fabrication involving long metal cylinders is . . . er . . . dimensionally unforgiving. It's gotta be the right length.

You could use your hacksaw and miter box, then true up your dimensions and dress your edges with emery cloth, needle files, the Leveler (you'll learn about this shortly) and a set square, or you could use one of these while drinking a cocktail. **[Figure 01.04]**

It's your call.

Whetstone (and the skills to use it properly) Sharp tools are happy tools.

Measuring

Quilter's measuring gauge Seek out a sewing supply store and be *amazed* at the variety of efficiently designed drawing and measuring tools. The needle and thread community *know* measuring. This 2" x 2" square of metal gives you accurate right angles and measurements from ⅛" to 2" in ⅛" intervals. **[Figure 01.05]**

12" carpenter's square I soundly encourage a non-Euclidean approach to life. That said, a majority of mechanisms are generally more comfortable with a "right angles/straight lines" kinda thing. Use appropriately. **[Figure 01.06]**

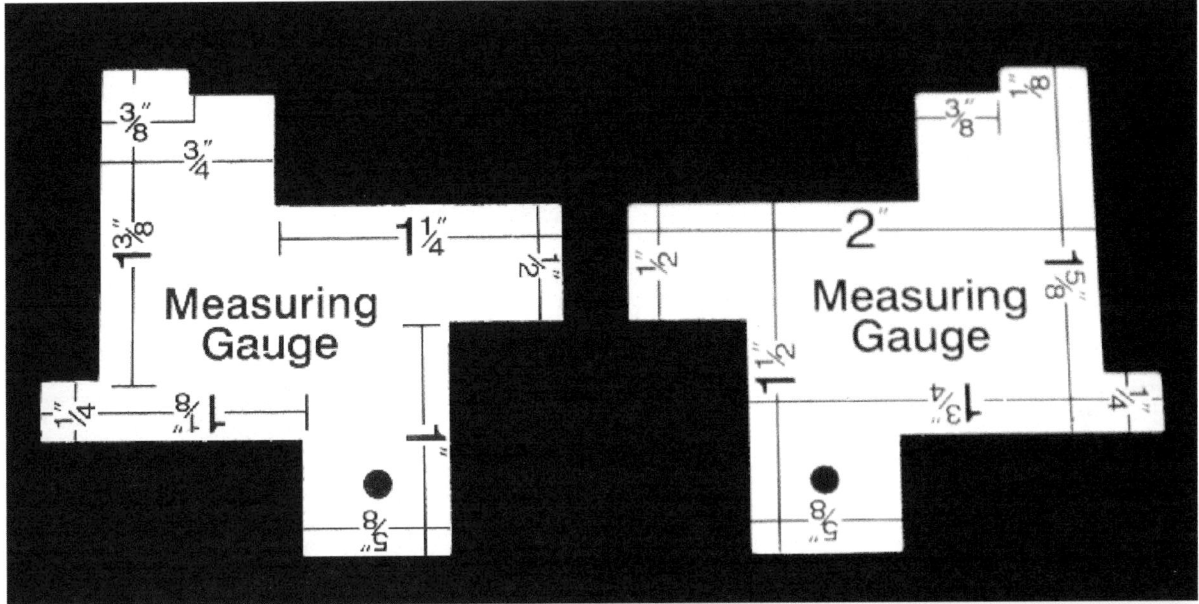

Figure 01.05: **Quilter's measuring gauge. Crafters have the coolest tools.**

Set Square Accurately setting up your power tools helps achieve the aforementioned "right angles/straight lines" environment.

Calipers Inside *and* outside. Transferring a measurement directly to the stock as a physical analog is inherently more accurate than the multiple format changes a dimension goes through when a ruler is involved. Get them at a swap meet from the same guy you buy your needle files from.

Protractor You can get away with using the one from your grade school math set, but use something more accurate if you can get one. All you're really looking for is an accurate angle measurement to check your cuts against. About five years ago, I dug a very slick little laptop drafting table out of the dumpster behind a thrift shop. I use its protractor function in the shop for angle checking. Yes, there are better ways. No, I can't see myself changing.

Compass For drawing circles — knowing where magnetic north is rarely important during the fabrication phase of a project.

French curves Before the advent of spline curve based digital drawing, the French curve was the go-to tool for

Figure 01.06: **Squares and other measurers**

drawing smooth polyradial curves. Now, do not mistake me for a Luddite in any way, shape or form; I do 95% of my design work digitally. The other 5%, where I'm finessing the visual aesthetic and trying to make a curve work with the grain and texture of a specific material, I use a French curve. You're a CAD uberuser with no pretension towards artsy-fartsy nonsense? You don't need it. [Figure 01.07]

But if you had one, you'd use it, because it's handy.

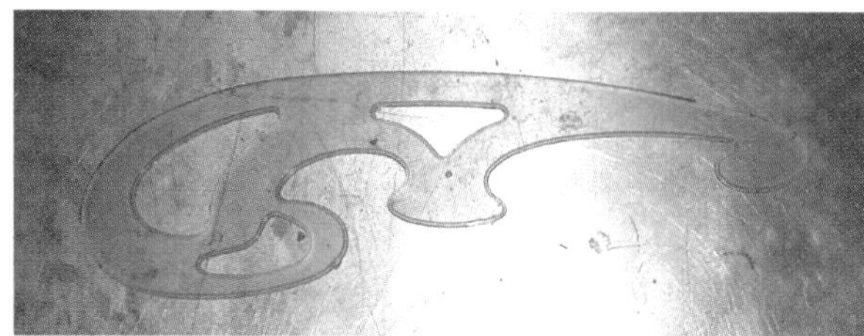

Figure 01.07: **Ooh (as zey say) la la: the French curve**

Sticky Stuff

Wood glue Real wood glue, dammit. Not that minty fresh white stuff preschoolers eat.

Double-faced tape The regular stuff and the foam-backed stuff.

Thread adhesive Think "chemical lock washer." I use the semi-permanent stuff from Loc-Tite. It's pink, and smells ghastly, but it *does exactly what it is intended to do*, which makes it easy to overlook the hideous odour.

Well, almost easy.

Aerosol stencil adhesive This is amazingly useful stuff. I use a no-name dollar store brand that sets up to about the consistency and tackiness of the adhesive on a sticky note. It adheres solidly enough to hold two flat surfaces tight during fairly rough handling, and it's easy to remove with minimum residue.

Aerosol contact cement Stencil adhesive's tough-ass brother who was in the Marines. Make adhesive sanding discs, veneer with impunity, stick stuff together with child-like enthusiasm. Glue hairless animals to the wall.

Abrasives

Sandpaper 60, 100, 150, 400 and 600 grit. For hand sanding, making your own sanding pads is the only rational approach. I really like the dense plastic foam they extrude those pool noodle thingies out of — you can carve it easily to whatever profile you need using knives, hot wires, or power sanders, then use aerosol stencil adhesive to glue on the abrasive surface of your choice.

As an aside, I recently came into a supply of the most intimidating sandpaper ever produced. It's labeled as 40 grit, which is a grossly conservative assessment of its coarseness. Imagine the roughest gravel road you ever found yourself lost on. Now laminate it onto a sheet of paper with brick-red resin, and that is a close approximation of the awesome abrasive might that is contained on these sheets. I'm using it with extreme caution.

Figure 01.08: **Little sanders**

Emery cloth/paper 80, 150, 400, 600, and 1500 grit. Proper cloth for the coarser grits, wet and dry paper for the finer ones.

Manicurists' emery boards are also pretty handy to have handy for quick surface touchups and localized special attention, but be aware that all emery boards are not created equal. Brave the cosmetics section of your local pharmacy and engage the salesperson in meaningful technical discourse regarding the abrasive qualities of their emery board selection.

I'm serious.

Steel wool Medium, fine, and extra fine.

A dead-flat sanding surface You probably don't have one of these, but if you had a can of aerosol stencil adhesive and the abrasive paper of your choice, all you'd need would be a really flat surface. Marble cutting boards are okay, although I've seen some that were a little convex. Personally, I use a piece of 5⁄16" mirror, with the theory being that any

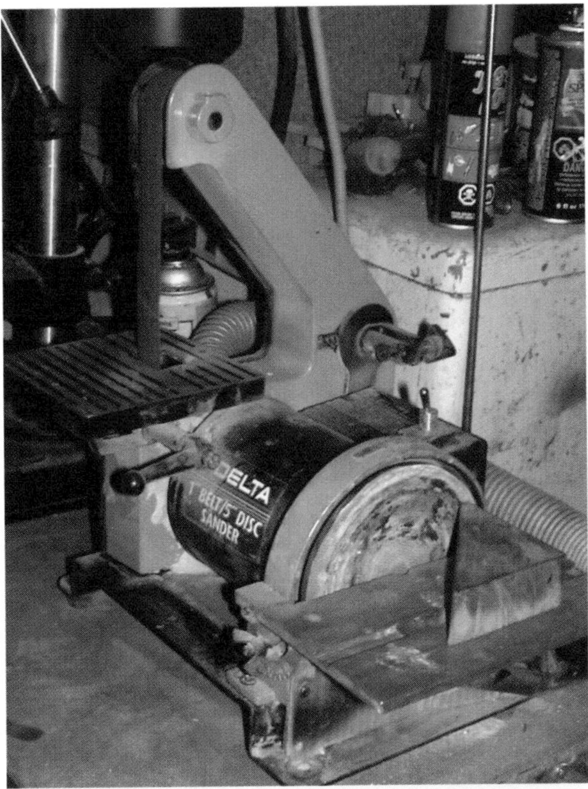

Figure 01.09: **This belt sander has saved my ass countless times.**

imperfections in flatness will show up as distortions in the reflections . . . yeah, right.

Seriously, it's a worthwhile tool to build. Use the lightest possible coating of stencil adhesive on your abrasive paper, and a sheet of glass to press it completely flat onto your official surface. The stencil glue makes it easy to change abrasives. You can do thickness sanding by hand with 50 grit (there's a certain Neanderthal pleasure in making that much sawdust manually), and put a mirror finish on brass plate with 15 micron polishing paper.. I use mine a lot to true up miter cuts and get nice flat surfaces after glue-ups. I call it "the Leveler."

Sanders You need a ⅓-sheet pad sander to flatten and smooth out wood surfaces. That's all there is to it. You might also consider one of those cute little detail sanders, but I gotta confess that I have yet to see one of these things from *any* manufacturer that was really well designed. It's like the guys who did the I.D. on them (yeah, all of 'em, every single one) thought the term "woodworking tool" was a colloquialism for "sex toy." Sheesh. Ergonomic and industrial design issues aside, they're really quite useful. **[Figure 01.08]**

Belt/disk bench sander Personally, I prefer a sanding belt running in the vertical plane. My little Delta 1" belt/5" disk model cost about 80 bucks at Canadian Tire. The cool thing about this wee beastie is the ability to remove the back plate from the belt path, leaving you with an amazingly useful flexible sanding surface. Curves can coexist with right angles and straight lines, and this tool lets you approach forming curves in a very controlled freestyle manner. The stick-on abrasive discs are invariably optimistically priced by the retailer. See: Sandpaper, Aerosol contact cement, Razor knife, and Compass, and make your own. **[Figure 01.09]**

Bench grinder Removing large amounts of metal? Buffing up a high gloss? Save time: get one of these; collect every overachieving wheel, pad, and brush you can find for it; and spend the time you save foraging for components.

Dremel Oh, alright . . . if you have to. But build a foot pedal speed controller for it, wouldja? (Conveniently, there is a how-to on the subject contained in this very book. See Chapter 9.)

Needle files I paid 10 bucks per set at a swap meet. Ten different profiles in a set, and they're made to cut with the edges as well as the face surface. They are exceptionally useful tools. Jewelry makers use them to finesse intricate gold castings, and they're the gunsmiths' tool of choice for filing a hair trigger. Each file in the set has a different profile: various radii, assorted acute angles, flat, cylindrical . . . you get the idea. It's a well-thought-out collection of shapes for finely detailing metalwork. Think of a Dremel grinding bit as a being a chainsaw; these are scalpels. **[Figure 01.10]**

Hold 'ems

Jigs Jigs are our friends — there is no better way of ensuring accurate, repeatable assembly glue-ups, cuts, and hole positioning than by using a jig, and the real joy comes from the fact that they are so damned easy to make. (And see the nano-project at the end of Chapter 2 for instructions for making an endlessly adjustable one of your own.)

Clamps You will reach a point where you absolutely cannot have enough clamps. Collect multiple styles and sizes, but at the very least have four 18" bar clamps, four 6" C clamps, and a drawer full of those black-and-orange clothespin-style ones. **[Figure 01.11]**

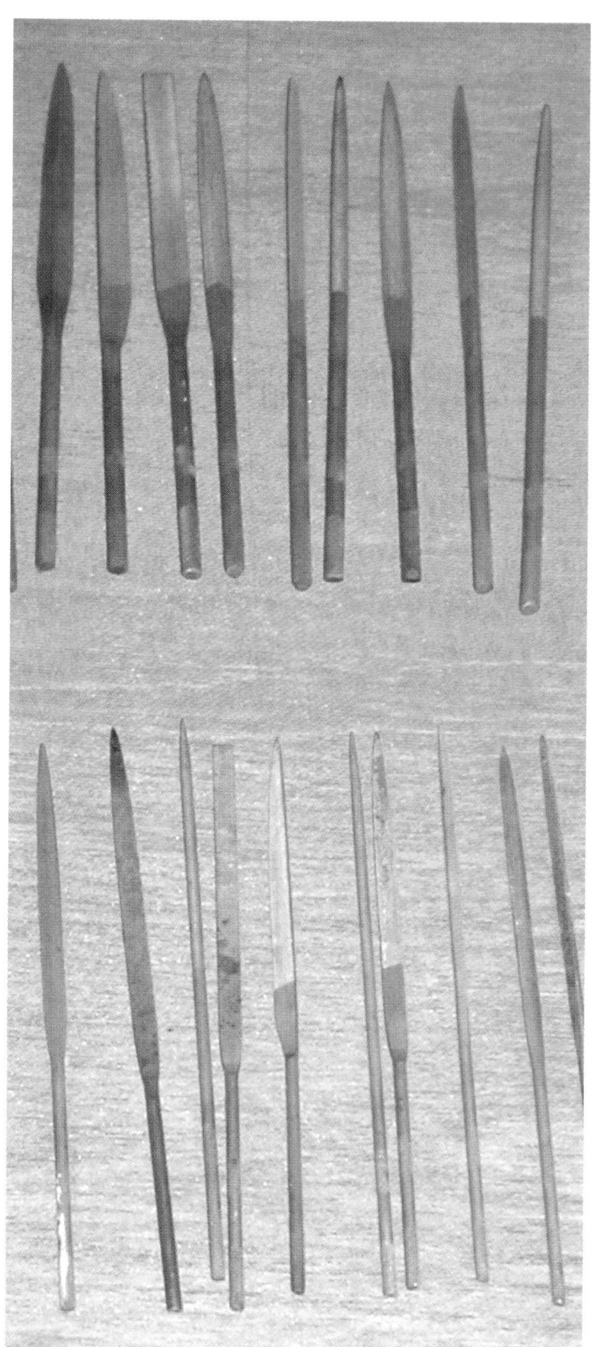

Figure 01.10: **Jewelers' needle files: the Maker's secret weapon for fine-tuning a mechanism.**

Figure 01.11: **The clamp food chain illustrated**

Figure 01.12: **My secret vises**

Dressmakers' elastic Once again, the needle-and-thread contingent comes through with an amazingly useful product (even if we *are* repurposing a tad). I found this stuff at the local sewing supply shop in widths from ½" to about 4", priced at around three bucks for a hundred-foot roll. Picture a near-endless piece of elastic waistband from industrial strength boxers and you've got it. Clamping an irregularly shaped glue-up? Need even pressure applied all the way around? This stuff is the answer. Wrap the WIP (work in progress) in question in this stuff, from every direction, and wait for nature to run its course on the glue consistency. I find 1" and 3" widths to be the handiest.

Numerous vises Bench vise, drill press vise, woodworking vise, tilting vise, jewelers' vise — you can never have too many ways to hold your work solidly in position while you do stuff to it. I'm a bench vise traditionalist, for the most part. Gimme "Strong Like Bull" over "Gosh, Aren't I Clever and Versatile" any day of the week. That said, I have an unseemly number of vises in the shop.

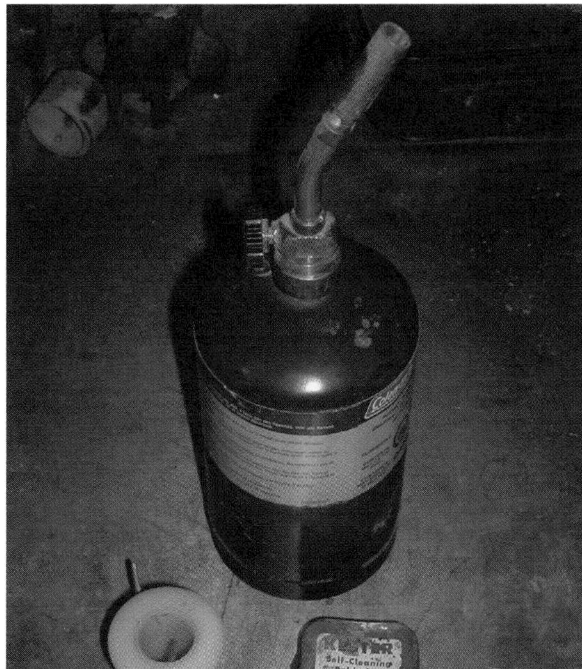

Figure 01.13: **A typical no-frills propane torch. Because your expensive Weller soldering iron with interchangeable tips and precision temperature controller can't solder pipe.**

Use whatever you like, but use *something*. You'll need to make some wooden or leather covers for the jaws if you don't have something appropriate already, to protect the surface of whatever slab of expensive wood/metal that ends up clamped in them from getting chewed up. If I catch you going out and *paying* for jaw covers, expect an interesting late-night visit from tool ninjas. **[Figure 01.12]**

Other

A couple more.

Propane torch Just yer basic propane torch, with a tin of plumbers paste flux and a spool of joint solder. **[Figure 01.13]**

Rubber mallet Our old friend, the blunt instrument.

The Right Stuff . . .

A big factor in Improvisational Fabrication is material selection: the right stuff for the task at hand, as it were. Knowing material properties and being able to adapt both your design and fabrication techniques to make effective use of the materials at hand are two of those essential skills that make a Maker. Most of the lore involved is common sense, tempered by a strong sense of compromise. It'd be nice to be able to use advanced carbon fiber and nanomaterial technology on every project. Realistically, you're gonna use whatever you can find on sale, dig out of a dumpster, or find in a shoebox in the attic. Here are some useful thumbnail guides to material selection. No, they are not overwhelmingly comprehensive. Yes, they are useful.

MDF (Medium-density fiberboard)
Advantages: Cheap, available, easy to work with.
Disadvantages: Not particularly strong, not particularly water-resistant. Ugly as sin.
Uses: Big, flat surfaces; jigs.

Plywood
Advantages: Ubiquitous. Comes in lots of flavours, grades, and thicknesses. Generally quite flat.
Disadvantages: None, really — as long as you remember that it's plywood and treat it as such. Which means it ain't pretty, has challenging end grain issues, and delaminates at the least appropriate times.
Uses: Big flat surfaces of varying thickness where end grain is not an issue.
Softwood (Basic 2' x 4', for example)
Advantages: Cheap, available, easy to work with.
Disadvantages: Soft: the surface damages easily, and long

lengths are prone to warping. Appearance varies, but can turn into a "50s rec room" knotty pine horror with alarming ease.
Uses: Framing, internal support structure, jigs and fixtures, test cuts.

Hardwood (Maple, birch, oak, walnut, countless other species)
Advantages: Hard, resilient, Looks like real wood because it is. Comes in a mind-blowing array of colours, grain structures and resiliency.
Disadvantages: Expensive, tougher to work with than softwood. Proper finishing can be a righteous pain in the ass.
Uses: Personally, just about everywhere. Maple is my go-to material for a lot of stress-bearing components, and I'm not just saying that because I'm Canadian.

Brass
Advantages: Easy to work with, resilient, widely available in an inspirational variety of form factors. Learning how to look at plumbing fittings and not see "just plumbing fittings" is absolutely epiphanous. Thermally and electrically conductive. Buffs up all pretty like.
Disadvantages: Soft.[1] Tarnishes at an appalling rate.[2] Won't hold an edge.
Uses: Mechanism components. Moderate load structural components. Connectors.

Copper
Advantages: Thermally and electrically conductive, easy to work with. Ubiquitous in a variety of form factors, most usefully pipes, tubes and sheets. Solders easily.
Disadvantages: Soft. Really, really soft. Tarnishes easily. Becoming ridiculously expensive. Won't hold an edge.
Uses: Moving electrons, heat, fluid or gas. Ornamental cladding. Big shiny cylinders that *aren't* PVC drainpipe.

Aluminum
Advantages: Lightweight, easy to work with, strong alloys readily available. Cast and extruded components widespread in countless form factors. Inexpensive. Thermally and electrically conductive. Can be melted and cast easily. Polishes to a mirror finish. Ubiquitous. Weldable .
Disadvantages: Some alloys have brittleness issues; cast pieces in particular can shatter under impact. Corrodes easily and unattractively. Not easy to weld. Won't hold an edge.
Uses: Just about everything. It's a versatile material to begin with, and the enormous range of preformed shapes you encounter at scrap yards makes it *damned* inspirational.

Stainless steel
Advantages: Strong, corrosion resistant, most alloys are nonmagnetic. Weldable. Holds an edge while still being readily sharpenable.
Disadvantages: Difficult to work with. It's a tough but prissy metal: a challenge to weld, discolours under excessive heat, beats the shit out of your tools. Requires skill and finesse to do it justice.
Uses: Limited from a general-purpose fabrication standpoint. Use where its particular material properties are needed, or if you find a component preformed that will repurpose easily. Generally a pain in the ass.

Other ferrous metals
Reg'lar folks' steel and iron. Magnets stick to it, rusts like crazy, about a bazillion different alloys of varying provenance and properties. Iron is the metal that changed civilization: tough, versatile, universal. Not an easy material to work with any precision without Spending Money On Tools.® I use it where needed for strength.

1 Not "soft like softwood," but "soft compared to other metals." I generally do not recommend using brass rod as an axle or pivot point in a high-load situation due to the extreme risk of it bending. Harness the inherent softness of brass constructively by using it as bushing material to separate harder metals from the delicate fiber of wood. A properly sized and polished bushing is nearly as effective as a bearing race in terms of reducing friction.

2 There's a reason that brass musical instruments are heavily lacquered, and this is it. Hours of elbow grease expenditure lapping and buffing brasswork up to a near gilded gloss disappear before your eyes as the powers of oxidation exert themselves and turn the damned thing green overnight. This is crazymakin' in the extreme, which means that having a good brass polish close to hand is essential. Personally, I use "Flitz," which is this weird blue goop in a tube. It's of Teutonic origin, so local availability may be problematic, but it's well worth seeking out.

. . . for the Right Purpose

There are other approaches to material selection. It's immeasurably handy to know in advance what material works best for a given application. I do strongly advise you to start a list of material/specific task correlations that you find workable.

Here's a list of generally useful materials I keep around the shop in varying quantities, and why:

- **Glove leather** Linings.
- **Belt leather** Straps, impact padding, feet, heavy gaskets, and seals.
- **Cork sheeting** Insulation, noise abatement, gaskets, seals.
- **Craft foam sheets** Heavy duty stencil material, insulation.
- **Threaded rod (a.k.a. "all-thread")** Threaded steel rod in multiple dimensions is infinitely useful.
- **Craft felt** Linings, nonscratch surfaces.
- **Inner tubes** Gaskets, air seals, diaphragms.
- **Neoprene pipe insulation** Padding, vibration dampening, noise supression.
- **Bicycle brake cable** Actuators and linkages.
- **Guitar strings** Really lightweight actuators and linkages. Springs.
- **Aquarium air line (in lots of diameters)** Gas and fluid transfer.
- **Hardwood dowel (in lots of diameters)** Pinning joints, plugging holes.
- **Bamboo skewers** Stripped-screw hole repair, mixing epoxy.
- **Playing cards** Temporary shims, epoxy mixing surface.
- **Teflon cutting board** Low-friction surfaces.
- **Thrift shop rollerblade wheels** Ball-bearing races.
- **Bead chain (in various dimensions and materials)** Low- to medium-load linkages.
- **Drum heads** Tough-ass Mylar sheeting for low-friction surfaces, heavy-duty membranes.
- **Lead** Counterweights.
- **Mouse pads** Nonskid surfaces, gaskets, seals, impact padding.
- **Thrift shop wetsuit** Big non skid surfaces, gaskets, seals, impact padding.

This list grows intermittently as I come across new uses for old materials; I still get a visceral thrill out of figuring out a new and effective material substitution.

Yeah, I do probably need to get out more.

Getting Stuff

I'll flat-out admit it: I really love the thrill of the chase when it comes to raw materials. Most of my best pieces directly result from particularly evocative components I dig up at scrap yards, and I'm on a first-name basis with the staff of countless thrift shops and swap meet tables.

Improvisational Fabrication requires a certain mindset when foraging for components. Once you've defined the subassembly mechanisms of the . . . er . . . *thing* you're building, start foraging for general mechanisms, rather than individual components.

Hypothetically, if I set out sourcing, say, "airflow, a fluid reservoir, rotary motion, and mesh," I could come home at the end of the day with an RC car, a Todd Rundgren 45 record, a loaf pan, and a hair dryer.

I could also just as easily return home with a windshield-wiper motor, an innertube, a barbecue rotisserie drive, a canteen, and some expanded aluminum.

Either way, I'd end up putting together a bubble machine.

In the first instance, I happened to notice that the wheel of the RC car was a pretty solid fit in the centre of the 45. I built a little jig for the drill press to help space a pattern of ¾" holes around the surface of the record disc, rendering it mesh-like. I needed a fluid reservoir about 7" x 3". It took about 30 seconds to find a very nice seamless aluminum loaf pan that was in the ballpark, dimension-wise. The hair dryer was a pathetically weak "plug it into the lighter socket of your car" model, of occidental origin. Bodged it all together with hot-melt and pop rivets into a milk crate, and MacGyvered a cutesy three-position switch onto the steerable front wheels of the car, to give me radio control of the hair dryer's off/low/high function as well. I disabled the heating element in the hair dryer, too . . . hot bubbles don't last very long.

Total fabrication time? About 90 minutes.

Total cost? I got change back from a ten.

In the second instance, I found the wiper motor first. The reciprocating action still worked, but the actuator arm had been snapped. I decided to build a two-chambered bladder pump with a reservoir as the air supply, using an innertube as source material for both the bladders and the reservoir. I bought enough expanded metal to fabricate the mesh wheel and the mounting framework.

The canteen I cut in half lengthwise and I pulled a suitably dangerous-looking power switch for the rotisserie motor out of my parts bins. The only other nuisance was the ball valve manifold for the air pump, which I fabbed out of a block of maple on the drill press. I used squash balls for the checkballs. The whole thing bolted together pretty quickly once the fabrication was done.

Total cost? I got change from a ten.

Total fabrication time? 40 hours or so. It took me a while to figure out the best way to disperse the air from the receiver.

My point? *Plan* on improvising during sourcing. It adds character to the build, and will lead you down previously unconsidered paths.

It can also add extra trips out onto your build schedule. When you start improvising, your parts requirements can change in the wink of an eye, leaving you with a benchful of purposeless components. Store them away nicely. Start a database of your inventory, if you have the time. You're going to be accumulating usable components at an impressive rate, and knowing what you've got and — more importantly — where it is will save you many, many hours.

Interestingly, how you sort and store your inventory can have a strong influence on how future projects evolve if you eschew standard or traditional categorization. I try to avoid microcategories as much as possible, and embrace unexpected generalizations where ever I can so that, as an example, when I open a bin labeled "Motion," I'm stared in the face by electric motors, springs, rubber bands, string, solenoids, bearing races, pumps and fan assemblies. Having preprogrammed random inspirational events like this dotted along your build path is a real good way to ward off "Maker's block" and keep the build interesting. I can't tell you how many of my pieces have resulted from randomly intersecting components I stumbled across during the course of a completely different build.

Freestyle sourcing relies heavily on your knowledge of what's under the hood of just about everything. Learn the various processes at work inside a piece of technology, and the means by which they're accomplished. Take a lot of stuff apart; see how it's built. See what it does. See how it works. See what it's built from. Consider new applications.

Here's an exercise that oughta be mandatory for Makers. Free up a Sunday afternoon. Go to a thrift shop and buy a $20 typewriter. Bring it home and take it apart. Every bit of it. Properly disassembled right down to basic components. If you pay attention, you will learn a *lot*. Typewriters are amazingly complex mechanisms — there's lots goin' on when you press a key or hit the carriage return lever, and these things were built to take a beating, so you're looking at very resilient engineering. There's a lot of UI occurring, too, with control placement being completely dependent on mechanical linkages. To the digital UI contingent who agonize over pixel placement and menu hierarchies, I say "Gimme a call when you have a real problem." Seriously, the guys who did the engineering on manual typewriters were unsung heroes of the mechanical age, and every true Maker should take the time to appreciate the sheer density of their achievements.

You'll also score about four shoeboxes full of mind warpingly useful-in-some-way-you-are-currently-unaware-of mechanical components in the process.

I fully disassemble and harvest the components from stuff almost daily. Most recently a weed-whacker, a VCR, and a rice cooker (which contained the cutest little retractable AC cord you've ever laid eyes on).[3]

This is kinda like a post-millennial version of native wood lore, and the most potentially invaluable modern day survival skill I can think of.

Scrap-Fu: The Way of the Yard

Hiiiiiiiiiiiiiiiii-YAH!

Enter the scrap yard.

Oh, all right. Enter the "metal recycling facility," if you absolutely insist on using the current politically and environmentally correct terminology. Call them what you will, but enter them you must: they are the wellspring of arcane components and mysterious metals you need to complete your endeavours.

You must be wary. The scrap yard is a perilous and mysterious land of unknown wonders and horrors, its treasures protected by formidable and inscrutable metal monks. Mastering the ancient art of scrap-fu gives you the undefeatable skills you need to emerge victorious.

You must practice your scrap-fu skills for many hours. Watch, listen, and remember. Celebrate your victories with rice wine. Bind your wounds and learn from your defeats.

Become one with the scrap yard, but be forewarned: not all yards are created equal, nor the denizens who serve it. Knowing the yard and respecting the priests enhances your experience a hundredfold, optimizes your chances of fulfilling your quest, and reduces your risk of meeting a horrible doom at the gaping maws of the beastly Iron For-Klift, or becoming

3 In a quite stunning segue, I'd like to point out that there's a quick 'n' dirty how-to in this very book (see the tail end of Chapter 5) detailing the conversion of a harvested cord-reel mechanism into a 1⁄20th-the-cost-of-a-similar-thing-from-the big-box-Home-Centers retractable extension cord. Go figure.

lost on the desolate plains of Ex Tru Sion.

Now pay attention, grasshopper. Class is in session

Understanding a scrap yard means understanding the scrap they deal with. Some yards are general-purpose, some are more specialized. Some are huge industrial yards that deal with hundreds of tons of one or two specific kinds of metal daily. Other yards are more like a neighborhood junkyard repurposed into a thrift shop. Both have their merits, but a smaller "mom and pop" yard is more likely to have trippy cast-off arcana from unexpected sources. Scout out a few different flavours of yard and get a feel for each. You'll eventually end up needing the services of all of them, if you're halfway adventurous.

Scrap Metal at a Glance

There are four main commodity metals traded regularly at scrap yards: copper, brass, aluminum and stainless steel. There are a bunch of different grades of copper and aluminum and a few flavours of brass and stainless, and each of them can be found in various subgrades. Each is bought and sold at a different cost per pound, which can quickly become confusing when it's time to cough up the cash. Local scrap yards make money in a pretty simple way: buy metal cheap, clean it up and sort it out, then sell it in quantity to a larger broker upstream in the commodity chain. If you're selling to a yard, you can optimize your return by sorting and cleaning it beforehand. If you're buying metal or wire, you'll be paying roughly the same rate the yard gets when they sell their metal upstream, but you'll find that being a regular is often reflected in a more favourable rate of exchange. Buying salvaged components and artifacts brings other pricing considerations into play; I'll deal with that in detail later.

Other common metals like lead, tin and zinc are daily staples at 'yards, but if you need something from a less well-traveled portion of the periodic table, like bismuth or titanium, your search may be thwarted.

Steel and iron are kinda like the redheaded stepchildren of scrap yard metals: they're *there*, but they're not afforded any respect due to their low (in comparison) commodity value. Current (mid-2007) street-level value of steel is about $40 a ton. Mid-grade copper is about $2.50 a pound. Turning a profit from recycling steel requires a large-scale industrial operation that can handle hundreds of tons a day. Every city has a big steel yard or two, and it's a fascinating field trip to see the inner workings. They're generally lacking in personality, and safety-wise not the best place for lone Makers to be poking through tubs of metal. Unless you're fabricating a lifesized model of the Nimitz and need a lot of structural steel plate and 18" I-beams, you're better off finding and frequenting a local scrap yard.

In addition to the various commodity metals, most scrap yards salvage artifacts, componentry, and technology for resale.

What kind of componentry?

Damned good question, Billy. To answer it, you need to answer the main question people ask when they first visit a scrap yard: "Where the hell does all this shit come from?"

Seriously, every yard I've ever been in is for the most part a chaotic mass of twisted copper plumbing, piles of aluminum window frames stacked like cordwood, huge drums of snarled CAT5 cable and fetid mounds of decommissioned commercial kitchen equipment. Scrap yards are filled with the metal from demolition jobs, leftover supplies from construction sites, scrap and cutoffs from manufacturing firms, obsolete industrial equipment, and the contents of hundreds of garages and basements.

Which is to say that on any given day, you run the possibility of finding *anything*.

The kind of stuff that gets salvaged depends on the stuff that comes in, and how hip the staff of the yard is. You'll see a lot of plumbing and electrical supplies, and stuff that reflects the local industrial landscape. Vancouver, where I live, is a port town, so there are a lot of marine fittings and commercial fishing–related stuff coming into yards. Machinists' metal stock, and fabrication-grade box channel, tubing, and plate can be found, but rarely in useful size and quantity. A surprising amount of functioning machinery finds its way into scrap yards. It's generally one or two generations old, and being scrapped to make way for new 'n' improved gear. Big industry doesn't often waste time and money disposing of old kit on eBay or Craigslist. To them, it's depreciated to the point of having no value, so it gets scrapped. Once it's in the yard, it'll either have all the easily accessible commodity metal stripped from it, with the bare carcass being tossed into the metal ghetto of "the Steel Bin," or it'll be kept in hopes of resale, either intact or parted out.

Makers in the know rub their hands together gleefully at this, because what's "scrap" to industry and "metal" to scrap yards is "componentry" to us. Finding cool tech just *waiting* to be harvested for functioning subassemblies is kinda like ChristmaHanuKwanzakah, your birthday, and a date with a leggy supermodel all at once.

Really. It's that good.

I recently happened upon a decommissioned medical imaging device called a UroView 2500 at North Star Recycling. It was in three pieces, sitting in between a stack of benches recently removed from a shopping mall, and a three-ton tub of elevator wiring harness. I had a quick chat with yard owner and scrap-metal ubermensch Phil Watson, then proceeded to harvest the carcass of the UroView (yup, "Uro" as in "Urology." I had a moment of chilling discomfort when visualizing the large and dangerous-looking mechanism being used in close proximity to my . . . well, my urinary tract) for four precision 16" linear actuators, a handful of microswitch-based motion limiters, half a dozen low-speed/high-torque gear motors and an assortment of drivetrain components. Total elapsed time, 20 minutes; total cost, 20 bucks and a coffee.

My scrap-fu is *strong*.

Notable tech left behind for the next adventurer to encounter in the corpse: a digital rotational encoder accurate to three decimal places, the Fuji hi-res video camera and image intensifier circuitry, and all the motor control circuitry. A couple of days later, when the yard grunts got tired of tripping over the remnants, the once proud UroView 2500 was unceremoniously consigned to the Steel Bin, signaling its impending return to molten metal.

During the same expedition I picked up some sheet brass and 3⁄16" brass roundbar that had come in as scrap from a local machine shop, a motorized flow control valve that had been part of a plumbing contractor's weekly "beer run" transaction, and a spun copper planter brought in by a retiree cleaning out his basement that became the motor housing for the hypnodisc I made for David Pescovitz.[4]

Damn, I love scrap yards.

Anyway, my point is this: if you can master the skill of "seeing at a component level," you have begun your journey towards scrap-fu mastery, because at a scrap yard, components are *everywhere*.

The Secret Language of Scrap Yards

Similarly to the Inuit having multiple words for "snow," scrap yard metal nomenclature is both specific and cryptic. Here's a brief translation guide to common scrap yard commodities:

#1 Copper The king of metals right now, currently being bought at about $2.80/pound CDN as a result of recent studies indicating that there is insufficient copper metal *on the face of the earth* to wire up China and South Asia's networks with CAT5 cable. Corrosion- and solder-free copper plumbing, sheet-copper cladding, and stripped industrial gauge electrical cable are considered "#1 copper" at scrap yards, and you will pay top dollar to buy it. Unless you're dead set on a particular pristine piece of metal, you're better off buying something lower-grade and cleaning it up at home with emery paper and steel wool.

4 *Boing Boing* editor and contributing editor to *MAKE* magazine.

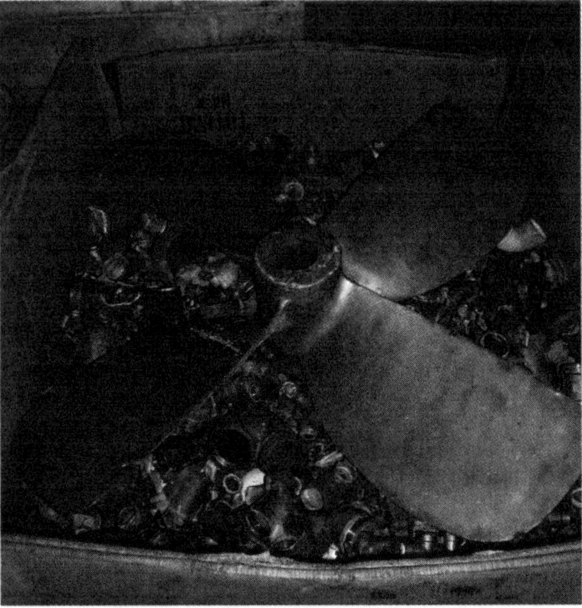

Figure No. 01.14: **You see a lot of *big* cardboard boxes at 'yards. They're called "Gaylords." I don't know why. This one is full of red brass, and features a 240 pound marine propellor as its main attraction.**

#2 Copper The next most valuable: copper plumbing, sheeting and bare wire with corrosion, bits of solder, and impurities of dubious provenance. Price-wise, this is a better bet.

#1 Copper wire This is thick stuff. Insulated uniconductor household wiring is an example. Contractors often sell leftover rolls of this stuff for beer money. If you're doing some home improvement, you can save a ton of money scoring your wiring supplies at a scrap yard.

Burnt copper wire This comes from the windings of overheated transformers and industrial motors. It's worth money to sell to a yard, but I've yet to find a use for the stuff in the shop. Gag-inducing aroma, often covered in flaky detritus like a cross between mica and glitter that will make your skin itch for days. Avoid at all costs.

#2 Copper wire Multistrand consumer electronic wiring: AC cords, audio, CAT5, and other data cable, that kinda stuff. This is another commodity that often comes into a yard in full roll quantities that are an absolute bargain if you do a lot of cable runs. I hit Capital Salvage on a good day once and got 100 yards of high-end Belden three-conductor-plus-woven-shield audio cabling for a ten-spot. Lost the next three days obsessively designing, fitting, and soldering up a custom wiring harness for my V-Drums, but that's another story.

BX wire This is #1 copper wire in that flexible aluminum armour. Gives a nice Mad Max vibe to your wiring projects, and the empty aluminum cladding is useful in countless other applications.

Brass Comes in innumerable yellow and red alloys. The price the yard buys at varies on how much other stuff has to be removed to leave clean (read: "no other metal attached to it") brass. The selling price is generally at a par with the yard's upstream selling price. Plumbing fittings, ornamental household items, marine instruments, arcane componentry that defies logic and imagination . . . it's all at a 'yard, and it's made outta brass.

Cool.

FWIW, cymbals are treated as brass, rather than the bronze they truly are. There is (for a drummer, anyway) no greater thrill than paying $2.50/pound for a beautifully aged, lovingly maintained Paiste Seven Sound series 18" flat ride.

Been there, done that, still grinnin' like the butcher's dog.

Stainless steel Comes in about a million alloys, not all of which are nonmagnetic. Surprisingly cheap for the longest time, it's recently become "dynamic," as they say in the commodity metal trade.

The king of stainless alloys is 316L: yer A-1 Primo Surgical grade metal of choice. You can use it to fabricate the scalpel you'll need to remove the arm and leg you'll be using to pay for it. If you can find 316 in 3⁄32" plate, it makes for an effective guillotine blade.

Just sayin'.

The vast majority of stainless that enters scrap yards is in the form of food industry equipment, which, beneath the inevitable thick coating of deep-fryer grease, also contains useful industrial-strength mechanisms like compressors, chain drive trains, high-torque gearboxes, and the like. If you can steer your nose around the odours, you can scoop up quality mechanical schwag for cheap, because the guys who work in scrap yards would much rather have you disassemble the stuff than suffer the task themselves.

Figure No. 01.15: **A "scoop" of assorted aluminum extrusion.**

Figure No. 01.16: **Gauges, meters, door and window hardware, assorted plumbing and locksmithing arcana.**

Figure No. 01.17: **Far too many industrial strength stainless steel hoseclamps to count.**

Figure No. 01.18: **600 pounds of aluminum punchouts. If you can think of a use, I can get 'em for you wholesale.**

Aluminum is a brutally diverse metal in the eyes of a scrap yard, with the buy/sell prices being just as confusing:

Extruded Window frames, structural pieces, box channel, that kinda stuff. Aluminum extrusion comes in a range of profiles that staggers the imagination: you name the shape, and I can guarantee that some manufacturer somewhere has found a need to extrude aluminum with that particular profile. Seek out the extrusion stacks at a scrap yard and spend some time pondering the shapes and sizes you encounter. It almost requires a full-on meditative trance state to open your mind up to the potential of intricately profiled extrusion, but I can assure you of the value of such consideration.

New aluminum Heavier-gauge machine formed metal: plate, pipe, fabrication-grade metal. Machine shops sell their scrap regularly, and depending on the jobs they've been working on, their scrap can include regularly shaped cutouts/cutoffs/punchouts in quantity. As an example, I have a couple of five-gallon pails of circular ¼"-plate cutouts ranging in diameter from one to ten inches. At some point in time, I'll actually find a use for them.

Cast aluminum What it says. As a material, it's brittle and the surface is generally unfinished, but cast aluminum comes in shapes ranging from commonplace (barbecue grill hoods) to being completely alien in topography (I've built home décor items from electric motor housings that would not look out of place on the bridge of a Klingon battle cruiser). If you're prepared to spend time on surface finishing, scrap yard cast aluminum is a limitless source of Dali-esque project boxes and enclosures.

Old aluminum
Thin-gauge metal: rain gutters, siding, that sort of thing. A good source of easily workable faceplate material.

Dirty aluminum Treated with disdain by the yard grunts: Their attitude is, "Well, there's aluminum in there somewhere, but it's a pain in the ass to clean it up." The disdain is, for the most part, well-deserved. It's the category of aluminum that also includes "cast, with brass bushings and/or steel bearing races still in place," though, which means there's always potentially something useful.

Figure No. 01.19: Antique phones, bellows cameras, analogue test gear and other WTF-grade tech salvage. Not shown: The Flux Capacitor bin.

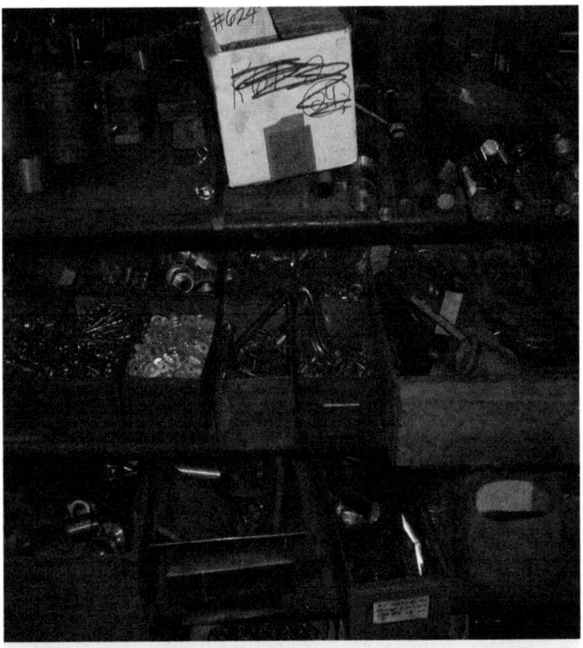

Figure No. 01.20: Fasteners, metal stock, assorted gewgaws and gimcracks.

ACSR This is industrial-gauge aluminum wire with a steel reinforcing core; comes clad or unclad. They don't pay much for it, don't charge much for it, and any prospective usage has thus far escaped me.

As mentioned, there are likely other common metals around somewhere — ask a yard grunt. Despite my previous caution about the availability of exotic elements, don't be afraid to ask about them, either. On a given day, the grunts in a scrap yard have no idea what's gonna come through the gates on the back of a truck, and you may get lucky. The thing about scrap yards is that there is *huge* turnover of inventory on a weekly basis, and being a regular is the only way to grab the good stuff before it gets crushed into a bale and shipped to the Pacific Rim.

Regular steel and iron is priced either by weight or by item, if you're buying. Most yards salvage common steel and iron items like angle iron and rebar when they come in, but demand is high and it seldom lingers on the racks for long. The real treasure trove lies in the bins of steel yards accumulated through "courtesy disposal" for clients, which often contain *spectacularly* cool artifacts you will feel compelled to own. Accessing the bins and recovering the goodies is an adventure often fraught with peril, and requires powerful scrap-fu.

The Way of Scrap

To understand the Way of Scrap, think of a scrap yard as an semi-organic mechanism tasked with sorting all the crap that gets hauled in through the gates into the aforementioned categories. When enough of a certain flavour of metal accumulates and the price is right, they ship it upstream in the recycling hierarchy to a metal broker and turn a reasonable profit. There's a place for everything, and everything gets to its place eventually — ask the guy at the scale where stuff is. To you, it's an invaluable component in your next build; to them, it's just metal to be moved around.

Despite my referring to them as grunts, on't make the mistake of assuming that these guys are clueless. They spend their workday dealing with a mind-boggling array of mechanisms and materials (and the people who use them), and they pay attention. The collective knowledge and experience of a scrap yard crew gives 'em an unparalleled ability to spot the good stuff from whatever technical discipline they happen to be dealing with.

Treat a trip to a scrap yard with the same attitude as a trip to a technical consultant: assume that (at the very least) they are as knowledgable as you are regarding whatever it is you're looking for.

Earn extra points by asking for what you want with reasonable, but not extreme specificity: one surefire way to annoy yard staff is to come through the gate and say "I need leetle piece metal" while holding your index fingers in the air demonstratively. Another way is to ask for "3/8" polished aluminum checkerplate 14 7/8" x 29 13/16" . . . I can go as high as 29 15/16", but you'll need to knock a buck or two off the price." (These are verbatim requests I have personally fielded during my time as a yard grunt at North Star recycling.)

Once you're pointed in the right direction, proceed with caution and keep your eyes open. A yard is full of pointy metal, large weighty things on forklifts, and unnaturally strong men carrying heavy loads. Having your path intersect *any* of these things will invariably result in injury.

In a scrap yard, you're gonna be faced with containers of metal. Really big containers. The stuff you want is likely on the bottom. Ask before climbing in, and put back everything you displace in the process. A lot of metal in a yard is moved by hand, and making more work for the previously noted unnaturally strong men is generally not a good idea.

Bring your dimensions with you, and bring a tape measure and/or calipers. Scrap yards *may* have such things available, and they *may* let you borrow them, but it's a sign of professionalism if you come prepared.

Bring a few useful tools with you, in case you discover something worth harvesting. I can get by with a multi-screwdriver, adjustable wrench, locking pliers, and wire cutters. Your needs may vary. Whatever you do, *do not* just start taking something apart. Show the guy at the scale what you're interested in, explain what you're planning to do with it, and negotiate both permission and price. Because these things get priced on the fly 99% of the time, the way you relate with guy at the scale directly determines both the price and the possibility of you getting clocked on the head with a baseball bat for being an asshole.

Finding the stuff in the first place is dependent on your relationship with the yard grunts. The owner/manager/guy at the scale may handle the money, but the guys in the yard move the goods around and know *exactly* where it is. Be polite, become a regular, and show them proper respect. The occasional box of Krispy Kremes wouldn't hurt, either. If you're on good terms with the staff and you come in frequently, they'll often keep an eye open for stuff on your "gotta get" list.

It's worth the effort. Stuff I've come across at yards recently, over and above the now-legendary UroView 2500? A full set of ding- and crack-free Zildjian and Paiste cymbals, 1500 LCD862 PIC controllers, rack-mounted HP EEG and ECG monitors, otherworldly cast aluminum casings from mid-50s microscope projectors, a belt-drive dental drill, a surgical electric scalpel/cauterization instrument, and a metal-bending tool set that looks like it came from Fred Flintstones' garage. I spent less than 60 bucks Cdn.

I have the lift mechanism from a dentist's chair, currently poised to become an in-workbench hoist system.

Now go, and practice your scrap-fu. Practice relentlessly, with great power. Bring your village great happiness.

2 Active Deskchop: Your Personal Guillotine

I started building guillotines by popular demand. I guess the trebuchets I'd built got people thinking about launching severed heads over castle walls or something, but within a six-month period I had at least a hundred people say "Dude . . . you gotta build a guillotine" to me. It was actually getting a little creepy, so I did, just to shut 'em up.

There's a lot to be said for heeding the voice of the people: guillotines turned out to be my most popular product line. Go figure.

What We're Building

As specified by the French, a guillotine was 14 feet high, with an 88-pound blade and a razor-sharp 45-degree cutting edge. All quite . . . er . . . revolutionary in its time, as it was the first scientifically researched device for the administration of capital punishment and all.

"Crude but effective" is a phrase that springs to mind. Early records show guillotine-like devices (or *gibbets*) in use in Ireland in the early 1300s. By 1792, the guillotine had evolved to the form we're now familiar with and — unbelievably — was used sporadically until 1977. It's still pervasive imagery, which speaks volumes about humanity's fascination with killing machines.

As attractive as the proposition may be, fabricating a full-sized decapitation machine in your backyard is impractical in all but the most enlightened communities. Scaling the guillotine down to desktop size still presents a few challenges. Forty kilos of blade plummeting from a giddy height is gonna take your noggin off, regardless of edge sharpness, but at 1/12th scale, you're dealing with exponentially reduced potential energy in the blade, which means getting creative if you want to produce a device that can chop the end off a cigar or dismember vegetables with any degree of authority. Creativity, in this case, manifests itself as a block of lead bodged onto the blade.

CAUTION: Yes, you are going to be fabricating a device with a heavy sharp blade that has the potential to cause grievous bodily harm. The tools you will be using to make this have the same potential. Do not forget!

Now, truth be known, I've fabricated a *lot* of guillotines and I'm getting a little sick of 'em.

I designed the first one on the bench from a fairly conservative viewpoint, and the majority of the subsequent pieces were variations on that basic theme: I build to order, and clients tend to want something familiar. Keeping the builds interesting is always a challenge, and is particularly frustrating when you're working with a mechanism that can be executed (pun intended) in so many different styles that just aren't in demand.

Fortunately, the form factor we're using here is infinitely flexible from an industrial design perspective, and can be adapted to just about any potential deployment. By all means, feel free to adapt, modify, hack, repurpose, and improvise. After all, it's not like we're dealing with an overly complex mechanism. Let's look at the subassemblies involved. There's the stuff associated with the *chopper* (blade, weight box, trestle, and pulley), the stuff associated with the *choppee* (the lunette and the bed), and a nice solid base to hold the lot of them in position.

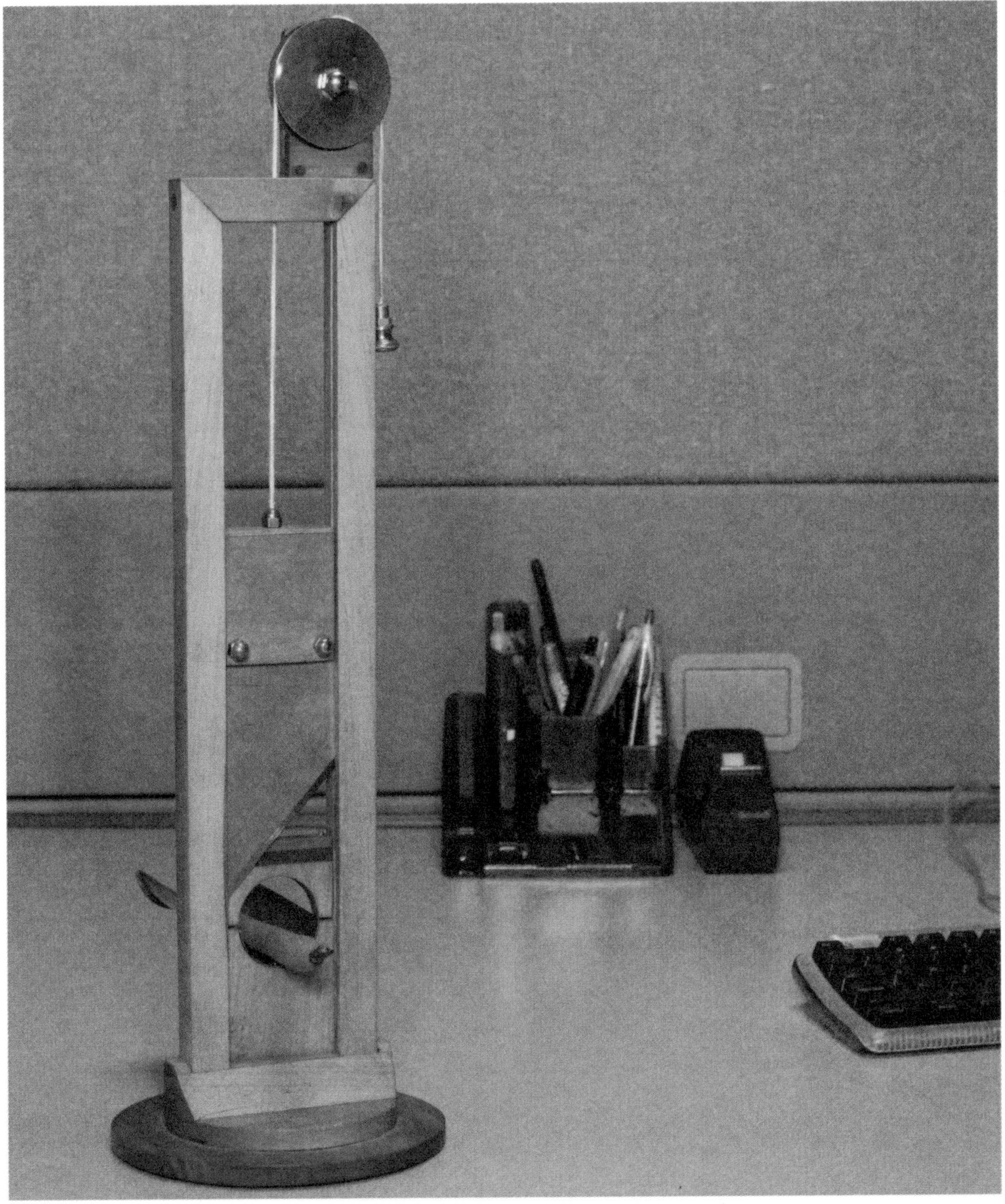

Given the "cubicle-friendly" mandate of this series of projects, the footprint of each individual unit is an obvious concern. It's a foregone conclusion that desktop real estate is always in short supply. We're going to approach this design exercise from a decidedly minimalist direction and get all postmodern with the bed, cantilevering support for it up from the circular base assembly. It was a bit of a balancing act getting the center of gravity to cooperate with the minimalist footprint, but the result is actually quite slick.

What You Need

Here's your shopping list:

You'll need some hardwood. If you have a table saw or a band saw, you can rip everything you need from 2 feet of 1" x 6" clear (knot-free) maple, which should set you back less than a sawbuck at your local lumberyard. If you're of an "alternative sourcing" bent, you're looking for a chunk of *solid* hardwood — veneer over MDF ain't gonna cut it. Softwood won't do either: if it smells like Christmas trees or pencils when you cut it, keep looking.

If you're more comfortable working with premilled stock, big-box home centres usually have a selection of what they call "hobby wood" available. You'll need 4 feet of 1" x 1" (which is actually about 7/8" x 7/8"), and a couple of feet of 3/8" x 4" or similar.

You'll also need:

- A decommissioned 10" table saw blade, or a piece of 1/8" plate steel, about 3x6". If you've taken the time to earn a black belt in Scrap Yard, you should have no trouble sourcing a piece of 316L alloy surgical stainless steel, which is the absolute business as a material for frighteningly sharp blades.
- A foot of 3/16" hardwood dowel for pinning joints.
- An inch of 1/4" ID brass tubing and an inch of 5/16" ID brass tubing. It's fairly critical that the two different diameters of brass tubing nest together smoothly. We're making bushings, doncha know.
- An inch of 1/4–20 all-thread and 2 acorn nuts.
- 3 inches of 3/8 all-thread and 5 acorn nuts.
- A pound of lead.[1]
- 6" x 6" of 18 gauge sheet brass or aluminum.
- 6" of 1½" brass pipe.
- 12" of 1/8" brass rod.
- A few other miscellaneous screws, nuts, and bolts.

Or not. We're working on our improvisational skills, so feel free to redesign/respec on the fly.

The Prebuild Pep Talk

You don't need to be "good with wood" to complete this build, although it may help somewhat. My personal approach to traditional woodworking is oblique at best, but as with most things, common sense and adaptable basic skills go a long way towards bridging the gap towards competency.

Human Resources people treat my résumé like it's toxic. I've worked in an *ambitious* number of fields. After you've learned the tricks of enough trades, you start to recognize basic skills and practices that are valuable — regardless of the actual endeavour. If you have these, you can build this project. If you don't have these basic skills, learn them real soon.

1. **Protect yourself.**
   Know your tools, know your materials, know your environment, and know what you're making. Know how they can hurt you. Know how to prevent it. Show them respect.

2. **Do #1 all the time.**
   I mean it, dammit. Don't make me come over there and whack you in the belly with a trout.

3. **Understand what you're doing.**
   Knowing the purpose of the components as well as the overall *gestalt* of the finished thing is a step toward achieving that one-with-the-project Maker Zen we're all trying to experience again.

4. **Be efficient.**
   Jigs and templates are our friends

5. **Measure twice.**
   Before cutting or gluing. That includes knowing how to accurately read and mark a dimension, and knowing how

1 Wanna get adventurous and try doing the "melt and pour" thing? You can likely scrounge up what you need with a trip to the service station to cadge a handful of old wheel weights. Those of you with less of a devil-may-care attitude towards heavy metals can make do with a sack of lead birdshot from BillyBob's Burger, Beer, and Bullet Barn. You won't be able to get as much weight onto the blade assembly as with a solid-cast block, but you won't be dealing with the inherent risks of working with molten metal either. Weigh the advantages.

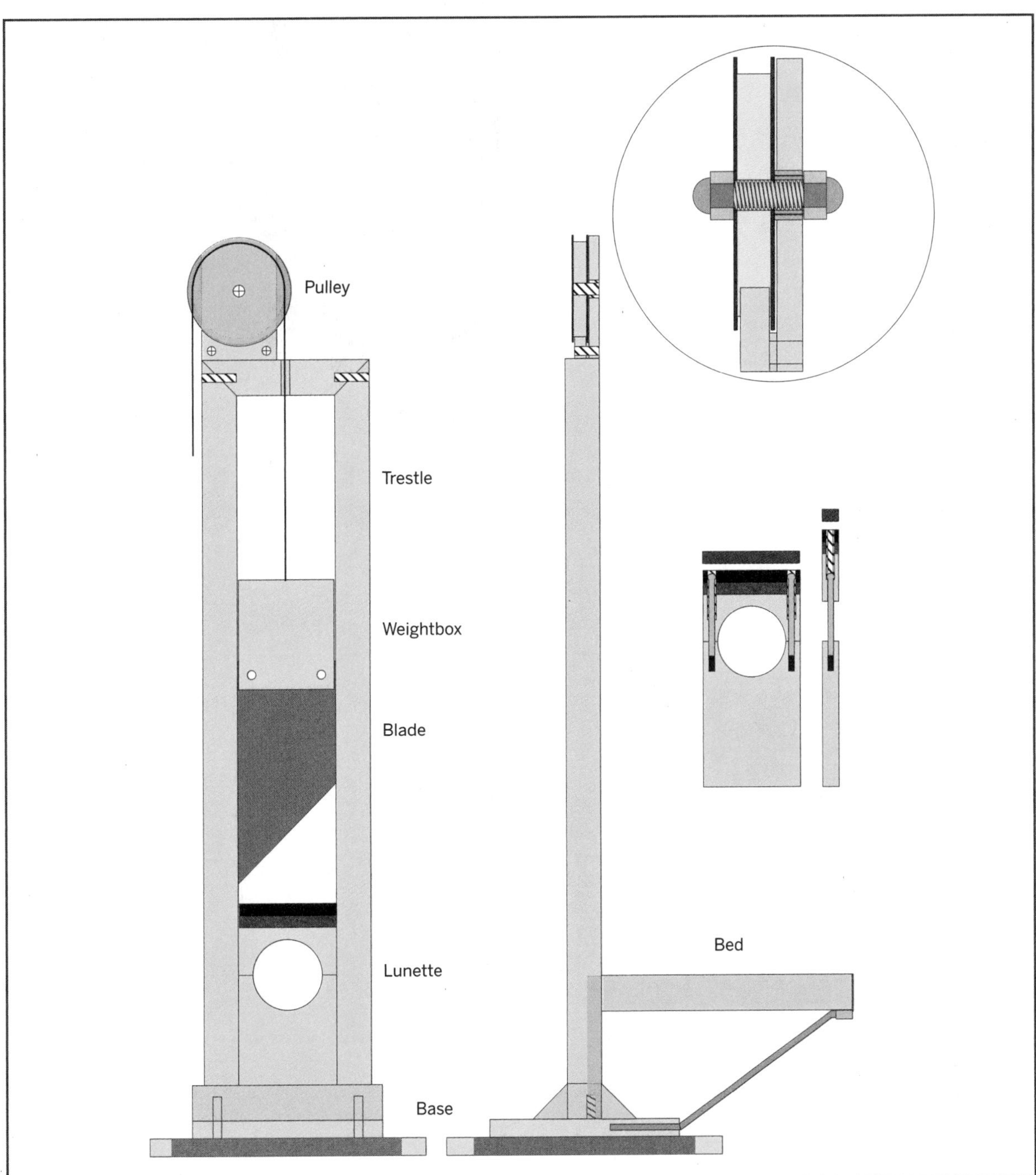

Figure 02.01: **Illustrated guillotine nomenclature, plus fabrication details.**

to accurately set up your tools and use them to spec. Do not take an angle for granted. Check your work. Put it together properly. The right bits in the right spot. Check your angles. Use clamps.

6. **Know when you're right.**
   Errors happen. Check your work against the drawing, check the drawing against common sense. Go with the *right* decision.

7. **Plan ahead.**
   Understand the sequence of events. Optimize it. This makes #8 easier.

8. **Be patient.**
   With the right attitude, it's all just measuring, cutting, and gluing. Just like kindergarten.

Now hit the shop and build a guillotine.

Figure 02.02: Tablesaw, featherboard and white maple. (Coming soon: sawdust.) Leave your blade guard and kerf splitter in place, kids...safety first, remember?

The Build

We'll work through this one subassembly at a time, starting with the main trestle structure.

I'm using maple that I milled out of a shipping pallette. "Skid wood" is a time-honored material source for improvisational fabrication. The base-level quality has gone downhill in recent years, but if you pay attention, you can recover a lot of good quality local hardwood lumber from skids you pull out of dumpsters. Notice the term "local hardwood." It's amazing what they make skids out of in other countries. Besides the ubiquitous maple,[2] I've had oak, birch, some tropical variant of walnut, and Brazilian cherrywood (aka Jabota) come through the shop in the past six months — well worth the time and effort spent in disassembly, nail pulling, and milling. If you're using premilled stock, you lucky devil, this is the fun you're missing.

If you buy planked lumber, say, 1" x 5" white maple, at a retail outlet, the first thing you'll notice is that it's not actually 1" x 5". That's right: the guy at the lumberyard lied to you. Or maybe the idiot at the mill that sawed it couldn't use a tape measure. Either way, you got screwed, and dammit, you're gonna sue!

No, not really. The wood *was* 1" x 5" when they milled the plank green out of a recently-deceased-and-still-drippin'-with-sap maple tree. By the time that it kiln-dries down to 6–12% water content, it's shrunk a tad. There are different standard dimensions (both nominal and actual) for hard and soft woods, which adds further confusion, and the residual moisture content (and shrinkage/expansion factor from nominal) in the chunk of wood you're holding in your hand is directly related to the local environmental conditions. Cutting to the chase, the moral of the story is "measure twice, cut once, and your chunk of wood is likely 4¾" x ⅞" x 43½" long with neither edge being particularly well dressed."

If you're using a table saw, I assume you've done an accurate setup on it for blade and fence angle, fence gauge accuracy, and miter gauge accuracy. If you haven't done that yet, go do it now.

But first, let's talk about *glue*. You've got some, and you're gonna use it. You specifically acquired wood glue — real carpenters' wood glue. Not "glue-all," not rubber cement, not "Kray-Z Gloo," not mucilage, not paste. Not *anything* that is not specifically wood glue. Got it? Now take some time to learn about it.

Test the glue on scraps of your stock. Try different quantities of glue and different grain orientations, and clamp them up properly. When you're tightening the clamps, watch to see if the joint "skates" out of alignment on the glue as it disperses. Some glues are better than others at avoiding this, and old glue that's thickened a bit from

2 As a citizen of the Great White North, I am legally mandated to cite recognized Canadian Cultural Identity Icons at intervals proscribed by the Ministry of Trade, Culture, and Northern Affairs. Coming up this hour: Back Bacon, Hockey, and the drummer from Rush.

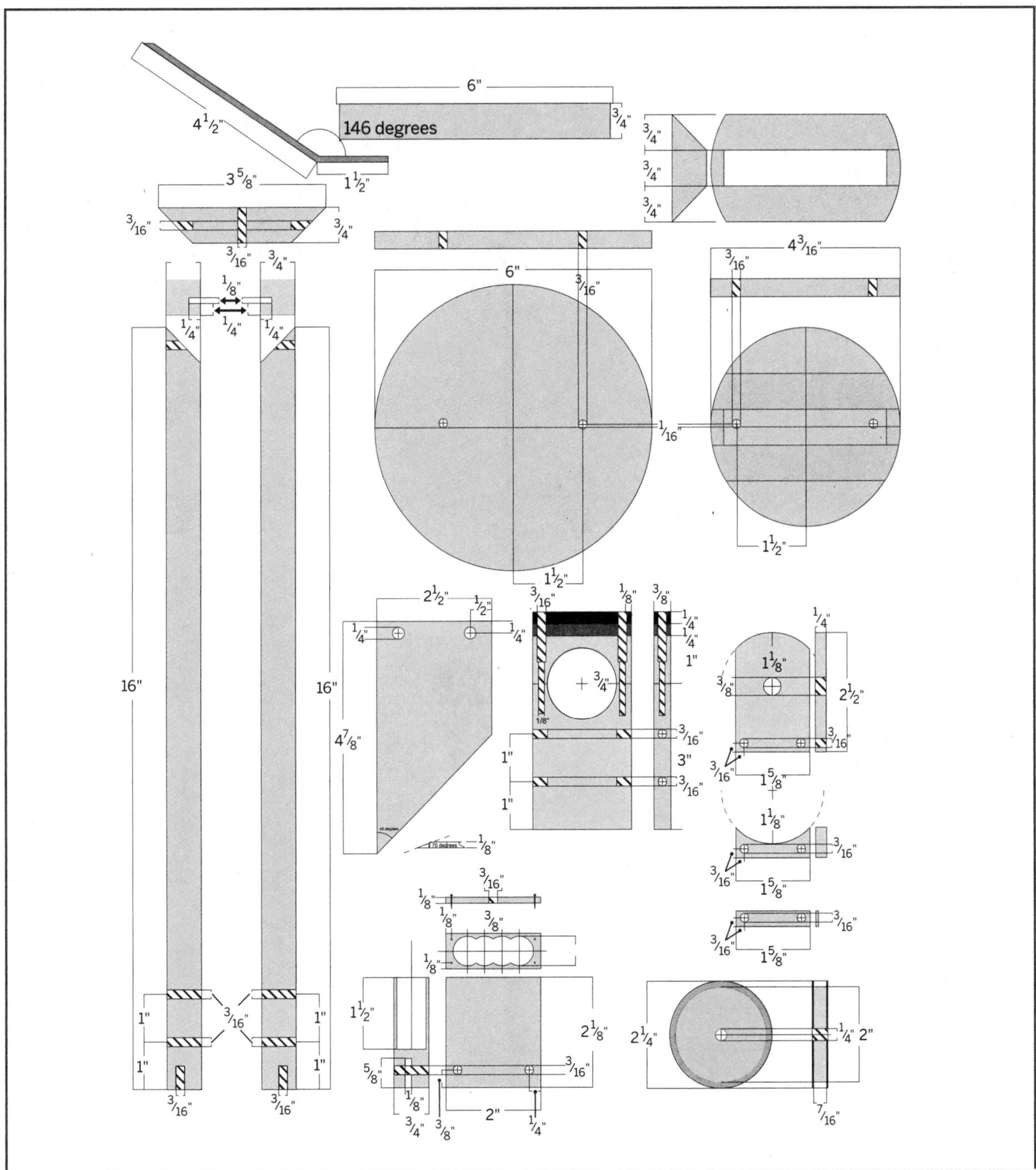

Figure 02.03: Trestle riser and cross-piece cutting diagram

Figure 02.04: **Standard-issue dirt-cheap-but-surprisingly-accurate mitering saw, which totally pwns the traditional miter box/handsaw combo most people use.**

water loss is *really* prone to it. As long as you're aware of the potential problem, you'll be able to catch any dodgy alignments before they're irreparable.

You should be able to handle the joint safely after two hours, but full curing takes overnight or longer. We get about seven straight months of rain in Vancouver. The relative humidity is pinned at 100% from October 'til April, and there are times when it takes *days* for glue to cure properly. Know your environment, and know your glue.

When your test joints are out of the clamps, check a few of them for rogue glue drips, and see how hard it is to sand them out. Leave a few spill points in place until curing has finished, and compare removing them. Sometimes it's easier one way or another, and it's good to know. Check the joints for discolouration, too. I've seen cases where the glue reacts with the wood and leaves stains that just won't sand out, sometimes in funky colours. I once had a piece of oak turn teal blue on me because of some supposedly miraculous eastern European cabinetmakers' glue. The discolouration did not sand out. So much for the miracles of eastern European cabinetmakers.

Anyway, we gotta cut some wood. Here's my setup for what we're currently doing. I've taken off the blade guard and kerf splitter assembly so you can see what's going on, which means there's not a whole lot separating my fingers and a really sharp

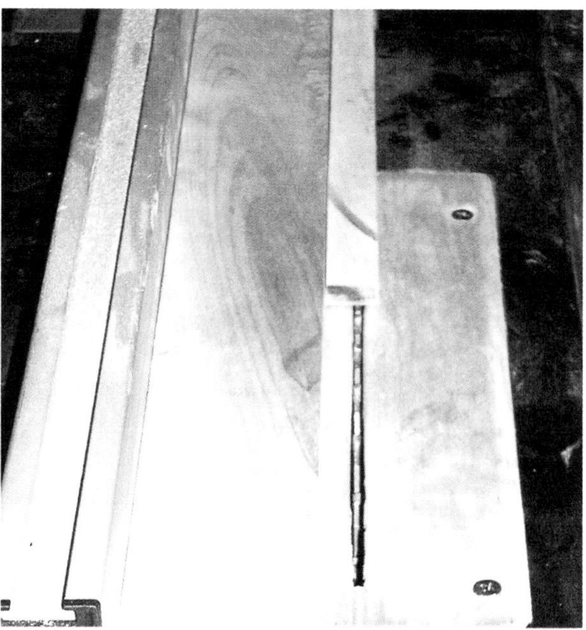

Figure 02.05: **Cutting the blade guide grooves**

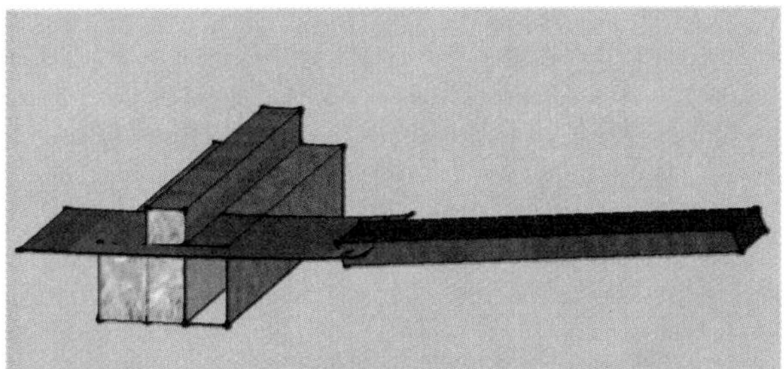

Figure 02.06: Guide blocks + kugihiki = symmetrical slat cutting fiesta time.

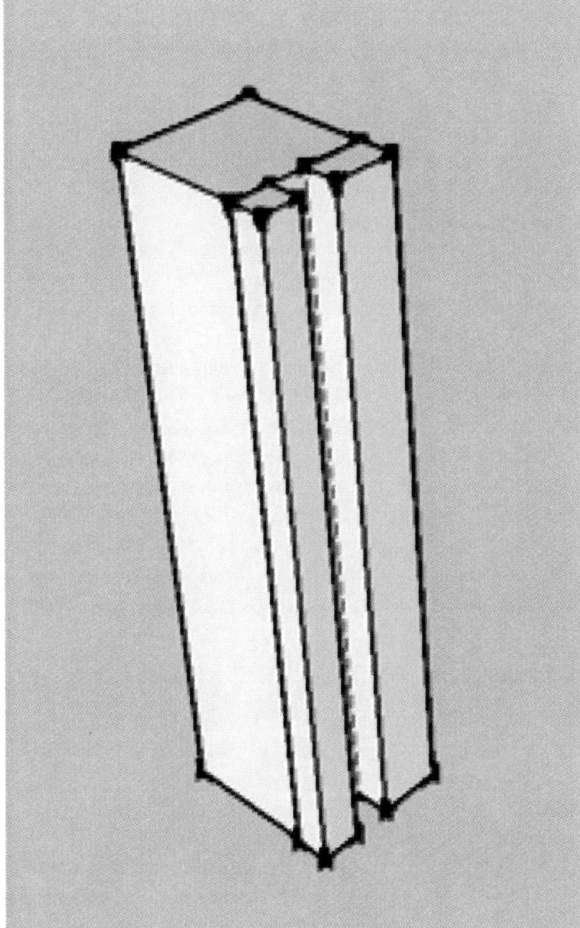

Figure 02.07: Slats + riser + spacer + glue = blade guide grooves

saw blade moving at 5200 RPM. I'm a reckless daredevil who'll do anything for a good picture. Don't try this at home.

Notice the featherboard on the lefthand side of the blade. It's there to hold the stock stable during the cut. They're easy enough to make, and because I am a pleasant and amenable fellow, I have conveniently included a short tutorial on the subject at the end of the next chapter. I have mine clamped onto the sliding miter table on my table saw, which is apparently a feature found only on one manufacturer's machines. Everyone else can just C-clamp the 'board onto the deck of the saw.

Let's rough this out slowly. After ripping ½" from either side to clean up the edges, I'm left with a 3¾" x ⅞" x 45" plank. I set the fence at ¾", make a cut, then run the resulting stick of wood through the saw again — now rotated 90 degrees around the short axis, giving me a nicely dressed ¾" x ¾" piece of stock. The trestle risers and cross piece are cut to dimension as/per the cutting diagram, either on your table saw, or with a mitering saw, or a miter box and handsaw. Use the most accurate one in the house: the 45s you're cutting here are *the* important cut of the whole project. Measure *twice. Cut* once. **[Figure 02.03]**

True up your angle cuts with a protractor and your dead-flat sanding surface, drill the hole for the hoist cable in the crosspiece as detailed, then give 'em all a light sanding with 150 grit.

The risers require a bit more saw work. Depending on your available toolage, you may soon be acquiring a fresh set of cuss words.

Table sawyers will need a zero clearance insert for their saws. Again, easy to fabricate, again, useful how-to helpfully provided by the guy writing the book, at the end of the next chapter. **[Figure 02.04]**

We're gonna need to run grooves down the length of the risers for the blade drop path. Set your blade depth to ¼", and clamp your remaining big piece of wood to the fence to give yourself some finger clearance from the blade path. You want to run a shallow kerf down the length of each riser, 3⁄16" from the *front* of the piece. Practice the cut on some scrap a few times, and pay attention to the orientation of the stock when you feed it into the blade path. It's easy to put your cut in the wrong place. (Been there, done that, trashed about 20 dollars worth of beautiful birdseye maple.) When I'm milling stock out of a larger piece of wood, I usually use the same setup to cut some practice stock out of a piece of softwood 2" x 4", just so I have an exact analog for test cuts.

Those of you without a tablesaw have a few more hoops to jump through, unfortunately. You can form the blade guide groove by cutting and gluing narrow slats of wood onto your main trestle riser. Crude, but effective. **[Figure 02.05]**

A Kugihiki and two guide blocks are the secret to cutting

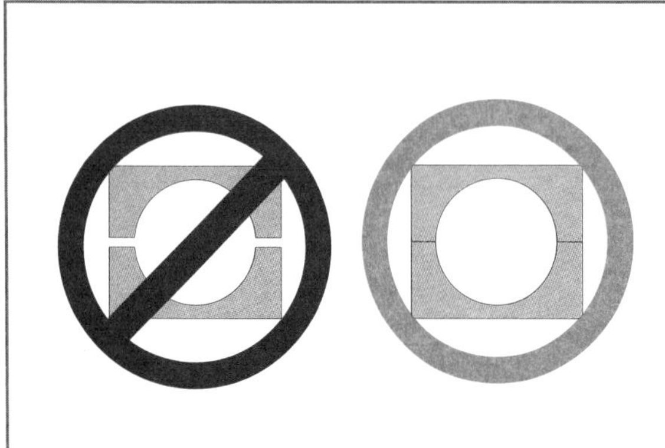

Figure 02.07: **Say "yes" to circular lunette holes.**

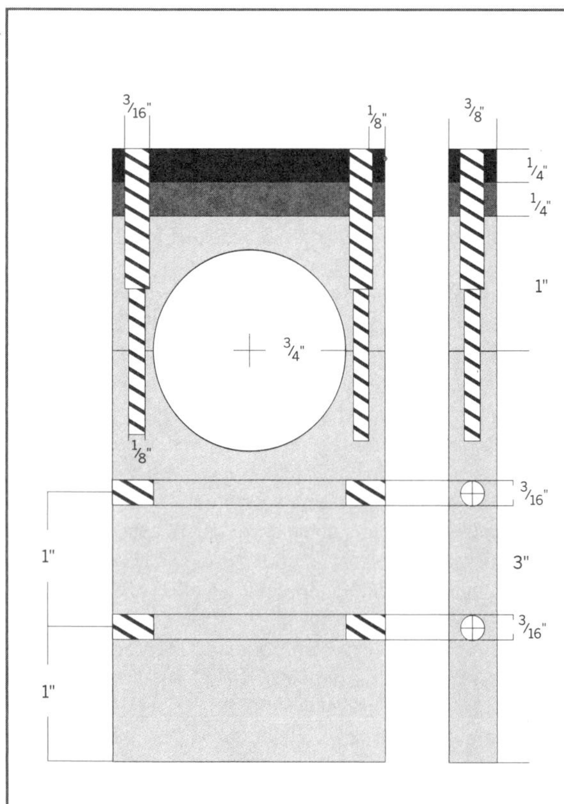

Figure 02.08: **The lunette assembly in detail**

nicely symmetrical slats by hand. Do the glue-ups in stages to ensure solid, flush alignment of one slat with the main riser of the trestle, then attaching the second slat, using scraps of the metal you're using for your blade as spacers. **[Figure 02.06]**

Wrap each spacer with a single layer of masking tape to provide a bit of blade clearance after the fact. Use a reasonable number of clamps, deal with glue spills promptly, and remember to adjust related measurements appropriately to compensate for the modified dimensions. That thing on a guillotine that the poor sod's neck goes into is called . . .

The Lunette

Fabrication requires you to rough out both the top and bottom sections of the assembly, then temporarily join the two before drilling the main lunette opening and the guide holes. **[Figures 02.07, 02.08]**

Why? A true circular hole looks better, which means "remove the kerf *then* drill the hole." Some folks would call it nitpicking. To me, it's attention to detail, and in this case it's not a difficult thing to achieve.

Sand out any machining marks and surface blemishes on the lunette components with 150-grit sandpaper, then glue up the trestle assembly. **[Figure 02.09]**

I will not insult your intelligence by reminding you to use a square and many clamps. Put it aside to cure overnight, and carry on. When it's out of the clamps, mark and drill the holes for the dowels that strengthen the riser to crossbar joint. Cut the dowel pins a bit long, and taper one end slightly for easier insertion. There's no end of suggested methods of applying the glue to dowel pins. I usually drop a dot of glue onto the back of a playing card and roll the pin through it a few times to pick up a thin coat, then tap it into place with a leather-padded hammer. Let the glue cure, then cut the dowel flush with your Kugihiki and sand out any surface irregularities. **[Figure 02.09]**

The Baseplate

The baseplate of the mechanism is composed of big flat wooden planes. You'll need circles 6" and 4" in diameter x 3/8" thick. How you come up with these bits is entirely up to you. With a bit of redesign, you can eliminate them altogether, but what fun is that? I approached the matter by ripping a section of my remaining stock edgewise; after sanding (and accounting for the width of the kerf removed), I had two pieces of maple 3/8" x 3½" x 12". I could just as easily have ripped a succession of 3/8" x 12" x 7/8" slats from the edge of the stock, but I liked the grain structure of the face of the stock.

Either way, glue-up is necessary. If this were a full-size

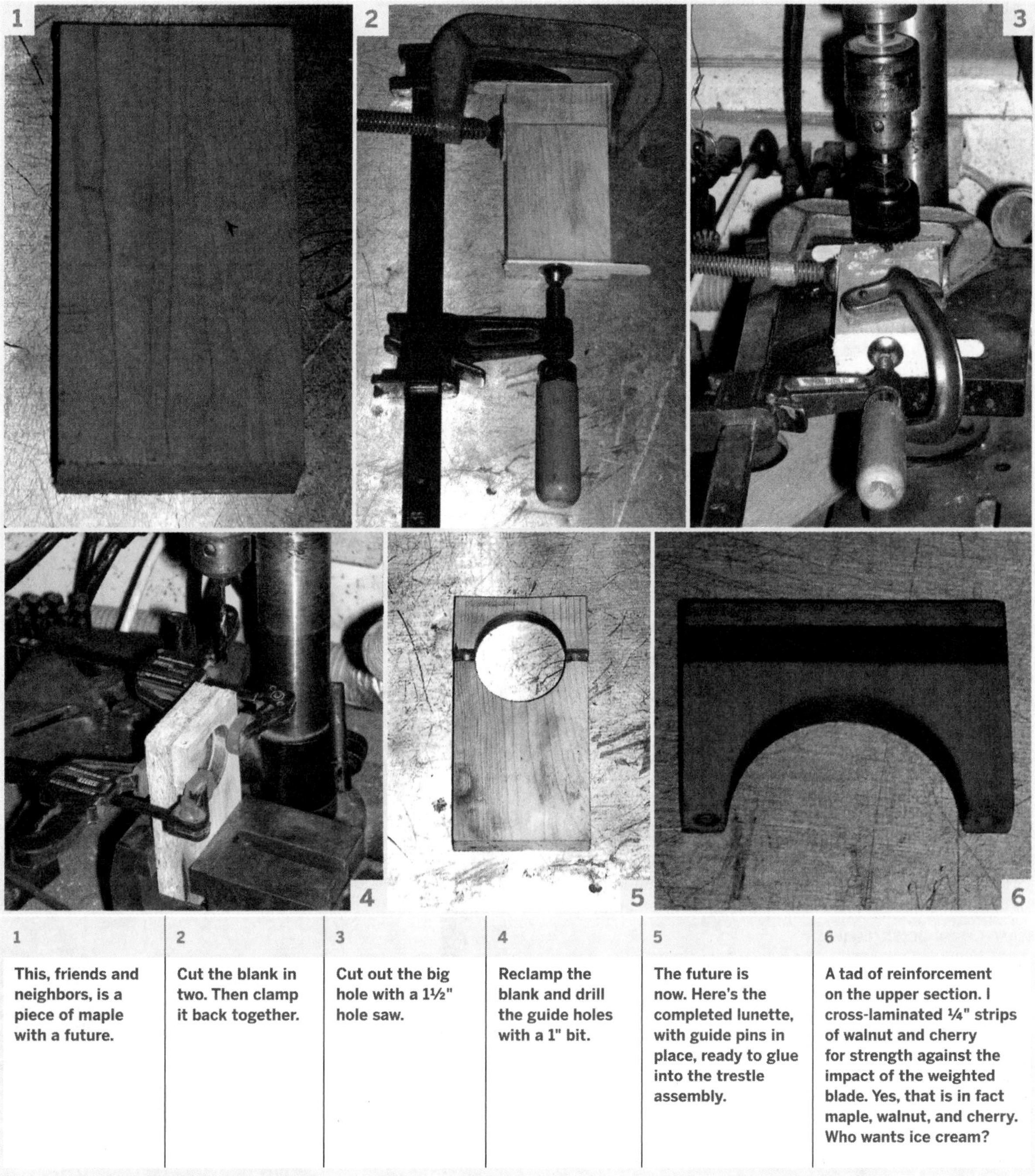

1	2	3	4	5	6
This, friends and neighbors, is a piece of maple with a future.	**Cut the blank in two. Then clamp it back together.**	**Cut out the big hole with a 1½" hole saw.**	**Reclamp the blank and drill the guide holes with a 1" bit.**	**The future is now. Here's the completed lunette, with guide pins in place, ready to glue into the trestle assembly.**	**A tad of reinforcement on the upper section. I cross-laminated ¼" strips of walnut and cherry for strength against the impact of the weighted blade. Yes, that is in fact maple, walnut, and cherry. Who wants ice cream?**

Figure 02.09: **Creating a lunette.**

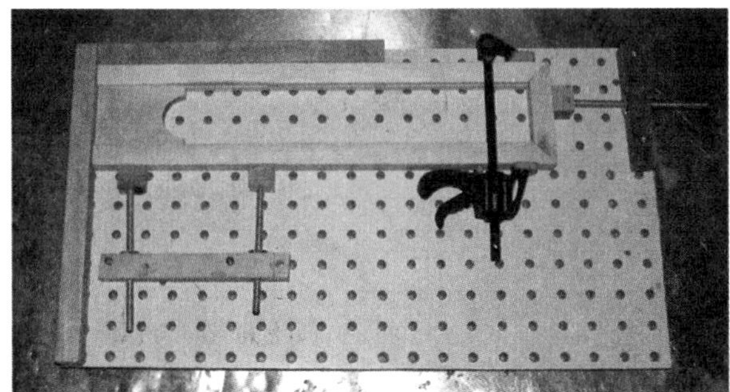

Figure 02.10: **The trestle glue-up. Note the use of the Hand-E Dand-E Eccentric Genius clamping jig construction set. (See the end of this chapter.)**

project with inch-thick slabs of wood to be joined, we'd be using a planer/jointer machine and all manner of pegs and biscuits to ensure a solid set of joints. At this scale, all we need to do is true up the facing edges, apply glue, and clamp 'em up nice and tight.

There are a few pitfalls lying in wait when you're gluing up large flat planes, not the least of which involves the challenge of keeping your large plane flat. Using glue-resistant battens as illustrated wards off the problem. What's that, you say? You don't have any glue-resistant battens? [Figure 02.11]

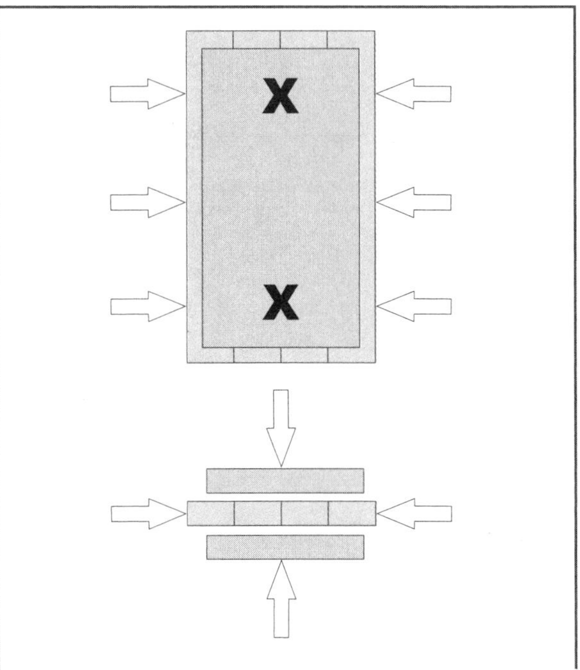

Figure 02.11: **Battens + clamps = nice flat glue-ups**

Sure you do. On my homeworld, we call it "wax paper and scrap plywood." Wipe down the plywood with a damp sponge and harness the surface cohesion of the water to hold the wax paper in place. A more permanent solution to the problem of glue-resistant surfaces (essential for jig making and the like) is Formica-laminated MDF . . . your basic dirt-cheap kitchen-cupboard doors. Avoid antagonizing your mate and/or landlord and resist the urge to plunder the kitchen for your supply of such materials. You're on much safer ground foraging in dumpsters and demolition sites, or looking for sales at your big-box outlet.

Whatever method you opt for, use it *now* and glue up the blank for the two base components. [Figure 02.12]

Figure 02.12: **A daring unassisted circularity correction on the woefully underappreciated Delta 5" belt/disc sander. Degree of difficulty: 4.3. Artistic impression: low 7s.**

After glue-up I had a nice piece of *almost* book matched maple 7 x 12 x +/–3/8". I sanded both sides dead flat with 100-grit paper, marked the center for the two discs that I needed and drew the circles with a compass. I did the cutting on the scroll saw, then trued up the circles with the disk sander, but it would have been almost as easy to do it by hand with a coping saw. Drill the mounting hole for the bed support rod in the 4" disk, then sand out both disks with 150 grit and put them aside until you're ready to glue things together. [Figure 02.13]

The design of this mechanism calls for a tad of hoopjumping

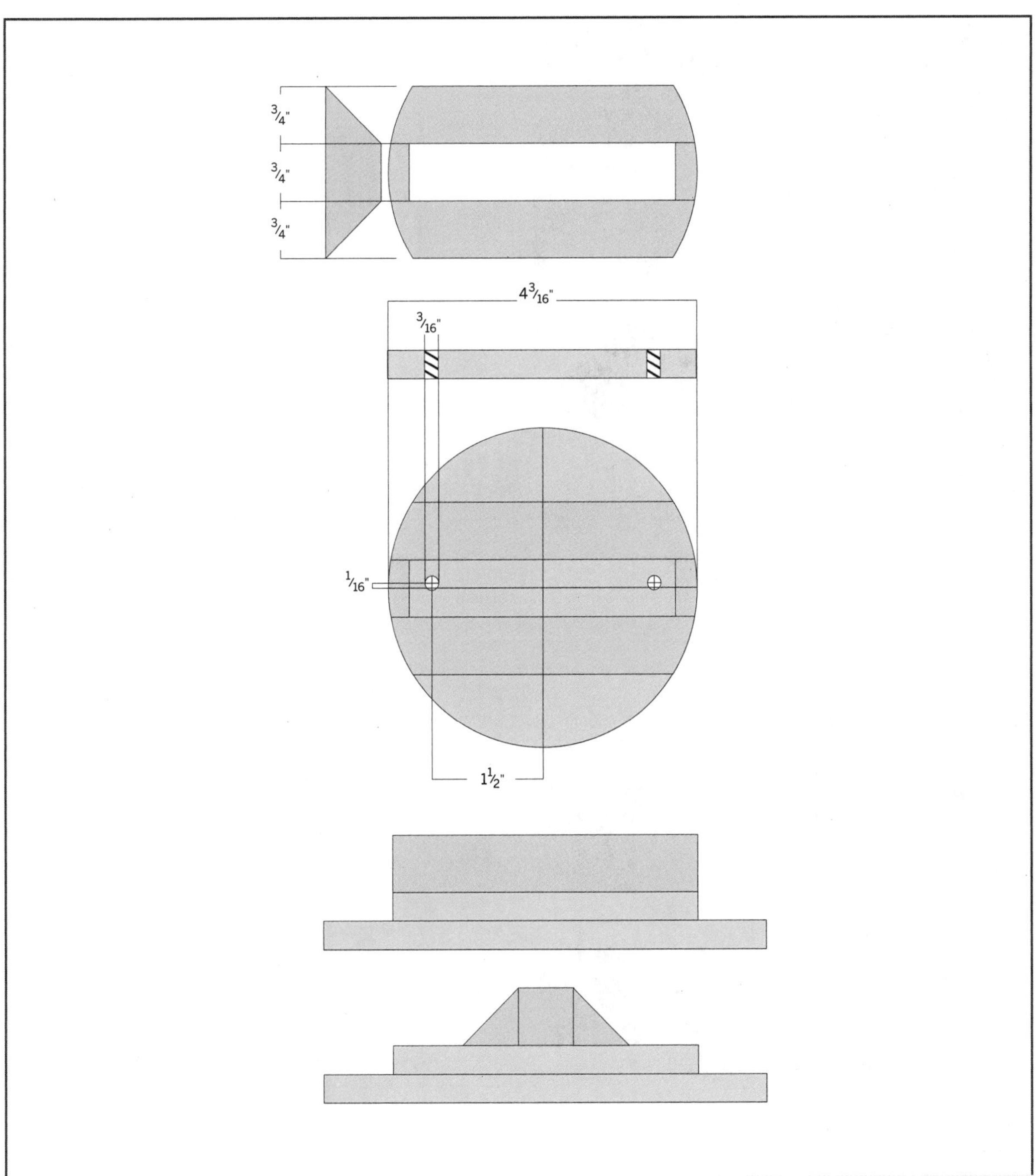

Figure 02.13: **The baseplate and trestle pocket, in modest detail**

Figure 02.14: **The baseplate glue-up in process**

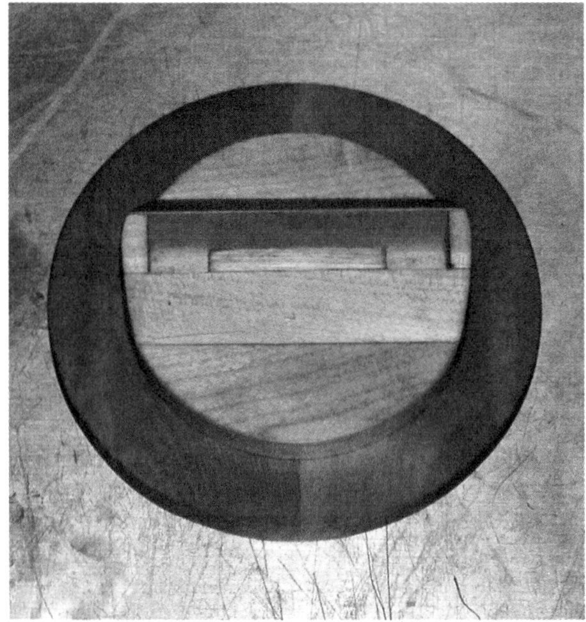

Figure 02.15: **Bueno! Los baseplatos finito!**

to accommodate removal of the blade for sharpening. It's nothing insurmountable, and is definitely made easier and more reliable by framing a pocket for the trestle assembly to slot into and attaching it to the baseplate. This lets you securely and solidly mount and dismount the entire trestle assembly with just two screws, giving you reasonably quick access to the blade for cleaning and sharpening. I had some 45-degree beveled 3/4" maple scrap in the wood crib that I used to form the pocket. Feel free to improvise like crazy.

Once the base glue-up is properly cured, scope it out for errant traces of glue, sand it down to *at least* 320 grit and give it a light once over with extra-fine steel wool and a tack cloth. You're close to being able to apply a finish now: for mine, each of four light applications of boiled linseed oil was allowed to cure overnight, then hand-rubbed to a nice organic glow. **[Figure 02.14, Figure 02.15]**

The Weightbox

The weightbox is a simple affair: size a solid block of maple to fit, and run a 5/8" deep kerf across the bottom, positioned as shown to accommodate the razor sharp chunk of metal what's gonna be doing the actual chopping. **[Figure 02.16]**

Drill the blade mounting bolt holes, then hollow out the remainder of the block. Forstner bits let you drill overlapping holes with comparative ease, so I chucked a 5/8" bit into the drill press and drilled a series of 1 1/2" deep holes. Your toolage/technique may vary, but the goal is the same: make space in the wood for lead. If you've opted to use lead shot as mass, it's just a question of pouring it in and sealing it up. **[Figure 02.17, Figure 02.18]**

CAUTION: If you're planning on pouring molten metal, exercise proper caution: Lead melts at *stovetop temperatures* (327.5 °C, 621.5 °F) but it's a scandalously toxic substance prone to accumulation in our body tissues. Get a portable hotplate and do the melting outdoors, or under an industrial-strength fume hood. I use a thick-walled stainless steel sample jar as a crucible; a small capacity cast iron pot would do the job too. You're looking for something you can pour from accurately. Inspect your crucible before each melt since burning through the bottom of your pot is always a possibility, and generally an unpleasant event. Lead is *eutectic*, meaning it changes state rapidly: from solid to liquid and back in a fraction of a degree temperature range. It also retains heat like a demon: Just because it's back to being solid doesn't mean it's not still flesh charringly hot.

Be careful.

Let me repeat that: *Be careful.*

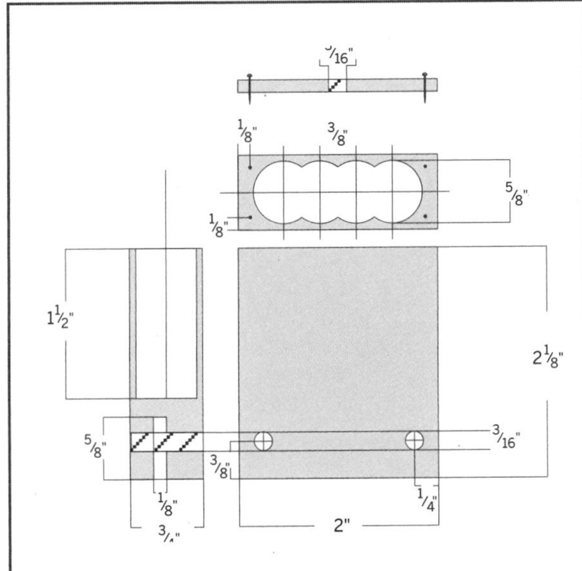

Figure 02.16: **The weightbox in detail: start with a solid block of maple and apply drills and saws to taste.**

Figure 02.17: **The hollowed-out weightbox: little does it suspect the horrors soon to befall it at the hands of a crucible full of molten lead.**

Figure 02.18: **The weightbox, post-pour. It'll take at least 30 minutes to cool to the point where it can be comfortably handled. Patient: be the adjective, or be the noun.**

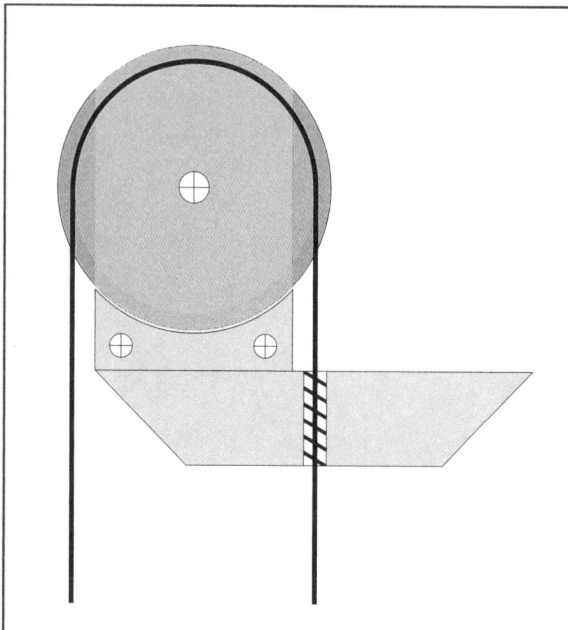

Figure 02.19: **The pulley assembly, in theory**

Figure 02.20: **Kwik-N-Ezee Guillotine rigging, courtesy of one honkin' big pulley.**

As shown, clamp your weight box into a vise for stability. As an added bonus, the vise jaws act as a heat sink and draw off some of the heat of the metal, which helps prevent scorching. Wear appropriate protective equipment, and take the job seriously. You've seen that guy on the talk shows flipping molten lead out of the crucible with his bare hands? You're not him. Don't be stupid.

Once you've weighted the box, glue and brad the top in place and put it aside for final finishing.

The Pulley

We need a pulley to guide the cord used to raise the blade into "armed 'n' dangerous mode." Fortunately, this is another dead-simple bodge. I've previously used as many as four pulleys on a guillotine, resulting in picturesque but needlessly complex rigging. In this case, we're using a single honkin' big one to get the job done. Now, your basic retail pulley is somewhat of a cipher: often elusive, usually priced like it's made of precious metal, and rarely stylin' in any way, shape or form. If the sourcing deities smile on you in the form of a suitable cable guiding system, honour them with a high-quality goat sacrifice. The rest of us have to fabricate from scratch. Lathe owners, or those among you who have successfully navigated the fabrication path of the Drillpress Lathe described at the end of Chapter 7 can get on with the task of custom-turning your pulley. The dimensions are detailed here, and on the cutting diagram. If you've changed the trestle width, adjust the diameter accordingly. **[Figure 02.19, Figure 02.20, Figure 02.21]**

But you knew that.

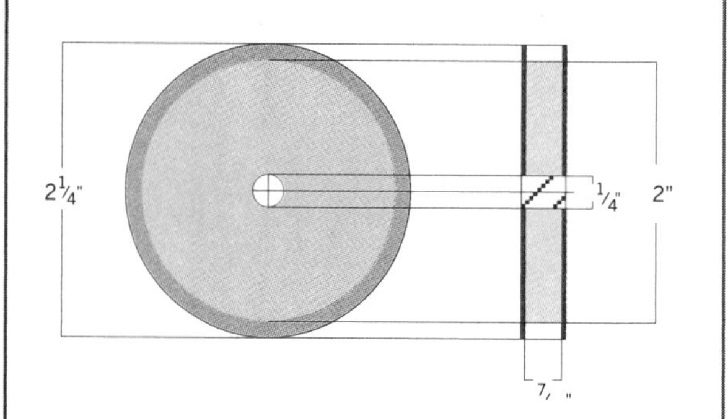

Figure 02.21: **Pulley dimensions that work, providing that you haven't changed the overall width of the trestle, blade and/or weight box, in which case you'll have to adjust accordingly or it just plain won't function, Bunkie, so don't come crying to me if it doesn't and don't say I didn't warn you, because I did.**

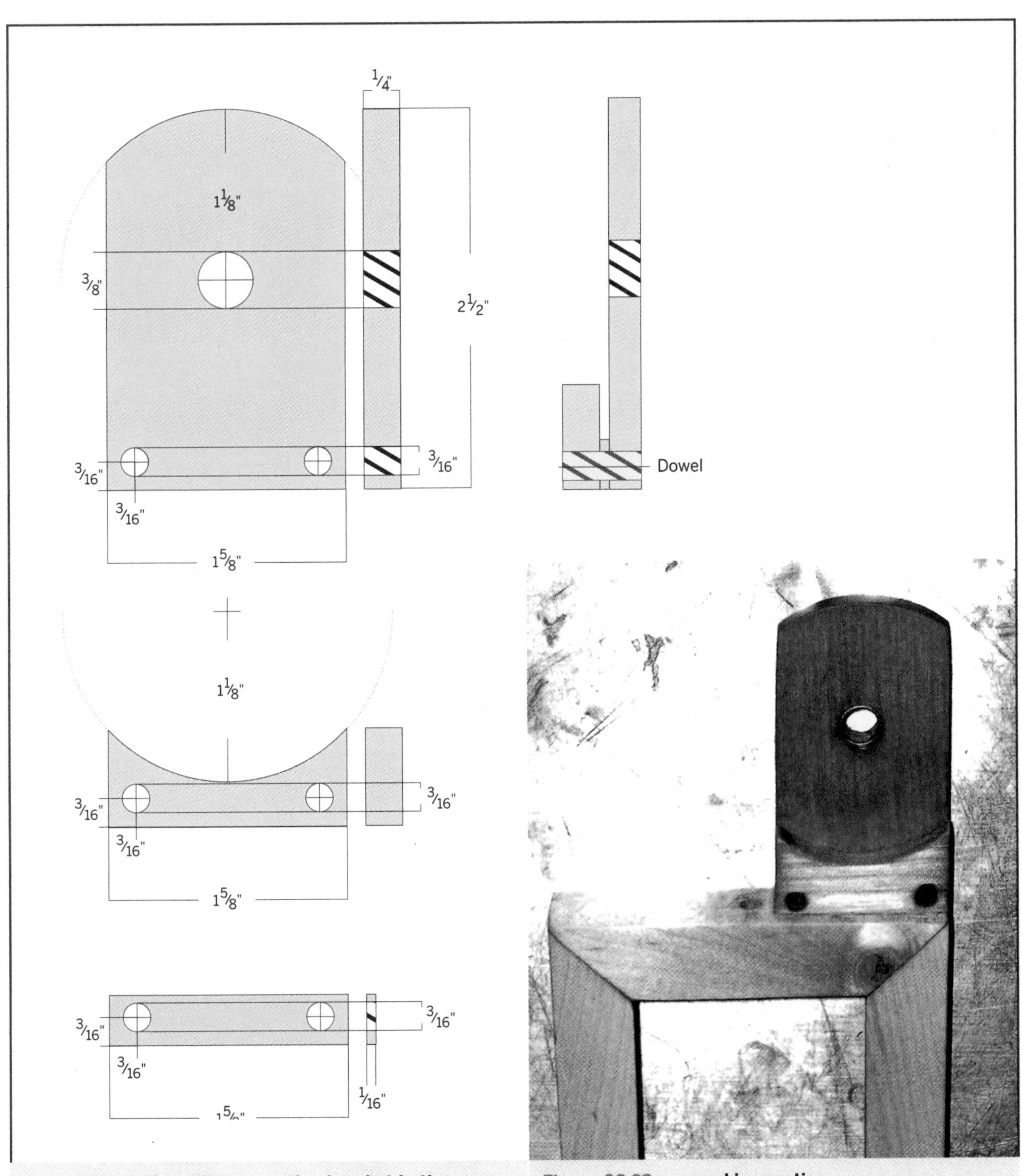

Figure 02.22: The pulley mounting bracket in theory . . .

Figure 02.23: . . . and in practice.

Lacking a lathe, chuck a 2" hole saw and cut a circle out of 1⁄2" (or thereabouts) maple. There's the core of your pulley, about 1 15⁄16" diameter, complete with perfectly centered 1⁄4" mounting hole. If you want to proceed with an all-wood pulley, at this stage you can secure a 1⁄4-20 bolt through the mounting hole with two nuts and a lockwasher, chuck it into your drill, and grind a shallow groove into the circumference of the wooden disk with your choice of abrasives. It doesn't need to be excessively deep: 1⁄16" is enough if it's well defined. Alternately, you can use a 2 1⁄4" holesaw to cut two larger disks from 3⁄16" plywood and sandwich all three together to form your pulley. Feel free to improvise.

I like brass, so I went with a brass-wood-brass sandwich. I marked the center points of a pair of 2 1⁄4" circles onto a piece of 18-gauge brass plate, traced the outlines with a compass, and cut them out on the scroll saw. I assembled the sandwich using two-part epoxy glue, and clamped it in my wood vise until it was cured. This design gave me the aesthetic I was after with relative ease, and let me get a tad fancy with the next step of the process.

The Pulley Mounting Bracket

It's another wood sandwich kinda thing, designed for stability and smooth operation. Quarter-inch ID brass tubing is used as a bushing to minimize friction: Cut it about 1⁄32" longer than the thickness of the main bracket component and epoxy it into place with the excess protruding towards the pulley side where it can act as a spacer and keep the pulley surface from contacting the bracket. The curved lower portion is cut from the piece of wood you cut the pulley core from, with the thickness reduced a tad with a bit of judicious sanding. I used a section of a fudgsicle stick for the middle spacer, and held the whole thing together with glue and a pair of 3⁄16" dowels. There's a lot of finicky little detail sanding needed on this assembly, which I advise doing as you shape each component; that way is *lots* easier than trying to negotiate the nooks and crannies after glue-up. When the assembly is complete, position and glue it in place on the trestle. I set a couple of finishing brads through the spacer section into the trestle crosspiece to really secure the joint, but frankly, it was overkill. Once again, consult the cutting diagram or your workpiece for specifics. **[Figure 02.22, Figure 02.23]**

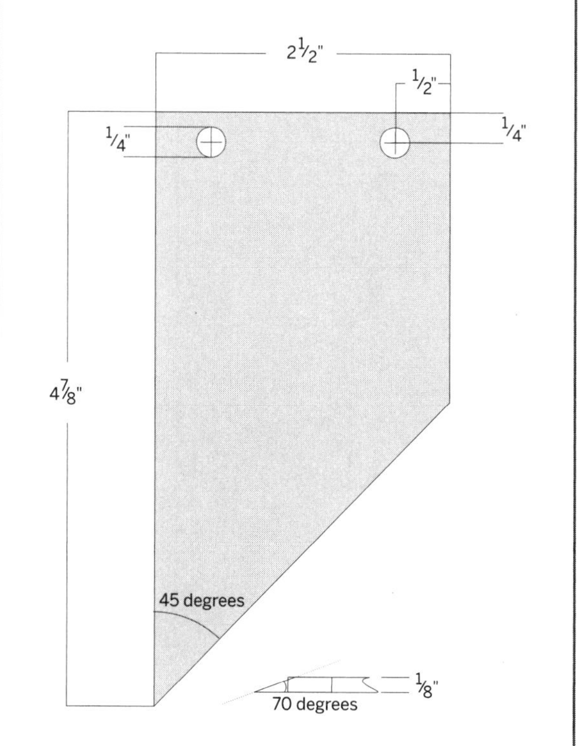

Figure 02.24: **The blade: the crux of the guillotine biscuit, as it were. Your dimensions may vary.**

The Blade

Rough out the blade with a hacksaw or the ubiquitous Dremel. You're cutting exceptionally hard metal, so work slowly, and avoid excessive heat-of-friction accumulation, which could break the temper of the metal and diminish its strength. True up the dimensions and angles of the rough blank with patient, determined filework, and slightly round all edges and corners except for the cutting edge. When the blade drops during use it is essentially in freefall; you can go a long way toward minimizing friction and resistance by simply smoothing out the rough edges. **[Figure 02.24]**

The cutting edge that you'll be forming is similar to a chisel's: one side gets a 70-degree angle. Rough in the bevel with a coarse file, then gradually refine the edge with progressively finer abrasives. The angle isn't *critically* important, but the closer you get to it, the better for making mit der awezumslicenchoppen. **[Figure 02.25]**

Surface finishing the rest of the blade is optional: I generally

Figure 02.25: **The blade**

content myself with achieving that brushed metal look popular with mid-70s consumer electronic products, using medium steel wool and a bit of elbow grease. A mirror-finish buff-up is entirely possible with the expenditure of prodigious time and energy.

The Bed

The bed is cut from a 6" piece of 1½" brass tubing. I used a piece of a scrapyard kitchen sink union. Mark lengthwise cut lines at 0 and 180 degrees as shown, and make your cuts with the metal-separating tool of your choice. **[Figure 02.26, Figure 02.27, Figure 02.28]**

The bed support bracket is nothing more than 6" of artfully bent ⅛" brass rod. One end fits into the mounting hole that you drilled into the 4" base disk, the other end slots into the piece of ⅛" ID brass tube you're about to solder onto the rear of the bed itself.

A propane torch, acid flux, and plumber's solder combo is the de facto standard method of soldering brass together. An electronics soldering iron isn't up to the task, due to the heat-sinking properties of large masses of metal, which suck heat away from the site as quickly as your 20-watt pencil can produce it. I managed to get a workable solder joint on a test set-up with one of those Weller pistol-grip soldering guns, but it took about 20 minutes to get the bed area hot enough to pre-tin. It's doable, but why bother, when a proper torch is cheap, easy, and useful for so many other things (plumbing repair, paint removal, caramelizing your crème brûlée . . . the list is endless).

Cut your ⅛" tubing to length, clean both surfaces with a bit of emery cloth, and apply a *small* dab of flux to the target area. (See **Figure 02.29**, and be careful with that clamp, Eugene... crushed tubing is never pretty.) Clamp the components together *snugly* (brass is soft — don't crush your bits), apply heat from the underside of the material until the flux smokes off, then touch the tip of your solder wire to the hot metal surface. It'll flow where it's needed. You're not welding here: this is *not* a strong-like-bull joint, but it's enough for our purposes. **[Figure 02.30]**

Let the joint cool and clean off the the remnants of the flux with a toolbrush and a bit of damp baking soda. You'll need to drill a small-diameter hole where the bed intersects the curve of the lunette for mounting purposes, then get ready to buff it up. **[Figure 02.31]**

Finishing

Glorioski! We've run out of stuff to fabricate (mostly). All that's left is getting the surfaces looking good, and putting the whole thing together.

Spend as long as necessary finishing the wood. Two coats of Uranium Yellow spraypaint and a Half Life logo sticker on the weightbox oughta take a few hours at best (but will non-the-less rOxxOr at your next LAN party). Full French Polishing will keep you occupied for several months, and cost you the love of a good and decent woman.

Good surface preparation is the secret to a good wood finish. How you prep for finishing is dictated by your choice of wood and finishing compound. Libraries' worth of instructional books have been written on the subjects, and knowledgable opinions on same are everywhere. One universally agreed-upon consensus regarding surface preparation is that fresh sandpaper is essential. Keep a full range of grades in stock, and use it and toss it frequently. Surface prepping's secret weapon? Scrapers are *the* unsung hero; the learning curve can be frustrating — but once mastered, they can cut your prep time in half. And unlike sandpaper, they can be resharpened.

In the case of this piece, done in maple, I sanded all surfaces down with 320-grit aluminum oxide sandpaper, then

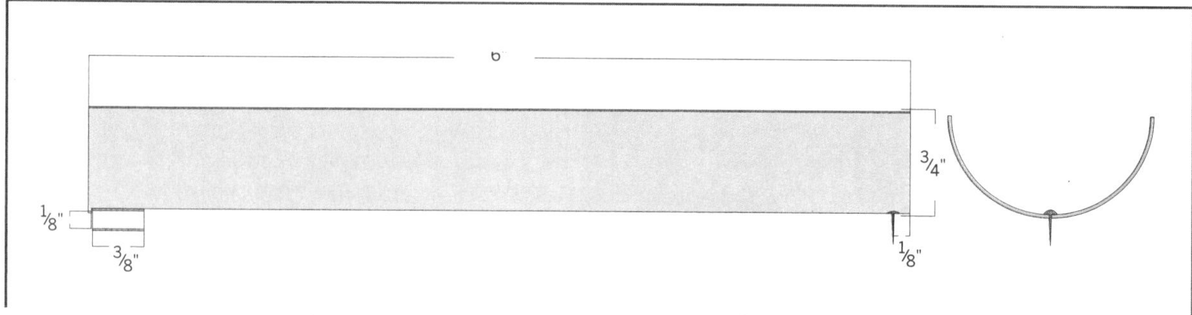

Figure 02.26: **The bed, in detail**

Figure 02.27: **Marking the cut lines needed to accurately perform the tubing bisection**

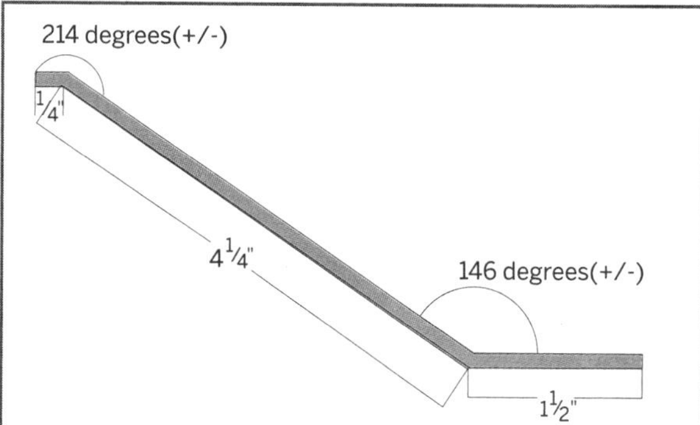

Figure 02.28: **The bed support bracket**

gave the wood a light once-over with extra-fine steel wool.

The finish I used was four light coats of boiled linseed oil, with 24 hours cure time, a light steel-wooling between each coat, and a final hand buffing. If you're not sure what to use, ask the oldest guy at the counter of your local paint store what *he* would suggest, then follow the instructions on the package. I've detailed my personal approach to finishes in Chapter 11. Surface prep is just a matter of patience, fresh sandpaper at regular intervals, and a light touch.

I have a fairly standard routine for finishing brass that makes it look the way I expect brass to look. Your expectations (and results) may vary. As with wood finishing, patience and a light touch are essential.

You'll need lacquer thinner, steel wool in a variety of grades from medium to extra fine, emery paper in a variety of grades, a tube of regular white toothpaste and an old T-shirt to use as rags.

Unlacquered brass can be cleaned of corrosion with medium

Figure 02.29: **Clean and flux the facing surfaces, then clamp the tubing to the bed.**

Figure 02.30: **Heat from the underside with a propane torch, then apply plumbers' solder to the fluxed area.**

Figure 02.31: **Cool, clean, and pat yourself resoundingly on the back.**

steel wool. With repurposed brass, there's a good chance that it's been heavily laquered to preserve that blindingly bright gloss. It's gotta come off. Reach for the thinner.

If you can fully immerse the brass, more the better; otherwise make do with medium steel wool soaked in thinner. It'll take several cycles of "soak steelwool, rub like crazy, soak steelwool" to lay bare the alloy, but perseverance and a light touch will be rewarded.

Once the bare metal is exposed, clean up any surface imperfections (and there are bound to be a few . . . besides resisting corrosion, lacquering is used to effectively conceal any number of manufacturing sins) with the finest-grade emery paper possible, and give the metal light but thorough rubdowns with fine and extra-fine steel wool. You should now be able to use a rag and small amounts of buffing compound (okay, toothpaste) to bring a near mirror finish to the metal. Work small areas at a time, and be patient; the results are very satisfying.

Of course, a cloth wheel on a bench grinder with commercial rubbing compound will get the job done in a flash with admirable results as well. There's a really gloopy Turtle Wax rubbing compound I highly recommend, if you're of a commercial bent.

Once the surfaces are as shiny as you want them to be, you can apply a protective coating to ward off the evil forces of corrosion. You may want to try a few coats of clear lacquer. Personally, I've never been fond of the look. I'll use a quick hit of an acrylic floor polish if I want that "Brite 'N Shinee" thing. I prefer a quick wipedown with WD-40 for inhibiting corrosion, which leaves the metal surface looking more like metal and less like some space-age plastic.

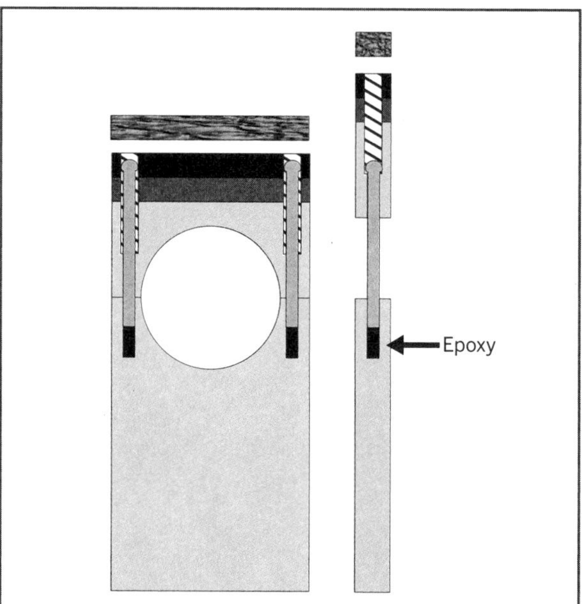

Figure 02.32: **The hidden mysteries of the lunette revealed!!**

Assembly

Putting this thing together is a piece of cake if you paid attention during fabrication and made all the bits the right shape and size. If not, you're hooped. **[Figure 02.32]**

Cut two pieces of brass rod 2⅛" long. These are your lunette guides. Use a small hammer to peen a dome onto one end of each; your aim is to widen and round out the top slightly. The brass is soft and will cooperate with you. Why are you doing this? To capture the upper section of the lunette. Use two-part epoxy adhesive *sparingly* to lock the guide pins in place on the lower lunette section, and cap the upper section with a strip of belt leather attached with double-faced tape. This cushions the impact of the blade and weightbox during use.

The blade must be positioned in the guide slots before mounting the trestle assembly into the pocket on the base. Use countersunk 1¼" #6 brass screws through the bottom of the base to secure the trestle. **[Figure 02.33]**

In a burst of artsy-fartsy nonsense, I used 8-24 threaded rod and acorn nuts to attach the weightbox to the blade. Notice the orientation of the blade: the bevel of the cutting edge is on the outside, the flat side flush to the lunette. **[Figure 02.34]**

Cut a piece of ¼" ID brass tubing to length. What length? You want it about 1⁄32" longer than the piece of tube you've already set into the pulley mountng bracket. Brass on brass bushings are a surprisingly effective substitute for a traditional ballbearing assembly (called a "race" by those who oughta know). You'll be amazed at how smooth and solid the action is when you get it set up right. **[Figure 02.35, Figure 02.36]**

Stringing the hoist cord is next. I use a length of the 70/30 cotton-polyester handyman's chalkline that I normally use to string the torsion skeins of ballistae and mangonels.

In keeping with the minimalist aesthetic of this enterprise, there's no trigger mechanism involved: just a cord attached to the blade with a knob on the other end to hold onto. Get artistic with your choice of knob. I'm using a knurled brass thumbnut that originated on a thrift-shop pepper mill.

Here's a neat trick for doing a blind attachment of a cord or cable. You can use it on both ends of the hoist cord. Drill through the end of an acorn nut with a hole slightly larger than the diameter of the cord you're using. Run the cord through the hole, and tie a *large* retention knot to prevent the

Figure 02.33: **Position the blade in the guide grooves, then slot the trestle assembly into the pocket on the baseplate. Nice burst of jargon, huh?**

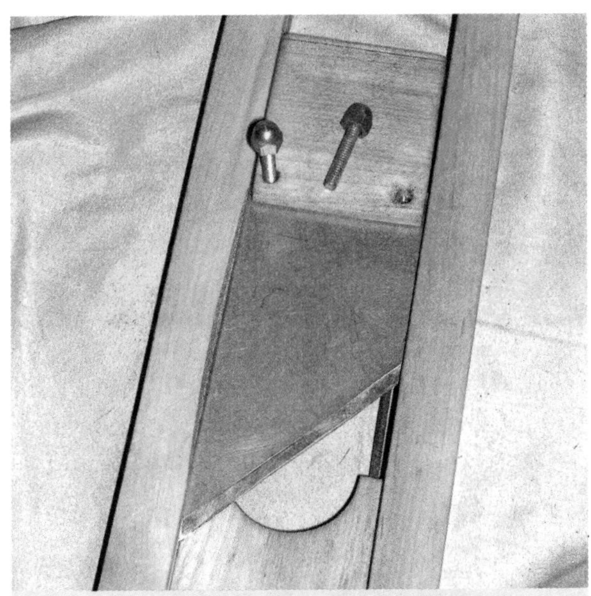

Figure 02.34: **Bolt the weightbox onto the blade.**

Figure 02.35: **Bushing, yes! Bearings, no! Pulley and bushings prior to mounting.**

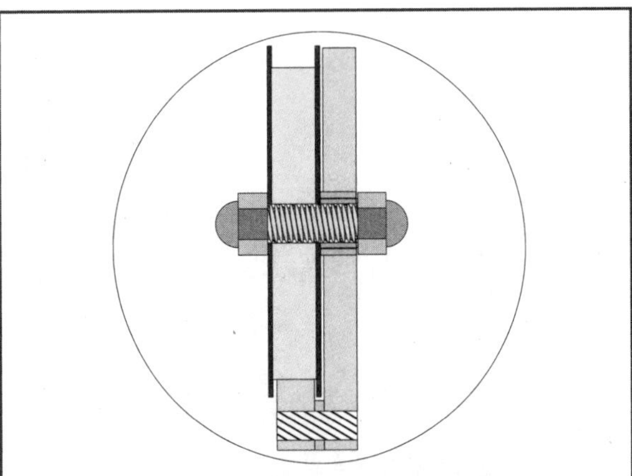

Figure 02.36: **A close inspection of the illustration reveals the details. The bushing tubing is in green. The nested tubing keeps the pulley and rear nut from contacting the mountng bracket, and all moving surfaces are brass on brass, for minimal friction. Plan on spending a bit of time with a manicurists' emery board finessing the lengths of the tubing. Once you're satisfied with the bushing action, mount the pulley.**

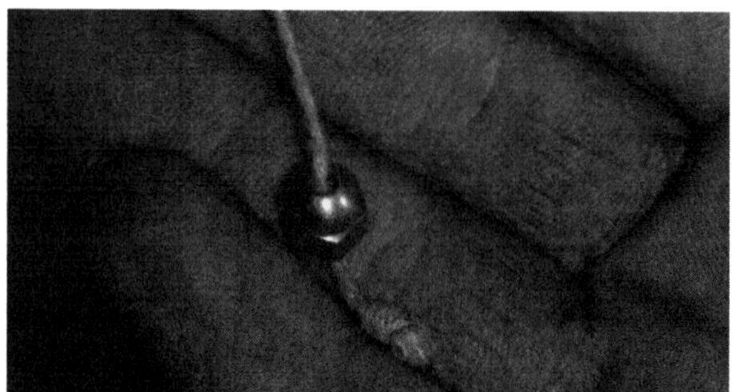

Figure 02.37: **Drill through the acorn nut, thread the cord and tie a retaining knot.**

Figure 02.38: **Screw in a short length of threaded rod.**

Figure 02.39: **Screw the threaded rod/acorn nut/cord assembly into the weightbox. Repeat the process to attach the handle of your choice to the other end of the cord.**

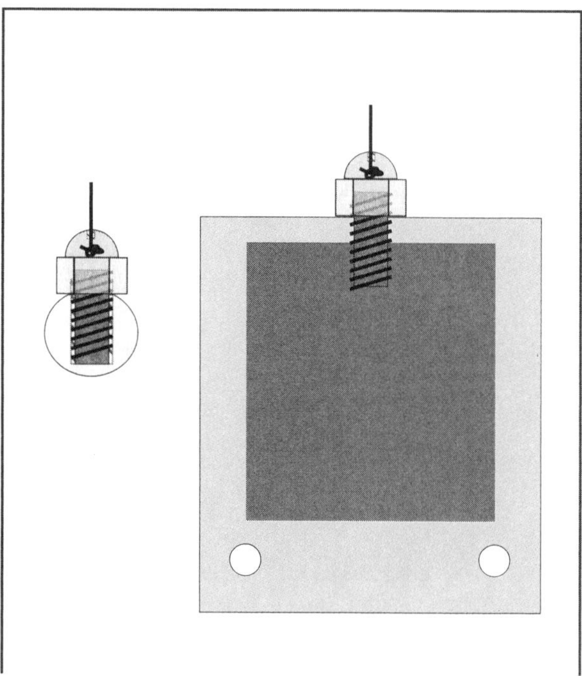

Figure 02.40: **The quite clever blind cord attachment bodge**

cord from pulling back through. Screw a length of threaded rod into the acorn nut, locking it in place with thread-locking glue or cyanoacrylate. It's clean, dare I say "elegant," and has a solid 7.8 WTF factor. **[Figure 02.37–Figure 02.40]**

The bed attaches to the lunette with double-faced tape and a single ½" finishing nail. (Drill a pilot hole! The last thing you need at this point is to split something open trying to force a nail into place.) Finesse the fit of the artfully formed brass support rod detailed in the cutting diagram, slip it into place and you're done. Now, *chop something*.

To use:

1. Pull cord down.
2. Insert unsuspecting object into lunette.
3. Let go.

Watch your damned fingers, would ya?

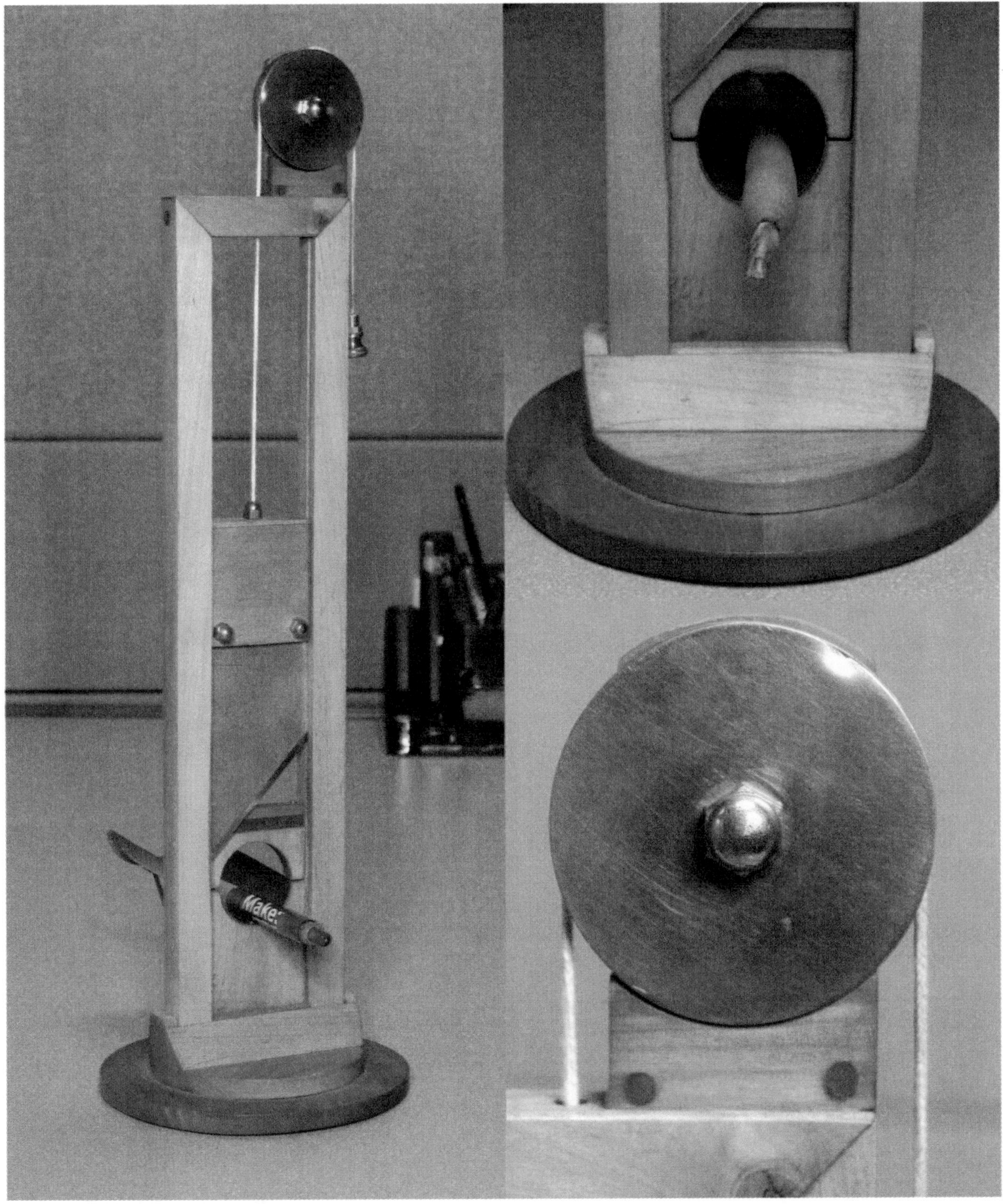
Maker

‹ Nano-Project › Clamping Jig Construction Set

This is probably the most useful two hours of shop time you're going to spend this year. Jigs are our friends, and they're easy friends to make. What we're doing here is kinda like a breadboard clamping system, using reinforced pegboard as a "breadboard," with movable stop blocks and vise components made using threaded rod and T-nuts. We're just doing the very basics: once you get a feel for the overall Zen of the system, you'll be cobbling together your own jigwidgets, jiggadgets, and jiggewgaws for it at the drop of a hat.

Here's what you need:

- **Pegboard**
  Say 1' x 2' ft. You can always go large later.
- **¼" MDF**
  Ditto, plus some scraps to cut stop blocks.
- **Scrap wood about 1"x 1"**
  At least 6' of it. Solid wood, please. Plywood isn't up to the task.
- **¼-20 T-nuts**
  Get at least a dozen.
- **¼-20 threaded rod**
  They sell it in 3-foot lengths. Get three or four lengths; it's really handy stuff.
- **15/64" drill bit**
- **5/16" drill bit**
- **¼" drill bit**
- **A few clamps**
  Well, more than a few. But not a lot.
- **A hacksaw**
- **Needle files**

Most of the quantities I'm leaving up to you. This is an open-ended system that can expand indefinitely if you let it. I'm reproducing here what I started out with when I first prototyped the idea; you'll find yourself adding new fittings all the time as you adapt the kit to each new project. The beauty of this design is that the tolerances are, for the most part, pretty loose. As long as you get your base right angle accurate and pin spacing in the ballpark, everything else flexes to accommodate the gig.

My basic kit is about 20" x 11". It's what I happened to have on the top of the wood crib when I went looking for supplies. You need identically dimensioned pegboard and 3⁄4" MDF for your base, and some smaller squares of MDF for positioning blocks. I also cut a 6" diameter circle, a 30/60/90 triangle, and a 45/45/90 triangle, all of which are useful angles to have at your disposal. The 1" x 1" is cut to workable lengths. I started out with mostly 8" and 4" lengths, plus two pieces long enough to give me a nice, solid right angle permanently attached to the base, and a dozen 1" x 1"s for "jaws."

You want all the exposed wooden surfaces to be glue-resistant, else jig and jiggee become one during use. Enamel paint does the trick, as does a linseed oil finish, but a healthy coat of acrylic floor polish is the quickest way I can think of to ward off the evil forces of adhesion if you're looking for immediate gratification.

There are two glue-ups: the pegboard and MDF base components are squared up and glued. Clamp 'em up realistically and let set for a couple of hours. Spend the time cutting your threaded rod into 6" lengths, and thinking about what kind of actuators you want on the ends. These are the things you're going to be turning to tighten your clamps. On mine, I just cut a slot for a screwdriver into one end. Feel free to consider Plans B, such as knurled knobs or hex heads when doing your UI (user interface). **[Figure N2.01]**

Yes, it's a UI.

You'll also need a handful of 1½" sections of ¼-20 threaded rod. These will be the positioning pins that hold your components in place on the base.

The second glue-up creates a solid, accurate 90-degree angle at one corner of the base. Accuracy of the right angle is absolutely essential. Align the first component of the angle flush to the bottom of the base, and glue it up. The pegboard I'm using came out of a dumpster (where else?), complete with a rock-hard coat of some kind of enamel. I'm assuming its Tremclad, or some other rust/acid/glue/nuclear-strike-resistant paint, because it took me about 20 minutes to sand bare the glue area for the right angle barrier. Flush the other piece of the angle against the vertical edge as illustrated, true up the angle with your carpenter's square, and set your clamps. **[Figure N2.02]**

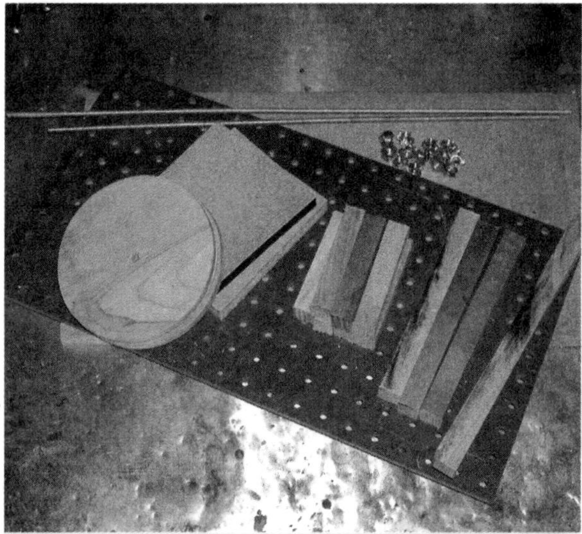

Figure N2.01: **The pieces.**

Figure N2.02: **Stiffening the pegboard.**

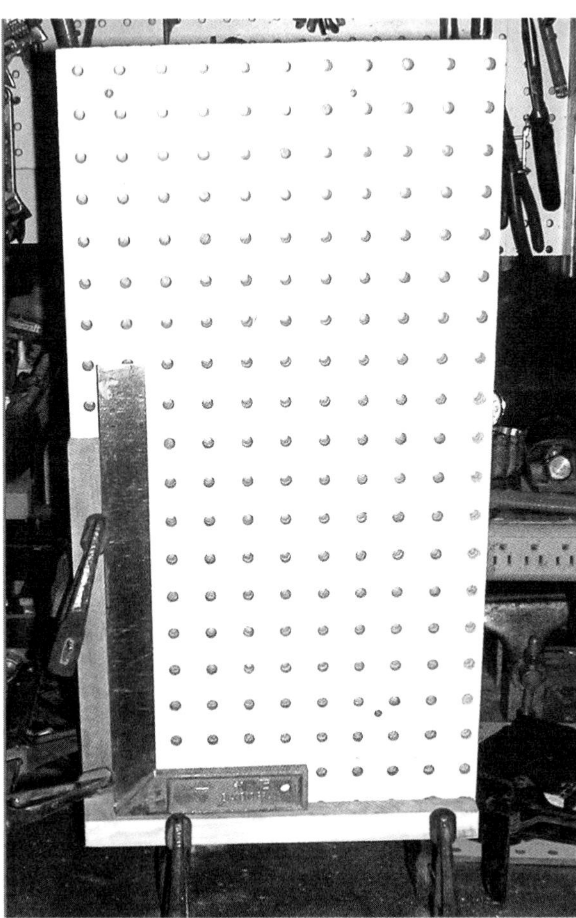

Figure N2.03: **Turning the corner on the second glue-up.**

If I were you, I'd head out for a cocktail while this particular glue-up is setting. There's a character-building experience looming on the horizon.

When the clamps come off, the fiesta begins. Drill out the holes in the pegboard/MDF sheet that you just laminated to a depth of 3/4" with a 1/4" bit in the chuck.

A drill press looks like a much more attractive purchase right now, doesn't it?

In this example, use a 1/4-20 T-nut with a 5/16" OD and a toothed shoulder. Drill the hole, set the nut with a quick squeeze in the vise or a solid whack with a rubber mallet, and you've just made yourself one of them IKEA höle thingies. In this instance, we're using the T-nuts to make vise mechanisms that'll be repositionable anywhere on the surface of the pegboard. **[Figure N2.03]**

Chuck your 5/16" bit, then find and mark the T-nut holes as indicated. **[Figure N2.04]**

While you've got the bit in the chuck, drill to a 3/8" depth dead center on one face of each of your 1" x 1" pieces to act as a receiver for the threaded rod. **[Figure N2.05]**

Bung the T-nuts into your freshly drilled holes with your choice of percussive manipulators; they should anchor in tightly, flush to the surface of the wood. **[Figure N2.06]**

Believe it or not, you're almost done. All that's left is to drill the pin placement holes through the bits of wood what's got the T-nuts in them. You want your T-nutted blocks to be attachable to the pegboard straight across and at a 45-degree angle, which makes accurate spacing of the holes one of those mission-critical operations. **[Figure N2.07, Figure N2.08]**

Pegboard holes are 1/4" spaced, 1" center to center, which makes the 45-degree diagonal spacing 1.41". **[Figure N2.09]**

Damn you, Pythagoras.

The previous diagram details the hole placement, but you may wanna hedge your bets on accuracy of that nasty little

Figure N2.04: **Behold, the mighty T-Nut. Ikea's hidden secret.**

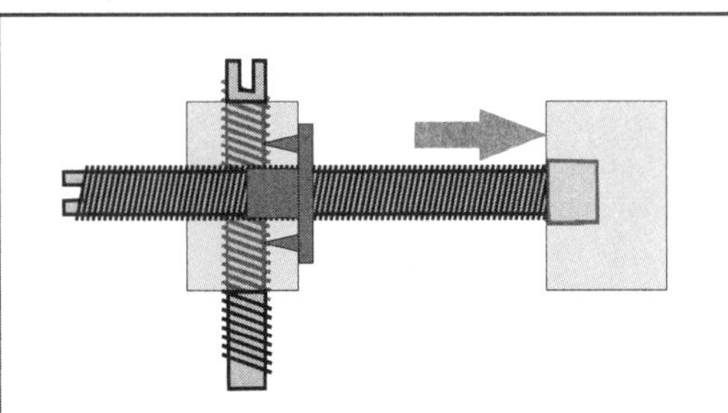

Figure N2.05: **The working end of a clamp.**

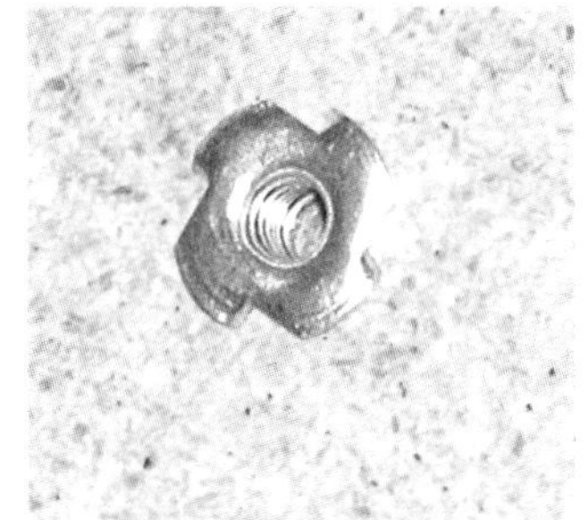

Figure N2.07: **A mighty T-nut bunged in place.**

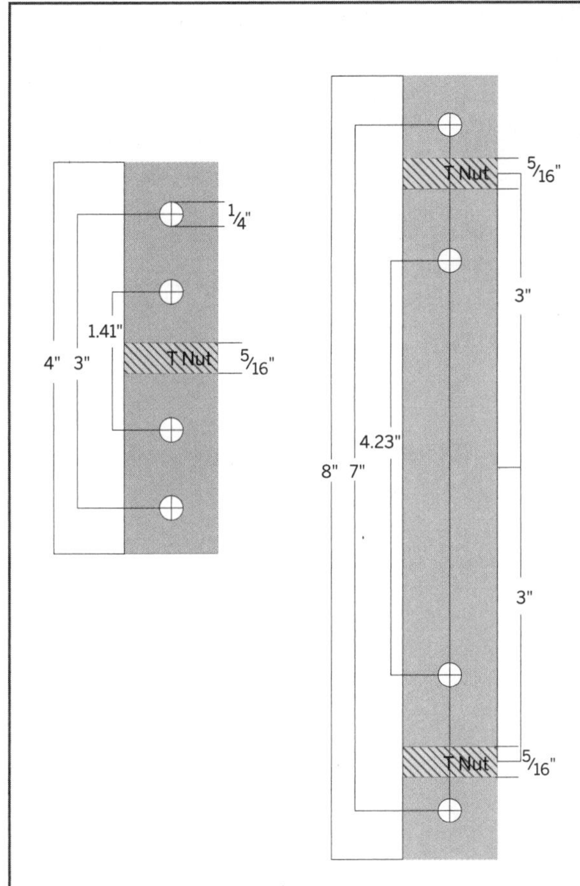

Figure N2.06: **T-nut holes.**

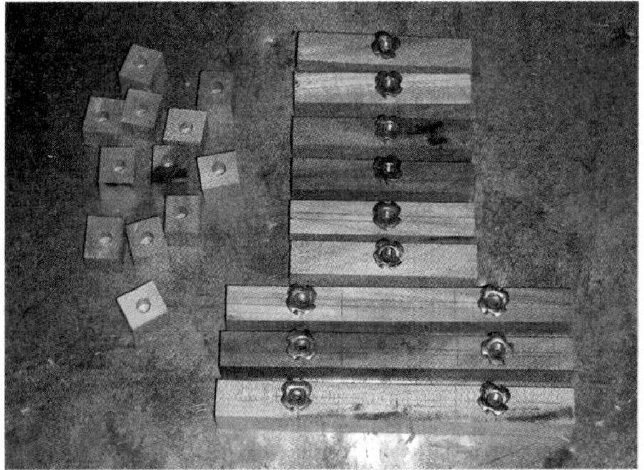

Figure N2.08: **Clamp pieces.**

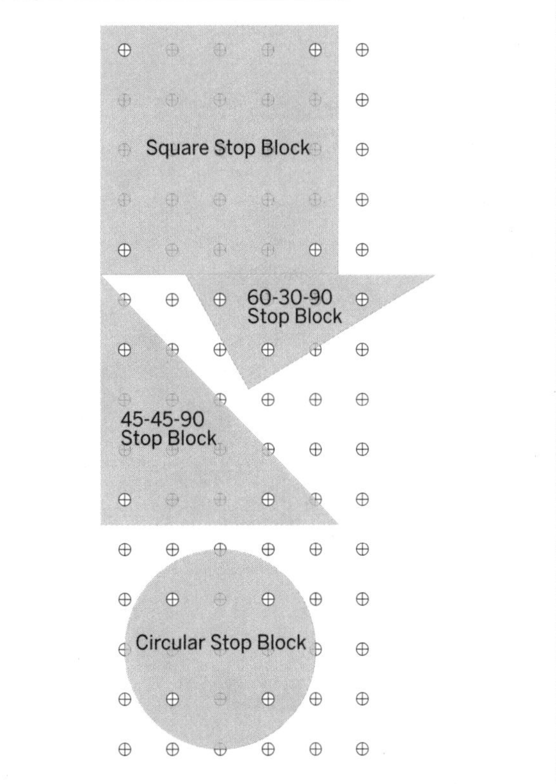

Figure N2.09: **Stop blocks.**

1.41" dimension by cutting position templates from a scrap of pegboard. **[Figure N2.10]**

Cut a single row of holes straight across, and at a 45-degree angle. Those are the only angles that you really need to accommodate on the vise equipped pieces, as you can cut custom-angle jaws and inserts to shim together whatever other angles you need in the future. The whole idea behind this project is flexibility and adaptability.

Give your positioning templates a quick spray of stencil adhesive, let it set up (about two minutes), then repeat. This step leaves enough adhesion present to hold them solidly in place while you drill the positioning holes in each vise component. Make sure that they're absolutely vertical through the plane of the wood. Deviation from this is . . . let's just say it's not good.

The stop blocks need positioning pins, too. The pins have to be precisely square to both the stop block and the base plate. The diagram should give you an idea of what's needed.

Philosophically, isn't it amazing how so much (accuracy) depends on literally nothing (your holes)? Context: gotta love it.

The next step is technically a misuse of toolage. Live with it. Dig out your 1/4-20 thread tap, and run it through each of the positioning pin holes you just drilled. According to standard woodworking practice, you are not supposed to use machine taps in wood, but in this case, it's a perfectly valid way to ensure a solid fit for the 1½" threaded rod pieces you cut about two hours ago.

It's like Lego with movable pegs. Grok the concept, kids!

Anyway, you're done. Now play with it and see how it functions. Orientation of the T-nuts in relation to the force vectors is important (as shown, although it oughta be apparent). **[Figure N2.11]**

You can begin modding at your convenience. **[Figure N2.12]**

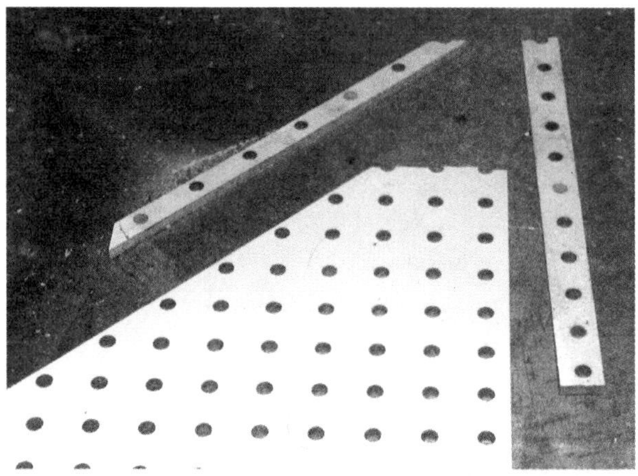

Figure N2.10: **Using the pegboard as a template.**

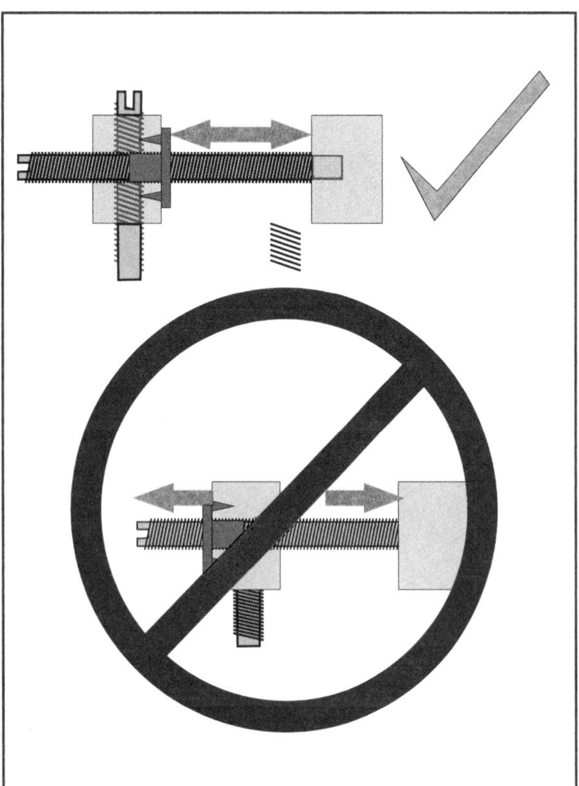

Figure N2.11 : **It's important which side the T-nuts go on.**

Figure N2.12: **Use like so.**

3 BallistaMail: Projectile-to-Peer (P2P) Intercubicle Messaging

Remember those wind-up balsa airplanes you flew as a kid? Wind about a hundred turns of the propeller onto the nearly-impossible-to-replace-when-it-breaks rubber band, chuck it into the air, and watch it soar majestically onto the roof of your house? Snickering as your dad almost falls off the ladder rescuing it?

That's torsion energy at work, kids, and it's woefully under-appreciated as an energy storage medium.

Ballistae work on the same principle. Picture a big-ass crossbow with twisted skeins of cord providing tension to the movable arms that connect to the *bowstring*. Despite — or perhaps because of — the simplicity of concept, this is a *massively* powerful mechanism. Full-scale ballistae (say, 12 feet high) once chucked regulation-sized javelins about 300 feet with enough wellie to impale two (purportedly armored) men. Call it a Greco-Roman cruise missile: the most formidable weapon of its time. Unlike gravity-powered early weaponry (which lose power exponentially as size decreases), the mechanism retains substantial guts and balls when scaled down.

CAUTION: Torsion springs like we're making here store a lot more energy than you might think, so property damage and/or personal injury are distinct possibilities for the unwary. You've been warned. And quite probably encouraged. Bueno!

Let's flash forward in time about 1900 years, and consider *Rocket Mail* — delivering mail via rocket or missile. From early 1930s Germany to the present day, sporadic attempts have been made by various postal services worldwide to harness the motive power of missiles to deliver the mail, using everything from gunpowder-fueled fireworks (Indian Airmail Society, 1934) to submarine-launched refitted guided missiles (USPS, via *USS Barbero*, 1959) to piloted reusable craft (an XCOR Long-EZ piloted by "things that fly" legend Dick Rutan, 2005). On paper, it's a brilliant concept: the next logical advancement from Airmail. Sadly, for some unknown reason, it still hasn't caught on, although full props go to the persistent few who Know A Good Idea When They See One© and fight the good fight to bring this innovation to market.

We're gonna join this particular fight, though on a somewhat more modest scale.

I've built a lot of desktop ballistae, with aesthetics ranging from the traditional and brutishly utilitarian model commissioned by a local motorcycle enthusiast shown in **Figure 03.01** to the black walnut Art Deco number shown in **Figure 03.02**, inspired by Agatha Christie's Hercule Poirot. It's a flexible form factor.

Regardless of the styling, the purpose has remained constant: launch Spinnin' Metal Tubes o' Death™ (see sidebar on page 59) with the intent of penetrating some innocent surface.

One-trick pony? Hell yeah. But it's a great trick.

Now, though, in a tribute to the great Rocket Mail pioneers Zucker, Smith, and Summerfield,[1] we take up the gauntlet

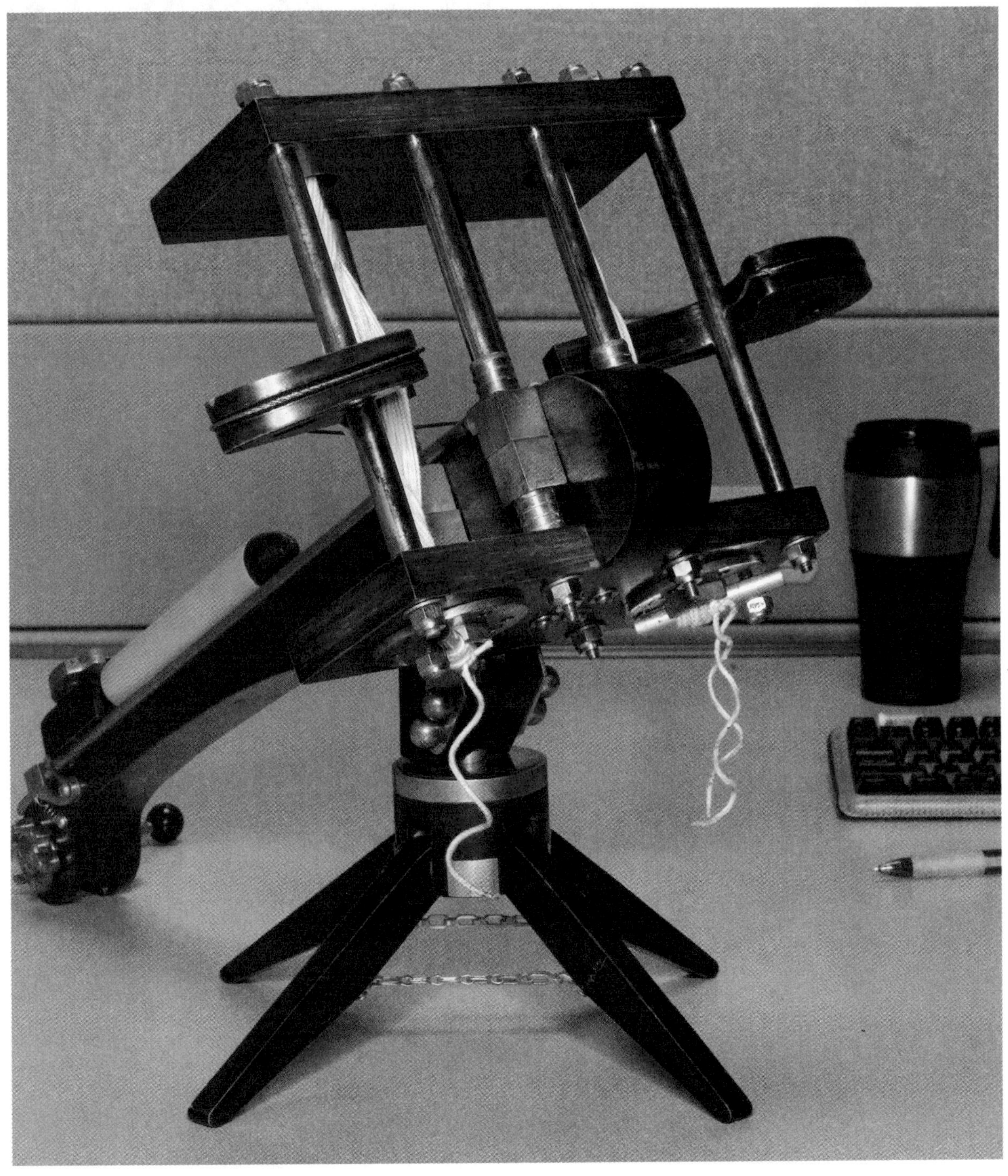

Figure 03.01: **A more-or-less traditionally styled ballista**

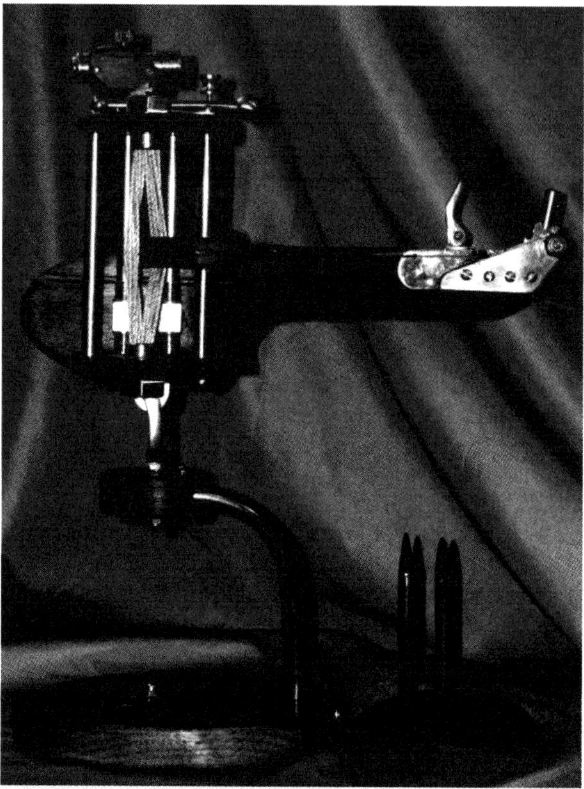

Figure 03.02: **The oh-so sophisticated Art Deco–influenced ballista**

and bring BallistaMail to cube farm communications. Mail server down? Need to get that expense account requisition

1 In 1934, German expatriate Gerhard Zucker conducted the United Kingdom's first experiment in rocket mail, using a small gunpowder-fueled rocket in an attempt to launch 1,200 letters from one Hebridean island to another. It blew up.

A few months later, Stephen Smith, an official of the Indian Airmail Society attempted much the same thing in (you guessed it) India. Surprisingly, it did not blow up. Over the next few years hundreds of rocketmail launches were successfully completed in India.

Then they stopped.

Arthur E. Summerfield was U.S. Postmaster General in 1959, when the submarine *USS Barbaro* successfully delivered ship-to-shore "missile mail" via a denuked Regulus guided missile. Summerfield was effusive in his praise of the endeavour, declaring it to be of "historic significance to the peoples of the entire world."

Shortly afterwards, they stopped too.

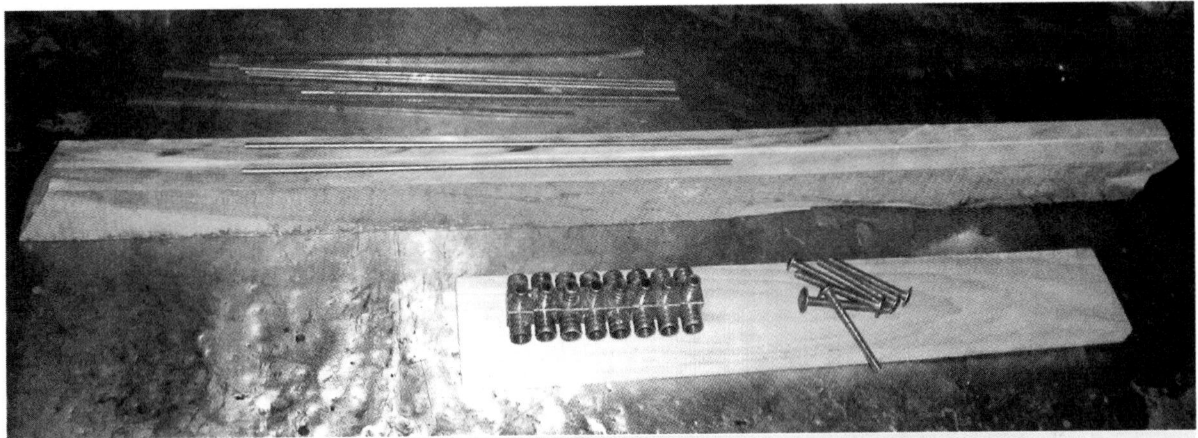

Figure 03.03: Some likely material candidates. Your results may vary.

from IT to Accounting A.S.A.F.P.? Turn to BallistaMail. A dark ops agent in inter-office political intrigue? Need a secure comm link for transmitting high-quality dirt on the H.R. intern? BallistaMail is there.

This new role requires some adaptive design. Primarily, it's gonna be bigger than those candy-ass little buggers I usually build, to allow use of a larger projectile with a reasonably sized payload. To this end, this build is going to venture into the realm of "working without a net," and I'm going to design on the bench.

What You Need

Figure 03.03 shows the results of three minutes spent rummaging for initial components. This will get us started:

- A piece of unidentified *skid wood* (see "Skid Wood Defined") about a yard long and 2¾" x 1 .
- 23 inches of poplar ¾" x 3½".
- Some brass PEX T fittings, intended for connecting household PVC plumbing pipe.
- A few 5⁄16"–18 toilet mounting bolts.
- A handful of 3⁄16" brass rod and ¼" square bar.
- About 8 feet of ¼" OD brass pipe (not pictured), which interfaces nicely with the pipefittings

Frankly, the skid wood ain't pretty — scars, gouges, and nail holes, the ends inexplicably cut to odd angles. Casting a practiced eye on the beleaguered chunk of tree, I estimated the best possible scenario for the shape/size of the body, cut the stock to length, and then dressed each face with a quick pass through the table saw. We're looking at a total body length of +/–20". **[Figure 03.04]**

The Humble Shipping Pallet: Skid Wood Defined

Skid wood is a legendary material for woodworking guys of all ilk. Shipping palettes can be found in an amazing variety of woods, from essentially raw, fresh-cut pine to exotic hardwoods such as Jatoba (Brazilian cherry wood), depending on the point of origin of the skid. Working with skids is fraught with danger and disappointment. Finding and removing hidden nails and nail fragments is essential for subsequent safety when milling the wood. Apparently pristine chunks of stock are frequently revealed to be structurally flawed when subjected to the Table Saw of Truth.

The Body

Yes, we're designing on the bench. No, it isn't scary. All of my design decisions are based on material I had at hand, but none of the stuff I happened to use is particularly exotic

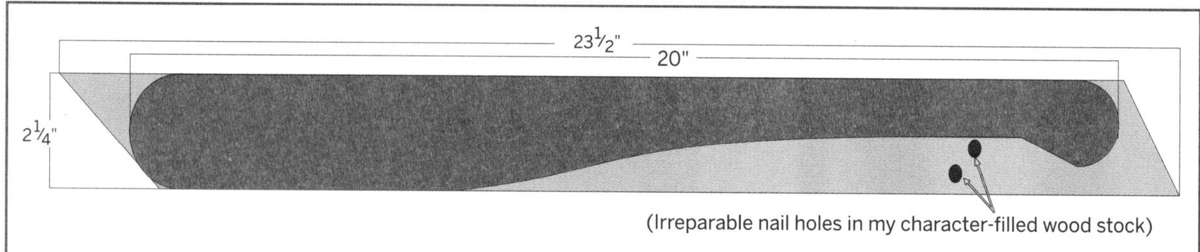

Figure 03.04: **Working with what ya got: fitting the requisite body shape onto less-than-pristine stock**

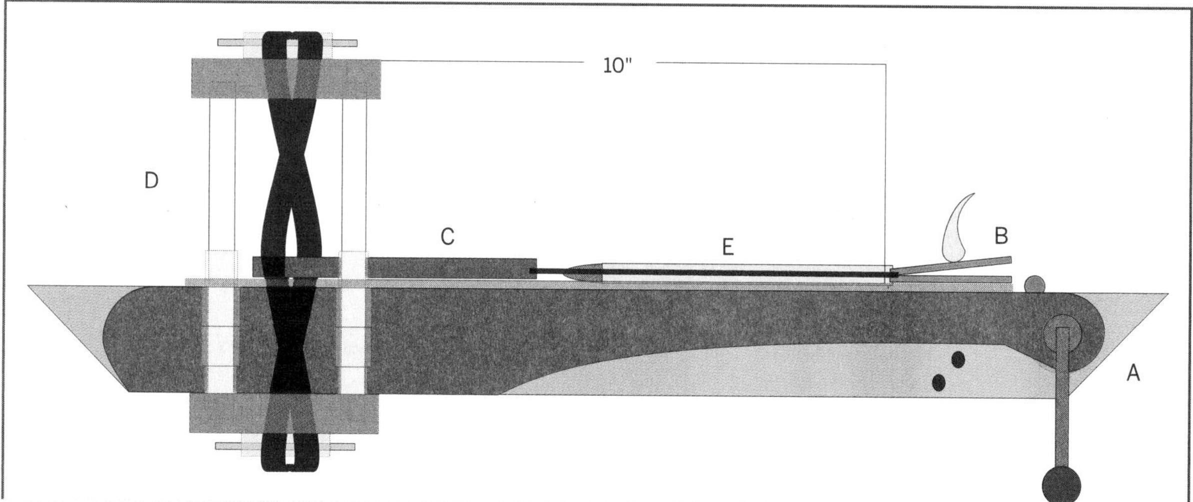

Figure 03.05: **Yumpin' yiminey! Look at all the crap we have to bung onto this flippin' thing.**

Figure 03.06: **Forming the skein plate pocket. A few scraps of skid wood will do to rough it in.**

A Note on the Term "Ballistae"

Technically, the Romans attached two different names to essentially the same (swiped from the Greeks) mechanism, depending on the projectile being ... er ... projected. A *catapulta* threw arrows, and a *ballista* threw stones. When I started selling these things, my target demographic was North American and, thanks to poorly researched mass media, used to applying the word *catapult* to the "improbably flexible tree trunks with a big spoon on the end" you see in Road Runner cartoons.

So I marketed 'em as *ballistae*, which some people recognized and some people asked about. Either way, it was better than having them think I had a ready source of really rubbery trees.

Feel free to use the word *catapulta*.

Figure 03.07: **I used a piece of my 3½"x ¾" skein plate stock to space the pocket accurately while the glue sets.**

in nature. On-the-fly component and material substitution is Standard Operating Procedure during improvisational fabrication; expect your results to vary. Successfully winging it just means being cognizant of the purpose and function of each individual subassembly, and matching the material(s) used to the physical needs of each component.

No biggie. Using a compass and a French curve, I sketched out a rough body shape that ended up looking half cricket bat, half bowling pin. The bulge needs to be present at the skinny end so we can build the windlass into it, and the wide end needs to be wide to accommodate nice, long skeins. Keeping the tail end light right from the beginning also goes a long way toward keeping the balance of the completed project controllable on the tripod.

In order to actually accelerate a projectile (E), we have to cram onto the body a windlass (A), a trigger mechanism and guide rails (B), and a bow assembly (arms and bowstring, C) attached to the torsion skein rack (D). **[Figure 03.05]**

This leaves us with a potential draw of 10". We'll wait until the majority of the build is completed, *then* [Figure out how long the bow arms need to be to provide us with an optimally sized bowstring.

The rack that supports the torsion skein takes a serious amount of stress, both from the tension wound into the cord — which wants to pull the top and bottom plates together to meet in the center in a horrid, tangled mass — and from the pull of the bowstring — which wants to horizontally displace the skein backward to meet the trigger mechanism in (you guessed it) a horrid, tangled mass. **[Figure 03.06, Figure 03.07, Figure 03.08]**

Can't have that. We'll add strength to the bottom plate

Figure 03.08: **The joints are finished by setting a few dowel pins.**

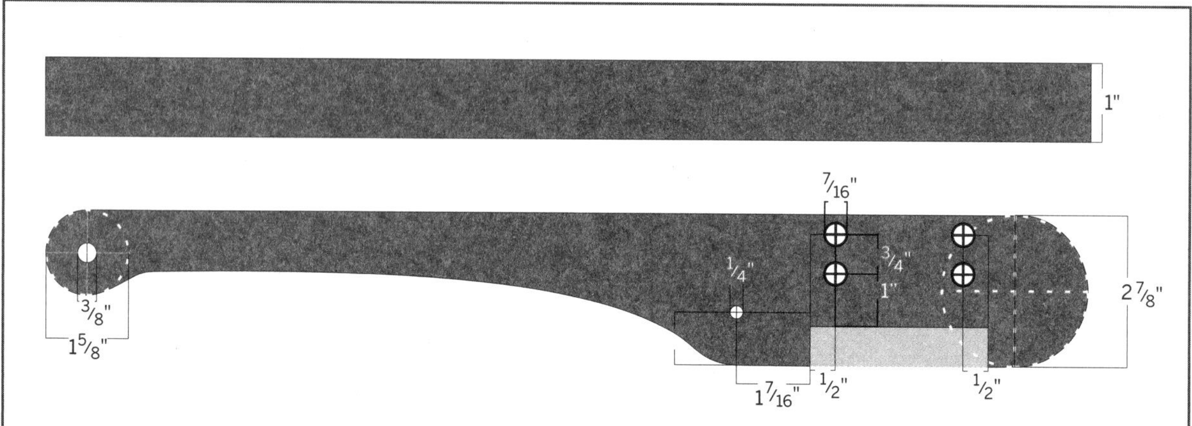

Figure 03.09: **Finally! The body in detail.**

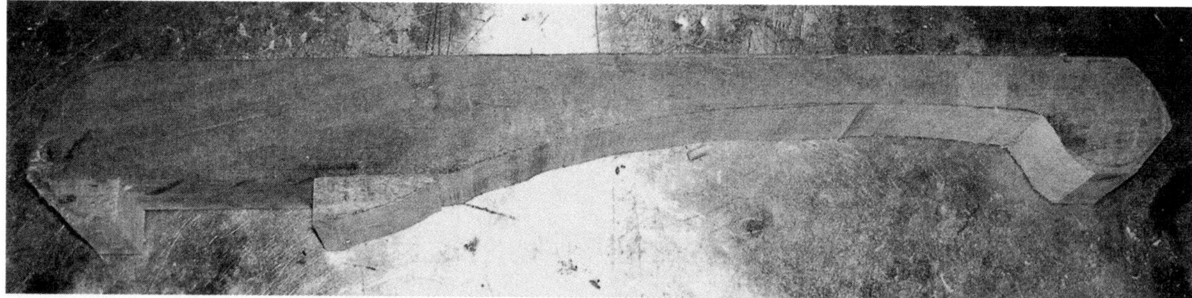

Figure 03.10: **The body blank, awaiting frenzied holezdrillen**

attachment by gluing and dowelling some additional wood onto the body blank to form a pocket for the skein plate to slot into, then adjust the shape of the body appropriately. **[Figure 03.09, Figure 03.10]**

This is workable. Time to rough in the body a bit more, so we can start figuring out how to get the other stuff to fit in.

We're looking at a finished body about 20½" long, 3" high, and 1½" thick. The 1½" thickness is reasonably critical in this project, as BallistaMail is scaled to launch less-than-svelte 1" diameter projectiles. Feel free to laminate two pieces of ¾" hardwood stock to get the required width.

I've drawn up the cutting diagram based on the 1½" width. If you decide to scale down your intended projectile to something more sleek and lethal, the only *really* critical measurement changes you'll need to consider involve the placement of some of the vertical support mounting holes on the skein rack plates. There's no rocket science involved adapting the skein plates to a narrower body width; it's just something you need to be aware of before you start drilling holes in stuff.

Skein Plates, Supports, and Their Attendant Mysteries

We're gonna be using ½" OD brass tubing as vertical support components for the skein plates, with ¼-20 threaded rod running internally top to bottom to tie the whole thing together. Positioning the supports to allow maximum bow arm movement while warding off collapse under stress

Spinnin' Metal Tubes o' Death™

When I first started making these things, I put a stupid amount of effort into determining the (theoretical) most effective projectile (officially called a *dart*). Stability in flight was the main problem to overcome. There's not really enough room for full-scale fletching on a pint-sized ballista (at least not on the ones I build), so I resorted to trying to tune the center of gravity on the darts so that they could take a huge push from the rear without wobbling out of control once they left the guide rails. To that end, I put together some test projectiles out of 3/8" brass tubing with 1" wooden balls as the "arrowheads," the plan being that I'd be able to press-fit balancing weights up the length of the tubing to manipulate the positioning of the C. o' G.

What the hell was I thinking?

Take my word for it: making a safe high-performance ballista projectile is *not easy*. Compensating for both the mass and aerodynamic effect of a honkin' big ball of wood stuck on the end of your projectile is like trying to straighten out a Phil Niekro knuckleball. The same airflow patterns around a nonspinning sphere that make a knuckler jump around, seemingly at random, as it heads to the plate are the factors in play here, and without some kinda rotational gyroscopic thing going on, you're more or less going to have to live with a bit of wobble. Ballistics is an unforgiving science. Putting a rifling twist on 1/4"-high fletching down the whole length of the shaft is about the best solution I could come up with, but even then, it's a compromise. Pain in the ass to fabricate, too.

***Unsafe* high-performance ballista bolts are an entirely different story. Just by losing the end caps and using a Dremel to shape an aerofoiled set of rotation-inducing blades on the front end of the length of brass tubing, you're left with a superbly aerodynamic spinnin' metal tube o' death, not unlike that *tubular penetrator* armor-piercing ordinance used to such great success by various bellicose nations.**

I bet if ya made one of those out of 316L alloy surgical-grade stainless-steel tubing, it'd go clear through a piece of 1/4" plywood.

Just sayin'...

requires sacrifice of high-quality goats, a bit of common sense, and the assistance of big chunks of metal.

Bracing the rack to deal with lateral stress introduced into the geometry when the bowstring is drawn back is typically accomplished by running rigid support struts between the rear edge of the top skein plate and the back end of the body near the windlass location. This approach works like a charm on full-sized pieces, but it makes for cramped quarters and awkward ergonomics at the rear of a scaled-down mechanism. Cue Plan B. **[Figure 03.11]**

The spacing of the supports closest to the body is dependent on the brass PEX pipe fittings noted earlier. With a bit of tweezing and some artfully placed holes, these fittings anchor the four inside supports vertical to the body and brace the skein rack against lateral movement. **[Figure 03.12]**

I used 1/2"–1/4" T Junctions. They pass 1/2" OD tubing through the wide bits, 1/4" through the narrow one. If we cut off one of the large-diameter extensions on each fitting, two of them butt together and fit nicely on the body, providing excellent... er... support to the supports against horizontal stress. **[Figure 03.13]**

Mark the body holes for them carefully, and drill straight through the body with a 7/16" bit. The PEX fittings will press-fit into place snugly. **[Figure 03.14]**

Cut the skein rack plate blanks to size from 3/4" hardwood. I used poplar because I had some sitting around the shop, but maple is actually better.

Stack the two plates together with two-sided tape; purists may call it cheating, but it's the best way to get absolutely identical top and bottom support locations. **[Figure 03.15]**

If you're using a different body width, *this* is where you'll need to adjust the positions of the inner support struts to ensure the holes in the plates line up with the brass

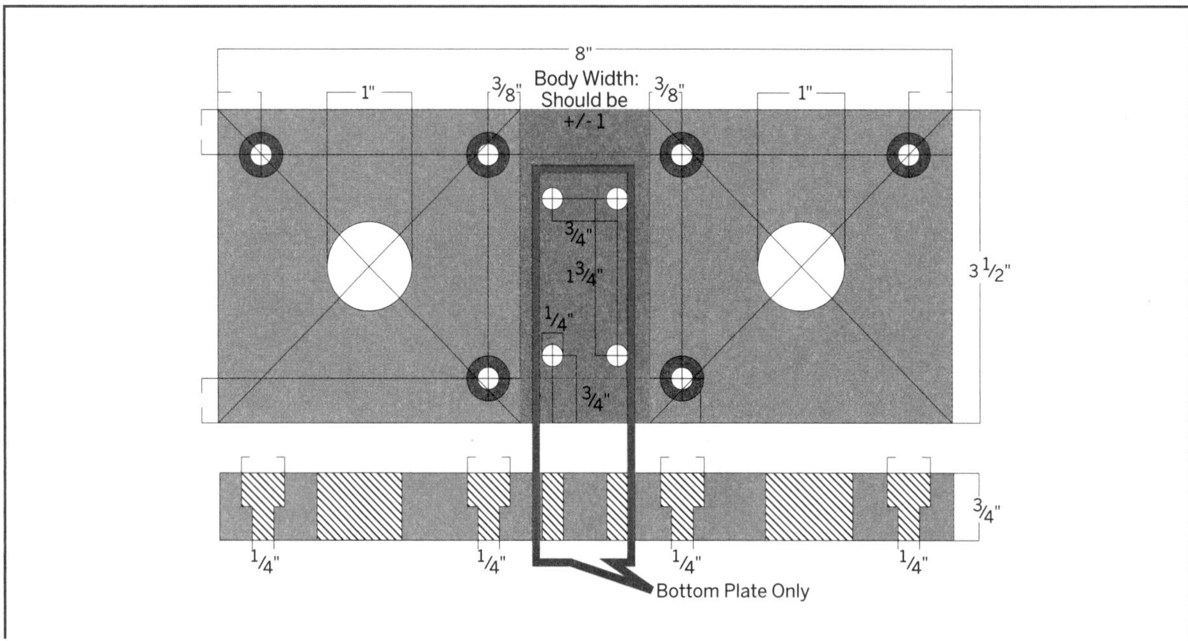

Figure 03.11: **Skein plate cutting diagram**

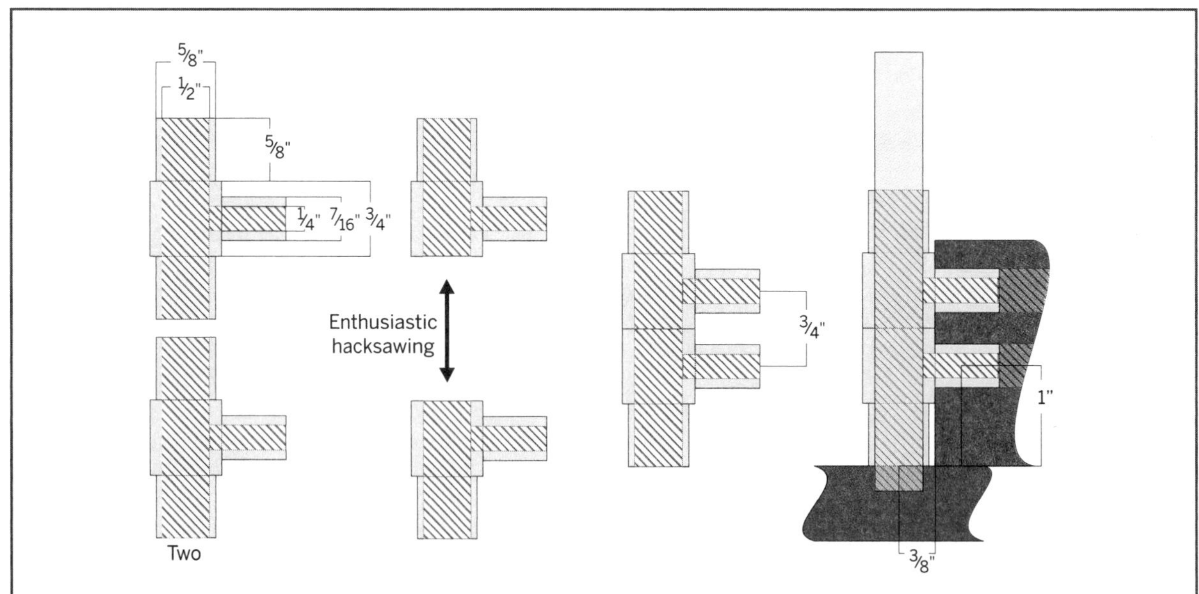

Figure 03.12: **The PEX fitting-to-skein brace conversion**

Figure 03.13: **The remarkably useful PEX fittings. Plumbers hate 'em.**

Figure 03.14: **Accuracy counts here if you want a solid, properly aligned fit.**

lateral bracing fittings on the body. Once you're sure of the positioning, mark and drill 3⁄32" pilot holes at the support tube locations. Separate the plates, chuck a 1⁄2" Forstner bit, and drill out the pilot holes to a depth of 3⁄8" into the top surface of the bottom plate and the bottom surface of the top plate. **[Figure 03.16]**

Determining the height of the supports is more than just

Figure 03.15: **The (mostly) completed skein plates**

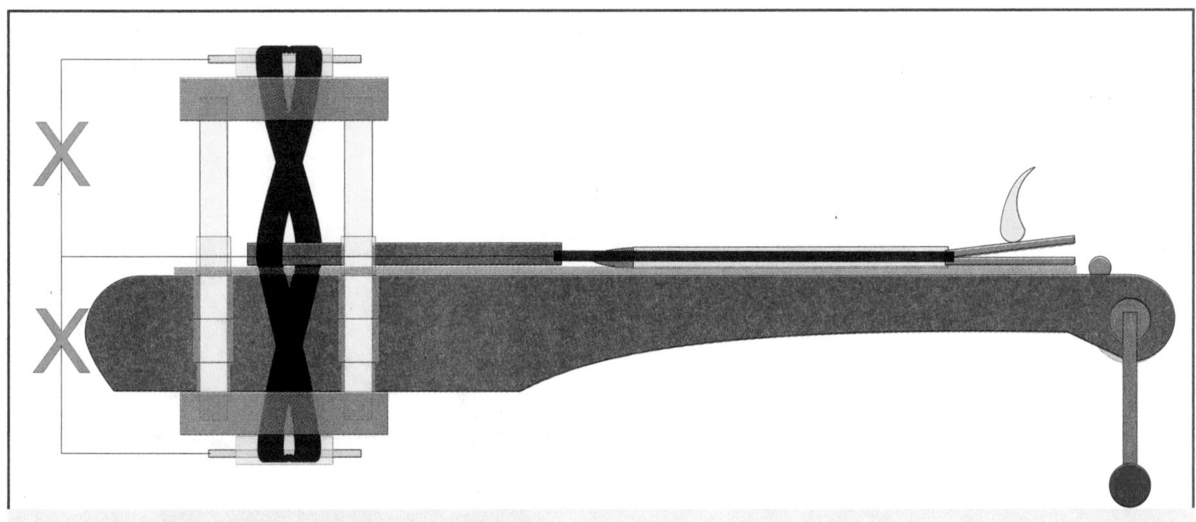

Figure 03.16: **Balanced skeins are happy skeins.**

a matter of "whatever looks right." To achieve the much desired *balanced skein*, the bow arms are ideally located at the midpoint of the torsion skeins, such that the bowstring runs parallel and adjacent to the dart guide rails. Getting the midpoint of the skeins *there* calls for us to know where exactly *there* is — which means having the guide rails in place and some of the winch components sized. **[Figure 03.17]**

So, we gotta build some more stuff before we can proceed

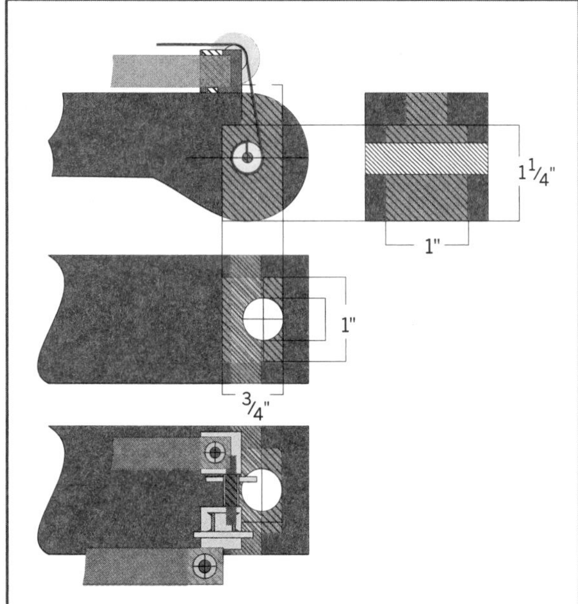

Figure 03.17: **Examining the complexities of the windlass cavity and guide rod mounts**

with the skein rack. The winch (*windlass*, actually) is gonna be hidden in the circular bit at the end of the body, with the cable feeding out of a hole in the top of the curve. Find the center of the circular rear section of the body, and drill it straight through the body to ⅜". Then, flip the body to expose the underside and plot the mayhem required to form the winch cavity. **[Figure 03.18, Figure 03.19]**

As you can see, I took a fairly cavalier approach once I'd drilled through the body with the main *cable exits here* hole. I removed most of the material with Forstner bits, then tidied up the edges a bit with a high-speed cutting bit chucked into the drill press before pulling out the chisels and getting the cavity to look somewhat presentable. **[Figure 03.20]**

The Guide Rail Mounts

Remember those funky brass PEX T fittings we used to brace the skein rack supports? We'll use four of the next size smaller. These fittings are centered around ½" brass cubes and are intended for use with ¼" tubing, but with a bit of drilling they'll accept ⅜" OD tubing, which is what we'll be using as guide rails. Cut off all the extensions, leaving just the brass cube. True up the cut edges, drill out the crossing hole to ⅜", and drill a 3⁄32" pilot for the mounting hole down through the other axis. **[Figure 03.21, Figure 03.22]**

The guide rails need to run from just in front of the windlass cable opening on the top face of the body down the length of the body to somewhere in the middle of the skein rack — in this case, 17" in length. So, rustle up some ⅜" OD tubing and cut two 17" lengths. Slide your guide rail end blocks into place on each end of the rails; then use the block pilot holes as guides and drill though the rails with a 3⁄32" bit. **[Figure 03.23]**

The top faces of the front blocks need to be rounded out

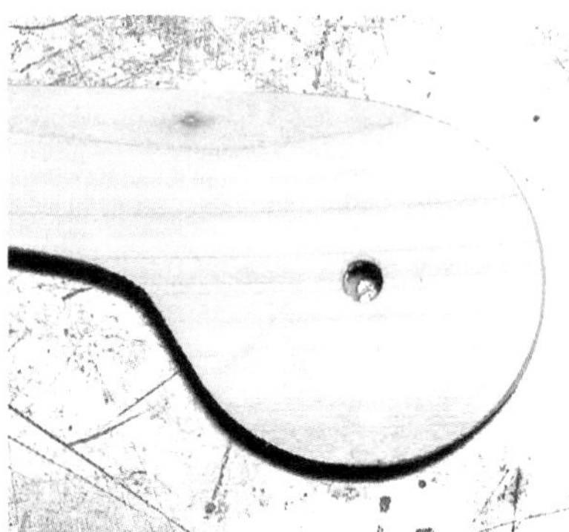

Figure 03.18: **The windlass axle hole**

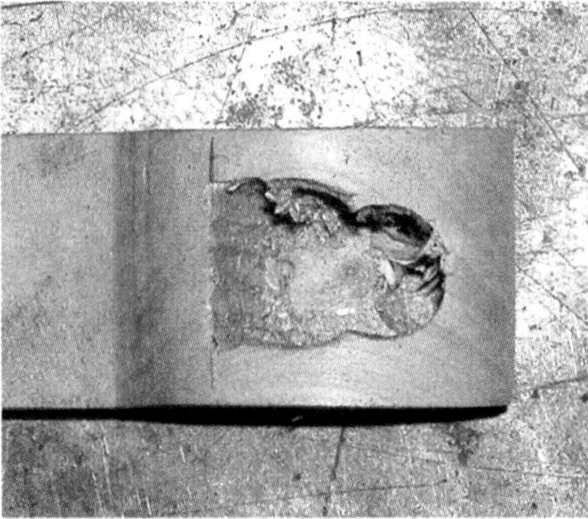

Figure 03.19: **The winch cavity roughed out . . .**

Figure 03.20: **. . . and cleaned up.**

Figure 03.21: **More PEX fittings, modified to within an inch of their lives.**

Figure 03.22: **Round off the front guide rail mounting blocks.**

Figure 03.23: **Guide rail placement**

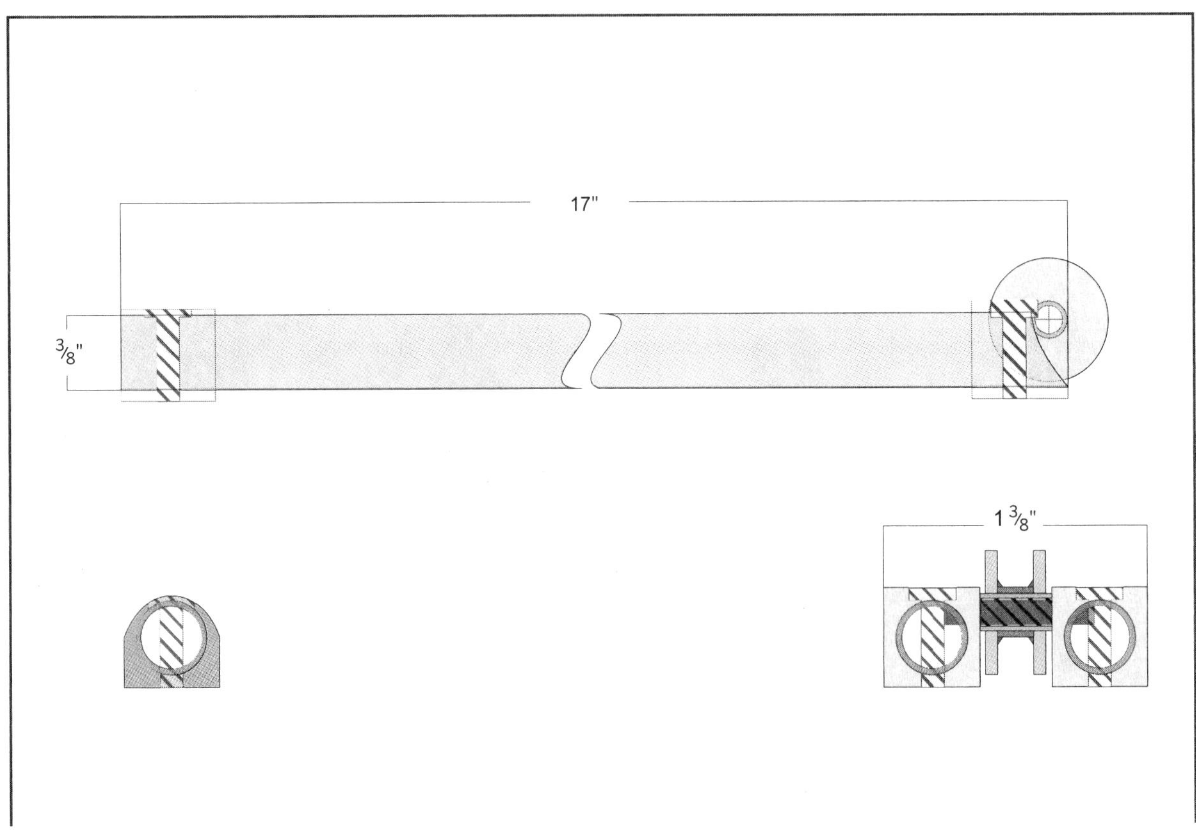

Figure 03.24: **Guide rail and block mounting spec**

and lowered as much as possible to reduce the potential speed bump effect they'll have as the projectile passes over them.

Enlarge the hole on the top face to 1/4" so that the head of the mounting screw can pass through the block and secure the rail/block assembly to the body using the bottom face of the guide rail only. **[Figure 03.24]**

Unnecessary? More or less. I went this route to maintain the conceptual continuity of the aesthetics, as is the wont of those endeared to artsy-fartsy nonsense. For those of a more utilitarian nature, the front rail block assemblies can be replaced by just a screw and spacer to keep the rails parallel to the body. The rear rail blocks are pretty much mandatory, though, as we need to have somewhere to mount the winch pulley.[2] **[Figure 03.25]**

To get the windlass cable out of the hole and into a position that it will actually be able to pull on stuff requires a pulley. Which we're gonna have to fabricate from scratch.[3] **[Figure 03.26]**

The Windlass Pulley

You need two 5/8" brass washers with a 1/4" hole, a 3/16" long piece of 1/4" OD brass tubing, and a 3/8" long piece of 3/16" OD tubing to use as a bushing. If you source your tubing at a hobby shop, you'll be thrilled to discover that the two diameters nest together perfectly. If you're scrounging stuff from scrapyards, you may need to hunt a bit to find the right dimensions. When you *do* find nesting brass tubing, buy it in

2 WINCH PULLEY??!!?? Yeah, winch pulley. Don't panic.

3 I have no doubt that some of you will now fire up your CNC minimill and machine a perfect pulley out of a block of metal in less time than it takes me to write down my so-called quick 'n dirty pulley bodge. Yeah, Nick Carter, I'm talkin' to you.

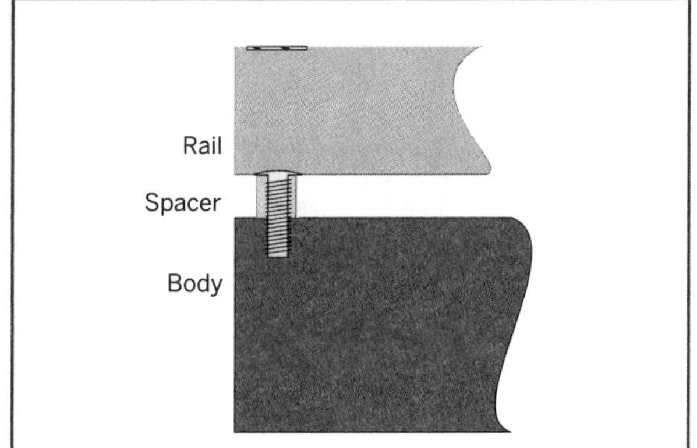

Figure 03.25: **An alternative front guide rail mount**

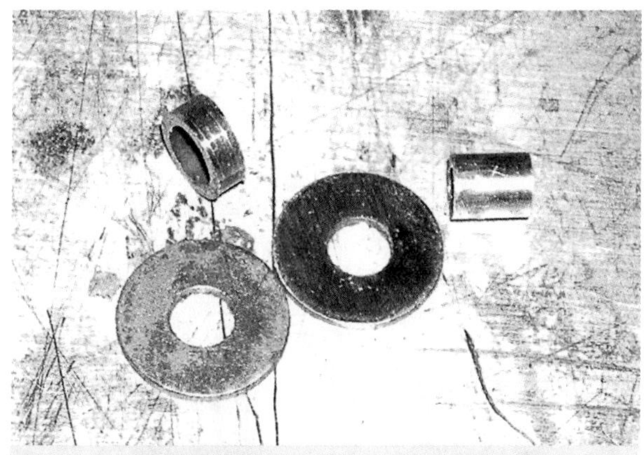

Figure 03.27: **Needful pulley bits**

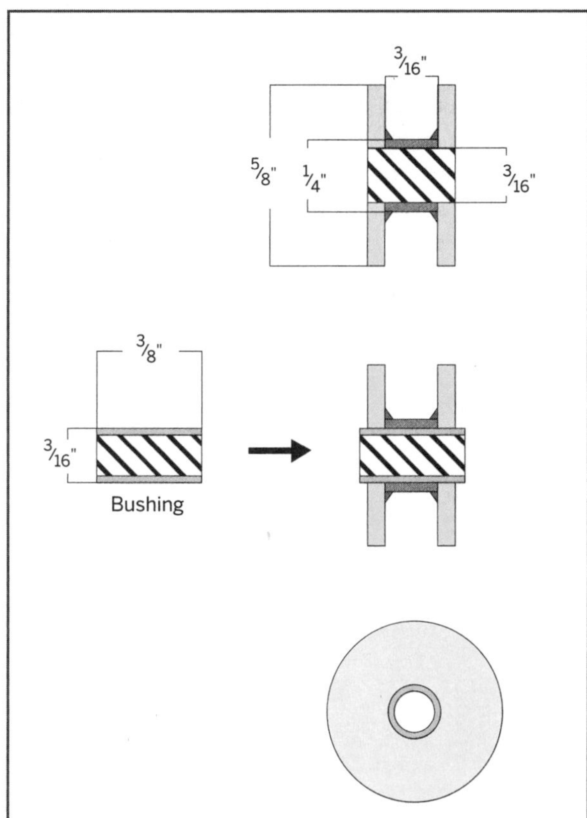

Figure 03.26: **The pulley bodge**

Figure 03.28: **Cleaned, fluxed, clamped, and waiting to be soldered**

quantity, if only for its usefulness as bushings. [Figure 03.27]

Clean the facing surfaces of the washers and 1/4" ID tubing, and carefully flux up the contact points. Use a length of 1/4-20 threaded rod and two nuts to clamp the lot of them together. Then, fire up the torch and solder the joints.

When the metal has cooled, clean up the surfaces with a wire brush and insert the bushing (that's the 3/16" OD tubing, for those of you who might have dozed off). It ain't pretty, but it's a pulley, dammit, and it's gonna do the job just fine. [Figure 03.28]

Install the pulley axle by drilling 1/8" holes located as shown

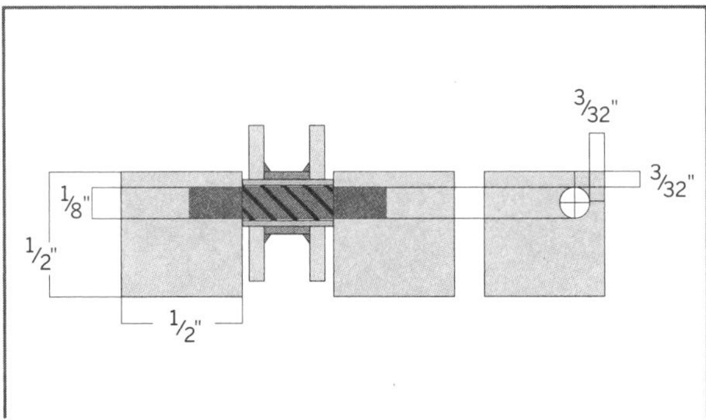

Figure 03.29: **Fitting the pulley**

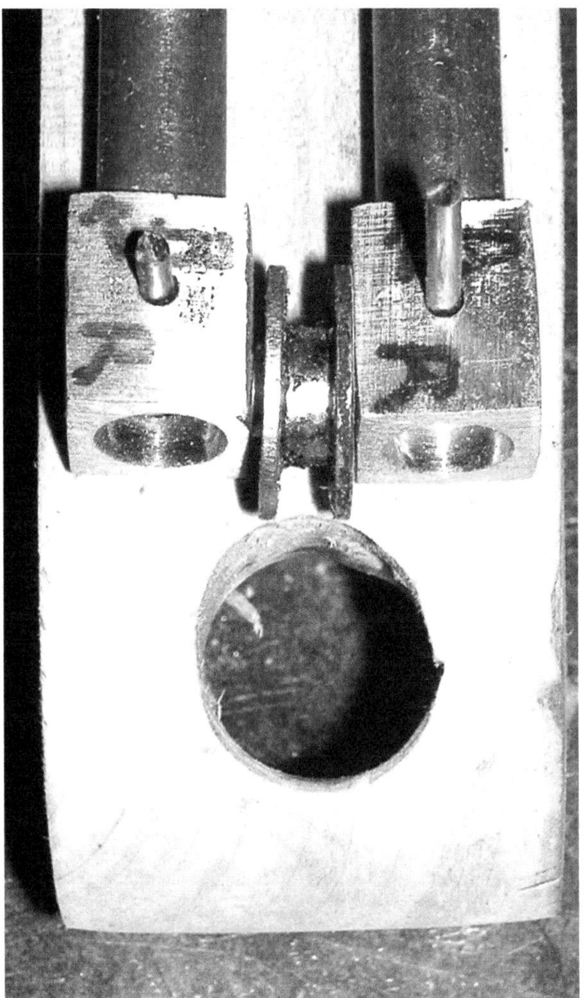

Figure 03.30: **The pulley and rear guide rail mounting blocks properly positioned**

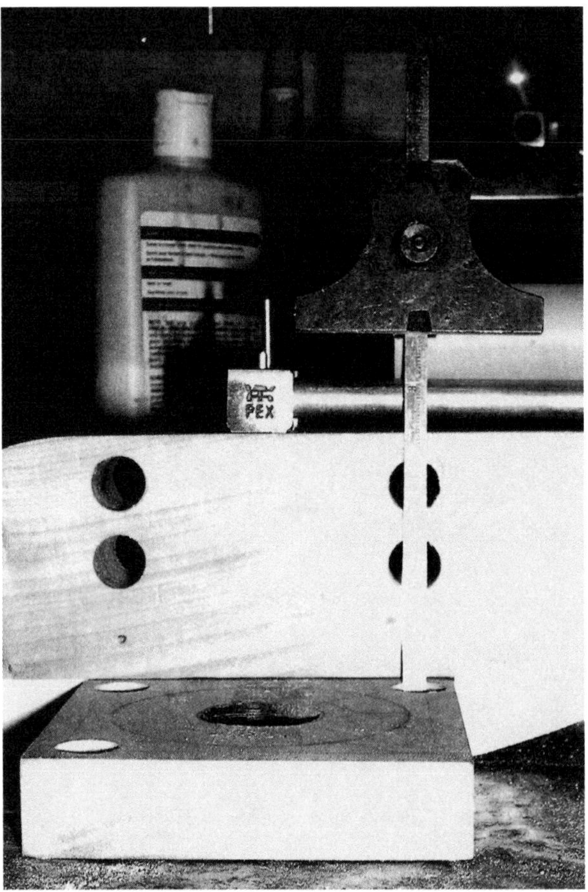

Figure 03.31: **At last! The critical skein balancing dimension revealed.**

in the two rear rail mounting blocks. Use a short length of 1/8" steel rod press-fitted into these holes to mount the pulley. **[Figure 03.29]**

Finalize the positioning of the guide rails and drill pilot holes in the body for the mounting screws. Mount the rear blocks first, such that the spool of the pulley *just* clears the edge of the winch cable exit hole in the body. The rest of the locations happen in context of that position. The guide rails are centered on the top of the body, spaced 7/8", center to center. They *need* to be parallel, to each other *and* to the body. **[Figure 03.30]**

Measure twice, drill once!

Finalizing the Skein Assembly

Now that we've finished fabricating the rails and pulley, we can get a pretty good idea of where the bowstring is gonna have to sit to notch properly into the dart.

To ensure lots of room for multipage missives and the occasional thumb drive, I spec'd the darts for BallistaMail out of cheerful orange PVC sprinkler pipe 1" in diameter. With a sample of the material in question positioned on the rails (tack them in place with bit of brass rod) and the bottom rack plate in place, my depth gauge gave me a distance of 3½" from the bottom of the support hole to the midpoint of the pipe. **[Figure 03.31]**

Thrilled by my knowledge of this, I snatched up a pipecutter and cut six 7"-long pieces of thickwalled ½" OD brass tubing. When I fitted together the bits and pieces scattered around the bench, it looked like **Figure 03.32**.

My glee was infinite.

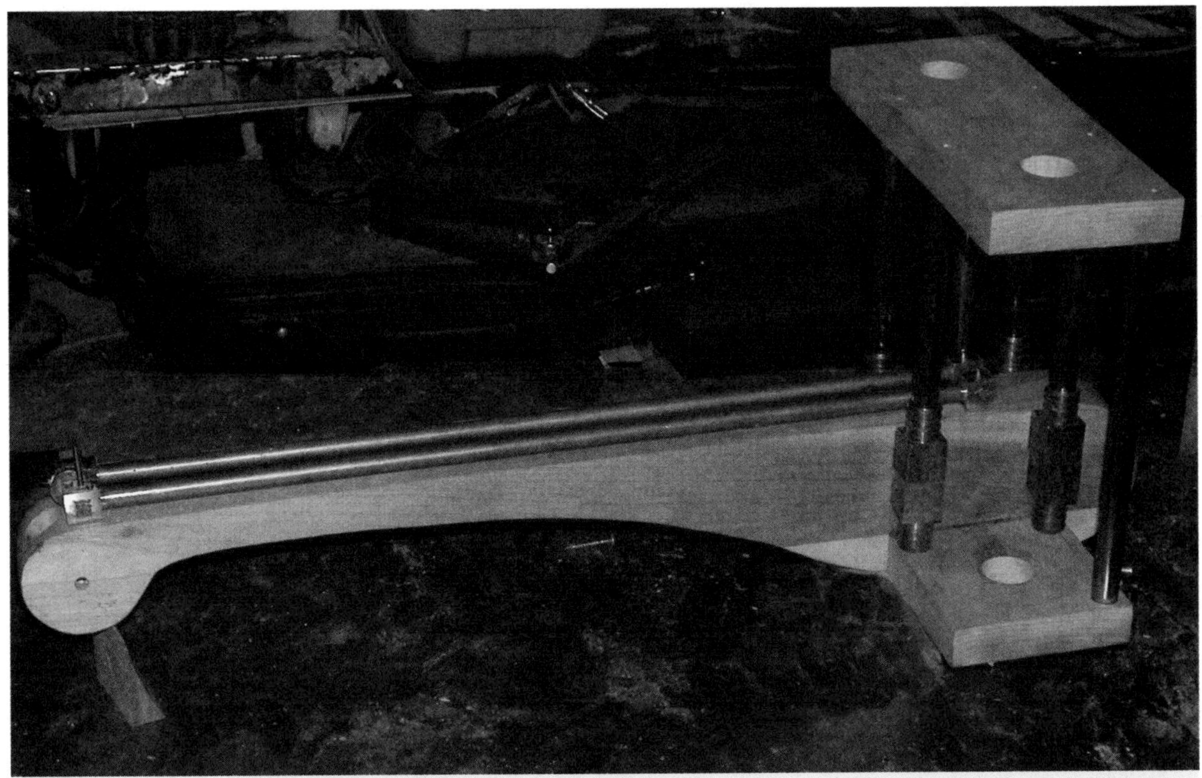

Figure 03.32: Hot damn — it's starting to look like a ballista.

Foreign Words: Fabricating the Epizygis and Modiolus

The traditional tensioning mechanism for skeins consists of components with names like *epizygis* (lever) and *modiolus* (washer). Now that you know the names, we can all cease to refer to them.

Washer is easy enough to deal with. Pictured are four honkin' big ones dug up at Capital Salvage: brass, ⅛" x 2½", with a 1" hole. Origin? Beats the hell outta me, but similarly sized items are readily available in galvanized steel, which is actually the more suitable (read "stronger") choice. **[Figure 03.33, Figure 03.34]**

Back to the epizygis/modiolus[4] assemblies. You need four of 'em: top and bottom, left and right. The modioli have equally spaced holes around them, tapped to accept threaded rod posts to lock the epizygis in position after the skein's been torqued up. Drill out the skein tension retainer holes in the oversized washers to 13/64". They're spaced 60 degrees apart, 5/16" in from the outer edge. Tap these six holes with ¼-20 threads.

Drill two mounting holes ⅛" in diameter, ⅛" in from the inner edge, 180 degrees opposed. Add a ¼" countersink to these holes to let the mounting screw heads lie flush with the surface. Use ½" #8 flathead screws when it comes time to mount the components.

Position the washers on the rack plates, mark all hole positions accordingly, and drill 'em out. The tension retainer holes are drilled to 7/32" at a depth of half an inch, and the mounting holes to 7/64" at the same depth. **[Figure 03.35]**

Plumbers get the coolest parts to play with. Appreciate the snazz on these suckers: the OD of the threaded part is 1" and the ID is ¾". The unthreaded bit on top of the hexnut is ½" ID. A plumber looks at these things and sez, "brass ½" to ¾" reducers." I look at 'em and say, "these will be epizyges in a very short time." **[Figure 03.36]**

I'd make a lousy plumber.

Here's the reducer-to-epizygis conversion process.

Lop the threaded part off with a hacksaw, smooth out the cut surface, and grind out the hole to ¾" all the way through. This isn't as big a job as you'd expect. After removing the extended ½" section of the reducer, there's about 3/16" left on the fitting at the smaller diameter. It took about two minutes with a grinding stone chucked into the drillpress to get the entire fitting up to ¾" ID.

4 Yeah, I know. We weren't gonna use those names any more. But they roll off the tongue so smoothly, I can't resist the urge.

Figure 03.33: **Four honkin' big brass washers, soon to be four honkin' big modioli.**

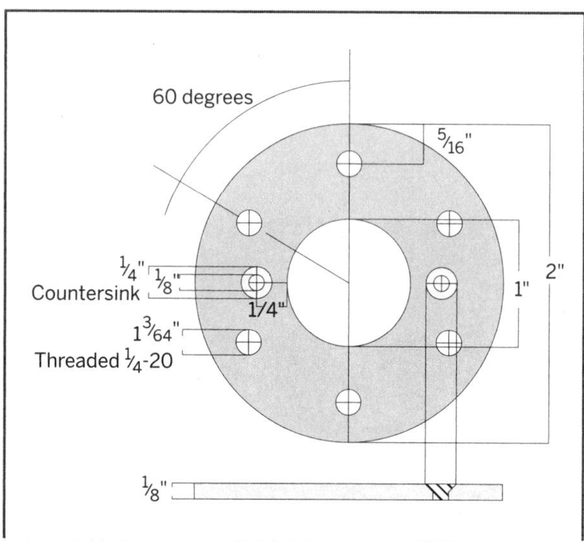

Figure 03.34: **In detail: the modiolus formerly known as washer. You'll need a quartet of the little buggers.**

The shortened, bored-out fitting sits comfortably in the modiolus, and — because it's polished brass on polished brass — rotates like it has bearings. **[Figure 03.37]**

Next, use a round file or dremel-like device to carve a 5/16"-wide notch 3/16" deep across the diameter of the hex head, as illustrated. Make sure both sides are carved to the same depth. **[Figure 03.38]**

You can see where this is going, can't you?

You'll need to rustle up 10" of 5/16" steel rod to complete the epizygis fabrication. Cut four 2½" lengths. These components slot into the notches in the epizygis and serve as the winding posts and tension levers for the skeins.

Material selection can be an issue here. The rod has to withstand the vertical strain imparted by the skein

Figure 03.35: **Position the modioli on the skein plates, mark the hole positions, then drill 'em out to spec.**

Figure 03.36: **Primary raw material for epizygis fabrication: the quite splendid brass ½" to ¼" reducers.**

Figure 03.37: **See — it fits into the modiolus like it was made for it!**

Figure 03.38: **Form a notch across the diameter of the hex head.**

Figure 03.39: **Just add steel rod, and the modified brass reducer achieves full epizygal functionality.**

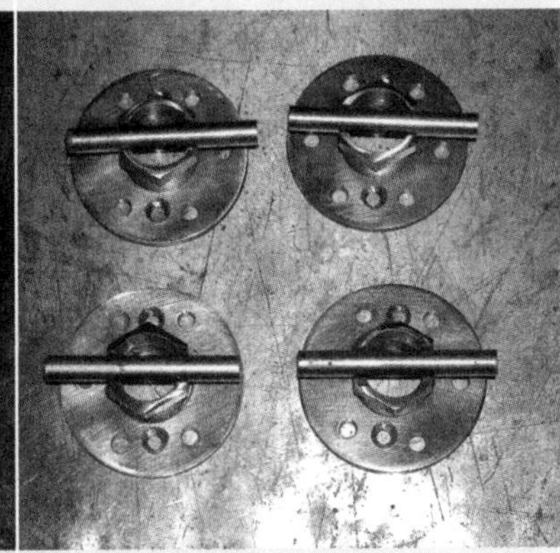
Figure 03.40: **A matched set.**

shortening as it's twisted, as well as the torque strain of the twist itself. Brass would *likely* be strong enough to take the stresses the rod is subjected to under load, but this is clearly a "better safe than sorry" situation, so let's opt for caution. **[Figure 03.39]**

Now do that three more times, and adjourn for a quantity of celebratory libation. Entertain the cocktail waitress with your intrepid tales of epizygis/modiolus fabrication. Stop drinking when you can no longer pronounce the words clearly. **[Figure 03.40]**

Bow Arms

I've put off doing the trigger, because it's the toughest part of the build. There's still the winch mechanism and the bow arms to suss out. Making with the virtual coin flip, it comes up heads and I'm digging in the wood crib looking for something to make bow arms out of.

Look at any of the historical recreations of ballistae and you'll notice that the bow arms aren't much more than steroid-enhanced sticks with a bowstring tied onto them. When I first looked at the mechanism and started figuring out exactly what goes on during a firing cycle, it bugged the hell out of me for some reason I couldn't put a finger on. The first few prototypes I built went the traditional route, with slightly tapered straight bow arms. They still annoyed me.

When I finally reached the point where I was comfortable with the basic mechanism, I started doing some tests on the power curve of torsion bundles. Nothin' fancy — basically,

I clamped a finished model into the vise, hung a bucket on the bowstring, and started adding water to the bucket. A pointer on the bucket let me mark the amount of *draw* gained by each quart (about two pounds) of water added to the bucket.

No surprises here: the amount of resistance provided by the skeins increased exponentially with the length of the draw. The graph was picture-perfect; it looked like something out of a first-year physics text and indicated that there was *lots* more energy being applied to the dart at the start of the shot than there was as the arms reached the end of their travel. **[Figure 03.41]**

Well, duh.

So I got to thinking about working some cam-like geometry into the bow arms to increase the bowstring forward velocity as the bow arms moved through their motion range. Now, do *not* ask me for the math: cam geometry is about as arcane as 2D math can get, particularly when implemented in a physical mass/force/velocity environment. I'm a pretty clever fella, but this shit is complex enough to have caused me significant loss of sleep just trying to wrap my brain cells around the numbers. Instead, I invoked Occam's Razor[5] on the issue, and realized that the main concern was ensuring that the bowstring always wants to move faster than the projectile at any point in the firing cycle. **[Figure 03.42]**

There's a lot of experimentation potential in this simple addition to the basic ballista concept. The design illustrated has so far served the purpose well — preventing the projectile from outrunning the bowstring and ensuring maximum energy transfer — but I'd be thrilled to get some more thoroughly researched input from those schooled in mathematical arcana.

There are a couple added benefits to this design. First, it allows the bowstring to be secured by running it *through* the body of each bow arm rather than simply tying it onto

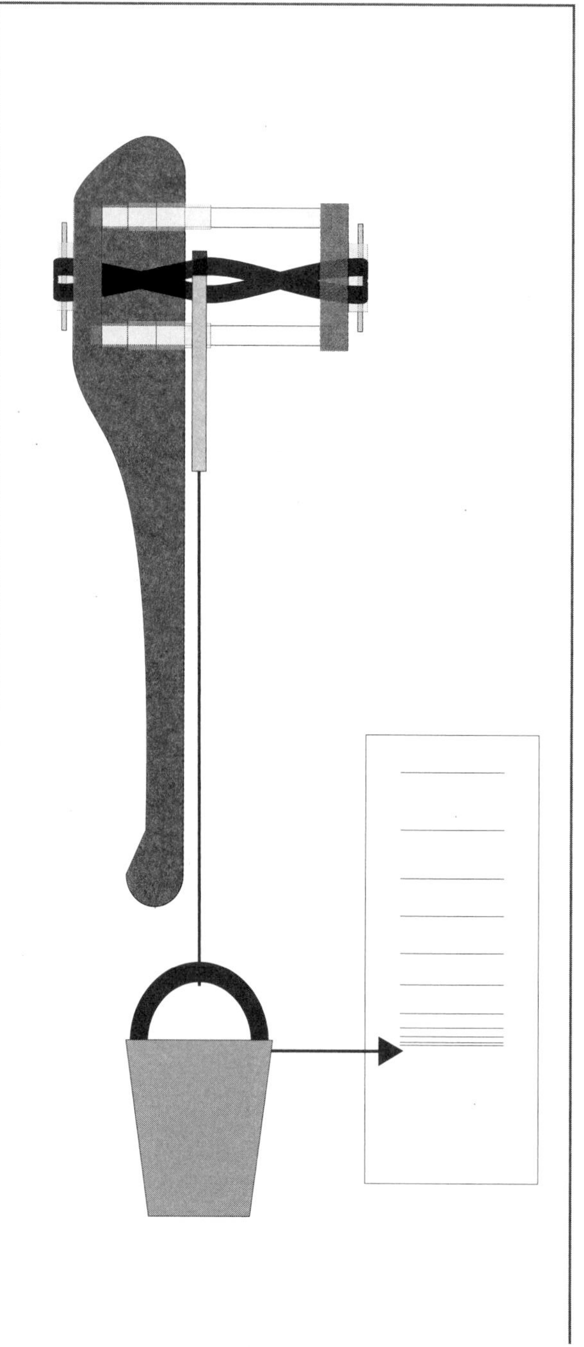

Figure 03.41: Testing the torsion skein power curve

5 William of Occam, 14th-century Franciscan friar and stone-cold logician, originally postulated, "Entities should not be multiplied unnecessarily."

Huh?

Okay, try this: "When you have two competing theories which make exactly the same predictions, the one that is simpler is the better."

Clearer, but still lacking in *essence*.

How about: "The explanation requiring the fewest assumptions is most likely to be correct."

Now we're gettin' somewhere.

Refining the essence of the postulation to a self-realizing term: Keep It Simple.

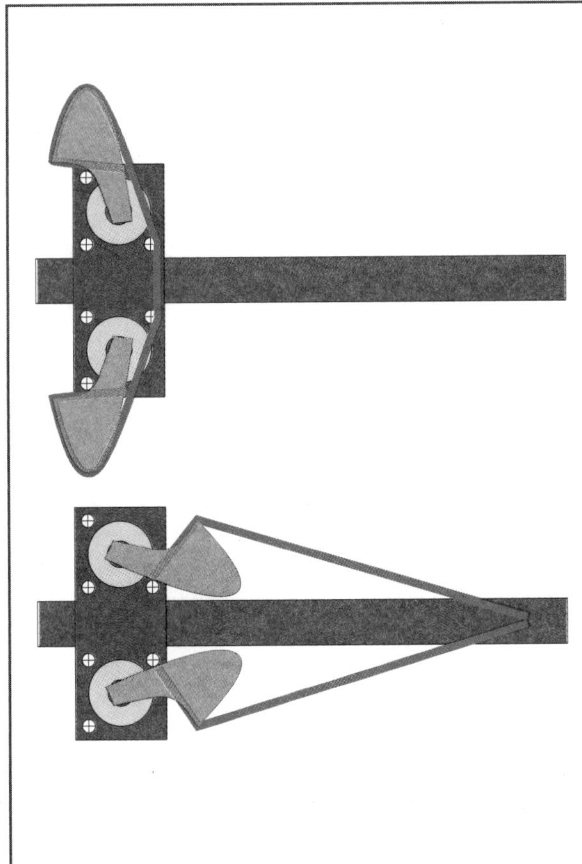

Figure 03.42: **Cammed bow arms for enhanced power curve goodness**

Figure 03.43: **Arm blanks**

the tip of each arm. This design permits an extended range of retraction without risk of having the flippin' bowstring slip off the end of the arms in mid-demonstration. Serendipitously, the bowstring also acts as a shock absorber, cushioning the impact of the bow arm against the support column during operation.

Shown is stack of two three-ply bow arm blanks; they're laminated from 1⁄4" poplar, red oak, and poplar again, with the grain of each ply running about 15 degrees off parallel to add a bit of strength. The blank is about 67⁄8" x 23⁄4". You can use solid, unlaminated hardwood if you want. The grain strength improvement from lamination is a nice bonus, but not necessary if you use clear, straight-grained maple. Draw your arm onto the blank, and drill the bowstring holes before going any further. **[Figure 03.43]**

I roughed the arms out with a coping saw. The discoloration you see in the wood is from the appalling amount of sweat generated by the process. The curve geometery came from using a French curve to connect a few circles, and I used the entire length of the blank, which leaves room to install an arm position stop once the bowstring length has been sussed out. **[Figure 03.44]**

I had a bit of concern about the overall mass of the arms, so I drilled out some material on each arm. I then used a spherical high-speed cutter about 3⁄16" diameter to form a shallow groove in the middle ply to act as a string guide; the groove runs most of the way around wide curvy part of the arms. **[Figure 03.45, Figure 03.46]**

Scaling the bow arms to allow for a bowstring that exactly meets both limit-of-travel criteria (full draw and at rest) takes a bit of trial and error working with arms, the skein rack, and the bowstring on the actual body of the mechanism. We'll do that later. Think of it as a challenge to look forward to.

Winch, Windlass . . . Whatever

The winch mechanism is a pretty cunning bodge. Let's consider the components required: axle (A), spool (B), handle (C), ratchet (D), and pawl (E): **[Figure 03.47]**

Axle? 5⁄16" – 18 brass toilet bolt. Check. **[Figure 03.48]**

Spool? 5⁄16" ID thick walled brass tubing, internally threaded at 18 threads/inch. Check. **[Figure 03.49]**

Handle? 6" brass truck tire valve stem. Check.

NOTE: Don't freak. They're not hard to find.

Ratchet? Modified brass pipefitting. Check. **[Figure 03.50]**

Pawl? Carve one out of 1⁄8" brass plate. Check. **[Figure 03.51]**

Some of the components are pretty self-explanatory: I mean, what's complicated about a 5⁄16-18 bolt other than cutting it off at the right length?

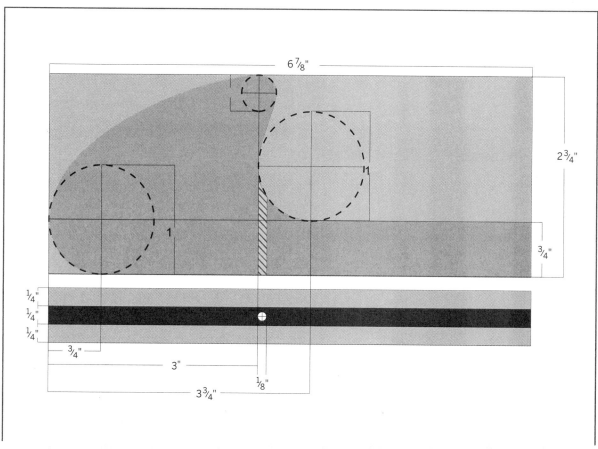

Figure 03.44: **The bow arm in modest detail: two required (see text for the fine points).**

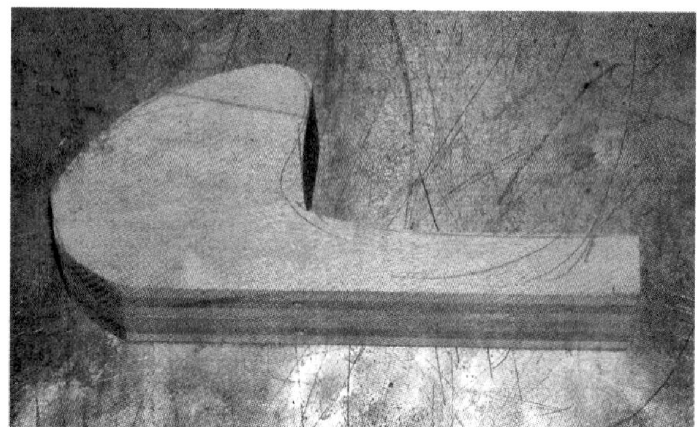

Figure 03.45: **Bow arm roughed out**

Figure 03.46: **Jolly good! Two bow arms!**

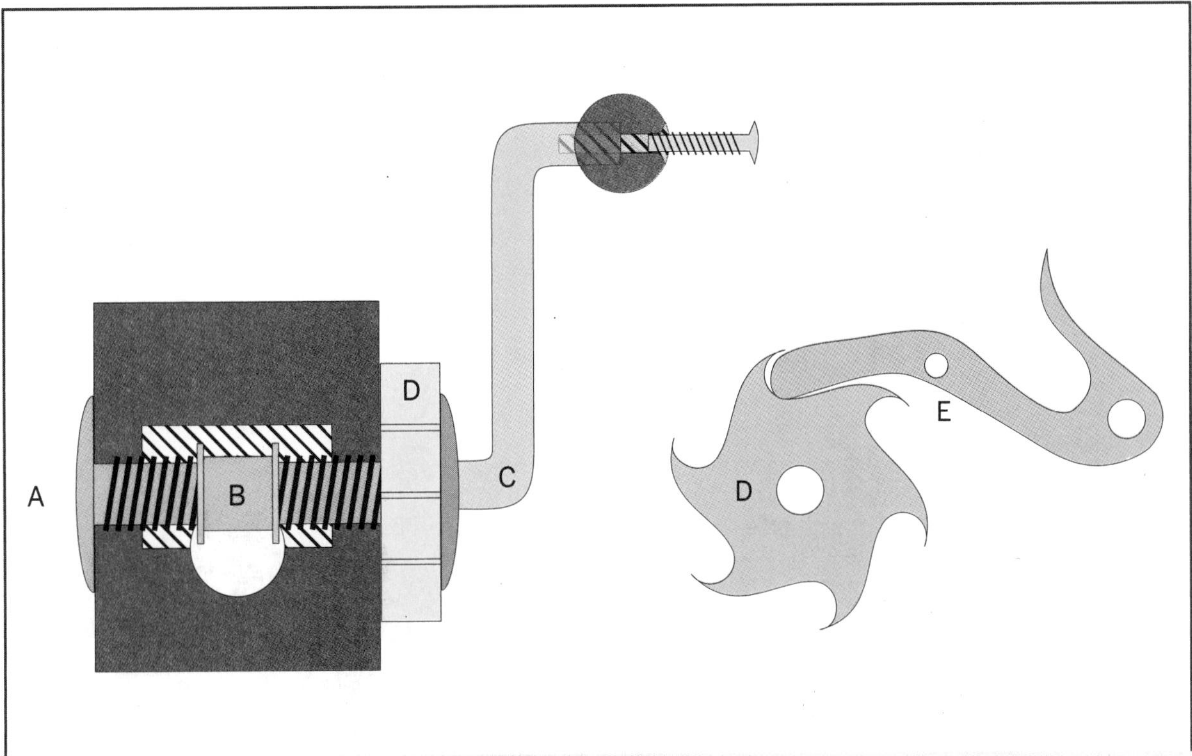

Figure 03.47: **The ABCs (and Ds and Es) of windlass componentry**

Figure 03.48: **Toilet bolt**

Figure 03.49: **Spool tube**

Figure 03.50: **The aforementioned potentially freak-inducing brass valve stem**

Figure 03.51: **Started life as a humble 1" threaded brass end cap, believe it or not.**

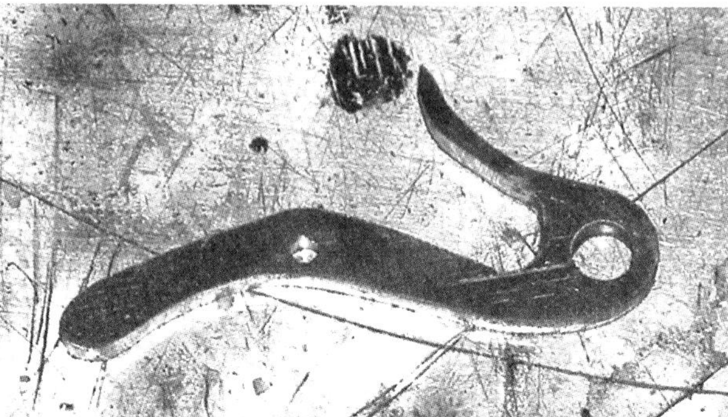

Figure 03.52: **Yeah, it's a ratchet pawl.**

Others require a bit more of an explanation. The ratchet is fabricated from a 1" threaded brass pipe cap. We're using the 1 3⁄8" hex head portion of the fitting, so out with the hacksaw and cut off the threaded bit. Locate and punch-start the seven holes and drill 'em out. The center hole is sized to 17⁄64" and gets threaded to 5⁄16-18; the perimeter holes are 5⁄16" and get abused mercilessly soon after being drilled. **[Figure 03.53]**

NOTE: Take your time; get it right.

The white lines on the diagram indicate cut lines. You're cutting through 5⁄16" metal, which is far beyond the capacity of a rotary hobby tool. Fortunately, the metal is brass, which makes it a less formidable task. I like those little *junior* hacksaws for this size of cutting. They're more

Figure 03.53: **Start with one of these.**

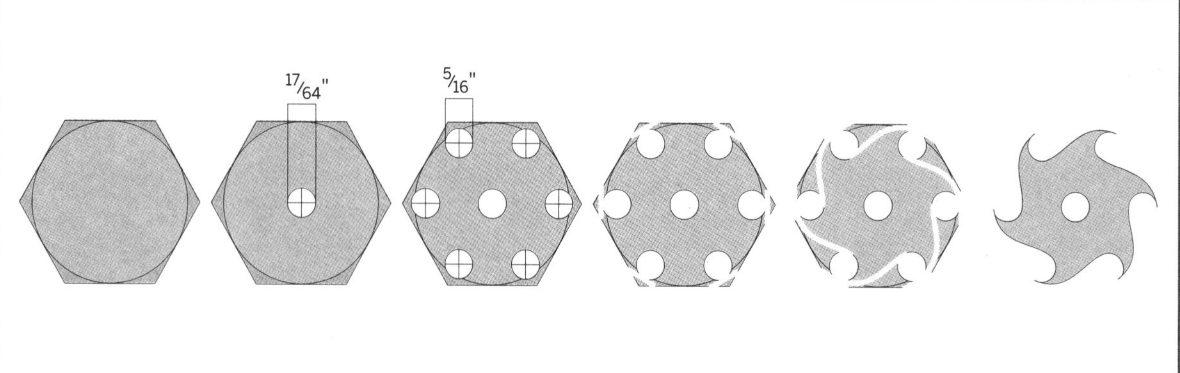

Figure 03.54: **Do all this stuff to it.**

Figure 03.55: **End up with one of these.**

robust than a jeweler's saw, but the blade is still narrow enough to let you cut in close quarters. They get the job done as long as you remember to change the blade frequently. **[Figure 03.54]**

Mark your cut lines carefully with a scribing tool, and make the cuts; precision isn't super essential, as long as you *stay inside the lines* when you're sawing. That said, the closer you are to the lines, the less metal you'll have to remove with needle files after the fact.

Lop off the corners of the hex head first to open up the holes; then, make the angled cuts. Finish shaping the ratchet with files or a dremel, then polish out any tool marks with emery cloth. You can buff up a mirror finish on the entire surface of the component if you want, but it'll be a time-consuming proceedure. **[Figure 03.55]**

To put the issue of brasswork surface preparation and buffing in perspective, **Figure 03.56** provides a look at *most* of the brass componentry of BallistaMail. A dozen ¼-20 acorn nuts aren't pictured.

That, campers, is a *prodigious* amount of metal to polish: 50 separate structural components and about 30 machine

A Point Regarding Thread Direction

The geometry of this particular winch is configured so that any load on the mechanism acts to *tighten* threaded couplings. The direction of the ratchet (and its placement on the right side of the body) is such that pull on the winch cable tightens the ratchet threads onto the axle when the pawl is engaged.

Similarly, the handle placement on the left side of the body tightens the handle onto the axle threads during winding. I'm left-handed, so for me, the ergonomics of this arrangement are ideal. If you *absolutely* need to have the winch handle on the right and the ratchet on the left, use rolled pins or keyways to secure the ratchet and handle on the axle shaft.

We now return to our regularly scheduled fabrication.

screws, nuts, and washers for assembly. Total weight, about 7 pounds.

I shudder to think of the surface area represented. Adopt a realistic benchmark for metal polishing right from the start, or you'll develop a nasty obsessive-compulsive jones in no time flat.

For the record, it took me two freakin' 11-hour days to get a *reasonable* buff job applied to that lot in the photograph.

Holy Toledo! You're looking at *damned* useful things in the next figure: brass valve stems intended for use on particularly manly commercial vehicles. Pictured are French-made Schrader clamp-in stems. I got a handful of used ones at a tire repair shop for $5 and a cup of coffee; they were destined for recycling. I've since seen them advertised at online auction sites for around $1.50 a pop. There's 6" of thick-walled 5⁄16" OD brass tubing extending at a right angle from the base flange; the base is threaded internally to 1⁄4-20, and the chromed washer thingie that forms the flange rotates freely. The open end is threaded internally to accept a standard tire valve core, and externally to accept whatever flavour of pimped-out valve cap you wanna dress your ride with. **[Figure 03.57]**

Yo.

Figure 03.56: **There is potential for madness when faced with a massive pile of brasswork in desperate need of buffing and polishing. Know your limitations.**

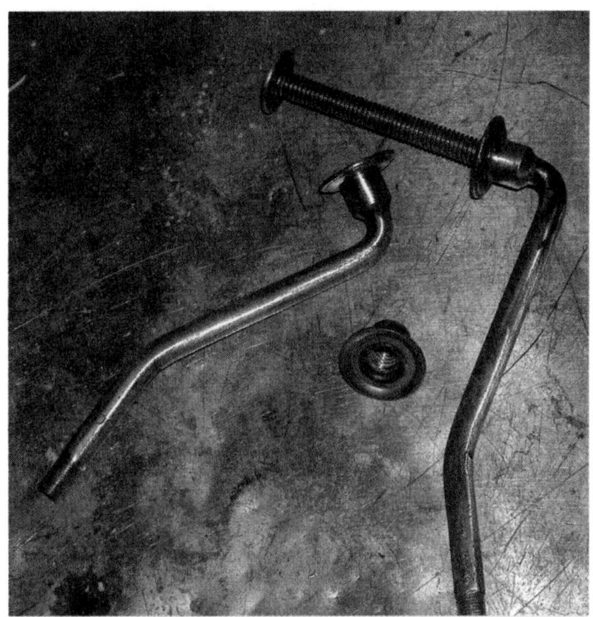

Figure 03.57: **6" Schrader clamp-in valve stems. C'est bon, mon ami.**

Figure 03.58: **Fugly? Uh huh. Useful? Yeah, that too. Recognizing potential alternative uses for garden-variety stuff is an essential part of improvisational fabrication.**

Modifying one of these to serve as a winch handle was remarkably easy. I retapped the threads in the base end to 5⁄16-18 (there was ample material there to form solid threading), packed the tubing with sand (to prevent crimping), and bent the 22.5 degree midlength offset to a full 90 degrees. **[Figure 03.58]**

I fashioned a knob for the handle out of a 3⁄4" wooden craft ball. I drilled one side to 5⁄16", countersunk the other to accept a 3⁄4" 8-32 machine screw, and tapped the end of the brass handle to 8-32. It took about five minutes total and gave me a fairly slick-looking knob.

NOTE: Attention to detail doesn't always take hours. The results are invariably gratifying.

Of course, you're welcome to assemble any manner of winch handle you like during the course of *your* build, but as I undertook this fabrication with a "design on the bench" philosophy, this is what I used, because it was *there*. **[Figure 03.59]**

The tubing I used for the windlass spool is that pretty standard issue 3⁄8" OD/*A Hair Over* 1⁄4" ID brass stuff that's used in a lot of thriftshop decorator accents. This particular chunk previously saw duty as part of a desk lamp. It's threaded internally to 5⁄16-18 and cut to 1-9⁄16" . The length assumes a 1½" body width, plus 1⁄16"" extra to stand off the handle and ratchet from the body. **[Figure 03.60]**

Take a minute and drill out the windlass axle hole in the body to 3⁄8".

Sculpting the ratchet pawl lets you indulge your inner arteest. Start with a 3⁄4" x 2" piece of 3⁄32" brass plate and remove the bits that don't look like a ratchet pawl. It's easier to do if you have the mounting holes for the pawl and tension spring already positioned on the body and the pawl stock. The pawl needs a spring attached to latch it properly into each tooth of the ratchet and ensure a fully satisfying rakataka-rakataka noise during winding. Adding a lever to disengage the pawl when unwinding the cable is a nice ergonomic touch. **[Figure 03.61]**

Thread the bolt through the ratchet, then thread on the spool tube. Loctite on the threads wouldn't be amiss here.[6]

6 I favor the pink semipermanent variety. The "semipermanent" feature is the big deal here, as it releases before the torque gets high enough to induce material twist and the potential for snappage (which is always a big deal when you're dealing with brass).

Drill a 3⁄32" cable attachment hole through the midpoint of the axle and spool.

Got your ratchet/axle/spool assembly?

Got yer handle/knob assembly?

Got yer ratchet pawl?

Dude, it's a windlass — or at least all the parts needed to put one together. Lemme hear ya say, "Yeehah!" **[Figure 03.63]**

Now, for the trigger.

Trigger

A ballista trigger has to grip the bowstring securely at two points, leaving an exposed area of string open to notch the dart into. Because drawing the bow involves the use of a windlass, the string-gripping trigger has to ride on a sled that slides up and down the same rails that guide the trajectory of the dart.

The trigger build isn't particularly challenging, but you need to get the measurements right in context of *your* project. I started by rough-shaping the basic sled to the point where I had a low-profile piece of wood that fit on the rails and moved smoothly. I formed the guide rail slots on the table saw, but could just as easily have glued the whole thing up from blocks and strips.[7] **[Figure 03.64]**

The cutting diagram provides all the gory details. **[Figure 03.65]**

Here's a walkthrough. It's a cam-locked pinch mechanism,

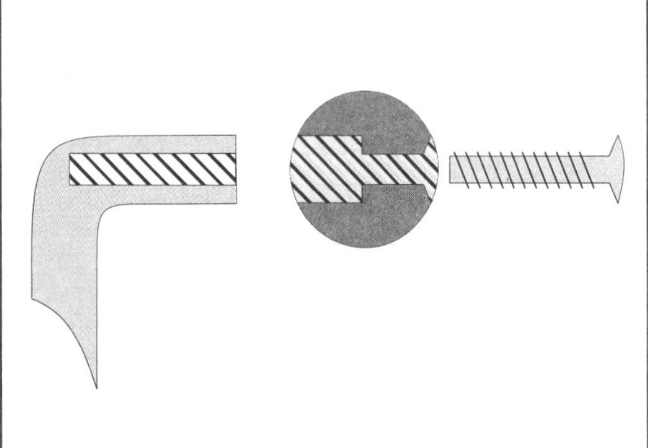

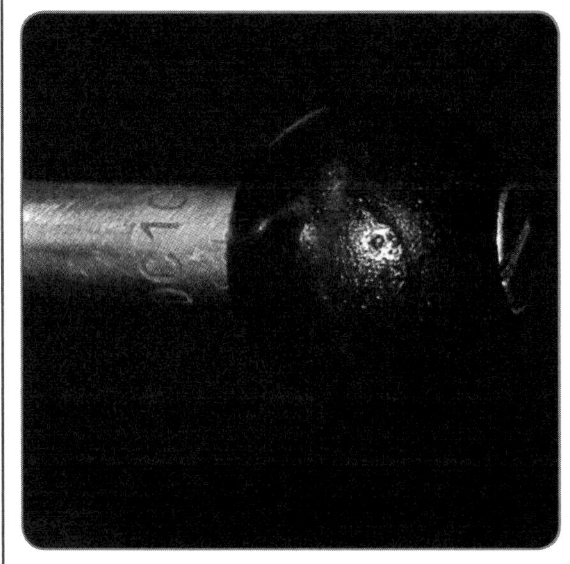

Figure 03.59: **The three-minute knob handle**

Figure 03.60: **Cut the internal threads through the entire length of a 2" piece of tube. You can cut it to size later.**

Figure 03.61: **Position your pawl stock in context of the ratchet assembly and rough sketch the outline of the pawl. Cut it to shape with the metal removal tool of your choice, then fine-tune the fit with needle files.**

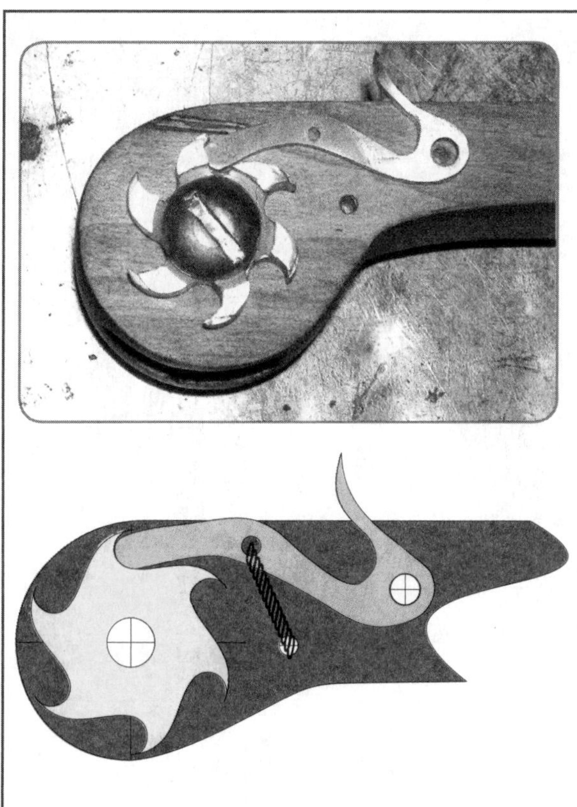

Figure 03.62: **The ratchet pawl in principle and practice**

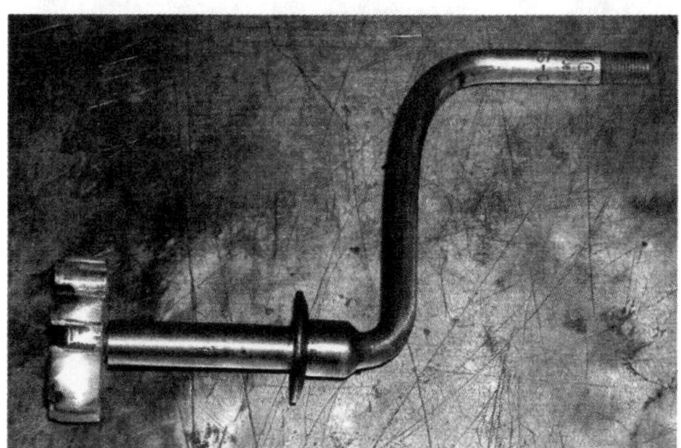

Figure 03.63: **Most of the winch subassembly. Not shown: the ratchet pawl and tension spring. Also not shown: the ballista the whole lot will be attached to.**

Figure 03.64: **The seamy (and accurately notched) underbelly of the trigger sled revealed.**

consisting of two PacMan-shaped plates (more of those honkin' big brass washers we're also using as modioli, modified to within an inch of their lives), a wooden sled notched on the underside to straddle the guide rails, and a cam lever/bolt combination. The plates are grooved on either

7 Either approach works. Your only mandate is that it rides smoothly on the rails and sits at a height that places the upper surface of the bottom metal jawplate parallel to the bowstring (that's the measurement we sussed out). The overall shape of the sled is immaterial, but try to keep it as short as possible to allow for maximum draw length of the bowstring.

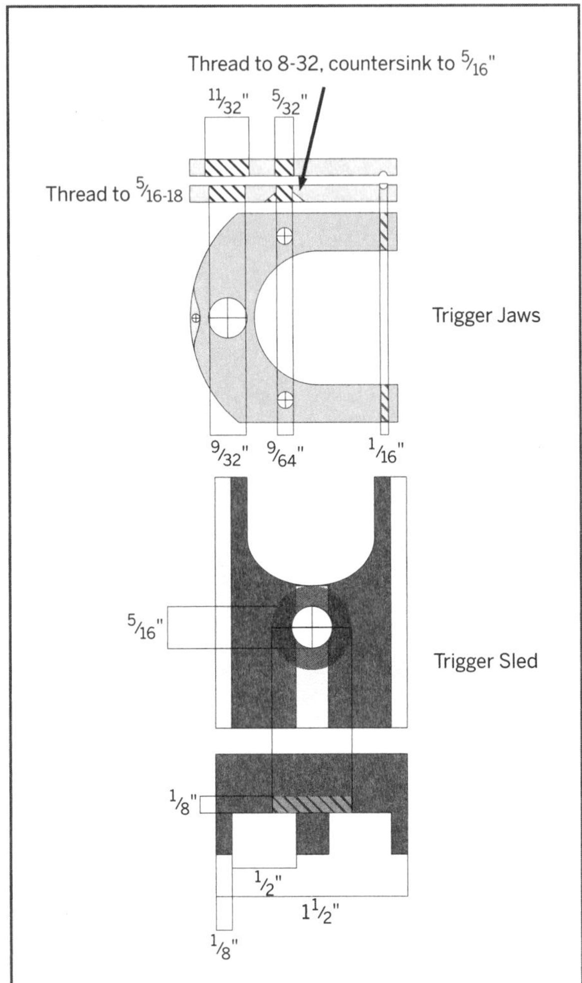

Figure 03.65: **The trigger jaws and sled in modest detail.**

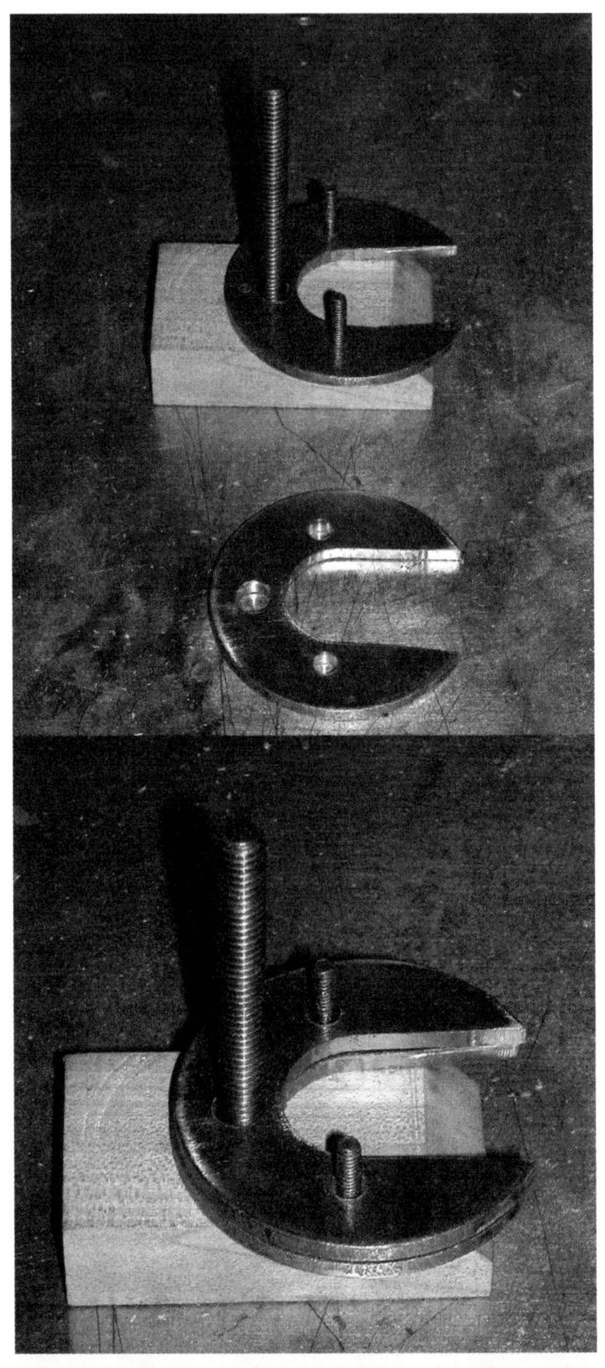

Figure 03.66: **The sled blank and lower jaw plate with the top jaw plate positioned**

side of the inner faces of the jaws to fit the bowstring and kept in alignment by two 8-32 bolts tapped into the lower plate.

The cam bolt threads straight through the sled and lower plate. The bolt and alignment holes on the upper plate are slightly oversized, so that when the cam is released, the two plates separate smoothly, opening the jaws and releasing the string.

Stack the washers with double-sided tape and modify them in tandem. Cut the opening with a hacksaw and then true up the edges with a file. Mark the positions of the holes and drill 3/32" pilot holes through both plates simultaneously.

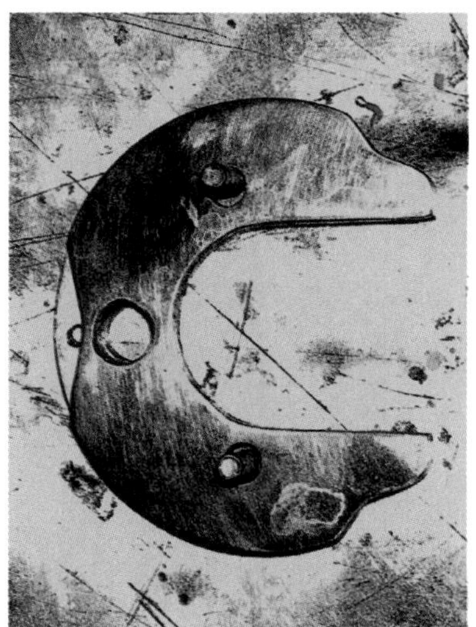

Figure 03.67: **The finished jawplates, guideposts removed**

Figure 03.68: **Big-assed countersink in the underside of the sled to accommodate the head of the toilet bolt used as the trigger bolt.**

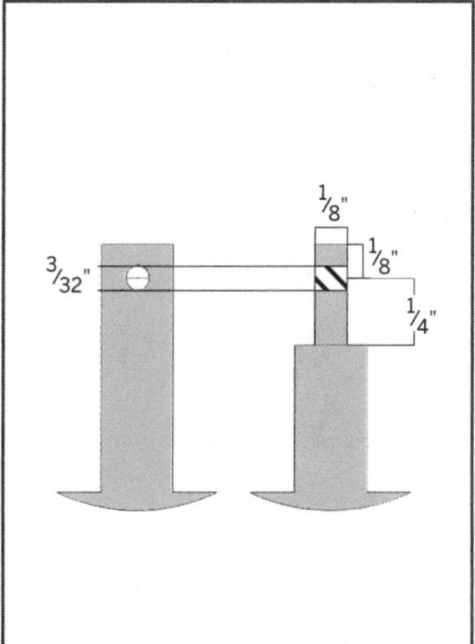

Figure 03.69: **The trigger bolt modded to accept the cam lever. Your measurements will vary in context of your particular cam lever specifications.**

Only the bottom plate gets drilled for the cable attachment point. **[Figure 03.66, Figure 03.67]**

Once the holes are drilled, finish the basic shaping of the plates and then separate them. The alignment holes and cam bolt hole on the top plate are drilled out slightly oversized. Grind the threads off the exposed sections of the 8-32 alignment screws to ensure smooth release action.

The windlass cable attaches to the bottom plate via a 3/32" hole drilled just aft of the cam hole. The top plate is notched away at this point to expose this hole, and there's a shallow groove carved into the body of the sled for the windlass cable to run along. **[Figure 03.67]**

Form the string groove with caution, making it straight, parallel on each side of the jaws, and sized for a *comfortable* but not *roomy* fit. Bicycle brake cable is the bowstring material of choice. Fiber-based strings just don't have the resilience to withstand long term abuse in a high-load/high-abrasion setting like this.

The cam bolt is a modified toilet retention bolt. These suckers have massive heads that you'll need to accomodate in the underbelly of your sled with a strategically placed counter sink hole. **[Figure 03.68]**

The cam itself is shaped from a scrap of 1/2" brass bar stock. **[Figure 03.70]**

I cut the basic shape slightly oversized with a hacksaw and formed the bolt slot by drilling a 1/8" hole at the top of the slot position, then cutting out the rest of the slot with a hacksaw. I drilled the pivot hole on the cam itself first, after roughing the toilet bolt to length and filing opposing faces flat to fit the slot in the cam. **[Figure 03.69]** I drilled the corresponding hole in the bolt after I'd done some test fitting and determined the proper height. **[Figure 03.71, Figure 03.72]**

As with all ~~homemade~~ hand-fabricated cam mechanisms, count on spending some quality time with needle files and shim stock to get a tight, smooth action. The axle pin for the cam needs to be as strong as possible, due to the force potential inherent in cam mechanics. I used a short section of a broken 3/32" drillbit and peened heads onto each end to hold it in position during final assembly of the trigger. **[Figure 03.73]**

Which ended up looking like the illustration. **[Figure 03.74]**

Anyway, there I was, happy as a clam, ready to start final assembly when I suddenly realized I'd forgotten about the damned tripod.

"Flibbertygibbets," I said. Rather forcefully.

Tripod, A.K.A. THE 'POD

Tempting as it is to finish the build around the aesthetics of a handheld ~~weapon~~ message delivery system, the pinpoint

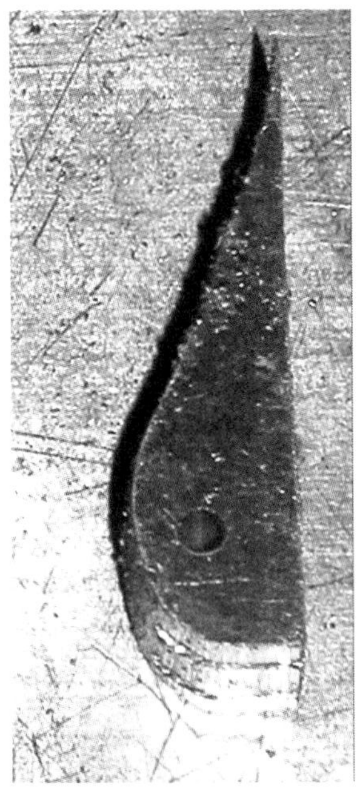

Figure 03.70: **The roughed out cam lever**

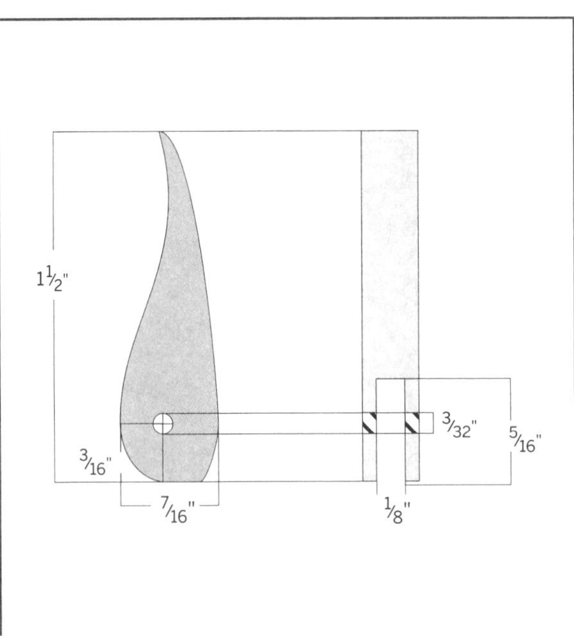

Figure 03.71: **Again with the cams — the trigger lever in detail**

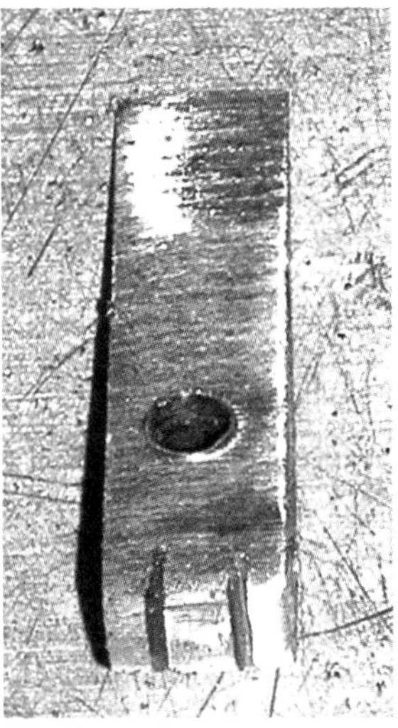

Figure 03.72: **Drill out the top end of the bolt slot with a 1/8" bit, then carefuly cut out the rest of the slot with a hacksaw.**

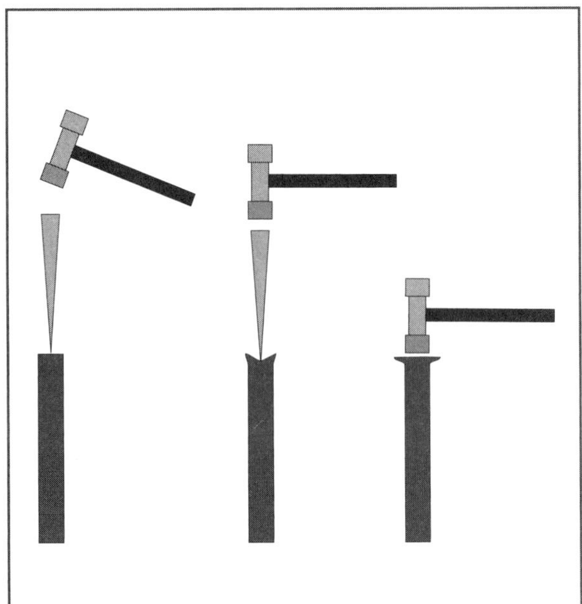

Figure 03.73: **Peening simplified**

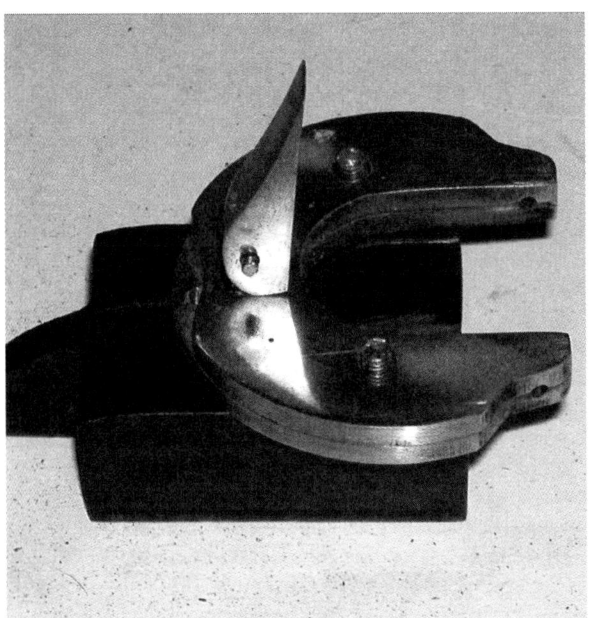

Figure 03.74: **The finished trigger**

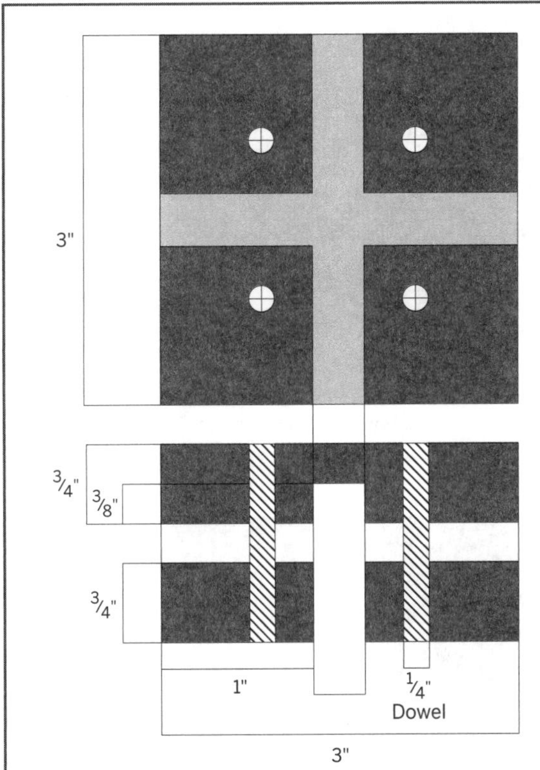

Figure 03.75: The 'Pod Legblock glue-up, with guest fasteners the Fabulous 1/4" Dowels

Figure 03.76: The requisite bits . . .

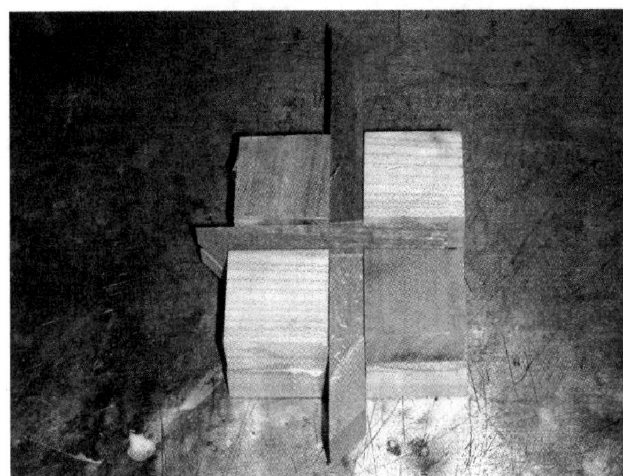

Figure 03.77: . . . adroitly spaced with scrap stock

Figure 03.78: Out of the clamps with the leg axle holes positioned and drilled

accuracy (or facsimile thereof) required by BallistaMail calls for solid, repeatable target vectoring capabilities. Under the circumstances, this translates to "Build the damned tripod, Kaden".

I started with a 3½" square block of ¾" poplar and used the table saw to cut ½"-wide dadoes ⅜" deep, crossing from the midpoint of each side. **[Figure 03.75, Figure 03.76]**

I cut 1½" squares from the same stock, spaced them out with ½" scrap and glued it up. **[Figure 03.77]**

When this receiver block was out of the clamps, I marked the center point of each exposed cube face formed by the glue-up and drilled 3/32" pilot holes. **[Figure 03.78]**

You likely don't need to go to this extreme, but I felt the need to reinforce the leg receiver and add some aesthetic conceptual continuity to the build. **[Figure 03.79]**

I rummaged around in the parts bins and found a 2¾" x ½" cast brass disk that had previously seen duty as a decorative flange on a truly hideous swing-arm sconce lamp

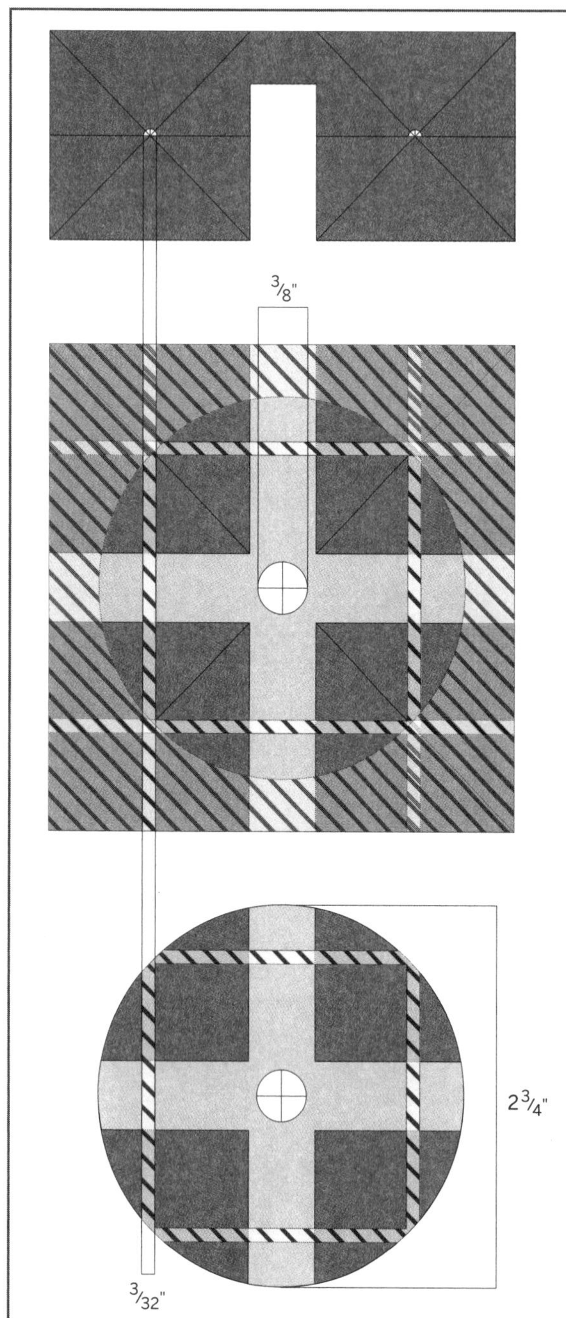

Figure 03.79: **The continued evolution of the leg mounting block**

Figure 03.80: **Artsy-fartsy nonsense meets structural reinforcement in the form of added brasswork.**

Figure 03.81: **What's a pod leg receiver block without pod legs to receive?**

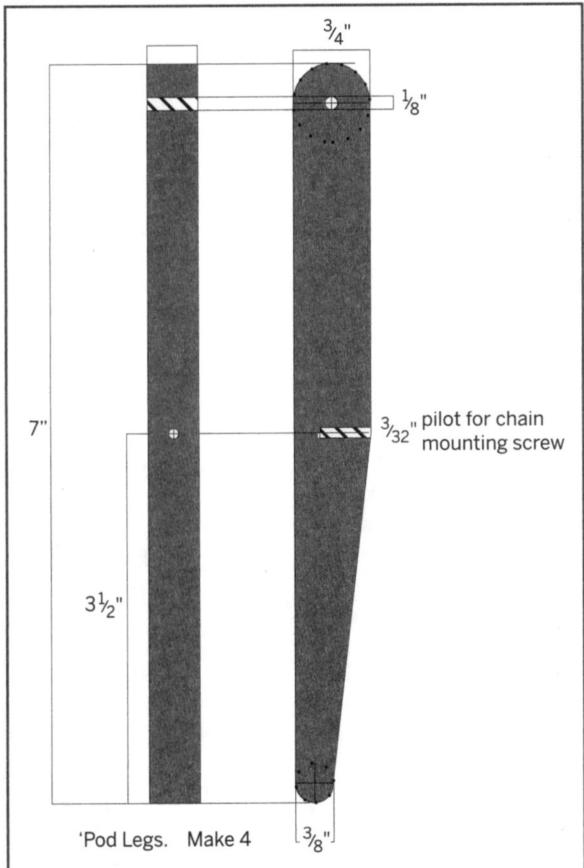

Figure 03.82: **The legs in detail. Your results will most certainly vary, but do please heed the pivot hole placement and related radial shaping of the upper leg.**

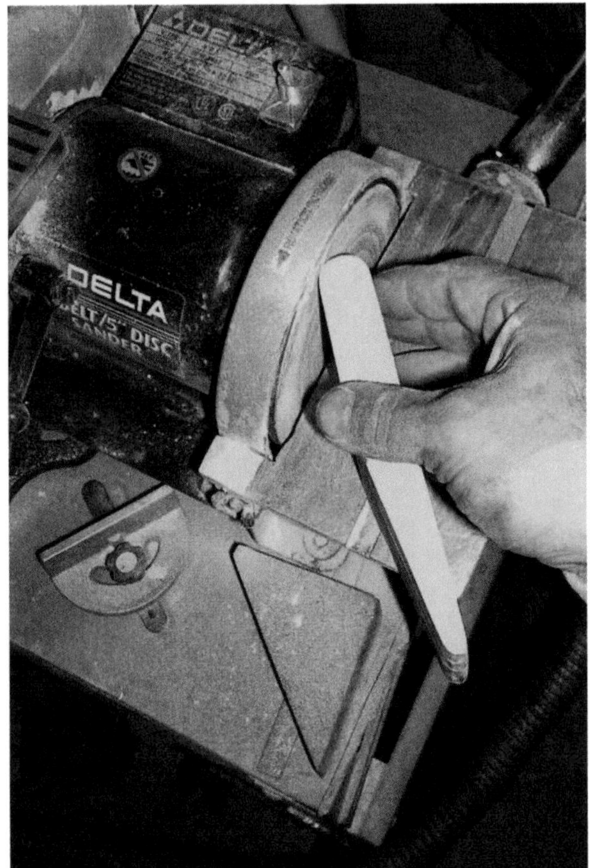

Figure 03.83: **Shaping the stack of leg blanks. Double-sided tape is our friend.**

in a (formerly seedy, now upmarket and boutique as all get out) Vancouver hotel. I fired up the scroll saw and patiently shaped the leg receiver block to match the diameter of the brass disk, then marked and drilled the pilot holes for the attachment screws. I drilled out the center point of the block to 3⁄8" to accept the brass bushing tube we'll be using for friction reduction in lieu of completely denuding your Mom's rollerblades of bearing races. **[Figure 03.80]**

Stock for the legs required another scrabble through the wood crib. I found some 7⁄8" x 1⁄2" sugar maple and cut four blanks about 7" long, stacked them with double-faced tape and shaped them en masse on the disk sander. The width went down to 3⁄4", with the top rounded and a taper from the midpoint to the foot. I drilled the centerpoint of the top radius to 1⁄8". **[Figure 03.81, Figure 03.82, Figure 03.83]**

For those of you keeping track of the various woods used so far on this project, it's mystery skidwood, red oak, poplar and sugar maple. This thing is turning into a real mutt, innit? Let's run with *that* concept, and add another flavor of maple to the mix. The pan/tilt block is shaped out of two pieces of white maple heartwood glued and doweled together. I needed a piece of stock resilient enough to let me get fancy with the shape of the block while still maintaining enough structural integrity to support the hulking monstrosity of the ballista itself. **[Figure 03.84]**

Drill down through the center of the top face with a 7⁄32"

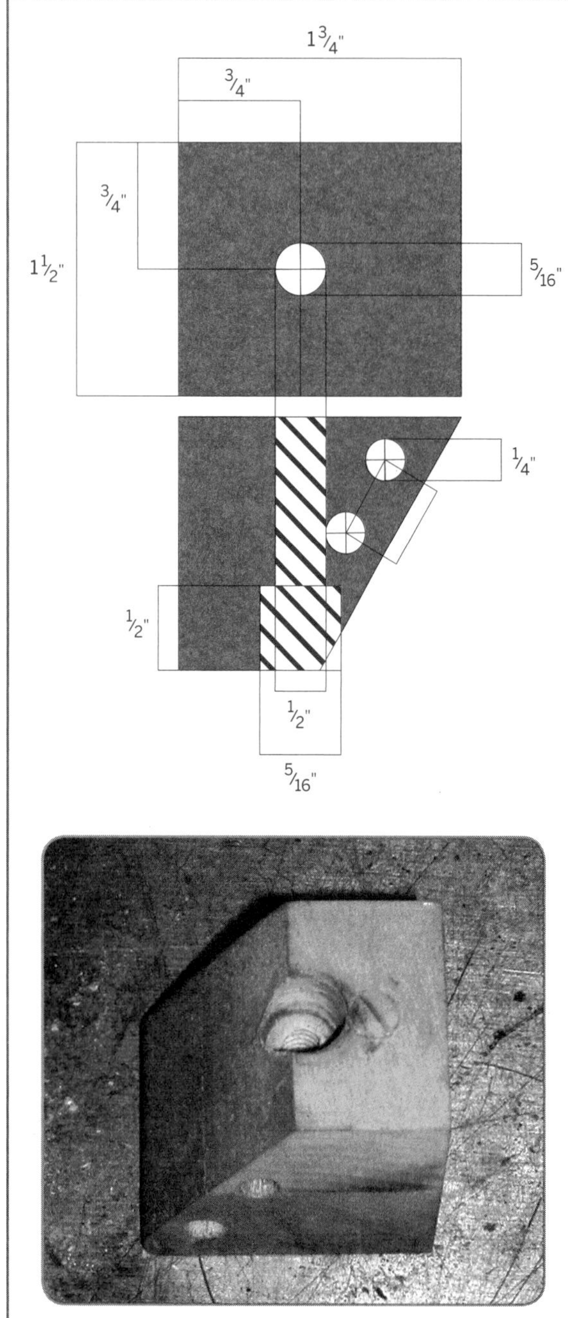

Figure 03.84: **The pan/tilt block in theory and practice. Use manly wood; it needs to be tough.**

bit and tap the hole with 5/16-18 threads. If you don't trust the wood to hold threads securely enough, you can countersink a 1/2" hole 3/8" into the top to accomodate a nut (for the toilet bolt you'll be using as an axle to enable the pan motion in the pan/tilt head).

Drill out the axle hole on the bottom face to 3/8" at a depth of 1/2" to receive the axle bushing and then drill the mounting holes for the tilt mechanism support struts. **[Figure 03.85]**

Cut the brass struts for the pan-tilt mechanism from 1/8" plate. The geometry is part artsy-fartsy nonsense, part necessity. The ballista itself is gonna end up being front-heavy from the sheer mass of brasswork involved in the skein rack, so the pan-tilt head is made to provide a bit of a shelf to limit the forward tilting range of movement. **[Figure 03.86]**

The strut geometry ended up being a compromise shape

Figure 03.85: **Once again the humble 5/16-18 toilet bolt proves its worth.**

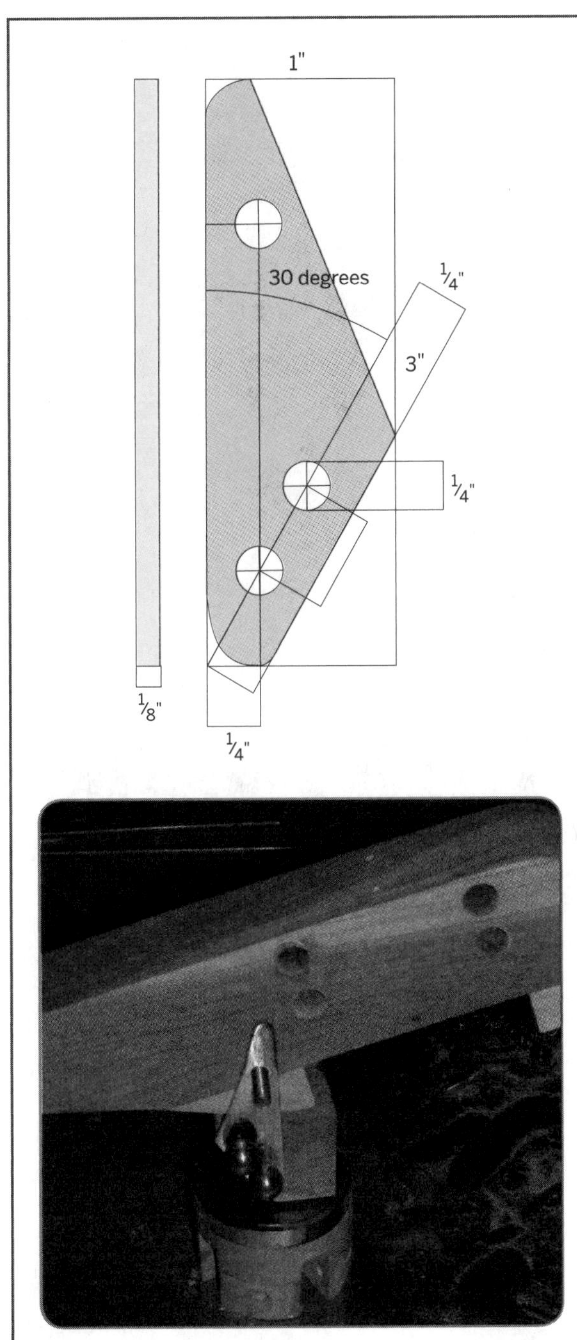

Figure 03.86: **Pan/tilt support brackets: two, please, from 1/8" plate brass.**

to accommodate the mechanical requirements, given that I was cutting the struts from a piece of scrap plate a little over 2" x 5". If you've followed along with any degree of accuracy, it shouldn't be hard to find a spot for the tripod mounting bolt hole that will provide a reasonably balanced mechanism with about 55 degrees of vertical movement. Use a length of 1/4-20 threaded rod and two thumbscrews or wingnuts to mount the body to the *'pod*.[8]

Here are the bits that comprize the 'pod, post woodfinishing. If you assemble the 'pod first, you'll have something to hold the main body of the ballista while you complete final assembly. **[Figure 03.87]**

The (optional) brass plate attaches to the leg block with four 1/2" 6-32 machine screws, then it's just a matter of threading the pan/tilt block onto the bolt and bushing as shown. **[Figure 03.88]**

I padded the bottom face of the block with a craft felt slip

8 It has four legs, so we can't call it a *tri*pod, can we? Dang. *Tetrapod* sounds like a juice container, and *quadrapod* sounds like it refers to alien taxonomy. I'm sticking with *'pod*. Apple's gonna sue me for sure. Bring it on, Jobs!

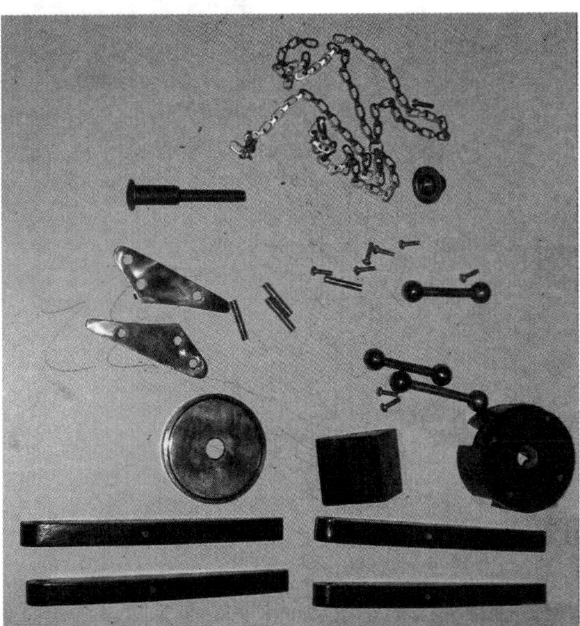

Figure 03.87: **Pieces of 'pod. I'm always amazed at how quickly the parts count skyrockets during the course of a build. Sometimes, attention to detail can get component-intensive.**

Figure 03.88: **Bolt, bushing, receiver, block. Not shown: optional retention nut.**

Figure 03.89: **Craft felt: friction reduction on the cheap.**

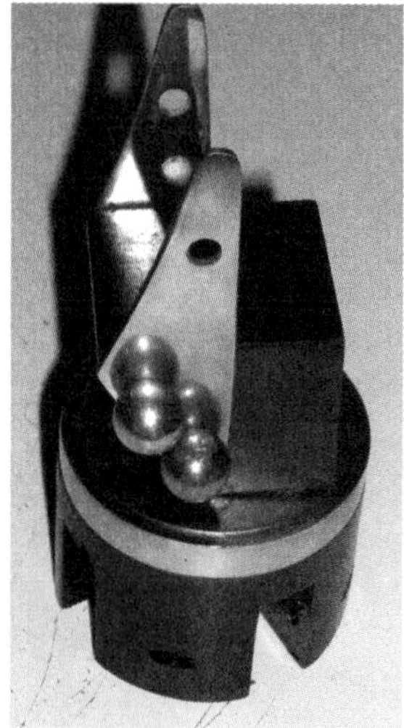

Figure 03.90: **A satisfyingly sturdy pan/tilt mechanism.**

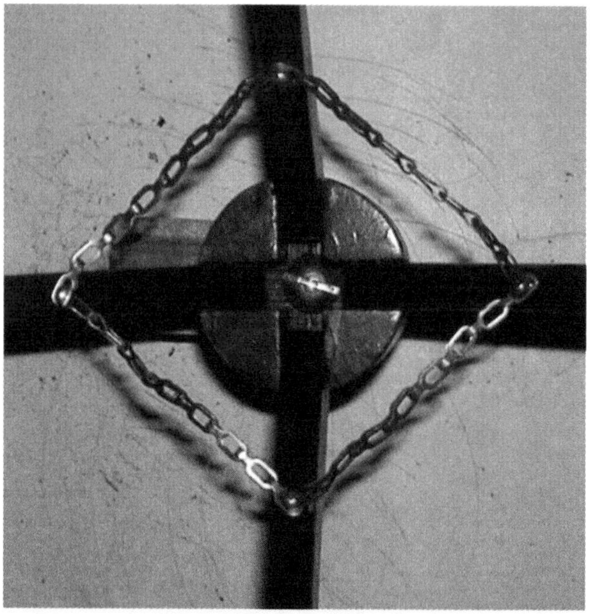

Figure 03.91: **Leg bracing in detail. Gotta love the folded interlocking link structure of toilet chain.**

Figure 03.92: **The finished 'pod**

pad to keep friction to a minimum. **[Figure 03.89]**

The tilt support struts are attached with ¼-20 bolts (yes, that's more artsy-fartsy nonsense visible in the form of threaded brass balls as nuts). The legs attach using 1" lengths of ⅛" brass rod press-fitted into the holes in the leg receiver block, through the pivot holes in the legs. **[Figure 03.90]**

To brace the legs, I pressed into service yet another plumbing supply staple — brass toilet chain, attached to the legs with ½" #6 roundheaded wood screws. **[Figure 03.91]**

In far less time than it took me to document the process, I had a splendidly functional 'pod sitting on the bench. **[Figure 03.92]**

You can conceal the exposed leg axle holes in any number of ways. I cut cover plates from brass shim stock and stuck 'em in place via the crude but efficient double-sided tape method. [Figure 03.93]

After attaching the bottom skein rack plate to the main body of the ballista with four 1" #8 screws, your 'pod is eager to be pressed into use. [Figure 03.94]

Assembly from this point onward is purely by the numbers: fit the strut support blocks in place and then slot in the support struts. [Figure 03.95]

A Warning to Woodworking Purists

Woodworking purists may want to skip over the next paragraph or two. We're talking about woodfinishing and, once again, I have committed unnatural acts.

There ended up being an unseemly variety of woods used in this build, which had a variety of raw coloration ranging from khaki green to muted red. A *traditional* wood finish was clearly inappropriate, so I started mucking about in the kitchen. I found a bottle of alcohol-based electric blue aniline wood dye on the back of a shelf and tested it on samples of the various woods involved, with mixed results. Feeling adventurous, I pulled out a pint of generic varnish inherited from who-knows-where and mixed up a bilious concoction with a ratio of 5 varnish to 1 dye. It looked like slightly thickened cuttlefish ink, but it went on smoothly and cured hard overnight to an exhilarating shade of *translucent electric teal*.

Jolly bloody good.

I applied three coats, giving it a light rubdown with fine steel wool and a tack cloth between coats and a final hand rubbing with the remnants of an old King Crimson T-shirt. The results are visually effective in context of the enormous amount of brasswork on the piece, as well as an effective distraction from the *cripes-how-many-kinds-of-wood-did-you-use-on-this-freakin'-thing* issue.

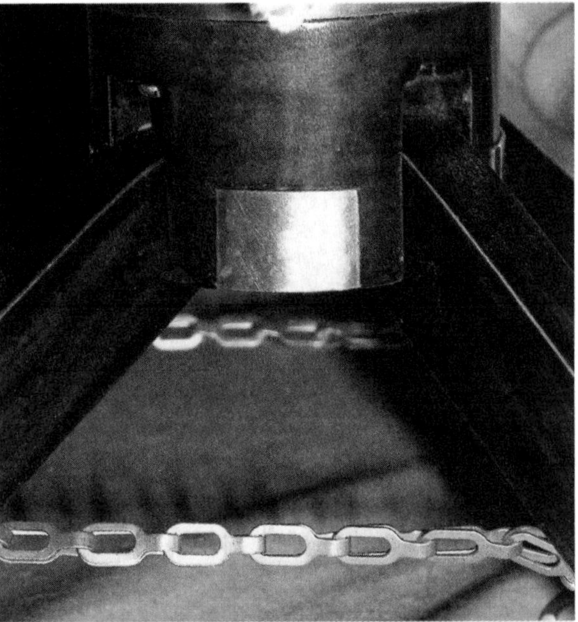

Figure 03.93: **Axle holes? What axle holes?**

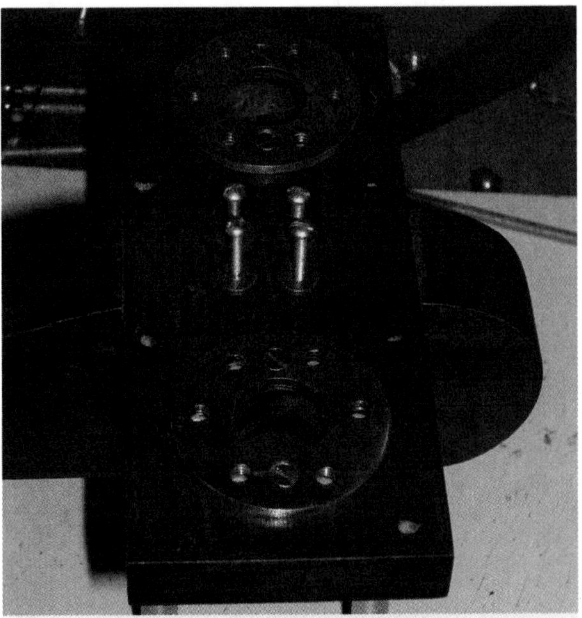

Figure 03.94: **Attaching the bottom skein plate to the body: 1" #8 wood screws with washers**

Figure 03.95: **Bod on 'pod: final assembly begins. It's about bloody time.**

Figure 03.96: **Strut supports and support struts positioned**

As tempting as it may be to drop the top skein rack plate into position next, you'd better attach the guide rails and pulley first. Use #6 round-head wood screws. **[Figure 03.96, Figure 03.97]**

Now position the top skein rack plate, and bolt the rack together with 1⁄4-20 threaded rod running through the support tubes, terminated in washers and nuts. **[Figure 03.98]**

Assemble the windlass, using a few drops of thread-locker to glue handle/axle threads and the knob screw. **[Figure 03.99]**

Install the ratchet pawl with a 1⁄2" 8-32 machine screw, using a #8 washer to stand the pawl off from the body of the ballista. If you're pondering what spring to use on the pawl, consider, if you will, the humble ballpoint pen as a potential source.

Stringing the Skeins

Hot damn, kids: it's time to string the skeins. You can make a foot-long needle with a large-scale eye to accomplish the task by flattening out one end of a length of 1⁄8" brass rod with a hammer and anvil and meticulously forming the eye with a dremel and needle files, or you can cheat and tape the string to the rod with electrical tape. **[Figure 03.100]**

NOTE: Don't make no nevermind to me.

Figure 03.97: Guide rails and windlass pulley

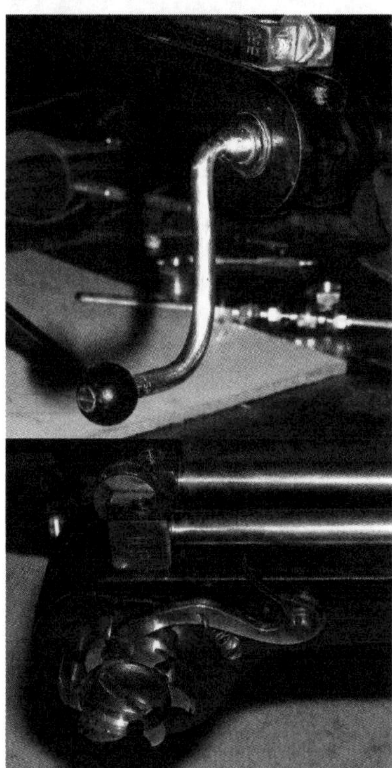

Figure 03.99: The windlass assembly. Don't forget the Loctite.

Figure 03.98: The modioli attached. The skein plates are bolted together with the ¼-20 threaded rod. This results in a strong skein assembly capable of delivering a startling amount of power.

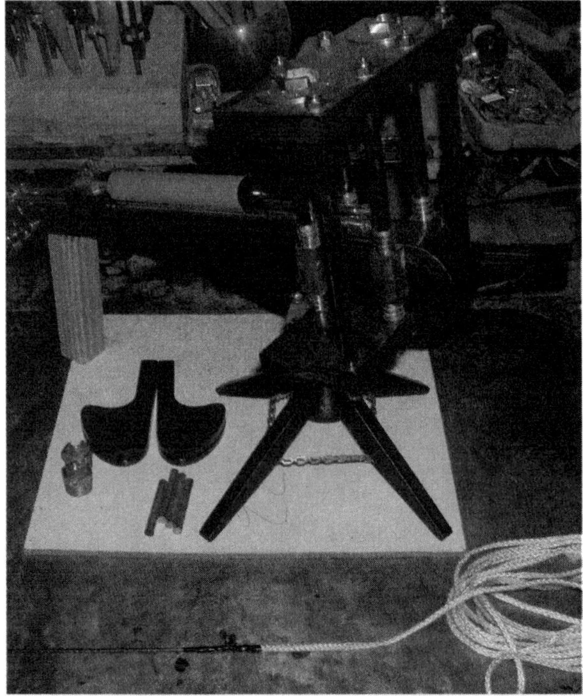

Figure 03.100: **Prepped for skein stringing. The excitement is palpable.**

Figure 03.101: **Epizygi in position**

Your choice of cordage to string the skeins is critical. For the record, the 1⁄4" braided poly macramé cord pictured turned out to be one of the *least* effective skeinfodders I've ever used.

NOTE: Live and learn.

A vastly preferable choice is twisted 70/30 cotton-poly blend sold in hardware emporiums as *chalkline*. It's about 3⁄32" in diameter and really packs a lot of potential mayhem into your torsion bundles.

There's a real art to stringing a skein. Tighter is better, and you want to layer the cordage onto the epizygis bars evenly.

Position the epizygis/bar assemblies into the modioli, with the bars aligned top and bottom. Tie the cordage with a half hitch to the bottom bar, and begin threading the cord bottom to top, top to bottom. [Figure 03.101]

When there are a few wraps in place to hold the bars in position, untie the cord from the bottom bar and tie it off out of the way around one of the support tubes. Pull each wrap tight, holding it in position with one hand while you thread the needle down the other side of the bar with the other. Repeat until you can't fit any more cord through the holes in the epizygis. With fine diameter chalkline on a skein of this scale, you should be able to wrap at least 40 feet of cord onto each skein. I managed to get 15 feet of the accursed elephantine cord pictured into each bundle with no small effort. [Figure 03.102]

Both skeins *must* contain the same length of cord and number of wraps, under the same amount of tension. Mismatched skeins are a surefire path to misfires and the dreaded *lateral trajectory*. Once each skein is wound, tie the ends together at the bottom of the skein rack, leaving a few inches hanging from each end for ease of adjustment. [Figure 03.103]

When viewed along the long axis of the bar, a properly wound skein will show a clear opening between the parallel bundles of cord. Insert the bow arm into this opening, and apply a small amount of torque to the skeins to hold it in place. In case it's not obvious, the skeins are twisted as shown. [Figure 03.104, Figure 03.105]

The bowstring threads into the arms as illustrated. Secure the ends by using a short length of 1⁄8" ID brass tubing as a crimp. Fold the end of the bike cable back through the tubing and give it a squeeze with vise grips; it won't be goin' anywhere. Thread both arms, but crimp off only one end of the string.

Figure 03.102: **Starting the wrap procedure**

Figure 03.103: **Inserting the bow arms.**

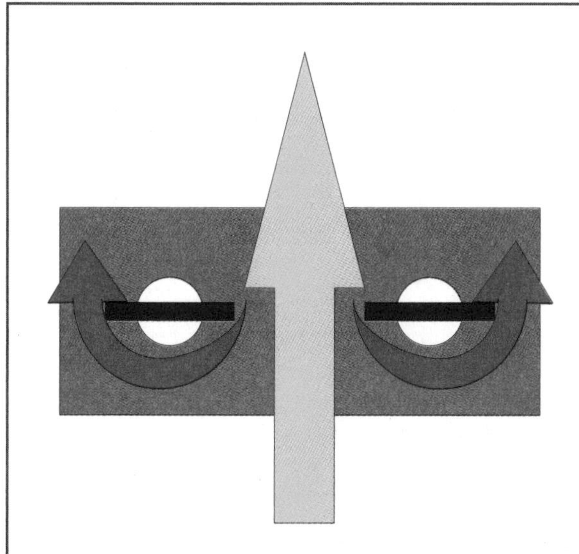

Figure 03.104: **Torque up the skeins in the right direction, wouldja?**

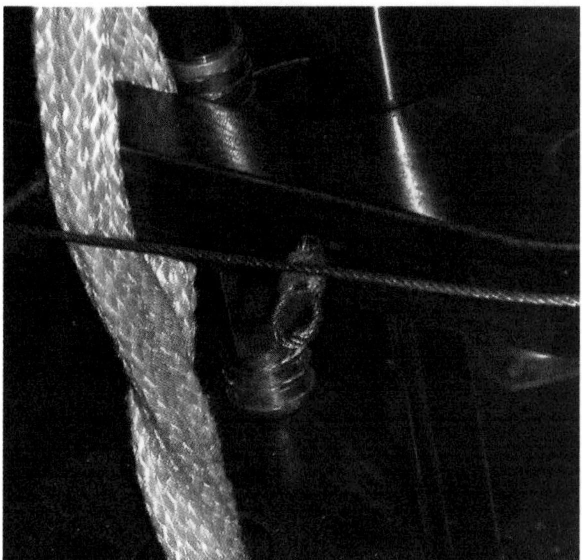

Figure 03.105: **Use brass tubing as crimps to lock the bowstring in place**

Figure 03.106: The bow arms at rest, showing the bowstring making firm contact against the rear skein plate supports.

The Harrowing Process of Optimizing Bowstring Length

CAUTION: If you want your ballista to shoot straight, Pay Attention!

Place your assembled trigger sled mechanism on the guide rails, lock the jaws around the bowstring and pull it back towards the rear of the ballista body while holding the loose end of the string in position on the bow arm. The arms will be pulled back under tension into their cocked position. When the sled reaches the back guide rail mounting blocks, adjust the string length so that the arms are in a fully retracted position. Cut the string to length and crimplock it. Release the string from the trigger and allow the arms to return to their resting position. **[Figure 03.106]**

Now, adjust the position of the arm shafts in the skeins inwards or outwards so that the bowstring is snug against the rear rack support posts.

Mark the position of the skein bundles on the arm shafts, and then drill and set a a short length of ⅛" brass rod into the middle ply of the arm shaft at that point, to serve as arm position locks. **[Figure 03.107]**

I used 100 lb.-test braided picture-frame-hanging wire to cable the winch. This is a more pliable material than the bike cable used for the bowstring, making it more suited to repeated winding/unwinding around the winch spool. It's less resistant to friction-related trauma, though, so resist the urge

Figure 03.107: The bow arm position locks: cunningly deployed bits of brass rod

to use it as a substitute bowstring. The pliability allows it to be easily knotted, which is the best way to secure it. Consult your Girl Scout knot-tying guide or Shibari Girl Scout tying guide for *surgeon's knot* instructions, and load up your winch with about 24" of wire.

You'll need four epyzigis lock bolts, which are just ¾" lengths of ¼-20 threaded rod with a thumbnut stuck in place on one end with thread-locking glue. Thread them into the appropriate holes on the modioli after skein tensioning to keep the bars from slipping and releasing tension. **[Figure 03.108]**

The projectile is a 6" length of high visibility orange 1" ID PVC sprinkler pipe with hardwood end caps spun with the invaluable drillpress lathe bodge (see Chapter 7). Aesthetically, it's kinda out of place in the wood 'n brass surroundings of BallistaMail, but the low mass improves efficiency significantly and the cheerful, eyecatching hue makes finding errant shots a lot easier. The endcaps press-fit

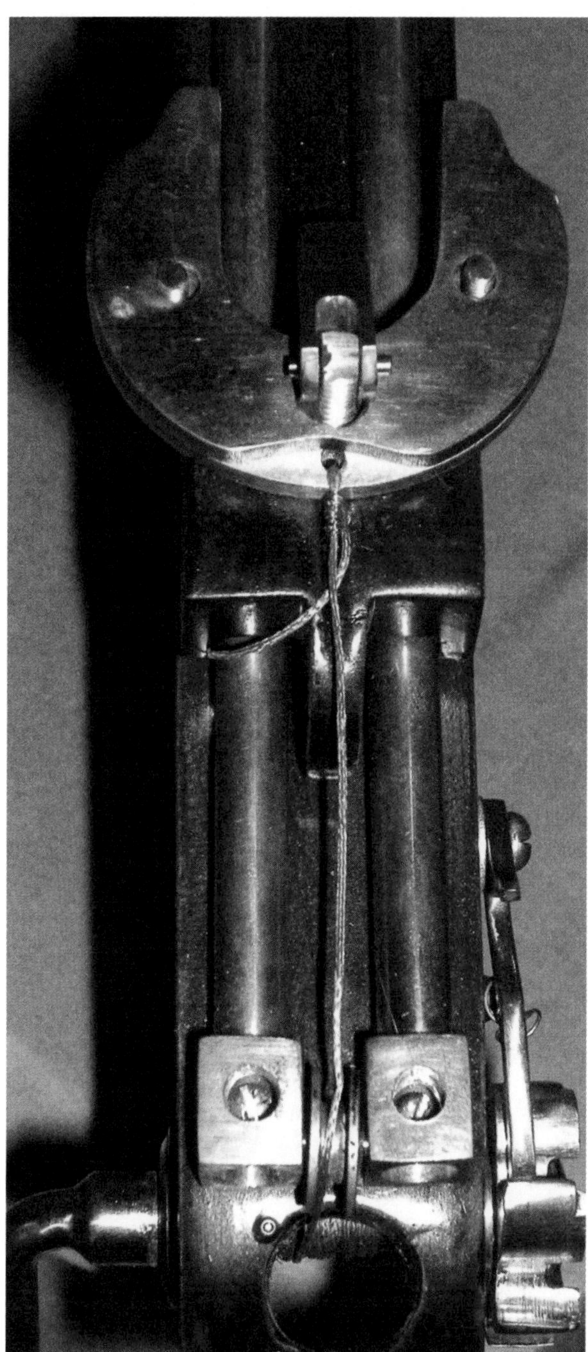

Figure 03.107: **High-test braided picture frame wire serves as the windlass cable.**

Figure 03.108: **Epizygis lock bolt in position. It holds the skein tension in place, dunnit?**

into place for ease of message retrieval, and a ⅛" deep notch for the bowstring is formed across the radius of the rear cap. **[Figure 03.109, Figure 03.110, Figure 03.111]**

Which brings us to the end of the build. There's nothing left to fabricate.

Use It

Field testing involves dialing progressively higher degrees of tension into the skeins (isometric tension is essential: top and bottom, left and right), releasing the winch cable to allow the sled to be positioned at the top end string position, locking the trigger jaws around the string, winding the sled back with the winch to cock the mechanism, notching the projectile onto the string, and releasing the camlock to fire.

The skeins stretch under use. Untie the cord ends and tighten the bundles as needed, and avoid storing the mechanism with the skeins torqued up.

You've build a robust mechanism. Frightening as the prospect may seem, it will withstand *lots* of torque on the bundles. A fully torqued pull in excess of 100 pounds is entirely possible. With a 10" draw and a 3-oz. projectile, I invite the mathematically inclined to *do the math* regarding potential performance.

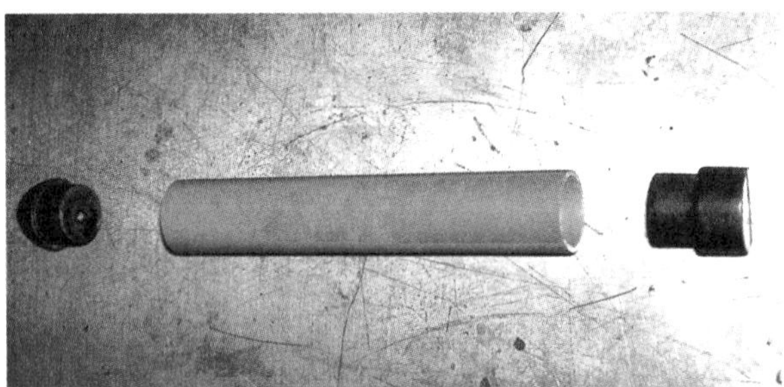

Figure 03.109: **Projectile components**

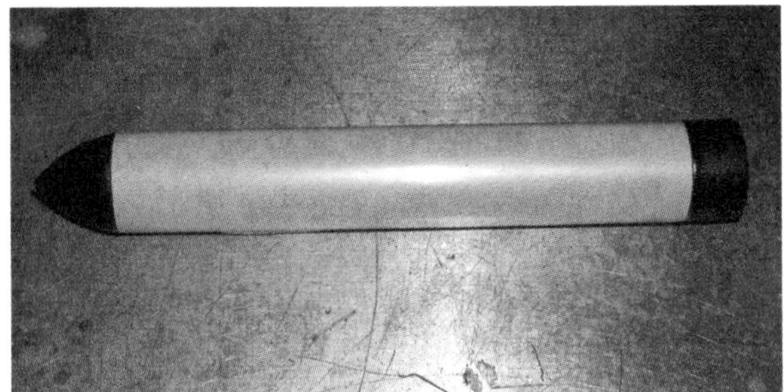

Figure 03.110: **The assembled projectile**

Figure 03.111: **The assembled projectile in position on the guide rails**

CAUTION: Exercise caution. It's all good clean fun until somebody loses an eye.

Now go and send someone special a pointed message. Muahahahahahah.

Figure 03.112: **BallistaMail assembled, tuned, and ready for operational deployment**

‹ Nano-Project › Table Saw Essentials

The Mysterious Featherboard

I repeat: Do tools have the *best* names, or what?[1] Featherboards are unsung but needful ancillaries for table saws. Their sole reason for existence is to ensure that your stock is politely but firmly held against the rip fence while making a cut. Make one *now*.

You'll need a couple of feet of ¾" x 4" wood. Solid wood, please; softwood will do. Plywood isn't suitable. **[Figure N3.01**

Miter one end to 45 degrees, then fire up the saw and cut 6" to 8" kerfs every ¼" or so. All feathery-like. Wasn't that simple? **[Figure N3.02]**

Now to use it. A picture is worth a thousand words, with the only needed warning being to ensure that the featherboard contacts your working stock *only* on the front side of the blade diameter. This prevents kickback and scorching by reducing stock contact with the blade surface.

The Zero Clearance Insert

Table saws are versatile, and that's a fact: rip cuts, end cuts, miter cuts, bevel cuts, beveled miter cuts, mitered bevel cuts, impacted cantilever cuts. Okay, I made that last one up, but you get the point. Being all things to all sawyers means compromises, which require a bit of work to overcome.

We can do that.

The slot that the blade protrudes through on yer basic table saw is as wide as it is to allow the blade to be tilted up to 45 degrees for the aforementioned beveled cuts. Unfortunately, having a half-inch gap between the blade and the surface of the insert makes cutting dimensions of less than ½" next to impossible.

Enter the "zero clearance insert." Endlessly useful, and bog simple to make.

Pull the regular insert from your saw: You need a piece of plywood exactly that size and thickness, but without the slot.

It's one of those trace/cut/sand/drill tasks imbued with minimum creativity/maximum utility.

Countersink the mounting screw holes to allow the screws to set flush with the surface. Got it? Good. Set your blade at 90 degrees, exactly, and lower it as far down as possible. Put your slotless plywood insert into the insert receiver and shim it until it's perfectly level with the table, if it isn't already.

Screw it down. Now turn on the saw, and slowly raise the blade to its highest position, which will cut a kerf-wide slot in

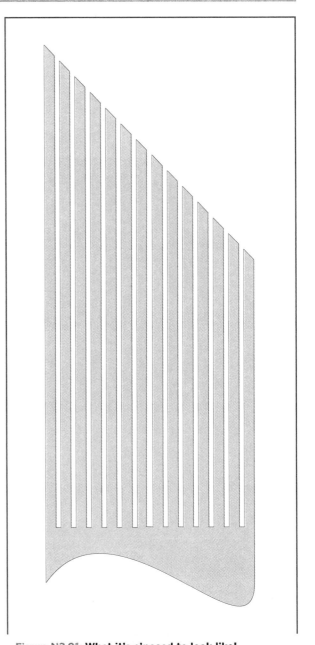

Figure N3.01: What it's s'posed to look like!

1 You did read the introduction, didn't you?

Figure N3.02: **Here's mine, clamped onto the sliding miter table of my saw, which is apparently a feature found only on this brand of saw. The rest of you can just clamp the 'board directly to the deck of the saw. You want it positioned so as to apply firm pressure to the stock (the "fingers" should deflect slightly as the stock is pushed bladewards) without rendering said bladeward motion difficult.**

your brand new Zero Clearance Insert. **[Figure N3.03]**

You're done. Cut something really thin, then go have a cocktail, once again proud in the knowledge of your `L337 w00dw3rxx0r 5kiLL5`.

Push Sticks

Count your fingers? Got some? Good.

Wanna keep 'em? Use a push stick when you're feeding your table saw. There's as many different designs as there are sawyers, but you need one for big pieces of wood, and one for small ones. **[Figure N3.04]**

There's no need to get fancy, no matter what the glossy woodworking magazines try to tell you. I cut mine out of 2" x 4"s or plywood scrap, use them until they start getting a bit frayed, then toss 'em and make new ones. Nothing fancy: just a large contact area for the surface of the wood being pushed

Figure N3.03: **Zero Clearance Insert in place. Original insert lying there.**

Figure N3.04: **A couple of push sticks.**

and a healthy, well-defined lip to grab the edge of the wood. **[Figure N3.05]**

They're your fingers: keep 'em clean, keep 'em dry, keep 'em attached to your body.

Carry on.

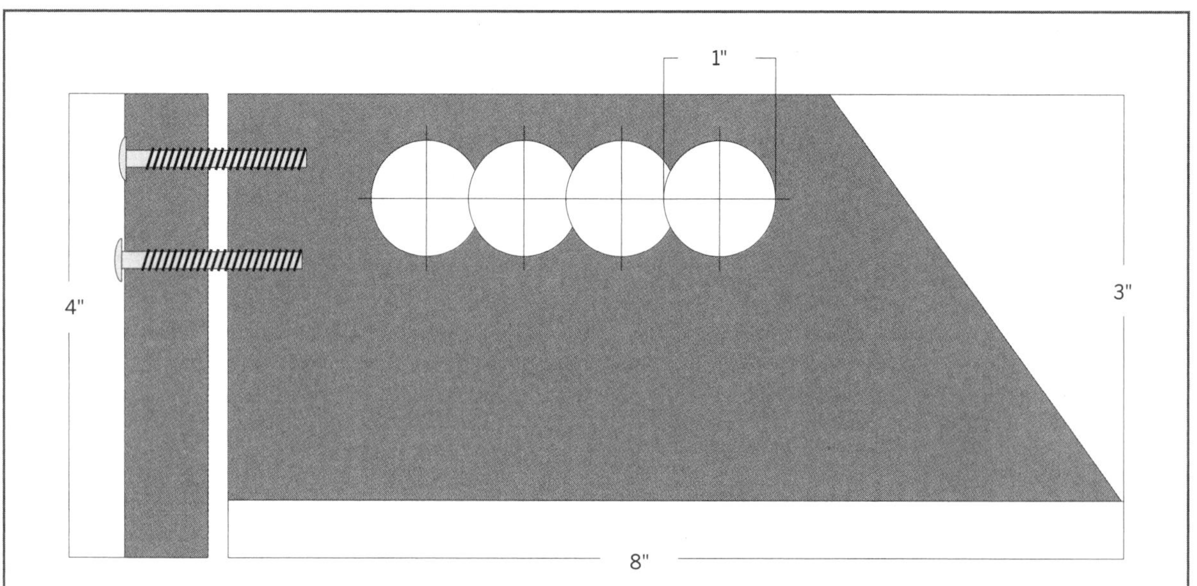

Figure N3.05: **Oh, all right . . . here's a diagram of one o' them fancy-ass pushers. Make it out of 2" x 4"s. The hand grip is made by overlapping holes with a 1" Forstner bit, and the replaceable grip lip is held in place with 1½" #8 wood screws.**

4 Maple Mike: The Desktop Driver

Help me out here: what is it about whackin' a little ball around a park that has made *golf* such an enduring accoutrement of *business*? Freud would have a field day analyzing the mano-a-mano symbolism of grown men, clubs, bags, balls, and holes. There's definitely something afoot here that (as a sworn nonparticipant) I'm completely (and, frankly, gratefully) missing.

I've always thought that golf was a game that would be greatly improved by the presence of shotguns: once golfer A has the ball in the air, the other members of the foursome (golfers B, C, and D, respectively) quick-draw 20-gauges from their golf bags and do their skeet-shooting best to blast it out of the sky. Think of it as upgrading the game for the FPS demographic.

Yeah, that's the ticket.

Golfers are uniquely obsessive with perfecting what is essentially a slightly complicated pendulum motion, a.k.a. "the swing." Convincing the human body to repeatedly and accurately perform the geometry needed to get the club head striking the ball at *exactly* the right angle and force *every time* is essentially impossible: "Close enough and often enough" is about the best *anyone* can hope for. A guy named Byron Nelson was *really* close, *really* often.

From an engineering standpoint, it's pretty simple to replicate the motion geometry of the Perfect Swing mechanically. Engineers (and golfers) being what they are, this was done in 1966 by a golf club manufacturer called True Temper.

They called the result Iron Byron. Iron Byron has hit seven holes in one.

We're working with wood, rather than iron. Let's call this one Maple Mike.[1]

This is an elegant mechanism with ruthless efficiency — and it scales well. There's a potentially lethal amount of energy even in desktop-sized models, so build quality is essential. This is not a device you want to see fly apart in use.

Remember, it's all good clean fun until somebody loses an eye (see Chapter 3).

Here's the motion we're going to produce. Siege engine aficionados among you will immediately recognize a variation on trebuchet sling geometry. Those with a background in recreational ice skating will more commonly suffer a traumatic flashback to "cracking the whip," and the winter you spent with a broken clavicle. **[Figure 04.01]**

The rotational energy needed can come from a torsion skein, springs, or bungee elastic. You're only dealing with about 180 degrees of useful rotation before making contact with the ball, so you need to get a lot of energy into the system quickly. To do this, we're gonna have to bodge some mechanical advantage into the mechanism somewhere, either with a cam or a lever. We're gonna have to think about a club for the little bugger, and decide on a standardized spherical projectile. I'd love to use mouseballs. Accelerating that kind of mass would call for a "Strong Like Bull" mechanism, but the results would be . . . er . . . dangerously gratifying. This application we're gonna work around ¾" wooden craft balls because they're cheap, in the right ballpark mass-wise, and easy to find. Feel free to experiment with other projectiles, bearing in mind the abuse that they'll be taking every time the club makes contact with 'em.

1 As noted previously, I am Canadian. The Federal Ministry of Trade, Beavers, and Northern Affairs requires me to cite notable Canadian cultural references at strictly monitored intervals or face penalties including fines, incarceration, and/or forced exposure to Nickleback's Greatest Hit. We tend to toe the line.

So who's this Mike guy? Mike Weir, born in Sarnia, Ontario. A nice Canadian lad. Won the Masters in '03, which officially makes him a Damned Good Golfer. Cheers, Mike.

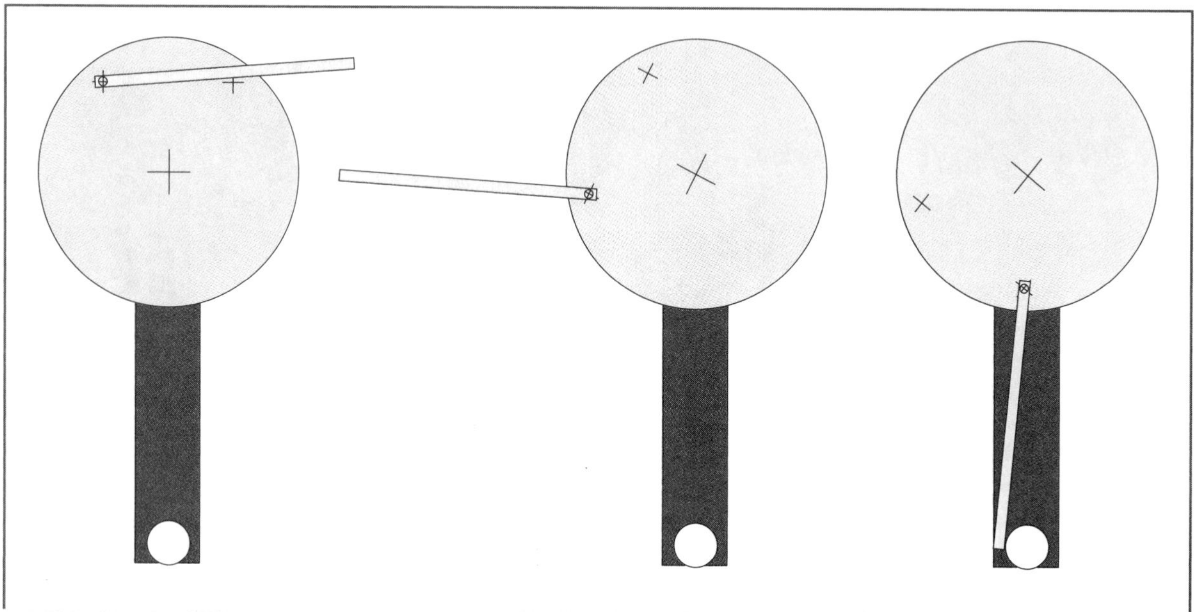

Figure 04.01: The almost sling-like nature of a golf swing. It's a pendulum wif a bit extra, innit?

What I'm sayin' is: no marbles, no cheese, no nuts, and no berries.

Other than that, knock yourself (and quite likely your co-workers) out.

Think of a golf swing as a fancy way of getting a really long hammer to whack the hell out of a little ball. That said, to golfers, the geometry of the motion is critical. The backslope angle of this particular swing plane (ooh! ooh! I used an official golf term!) is 30 degrees, which is spec'd more for ease of fabrication than for any resemblance to actual golf swing geometry. I did however, set the club shaft to radius ratio within reality-based measurements.

No shit: golfers take their kit *damned* seriously. Researching this build had me elbow-deep in golf club technical minutiae for about 10 days. Some of the propaganda being thrown around had obviously sound physics behind it, other bits of it was such blatant balloon juice as to make high-end audiophile gear appear scientifically realistic ("These $300 petrified oak volume knobs will maximize your overall sound field imaging clarity and impart a subtle implication of amber to bass clarinet passages").

Anyway, between referencing innumerable pages of learned discourse, marketing poopsheets, and whiny blog entries, and two days spent measuring swap meet golf clubs, I arrived at 43" as being "yer average shaft length." Oddly, golfers don't seem to consider girth to be an issue. Further research into human anatomy (me, a tape measure, and every poor sap who walked through my door for a week) arrived at 34" as "yer average reach," from the center of the shoulders to the knuckles of clasped hands extended forwards, for an average arm-to-shaft ratio of +/− 1:1.25.

The pitch of the clubface (the amount of backslope on the bit that actually hits the ball) is a club-specific variable related to the amount of loft provided. (Loft as in "angle of ascent," not as in "overpriced attic in Manhattan.") I saw numbers ranging from 7.5 degrees for a right proper "manly" wood ("ladies" can apparently enjoy as much as 31 degrees of ascent-producing goodness) to more than 60 degrees for specialty wedges. The ambitious among you may want to consider fabricating a variable-geometry clubface to address the entire range of options. Because Maple Mike is nothing if not manly, I picked a value of 7.5 degrees, on the assumption that altering the tee height and point of contact in the overall arc of the swing can geometrically provide real-time variation during usage.

Yeah, you'll need to do some math, but it'll be good practice for playing Brain Age.

From a design perspective, the mechanism is based around a wooden chassis onto which are bodged the club

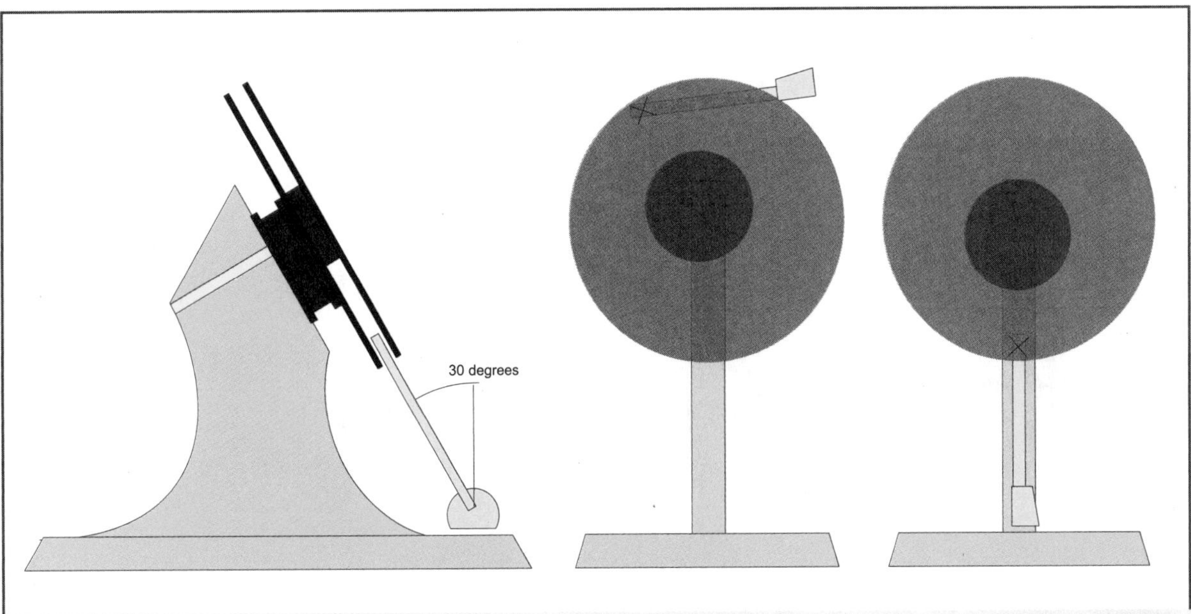

Figure 04.02: **The skeletal Maple Mike.**

assembly, trigger mechanism, and bungee tensioning system. The chassis mounts onto a baseplate sized to provide proper stability on your desktop. There's a lot of room for design mods in this form factor; the next one of these I build will incorporate a turntable mechanism into the base plate to facilitate targeting, quick-change club heads, and a flexible club shaft.

And it's gonna be bigger. W-a-a-ay bigger. *Overscale* bigger. I'm thinkin' powered-by-garage-door-springs-with-softballs-as-projectiles bigger. Five-pound-club-head bigger.

I digress.

Prior to fabrication I had a number of distinctly different tangents for the build on the drawing board; one used components mostly harvested from a bargain-basement drum kit kick drum pedal, and had a distinctly mid-50s Eastern bloc weapons research lab design aesthetic. As is the wont of most musicians I know, I have no small number of such things strewn casually about my flat. Recognizing the fact that not a lot of you share this circumstance, I opted for my plan B design, which relies on more accessible components such as wood, brass, springs, and bungee cords. The design aesthetic of *this* concept more closely resembles an early eighteenth-century maritime navigation device. At this stage in my career, I cannot foresee ever being at ease with designing something that *doesn't* look like it's supposed to be something else entirely. Be aware of this potential pitfall-ridden path: you may choose to embrace it or eschew it, but be cognizant of it during your design phase. **[Figure 04.02]**

Once again, I digress.

You'll drop the majority of your money shopping/foraging for this build at lumberyards and scrap yards: You'll need four feet of ¼"x4" hardwood (I used poplar), four feet of 1" x 4" hardwood (which will measure out to a little over ¾" thickness, despite what the label says at the lumberyard), and a foot or so of hardwood 2" x 4", which you'll likely end up having to laminate together from 1" x 4". I used maple for these last two items, fulfilling the "Maple Mike" monicker. At the scrapyard, pick up a few inches of 1" brass rod, a foot of ¼" brass rod, and a 6" x 6" piece of 3⁄32" brass plate, then hit the hardware store for some ¼-20 threaded rod, half a dozen acorn nuts, and some ¼" hardwood dowel.

Make a quick swing past the thrift shop for a pair of budget rollerblades (unless you've already accumulated a usable stash of bearing assemblies). You'll be making another purchasing pilgrimage later in the build when it's time to source some elastic to power Maple Mike. Bungee material works, but you may want to explore other options such as rubber

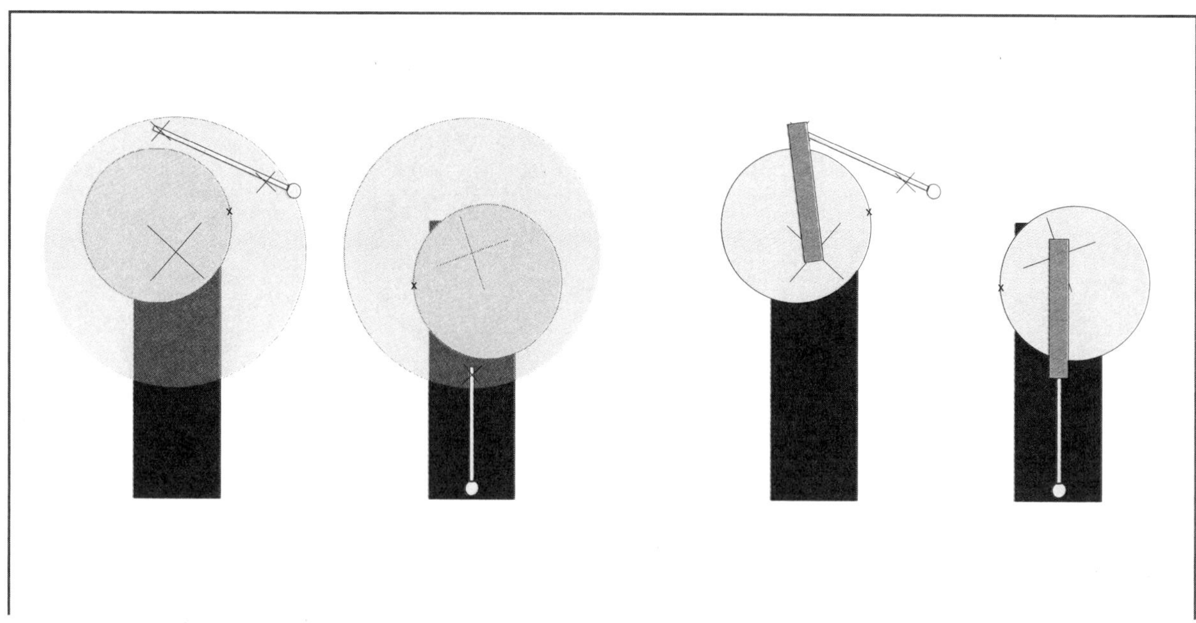

Figure 04.03: **A fully circular club holder provides more club position options than a simulated arm radial bar.**

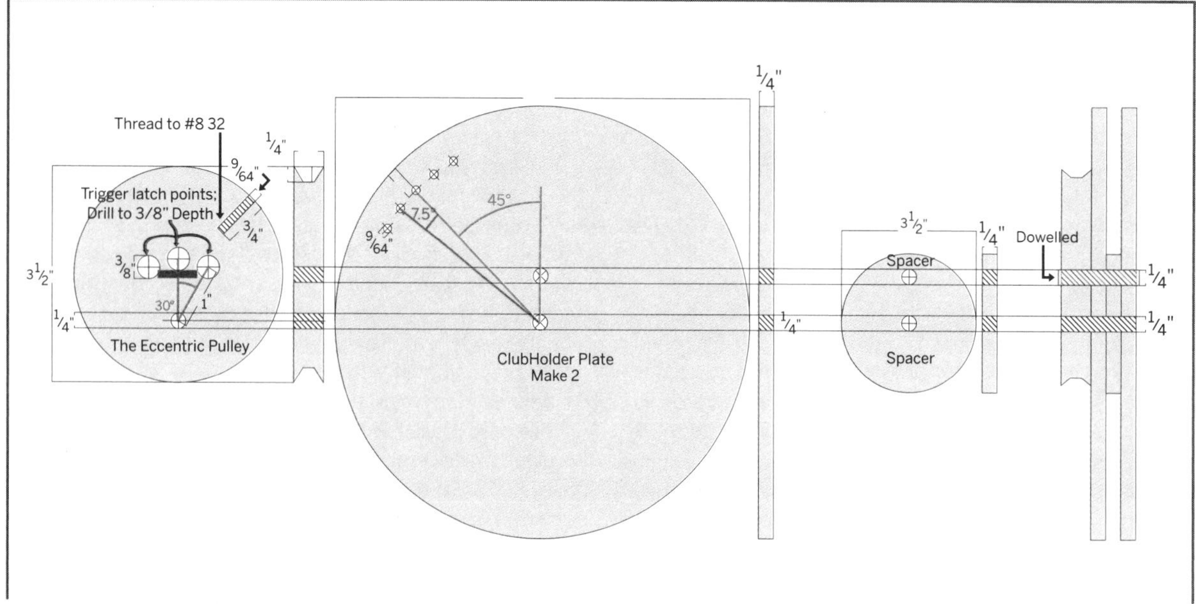

Figure 04.04: **The club holder assembly in excruciating detail**

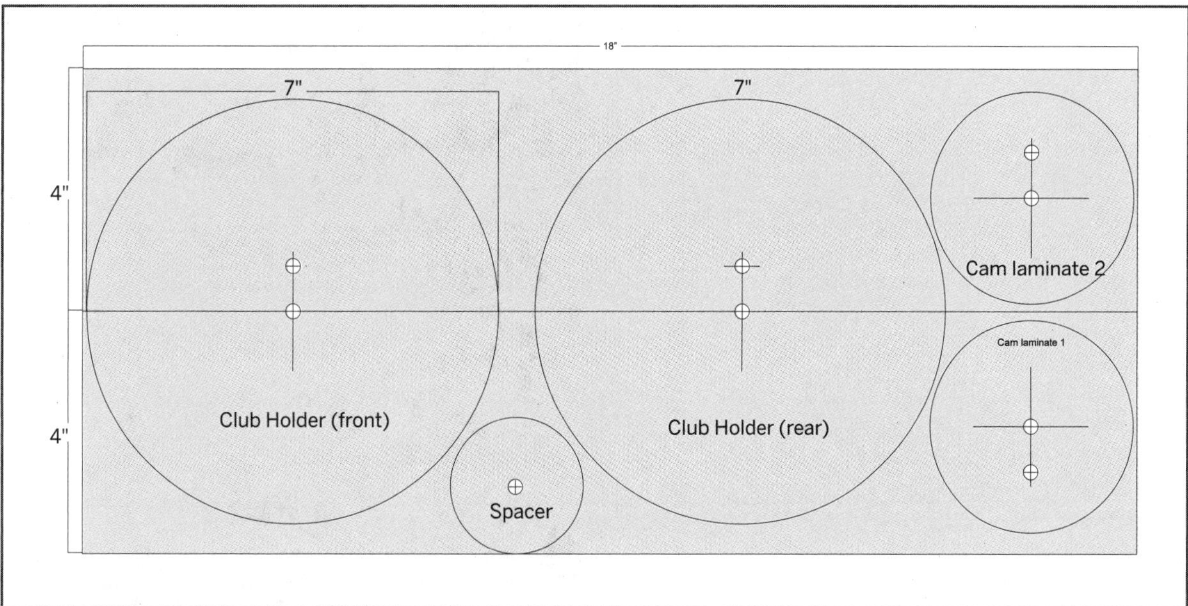

Figure 04.05: The bits you need to cut from your freshly glued up ¼" x 8" x 18" blank.

surgical tubing or some of the more industrial strength elastics available at sewing supply emporia.

We've already parsed the subassemblies: clubholder assembly with club, trigger assembly, tension assembly, and chassis. Feel free to substitute your own thematic variations on any of these submechanisms at will.

I dithered over the form factor considerably during this build.

Theoretically, the dual-circle assembly to which the club assembly is attached can be condensed down to a single arm-like bar positioned as the radius of the hypothetical circular swing, which would eliminate much of the inertial mass from the equation and give improved efficiency. This improvement in efficiency comes, unfortunately, at a cost in club position adjustability that irritated me. Plus, the form factor didn't look anywhere near as eighteenth-century. **[Figure 04.03]**

Do the math, and make your own decision.

True to my nature, I opted for adjustability and proceeded accordingly.

The Clubholder Assembly

The clubholder assembly is the nexus point of energy transmission. There's a lot of oomph at work here, so building for strength is essential. The basic structure is a stack of wooden disks: two large ones separated by a ¼" spacer disk that serve as a secure fore-and-aft mount for the club assembly, and a thicker pulley disk that's offset from the center axis to provide a cam action to the tension of the bungee cords. **[Figure 04.04]**

You're cutting 7" disks: cut your ¼" x4" stock into two 18" lengths, and butt-join them with glue and many clamps.

Stop snickering.

The subtleties of simple butt joints and the prominent role of glue-resistant battens in the successful execution thereof are documented in the Active Deskchop build log in Chapter 2. I heartily recommend perusing this short but informative section before you proceed. **[Figure 04.05]**

Cure the glue overnight, then scribe and cut your circles. I started with 8" x 8" blanks stacked securely together with double-faced tape, then rough-shaped both disks simultaneously on the scroll saw. Drill out the centers with a ¼" bit *before* you cut and finish the disks, but don't worry about the club-mounting holes. I realized well after the fact that they're better off being drilled post glue-up. **[Figure 04.06**

True up the circularity by threading a couple of inches of threaded rod through the center hole(s), with a washer, lock-washer and nut on each side. Chuck the rod into your electric drill or drill press: a quick spin and an artfully applied 80-grit sanding block will leave you with perfect circles and a dense layer of sawdust covering a 6' radius. I cut the spacer disk with a 2¼" holesaw, then stacked and glued the whole shebang using ¼-20 threaded rod and nuts and some extra 2¼" disks to really clamp the pieces together tightly. A word of warning: once this lot is glued up, your chance of applying a proper finish inside the gap is next to nil. You can prefinish the inner surfaces of the 7" disks now if it's an important factor; I missed this wee inconvenience until well into the process, and by then it was too late. So sue me.

Let's take a moment to consider cams. Consider them irregularly shaped wheels. In their simplest forms, they're a circle rotating around *not* its centerpoint. The technical term for this motion is *eccentric*, which may in no small part explain my affection for the damned things. Taken to ambitious extremes, they can be shaped to provide startlingly complicated periodic changes in a mechanism.

That's just one particular application. An equally strong suit for cams is providing mechanical advantage. In a particularly overt segue, I'd like to draw your attention to the short discourse on "Bicycle Hub Cam Lock Hack" (located at the end of this chapter), which is a useful primer on the usage of cammed levers in clamping mechanisms. It's not really essential reading for this build, as both the clubholder drive pulley *and* the trigger mechanism that we'll be building in about five pages harness the sublime charms of the cam in other ways, but it *is* another example of the versatility of the mechanism.

Camming the pulley that takes the bungee tension onto the clubholder lets you play with the power curve like crazy. When combined with variable positioning of the club around the radius of the swing arc and multiple latch points for the trigger, you get an extremely flexible "test bench" mechanism for elastic-based power systems.

Plus, you can really torque the bugger up for maximum destructive power . . . not that that's important or anything . . . nope . . . not at all.

The ¾" eccentric offset of the pulley component stretches the bungee considerably during the first 90 degrees of rotation from a fully slack state, then rather less so during the final 90–100 degrees. The nature of the elastic is such that the tension increase per inch of stretch rises almost exponentially; the end result when camming is factored in is a significantly more evenly distributed and efficient delivery of power into the system.

We need to fabricate the aforementioned cammed pulley component. The cutting diagram details the two 3½" discs that you'll be laminating together to form the blank for the cam; you'll only need to drill out the center hole for the moment. Rough out the disks, glue 'em up, and leave 'em in the clamps overnight. **[Figure 04.07]**

Figure 04.06: **The rough-cut club holder disks**

A lathe would be helpful in rounding out your cam blank and forming the groove, but it's not really necessary. If you have a drill press, now might be an appropriate time to consider fabricating the lathe attachment detailed at the end of Chapter 7. Failing that, run threaded rod through the center hole, add lock washers and a few nuts, and chuck it into your drill/drill press: a steady hand and 40-grit sandpaper wrapped around a piece of ¼" wood stock will shape the requisite ¼" deep groove in short order. Be patient, and refresh your sanding surface frequently until you're at the right depth, then smooth out the surface down to 150 grit. Remove it from the chuck and drill a ¼" hole ¾" off center. This is the new and eccentric rotation point of the pulley.

Drill and tap the hole for the bungee tether point into the rim of the disk as shown. It's threaded #8-32, and yes, you *can* use machine taps to cut threads into hardwood. **[Figure 04.08]**

Double-check your component orientation and alignment before attaching the eccentric pulley to the back face of the clubholder permanently. The original center point of the pulley is a now a dowel point to strengthen the entire assembly. Use it as a target and drill through the assembly with a ¼" bit.

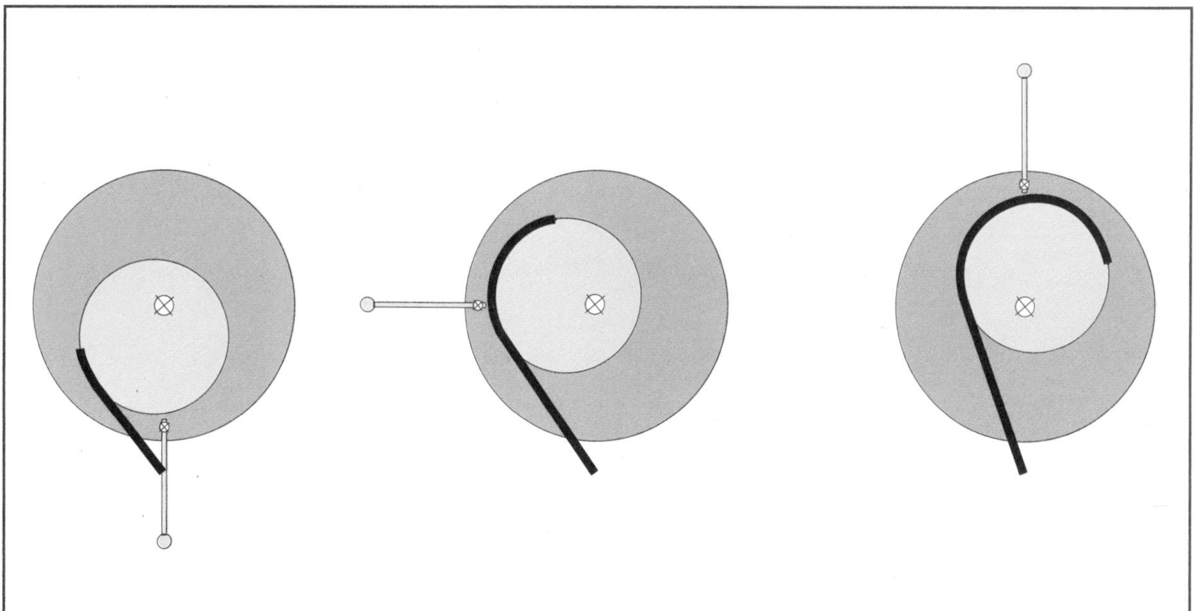

Figure 04.07: **A Young Person's Illustrated Guide to the Tension Advantage of the Eccentric Pulley**

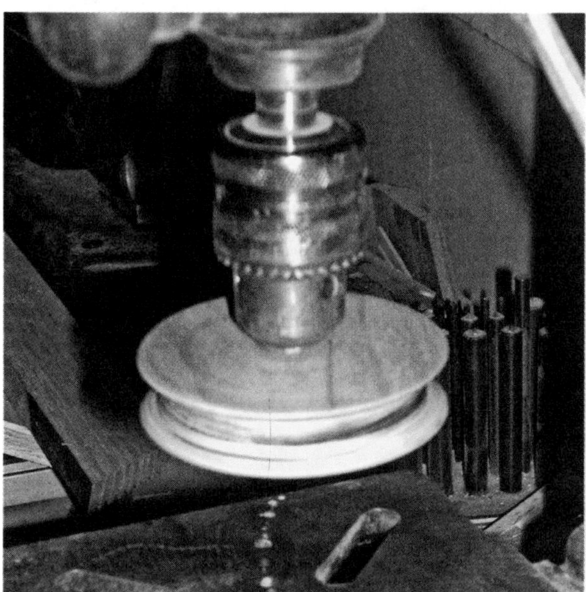

Figure 04.08: **Back to the drill press: cutting the bungie guide groove into the cam wheel. (Not shown: asthma inducing cloud of sawdust.)**

Set a dowel, reclamp the assembly and set it aside to cure. **[Figure 04.09]**

When the finished clubholder assembly is out of the clamps, clean up the dowelling, then mark and drill out the mounting holes for the club shaft and the trigger latchpoints. Drilling holes is a lot like real estate, when ya think about it. The three most important factors in each? Location, location, location. **[Figure 04.10]**

Figuring out where to put the holes danged near caught my brain on fire. My master reference point for the entire process was the line running center-to-center between the cams' original midpoint, and the off-axis hole that provides the eccentricity.

The hole positions and alignment of the cam on the clubholder were determined in context of the long and short of the cam. **[Figure 04.11]**

To maximize the advantage provided by the cam, the dead bottom of the club movement was offset 45 degrees from the long point of the cam. The bungee attachment point came next, calculated around the stretchability of the material; I wanted to max out the stretch of the "at rest" length of bungee in 180 degrees of rotation (give or take).

With the attachment point sussed out, I built in a bit of adjustability by adding three different trigger latchpoints

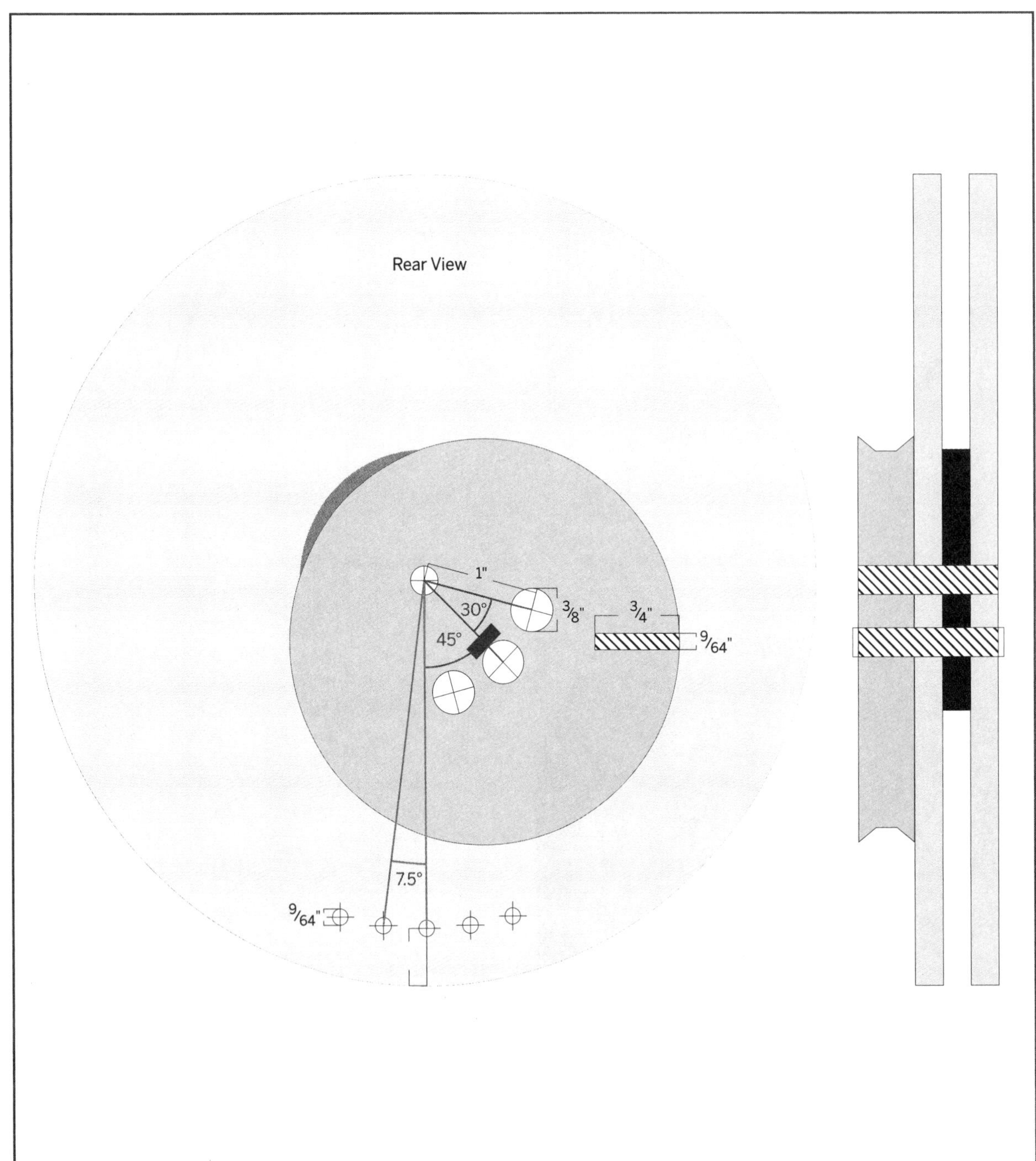

Figure 04.09: **Clubholder assembly/bungie cam detail: Holes! Angles! Distances! Each and every one is critical, and the fate of the free world depends on your accuracy.**

Figure 04.10: **Out of the clamps and ready to drill: the nearly completed clubholder assembly**

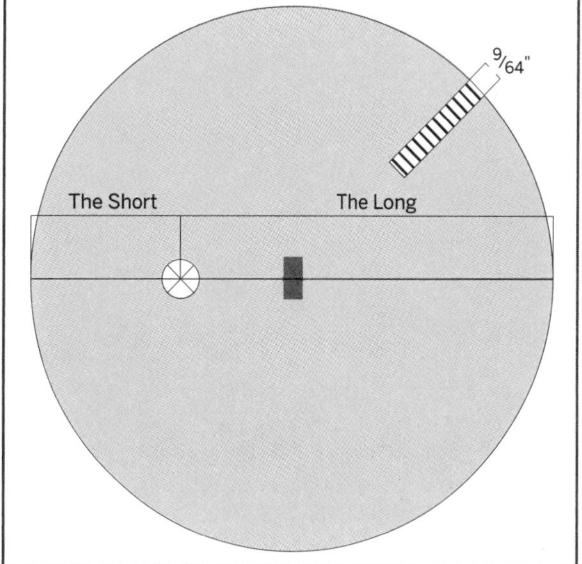

Figure 04.11: **Reprazentin' da long an' da short . . . yo.**

spaced at 30-degree intervals. Maple Mike has a trigger based on a spring-loaded 1⁄4" brass rod that slots into a latch hole when the mechanism is locked 'n' loaded. Retracting the rod releases the mechanism. The three latchpoints allow a modicum of control over the range of motion of the clubholder.

Effective, and 45 percent less crude than usual.

As noted, I'll generally take adjustability wherever I can find it: five club mounting points spanning either side of dead bottom bring a bit more control over the power stroke into the mechanism. You could easily increase that number/range should you feel the urge, but I don't recommend spacing the club mount holes any closer than 71⁄2 degrees: The possibility of material failure and subsequent high-speed club displacement through your brand-new 30" monitor isn't worth the risk. (But if by chance it does happen, try to get video, wouldja?)

Due to the stress on the materials under load, I would *not* advise adding more latchpoints for the trigger.

Assuming that workshop pixies didn't mess things up when you weren't looking, you have a near-complete clubholder assembly with the bungee mount point situated where it oughta be, contextually. If not, feel free to utter many cuss words as you attempt to redrill the mount hole in the right spot.

The club mounting holes occur at 71⁄2 degree intervals inset half an inch from the rim.

You *did* remember to mark dead bottom on the clubholder, didn't you?

Approach the task of drilling the club mount holes in whatever manner you prefer, bearing in mind that it's essential that they are absolutely perpendicular to the face of the clubholder, and pass cleanly through both faces of the assembly: Personaly, I marked out the angles, jigged the clubholder to the table of my drillpress with a piece of threaded rod, and had the holes drilled in about five minutes.

Heretically,[2] I cut #8-32 threads into the mounting holes. When the club is mounted properly with a machine screw and nut it's a *very* secure attachment. **[Figure 04.12]**

2 As mentioned, cries of outrage from the traditional woodworking community aside, cutting threads into hardwood with machine taps is an entirely workable solution. My experience has been that cutting the threads, as opposed to pressure forming them with a woodscrew, ends up being a more resilient method. The fibre mashing caused by a woodscrew compromises the material integrity in a wider radius.

This works in endgrain, too. Really want a strong-ass endgrain cinch with a machine screw? Cut your wood glue with 30 percent water and plop a drop into the hole before you set your screw. The dilution helps penetration, and when it's set, you have a *mighty* grip, as the grain structure has been plasticised by the glue.

The distance between the latchpoint centers and the rotational centerpoint of the assembly is determined by the location of the axle and trigger on the chassis. If you followed my drilling guide for the chassis, the latch points are 1" out from the center of rotation, center to center, positioned as illustrated on the detail diagram. If you changed the chassis dimensions in a fit of improvisational legerdemain, adjust the position of the latchpoints accordingly. The latchpoints are drilled at ⅜" to a depth of ⅜". Drill 'em out, then hit the driving range for a celebratory bucket of balls. The clubholder assembly is now complete.

Figure 04.12: Drilling the club attachment holes along the circumference of the clubholder assembly

The Baseplate and Chassis

I sized the base plate in this build "to fit." The width dimension is what I got when I butt-joined two pieces of in-house maple ¾" x (almost) 4" together (I said stop snickering, dammit), and the length dimension is what was needed to accommodate the footprint of the chassis and club head once the edges were beveled to 45 degrees. This came out as 6¾" W x 9½" L, which is a generally reasonable footprint for a desktop mechanism.[3] You pay an arm and a leg for solid plank hardwood more than 4" in width: save your money and glue up the wood for your base. **[Figure 04.13]**

If you're using a table saw, drop a strengthening spline into the joint by setting both your blade height and fence position to ½". True up the facing edges of your two pieces of stock, then run them edgewise through this setup, cutting a ½" deep kerf ⅛" wide. Back your fence off ⅛" and repeat the process, which gives you a neatly aligned ¼" slot in each piece of stock. Cut a 1" wide slat of ¼" stock, do a test fit of the joint and adjust as needed, then spread on the glue and clamp it up. You and your `L33t w00dw3rx0r 5k1lLL5`. **[Figure 04.14]**

Once the glue has cured, cut the blank to size. Try to keep the glue joint centered on the finished base. I mitered the sides 45 degrees; it's a nice touch, but not necessary (as is so often the case with artsy-fartsy nonsense). Use your own discretion. Realistically, as long as there's a flat spot under the clubhead, the rest of the base can look like whatever you want as long as stability isn't compromised.

The chassis mounts to the base with glue, and six ¼" dowel pins for reinforcement. Mark and drill the dowel holes in the base as illustrated, then put the (now completed) base aside for the moment.

The chassis component needs a bit of finesse to accommodate the geometry of the club assembly and still have a reassuring degree of structural integrity. If you want to duplicate the hipster po-mo curvilinear swoopiness of my chassis form factor, be prepared to become familiar with the singular creative joys of the French curve. Alternatively, basic functionality can be achieved with two lengths of 1" x 3" dowelled together and lopped off top and bottom at 30 degrees. **[Figure 04.15]**

The swoopiness started with an attempt to superimpose a pair of circles onto the basic form, which proved to be unsatisfying, for various nonspecific reasons. Tweezing the initial effort with judicious use of the aforementioned French curve provided a more satisfying result to my eye, but you're welcome to go in any direction you personally want to pursue. **[Figure 04.16]**

I strongly recommend fabricating the ancillary mechanisms to a semifinished state before you indulge your inner sculptor, though, primarily because drilling the requisite mounting and positioning holes in the chassis is a royal pain in the ass when performed on curved surfaces. Swoopi-

3 A random sampling of telephones on sale at the Vancouver Flea Market returned an average width of 7", and an average length of 8 5/16". Good dimensions to know when designing ostensibly desktop-scaled things.

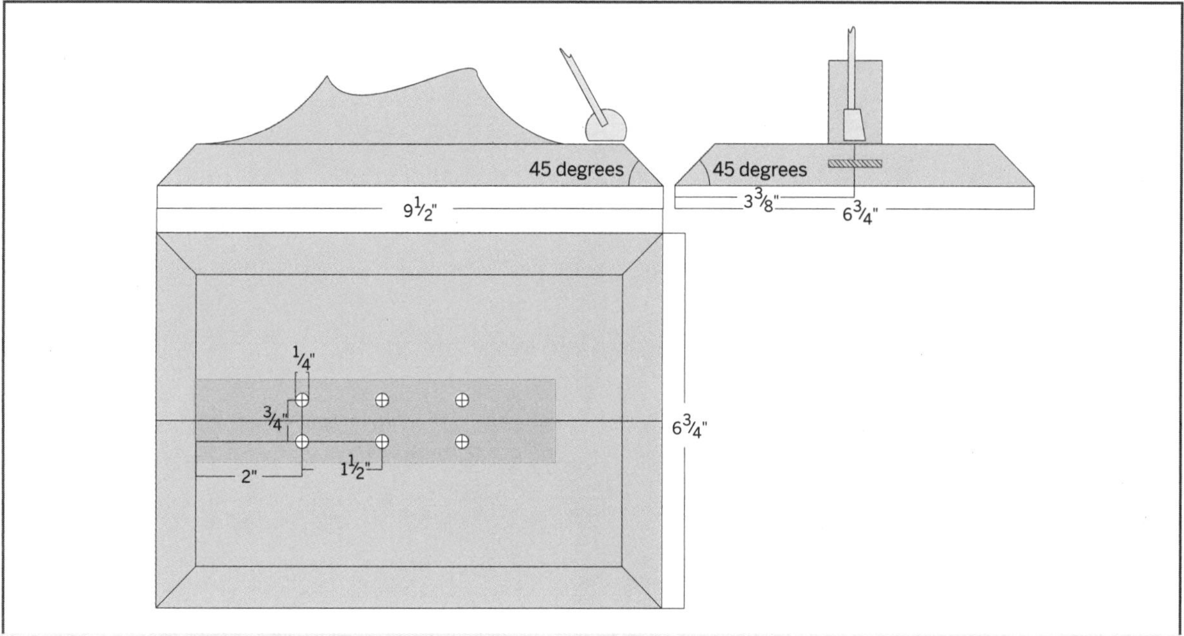

Figure 04.13: **All your base details are belong to us.**

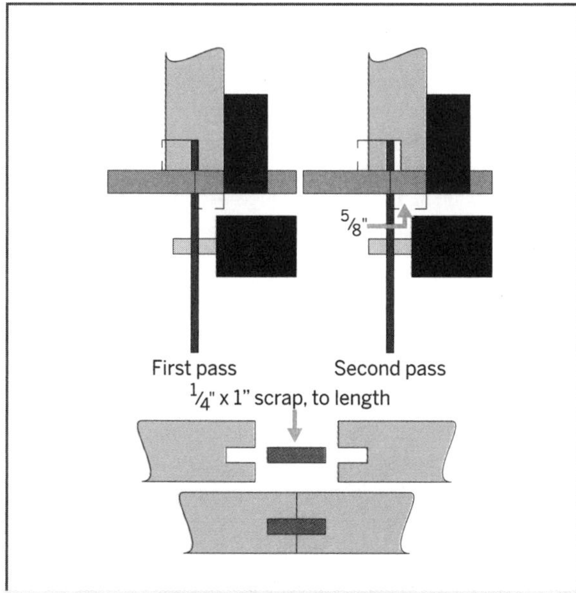

Figure 04.14: **The quick 'n' dirty tablesaw spline joint: showcasing your L33t w00dw3rx0r 5k1lLL4g3**

Figure 04.15: **The chassis in the raw: do please note the hipster postmodern curvilinear swoopiness.**

ness is also likely to require you to modify some of the hole depths detailed. Do not panic. By the time you're ready to actually drill 'em out, you'll have become one with the subassemblies, and the specific nature of the modifications will be easily recognized.

The cutting diagram shows the spacing, sizing and depths of the holes in question, as implemented sans swoop. There's a number of nested diameters to be drilled out with a certain degree of precision to ensure that the mechanisms work properly: unless you're particularly anal about sourcing your components precisely to what I used, you'll be substituting bits and pieces of your own into my ragtag collection of parts. This requires frequent bouts of adjusting-to-fit during the build. **[Figure 04.17]**

Drill the holes in decreasing order of dimension; Forstner bits are the drills of choice for these holes (smooth walls, flat bottoms, remember?). You can expect to do some sanding to fit, particularly when reinforcing the trigger pin hole with 1/4" ID brass tubing (an essential step to ensure strength and durability).

Yes, I'm being deliberately obtuse to encourage you to Think While Making.

CAUTION: While planning ahead is a given during *any* fabrication project, it's essential to be aware in real time of the cause and effect of each step in the build procedure. The success of adventures in improvisational fabrication relies *heavily* on your ability to integrate decisions made "on the fly" with the *entire* mechanism. Hence the importance of the credo "Think While Making."

Maple Mike is designed with the axle through the body, meaning that a bearing race is necessary on each end to keep things turning smoothly. The bearing race mounting holes are *the* critical consideration: if they're not absolutely parallel and properly centered on the axle passage, there's gonna be friction issues introduced into the mechanism. Accurate measurement and marking before drilling is essential if you plan on getting it right.

Drill the bearing mounting holes on each side of the chassis first, then complete the job by drilling through the body with a 3/8" bit to form the axle passage. Test-fit the bearings and axle to check the accuracy of your work: minor angular/alignment discrepancies in the bearing positions are more easily compensated for *before* the wood has been finished. You may find yourself having to enlarge one of the holes to allow the races to line up properly, in which case you can fill in any gaps that may result with wood putty well before starting your finishing surface preparation.

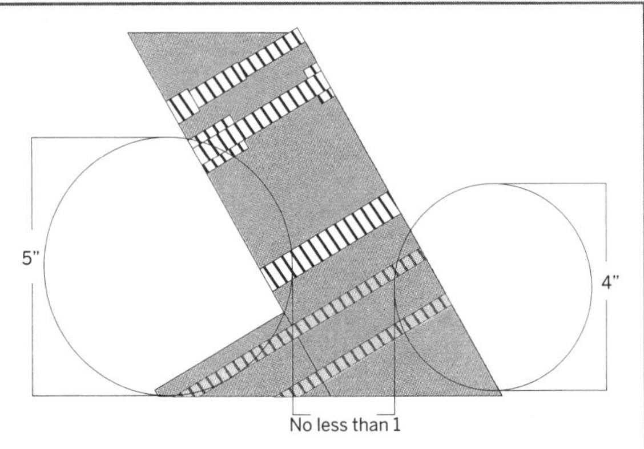

Figure 04.16: Form in context of function: the quest for swoopiness.

If, after drilling these holes, you decide to venture down the path of swoopiness, bear in mind that the rear bearing mount hole is almost certainly gonna take a hit, depthwise. Compensate for this impending loss while you still have the original hole in place as a pilot and deepen the mounting hole to post-swoop specifications. This is vastly preferable to having to try and center the bearing hole on the axle passage blind.

When I pieced together the unfinished woodwork on this piece the inherent nonmodernness of the form factor was apparent. I capitalized on this germ of an idea by using a router to make the decorative ogees around the chassis edges. **[Figure 04.18]**

Oooooooh . . . antiquey! Addition to functionality? Not a kipper. Addition to style factor? Huge. Attention to detail, kids; the little things count. Your mileage may vary.

A Brief Moment to Get Our Bearings

As noted, the clubholder assembly needs bearings to operate smoothly. We're using threaded rod as an axle, and it's gonna be under a lot of stress when loaded. The bearing system has to be done with a certain amount of care; otherwise, things start relinquishing their linearity.

Once again, we turn to thriftshop rollerblades as a material source. You'll need two bearing races, two spacer bushings, and one plastic shoulder washer. These things are all spec'd to receive a 1/4" axle shaft, so you'll also need a length of 1/4-20 threaded rod, a couple of washers, and some nuts. If you

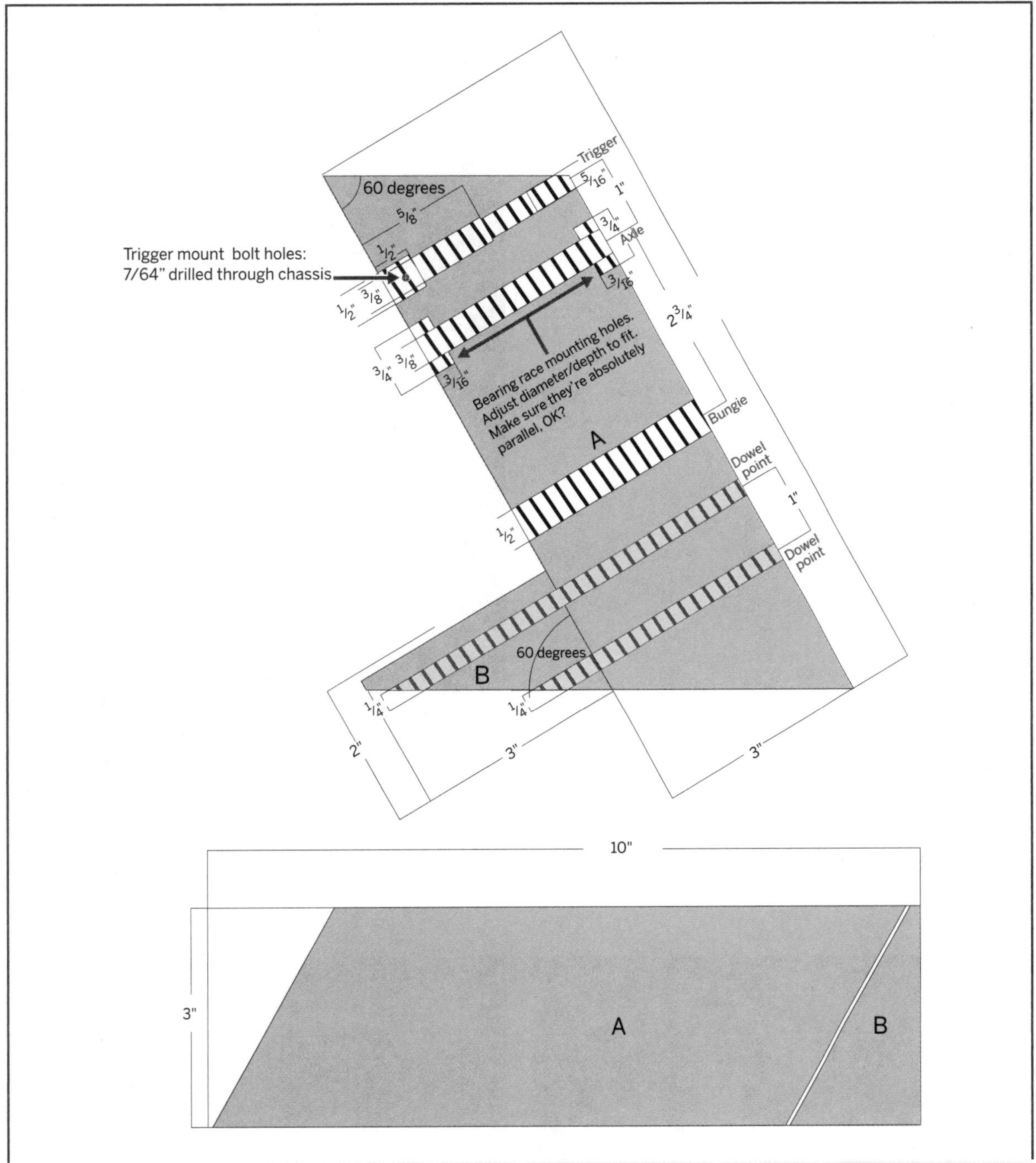

Figure 04.17: **The chassis in detail. Cripes, lookit all the damned holes.**

can lay your hands on a length of suitably dimensioned and threaded tempered steel rod to use as an axle, by all means do so: I've tried my damnedest to minimize the effect of off-axis strain on the assembly by providing extra support everywhere possible, but the axle is the weak point of the mechanism, and prone to bending under high tension. "Strong Like Bull" is a *damned* good way to approach the axle.

Pictured is the component chain both exploded and assembled; one bearing race goes on each side of the chassis, and the club holder assembly threads onto the righthand side, between the shoulder washer and the nut. The photograph shows acorn nuts and steel washers; the finished piece uses brass washers, an additional decorative brass disc, and . . . threaded brass balls as nuts. **[Figure 04.19, Figure 04.20]**

Install the bearing system in the chassis, and mount the clubholder assembly. It should spin effortlessly with no wobble. If it doesn't, check the chassis axle passage and bearing mounting cavities for binding. A bit of sandpaper action should set things right.

Leave the chassis/clubholder assembled for the moment to allow test-fitting of the remaining subassemblies as they're fabricated. Speaking of which . . .

Hey! Let's Build the Trigger!

The trigger latch mechanism uses a cammed lever to retract the springloaded rod that does the actual latching.

It only *looks* hard to fabricate. **[Figure 04.21, Figure 04.22]**

The cam lever is cut and drilled from brass plate. The design allows for a smooth ½" of shaft travel over a bit more than 90 degrees of actual rotation, terminating in a solid position lock at full open. The curve is based on a 1" diameter circle, but feel free to get artsy with the arc to achieve the performance you want. The reason we're building the damned thing is so that you have an incentive

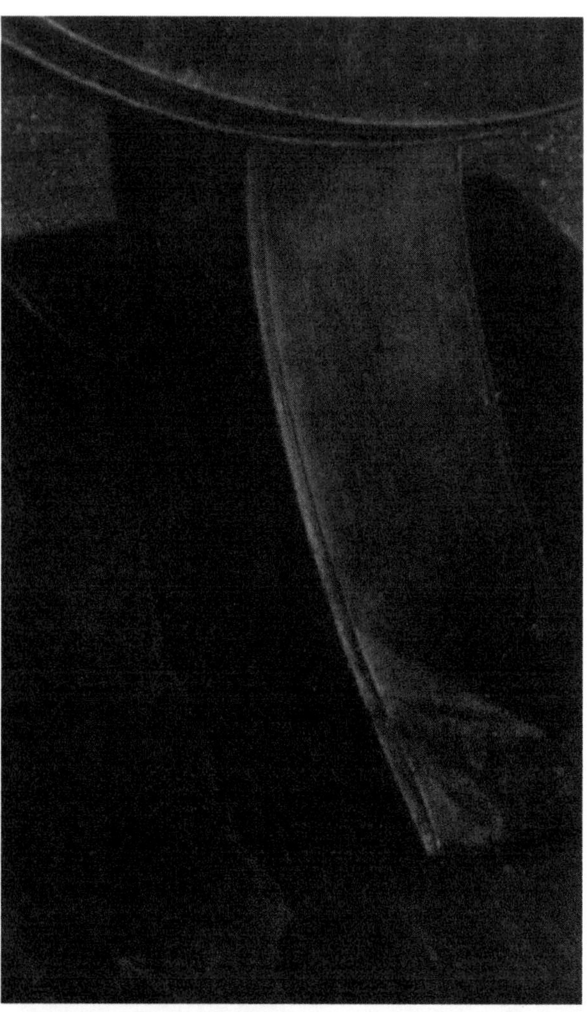

Figure 04.18: **Behold the evocatively antiquey might of the decorative ogee!**

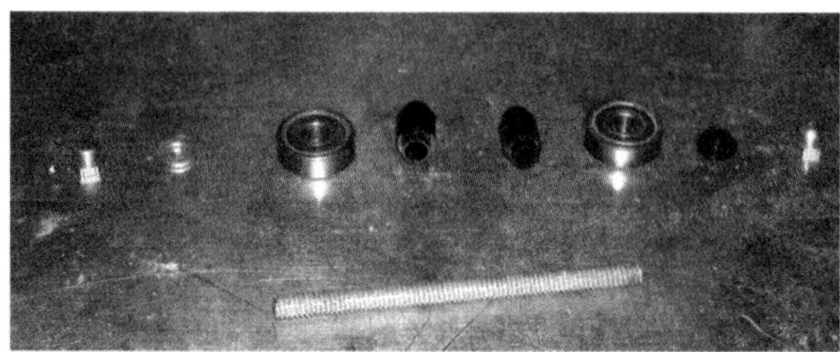

Figure 04.19: **The axle assembly revealed: all the needful bits laid out . . .**

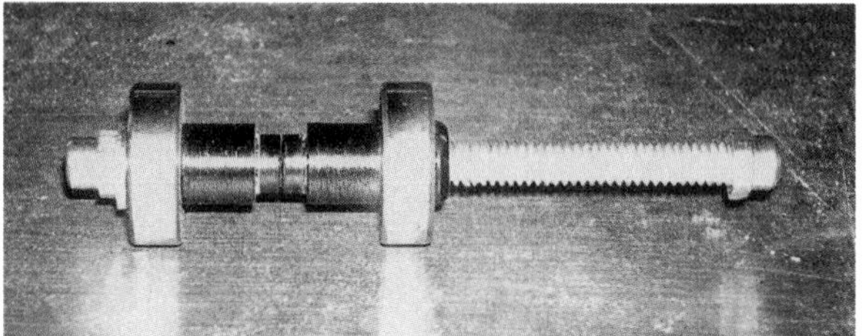

Figure 04.20: **. . . and fully assembled. Friction doesn't stand a chance.**

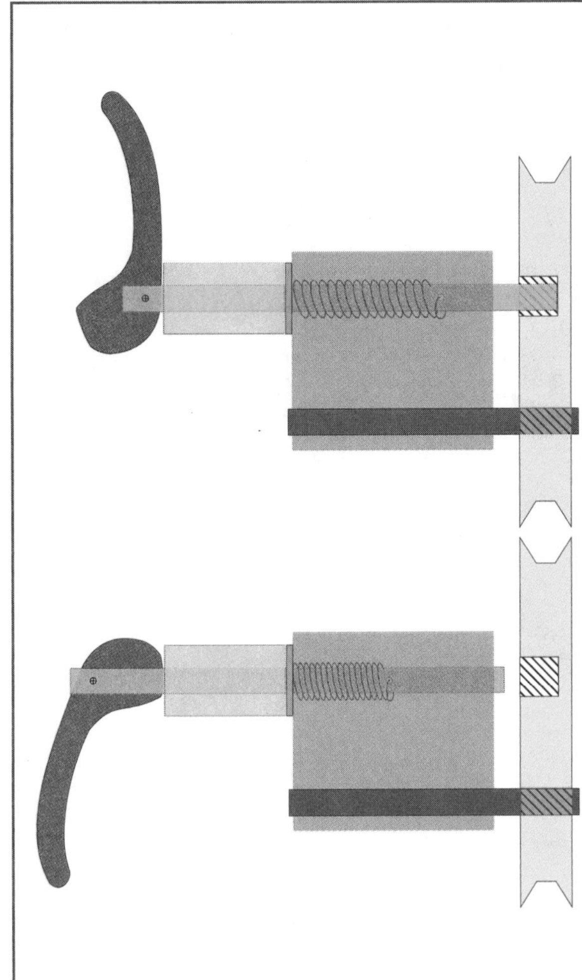

Figure 04.21: **The trigger: the graceful functionality of the cam in action**

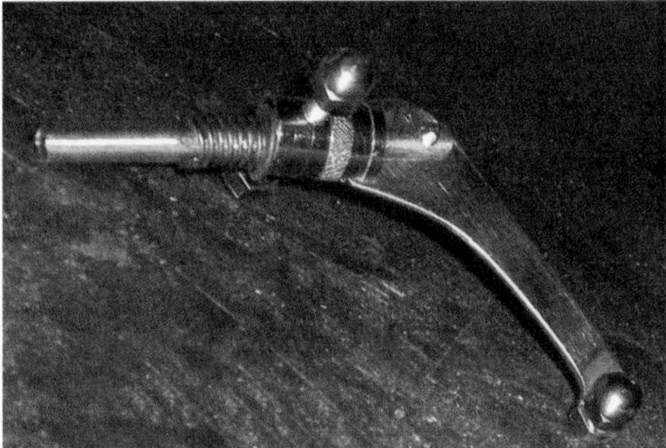

Figure 04.22: **The "only looks like a pain in the ass to fabricate" trigger in real life**

to achieve Cam Zen, and the only real way to do that is to wade in and start making 'em. **[Figure 04.23, Figure 04.24]**

Component-wise, here's a full list of what you'll need:

- 4" of 1⁄4" OD brass rod
- 4" x 2" 16-gauge brass plate
- One screw-on brass ferrule from an RCA plug
- 11⁄2" compression spring with ID > 1⁄4", OD< 3⁄8"
- Four 6-32 acorn nuts
- Two 2" 6-32 brass machine screws
- 11⁄2" washer with a 1⁄4" hole. Oddly, I couldn't find one in house for love or money, so was forced to drill out the hole in a "close-enough" diametered washer of European (read "metric") origin.

Start by drilling a 7⁄64" hole through the brass rod 1⁄4" from one end. Tap 8-32 threads into it, then carefully cut a slot 3⁄32" x just about 5⁄8" down the length, perpendicular to the threaded hole. Clean up the slot with needle files; the slot needs to be just wide enough to accomodate the cam lever, with enough clearance to allow it to rotate smoothly around the axle point. Cut a screwdriver slot into one end of a 1⁄4" length of 6-32 machine screw and mount the cam lever to check the action, dressing the metal where needed to ensure a smooth action. The handle of the cam lever is a short length of 6-32 machine screw with an acorn nut on each end. Use a drop of LocTite to keep it from unscrewing. **[Figure 04.25]**

The brass ferrule is one of those fortuitous happenstance discoveries that occurs while foraging for parts. It's a repurposed piece of a dollar-store RCA–RCA cable. (Gold-Plated! Audiophile! Multimedia Interconnect! 2M/6 Feet! Stereo! $1.00! That's less than 17 cents per exclamation point, which is a *damned* solid deal, even if the imperial to metric conversion is a bit dodgy.) Overall, it's 1⁄2" OD, with an ID a bit more than 3⁄8"; the end where the cable exits is capped, with a 1⁄4" exit hole. File that hole a bit larger to let the trigger pin move freely, then shape a shallow groove into the constricted end wide enough to slot the cam lever. The floor of this groove *must* be smooth and flat to let the cam lever slide easily over the surface. **[Figure 04.26]**

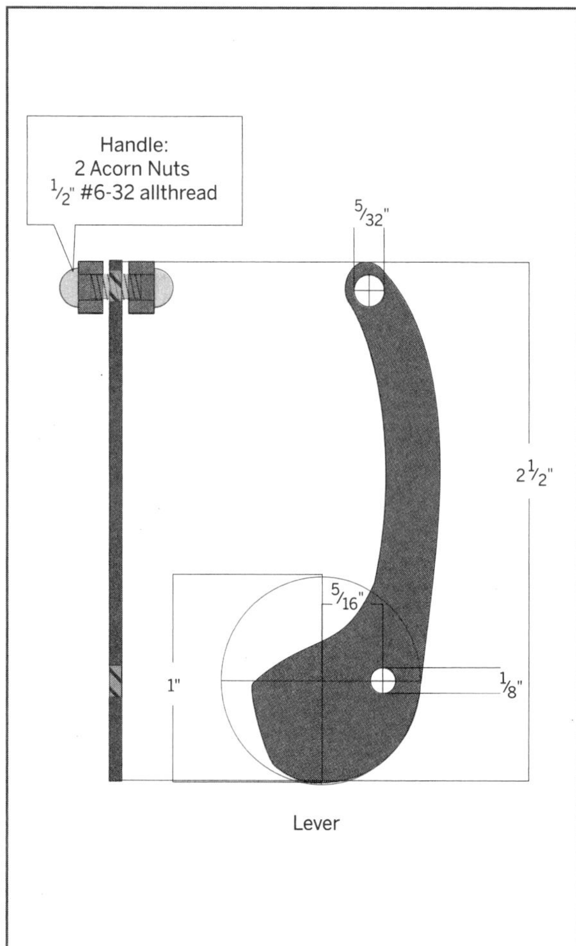

Figure 04.23: Revealed at Last! Cammed Trigger Lever's Shocking Details! "It's nothing but 16-gauge brass," says "close friend."

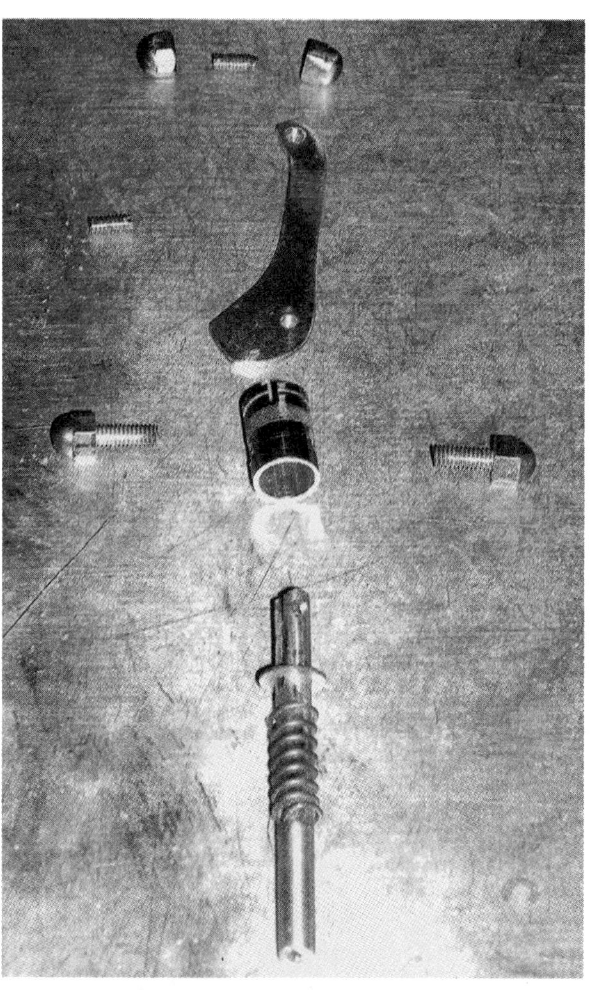

Figure 04.24: The exploded view of the trigger reveals yet another unavoidably high part count.

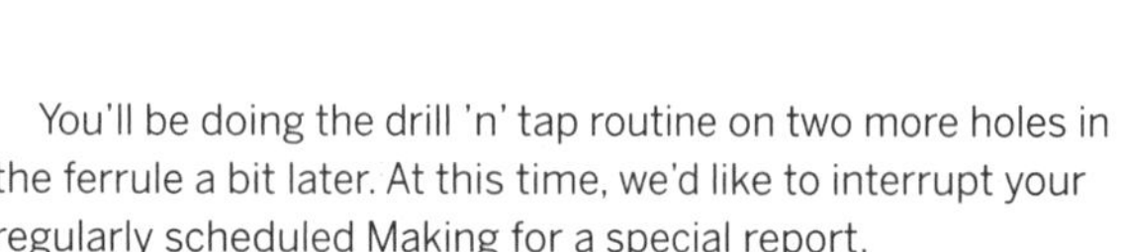

You'll be doing the drill 'n' tap routine on two more holes in the ferrule a bit later. At this time, we'd like to interrupt your regularly scheduled Making for a special report.

The Rites of Springs: Roll Your Own Boinginess

I *like* springs — there are three or four big bins of 'em in my parts archive, collected from everything I've disassembled over the last eight or nine years. We're at the point in this build where we need to consider the oh-so-critical trigger compression spring. I used one harvested from a late model Smith Corona manual typewriter,[4] although I've seen similarly spec'd items in use in early-edition VCRs. There are a number of different kinds of springs;

4 Disconcertingly, my memory is such that I can recall at a glance the provenance of about 99% of the components I have at my disposal. I still have trouble with my postal code after ten years, but by gar, I can tell you exactly where that black anodized 10-32 Torx head machine screw came from.

It's really freakin' annoying.

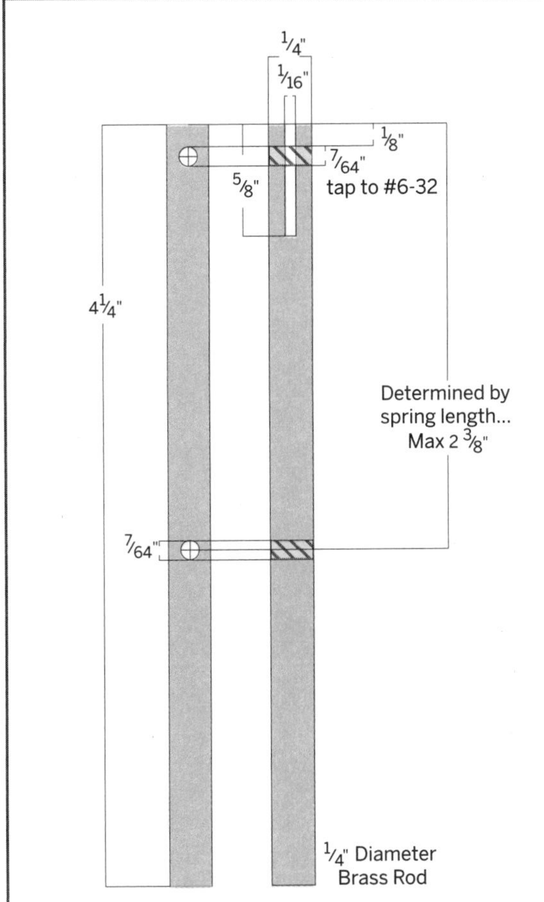

Figure 04.25: Fabricating the trigger rod requires lots **of finicky hole drilling and needle file work. It took me three tries to get it right...you should have no trouble getting it right in two.**

the coily ones we're most familiar with come in two flavours: expansion (pull on it and the spring pulls back, like on your basic articulated desk lamp) and compression (push on it and the spring pushes back, like in a ballpoint pen). You can make your own springs from steel spring wire by winding the wire tightly around a cylindrical form (coils touching for an expansion spring, coils separated for compression), anchoring both ends of the wire, then heating the whole shebang with a torch until the wire just begins to glow. The heating relaxes the tension in the wire to accomodate the cylindrical shape it's been wound

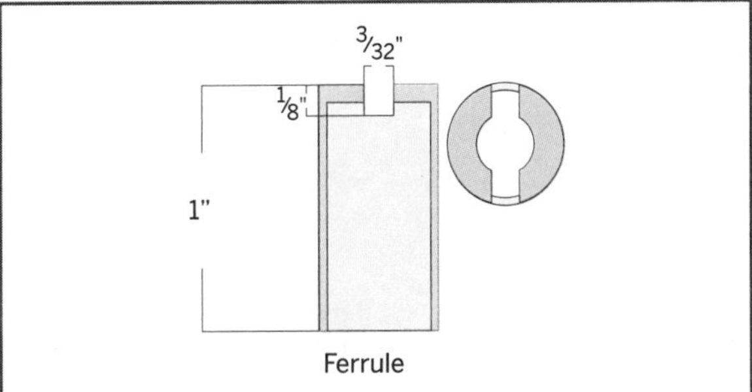

Figure 04.26: Today's featured oddball component: The heavily modified RCA jack ferrule.

around; the tension returns to the wire in its new form when it cools down. **[Figure 04.27]**

Where to get spring wire? Guitar strings are spring wire. Use the plain (unwound) ones for best results, and the heaviest gauge you can lay your lunch hooks on. How cool is that?

It's not *quite* as easy as it sounds. For one thing, it's an enterprise fraught with peril: until the spring wire has been tensioned properly in its new form, it's essentially a mechanical bomb waiting to go off. Lose your grip on either end of the wire and it'll uncoil explosively in a flurry of ninja-like cutting and slashing. Wear eye protection at the very least; work gloves and a leather apron, too, if ya got 'em.

For another thing, evenly winding even small-gauge spring wire is no picnic (it's spring wire — it's springy, dammit), and anchoring the ends is challenging. I've had success using an electric drill as a winder, with hole and slot anchoring. Chuck in brass tubing for the form when winding expansion springs, and coarsely threaded rod for compression springs (the spring wire slots into the thread grooves for nice, even spacing of the coils. Clamp the free end of the wire tightly into your bench vise, use the lowest Rs per M you can muster, and keep even tension on the wire as it winds onto the form.

Merely bending the wire into the slot at the end of the form isn't gonna work to hold the wound wire solidly in position. Clamp the spring wire to the form solidly with locking pliers at both ends, release the form from the drill chuck, and fire up the torch for the heat/cool cycle. Once cool, cut the spring wire at the point where it passes through the hole in the form on the (formerly) chuck side of the form; If you did the heat/cool correctly, the spring wire won't uncoil. If you wound an expansion (coils touching) spring on a smooth form, it should slide off the form easily. If you wound onto threaded rod for a compression spring you'll need to carefully cut the form at the base of each side of the slot

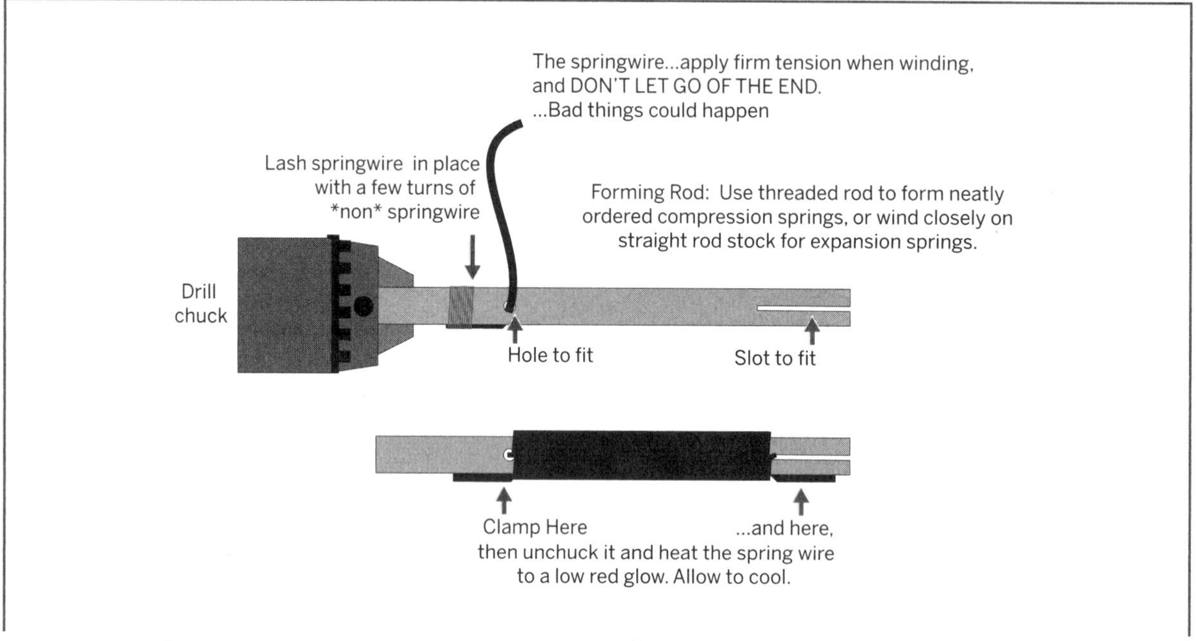
The springwire...apply firm tension when winding, and DON'T LET GO OF THE END. ...Bad things could happen
Lash springwire in place with a few turns of *non* springwire
Forming Rod: Use threaded rod to form neatly ordered compression springs, or wind closely on straight rod stock for expansion springs.
Drill chuck
Hole to fit
Slot to fit
Clamp Here
...and here, then unchuck it and heat the spring wire to a low red glow. Allow to cool.

Figure 04.27: **The Rites of Springs**

to free the spring wire crossing through and allow you to unscrew the spring off the form.

So now you know how to make springs. Need bigger-gauge spring wire? Check your local craft supply house for beaders *stainless steel* "Memory Wire." I've seen it up to about 1 millimeter, which is heavy enough to make a darned manly spring. You can check your local yellows for spring manufacturers/vendors, but if you're gona go the official route like that, you're just as well off buying the springs you need ready-made, rather than putzing around rolling your own.

CAUTION: Make sure the memory wire you get is stainless steel. There's memory wire available made from other alloys (I've seen it in weird tungsten and nickel/chromium blends) that performs the way *beaders* expect memory wire to perform, but is essentially useless for making springs.

As always, it's your call. We now return to our program, already in progress.

Back to the trigger at hand, I'm gonna assume you have a suitable spring in hand, and by "suitable," I mean "compression, fairly stiff, > ¼" ID." Use the shortest possible length that can attain 1/2" of compression, that bein', as you recall, the range of movement provided by the cam. Assemble what you've done so far: the cam lever attached to the trigger pin, with the pin running through the ferrule and the lever nested into the slot in the ferrule. Flip the lever to allow maximum extension of the pin through the ferrule, then slide the washer up the pin until it's flush with the ferrule. Using pliers, ensure that your spring is open at one end, and has the wire bent to cross the diameter of the spring at the other. Measure the spring lengthwise, then mark that distance on the pin measuring from the face of the washer down the exposed length of the pin. Drill a hole slightly larger than the diameter of the spring wire perpendicularly through the pin at that point, then work the spring down the length of the pin, starting with the open end of the spring. The crossing spring wire at the other end will resist your efforts in this regard, but gentle persistence will be amply rewarded when the end of the crossing wire passes through your freshly drilled hole.

Ta (as they say) da.

Aren't you clever! Your cam activated trigger is now spring-loaded and ready to install. On my homeworld, this is cause for a well-deserved cocktail. I'll have a Tanqueray martini, please. Dry, two olives.

I think that's another golfing term, innit?

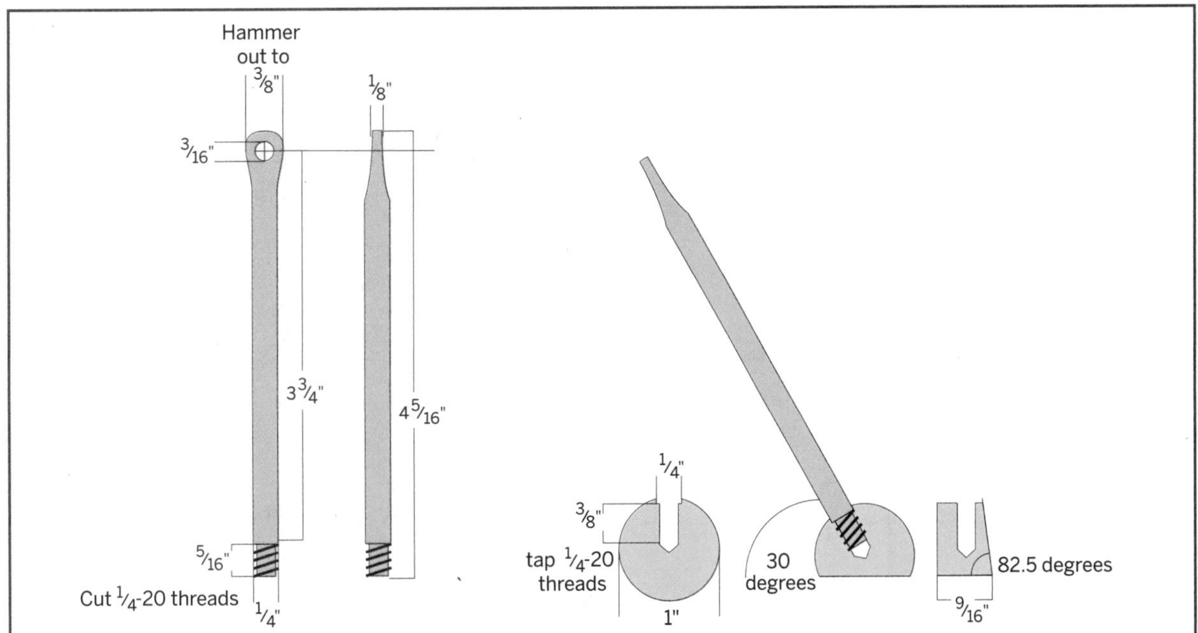

Figure 04.28: The handmade golf club is a tradition going back hundreds of years. They were not made like this.

The Club: Not That Thing You Clamp Onto Your Steering Wheel

The club is basic metalwork, nothing fancy; only three measurements you need to get right, and you're doing it in brass, so the material won't be fighting you to any great extent. Take the time to do it right (particularly if you're working with hand tools and not one of those rightfully droolworthy desktop milling machines) and your friends will view you as the second coming of Tubal Cain. **[Figure 04.28, Figure 04.29]**

You need about 3/4" of 1" diameter brass rod, and 4½" of 1/4" brass rod. And a fresh hacksaw blade or two. Get enough material to allow for a few retries.

This is a case where doing things in the right order makes the job significantly easier. Start with the shaft: using a hammer and anvil (you *need* an anvil, even if it's just a 5-pound jeweller's version) widen one end to 3/8", ensuring a symmetrical profile. Depending on the brass alloy, you *should* be able to accomplish this cold.If cracking issues develop, pull out the propane torch and try again after heating your stock to a low glow. Proceed cautiously, avoiding the urge to overheat the metal. Get someone to take pictures of you in blacksmith mode; you'll want them in your dotage to impress the grandkids. When the shaft is shaped, drill out the 3/16" hole for the mounting bolt and tap it for #8-32 threads, cut the shaft to length, and cut 1/4-20 threads 5/16" up the unwidened end. Use emery cloth to reduce the overall diameter of the shaft by a miniscule amount — less than 1/64". You want the shaft to fit easily into the gap between the disks of the club mountng assembly.

Cut a 9/16" length of 1" brass rod. This is your club head blank.

True up your cuts to 90 degrees (we'll add the pitch to the face in a later step), then drill and tap a 3/8" 1/4-20 threaded hole perpendicularly into the dead center of the length. Widen the top 1/16" of the hole to a full 1/4" as a countersink to accomodate the full unthreaded width of the shaft when it's threaded into place. When cutting threads into a blind (closed at one end) hole be prepared to deal with the metal cuttings produced by the tap: They have to go *somewhere*, which means drilling the hole you're tapping marginally deeper than you need, and removing the tap from the hole and shaking out the cuttings a few times during the thread cutting process.

In a perfect world, your shaft will thread into the hole in the club head and cinch in tightly with the mounting hole of the shaft exactly perpendicular to the faces of the club head.

It ain't a perfect world. Plan on adjusting the thread length of your shaft a few times until you're *close*, then rely on thread-locking glue or cyanoacrylate to chemically cinch your joint. Another option is to thread enough of the shaft to accommodate a locknut before the head is screwed on, then cinch down the locknut to secure the joint. I'm ambivalent about this method, due to the weakening of the shaft induced by cutting threads into it. It's your call.

The club mounts with an 8-32 bolt, which need a bit of modification. Run a 1" machine screw through one of the mounting holes in the clubholder assembly, with a washer fore and aft and a nut on the back face. Mark the section of bolt exposed between the two clubholder disks with a permanent marker. Remove the bolt, and file off the threads in the section that you just marked so that the club shaft swings freely on the axis of the mounting bolt.

Right now your club resembles a brass lollipop: a thick metal disk on a thick metal stick. You need to lop off the bottom part of the head parallel to the base, in context of the 30 degree backslope on the shaft.

What do you think the chances are of your assembled chassis/club holder assembly *actually* presenting a 30 degree angle vis-à-vis the horizontal plane of the base? Mine was pretty accurate at a bit under 31 degrees. The error is introduced into the system by the flex in the bearing races (small but noticeable over length) and the flex of the joint connecting the club shaft to the mounting assembly. Whip out your protractor and square and double-check the swing plane angle on the complete assembly, then mark the horizontal plane onto the face of your clubhead. You'll want at least ¼" of clearance available between the bottom of the club and the baseplate to allow for some kind of tee contrivance to hold the ball. **[Figure 04.30]**

Carefully cut the clubhead along the chord that marks the horizontal plane. Use a hacksaw to get close, then a file or emerycloth equipped disc sander to true up the angle. Once this horizonal plane is accurately established, go back to the file and/or sander to form the 7.5-degree loft angle into the leading face of the clubhead. In a real golf bag, a loft angle this low would normally be found on a driver, where an optimized energy transfer vector is preferable to a rapid ascent trajectory. If you're having trouble getting your shots up in the air and out of the extreme rough that is your cubicle, you'll want to look at increasing the loft angle substantially, up to as much as 60 degrees. As there's no one around to argue with me, I have determined this club to be a Brassy Cleek.

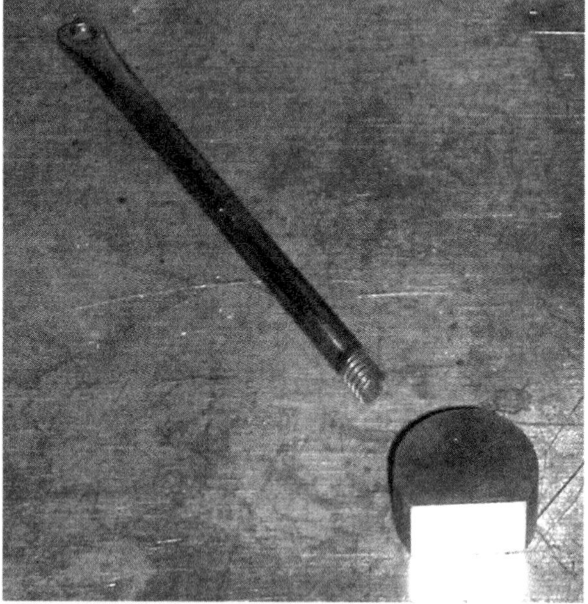

Figure 04.29: Brutishly elegant: The Eccentric Genius Brassy Cleek.

Anyway, once you're finished the shaping process (whatever that shape may turn out to be), lap the surfaces smooth and shiny with various grades of emery cloth, steel wool, and buffing compound.

Now, if you could make another one just like it, except about ten times bigger and equipped with a virgin eland skin leather grip, I have absolutely no doubt you could convince some fairway-bound richfella to part with about 800 clams for it. **[Figure 04.31]**

Nah. Too easy.

After that lot, the bungee tensioning mechanism is . . . er . . . a snap. I spec'd capacity for up to 5⁄16" diameter elastic into the original design, primarily because that was the largest diameter bungee I had around when I was drawing it up. The goal is to be able to guide the elastic onto the pulley, easily stretch tension into it, and securely lock that tension in place.

What I ended up with to perform this mundane but essential task is a truly classic overwrought "Eccentric Genius" bodge job execution of a basic screw-the-knob-down pinch mechanism. Illustrated are:

1. The bit you pull on to increase the tension: I used a brass end cap for ½" "PEX" PVC residential plumbing pipe with the locking ridges filed off; I drilled a 7⁄64" hole through the

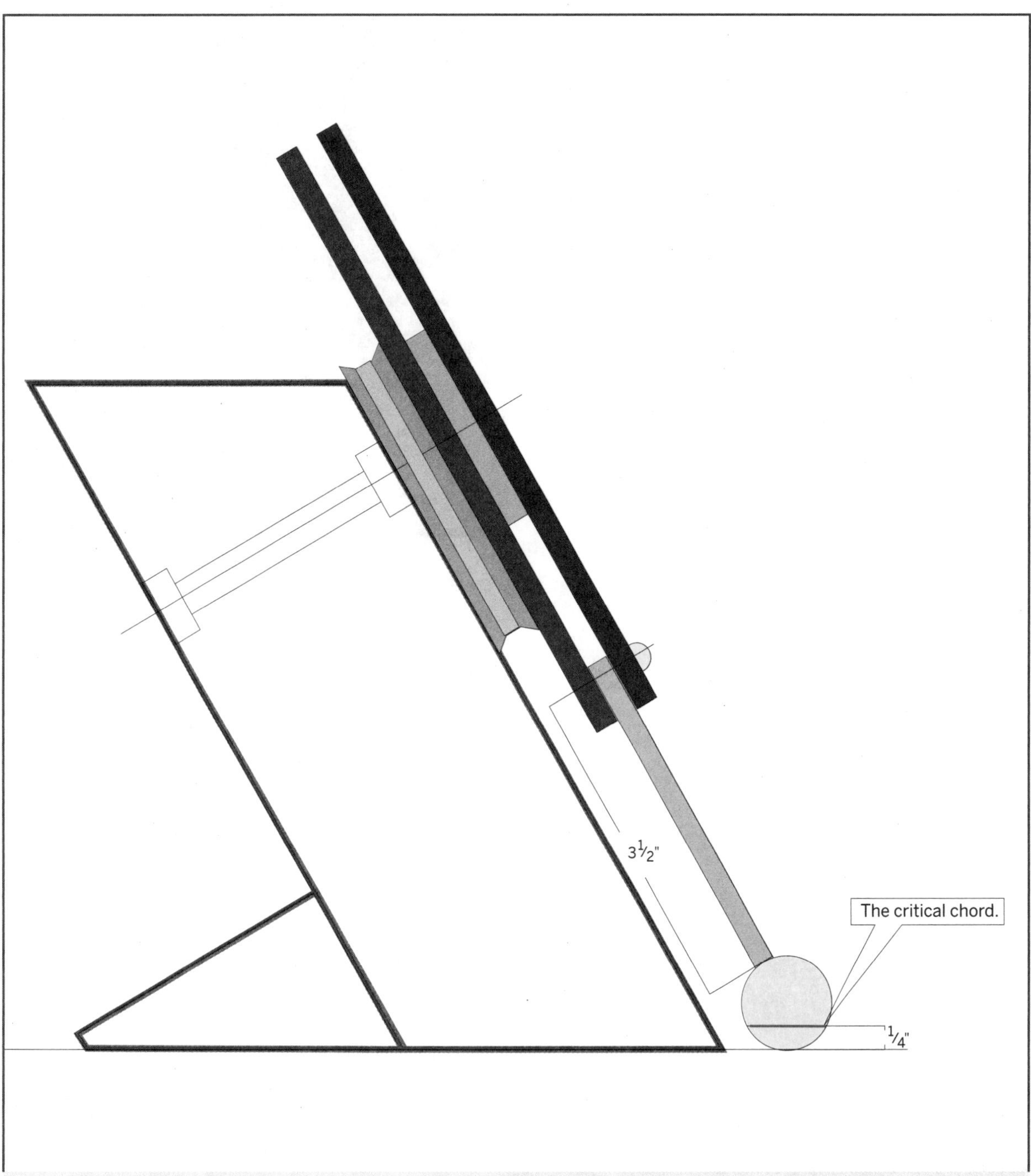

Figure 04.30: **How it lines up.**

fitting and pressfitted a length of ⅛" brass rod through the bungee elastic as a locking pin. A few drops of cyanoacrylate on the bungee fabric sheath prevents it from unraveling under stress, and the ends of the locking pin were filed and emeried flush with the curve of the fitting. This component can be filed under "Over-attention to Detail." It's not really needed, but makes a nice touch. The fitting was selected primarily because the ID matched the OD of the bungee I happened to use. Use whatever strikes your fancy. **[Figure 04.32]**

2. The tension lock itself, which doesn't need to be *anywhere* near as complicated as the one I ended up with: Depending on the diameter of bungee elastic you end up installing, your diameter requirements may vary, but it's in the best interests of tweezability, gusto, and really whacking the shit out of the ball that you at least give yourself the *option* of harnessing as much wellie as possible. **[Figure 04.33, Figure 04.34, Figure 04.35]**

To accommodate the widest diameter range of bungee elastic, you need a large-scale hole (obviously) with a large-scale spindle screwing into it. Through some bizarre component accretion process, I ended up with about ⅔ of the 7⁄16-18 threaded cartridge of a gas barbeque valve screwed into a hole I'd drilled and tapped into the compression nut from a ½" brass pipe fitting. Into this compression nut was pressure-fitted a piece of ½" OD brass piping, and the valve cartridge was topped off with a thumbwheel from an antique welding torch held in place by a copper rivet that took me two days to peen properly.

Make no mistake, campers: I can complicate *anything*. In your case, all you really need is something to keep the (taut) bungee elastic from being pulled back through the hole in the chassis.

Simple methods? Tie a damned knot. Poke a pointy stick through it.

Complicated methods? Well, you just learned how to make cams do stuff. That's one starting point to consider.

And lastly . . .

3. The front-side bungee guide: This is another "use what you want, but use *something*" situation: the component is present to ensure that the exit point of the elastic is exactly parallel to the pulley groove; the main axle of the mechanism takes enough abuse as it is without subjecting it to off-axis strain under load. I fabricated the component pictured from a ¾" piece of the same kind of PEX fitting I used on the bungee pull grip: The inner and outer diameters were just about perfect, and the ridges provided some textural detail to the part that made it not just another piece of brass tubing. I cut the piece to fit, then filed a nice smooth notch sized to accommodate the elastic into the rim. The component pressfits snugly into chassis, reinforced with my favorite ghastly-smelling-2-part-sets-in-about-90-seconds-startlingly-strong-dollar-store epoxy. **[Figure 04.36, Figure 04.37]**

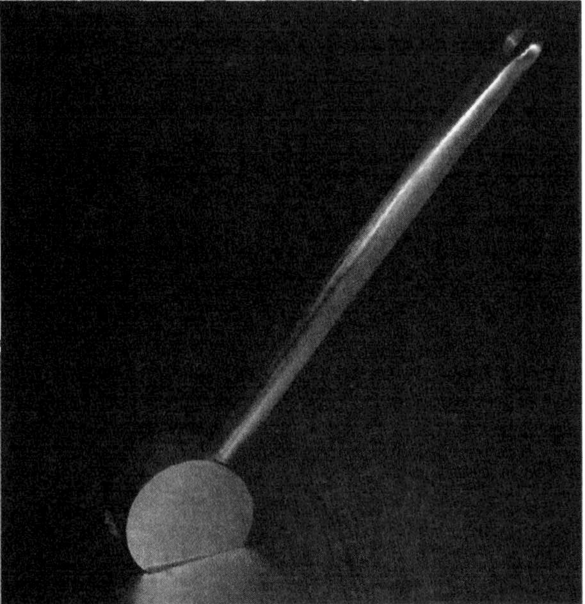

Figure 04.31: Hoot, mon, it's a bonny wee Brassy Cleek, Seamus. Can ye lend us a fiver 'til the end o' the week?

Figure 04.32: Bungee, guide and locking mechanism: Why did the bungee have to be pink?

Hey! You've made most of the pieces. Time to put it together.

Glue the chassis to the base. Once it's cured, use the pre-drilled dowel holes in the base as guides to drill ½" into the chassis. Set the dowels, let 'em cure, then cut 'em flush. See how easy it is to do with a Kugihiki? **[Figure 04.38]**

Golf Club Nomenclature: Old School versus New School

Drivers, 2 woods, 5 irons . . . golf clubs have standardized names and specifications (although there's a lot of variation from manufacturer to manufacturer), and there are stringently enforced rules about the number of clubs a golfer can carry. Such was not always the case. Back in the days when "irons" were actually made of iron, *all* clubs were custom-made, and a trip to the blacksmith was the equivalent of a trip to the pro shop.

Modern-day numbering and naming regulations painfully usurped the much more evocative nomenclature system used in those days. There's still heated uncertainty about the precise equivalencies of old-school vs. new-school club names, and as is their wont, golfing enthusiasts maintain their learned and passionate debate to this day. I spent a wasteful amount of time delving into the subject, and the closest thing to a majority consensus on the matter is this list. The old-school names take on new levels of hilarity if read aloud in a faux-Scottish accent. Loft angles included for your fabrication convenience, although the loft angle is *not* the only definitive factor in a club's designation. Shaft length, head weight, and the contour of the face also vary from club to club (and manufacturer to manufacturer). This list is by no means comprehensive, and many, many details of meaning to a golf enthusiast have been omitted.

Olde School	New School	Loft Angle
Cleek	Driver	7–13 degrees
Mid mashie	3 iron	20–24 degrees
Mashie iron	4 iron	24–28 degrees
Mashie	5 iron	28–32 degrees
Spade mashie	6 iron	31–35 degrees
Mashie niblick	7 iron	35–40 degrees
Pitching niblick	8 iron	40–45 degrees
Niblick	9 iron	45–50 degrees
Jigger	Wedge	45–60 degrees
Brassy	2 wood	12–16 degrees
Spoon	Wood	> 15 degrees
Baffy	Wood	> 30 degrees

See what I mean about golfers and technical minutae? Cripes!

Figure 04.33: **The tension lock up close 'n' personal.**

Figure 04.34: **The crudest of locking mechanisms, blatantly adapted from the much-beloved thumbscrew torture device.**

Figure 04.35: **The humble PEX end cap: loathed by plumbers, but endlessly adaptable in context of improvisational fabrication.**

Fit and install the brass reinforcing tube for the trigger pin exit hole. A press fit reinforced with a dab of cyanoacrylate will do. Shape the exposed tip of the tube to meet the chassis faces, then test mount the assembled trigger mechanism and ensure the trigger pin plays nicely with the reinforcing tube. With the trigger mechanism set to fully retract the pin, do a final fit of the ferrule into the backside of the chassis, ensure that the cam lever is properly perpendicular to the base, and mark the hole positions for the trigger mounting bolts using the predrilled holes in the chassis as guides. Remove and disassemble the trigger, drill the holes and tap them for #6-32 machine screws, then reassemble the mechanism and mount it in position on the chassis. On the example piece, I used acorn nuts and headless machine screws to give that much-loved light Victorian Industrial aesthetic. Feel free to improvise.

Position both sections of the tensioning mechanism, and (if you want to be *really* secure) drill the pilot holes for escutcheon pins to hold these components in place. If you do pin these components, remember to file the pointy bits of the pins flush with the inner walls of the components so the elastic runs freely through the holes. **[Figure 04.39]**

The bungee attaches to the pulley with a #8 machine screw through a #8 brass washer, directly through the bungee elastic if you're using thick-diameter bungee (reinforce the fabric sheath with a few drops of cyanoacrylate to prevent unravelling), or serving as a loop-around or tie-off point for thinner-diameter elastic.

You'll need a tee. I used a hex nut with the hole drilled out to a somewhat spherical shape to cup the ball securely, buffed up all shiny and purty like.

Tie it all together and fire off a few practice shots now, checking for bind points and misalignments. When you're happy with the performance, disassemble the beast, finish the wood, buff up the brass, then put it back together again. **[Figure 04.40]**

The example piece is finished with a bizarre combination of techniques I bodged together to give a "battered as hell, straight from the estate sale of Hamish McCrock, seven-time winner of the MacBeth Single Malt Invitational" kinda look.

After surface prepping the wood down to 600 grit, I started by dyeing the wood mauve with concentrated beet juice, then I dyed it again with stupidly strong black tea. After the wood dried out again and stopped smelling I went over the surface with fine-grade sandpaper, added equal portions of burnt umber and lampblack to 30 cut shellac and brushed on about 10 coats, with a light steel-wooling between each coat. After that lot set up, I buffed it out with a shoeshine brush, and finished with a light wipedown of a generic paste floor wax. It's a damned ugly finish, but contextually it rawks relentlessly.

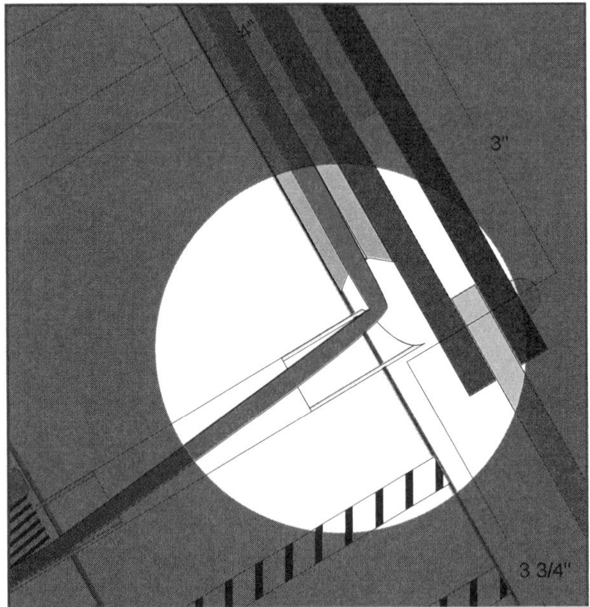

Figure 04.36: **Accurately shaping and positioning the front-side bungee guide is one of those "attention to detail" issues that enhances the strength and performance of the mechanism. Yeah, it's finicky, but much less of a pain in the ass than replacing the axle every couple of days due to excessive bending.**

Figure 04.37: **Vastly over-shaped, but nonetheless effective.**

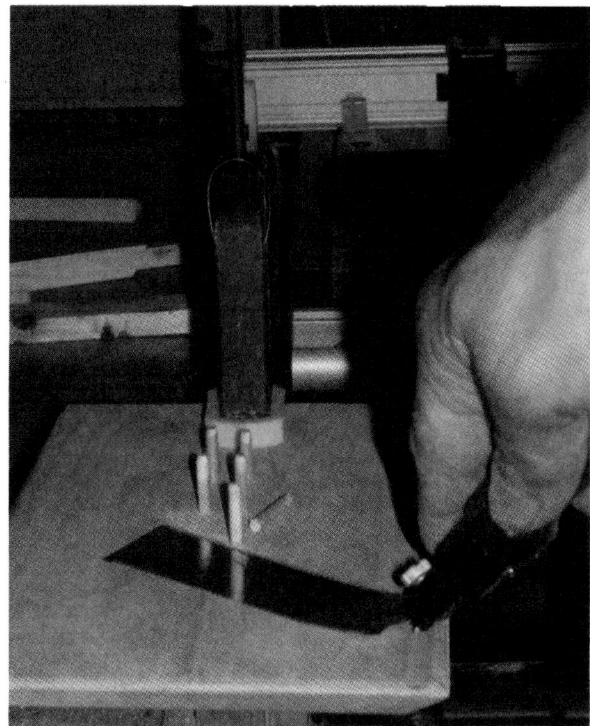

Figure 04.38: **The Kugihiki: subtle precision comes to flush cutting.**

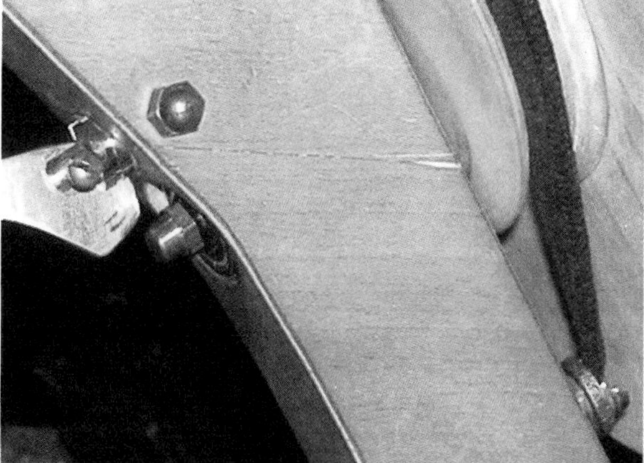

Figure 04.39: **Trigger mounting the Victorian Industrial way.**

Figure 04.40: **At this point, the build is considered ready to hit the 19th hole**

I categorically refuse to insult your intelligence by providing comprehensive instructions for use of this mechanism. To be frank, if you're smart enough to have built it, you're smart enough to know how to use it.

Which is what you should do.

You're done. Hit the 19th hole and celebrate. Order for me; I'll be there in ten minutes.

‹ Nano-Project › The Oughta-Be-More-Common Bicycle Hub Cam Lock Hack

In which our ribald workshop chicanery creates many tons of quick-release clamping pressure goodness with a handful of scrap yard bicycle components 'n' shit.

What we're bodging together here is commercially available, sorta. There's a lot of very innovative cam-based clamping solutions on the market. By all means, explore the wide variety available. Some of them are really quite useful.

The ones here are free. Which is *good*. When you see how much the commercial products cost, it's actually X-tra Special Super D-Lux Good. Plus, this is gonna get your brain thinking about cams in all kinds of other different directions, which is also good.

Time to get some stuff. Yes, you're going the scrap yard again. Unless you get lucky and find what you need in the dumpsters on the way there.

I'm such a kidder.

To make the best use of the bike bits that you'll be scavenging, you really need a tap and die set, but it's not absolutely necessary. I will be continuously prodding you until you do buy one though.

Pictured in **Figure N4.01** is what we're hunting: they're used all over the place on bikes these days. Cinch 'em up reasonably close with the thumbnut, then reach for the cam lever and get about 15 tons of pressure (really) with a flip of your finger. Absolutely bloody marvelous.

Primary mechanisms . . . ya gotta love 'em.

The trick is to make a custom nut for it that passes through or locks into the hold-down slot of the drill press table depending on the alignment. This approach is much easier than having to thread the thumbnut completely off the bolt shaft when installing or removing it. See how useful the tap and die set is? Custom-made nuts, cutting threads down the full length of the cam's bolt shaft. You could bodge around these jobs with mangled washers and spacer blocks, but it's just so much more *graceful* like this.

If you invest a bit of brainwork into pondering the mechanism at play, all kinds of potential uses will become apparent. Set some appropriately sized T-nuts up into the underside of your workbench surface and you'll have rock-solid hold-downs available just by screwing in a cam bolt equipped clamping jaw. They make a really useful retrofit (again with the T-nuts) onto the base of your jig construction set, and you

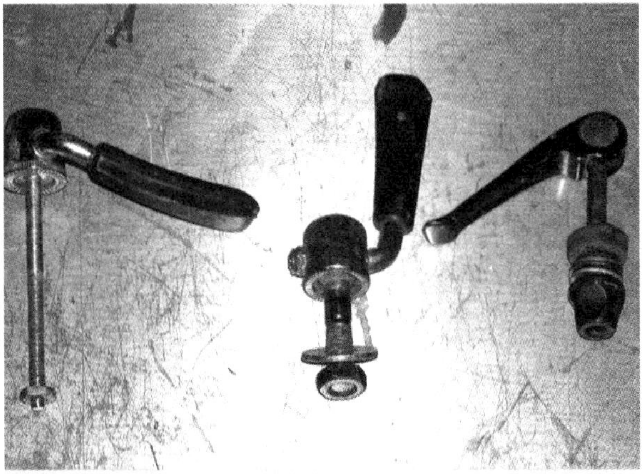

Figure N4.01: **Quick release cam levers, picked fresh.**

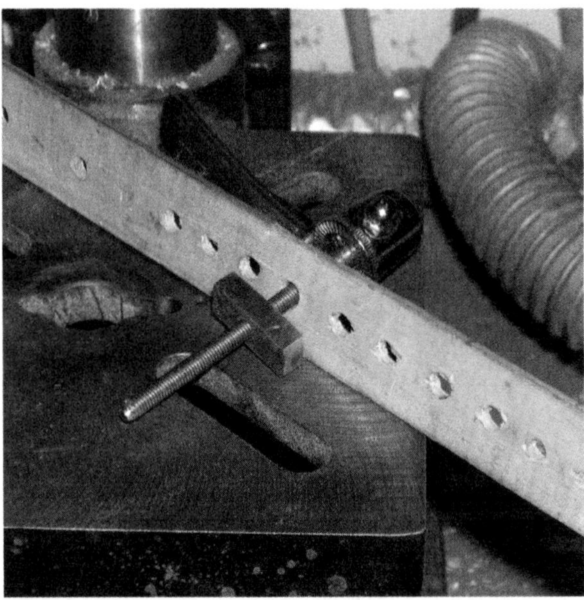

Figure N4.02: **The most obvious place for something like this is holding stuff tight on the table of your drill press.**

Figure N4.03: **View from the bottom.**

Figure N4.04: **In action.**

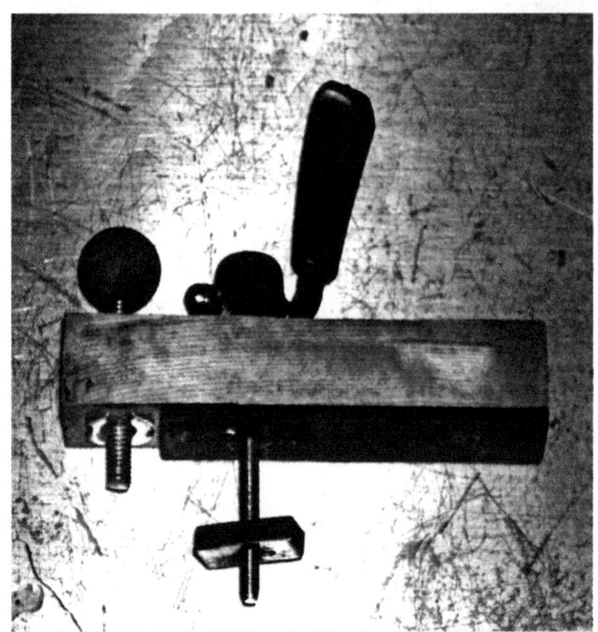

Figure N4.05: **Assemble like this.**

can use a pair of them and two rigid *anythings* to make a serious press clamp. **[Figure N4.02, Figure N4.03]**

Keep a handful around the shop for emergency klampenschtuff solutions that you haven't thought of yet. **[Figure N4.04]**

This is a pretty versatile drill press clamp that I bodged together in less than ten minutes and that will solidly position stock up to about 2" thick on my drill press table. Cutting a V-notch into the jaw to facilitate pipe clamping increases the useful factor even more. Here's what you need if you want to fabricate one:

- 6" of maple 1" x 1"
- A cam mechanism with a 4" bolt, rectangular nut
- A ¼-20 T-nut and about 3" of matching threaded rod

- 5" of 1" belt leather
- Some double-faced tape
- A wooden craft ball

Quick 'n' dirty? Guilty as charged. Does what it says on the packet? Yup! Hackable? That's the entire point, innit? **[Figure N4.05, Figure N4.06]**

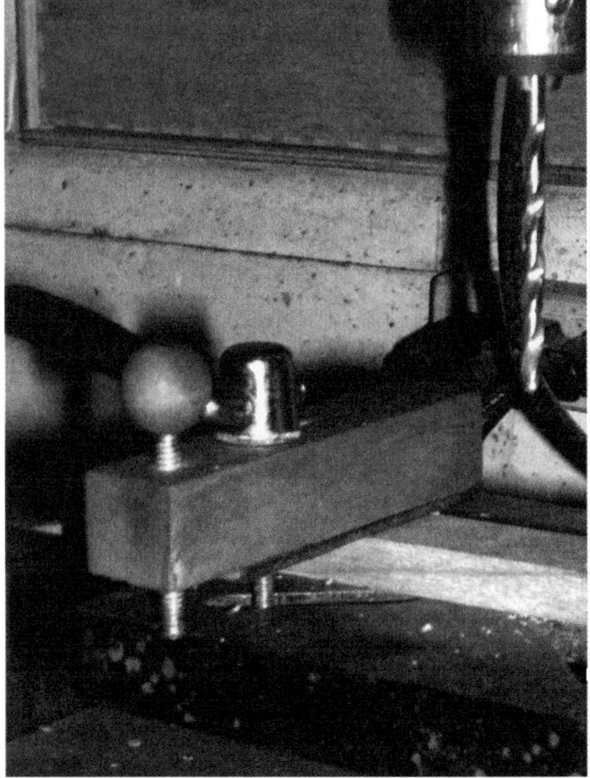

Figure N4.06: **Use like this.**

5 DeskBeam Bass: Don't Fret the Funk

Right at the end of the 60s, there was a hiccup in the timeline, and we got Craig Hundley, a skinny red-headed kid about 14 years old who played jazz piano like he was four times that age and a completely different colour.[1]

Sorta. Adding to the surreality was his previous career as a child actor.[2]

Burnout was inevitable. When next we heard of Mr. Hundley, he'd changed his last name to Huxley, had embraced avant-garde music making, and unveiled to the world The *Blaster Beam*, his personal take on Francisco's *Cosmic Beam*.[3]

The Blaster Beam was a gargantuan scale instrument: 18' long, with four piano wire strings and both magnetic and piezo pickups. Played with mallets, plectrums, and . . . er . . . marital aids, and fretted with a honkin' big piece of stainless-steel pipe, The Blaster Beam's extremely low-frequency output is easily recognized as the sound of V'ger in the first Star Trek movie and is infamously linked to instances of spontaneous orgasm in female audience members during live performances.[4]

Hundley/Huxley subsequently worked as a sound designer/composer on a number of movies through the 80s, then slowly descended into the murky depths of New Age multi-frikkin'-media DVDs. Which likely don't feature a whole lot of serious Blaster Beam action.

Bringing the Beam to the Desk

Anyway, we're not building one of those at the moment. As the theme of these instruments is "Desktop D 'n' B," we're more or less forced to scale the concept back a tad so that it fits on the titular desktop.

1 I owned Craig Hundley vinyl in the mid 70s. He was a skilled but polite player, kinda like the bastard offspring of Oscar Peterson and Dave Brubeck.

It gets better: he had his own teenaged jazz combo too! Gary Chase, a Louie Belson protégé drumming, and Jay-Jay Wiggins, who had a totally gnarly 'fro, on bass rounded out the trio.

They did not swing.

2 Among other things, two appearances in the original Star Trek series: as Peter Kirk in "Operation — Annihilate!" and as the deeply creepy Tommy Starnes in "And the Children Shall Lead."

3 Another musical curiosity from mid '70s California, Francisco was an odd combination of Maker, Musician, and Mystic. His Cosmic Beam featured driftwood stumpage as legs and was just one of many homebrew instruments in his arsenal. The Grateful Dead were enthusiastic first adopters of the Beam, at one time featuring two of them on stage to augment their acclaimed weenk weenk weedly weenky weenk musical stylings.

4 Your results may vary.

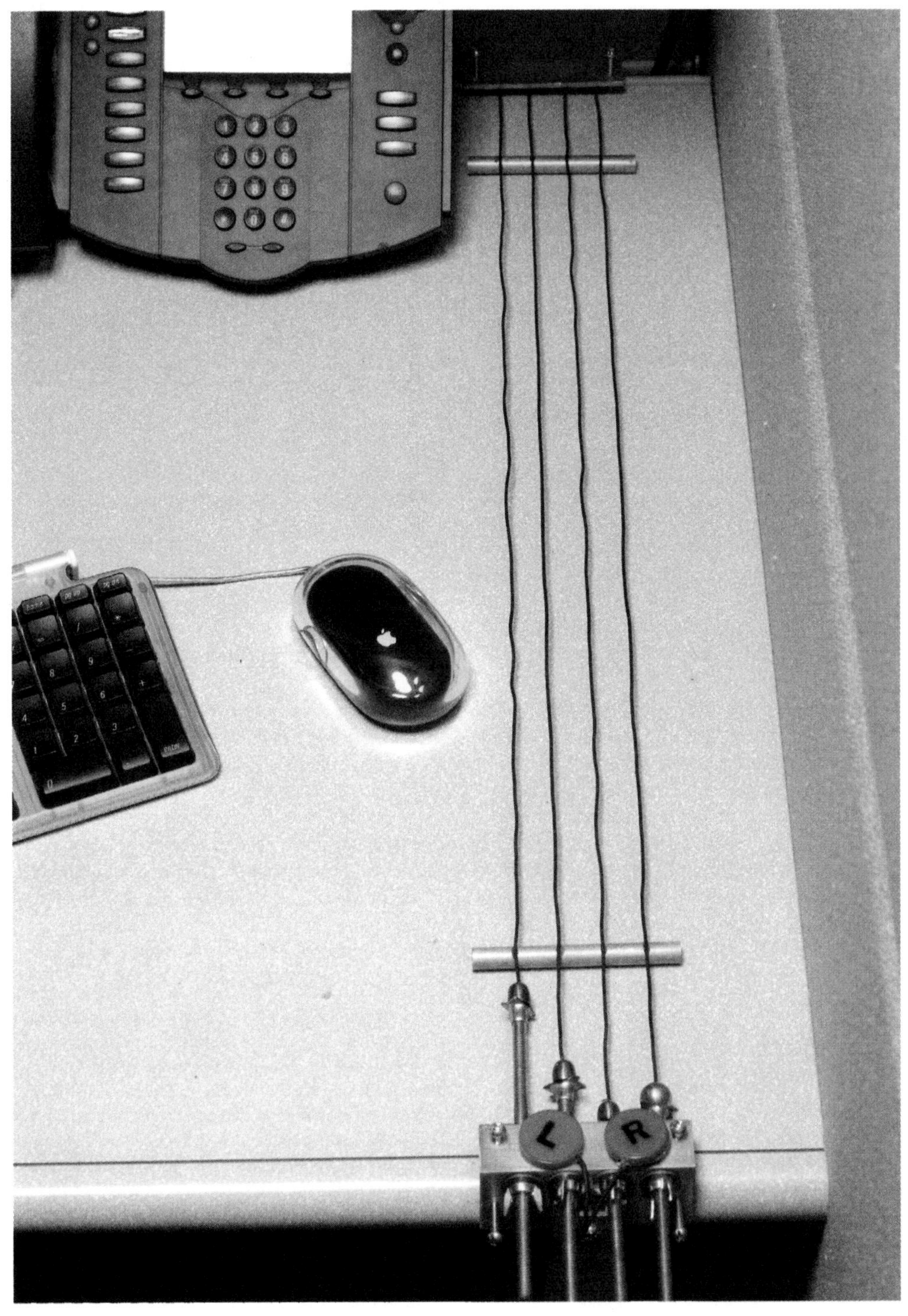
L
R

Actually, I have a confession to make. It's not just gonna *fit* on your desk; it's gonna *be* your desk. Or rather, your desk is gonna be it. We're making a bridge, tailpiece, and headstock to clamp onto your desk and turn it into an extended scale fretless bass.

How extended?

Therein lays the crux of this particular biscuit: you can make this little fella as long as it needs to be to fit your desk. As you (no doubt quite deservedly) rise through your corporate hierarchy to the point where you actually have a desk 18 feet long, the DeskBeam will be right there with you.[5]

Lacking the brobdingnagian magnitude of Craig's epic instrument, the DeskBeam is unlikely to stimulate more than the occasional butt wiggle (unless you're funkin' out like Bootsy), but it's still going to shake your cube, given the cunning way we're going to mechanically couple the string vibrations to the side panel of your desk and use it like a big-ass speaker diaphragm.

NOTE: So what if it's not exactly flat response? It's gonna move air. Which really is all that matters with bass, innit?

This is gonna be a pretty easy build: lotsa measuring, not much cuttin' and drillin', and generally easy-to-source components. Over the last six months, I've given every appearance of having a not unsubstantial *desk fetish* to friends, family, casual acquaintances and startled office workers, taking detailed measurements of every desk I happened upon in an attempt to arrive at an honest-to-goodness "one size fits all" design for this instrument. I was thorough and diligent, but I can't make any promises. Your employer may source his office furniture from an avant-garde European manufacturer who favours a non-Euclidean approach to linearity, in which case the onus is on you to suss out the design essentials of the DeskBeam and adapt them to work on your amorphous blob of a workstation.[6]

For added GarageBand fun, we'll equip the DeskBeam with a stereo pair of piezoelectric contact pickups, letting you capture every nuance of your dramatic reinterpretation of "Portrait of Tracy" directly onto your PC.

The DeskBeam in Principle

Let's look at the basic premise of the mechanism.

Think of the build as an effort to construct a polygon by defining the angles, then connecting them together with lines to complete the structure. The top two right angles are equipped with the headstock and tailpiece assemblies; the four wires that connect them across your desktop are the strings of the 'Beam. The bottom two right angles link to the upper corners with adjustable lengths of threaded rod but aren't *necessarily* connected together horizontally. Given a modest J-hook, they can just as easily hook onto the bottom edge of each side panel of the desk. [Figure 05.01]

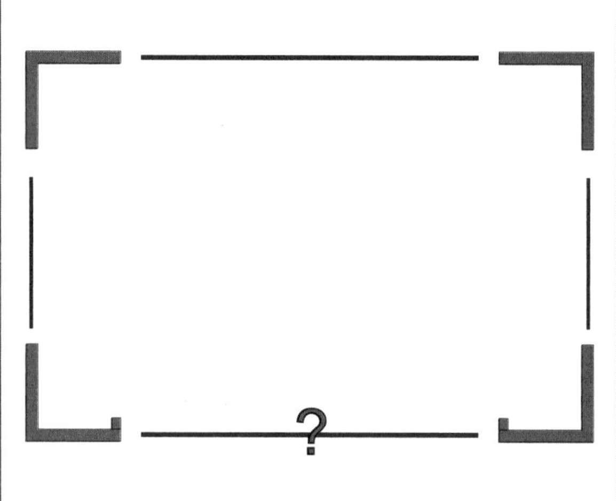

Figure 05.01: **The angles of the piece. Lower corners can be connected, or just hooked to the bottom of the desk.**

We're using the string tension to establish and maintain the structural integrity of the polygon, which results in the entire structure being resonantly *alive*. Depending on the style of your desk, one or both of the vertical connector rods is fitted with what amounts to a *sound post* to transmit structural vibrations to the desk end panels, energizing them acoustically. [Figure 05.02]

NOTE: The sound post is a critical component in both the structural integrity and acoustics of members of the violin family. It's a wee bit of spruce dowel wedged inside the body of the instrument between the bridge and the back. Besides serving as a support beam of sorts to prevent the body from collapsing, it mechanically couples the string-induced bridge vibrations to the back panel and modifies the resonance and sonority of the top and back panels. The placement, shape, and material of the sound post have huge impact on the voice of the instrument.

The DeskBeam uses a Flintstones-level variation on the Steinberger tuning mechanism,[7] tensioning the strings with a linear pull mechanism located behind the bridge. Nuts and

5 And at its full-scale length, your popularity with the female demographic of your workplace will *potentially* soar.

6 I don't envy you that, but I bet your desk is damned funky looking.

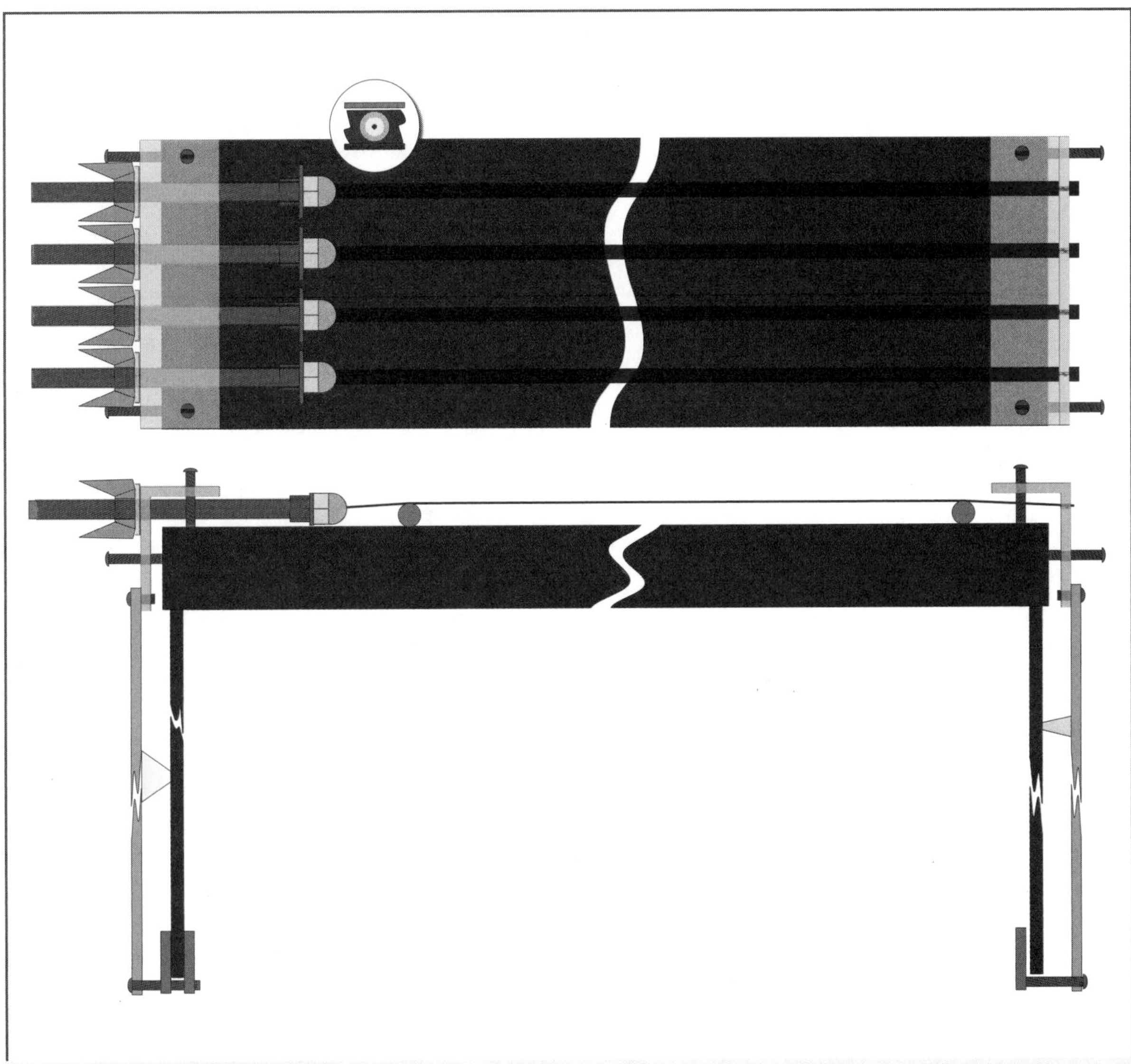

Figure 05.02: **What we're doing.**

7 In the late 70s, Ned Steinberger developed the first really new electric bass design since Leo Fender slapped thick strings on a log and called it the Precision Bass. Headless, tuned from the back of the bridge with thumbwheels, and formed from space-age carbon fiber–enhanced resin, the Steinberger bass got massive attention when it was introduced in 1980, primarily because it was so damned lightweight compared to the millstone-like heft of a P or J bass. After an initial flush of uptake by the likes of Geddy Lee, Andy West, and John Entwhistle, enthusiasm for the instrument and its similarly revolutionary six-stringed relatives waned, due in no small part to the aesthetics of the headless/bodiless design, which made the newly unencumbered bassists look like they were sprinting around on stage playing a toaster with an erection.

height/offset adjustment screws at each end of the string course are the only concessions to *setup variables* in the instrument. If you want more control over intonation, your best bet would be to cut individually positionable frets for each string and wedge them under the strings at the headstock end. This would take you about 10 minutes to accomplish, but likely wouldn't be worth the effort.

Material-wise, this could *easily* get complicated, depending on how just-like-a-real-instrument-ish you want it. If I were making a standalone 'Beam, this would be an issue I'd obsess over at the drop of a hat. For the purposes of this particular project extruded aluminum angle bar, ¼-20 threaded rod, and a motley assortment of nuts are core components.

Our material choices for stringing this monstrosity are many and varied. I've made 'Beam instruments in a number of different scales, and have strung 'em with everything from actual grand piano bass strings (Awesome, absolutely awesome. More awesome than you could ever hope to imagine. Really, *really* awesome. And expensive. Really *really* expensive) to 30-strand twisted-steel picture frame wire. (Not in any way awesome at all. Surprisingly pricey.) Somewhere in the middle of these extremes lies *stovepipe wire* — which is tonally rich, cheap as dirt, but prone to both breakage and stretchage — and *aircraft control cable* — which is kinda disappointing timbrally but can take a lot of abuse with nary a whimper.

I bet some of you are musicians, and likely quite experimental ones at that. You're doubtless looking at this project and wondering exactly how dorky you'll look hauling your office desk up on stage with you at the next Noise-a-palooza festival your band is booked to play.

Embrace your inner Pastorious, Bunkie . . . stop fretting.[8] There's a Plan B (and C, for that matter) that quite gracefully addresses your concerns.

The Previously Mentioned Plans B (and C)

With an eye to flexible implementation, I've laid out the headstock and tailpiece based on a 3½" width, which (not entirely coincidentally) is the width of yer standard 2" x 4". Any enterprising Maker with a mind toward a more portable version of the DeskBeam could easily modify the existing plans to take advantage of this fact, resulting in an instrument that would transport easily in a small gig bag and assemble on stage around a few pieces of lumber filched from a nearby construction site. **[Figure 05.03**

8 Musician jokes: gotta love 'em.

To make a reasonably warp-resistant neck/body, you'd have to knock together two 2" x 4"s into a *T* profile, which would mean carrying around a hammer and nails with you. You'd also need a drill and a ⅝" spade bit to drill holes in the lumber to accommodate the shafts of two tripod mic stands, if you didn't want to have to sit on the floor to play it.

Oh, and a handsaw to cut your purloined lumber to length.

All of this lies well within the realm of the do-able. You'd be sacrificing acoustic volume without the presence of the desk, which is probably for the best from a feedback perspective. Don't expect anything less than 18" and at least 800 watts of power to do an adequate job of enlarging the piezos' signal to acceptable levels. Reproducing the extreme low-end content of a 'Beam instrument eats up headroom on your power amp like nobody's business and entails . . . er . . . expansive speaker cone movement. If you're not using a Derek Smalls–scale backline, you're much better off running the 'Beam into the house system via a direct box.

Plan on buying a few beers for the sound guy, and don't be surprised if the lighting rig experiences a bit of brownout during your solo.

Overall, I tried to make this design as adaptable as possible. Another DeskBeam mod that performs admirably is the *table hack*, which requires pieces of three-ply plywood sized to slightly overspan the gap between the legs of your basic four-legged table. **[Figure 05.04]**

The plywood sheets act as speaker cones. They connect to the verticals of the DeskBeam with threaded rod and are held in place by the transmitted string tension. This configuration has the loudest acoustic reproduction of the lot, but is most prone to mechanical noise. Keep some strips of craft felt in your gig bag to pad away any obnoxious rattles and buzzes and you'll be fine.

I have no doubt that other variations will occur to you. Let's just build a basic four-string desk model for now.

Hunting and Gathering

On to the scrapyard. You'll need two 3½" lengths of aluminum angle with a minimum thickness of ⅛". The dimensions of the sides of the angle aren't overly critical, as long as they're over one inch. The pieces I used had one arm at 1" and the other at 1½". You might want to pick up a foot or so of 5/16" aluminum barstock or roundbar to cut your nuts and zero frets from, and you'll need about 5' of something rigid, metal, and about 1" x ¼" to carry vibrations to the soundposts. I used ¼" x 1" of in-house extruded aluminum to reduce the amount of stuff I'd

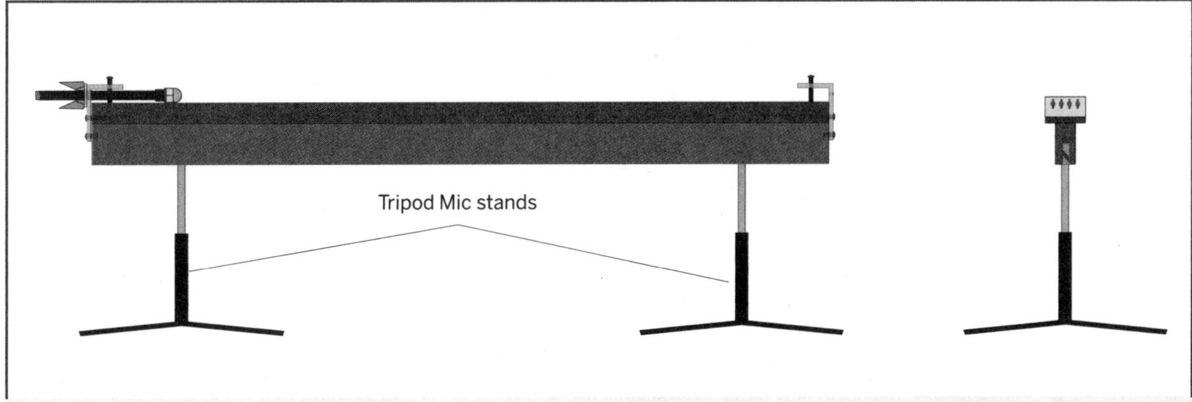

Figure 05.03: **Plan B: the 2" x 4" hack**

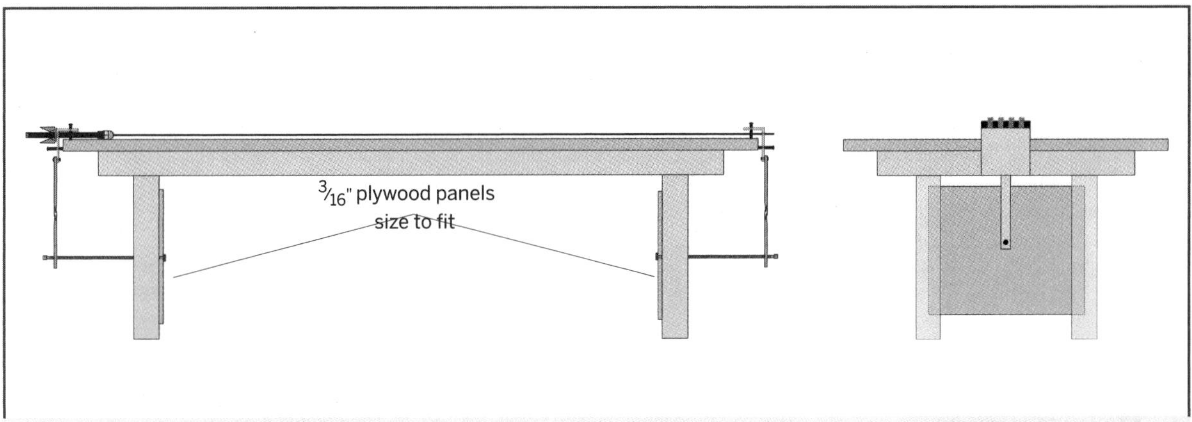

Figure 05.04: **Plan C: the table hack**

have to schlep home from North Star Recycling. Being decorative extrusion, it's not exactly flat-bar, having a profile something like a truncated *W*, which has the added bonus of increasing its rigidity.

At the hardware store, pick up two feet of 1/4-20 threaded rod, ten #8-32 x 1-1/4" machine screws, four T-nuts, four 1/4-20 wing nuts, four 1/4-20 acorn nuts, and four 1/4" washers. You'll also need four heavy-duty nickel-over-brass 1/4" eyelets and an eyelet-setting tool.

Lumberwise, it ain't much: a few inches of hardwood dowel to use as soundposts and that's about it. No one's gonna notice if the broom handle shrinks a tad.

But first, the electronics, such as they are.

Contact Pickups for Cheap: The Rightfully Revered Piezo Buzzer Bodge

Piezo contact pick-ups are the *absolute* business. They're dead simple to make, unnaturally useful, and if you fabricate 'em now, you can use them to record the machine noises of the rest of the build.[9]

Think of piezoelectric crystals as *two-trick ponies*. Push electricity into them and they vibrate. Vibrate them, and they push out electricity.

9 Because you've secretly always wanted to be an Industrial musician.

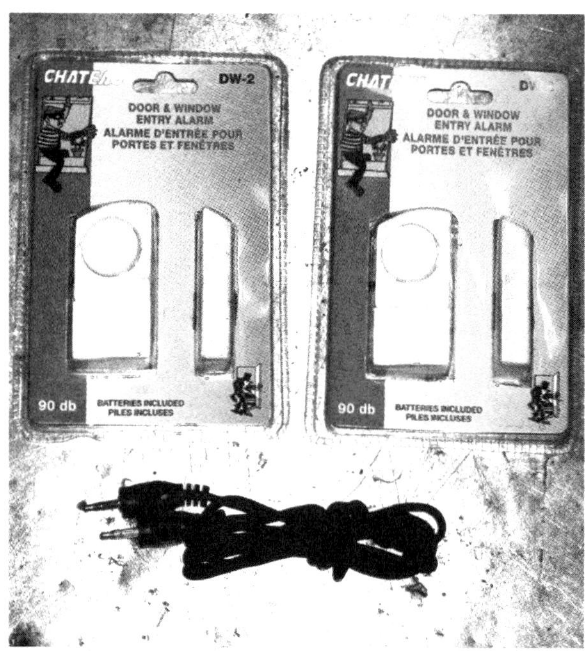

Figure 05.05: **Dirt cheap and really freakin' loud. The dollar-store window alarm is virtually indistinguishable from similar items sold in $15.99 packs of four by A Major Name In Home Security.**

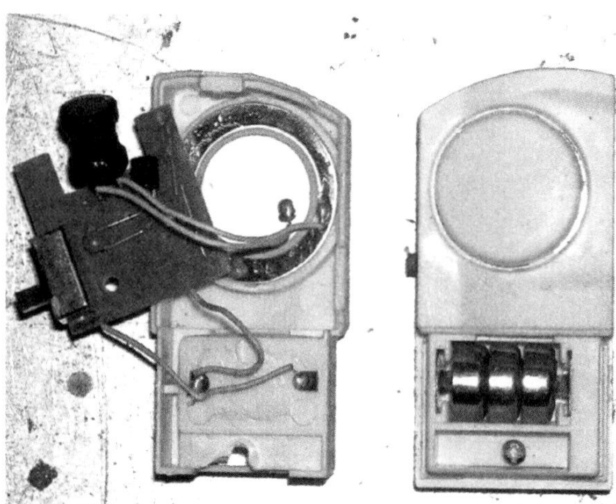

Figure 05.06: **Batteries, buzzers, magnetic vane switches... It's a technological bargain bonanza!**

That's the part we're interested in. Put a cable and plug on a piezo element and you have a *very* sensitive, reasonably flat response contact mic.

The pickup assembly is designed to be a standalone unit. Changing the location of the pickup points on the instrument can radically alter the timbre, with the added bonus of being able to use it as a stereo contact mic on just about anything that double-faced tape will stick to.

So we need some piezo elements. They've been the components responsible for the piercingly loud alarm tone in clock radios since the late 70s, and there's even been a particular school of thought that *vintage* piezos are highly desirable for use as contact mics, due to their larger scale and heavier coating of piezo crystals delivering a stronger signal. Personally, I'm ambivalent about that concept. Modestly driven contemporary piezos deliver in excess of 1,000 mA, which is a manly enough signal to drive *any* amplification system.

We could do a thrift-shop safari in search of a matching pair of 30-year-old Citizen brand clock radios, but a much easier solution to sourcing piezos calls for you to head to a dollar store and grab two window alarms. **[Figure 05.05]**

Pick up a ⅛" miniplug stereo cable, while you're at it. Length is up to you, but you need at least one male end on it.

If I find out you actually purchased a naked piezo element from an electronics supplier, I will seek you out and punch you in the brain. Cheap-ass alarms, like the one shown, use the same piezo elements as buzzers to generate their 90 dB of intrusion inhibiting might. **[Figure 05.06]**

Besides the piezo element, each alarm unit includes a separate stick-on magnet, three perfectly good AG-13 batteries, a weensy SPST slide switch, a magnetic vane switch, and a PCB sparsely populated with mystery capacitors and transistors. **[Figure 05.07]**

All this in a stylish white plastic case, with informative packaging, indicating its effectiveness at warding off both Andy Capp and ham-smuggling bellhops. It's a pretty good deal for a buck, innit?

Remove the piezo elements from the case with care. The crystals crack easily, and the disk they're layered on is shim-metal thin at best. Successfully wielding your trusty hobby knife on the glue line around the rim of the buzzer will reward you with an unbent, unscarred element.

You'll need two.

While the soldering iron is heating, snip off one end of the cable you bought, so that you have a length of 3 conductor wire terminating in a male ⅛" TRS plug.[10] Strip about three

10 TRS = Tip-Ring-Sleeve. The name refers to the three different contacts on the plug.

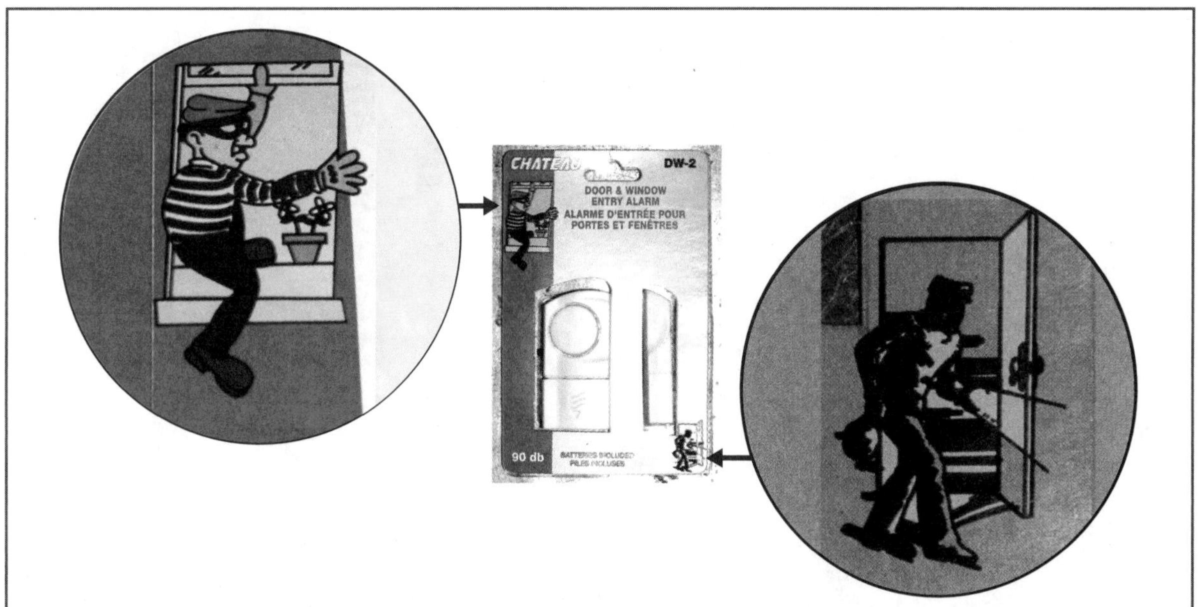

Figure 05.07: You don't just get cheap tech, you get stylish and informative packagin' too.

inches of the insulation from the bare end, which should expose two insulated leads and a stranded wrap that does double duty as ground wire and shield. Separate the ground wire into two sections, and shrink-tube each section; then bare and tin 1⁄8" of each of the (now) four exposed leads. Solder a ground lead (the ones you just shrink-tubed) to the metal rim of each piezo disk, and then solder a hot lead to the inner solder pad of each element. **[Figure 05.08]**

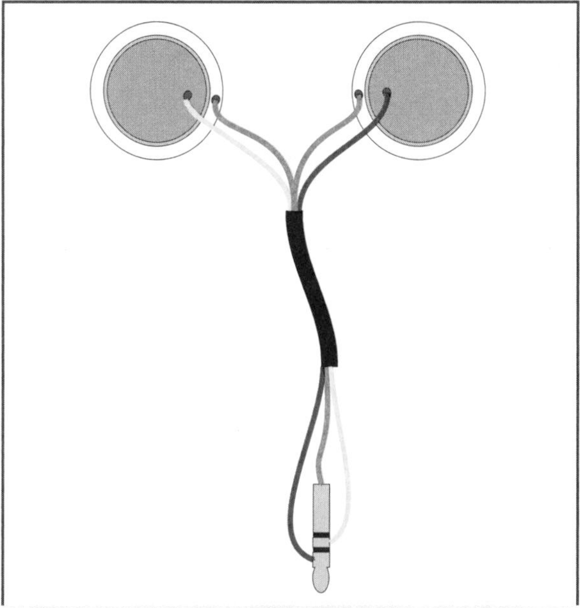

Figure 05.08: A non-rocket-science-related wiring diagram.

NOTE: Careful . . . if the metal disk gets too hot and expands, the crystals will crack, which is (of course) very much not good.

With the leads in place, you can now test the pickups. Plug the cable into the line in of your computer with the level fairly low and gently tap each element. You should hear clean channel separation between each element.

The piezo elements need protection. The screwoff lids from a contact lens case are the ideal size, and the Left/Right labeling on the caps will let you keep your channels straight. Hopefully the symmetry of using a *contact* lens case to encase *contact* mics has not been lost on you. You'll need to sand down the height of each cap to about 3⁄16" and carve a small notch to accommodate the cable. **[Figure 05.09]**

Believe it or not, this is a place where you can actually use a hotmelt glue gun without damaging your Maker street cred.

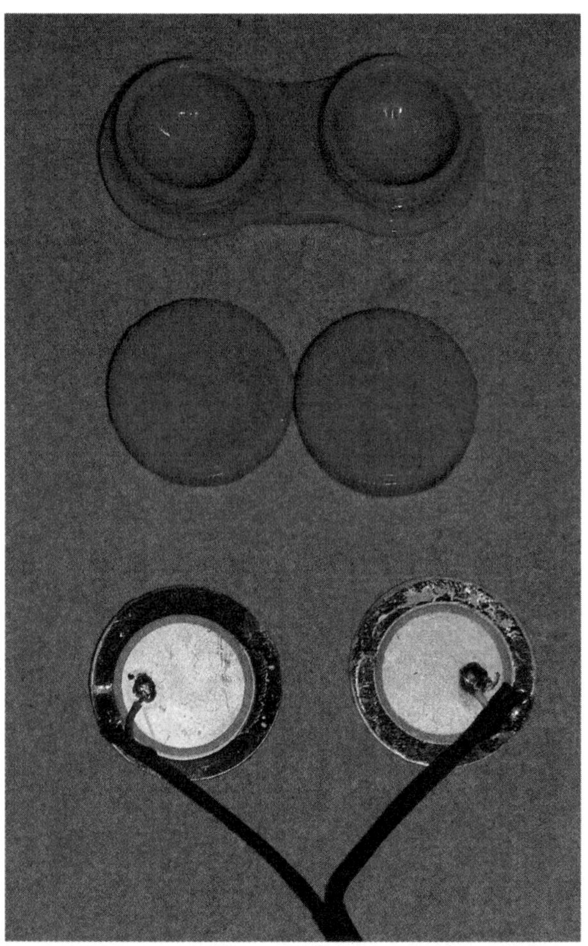

Figure 05.09: **You can see where this one's headed, can't you?**

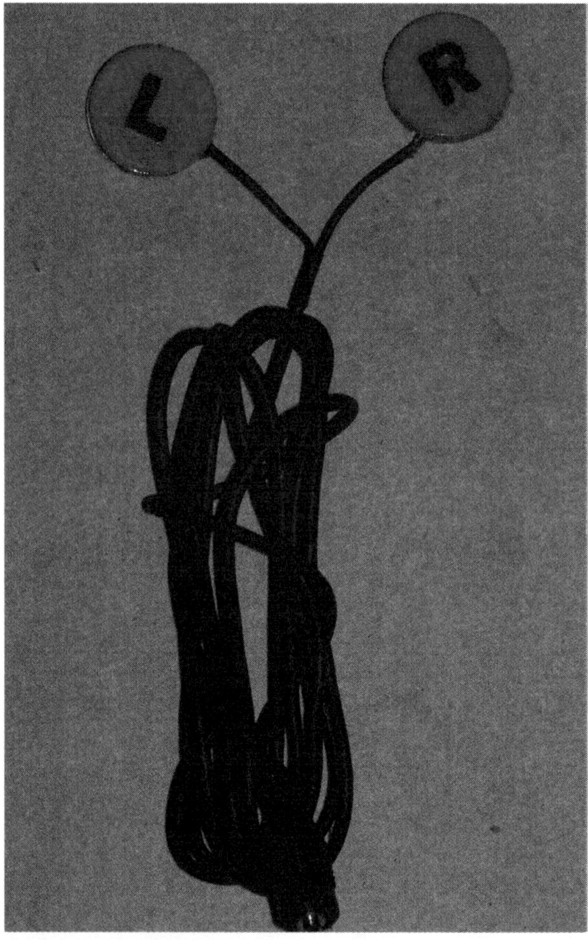

Figure 05.10: **The completed stereo contact mike assembly. Now featuring "Pink."**

Use a low-temperature gluestick, and fill the inverted cap with hotmelt before pressing it into position on the solder side of the element.

Trim off the leakage once the glue sets, and you're done. **[Figure 05.10]**

NOTE: If you've never used piezo contact mics before, take the time to mess around with them and find out what they're good at.

These things are unbelievably useful for recording things or helping make them louder, falling somewhere between a mic and an electromagnetic pickup. Use double-faced tape or BluTac to stick them onto anything that makes a noise, and then hit record; the results can be startling.

These are unexpectedly sensitive mics with a frequency response range that belies their modest origins. The output is surprisingly hot . . . you'll definitely wanna keep an eye on your input levels until you get used to the response, and don't be afraid to compress the input if you're expecting a big dynamic range from your source.

/audio geek

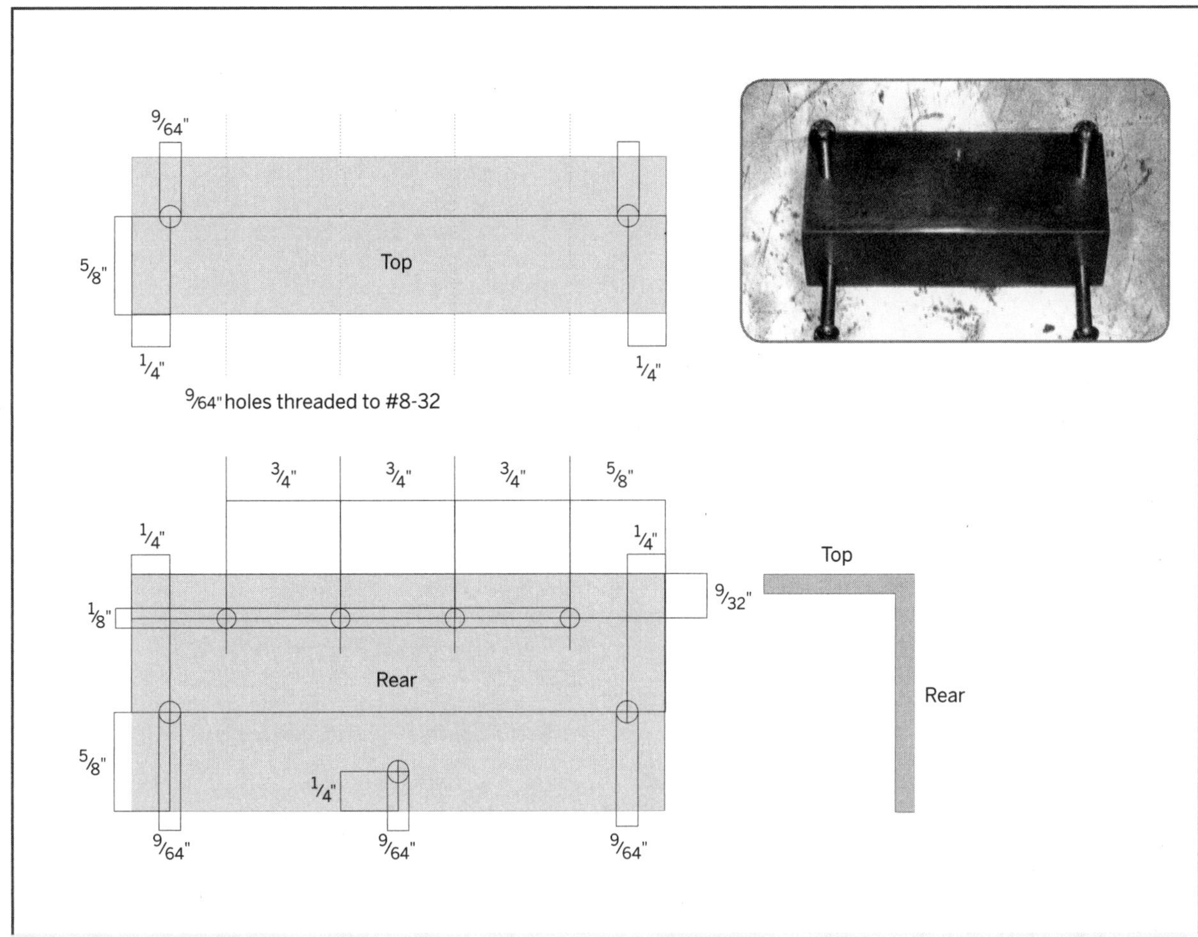

Figure 05.11: Headstock

On with the build . . .

The Headstock & Tailpiece: Bits of Aluminum with Holes Drilled in Them

The headstock is a chunk of angle aluminum with nine holes drilled in it: four for the strings to pass through, two on each face threaded to 8-32 for the positioning screws, and one to attach the vertical strut. Dimensions and positioning details are on the cutting diagram (**[Figure 05.11]**); please be accurate.

The tailpiece is identical to the headstock, except the four string holes are drilled to 9/32" and fitted with eyelets as illustrated. **[Figure 05.12]**

It's a pretty tight fit. I had to shave off a bit of material from the edge of the eyelets to accomodate the less-than-sharp inner profile of the angle in the aluminum, and I had to grind off a big chunk of my eyelet setting plate just to be able to position it properly for crimping. Unfortunately, the eyelets are essential if you want the tuning mechanism to function smoothly.

Speaking of tuning mechanisms (geez . . . nice segue, Kaden), let's examine the one in question. **[Figure 05.13]**

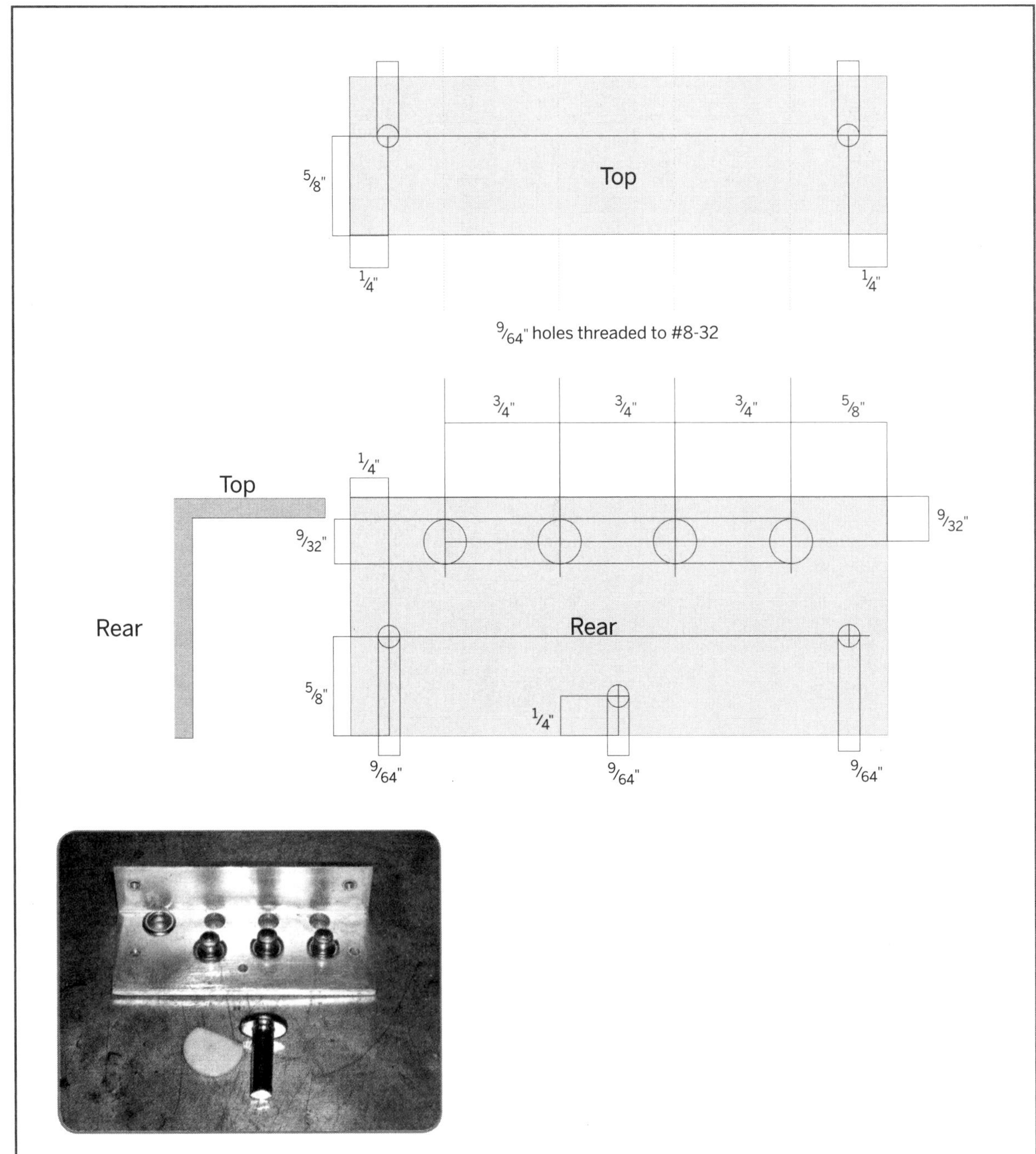

Figure 05.12: **Tailpiece**

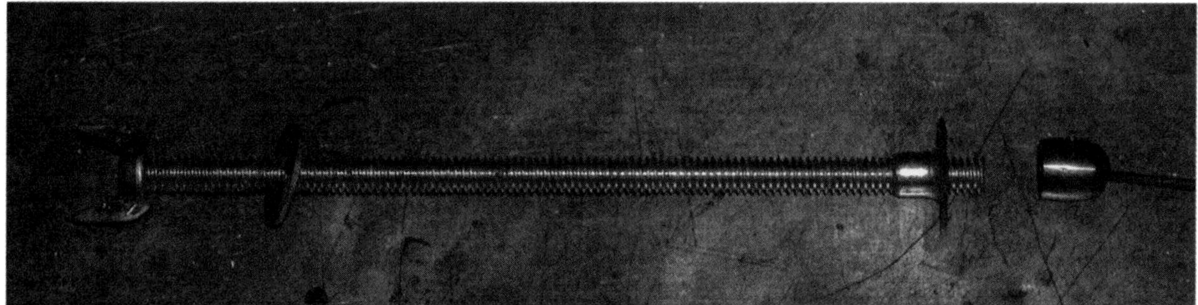

Figure 05.13: **I know, I know . . . it ain't a Schaller. An exploded view of a DeskBeam tuning head.**

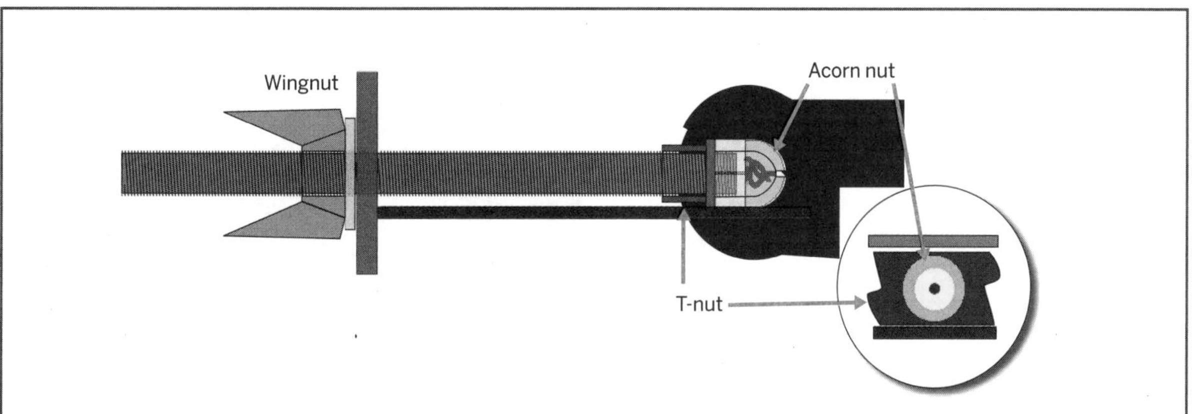

Figure 05.14: **See, I told you it made sense: detail of the tuning mechanism.**

In what has to be one of the most ridiculous displays of *really* low-level hardware modding ever committed to print, a DeskBeam string-tuning mechanism consists of 6" of threaded rod, a washer, and *three different styles of nut, each individually modified.*

Stop laughing. It all makes a certain amount of sense, and it's an easier method than fabricating the components by hand. **Figure 05.14** shows the overview.

Rather than wrapping slack string around a post like a traditional tuning peg or machine head, the DeskBeam tightens the strings with a direct linear pull. The pull is applied by screwing a wing nut down a length of threaded rod, pulling it through the back of the tailpiece; the string itself is attached to the other end of the rod.

When the wing nut is turned, the first instinct of the threaded rod is to turn right along with it (friction being what it is). A modified T-nut fixed near the other end of the tuning rod provides a flat surface contacting the plane of the desktop, preventing the tuning rod from rotating and allowing the wing nut to spiral down the threads.

Jolly good.

The string is attached to the threaded rod by means of a modified acorn nut, in a kinda ghetto improvisation of "bullet end" strings. The string passes through a hole drilled through the end of the nut, terminating in a knot to prevent it being pulled back out. The nut is then screwed onto the end of the tuning rod to complete the attachment.

It's another of those *crude but effective* moments.

Assembling the tuning rods is simple. It's a modest parts list, and the component modifications aren't rocket science. The ¼-20 threaded rod tuning shafts can be whatever length you feel necessary. I made mine 6" long to allow a bit of flexibility in the size of desk that a given set of strings could be installed on and to give some leeway to compensate for the inevitability of string stretching. **[Figure 05.15]**

The wings of the wingnuts need a bit taken off the sides to reduce the overall width to somewhere less than ¾". The string spacing of the DeskBeam is ¾", primarily to make it easier to fabricate. The nuts used to tension the strings have to be *less* than ¾" wide, for obvious reasons. Rather than mucking about fabricating knurled thumbwheels, I just mutilated off-the-shelf wingnuts to get what I needed. **[Figure 05.16]**

The fact that this makes the wingnuts look less like a Disneyland souvenir and more like little Viking helmets is an unexpected bonus. Because Vikings are cooler than both pirates *and* ninjas.

The T-nuts are modified from their original non-Euclidean footprint to be essentially rectangular; thinning both the top and bottom faces lets the T-nut pass under the top lip of the tailpiece angle for those moments of X-Treme Tuning. **[Figure 05.17]**

I filed off the hex of the string attachment acorn nuts, then reduced the overall diameter of the nuts on a bench grinder; bear in mind that the string height of the action is directly determined by the vertical dimension of the T-nut and acorn nut. The more you can reduce this dimension, the closer the strings sit to the desktop fret board, and the lower the action. Working with ¼-20 tuning rods is never gonna produce an action Chris Squire would be comfy with. If you *need* a lower action, you should by now have figured out the component changes needed to get it.

The tuners simply thread together to assemble, as illustrated, with the modded T-nuts getting a drop of cyanoacrylate thread adhesive to (semi) permanently set it in position with about three threads exposed. You want sufficient thread exposed for the acorn nut to get a good grip while still leaving enough room inside the acorn for the knotted end of the string. **[Figure 05.18]**

The sound post and vertical supports are the final subassemblies to be fabricated.

Degree of difficulty? Low 3s. You're in the home stretch.

The North American industry standard for desk height seems to be 28-¾". Dunno if this figure is the result of hundreds of man-hours of ergonomic research by highly trained office productivity solutions professionals, or a legacy height originally derived from an 1885 Ambrose Beal clerks' desk used by the Duke of Squatney when he penned his numerous (and notorious) ribald sonnets dedicated to his upstairs maid's flatulence, but it's How High Desks Are in the here and now.

Deskwise, while there's only one height, there are about sixty million styles. I designed DeskBeam around yer basic cubicle desk with end panels that stop about 6" from the floor, but cripes, even yer basic cubicle desk has eleventy hundred different designs, so plan on having to take a few measurements to get things properly sorted out here.

Figure 05.15: **Low tech with high hopes: the modest array of bits and pieces that make up the headstock and tailpiece.**

The vertical bars that stabilize the mechanism and transfer string vibrations to the soundpost need to clamp onto the bottom edge of the panels and be firmly held in position, parallel to the side panel.

Determine length X by first setting up the tailpiece on the edge of the desk and adjusting the positioning screws so that the T-nuts are touching the desktop, and the tuning rods run parallel to the desktop. The tailpiece should be square with the desk, with only the positioning screws and T-nuts actually touching the desk. Measure from the center of the vertical

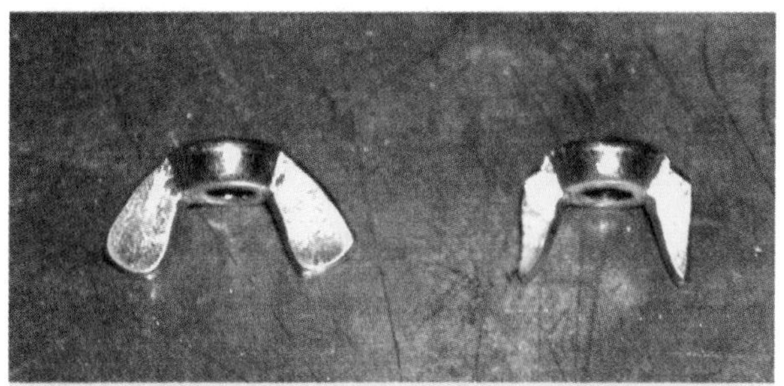

Figure 05.16: **Mickey no, Thor** yes! **The wingnut mod.**

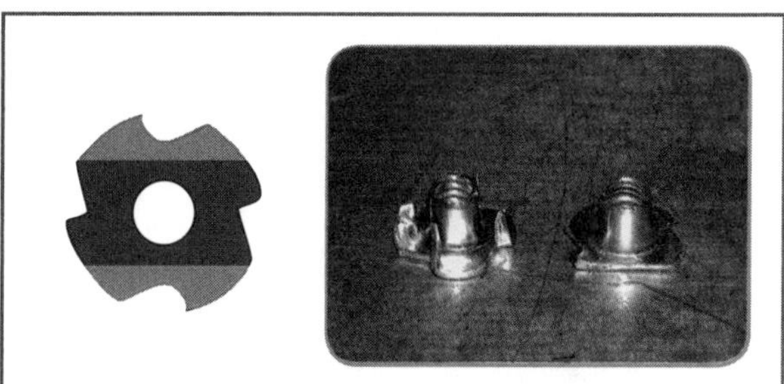

Figure 05.17: **The T-nut mod**

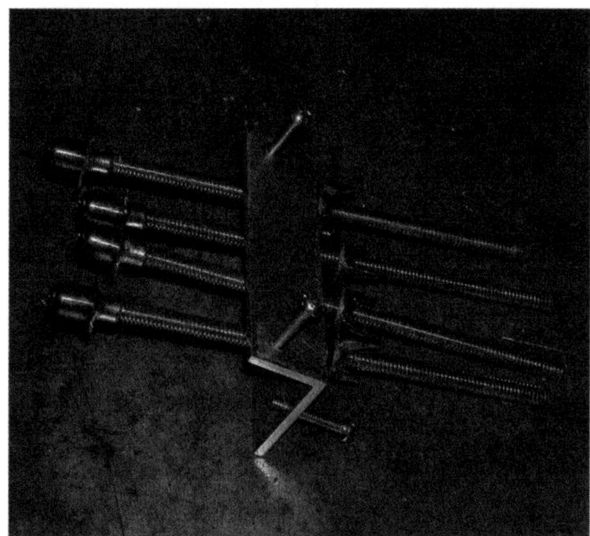

Figure 05.18: **The tuners, simply threaded together**

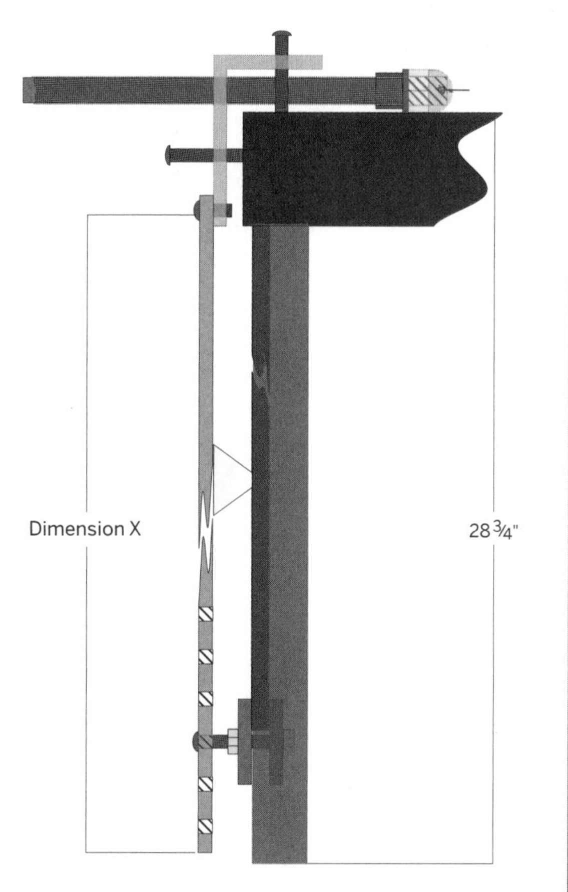

Figure 05.19: **The precise location of Dimension X. Memorize these coordinates, take the measurement, then eat this diagram.**

mounting hole to the floor, then cut your verticals to that length and drill the mounting hole ⅜" down from the top of the vertical. **[Figure 05.19]**

When mounted, the lower end of the vertical bar should be ½" from the floor. Mark and punch-start hole locations at one inch intervals starting ½" up from the bottom of each vertical to a height of, say, 12", then drill and tap the holes to ¼-20. **[Figure 05.20]**

This configuration should allow your DeskBeam to be properly fitted to about 99% of the world's cheap-ass "enterprise productivity furnishing solutions" without further modification. The verticals attach to the headstock and tailpiece with a single 8-32 machine screw each.

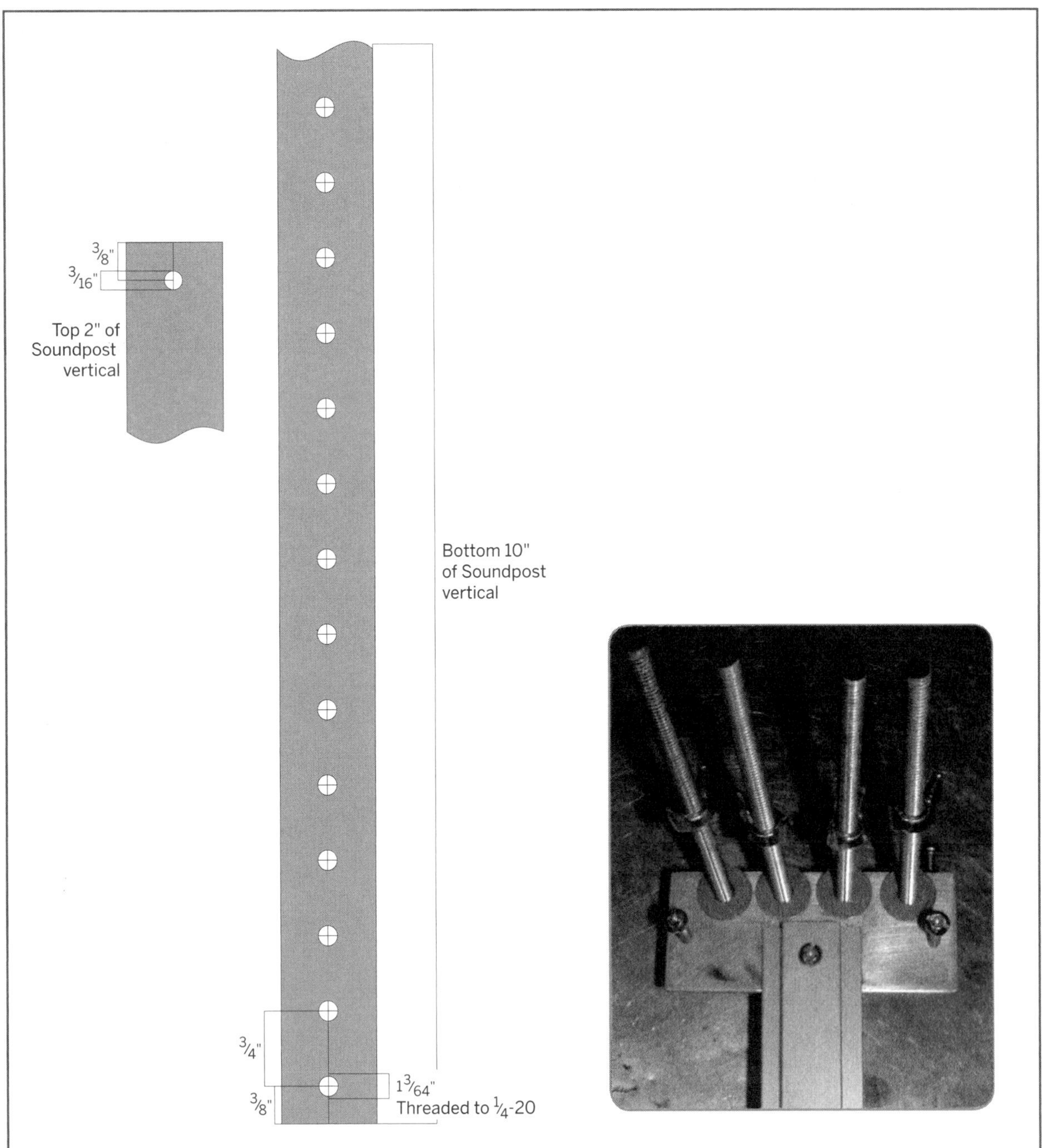

Figure 05.20: The vertical stabilizer bars attach to the headstock and tailpiece, then anchor to the bottom of the desk end panels.

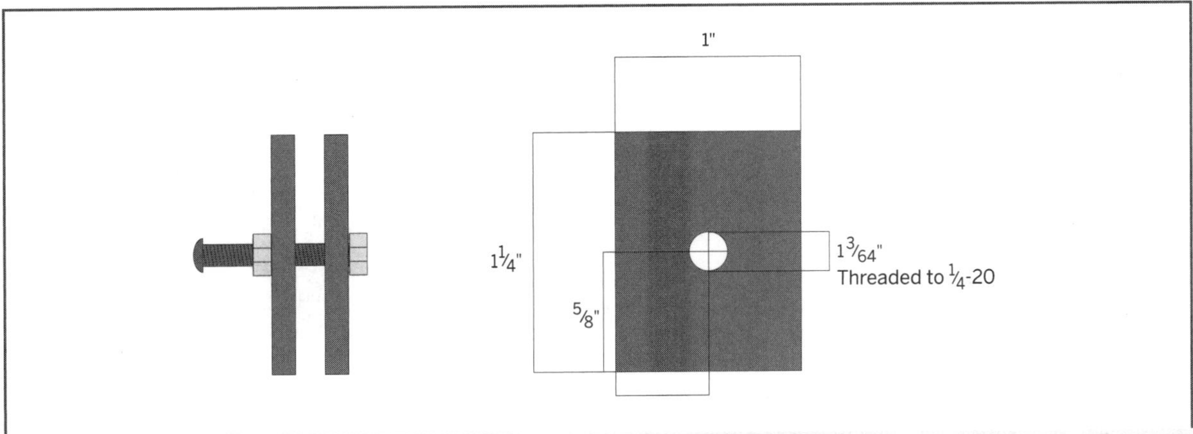

Figure 05.21: The end clamps in detail

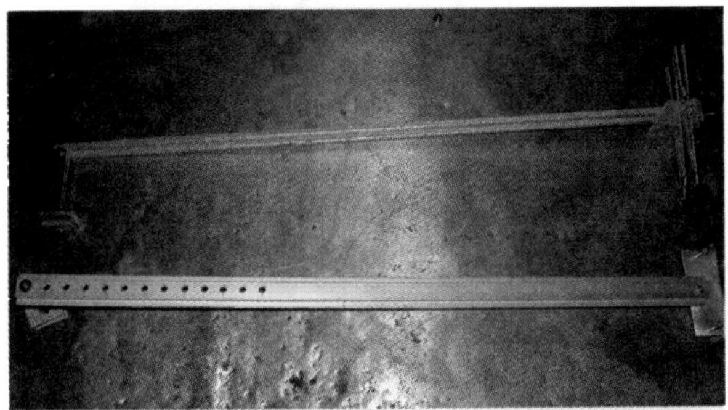

Figure 05.22: The end clamps on the completed tail and head assemblies

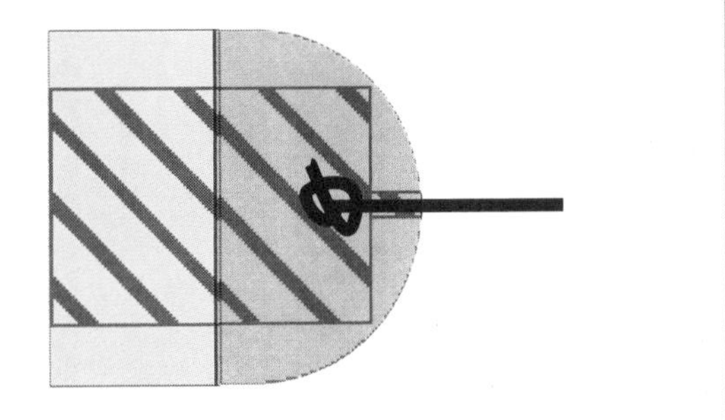

Figure 05.23: Thread the string wire through the hole in the retaining nut and knot it to lock it in place.

The clamping assembly is pretty self explanatory: a couple of 2" pieces of 1" x ⅛" aluminum flatbar, drilled and tapped to ¼-20, and 2 locking nuts. 3 inches of ¼-20 threaded rod are screwed into the appropriately located hole on the vertical, with the clamp components being threaded onto the rod as illustrated to provide the correct spacing and secure clamping action. You may need to pad the jaws of the clamp bars with a bit of craft felt to eliminate mechanical rattles if they prove to be an issue. **[Figure 05.21, Figure 05.22]**

Installing Your Instrument

You'll need to install the instrument on your desk before finishing the fabrication (read: cutting the nut and bridge). As mentioned at the outset, string choice is gonna be up to you. There are *lots* of options available, and you'll likely want to try 'em all. In general, thicker/heavier is better than thinner/lighter, but other than that, it's pretty much up to what your ears say is best.

Measure the length of your desk, add 2" for good measure, cut four strings to that particular length. Attach the modded acorn nuts to one end by running the string through the end hole of the nut, and making a knot, as shown. Thread the acorn nuts onto the tuning rods, and crank the tuning wing nuts all the way down the tuning rods. Attach the other ends of the strings to the headstock assembly the same way.

Get the strings in the right holes, OK? **[Figure 05.23]**

Mount the subassemblies on either side of your desk, using the vertical clamps to stabilize the positioning while you tension the strings enough to hold the whole mechanism in place.

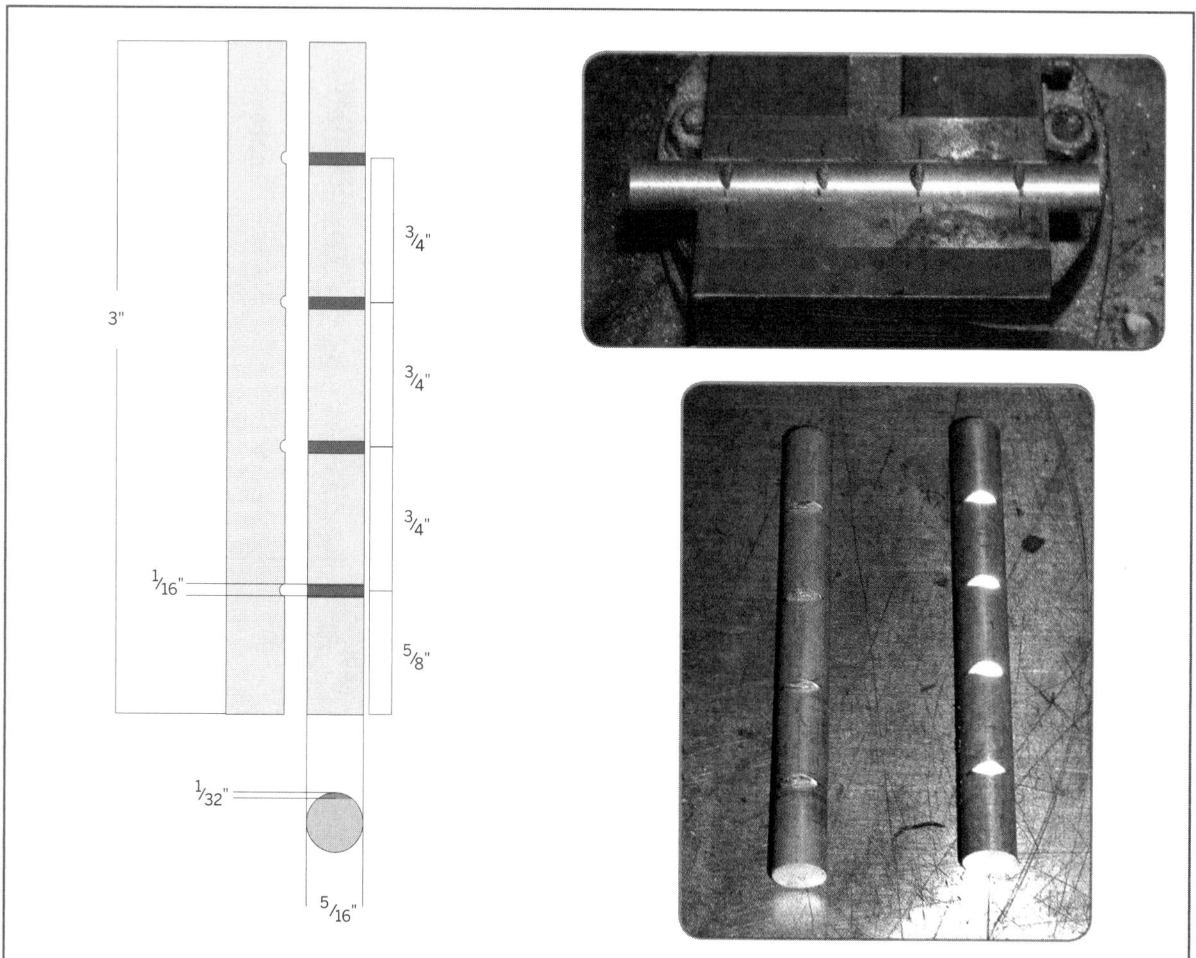

Figure 05.24: **The nut and bridge pieces are identical, so make two things that look like this. The string notches should match the diameter of your stringwire.**

The process of mounting and aligning the subassemblies on the desktop will have you jumpin' back and forth from one side of your desk to the other repeatedly, as you tweak the positioning screws and square up the string paths. For optimum acoustic/mechanical coupling, the DeskBeam should be centered on your desk. I hope you weren't planning on getting a whole lot done this afternoon.

With the strings positioned and approximately tensioned, you can cut and place the nut and bridge pieces. Length? 3½". Width? Not very. Height? Dependent on the string height. I used 5⁄16" aluminum rod, but you may want to experiment with various woods to see if they produce an audible variation in the timbre. (Spoiler: They do.) Rather un-Makerishly, they're simply wedged under the strings at either end of the string course for now; once you've finalized your string selection, you can file correctly spaced string grooves into each piece. **[Figure 05.24]**

The nut and bridge should lie at right angles to the strings, and be as low profile as possible while still maintaining firm contact with the strings. If you're planning on leaving the DeskBeam permanently attached to your desk, use double-faced tape to make the positioning semipermanent.

Positioning the pickup assembly is again a question of trial and error. Try it on the tailpiece, on the surface of the

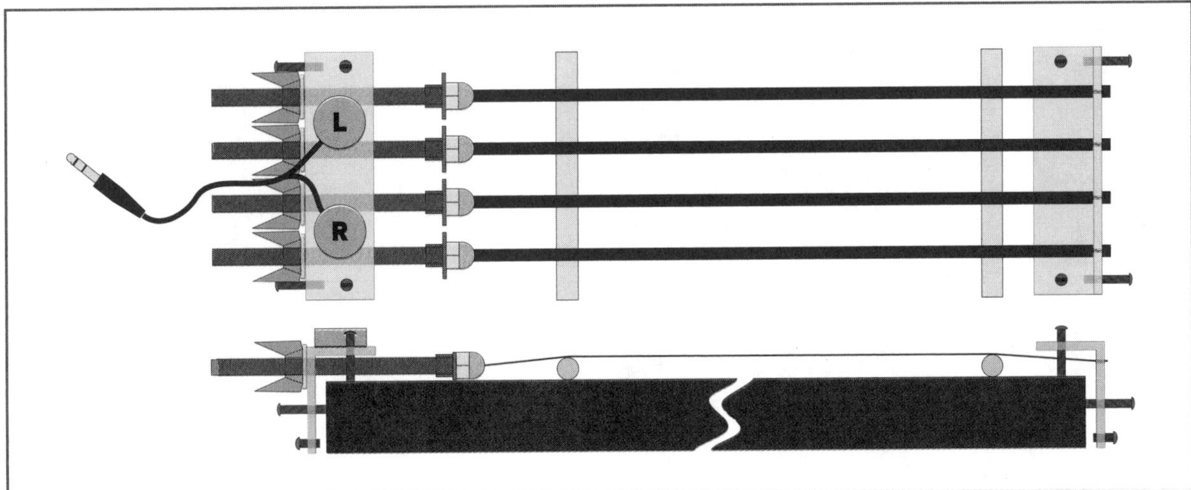

Figure 05.25: Positioning the pickups, bridge, and nut

desk under the strings and behind the bridge, or attached to the desk panel itself. Poster putty or double-faced tape are standard methods of stickin' piezo mics in position, but I've had pretty good luck with contact cement as well. **[Figure 05.25]**

The soundposts are another trial-and-error undertaking. I've had good results with tapered hardwood dowels sized to wedge *lightly* into position roughly at the midpoint of the desk panel, held in place with a bit of double-faced tape. And ⅞" maple dowel lathed to a point is a good start, but, as always, experiment with dimensions, shape, material, and positioning. **[Figure 05.26, Figure 05.27]**

If you want to forgo repositionability, the sound post can be made a permanent fixture on the verticals once the sweet spot has been located by drilling and tapping ¼-20 holes and using threaded rod as a tensionable sound post. If you go with this option, try capping the threaded soundposts with wood, leather or dense rubber, which will give you timbral variations in the acoustic amplification effect. Similar material usage under the bridge and nut inserts will also influence the timbre, with the effect being more audible through the piezos. **[Figure 05.28]**

Playing Your Instrument

You'll need something to use as a sliding fretbar. It needs to be heavy, with a smooth surface, and preferably round, so you can just roll it up and down the strings for those shimmering glissandi. Two-inch stainless steel roundbar works, but is tough to source.

From the "much easier to get yer hands on" file, if you were so inclined as to pour hot lead into a length of pipe you'd end up with a danged near perfect slide. **[Figure 05.29 to Figure 05.32]**

Tuning can be as wiggy as you want it to be. The E A D G of a standard electric bass, tuned down an octave (starting at E_0) is a "traditional" start, and I know guys who swear by tuning a bass in fifths like a cello (C G D A), which would give you a +/– 16 Hz low note (C_0)when adapted to the DeskBeam. **[Figure 05.33]**

The experimentally minded among you will definitely want to explore other options, given the Fretless-and-Gut-Churningly-Low nature of the DeskBeam. Good search engine terms to consider are "alternate bass guitar tunings," which should keep you busy for weeks, and "freeware instrument tuner," which will help keep you sane during the aforementioned experimentation.

Once you've finalized your actual scale length (the distance between the bridge and the nut), consult the intrawebs for fret-spacing calculators if you want to do a bit of cheating and mark some guidelines along the length of your ~~fret board~~ desktop to aid in pitch accurate fretbar positioning.

Here's a sample fret position guide for a 48" scale 12-tone tempered scale instrument, and a reference chart of 12 Tone Tempered scale note frequencies. **[Table 05.01, Table 05.02]**

At this point, you may wanna take a moment to kick back and relax with two or more vaseline-slathered groupies and

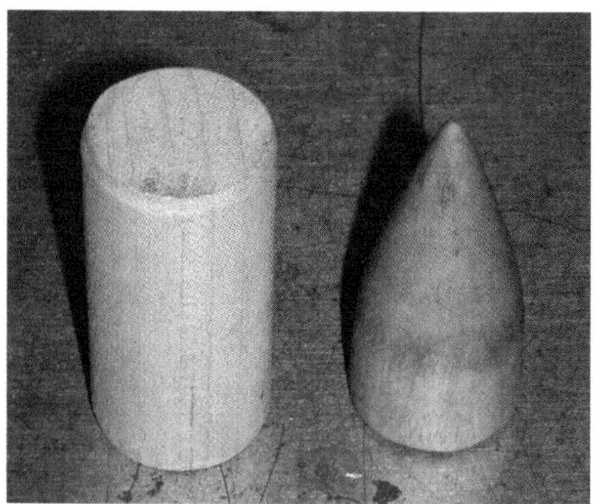

Figure 05.26: **The soundposts being shaped**

Figure 05.27: **The soundposts being finished**

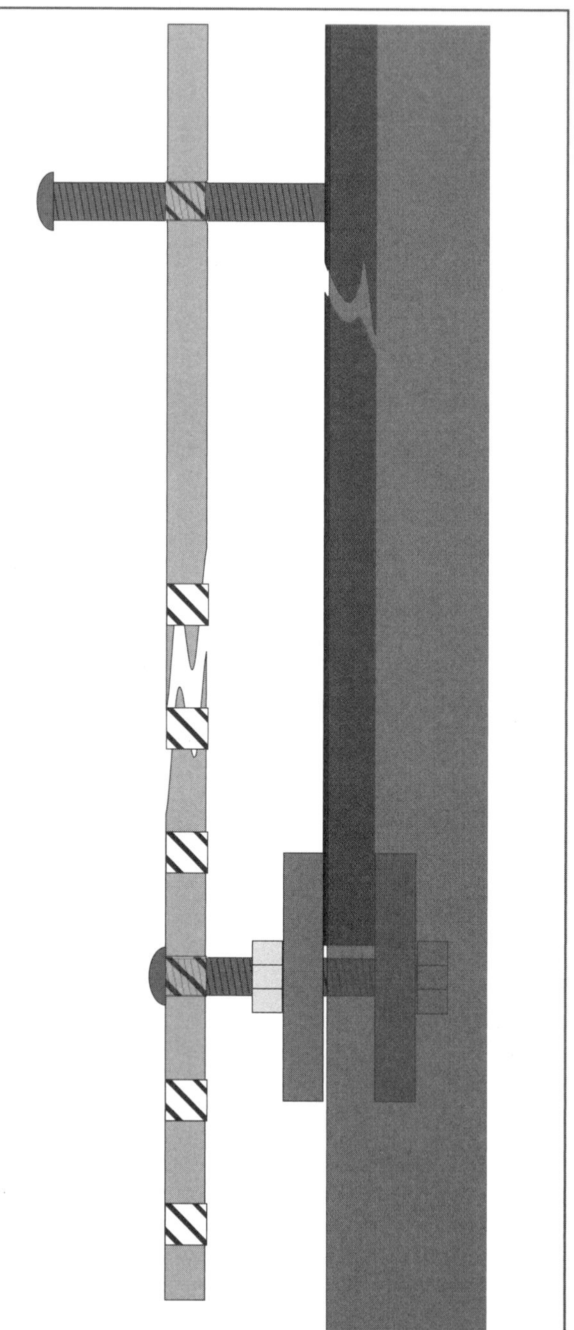

Figure 05.28: **The permanently positioned tensionable soundpost hack**

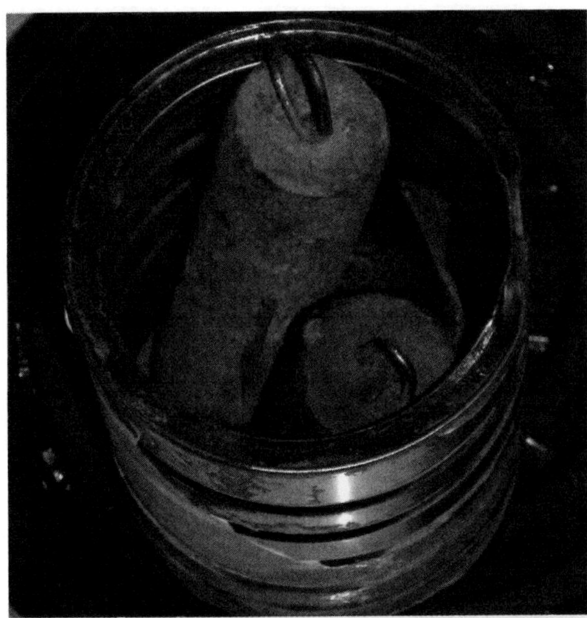

Figure 05.29: **Melting the lead in a bodged-together coffee can crucible.**

Figure 05.30: **The steel tubing is firmly clamped to my metal topped workbench, sealing the bottom and leaving an opening on the top for ease of lead pourin'.**

Table 05.01: **Sample fret position guide for a 48" scale 12-tone tempered scale instrument (inches).**

Fret	From Nut	From Bridge
1	2.6940	45.3060
2	5.2369	42.7631
3	7.6370	40.3630
4	9.9024	38.0976
5	12.0406	35.9594
6	14.0589	33.9411
7	15.9638	32.0362
8	17.7619	30.2381
9	19.4590	28.5410
10	21.0609	26.9391
11	22.5729	25.4271
12	24.0000	24.0000
13	25.3470	22.6530
14	26.6184	21.3816
15	27.8185	20.1815
16	28 .9512	19.0488
17	30.0203	17.9797
18	31.0294	16.9706
19	31.9819	16.0181
20	32.8809	15.1191
21	33.7295	14.2705
22	34.5305	13.4695
23	35.2864	12.7136
24	36.0000	12.0000

a bowl of brown-free M&Ms while your roadie tunes up your axe, because you're ready to rawk. Play the DeskBeam with your fingers, felt mallets, or rubber mallets made by forcefully intersecting 1" diameter rubber balls and chopsticks. If you're looking to produce digestion-enhancing low-frequency drones, stimulating the strings with a (heh heh) personal massager will give entirely satisfying results. **[Figure 05.34]**

As is the norm, experimentation is *expected*.

Now get out there, and rattle the furniture!

Figure 05.31: **Ooopsie — spilled a bit.**

Figure 05.32: **After cooling for half an hour or so, a bit of grinding wheel action followed by some coarse steel wool, and damned if it isn't a nice, heavy (though decidedly** not **Dickie Betts–approved) slide.**

Figure 05.33: **Right then: there's the lot of it, ready for installation.**

Table 05.02: 12-tone tempered scale note frequencies

Note	(Hz)	Note	(Hz)	Note	(Hz)	Note	(Hz)	Note	(Hz)	Note	(Hz)	Note	(Hz)	Note	(Hz)
C0	16.35	C1	32.70	C2	65.41	C3	130.81	C4	261.63	C5	523.25	C6	1046.50	C7	2093.00
C#0	17.32	C#11	34.65	C#2	69.30	C#3	138.59	C#4	277.18	C#5	554.37	C#6	1108.73	C#7	2217.46
D0	18.35	D1	36.71	D2	73.42	D3	146.83	D4	293.66	D5	587.33	D6	1174.66	D7	2349.32
D#0	19.45	D#1	38.89	D#2	77.78	D#3	155.56	D#4	311.13	D#5	622.25	D#6	1244.51	D#7	2489.02
E0	20.60	E1	41.20	E2	82.41	E3	164.81	E4	329.63	E5	659.26	E6	1318.51	E7	2637.02
F0	21.83	F1	43.65	F2	87.31	F3	174.61	F4	349.23	F5	698.46	F6	1396.91	F7	2793.83
F#0	23.12	F#1	46.25	F#2	92.50	F#3	185.00	F#4	369.99	F#5	739.99	F#6	1479.98	F#7	2959.96
G0	24.50	G1	49.00	G2	98.00	G3	196.00	G4	392.00	G5	783.99	G6	1567.98	G7	3135.96
G#0	25.96	G#1	51.91	G#2	103.83	G#3	207.65	G#4	415.30	G#5	830.61	G#6	1661.22	G#7	3322.44
A0	27.50	A1	55.00	A2	110.00	A3	220.00	A4	440.00	A5	880.00	A6	1760.00	A7	3520.00
A#0	29.14	A#1	58.27	A#2	116.54	A#3	233.08	A#4	466.16	A#5	932.33	A#6	1864.66	A#7	3729.31
B0	30.87	B1	61.74	B2	123.47	B3	246.94	B4	493.88	B5	987.77	B6	1975.53	B7	3951.07

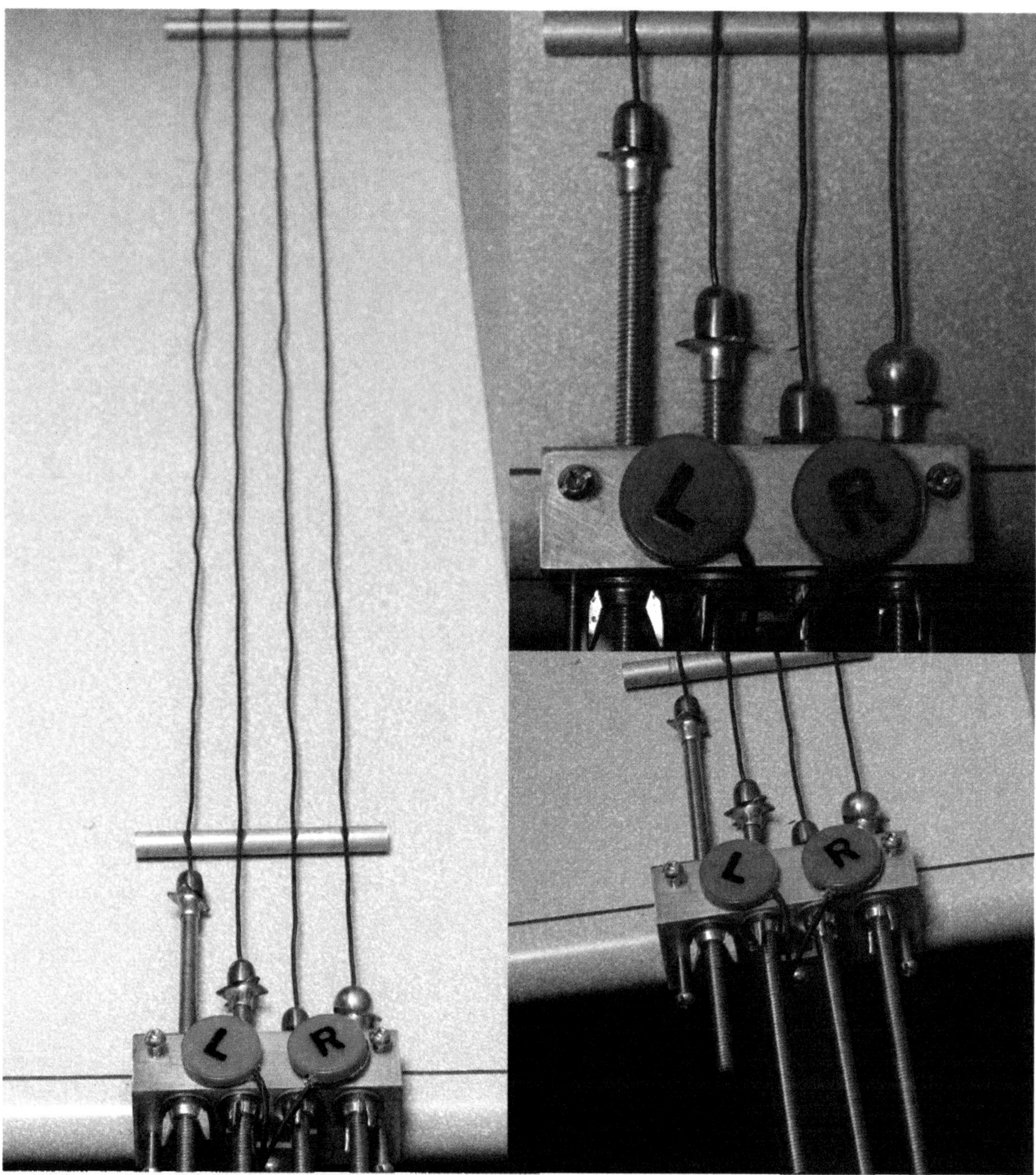

Figure 05.34: **Installed and ready to go (still needs tuning).**

‹ Nano-Project › Retractable Extension Cord

Look under the hood. I cannot stress it enough. There are tech treasures both high and low concealed 'neath the pressed aluminum covers of castoff consumer goods, as we're about to discover. I give you Exhibit A, a spring-loaded AC cord-retraction mechanism harvested from a vacuum cleaner that I pulled out of a dumpster shortly after 2 AM one night. The rug sucker itself was a honkin' big canister model from the early 70s that weighed about 30 pounds. Rather than haul it the 28 blocks home, I extracted the cord retractor on site with a Phillips screwdriver and a pair of locking pliers. Learning how to do quick 'n' dirty disassembly in the field is a good skill to develop.

Talk about useful: 25' of self-retracting conductive goodness in a 7" x 7" x 2" package. Any extension cord that you don't have to roll up by hand goes to the top of my "useful" list straight away. Lemme hear you say "Amen," brothers and sisters!! **[Figure N5.01]**

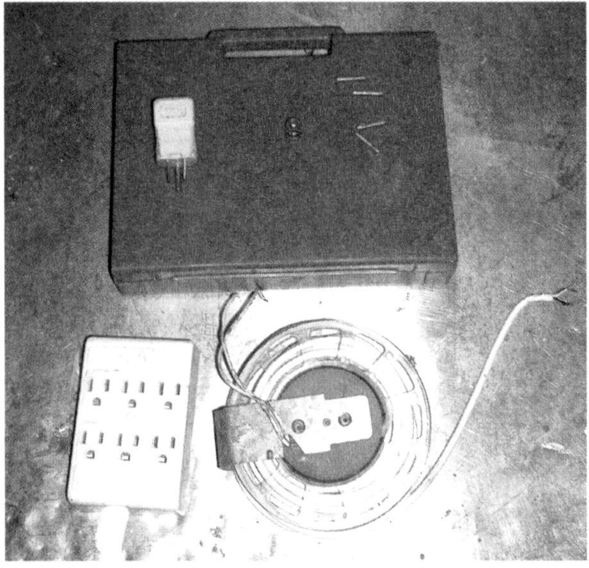

Figure N5.01: **The parts**

You don't actually need a lot of stuff to do this build. I'm using a 6-plug wall outlet multiplier, an OEM replacement AC plug, and a funky purple box from a thrift shop as a hard-to-miss-in-the-dark enclosure. That lot, a couple of bolts, and a few screws, and you're good to go.

When I pulled the retractor reel from the vacuum, I had to cut the male plug from the cord to release it from the hole it passes through, as the grommet thingie that locked it in place was surreally difficult to dislodge in the dark, in the rain. If you have to do this, remember to stuff a wedge into the cord reel to stop it from spinning off all its stored springage when you cut the cord. Replacing the male plug is a major step, and there's a decision involved: What end of the cord is gonna get the male end?

The mechanism we're working with is a conductor on a reel with bare leads at each end. Do you want to plug the retractable cord into the wall, and have the outlets attached to the reel mechanism, or do you want to plug the reel mechanism into the wall, and have outlets attached to the retractable cord? It's your call. Personally, I have these things all over the place: in the workshop, in my music gear road cases, hanging on the wall with other less dexterous cords, you name it. What I've found is that there's a case to be made for either approach. If you have a semipermanent location in mind where a handy extension would be universally useful, you want the male end on a short piece of AC cord extending from the chassis side of the mechanism,with the mechanism mounted on the wall near the outlet. If you're opting for portable, then have the reel assembly holding the outlets, and plug the retractable part into the wall.

Choose now, fabricate accordingly . . . and keep looking for more retractor mechanisms so that you can try it the other way too.

For illustration purposes, I'm making a portable one, so the male plug goes on the cord itself.

The secret to a retractable AC cord mechanism is the elusive rotary conductor: two circular conductive tracks on the spool, two flexible conductive wipers on the chassis. Simple, effective, and wildly dangerous from an exposed shock-hazard position. We need to shield this crucial component from prying fingers and the like. We also need to solidly attach our outlet module to the chassis. Golly, let's see about killing two birds with one stone.

Enter the funky purple box. The retractor mechanism mounts with two bolts: one through the axis of rotation, the other at the midpoint of the U-shaped piece of steel that holds it all together. Mark the location of the holes on your enclosure of choice and drill 'em out. **[Figure N5.02]**

The wall outlet multiplier has two sets of plug tines sticking out from the back, along with four convenient screw posts. Dunno how the screw posts could be of use if you were using the thing as originally intended, but for our purposes, they're

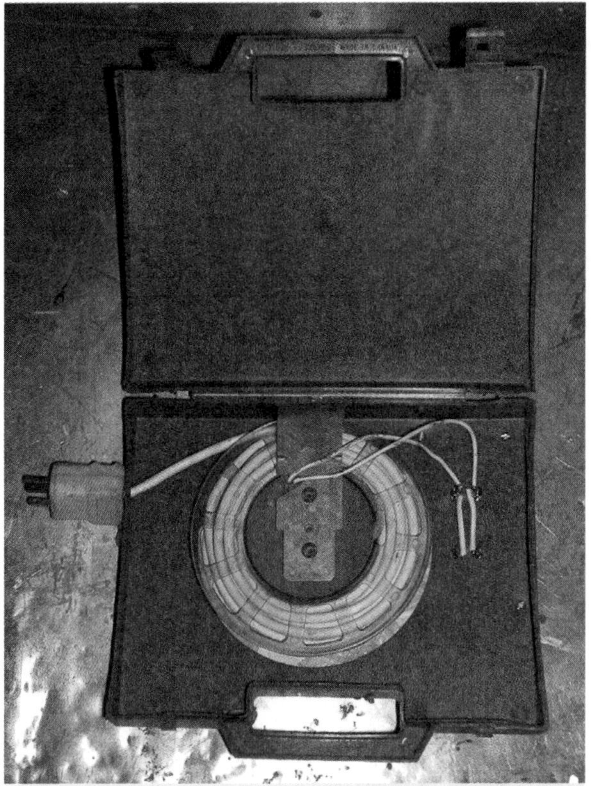

Figure N5.02: **The funky purple box**

ideal. Measure and mark the locations for the screw holes and tine slots, and drill or dremel them out. Insert the tines through the slots, screw the multiplier in place with four self-tapping screws, and wire it up.

Wiring is simple: run the leads from the retractor mechanism in parallel to each side of the circuit on the multiplier and solder them in place. Drill a suitable hole in the side of the box for the cord to pass through, run the cord through it and attach the plug assembly. **[Figure N5.03, Figure N5.04]**

Check your continuity, button up the box, and look for an excuse to go mobile with a corded tool.

Marvel at your extreme cleverness.

Figure N5.04: **Finito!**

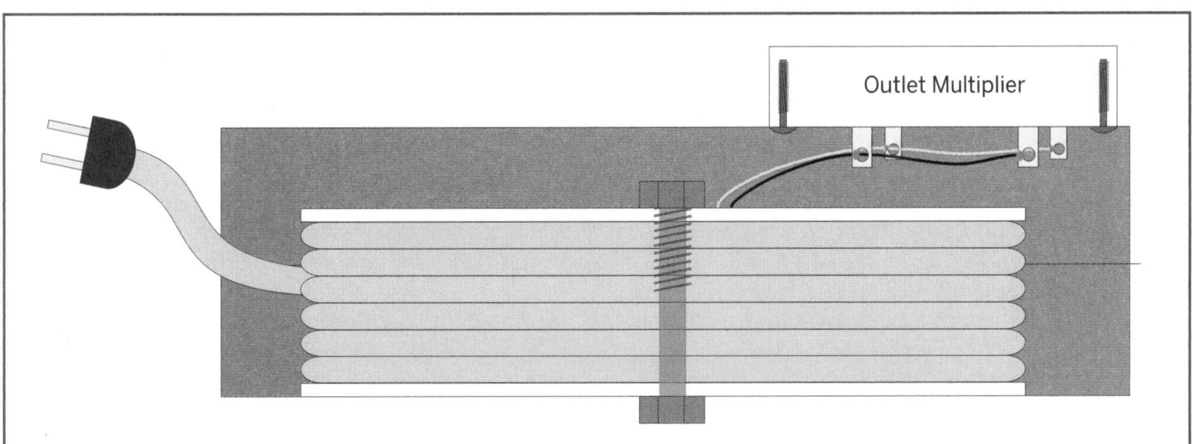

Figure N5.03: **Another less-than-complicated wiring diagram**

6 The Gysin Device

Earn Your MBA from Good Ol' Altered State

There's no shortage of hard evidence that photic stimulation of the optic nerve directly influences brainwave activity. Flash a light in your eyes at the right frequency, and weird shit happens inside your brain.

CAUTION: Before we go any further, something has to be made perfectly clear: this mechanism can trigger seizures in people prone to photosensitive epilepsy. The possibility is slim, but does exist. Be aware, be safe. Consult your physician or professional wellness facilitator. Warn your guests. Practice Safe Strobing. Carry on.

What we are dealing with here is a mechanism of (literally) biblical proportions. Based on his groundbreaking research into the modification and entrainment effects of strobing illumination on human brain waves, in 1946 Dr. W. Grey Walter[1] published a well-received paper which (among other things) postulated that the Old Testament "tree of knowledge" was a veiled allusion to the psychogenic impact of flicker effects caused by the sun through palm leaves.

That's right: enhanced creativity through visual stimulation.

We *definitely* wanna get us some of that action. Who needs corporate seminars and MSCIE certification for upward career mobility when you can harness your subconscious for enhanced creativity? Furnish your office cube with one of these suckers and lucid-dream your way into a corner office.

Here's the four-eleven: In the late 50s, Brion Gysin and Ian Sommerville[2] put W. Grey's research into practice by constructing "The Dreamachine." Despite Gysin's insistence on wrapping the entire endeavour in a thick coating of Sufic mysticism (as befits a defrocked surrealist), their intentions were clear: to create a mechanism to aid in achieving an altered state of consciousness (as also befits a defrocked surrealist). Strobe lights were generally unobtainium in 1959; the easiest way to achieve a reasonably controllable flickering illumination effect was by mechanically rotating a precisely perforated something-or-other in front of a light source.

Light sources we can do. Mechanical rotation we can do. Precise perforation we can do. More on this whole brain wave frequency thing later.

The basic plan, therefore, is this: get a record turntable, make a perforated cylinder to sit on it, then bung a lightbulb in the center. What could be easier?

Stable Illumination

Now, instructions for building the Gysin Dreamachine are all over the intrawebs, but I've yet to see a build diagram that elegantly addresses the lightbulb-in-the-middle issue: hanging a socket and bulb from a conveniently located ceiling receptacle is overly dependent on the presence of said ceiling receptacle. We're not even gonna consider that kind of kludge. Dangling the bulb from a snorkel-like thingie extending over the cylinder is effective, but frankly looks a little lame from an industrial design standpoint. Fortunately, a bit of creativity affords us a graceful solution to the issue with the added bonus of significantly enhanced evenness of illumination. **[Figure 06.01]**

1 Turns out that besides being a groundbreaking physiologist, ol' W. Grey (the W. stands for William) was also a pioneer in (dig it) autonomous robotics utilizing tube circuitry A.I.s, thereby making him one of the coolest guys ever.

2 Gysin and Sommerville are themselves the sort of legendary Beat Generation intellectuals who changed the world in no small way. Gysin was a self-taught painter, poet, and musician, Sommerville a formally trained mathematician and technologist. Individually, and in collaboration with William Burroughs, their work in visual arts, written and spoken word, and music set benchmarks for mash-ups and remixes that few contemporary artists are even aware of, let alone capable of challenging. Exceptionally creative fellas.

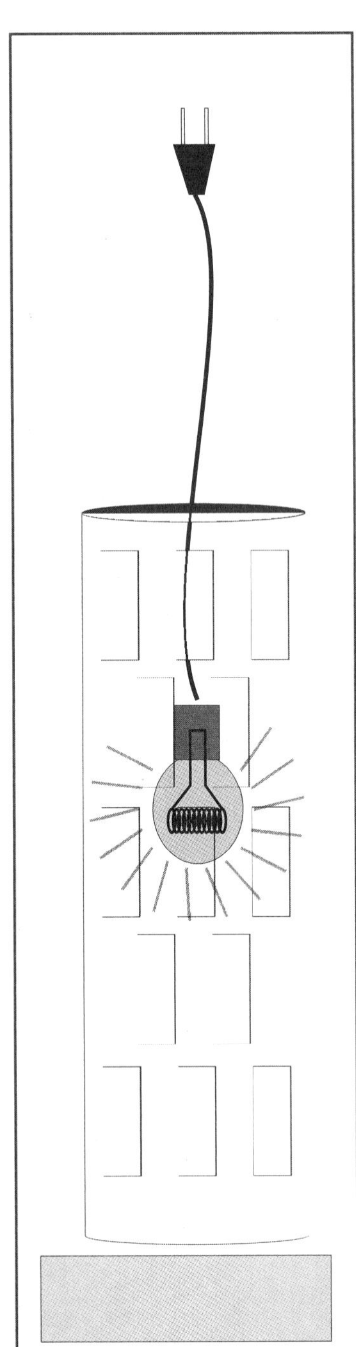

Figure 06.01a: **Inconvenient.**

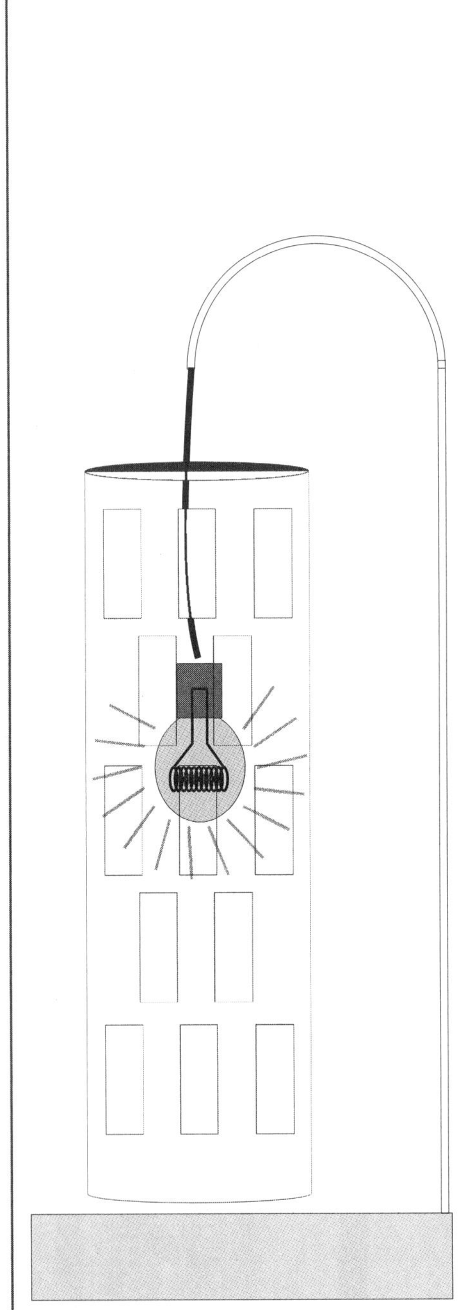

Figure 06.01b: **Stylin'? Hell no!**

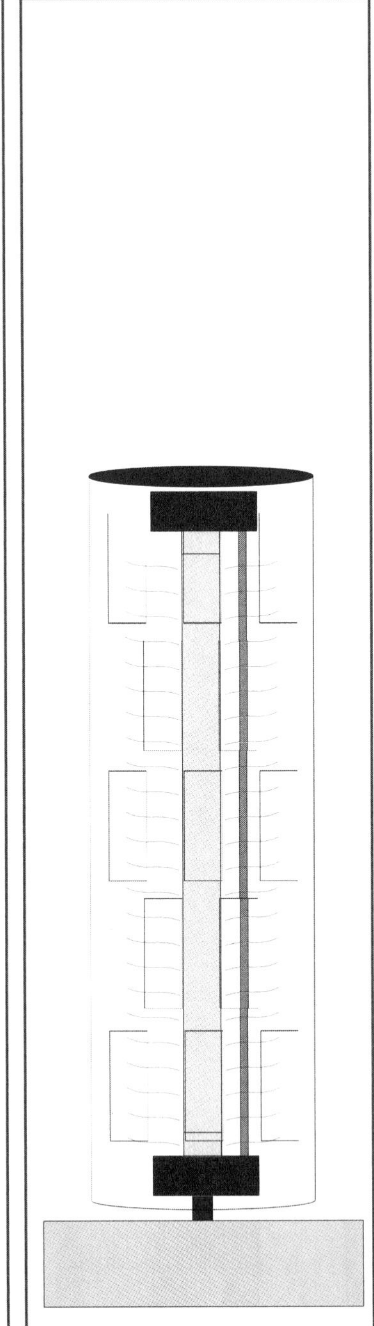

Figure 06.01c: **X-Treem Mo' Bettah!**

The mathematics for the perforated cylinder are optimized for use on a turntable spinning at 78 RPM. This is not a performance feature you'll find on a Technics 1200, which means you'll be venturing into flea market/swap meet territory for your main component.

Get a 'table with an automatic record changer mechanism, such as this 50s BSR direct drive unit. **[Figure 06.02]**

It's a pressed metal pan with a main axle and changer spindle, a drive motor, and a friction-based drive train to transfer the rotation to the removable platter. We only need the drive assembly, main axle, and the minimum speed control componentry necessary to lock the RPMs at 78. **[Figure 06.03]**

Removing the elongated spindle mechanism is as simple as pulling the pin on the underside of the carriage and removing the rod. (Other manufacturers accomplish the same effect with various combinations of split rings and threaded pipe.) **[Figure 06.04, Figure 06.05]**

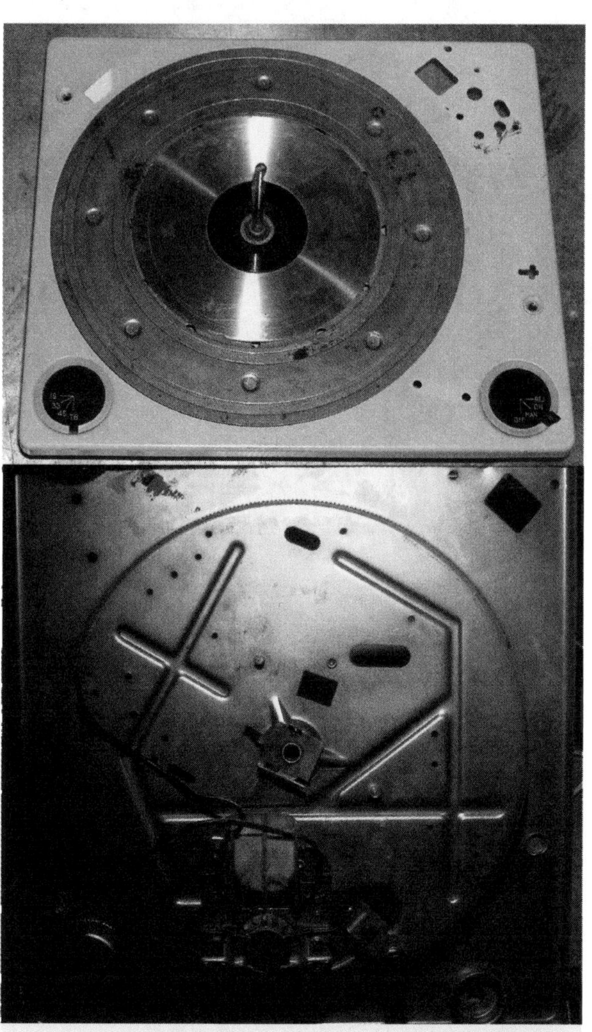

Figure 06.02: **Top and bottom of the unit, extracted from an abandoned console record player outside Capital Salvage in the middle of a torrential rainfall, using a dime as a screwdriver.**

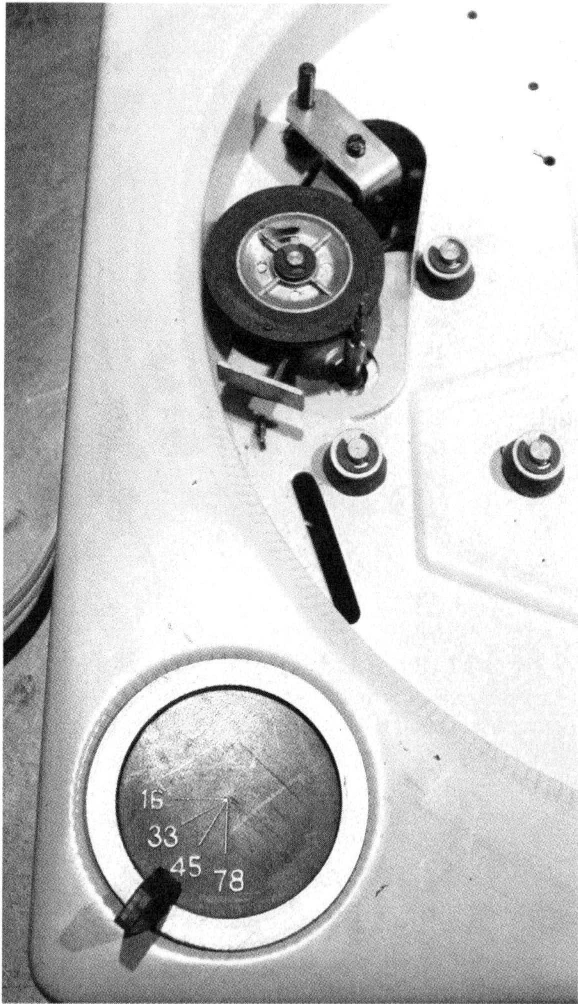

Figure 06.03: **It's not an overly complex mechanism, once you strip out the mechanical linkages and controls.**

Figure 06.04: **A stepped diameter shaft that rotates against the main drive wheel controls the speed; all that's needed is to lock the shaft at the correct height. For once, this proved to be exactly as easily done as said.**

Figure 06.05: **The nonrotating automatic changer mechanism is the key factor in the industrial design of this project. When confronted with such a mechanism, you may experience intensely traumatic memories of your mom and dad, their Walter Ostanek LPs, and the polka parties they used to host every month. I feel your pain.**

When the turntable platter itself is removed, we are left with a hollow nonrotating main axle that we'll tap threads into to secure the mounting system for a standard T12 fluorescent tube. Add a bit of imaginative wiring bodging and the end result is a smoothly rotating 78 RPM platter with a fixed position light source extending up from the center point.

Un morceau de gâteau, really. **[Figure 06.06, Figure 06.07]**

Gysin spec'd his cylinder at a height of 36", but he was using a hanging incandescent bulb as a light source. We're using fluorescent lighting, which raises a few issues.

The lampholder assembly can comfortably accommodate tubes up to 36" long, but requires at least a couple of inches of clearance top and bottom, raising the *minimum* cylinder height to 40" (which is actually about 6" too short to fully utilize the available lighting area).

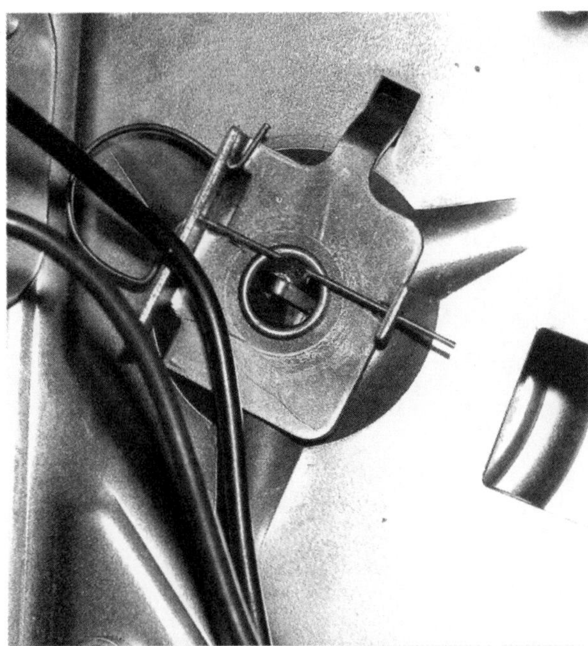

Figure 06.06: **Pull the pin to remove the rod holding the turntable spindle in place.**

Figure 06.07: **Hide the childrens' eyes, Mother; it's an exposed bottom. Admittedly, it's the bottom of a turntable, but the hollow axle is clearly visible. Shocking!**

I can state from extensive experience that this makes for a highly unwieldy build (and ensuing mechanism).

Cumbersome *and* wasteful? Not on my watch, Bucko.

Scaling the cylinder around a 24" fluorescent tube requires a bit of modification to the cylinder cutting diagram, but results in a cylinder with an overall height of 32", which makes use of the entire exposed lighting area. This is a vastly more desirable solution. **[Figure 06.08]**

What You'll Need

Build and test the fluorescent tube mounting system first. Here's your shopping/parts acquisition list:

- **1½" disks cut from ¾" plywood** You'll need a couple of them. I used a doorknob holesaw to cut mine. The ¼" hole left by the holesaw will be ok for the top disk. Drill the bottom disk out to ⅜" to accommodate standard-issue hollow lamp rod, with a shallow countersink at ⅝" diameter for the nut.
- **1½" disk cut from ¼" plywood** You'll need only one, for the bottom terminal mount. There's a certain amount of wood that needs to be chiseled away to allow the wiring to pass through the disks. The terminal itself is mounted to this disk, which is then fastened to the ¾" one.
- **Fluorescent tube terminals** You'll need two of them, with ½" woodscrews to hold them in place.
- **Around 8" of 1½" ID PVC piping** One piece 2" long; the length of the other is determined by the length of the fluorescent tube you're planning on using. To adequately support a 24" tube, use 4" of pipe for the bottom fitting. I'd suggest upping that to 6" if you opt for the longer tube.
- **One serious washer** 1½" diameter with a ⅜" hole.
- **½" escutcheon pins** Half a dozen.[3]
- Various bits of lamp rod, connectors, nuts and washers, and brass tubing.
- **A tap and die set** — essential. You might as well go out and buy one now; I'm gonna keep nagging you until you do.

3 Oy gevalt . . . such uptown terminology for what are essentially little thin nails.

The method illustrated provides solid freestanding vertical support for T12 tubes up to 36" in length by using 1½" ID PVC piping to house the tube terminal assemblies. The extended bottom pipe cradles the tube securely and houses the threaded adaptor used to mount the entire assembly on the turntable center axle. The upper terminal assembly slides onto the tube's lugs snugly and securely, completing the circuit with only a single conductor visible between top and bottom. This project is scaled for a 24" fluorescent tube: you'll need a 20-watt ballast to power it. You can safely use 16-gauge insulated wire for your harness, which will make for a comfortable fit as you snake it through the labyrinth. If you boldly decide to scale up to a 36" 30-watt tube, you'll need 14-gauge wire for your harness. **[Figure 06.09]**

The only potentially problematic aspect of this particular design is interfacing the light assembly with the turntable axle. Now would be the ideal time to spring for a tap and die set. The easiest way around the challenge is to tap threads into the axle hole, then cobble together an adaptor that will accommodate threaded lamp rod at one end and the threading of the turntable axle on the other. The turntable used in this build had an axle hole, which took a 5⁄16-24 tap to perfection (see sidebar). After tapping the threads into the axle, the search was on for a suitable adaptor: this turned out to be unobtainium, although I gotta admit, it was a pretty limited search. A general rule of thumb I *try* to adhere to when adaptor hunting (be they mechanical or electrical) is "Can't find it in 20 minutes? Put it together from spare parts." **[Figure 06.10]**

This circumstance is simple in theory: Get a piece of 5⁄16-24 threaded tube and a piece of lamp rod, and bodge them together. I made the 5⁄16-24 component by cutting threads onto a piece of 3⁄16" ID thick-walled brass tubing. The OD was a generous tad over 5⁄16". Pulling a lamp rod connector[4] out of a parts bin, I was thrilled to discover that my freshly threaded tubing press-fitted snugly into it. I pulled out the propane torch and plumber's solder[5] and three minutes later had a

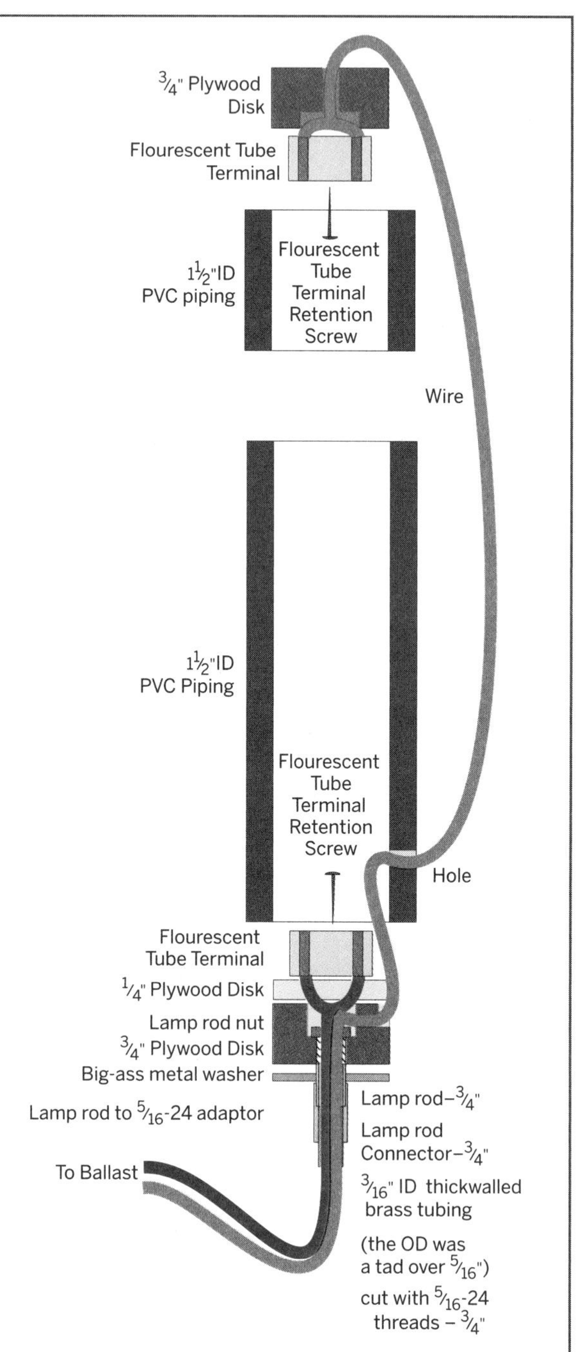

Figure 06.08: **The uncommon but still damned useful freestanding fluorescent tube mounting bodge.**

4 Lamp rod connector? It's a piece of brass tube about 3⁄4" long threaded to fit lamp rod all the way through: screw one piece in from the bottom, another piece in from the top, and voilà: connected lamp rod. Well, duh.

5 You *need* to know how to solder pipe joints. Anyone who has written a three-figure cheque to a plumber in exchange for him spending five minutes doing just that will agree. You need paste flux, plumber's solder, a propane torch, and some emery paper. Emery the surfaces to be joined down to bare metal, brush flux on both surfaces and fit them together. Apply the torch flame to the metal until the flux smokes off, then touch the solder wire to the hot metal. It'll flow to where it's needed, and set to a solid (but not "welded strong") joint. You are now a home repair deity.

The arcana of thread nomenclature.

What is a 5⁄16-24 bolt anyway? In the case of SAE (Society of Automotive Engineers) bolts and machine screws, for diameters 1⁄4" and over, the first part (5⁄16) refers to the diameter of the bolt hole. The second part (24) refers to the number of threads per inch. Adding to the confusion, smaller shaft diameters are defined numerically (as in #4-40, # 10-32, yadda yadda) according to the pleasingly arcane formula:

D(iameter)= N(umber) * 0.013" + 0.060.

Engineers...waddayagonnado?

The once-common numeric drill bit sizing convention still enjoys moderate popularity in the U.S. It's *kinda* analogous to numeric wire gauging, running from the smallest #80 (the spec actually defines sizes down to #97, I believe, though they are impractically thin for real use) up to #1, then proceeding though the alphabet following an apparently arbitrary scale. Madness, from my perspective, given that similar dimensional precision can be had using (as the rest of the world does) the metric standard.

Numerical Size	Diameter	Closest fractional drillbit that's actually gonna pass the shaft diameter
4	0.11	1⁄8"
6	0.14	9⁄64"
8	0.16	11⁄64"
10	0.19	13⁄64"
12	0.21	7⁄32"

Speaking of metric . . . don't ask me. Fractionally sized bits are fine for my personal purposes; even though I'm Canadian, and supposedly completely metrified, I've yet to find a valid reason to assimilate the lore for shop purposes. Likely something to do with every bit of my working experience having taken place under the banner of Imperial (i.e., fractional) measurement. Workplace unit conventions tend to have a lasting influence and produce some odd anomalies: I still reference font sizes in "points" and pressure in "PSI." Beer comes in pints, and I'm referring to a proper 20-ounce pint, not the 16-ounce heresy Americans are subject to (poor sods).

solid, reliable homemade adaptor. I threaded a 3⁄4" length of lamp rod into the open end of the connector, inserted *that* into the receiving hole of the bottom plywood disk and cinched on a retaining nut. Case closed.

Once that hurdle is cleared, it's full speed ahead. The wire leads get soldered to the copper contact strips on the bottom side of each terminal; you'll need to chisel or Dremel out channels in your plywood mounting disks to allow for passage of the wiring. Center the terminals on their respective disks and secure them with wood screws. **[Figure 06.11]**

Attach the 1⁄4" disk to the 3⁄4" disk with a pair of escutcheon pins, then assemble the top and bottom fittings as shown, securing the PVC pipe with two or three more pins. Temporarily wire up the assembly to the ballast and attach an AC cord to the black and white leads coming from the ballast. The top and bottom terminal assemblies slip easily over the pins of the fluorescent tube, and when you plug it into the wall, you will be rewarded with a blinding display of fluorescent illuminative might. **[Figure 06.12, Figure 06.13, Figure 06.14]**

Lemme hear you say "w00t!"

Turntable and Base

Now that the tough part is done, build a box for the turntable mechanism. For some ungainly reason, the turntable I used had main dimensions of 12 x 13 11⁄16" x 3" deep, when you factored in the drive motor and appropriate clearance.

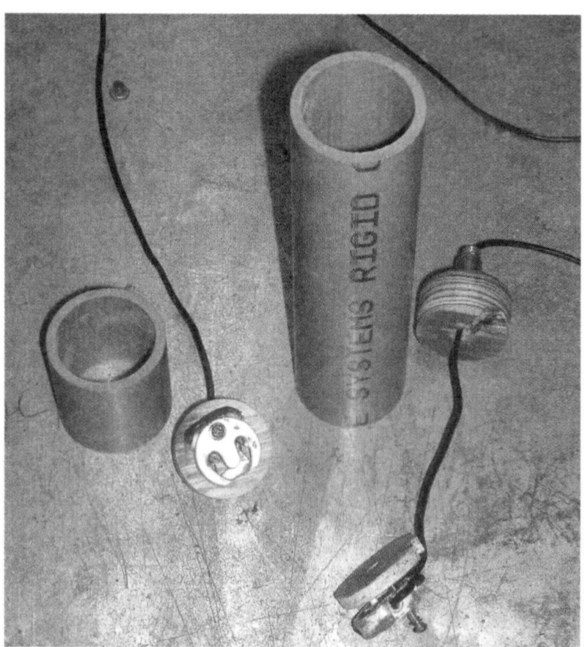

Figure 06.09: **All the requisite bits.**

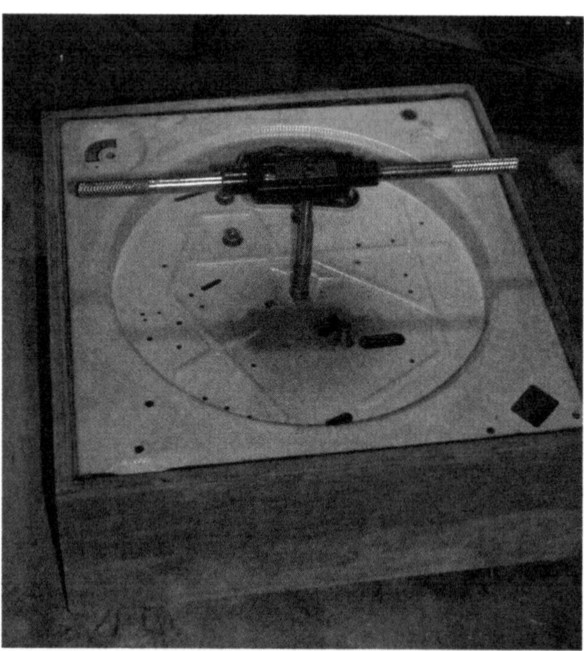

Figure 06.10: **Tapping the axle hole.**

Figure 06.11: **See that brass bit near the bottom? It's my homemade adaptor, punching in for the evening shift.**

Figure 06.13: **The terminal mounting screw revealed**

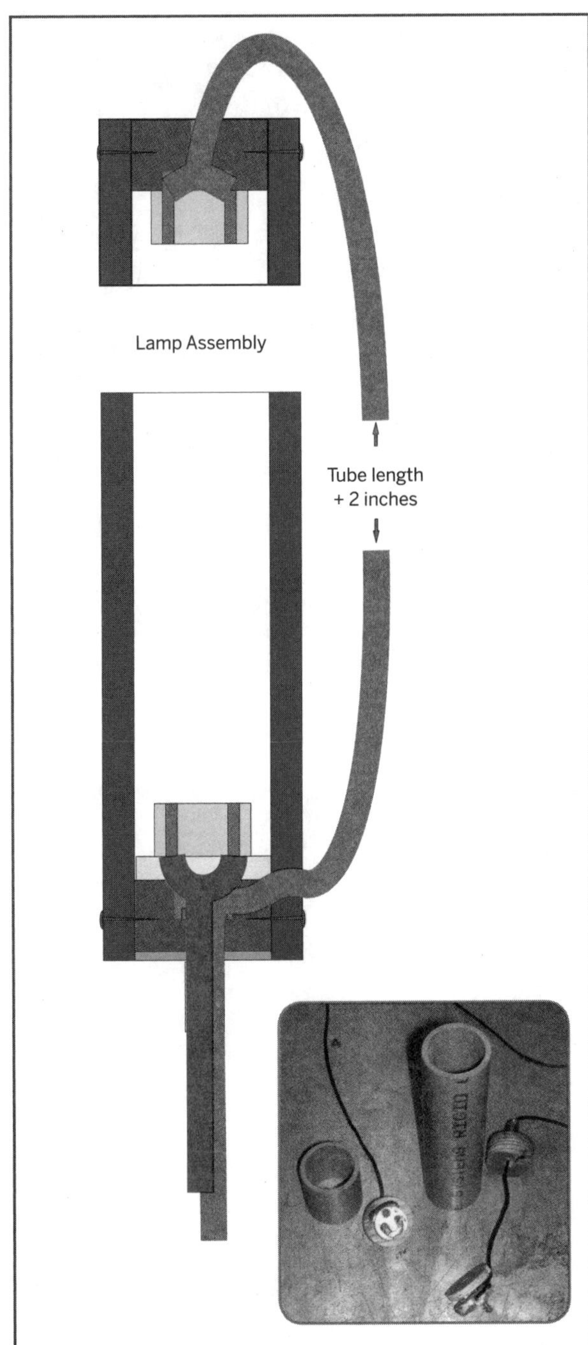

Figure 06.12: **Preassembly in real life**

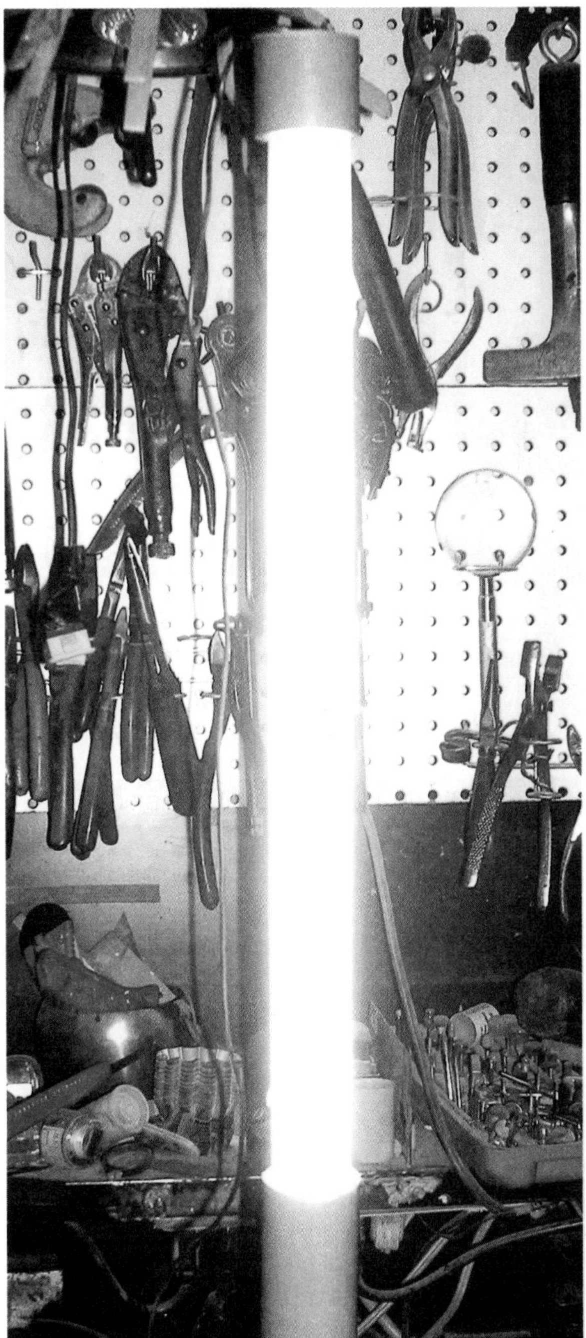

Figure 06.14: **It's alive! Actual fluorescing, right before your eyes.**

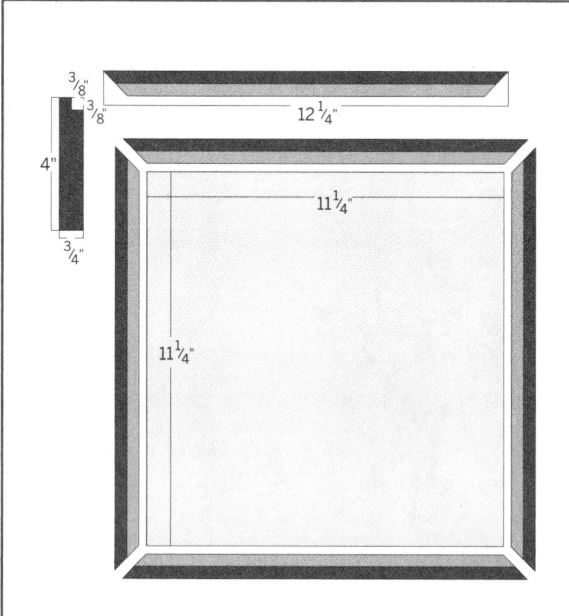

Figure 06.15: **The box. As mentioned, it's simple, and made of plywood.**

Figure 06.16: **Cork: an evocative but often overlooked laminate finish solution.**

Figure 06.17: **Watching glue set. Note the use of the Wile E. Coyote Memorial Anvil as a weight.**

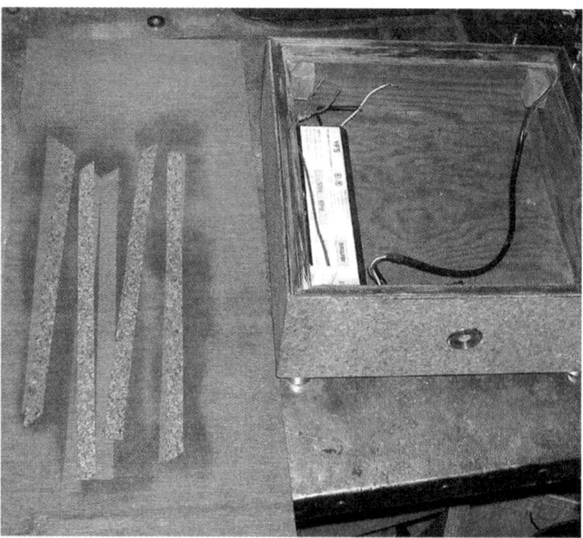

Figure 06.19: **Prepping the upper lip laminate glue-up.**

Figure 06.18: Two-inch dressmakers' elastic at work on the cork laminate glue-up. You really oughta get some of this stuff.

$13\frac{11}{16}$"?? WTF (as the kids say). Find the designer who spec'd that dimension and have words with him. What an appalling measurement to foist off on unsuspecting Makers.

Cripes. Dadblamed idjit galoots.

So I cut the tray of the turntable down to a more realistic 12" x 12". *Then* I built the box.

Use $\frac{3}{4}$" plywood to make a simple 12" x 12" x 4" box with a $\frac{3}{8}$" recessed shelf mortised into the top to accommodate the lip of the turntable tray. Those of you working without a table saw can accomplish the same goal (the turntable tray sitting flush with the upper rim of the box) with strategically sized and placed blocks of wood in each corner. **[Figure 06.15]**

The box goes together with simple 45-degree mitered joints and a base sized to fit inside the basic square of the box. Before assembly, drill the positioning holes for the AC cord on the rear face, and the power switch on the front face. Assemble the four walls around the square base piece, check the horizontal and vertical angles with a square, and leave it clamped overnight. In the morning, pin the joints for strength with $\frac{3}{8}$" dowel top and bottom and glue 1" x 1" blocks of scrap wood into each corner, flush with the tray ledge. These are the mounting screw receivers for the turntable mechanism.

You're done. This is pretty easy, isn't it?

As mentioned, finishing is your choice. I'd recently pulled a big roll of $\frac{1}{16}$" cork sheeting out of a dumpster, so I opted to go with a cork veneer look for the case. Cork sheet is easy to work with, as long as you have a sharp utility knife, and cutting it to size is made easier if you keep the blade lightly lubricated with a stick of paraffin wax. The wax reduces friction, which can sometimes cause tearing during cuts. I rough-cut cork panels to size and glued them to the box two at a time using contact cement. Apply a light coat to each surface, allow it to set for 15 minutes, then carefully position the sheets and attach them. I use a manicurist's emery board to spread contact cement. The abrasive action of the emery surface during application helps ensure solid adhesion of the cement to the surface being bonded.**[Figure 06.16]**

Use a rolling pin to firmly press the two surfaces together, then weigh them down for a few hours while the contact cement finishes curing. **[Figure 06.17, Figure 06.18]**

Lacking an anvil, 2" elastic is almost as effective for holding the laminate in position while the glue sets. It's available at dressmakers' supply outlets at surprisingly low cost. I got about 100 feet of it for under a fin Canadian, which is a damned good bargain, considering how useful the stuff is for both this sort of job, and for clamping irregularly shaped glue-ups. It's highly recommended; go buy some now.

For guys who feel that their masculinity may be challenged by beinging seen entering a sewing supply shop, I offer this: hot chicks shop there.

When the glue is set, tidy up your edges with a utility knife and repeat the process with the other two facing sides, followed by the bottom piece.

Once the corking is in place on the sides and base, do the exposed wood on the upper lip with thin strips and careful mitering of the corners. Dress the joint edges with a light application of 150-grit sandpaper (wear a dust mask or breathe through your ears; cork dust is nasty stuff to breathe), and you're done. **[Figure 06.19]**

Mount the ballast in the case with wood screws, and run the AC cord through the rear hole, tying a security knot to eliminate pullout. **[Figure 06.20]**

It's your decision with regard to feet. To me they fall into the category of "attention to detail, gotta have 'em." Don't buy them new, as buckets of such things are frequently found roaming at large in scrap yards. I used things that started life as expensive designer brass drawer pulls, but were languishing as mere chunks of yellow brass @ $1.50/pound at North Star Recycling when I rescued them. **[Figure 06.21, Figure 06.21]**

The upper surface of the turntable tray is gonna be some unpleasant "designer" hue from the 60s. You can repaint it

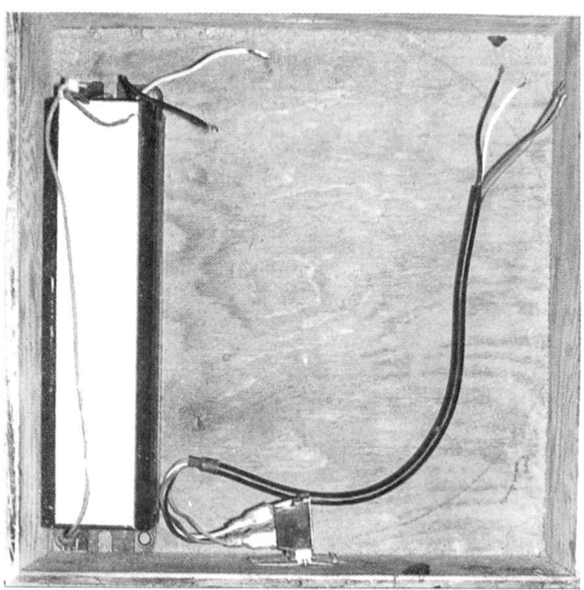

Figure 06.20: **Box, ballast, switch, cord. It's nice to have an uncrowded chassis for a change.**

Figure 06.21: **Feet!**

Figure 06.22: **The point of origin of the feet I used: A 5 gallon bucket of scrapyard yellow brass.**

(mask off the recessed drive mechanism bits), or surface it with the coverup of your choice. Contact cement will do the job of attaching it, but remember to account for the clearance the turntable platter will require to spin freely.

Replace the turntable platter and thread the leads from the light assembly through the threaded axle hole. Screw the lamp assembly into the axle hole, and carry on with the wiring procedure.

NOTE: Before the platter goes back in place, remember to clean any accumulated schmutz off the drive mechanism, and to lubricate the axle contact points. Powdered graphite dry lube is the recommended slickery of choice.

I salvaged a DPST power switch from a binned PC tower case, and used wire nuts (also called "marrettes") to complete the wiring. **[Figure 06.23]**

You can now button up the case, and secure the turntable tray in place with 1" #6 wood screws (or whatever works with your by-now-oughta-be-worked-out aesthetic conception, which will involve drilling mounting holes through the turntable tray.

My aesthetic conception included a dandy brass switch cap and bezel; the switch cap started life as a thumbnut for the top of a rococco pepper mill, and the bezel (basically a washer with self-important beveling) came from a box of random brass bits labeled "Random Brass Bits." I cut away the cork veneering to

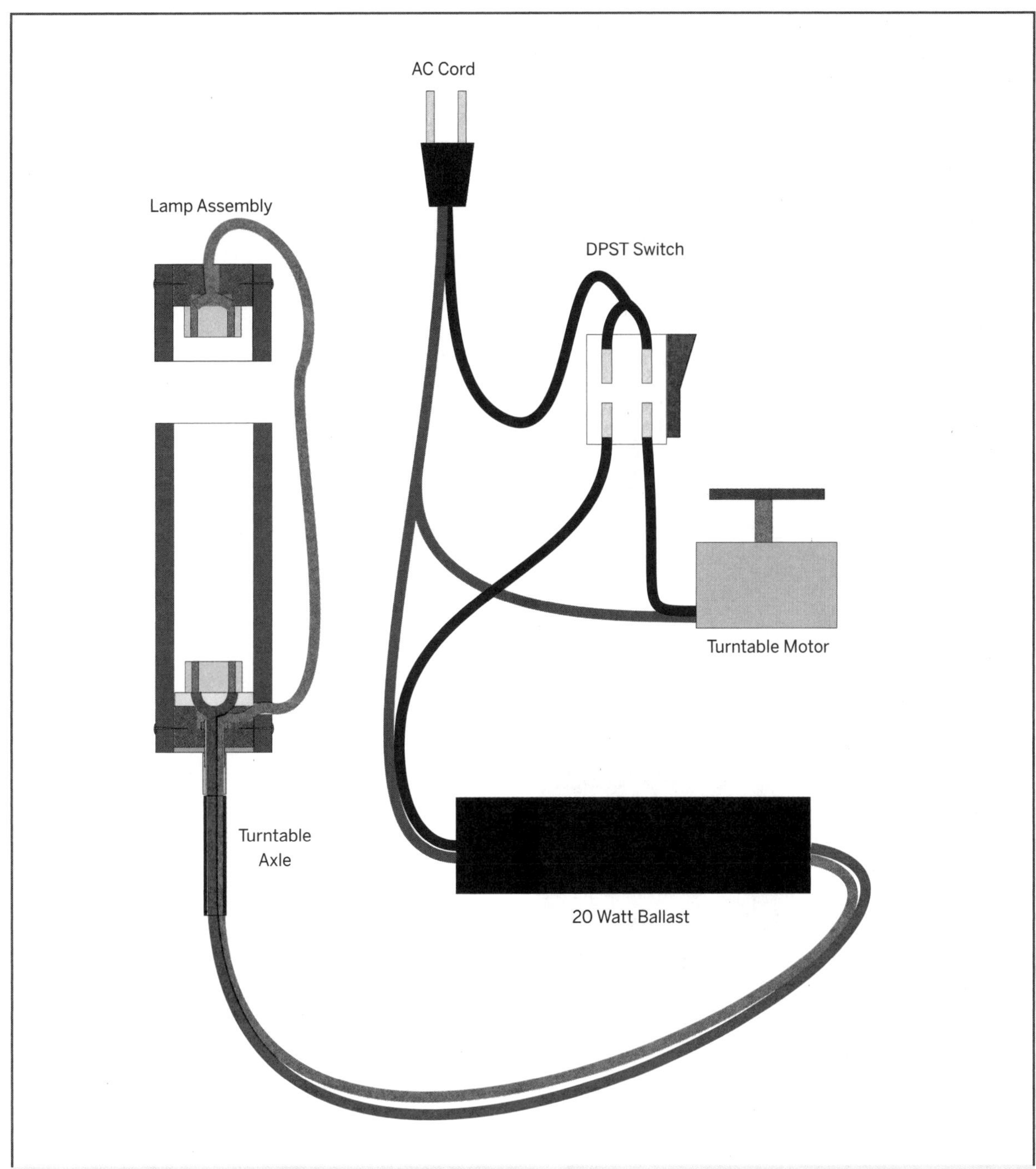

Figure 06.23: The wiring diagram. Not much to it, really.

Figure 06.24: **The power switch is ready for its close-up, Mr. DeMille.**

Figure 06.25: **A cork covered box with a spinning turntable on the top, and a vertical fluorescent tube stickin' up from the middle. If only I had an artfully perforated cylinder.**

inset the bezel, and stuck it in place with double-sided tape. The cap itself needed a little filing to reduce the diameter to a smooth fit in the case hole, but the threaded hole was the right size to tightly pressfit onto the switch actuator thingie. Sometimes, ya get lucky. **[Figure 06.24]**

The point is to think laterally in terms of components, particularly in context of U.I.s: rummage around for unexpected combinations from multiple sources, and have an open mind.

Slot the fluorescent tube, plug it in, and hit the switch. Wonder of wonders! A box with a spinning turntable and a light in the middle. **[Figure 06.25]**

Damn . . . aren't we clever?

On to the artfully perforated cylinder that this entire preamble build has been in support of.

Brain Waves

But first, let's talk about brain waves. EEGs have given us an accurate view of the "rhythm" of the brain: the frequencies of our brain waves when we're in various states of mind. Here's a quick thumbnail of what I'm talking about:[7]

DELTA waves: 0.1 to 3 Hz

Dead-to-the-world dreamless R.E.M. sleep.

THETA waves: 3 to 7 Hz

R.E.M. sleep: asleep and dreaming. The upper range is your go-to frequency for trance state.

BETA waves: –13 to 30 Hz

Your basic waking, doing, thinking frequencies.

ALPHA waves: 7 to 13 Hz

Relaxed, meditative alertness. The calm and creative mind.

Brain wave entrainment (what we're setting out to accomplish with this endeavour) is based on the theory that our brains will instinctively fall into synch with properly directed external stimulation. What's "properly directed?" Audio stimulation is one way, although delivering the stimulus is somewhat inconvenient, involving binaural simulation of the extremely (for audio, anyway) low frequencies involved. Photic stimulation of the optic nerve (what we're doing here) at similar frequencies is much easier on the budget to achieve, and gets the job done with some measure of efficiency. The only issue is

7 Yes, I am well aware that these are horrendously simplified definitions and delineations. At the very least, they will pique your interest in the subject and encourage independent research.

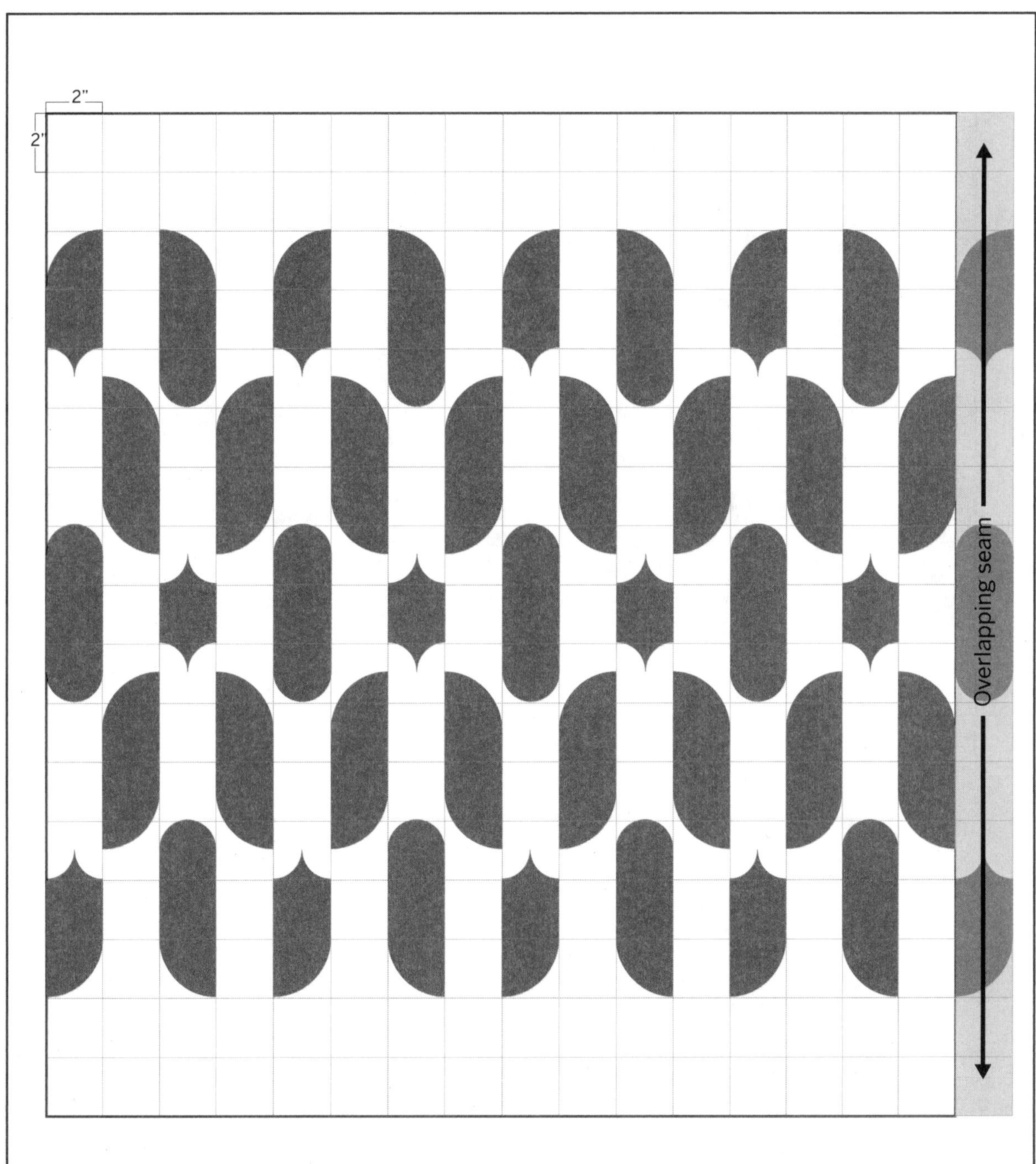

Figure 06.26: Gysin's original cylinder diagram: delivers photic stimulation @ +/– 20.8 hertz. Sorta.

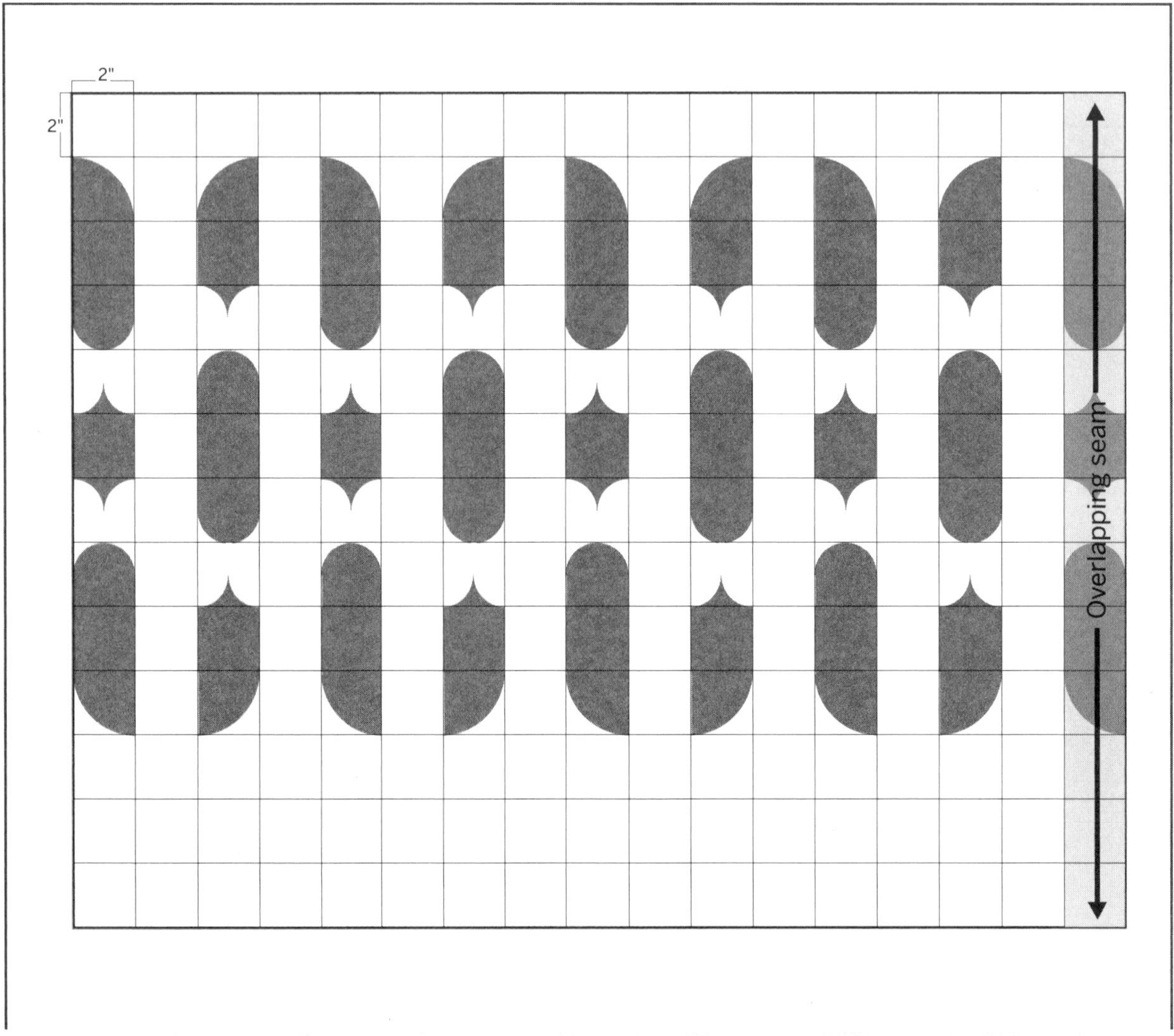

Figure 06.27: **My cunningly modified layout, which serves up a solid 10.4-hertz flicker for your alpha wave satisfaction, and coincidentally scales to our 24" tube length with admirable precision.**

getting the proper frequency, and that's just a matter of doing the math — which we're gonna do now.

Our turntable spins at 78 RPM, or 1.3 revolutions per second. Therefore, the frequency of flashing is $X * 1.3$, with X representing the number of perforations around the circumference of the cylinder. Our target frequency is the Alpha range of 7 to 13 cycles per second, so $X = 8$ gives a frequency of 10.4 hertz, just about midpoint of the alpha wave frequency range. Not coincidentally, a glance at Gysin's original cylinder diagram reveals that's exactly the number of openings per row in his cylinder.

I'm about to commit some kinda beat generation sacrilege and question Gysin's original concept. This has annoyed me for years, actually. Hear me out.

The offset of the alternating rows in Gysin's diagram is problematic, to my mind. At any viewing distance greater than rightupascloseasthis, you're receiving 20.8 hertz, which is decidedly *not* what we're looking for. There's some obviously

Figure 06.28: **Same size at the platter, innit?**

Figure 06.29: **Positioning magnets.**

intentional blurring of the flickers happening in the Gysin layout, which I have *no* idea the purpose of. Could be some transcendent analysis of brain wave function manifested in physical form, could be some of the aforementioned Sufic symbolism chucked into the mix for the sake of pure artsy fartsy nonsense. Lacking an EEG for comprehensive testing purposes, I'm hesitant to draw any technical conclusion. **[Figure 06.26, Figure 06.27]**

That said, from a purely neurological standpoint, with efficiency as the primary goal, eliminating the row offset means the device will deliver an unadulterated 10.4 hertz, which is what's needed to achieve the desired alpha state. I'm including in the download package layouts for the traditional Gysin cylinder, a truncated Gysin cylinder that works with a 24" fluorescent tube, and my modified one, as well as layouts for flicker frequencies targeted within other ranges for your experimental consideration. My personal research indicates more pronounced effect using the modified alpha frequency layout. The theta and low alpha frequency layouts have yielded promising results in achieving trance states of varying degrees, particularly when accompanied by second-party verbal guidance (which would be officially termed "hypnotic induction," for those of you with tendencies towards becoming Evil Criminal Masterminds commanding armies of hypnotized minions in a bid for world domination).

The Cylinder

Fabricating the cylinder is one of those deceptively simple trace-cut-glue jobs that works like a charm, provided that you've done your preparation thoroughly and with relative precision. In order for you to start out with something close to the original concept of the mechanism, we'll be using the truncated version of the traditional Gysin layout.

Start by cutting two 10-3/16" plywood discs, one from 3/4" stock, one from 1/4" stock. To accommodate a mathematically precise cylinder with a circumference of 32", the diameter *really* needs to be 10.185". Ya might wanna sand your disks down a tad to avoid the abject frustration inherent in trying to fit missized components together during final assembly. **[Figure 06.28]**

Turn the thicker one into a donut by cutting out a 6" circle from the center. This is the base of the cylinder, and the donut hole is for the fluorescent tube to pass through.

I spaced some *almost* flush-set rare-earth magnets around the bottom of the base, aligned with the conveniently situated indentations in the turntable platter, to position and retain the cylinder accurately on the platter. This involved a bit of careful marking, shallow holes drilled with the correct size Forstner bit, and a few dabs of two-part epoxy. The toughest part of this particular phase was finding the right size of magnets to interface with the dents in the platter.

The 1/4" thick disk is the top of the cylinder: You can skin the upper face of it with whatever you used on the turntable case to ensure, er, conceptual continuity.

The cylinder itself lives or dies based on your selection of material. Most readily available instruction sets recommend using Bristol board, like you used for your tenth-grade geography project on agricultural exports of Macedonia. Rightfully traumatized by *any* memory of that sordid experience, we're gonna cross that material off our list of potentials right from the start, and explore other alternatives. We need a stiff but formable material that can be cut with relative ease, and which will maintain its vertical strength with about 80% of the sheet cut away. It has to be light enough not to overtax the turntable drive mechanism, and it has to be affordable enough to let us make (purely for research purposes, doncha know) a bunch of different variations on the original concept without causing fiscal collapse.

Those of you with a larger fabrication budget than I have can rustle up a 34" x 27" piece of brass shim stock, send it off with the downloadable 1:1 cutting diagram to a waterjet cutting shop and receive back a mathematically precisely cut piece of metal that will bend to shape effortlessly while retaining admirable structural integrity. The last row of cutouts in the diagram overlaps with the first row to form your seam, which can be joined with contact cement or double faced tape. Form it around a piece of 10" OD PCV piping, slide it off, then position the top and bottom plywood discs with contact cement and escutcheon pins and you're done, you lucky bugger. **[Figure 06.29, Figure 06.30, Figure 06.31]**

The rest of us have more work to do. I traversed three rings of hell coming up with a solution that possessed the requisite physical characteristics without looking like a sheet of cardboard rolled into a tube. After exploring various wood veneer and plastic options (resulting in maximum aggravation and minimum satisfaction), I ambled into a sewing supply shop and I found stuff being sold as "Craft Cuts" that got me halfway to the goal. The material was similar to lightweight pasteboard on the back side, but with a shiny black PVC coating. 39.9" x 54", $1.99. Intact, it was ideal, strengthwise. With 40 big chunks cut out of it in a regular gridlike pattern, it assumed the physical characteristics of wet leather. Time to call in reinforcements. Reinforcement in this case takes the form of clear acetate sheeting used in the offset printing industry as film negative material. Luckily, I'm on a first-name basis with numerous dumpsters *and* warehouse managers in the field, and had suitable stock in hand within half an hour. The material in question came in sheets about 24" x 30" inches, which meant a bit of splicing was in order, but thankfully, I am possessed of the strength of ten and a pure heart. This proved to be an easy challenge to overcome.

Used negative stock *happens* in the printing industry, and is discarded daily. Making friends with local printing houses will ensure a ready supply of acetate sheets, which is incredibly useful stuff in many circumstances.

Laminating the acetate to the inside surface of the perforated cylinder (once again invoking the adhesive power of aerosol contact cement) restored the linear strength and

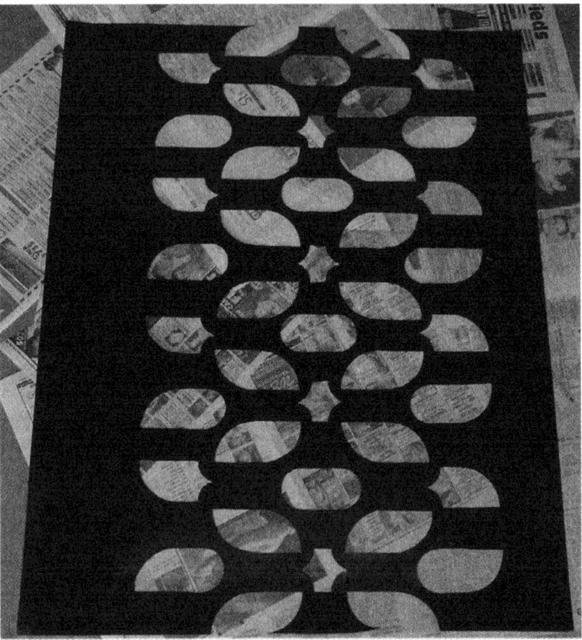

Figure 06.30: **The pattern**

gave a cylinder with a satisfying blend of structural integrity and aesthetic nuance.

But how did the perforations come to be made in the material? Alien technology? Voodoo? Pixies? Pixies with box cutters? Alien pixies with voodoo box cutters?

Nah . . . just me and an X-Acto knife and some carefully shaped templates.

Cut the individual templates from ¼" plywood and dress the edges with 150-grit sandpaper. You'll need to be fairly precise in shaping them. **[Figure 06.32]**

Conforming hole placement to the 2" x 1½" grid is of primary importance. The last set of openings on the diagram has to be accurate to form a precise seam when the cylinder is formed around the end plates. You can draw an accurate grid on the backside of your material to aid in placement, or bodge together a placement jig from a tape measure, carpenter's square and a T square. Change cutting blades regularly. There's a lot of knifework to be done, and a dull blade only makes the job more irritating. **[Figure 06.33, Figure 06.34]**

When the cutouts are done, laminate the acetate to the backside of the sheet, give both sides a wipedown with window cleaner (this is your last opportunity to *easily* clean

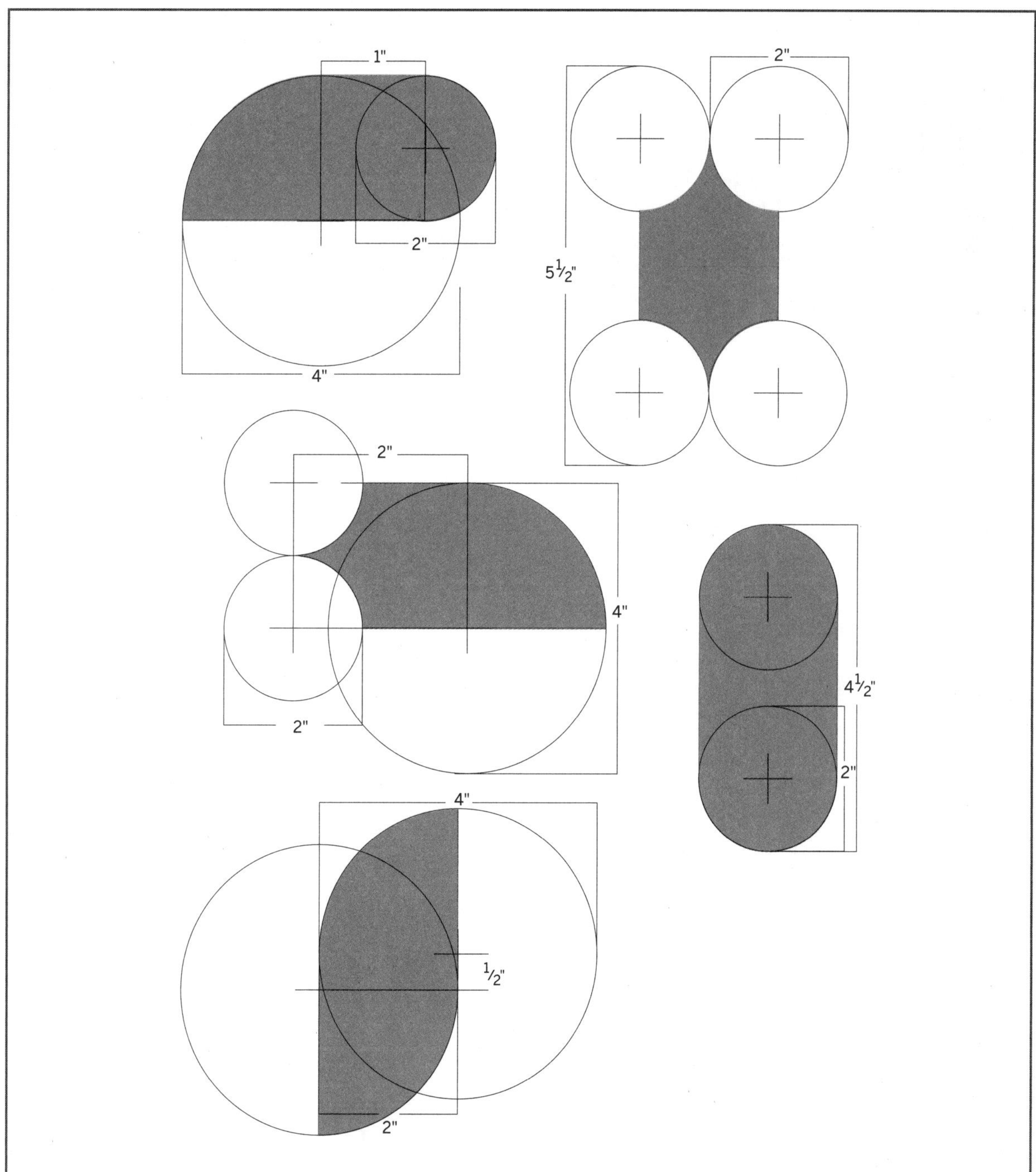

Figure 06.31: **Cutout templates for the truncated traditional Gysin layout**

Figure 06.32: **Lay 'em out on ¼" plywood and apply scroll/coping saw as needed.**

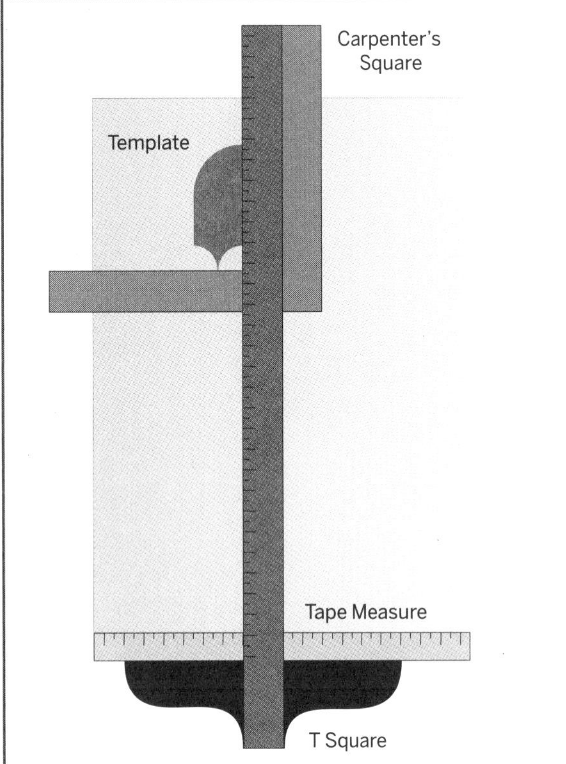

Figure 06.33: **The quick 'n' dirty template location jig**

the surface, so do a good job, okay?) and get out the double-faced tape.

My repeated attempts at forming the cylinder arrived at the following procedure. Apply tape to the bottom plate, the back side of the outer layer of the seam, and the front side of the inner layer. Peel the tape on the plate, and carefully roll the cylinder, starting at the right side (bottom seam layer) of the sheet. Roll the cylinder so that the seam is in contact with your work surface, and line up the overlaps accurately. Peel the tape one section at a time from the outer layer of the overlap, and seal the length of the seam. Repeat with the tape on the inner layer of the seam.

Take heart — you're only moments away from alpha wave nirvana.[8]

Practice placing the top plate in position a few times before actually using adhesive. The trick is to insert the plate fully into the cylinder at a slight angle, invert the cylinder onto the floor and press the top plate down flush with the edge of the cylinder, using a yardstick inserted through the donut hole. If your measurements and assembly to this point are accurate, it should be a snug fit that doesn't actually strain the seams; you can finesse the diameter of the top plate slightly if need be, but do try to keep it round. When you're comfortable with the process required, brush the inside of the top of the cylinder with contact cement and let it set for five minutes. Then, brush the outer rim of the top plate with contact cement, and quickly position the plate before the cement has a chance to set up. You'll still be able to press the plate into position without the glue grabbing excessively, and when it sets up you'll have a solid bond.

You'll also have a completed Gysin device, as soon as you place the cylinder over the fluorescent tube and center the doughnut on the platter. **[Figure 06.35]**

Instructions for use? Get comfy in front of it, turn it on, and close your eyes. Let the flickers knock on your eyelids, and, to quote one Mr. John Lennon, "Turn off your mind, relax, and float downstream."[9]

Lemme know what happens.

8 Perhaps a poor choice of terms. Urban legend has it that Mr. Kurt Cobain, leader of popular beat music group Nirvana, had been logging upwards of 10 hours a day using his recently acquired Gysin device in the days leading up to his unfortunate (and fatal) greenhouse incident.

9 "Tomorrow Never Knows" from *Revolver*, Lennon's acknowledged first psychaedelic song, and the only Beatles song to list Lennon as the sole songwriter. Aficionados looking for an energetically alternative interpretation of this timeless classic are well advised to seek out a recording of T.N.K. by the quite excellent Phil Manzanera/Brian Eno ensemble 801, from their *Live* album.

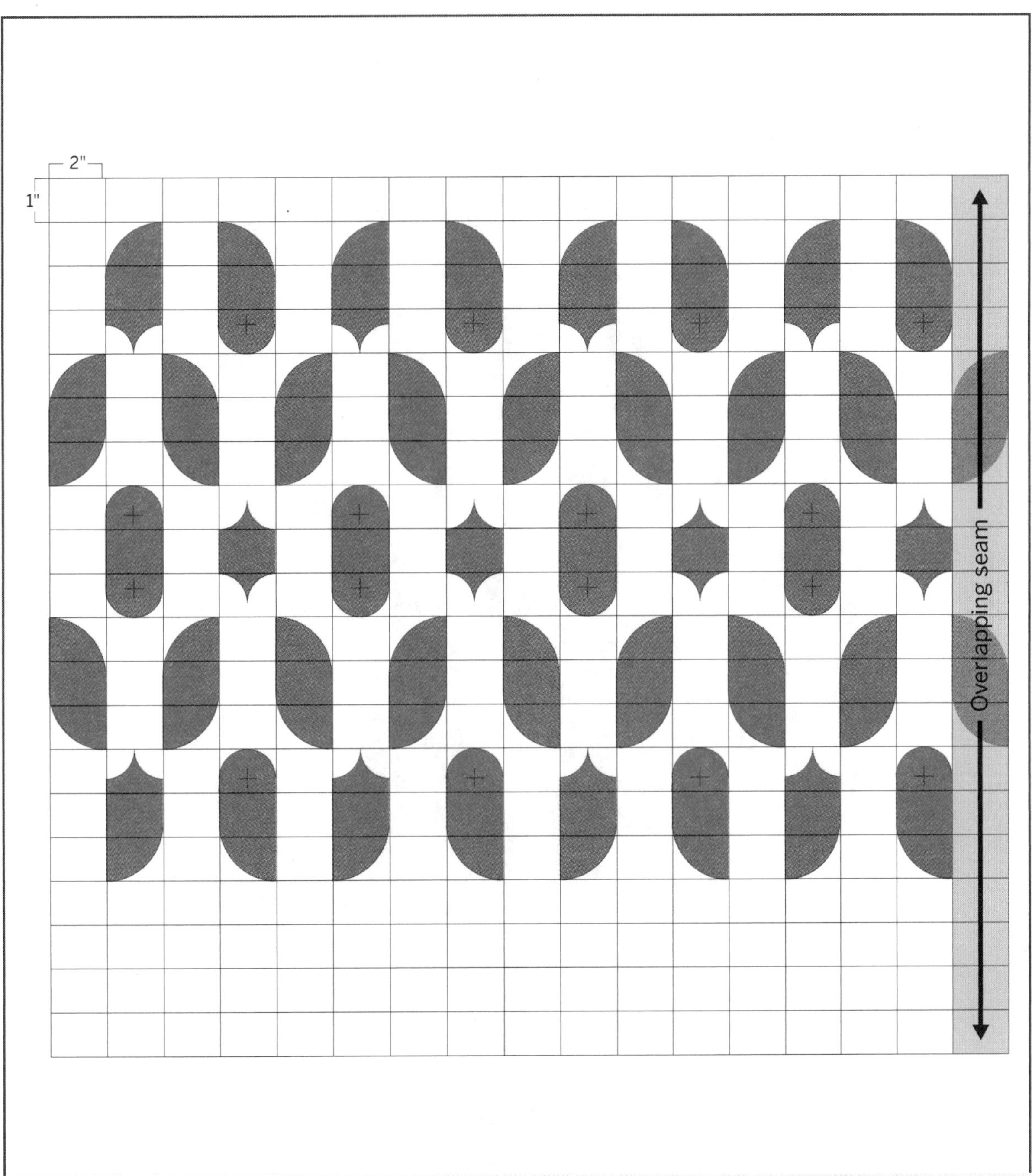

Figure 06.34: **Cutout locations for the truncated traditional Gysin layout**

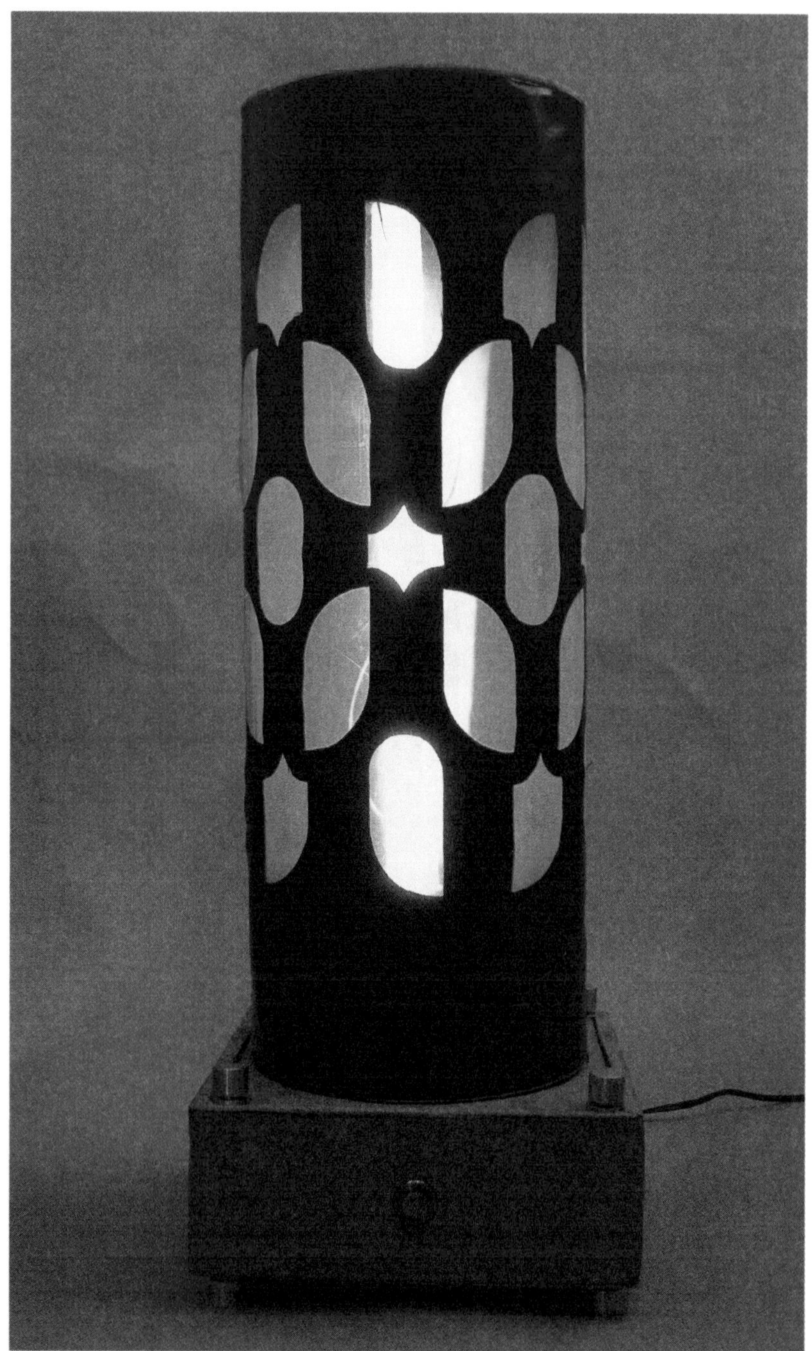

Figure 06.35: **What it is: the completed Gysin device**

‹ Nano-Project › Sewing Machine Pedal Hack: Speed Control, Cheap

Figure N6.01: **Illustrated are two random pedals I grabbed from my stockpile. The one on the left is from the early 70s, the one on the right from the early 60s. Both mechanisms are functional, but a look under the hood reveals some critical differences in technology.**

At last! Variable speed *everything*. Mostly.

Once again it's time for Makers worldwide to show proper respect to the Needle 'n' Thread community. So much about their art revolves around the efficient, precise use of purpose-designed tools.

Take the sewing machine for example: exact, versatile, built like the proverbial brick excretorium, and equipped with a magnificently hackable foot pedal speed control. You can easily find fully serviceable but unappreciated sewing machines at thrift shops and swap meets for under 20 bucks, which will net you a dandy little fractional horsepower electric motor, the aforementioned pedal controller, and the sewing machine proper. With a bit more rummaging around, you can often find just the pedal mechanism, alone, unloved, and priced under $5. Take a screwdriver with you when you're shopping so that you can have a peek inside. There are a few different variations on the speed control mechanism, and some are more appropriate than others for the task at hand.

The pedal on the left has a continuous sweepable resistance element ending in a "full on," while the older one uses cascaded resistance elements to give six discrete voltage positions (plus "full on"). It's your call as to what you'll find most useful. I've heard concerns that the graphite block used as the resistance element in the continuous controllers can degrade in quality of resistance and/or somehow cause damage to the motor it's controlling. I've had the same hacked pedal driving my Dremel for eight years, and both pedal and tool are doing just fine, thanks. **[Figure N6.01]**

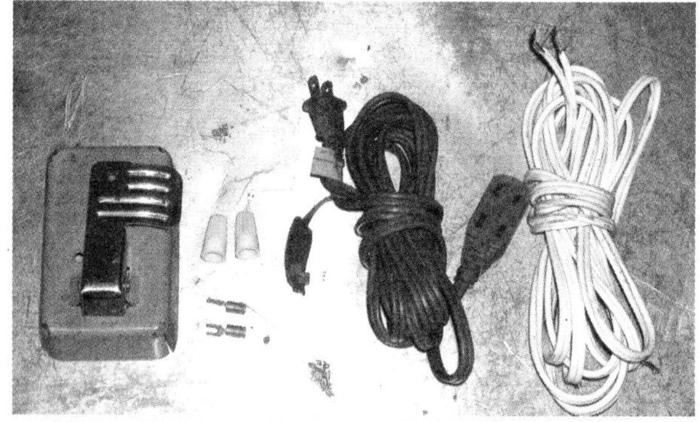

Figure N6.02: **What you'll need.**

Get yourself the pedal of your choice, ten feet of zip cord, a couple of twist-on wire nuts (Marrette connectors), a couple of crimp-on terminals, and a bog-standard dollar-store exten-

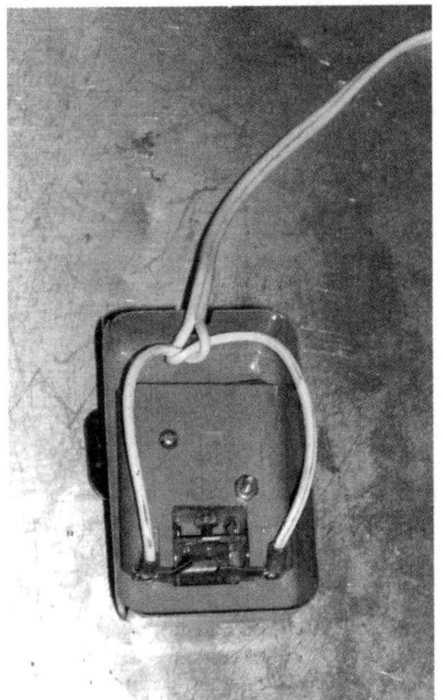

Figure N6.03: **Crimp some cord to your pedal contacts.**

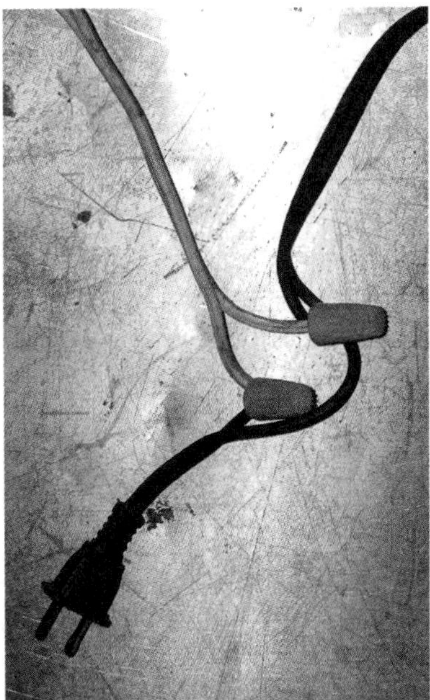

Figure N6.04: **Splice it into an extension cord.**

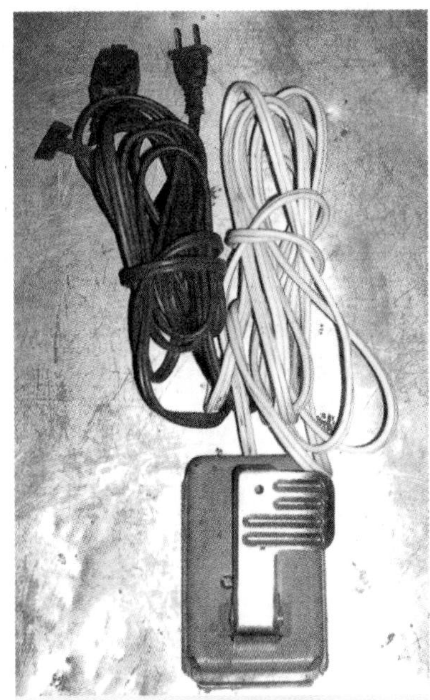

Figure N6.05: **You're good to go.**

sion cord. Toolwise, you'll need a utility knife, a screwdriver, and electrical tape. **[Figure N6.02]**

Strip half an inch on each conductor on the zip cord and crimp on the terminals. Tie a strain relief knot in the cord, and attach the terminals to the posts on the resistance element of the pedal. Button the pedal assembly back up and turn your attention to the extension cord. **[Figure N6.03]**

Split the two conductors of the extension cord about a foot from the male end. Cut one lead, and strip half an inch of insulation from each end. Strip the ends of the foot pedal zip cord, and use the wire nuts to splice the pedal leads in line with the extension cord. Tape up the splice with electrical tape and test the continuity and pedal resistance action with a multimeter. Plug the extension into the wall outlet, something motorized (say, your Dremel) into the extension, then stroke the pedal and wallow in some hot variable-speed action. **[Figure N6.04]**

Varispeeding a big-assed electric motor with this hack is likely not going to work: the start-up power required to get it spinning is gonna exceed the current the pedal is passing, and nothing is going to happen. Smaller motors (up to, say, the horsepower and current draw of the motor of the sewing machine that you harvested the pedal from) will work just fine, albeit with lowered torque at lower speeds. **[Figure N6.05]**

It's amazing how handy it is to use your feet.

7 iBlow Bubble Machine

When I was a kid I had this amazing pressed-tin ray gun that was a freakin' bubble machine. Pick a target, pull the trigger repeatedly (to energize a friction motor that powered the fan and perforated wheel), and holy Toledo, *bubbles*!

It didn't have much of a range, and the accuracy was subject to prevailing winds, but hot damn, did it ever drive the family dog nutsoid.

Around about the same time, *oberster käsemeister* Lawrence Welk and his Champagne Music Makers — the era's premier Family Television Entertainment™ superstars — were ushering in each wholesome episode of polkas, show tunes, and inspirational chorales with a perky cloud of bubbles (imaginatively intended to evoke the effervescent joie de vivre symbolized by overpriced carbonated plonk).

Fortunately, this abomination did not quench my enthusiasm for bubbles.

Occupying a position on the musical spectrum 180 degrees opposed to the musical horror of Mr. Welk and company were the surreally inventive Mothers of Invention, led by the anti-Welk, Frank Zappa, who frequently namechecked L.W. in lyrics and interviews. In 1974, their *Roxy and Elsewhere* LP was highlighted by a spirited performance of "The Be-Bop Tango," during which the great man himself was heard to intone, "Turn on the bubble machine."

Coincidence? I think not. These two disparate musical giants, so different and yet so eerily similar, recognized and paid homage to the irresistible entertainment power of the bubble machine.

Bubble machines transcend time, taste, and trends. They are the universal translation of "havin' some fun here, people — pay attention." Tireless bringers of smiles, giggles, and fond childhood memories, they are the ultimate morale boosters. Unless you were traumatized by too many episodes of *The Prisoner*.

A workplace without a bubble machine is like a payday without a cheque. So we'd better build one. Right freakin' now.

The operational concept is pretty simple: dip wand in bubble solution. Blow. Repeat. Serial bubbles ensue.

Hell yeah, we can do *that*.

Mechanizing the process of bubble blowing requires a fan to provide airflow, and an endless loop of wands dipping sequentially into a reservoir of bubble juice.

As noted elsewhere in this tome, there's no shortage of ways to accomplish this particular sequence of events; whatever path we take is gonna take some power, however, so we'll tap into one of your PC's USB ports for some battery- and wall-wart-free electrical goodness.

The fan? A 2" CPU fan. Sure, it's 12 volts (sez here right on the label), but even when powered by the 5v DC current delivered by pins 1 and 4 on yer basic USB port, it moves more than enough air to serve our purposes.

The perpetual bubble wand? An artfully perforated CDR on an axle driven by a bodged together reduction gear train powered by a small electric motor. Feel free to source in a retail gear motor if you want to avoid having to turn three pulleys out of acrylic; you're looking for +/− 5 RPM at 5v DC, which a quick online search reveals to be a fairly uncommon piece of kit.

Bubble juice we can either source commercially or brew up ourselves.

The bubble juice reservoir will be easily removable from the apparatus for draining and cleaning. It'll be fashioned from a

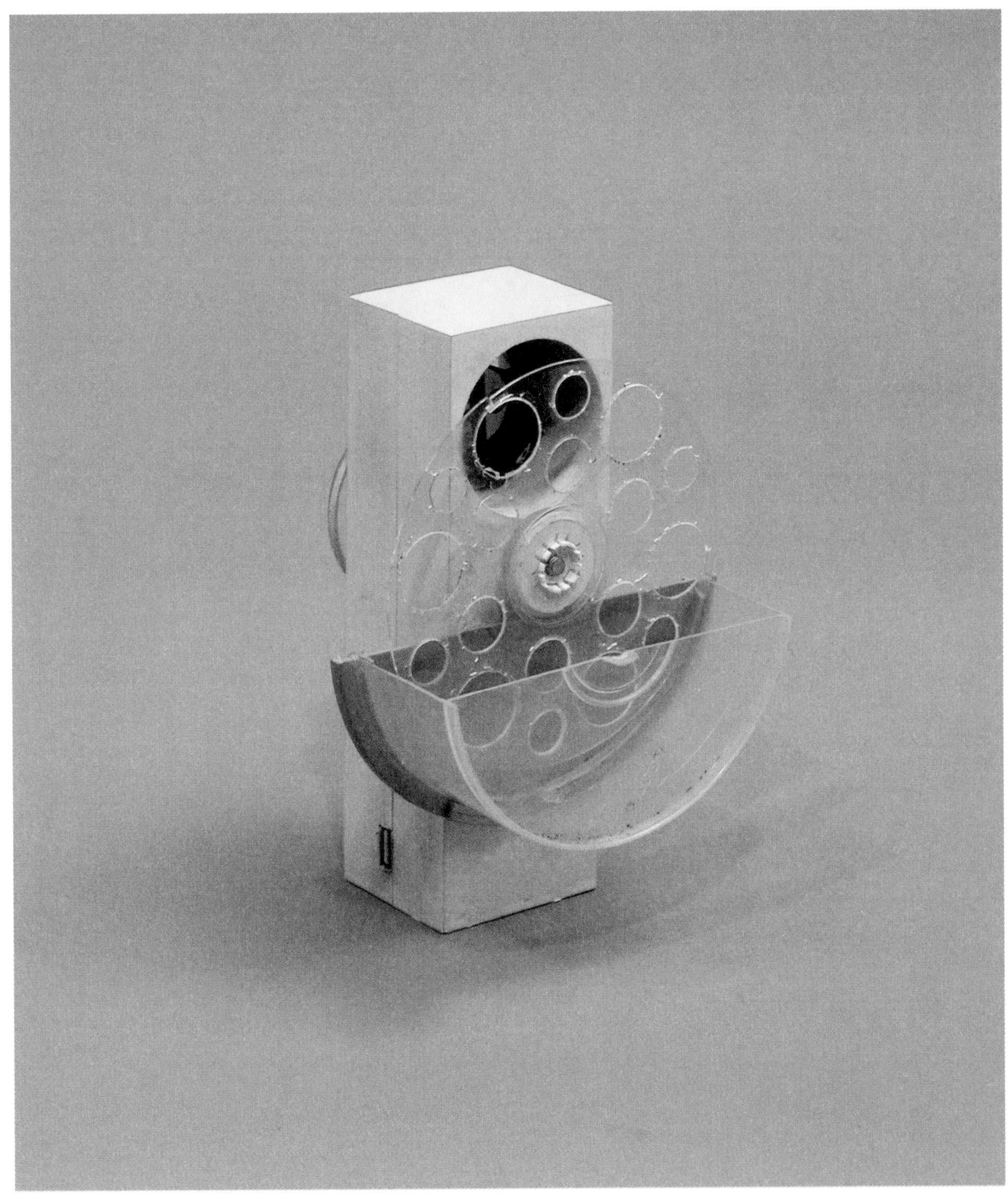

ritually dismembered CDR spindle case. We'll need to make some crucial material choices to deal with potential rusting issues as well.

If we design a mechanism that's simple and elegant from the ground up, we do an end-run around the need for a case to hide all the techy bits. Our mandate, therefore, is to do just that, and save ourselves the (in this case avoidable) pain in the ass of bodging together a housing for the machine. Do not be put off if this is starting to feel more like a pressure-filled product design course assignment than an entertaining DIY project. Stop for a moment and reflect on the fact that it's a bubble machine we're building here, and anything that involves a bubblemachine is *inherently* Fun.

Get on with it.

What You'll Need

There's not a lot of shopping to be undertaken. You might already have a 2" CPU fan stowed away in your "miscellaneous computer hardware" drawer, and the motor needed to drive the bubble wheel can come from a scrapped cassette recorder. We'll need:

- **6" x 6" of ¼" clear acrylic sheet** (if you're not feeling the need for transparency, substitute ¼" plywood)
- **A USB socket** I used a type A PCB mount number harvested from a first-generation PCI add-on card. I learned (much) later that A-to-A USB cables are somewhat rare: a couple of years ago I picked up an intestine-poppingly heavy box of assorted new-in-bag PC cables at a yard sale that included half a dozen cables each of every conceivable USB terminator combination, a resource most people lack. When it came time to cable up this build, I just grabbed what I needed out of "The Box," not realizing how anomalous the A–A terminator combination actually is in the wild.
- **Adhesive-backed hook-and-loop fastener**, like Velcro (a few inches)
- **1" medium-density fiberboard (MDF)** for the chassis
- **A subminiature SPST slider switch**
- **A 10-ohm ¼ watt resistor**

Other stuff you likely have squirreled away somewhere includes a few CD jewel cases, some uncoated CDR blanks that they top up spindle cases with, and an empty 25-disc spindle case.

You'll also need:

- **Brass or galvanized steel ¼-20 threaded rod** 3" worth
- **A cheap ballpoint pen**
- **A drinking straw**
- **A playing card**
- **Four 1½" #6 wood screws**
- **A 1" 6-32 machine screw**
- **Hookup wire and shrink tubing**
- **A tube of "automotive sealant"**[1]
- **A selection of rubber bands to use as drive belts**
- **6 large grapefruits**
- **A volleyball net**

Just kidding about the last two.

You may want to sacrifice a USB cord for testing purposes: Lop one end off and bare the ends of pins 1 and 4. Pin 1 is hot, pin 4 is ground.

Cooking your own bubble juice? You already have the dish-washing liquid in the kitchen, so you just need to grab a pint of glycerin at the pharmacy. Resist the urge to restock the supply of nitric acid you use in your Champlevé enamelling projects at the same time: otherwise, alarm bells will likely go off, followed quickly by an indefinite vacation in Cuba courtesy of the United States government.

The Drive Train

The basic mechanism is shown in the illustration. There are three pulleys to turn. Mark the outlines (the dimensions cited in the cutting diagram will get you close, but you may need to do some tweezing, depending on the speed your motor runs at. Start out with the blanks on the large side and fine-tune the operational diameters when you're forming the belt groove), rough-cut them with a coping saw or scroll saw and sand them to a close approximation of round with the disk sander that I finally convinced you to buy. Drill out the centers with 3/32" pilot holes, and (MA!!! He's doin' it again!!) tap the holes for 8-32 threads. **[Figure 07.01, Figure 07.02]**

NOTE: Use the slowest speed possible when cutting acrylic with a powered saw to avoid the thoroughly annoying "melted acrylic resealed my damned kerf" effect.

To finish the pulleys, chuck a length of 8-32 threaded rod into your drill or drill press, and thread on one of the blanks all the way up to the chuck jaws. Add a washer and nut as retain-

1 This stuff looks the same as, but is different from, silicon glazing compound. I used Automotive Goop, which is also popular in the Sk8tr community as a deck grip treatment. Comes in a purple tube resembling a toothpaste tube on steroids, smells horrid, sticks to world + dog.

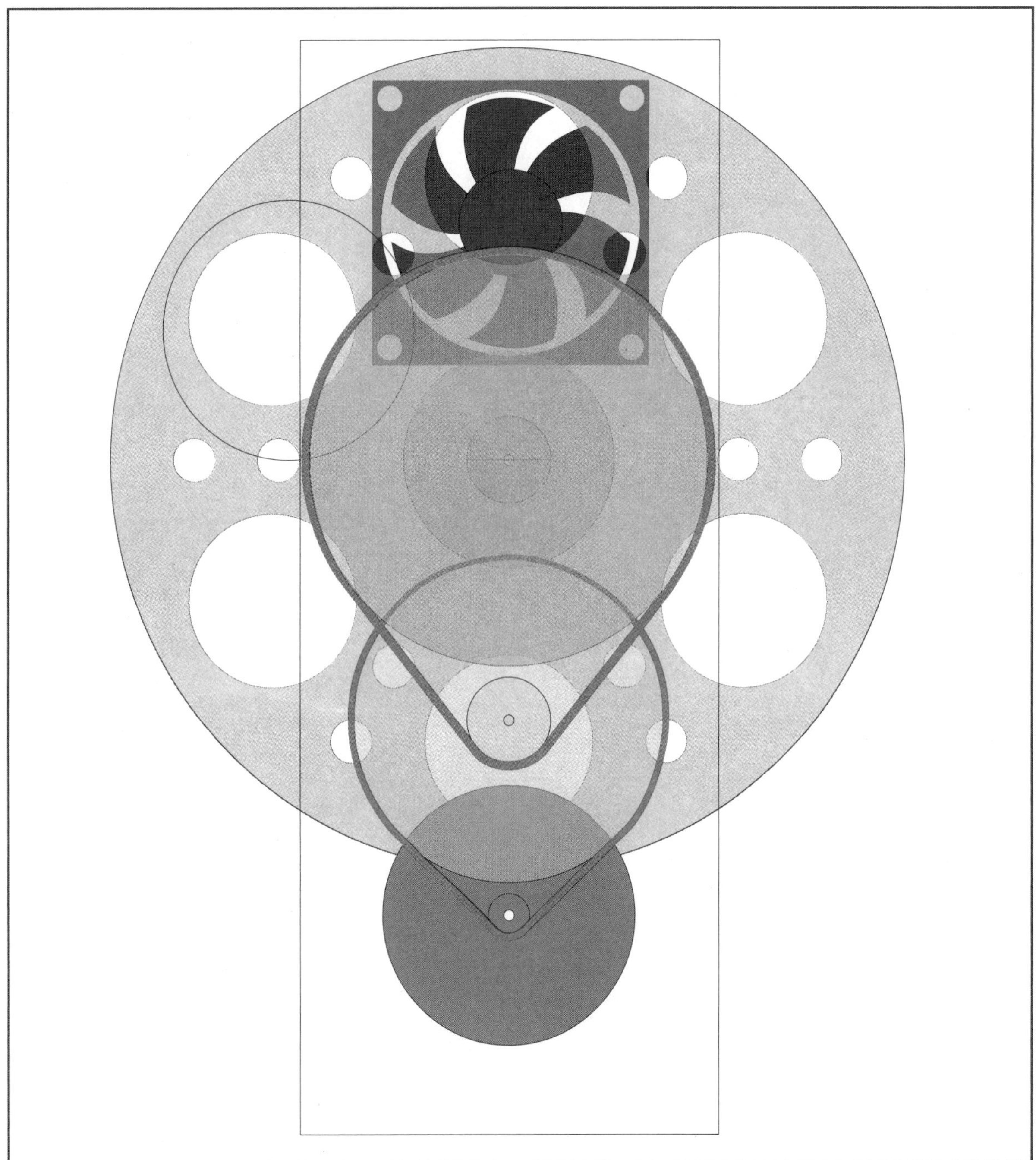

Figure 07.01: **The mechanism from the rear. Kinda looks like a crop circle, if you squint your eyes a bit, and imagine it laid out in a cornfield in Sussex.**

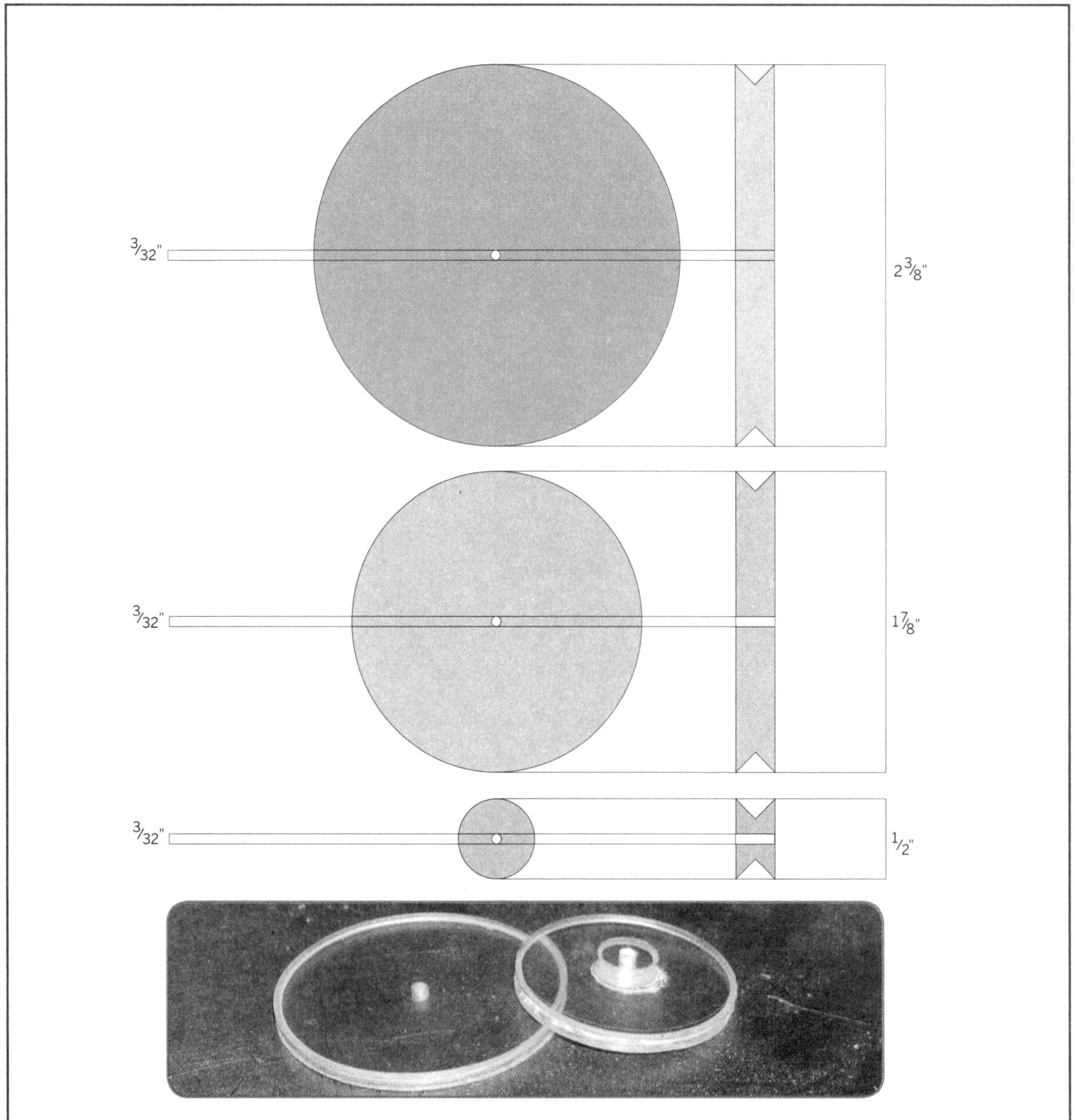

Figure 07.02: **Pulleys for reducing the motor RPMs. Getting the motor reduction ratio sussed out to spec will be part math and part voodoo ritual. Plan on prototyping and testing your drive train to get it right before you actually build the working model. The mathematics of gear ratios is covered pretty thoroughly in the Liquid Len Meets DiscoHead build log (Chapter 8). If you haven't made it to that project yet, definitely do a quick read-through of that section to pick up the lore.**

Figure 07.03: Lathing a teeny weeny acrylic pulley. Oooooh. Aaaaah. Oooooh. Aaaaah. (repeat)

Figure 07.04: Here's the rear view of my breadboarded drive train. Prototyping it like this let me get a feel for the aesthetics of the mechanism, as well as letting me check the reduction ratio.

ers, and your blank will be held firmly enough to let you spin up the drill and finalize the shape. **[Figure 07.03]**

Sand the blank to round with 100-grit paper, then carefully lathe in the pulley groove. I used real turning gouges to do this, because I have them to use. If you're improvising lathing tools, refer to the drill press lathe nano project (at the end of this chapter) for tips on DIY gouges, or take the *real* easy route and use the pointy end of a nail. This method is more effective than it sounds, because the tip of the nail is about the same shape as the groove you're forming. Get a firm grip on the nail with locking pliers, and use moderate pressure to shape the groove. Your initial groove should be no deeper than is needed to comfortably accommodate the rubber bands that you're using as belts. If necessary, you can deepen them to reduce the pulley dimension and increase the speed of rotation.

When the profile is where you want it, clean up the edge and groove with a bit of sandpaper, then repeat the whole dealie on the other two blanks.

To save space, we're stacking the ½" and 1 ⅞" pulleys: thread them both onto a piece of 8-32 rod, add a drop or two of cyanoacrylate, and cinch them together tightly to complete the bond. Thread the rod out before glue has completely set, and *shazzam!* — stacked pulleys.

I used the motor from a thrift shop cassette recorder. It's not your most high-performance piece of kit, but it came with a dandy wee 3⁄16" belt drive pulley already installed on it, and it was spec'd for a 9v battery. Driving it with 5v brings the native RPMs down a bit, which takes a bit of the onus for speed reduction away from the pulley system that we're fabricating. The accompanying decrease in torque will be offset by the low-gear drive mechanism it's gonna be powering.

As shown, the final rotation rate is about 15 RPM, which is a little fast for our needs. Fortunately, this figure doesn't take into account the mass of the bubble wheel, nor the effects of friction and hydraulic resistance imparted by the tank of bubble juice. After wet testing, it was still running fast, so I dropped a 10 ohm resistor into the circuit to lower the current a bit more and was rewarded with an acceptable 7 RPMs, and increased airflow from the fan. **[Figure 07.04]**

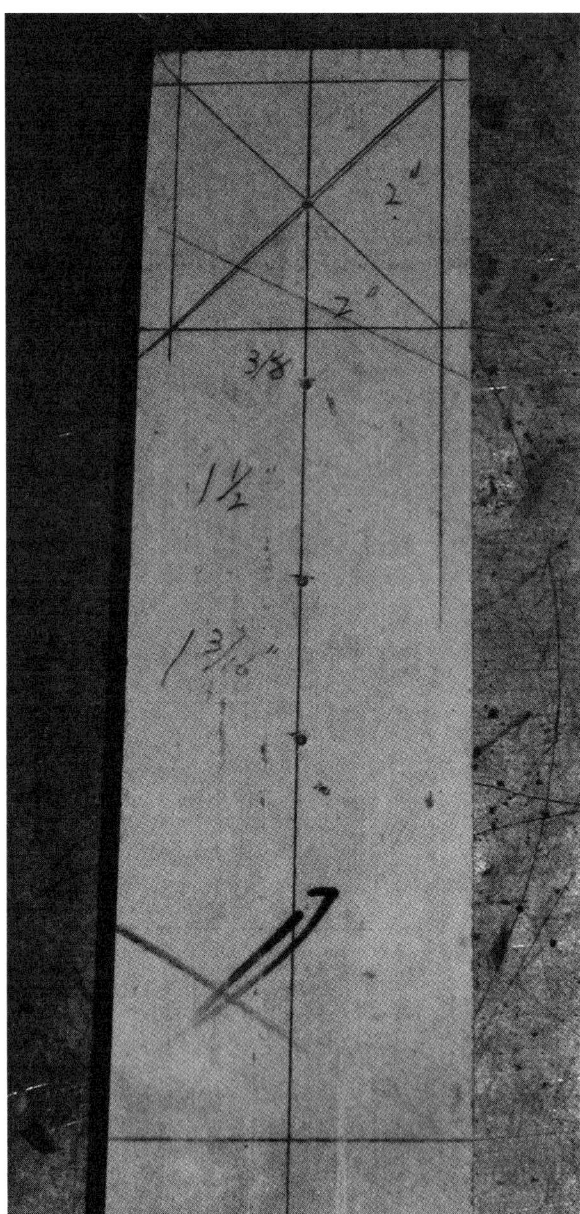

Figure 07.05: **The actual component layout on the build chassis pretty much reflects the breadboard version. The upper bit got stretched a few inches to accommodate the fan, but the footprint proved to be stable, even with a reservoir full of bubble juice hanging off the front face.**

Figure 07.06: **Mounting the fan**

Figure 07.07: **Squaring up the fan mount**

The wiring harness is minimal: the fan and motor are wired in parallel to pins 1 and 4 of the USB socket, which can fit just about anywhere, as it's an efficiently designed mechanical interface. The on-off switch goes inline on the hot lead, with the resistor inline on the lead feeding the drive motor.

The Chassis

The chassis is based on a sandwich of 1" MDF (the actual dimension is ⅞"). Sandwiching two pieces together lets us get fancy and hide the fan assembly and motor in the middle of the piece, so that only the pulley rigging and bubble wheel are visible from the outside. Cut two pieces 2⅜" wide. Length isn't a factor yet; we can trim it to size later. The minimum length needed to hold all the bits is 6". Temporarily join them together with double-faced tape and true up the edges, then mark the hole positions and drill 3⁄32" pilot holes through the back surface and about half an inch into the inside face of the front chassis piece. **[Figure 07.05]**

Drill the fan hole out with a 2" holesaw; take your time, and clear the sawdust from the circular kerf regularly. This is a pretty taxing job for your average holesaw. They're more comfortable taking out disks from ¼" thick door panels, and will generate huge amounts of heat-of-friction when faced with this kinda challenge. The heat is problematic, as the metal ring that makes up the cutting blade is gonna want to expand when the temperature rises, which increases friction, which causes more heat, which causes more expansion. You can see where this can get ugly (and smelly: charring MDF puts the hurt on your nose[2]). Take plenty of breaks during the drillout to let the blade cool down, and avoid damaging the ozone layer.

Mark the outline of your fan assembly on the inside face of the back chassis, then use either a chisel or a dremel circular saw attachment to define the outline into the MDF. You're aiming to form a square cavity in the chassis for the fan to slot into, and there are a few ways to do this: The most obvious way is with a chisel, maul, and extreme caution. Frankly speaking, MDF is a bitch to chisel, due in no small part to its eagerness to delaminate at the slightest opportunity. **[Figure 07.06, Figure 07.07]**

I took the easy way out and removed most of the material with a carefully wielded Forstner bit, then cleaned up the edges with a dremel high-speed cutter bit chucked into my drill press.

2 Frank Zappa, "Stinkfoot," from *Apostrophe* (1974): "Your stinkfoot. Put the hurt. On maaah Nose." F. Z. is referring to the exquisite little inconvenience of Bromadrosis, but trust me, charred MDF holds its own in the olfactorally offensive category.

Figure 07.08: **Same deal for the motor, but don't cut all the way through.**

Figure 07.09: **Properly fitting the fan and motor into the chassis. Take the time to get this right the first time, so you won't have to revisit the issue later.**

Figure 07.10: **The drill press as "almost a router": forming the slot for the USB socket**

The predefined straight edges made this almost easy. The corner angles get trued up with a small chisel, and the job's done.

We're gonna conceal most of the drive motor casing inside the chassis. Use a holesaw sized to the diameter of your drive motor to drill ¾" through the back chassis piece from the inside surface, then carefully remove the material from the core of the hole with a Forstner bit. There's likely an "Official Woodworker Guy's" method to accomplish this task that bears no resemblance to this technique, but dammit, it works, so I do it. **[Figure 07.08]**

Check motor for fit. I had to add a shallow notch to the hole to accommodate the protruding bit of circuit board that the motor leads were mounted on. I also had to enlarge the axle hole in the rear chassis face to accommodate the case geometry and positioning of the motor cooling slots. Admittedly, there's not much chance of an underpowered 9-volt DC motor developing overheating issues, but there's also no reason to take any chances. **[Figure 07.09]**

Shape the cutout for the USB port the same way. Draw the outline, shallow cut the straight lines, then router or chisel out the slot. **[Figure 07.10]**

The USB socket has 1⁄64" lips around the port to hold it in place. You'll need to be careful with your measurements and cutting to make proper use of them. The inner face of the front

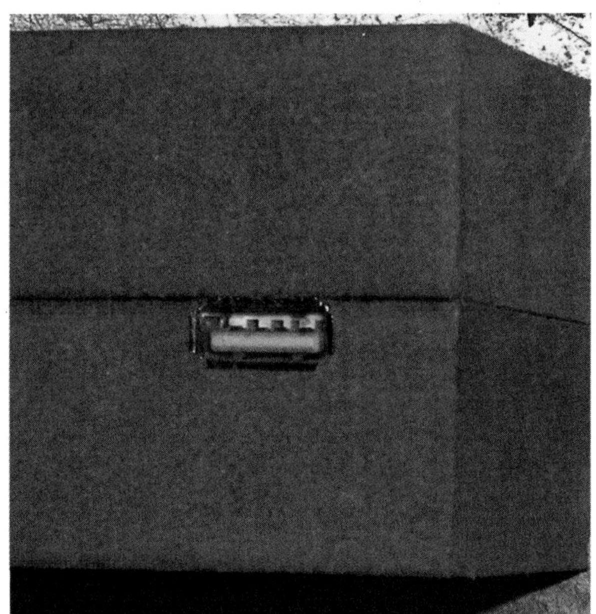

Figure 07.11: Sockets gots lips; account for them in your slot-forming ritual.

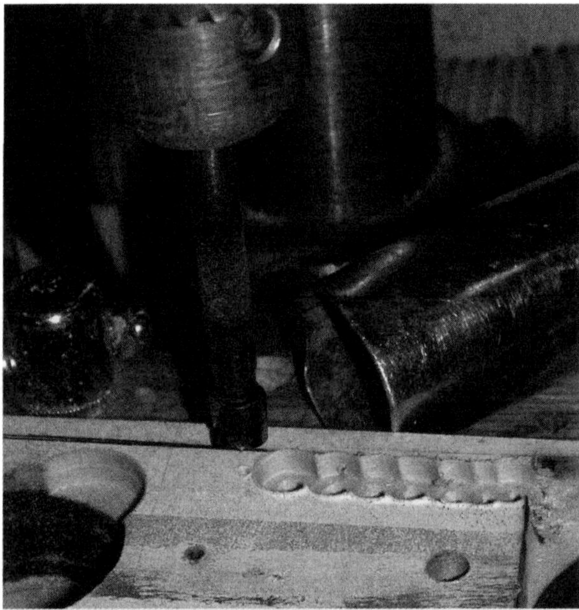

Figure 07.12: Roughing in the wiring harness channels

chassis will need a bit of sculpting to receive the topside profile of the socket — there's no need to be wildly precise. Just chuck a ¾" Forstner bit and make a hole for it to fit into. **[Figure 07.11]**

Carve out the wiring harness channel running between the fan and the motor. Clamp a guide bar onto the table of your drill press to ensure a straight line, set the hole depth to about half an inch, then remove most of the material with a Forstner bit before routering the sides of the channel smooth. **[Figure 07.12, Figure 07.13]**

The cavity for the power switch is formed the same way as the USB port. The switch I used was harvested from the same cassette player I salvaged the drive motor from. The actuator on the weensy little thing is about ¼" x ⅛" x ⅛", which meant that forming the access slot in the body for the actuator required the precise wielding of an X-Acto knife. Feel free to substitute the switching solution of your choice if you wanna forego *that* particular character-building experience. **[Figure 07.14]**

Now that you have the interior cavities formed, cut your chassis pieces to length. Use double-faced tape to temporarily join the chassis components together, ensuring that they're properly aligned; then true up the edges. Mark the locations of the four assembly screws at each corner of the back face of the chassis, ¼" in from the adjacent edges. Drill 3/32" pilot holes 1½" deep at these locations. **[Figure 07.15]**

Figure 07.13: Cleaning up the wiring harness channels

Figure 07.14: **The power switch cutout**

Figure 07.15: **Freeform interior cavities add wacky excitement to iBlow! (Sorry . . . my marketing department is field-testing catchphrases.)**

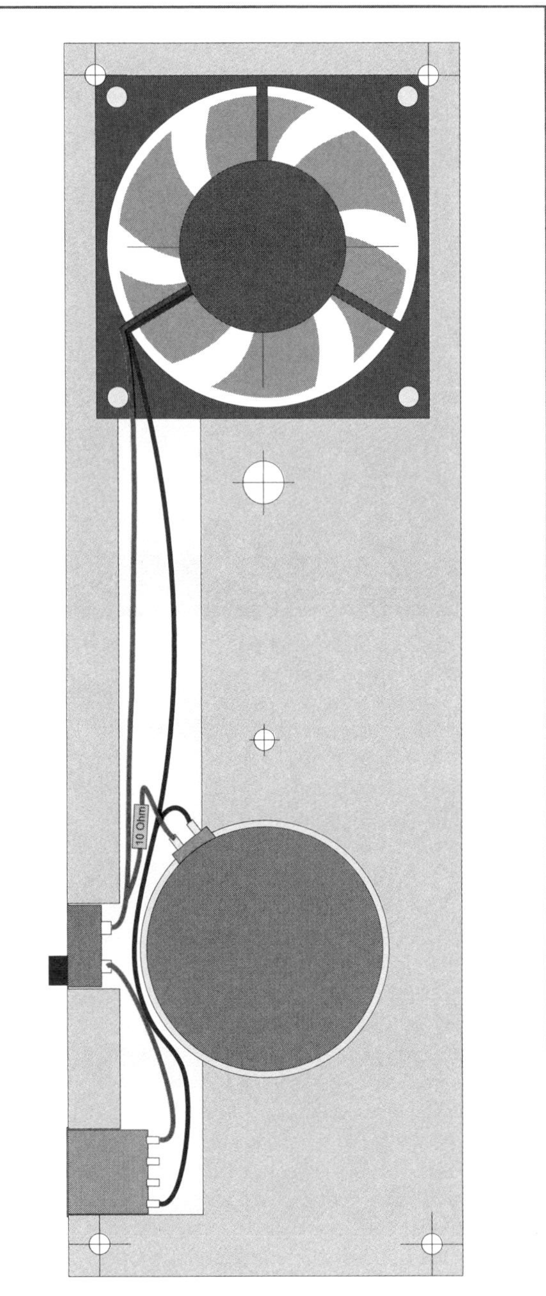

Figure 07.16: **The iBlow wiring diagram. Rocket scientists disappointed again: film at 11:00.**

Figure 07.17: **Live from Chopper 9: on-the-scene coverage of the wiring, as it unfolds**

Finishing and feeding

Zoinks! The internal stuff is almost done. Use a continuity tester to confirm the locations of pins 1 and 4 on your USB socket, and heat up your soldering iron. Connect the leads in parallel, and put the 10-ohm resistor inline on the lead feeding the drive motor to lower the current and slow the motor down a tad (as part of the quest for a 5-RPM wheel speed). **[Figure 07.16, Figure 07.17]**

Now that you've done all the mucking about with the wooden bits, you can ponder your finish options. It's something that needs to be done before final assembly takes place. A thorough sanding followed by a coat of 30-cut shellac and three coats of white enamel will do a pretty good job of capturing the iStuff aesthetic, if you want to pursue that line of visuals. Once you've done the surface prep, assemble the empty chassis with a sheet of paper separating the front and back sections, and mask off the installation points for the hook-and-loop reservoir attachments on the front face before proceeding with the paint application.

Fight the urge to watch the paint dry by making the remaining components.

The Bubble Wheel

As the bubble juice needs to age after mixing, brew it up now from this Quik 'n' E-Z Bubble Juice recipe:

- 1 part Palmolive dishwashing liquid
- 1 part glycerin
- 14 parts distilled water

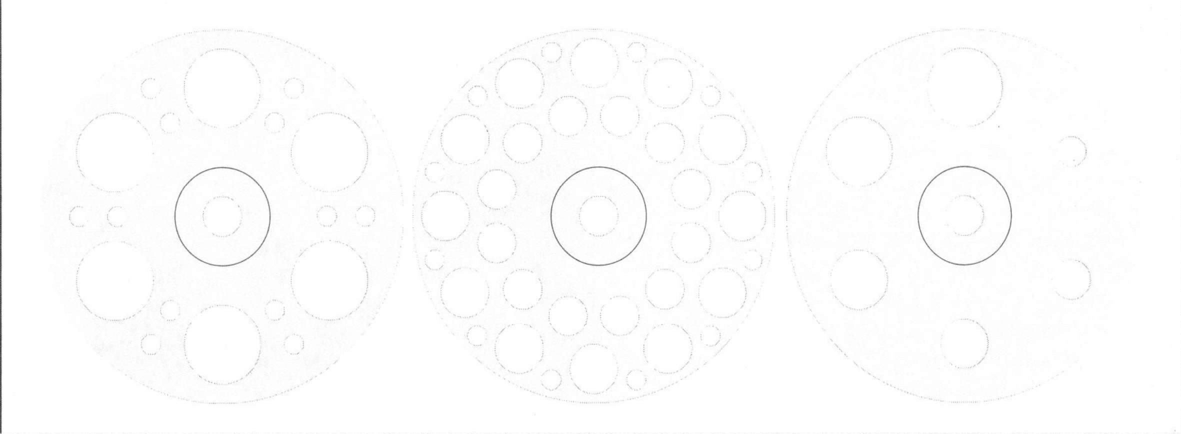

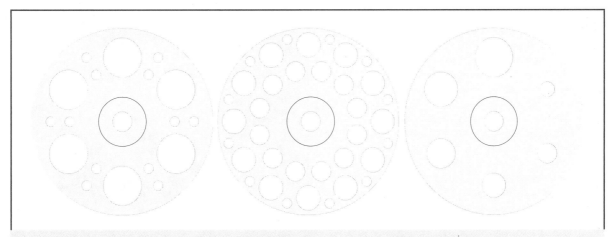

Figure 07.18: **Presented for your consideration: bubble wheel layouts. Improvise at your leisure.**

Figure 07.19: **Kludge yerself up a quick-change bubble-wheel mount from a CD case disc retention widget.**

Mix in a clean, dust-free environment, and let it "mature" uncovered overnight to let some of the detergent additives evaporate off. Bottle it up and set it aside.

Fabricate the bubble wheel from one of those uncoated CDRs that they use to pad out spindles. The material isn't as tough as you'd think, so exercise care when drilling out the holes. Forstner bits are *definitely* the drill of choice for the job. Regular drillbits at a 1" diameter are essentially unobtainium, and spade bits (however shiny, new, and sharp) grab the plastic like crazy, ripping it into dangerously pointy shards with little provocation. I found holes in the ½" to 1" range gave the best results. In theory, a symmetrical hole pattern will ensure smoother rotational movement by maintaining some semblance of balance to the wheel, but in practice, there's not enough mass involved to make a whole lot of difference. Feel free to mess around with the hole layout to give different results: A bunch of ½" holes scattered at random will produce a steady swarm of bubbles, while a geometrically precise series of graduated hole sizes will be more mannered in output, an effect I found funny, in a "locked in Fred MacMurray's lab waiting for a batch of Flubber to cook" kinda way. **[Figure 07.18]**

The drive axle for the bubble wheel terminates in an improvised quick-change holder. This makes testing different wheel layouts a completely pain-free experience. The

Figure 07.20: **Jigged bubble-wheel drillout. Sounds like it should be an automotive term, perhaps related to improved carburetion.**

Figure 07.21: **CD spindle case/2 + gOOp = reservoir**

Figure 07.22: **Harnessing the miracle of Velcro for reservoir mounting.**

bubble-wheel holder is made by cutting the disc retention widget from the center of a CD jewel case and epoxying it onto a scrap of ¼" acrylic. When the adhesive has cured, sand it to shape and drill and tap the centerpoint for ¼-20 threads. **[Figure 07.19]**

Fabricating the bubble wheel is *seriously* easier if you take the time to fabricate a drilling jig. Start with a scrap of ¼" plywood, and mark a 4¾" circle on it. Draw in concentric circles, decreasing successive diameters by ½", then use a protractor to divide the circles at 30-degree intervals to provide you with a usable array of nicely spaced hole targets. Harvest another retention widget from a jewel case, and set it at the centerpoint with double-faced tape (10 extra Maker points if you countersink the widget so that the plastic surrounding the retention clips is flush with the surface of the plywood). Trim the whole thing to fit the table of your drill press, and enjoy stress-free hole-drillin' thrills.[3] **[Figure 07.20]**

The bubble juice reservoir is a no-brainer, provided you have the right adhesive. We're using a CD for the bubble wheel, so we'll use a CD spindle case for the reservoir. To keep the center of gravity of the mechanism under control we'll need the shortest spindle case you can lay your hands on. Although the thought of an enormous reservoir may be comforting to some, hanging 2 pints of liquid from the front of the mechanism is gonna make balancing on a small footprint hard to achieve. I used a 25-disc spindle, bisected just short of dead center. Lay a bead of automotive sealant around the edge, and lock on the lid. Smooth out the bead of goop with your thumb and let it cure. Once it's fully cured, test the reservoir for leaks. **[Figure 07.21]**

NOTE: Try gluing or sealing the plastic they make spindle cases from. Cripes — none of the usual adhesives bond to this stuff, and it's *really* frustrationizing. Fortunately, the aforementioned automotive sealant, like Automotive Goop and its ilk, does a *splendid* job of sticking just about anything to just about anything else. It's nasty stuff to clean up though, so exercise caution in application.

Mounting the reservoir onto the chassis?

Velcro, daddy-o, Velcro.

Adhesive-backed hook-and-loop fastener tape is available at sewing supply retailers. It's another of those damned handy things the needle 'n thread folks try to keep secret from the rest of the world.

Use two ½" x ¾" pieces, positioned as illustrated. Leave the hook side attached to the loop side, and stick the Velcro

3 Under normal circumstances, drilling holes isn't particularly exciting, but this is a Bubble Machine, dammit!

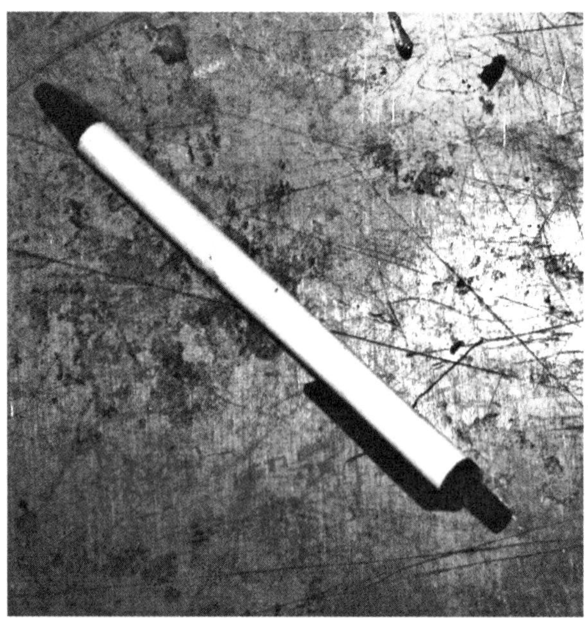

Figure 07.23: **Cheap-ass ballpoint pen.**

Figure 07.24: **Almost ready.**

onto the bare areas you masked off before finishing, then peel off the adhesive guard paper and position the reservoir onto *that*. **[Figure 07.22]**

However, not now. Wait 'til you've finished the rest of the assembly

The bubble wheel axle is a length of ¼-20 threaded rod. Use brass or galvanized steel; it's gonna be in contact with water, and rust is undesirable. We'll use a plastic bushing to shield the axle and reduce friction.

Rummage through your desk drawer and find a "budget" ballpoint pen — sorta like this one. **[Figure 07.23]**

The shaft tube from this fine writing instrument has a ¼" ID, an OD of 21/64",[4] and has been injection-moulded from a quite obviously space-age plastic.

Jolly good! A bushing!

4 21/64"? Oy . . . again with the ridiculous dimensions. Specs like this are clear evidence of alien life among us, because no *human* in a position of Industrial Design authority would ever say "Tell you what, lads; let's make the diameter of this pen 21/64", because it's the perfect ergonomic compromise dimension for comfortable penmanship."

21/64" is, in reality, *exactly* 10 G'cluurqs, a common dimension on Beta Reticuli 4.

Don't try to convince me that's a coincidence.

Drill out the axle pilot hole in the chassis to match the diameter of your ~~pen shaft~~ bushing tube, and cut it to length, extending ½" out from the front face and 5/16" out from the rear face (the extra lengths are clearance standoffs).

Drill out the pilot hole in the bubble-wheel drive pulley and tap ¼-20 threads, then measure and cut the threaded rod to length. You want to be able to thread on the pulley and wheel holder completely, with about 1/32" clearance between the faces and the end of the bushing.

Putting it all together

Great Googly Moogly!![5] The excitement is *tangible* as we enter the assembly portion of the build. Dress the wiring harness in the chassis with a few dabs of hot melt to hold the leads in the channel, and finalize the mounting of the USB port and power switch with two-part epoxy. If the drive motor sits less than firmly in the chassis, wrap it in electrical tape until it's a snug fit.

5 Yet another Frank Zappa reference: "Nanook Rubs It," from *Apostrophe* (1974), used denoting surprise and anticipation (and the impending injury of a fur trapper . . . whatever) although the term itself dates back to decadent and excitable early 50s bluesmen.

Figure 07.25: Up next: spinning, blowing, and bubble making.

Assemble the two chassis halves with 1½" #6 wood screws, countersinking the pilot holes so the screw heads lie flush with the chassis. Drill out the hole in the stacked drive pulley to 5⁄32", and cut a bushing to length from a thin drinking straw, "length" being just a hair longer than the thickness of the pulley, "thin" being 5⁄32".

Yeah, I was surprised that they were that skinny too.

Cut a spacer washer from a piece of playing card (punch the hole first, then trim to about 5⁄16" diameter), and install the stacked pulley (small pulley up) with the spacer between the pulley and the chassis using a 1" 6-32 machine screw. The pulley should rotate freely on the machine screw with minimal play.

What I'm sayin' here is "don't screw it in too tight" — capisce?

Thread the main drive pulley onto the all thread axle, using a drop of thread adhesive to prevent unscrewing. Install plastic bushing in the main drive axle hole, ensuring that the belt groove in the drive pulley lines up accurately with the groove in the smaller of the stacked pulleys. Fix the bushing in position with a drop of cyanoacrylate, then thread the bubble wheel holder onto the axle on the front of the chassis and secure it with thread adhesive.

You'll definitely want to have an assortment of rubberbands in different lengths and widths on hand to select your drivebelts from. They need to be a snug but not overtight fit over the pulleys. When you find a pair that work comfortably, slot a USB cable and test the operation. **[Figure 07.24]**

Spinning? Blowing? **[Figure 07.25]**

Bueno! *Now* you can install the Velcro, and subsequently the fluid reservoir.

Fill the reservoir with bubble juice and . . .

. . . wait for it . . .

. . . keep waiting . . .

. . . a little longer . . .

. . . okay, Don Pardo . . . hit it!

"Turn on the bubble machine!"

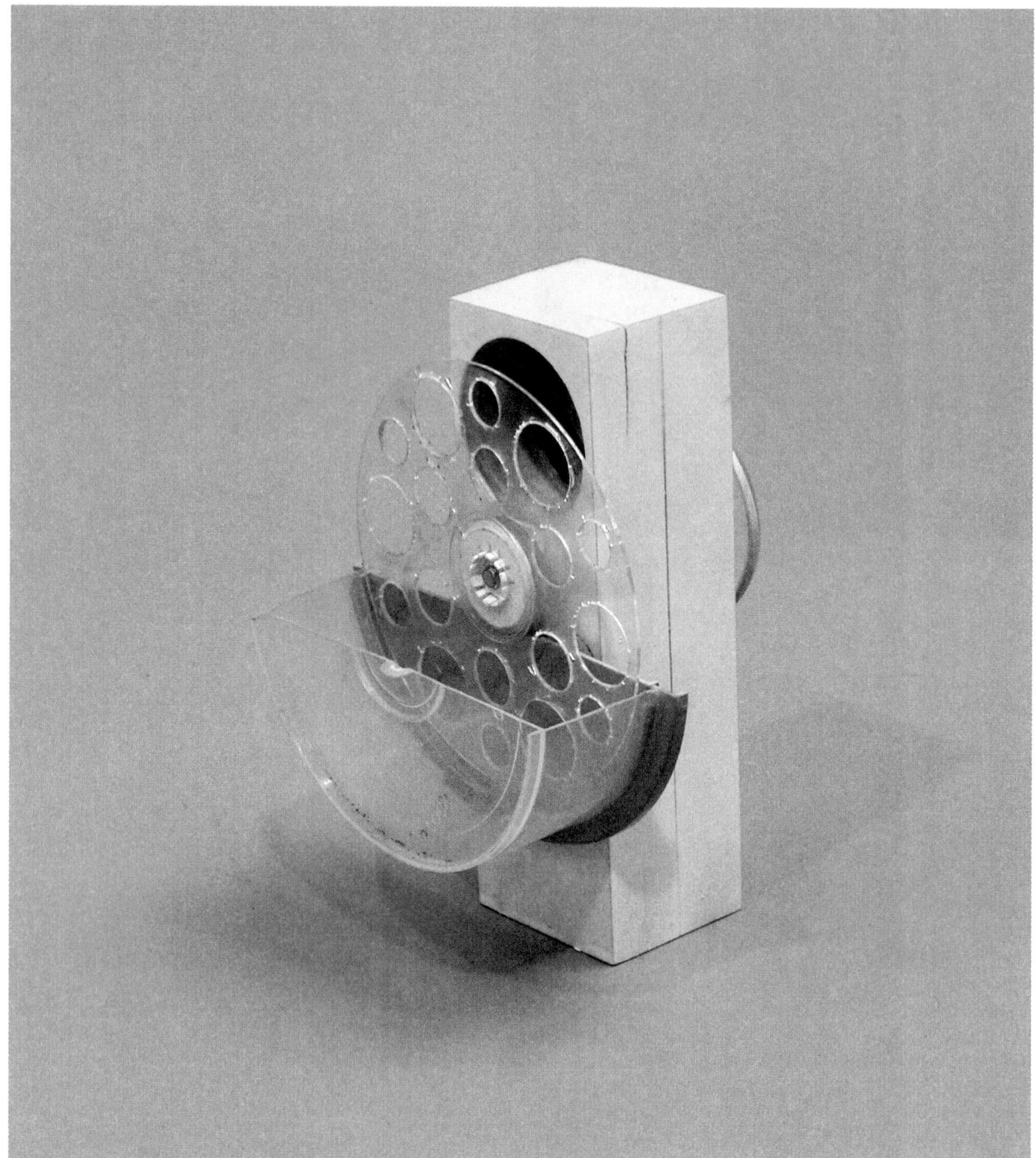

Figure 07.26: **Ready for action.**

‹ Nano-Project ›

The Drill Press Lathe

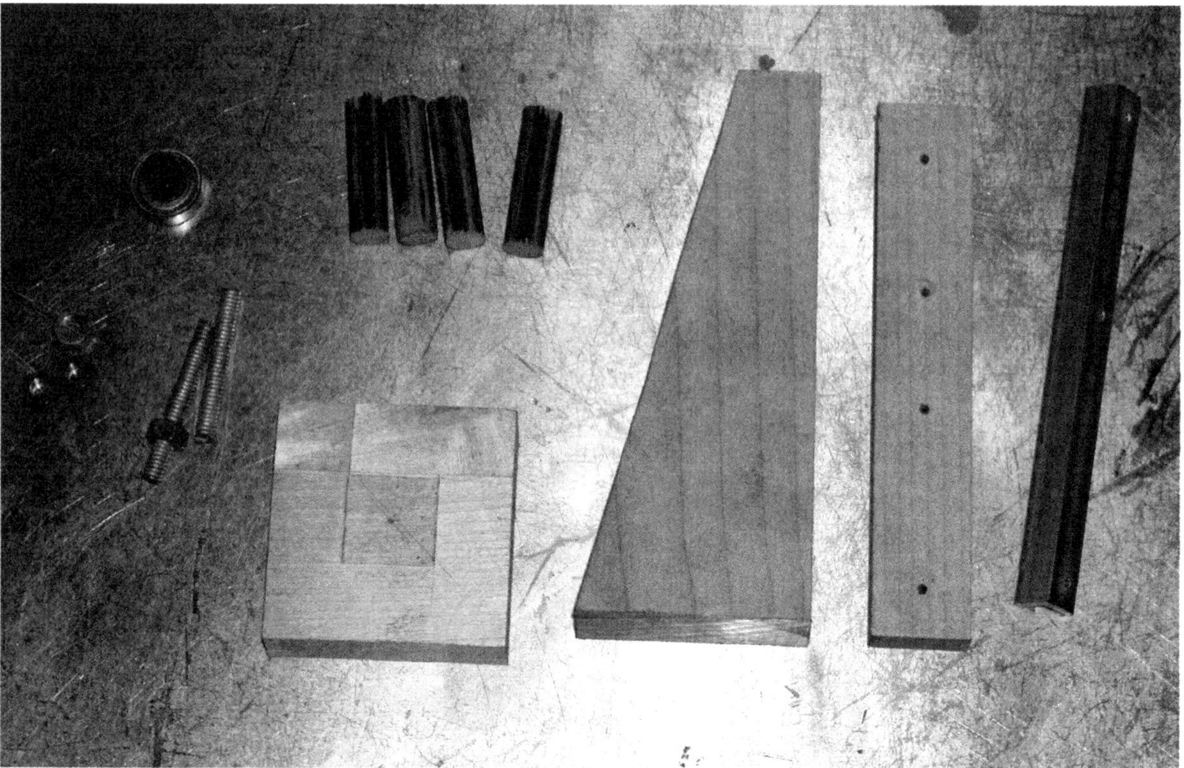

Figure N7.01: The pieces

Okay, so you won't be turning ornate cherry wood table legs with this wee beastie. For less-demanding tasks, though, this is actually quite useful.

We're going to make a vertical axis lathe attachment for your drill press, using the drill press chuck as the headstock and a kludged-together ball bearing–equipped tailstock on the drill press table. We'll bodge together a tool rest to clamp onto the press table, and you can hack flea-market screwdrivers and chisels into usable turning gouges.

Shopping? Let's get on it. You need a ball bearing race and shoulder washers sized for a ¼" shaft. **[Figure N7.01]**

Yeah, swap-meet rollerblades again.

Wasn't that simple? I'm assuming you already have a drill press. If not, you're gonna need one of those too.

Everything else you should have on hand. If you've got a few bicycle cam bolts tucked away in your (oughta be) by now overflowing box of jig components, you'll be able to figure out places to use 'em. Other stuff you'll need? Some ¼-20 threaded rod, a foot of ½" aluminum angle extrusion and a few scraps of maple 1" x 6".

Lathes are simple. Spin a chunk of wood at high RPM, use sharp metal implements of destruction to shave off the bits you don't want.

High RPMs? That'd be your drill press.

Sharp metal implements of destruction? The flea-market screwdrivers you do the "sharpen and pointy up" thing to.

There are only two flies in the ointment: holding the chunk of wood steady at both ends without having heat of friction

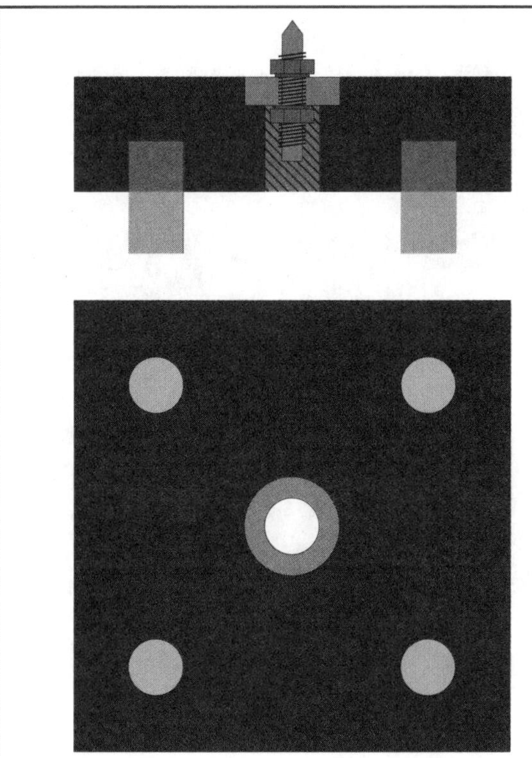

Figure N7.02: **The tailstock assembly. Locate the positioning pins on your drillpress table to center the bearing race/spindle under the chuck.**

Figure N7.03: **Drill out the bearing receiver hole to ½" to provide rotational clearance for the spindle retaining nut.**

initiate spontaneous drill press combustion, and holding the sharp-and-pointy metal in place so that it doesn't get ripped out of your hand before it gets a chance to shave the wood.

Which is where "making stuff" enters the equation.

To the workshop!

First, let's deal with friction. Cue up the "ball bearing" theme and dig out a piece of ¾" hardwood about 4" x 4". This will be the foundation for the tailstock of the lathe, and will hold the bearing race and spindle.

The bearing race I'm using is ⅞"x¼"; yours might not be, which will mean adjusting salient measurements to work with what you're using.

Find the center of your 4" x 4" x ¾" and drill a ⅞"x ¼" hole. A Forstner bit is ideal for this, due to the flat-bottomed, smooth-walled hole that it drills. The spindle that'll be contained by this cavity is in fact a length of ¼-20 threaded rod with a point ground on it, bolted through the hole in the bearing race. You'll need clearance for the retaining nut to rotate at the bottom of the hole you just drilled. Chuck a ½" bit and drill out the dead center of the hole, which will leave you with a solid 3⁄16" ledge supporting the bearing race. **[Figure N7.02, Figure N7.03]**

Once you've completed the drill out, leave the freshly drilled stock in place on the table with the clamps still positioned. Don't. Move. Anything.

Here's why. The tailstock gets clamped securely to the table of your drill press during use. Accurate vertical alignment of the tailstock with the headstock (the drill press

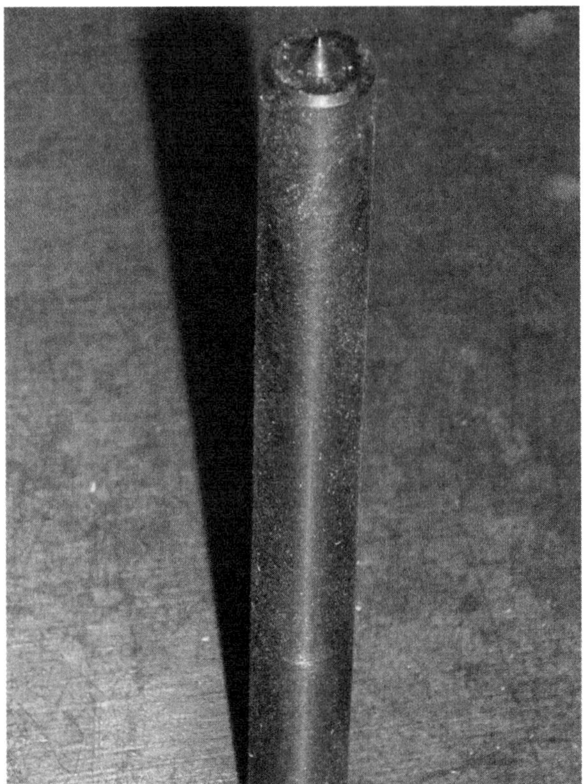

Figure N7.04: **A center punch**

Figure N7.06: **Making the spindle**

Figure N7.05: **What I'm talkin' about: the alignment pins ensure solid, accurate and (most importantly) easily repeatable positioning of the tailstock assembly on the drill press table.**

chuck, in this case) is *mightily* important for proper lathe-like operation. Attaching positioning pins that pass through the slots in your drill press table and into the bottom of the tailstock base plate is the easiest way to deal with the problem. The baseplate is currently *exactly* where you want it to be, makin' this the perfect time to install the aforementioned pins.

Which is what you should do.

The slots in my decidedly ghetto drill press table are ½" wide. I used ½" poplar doweling whacked into strategically placed holes in the base to make accurate, repeatable positioning essentially effortless. It's just a matter of positioning the holes accurately.

Lemme digress a tad: who among us has not used the term "center punch" at least once?

As in: "Yeah, he ran a red on Cambie in his El Camino and got center-punched by a runaway forklift."

Sure you have.

Guess what? If you actually *had* a real center punch right now, you could use it to position the alignment pins. Center punches come in sets, like drill bits. They're smooth-sided cylinders, accurately sized to specific hole diameters, with a punch point milled into dead center of one end. Need to mark dead center of a predrilled hole on undrilled stock? Position the two pieces of stock, stuff the right-sized center punch into the hole, whack it with a hammer, and your hole location is accurately marked and prepunched. **[Figure N7.04]**

You can't imagine how useful this can be.

The center-punch-deficient among you can get by with careful use of an appropriately sized drill bit.

Anyway, get some alignment pins in place. They can just be suitably sized scraps of hardwood glued onto the base, if you aren't feeling the love for dowelling. Once the glue has set up, the glue points can be reinforced with dowels or nails. Just make sure the fit is snug and secure and you're good to go. **[Figure N7.05]**

The spindle itself is a pointy piece of threaded rod. The point needs to be centered precisely on the long axis, which is actually easy to do: cut 2" of threaded rod, clamp it in the chuck of your drill press, and dig out your coarsest file. Turn on the drill press and spend the requisite 10 minutes letting it help you file a centered, symmetrical point. **[Figure N7.06]**

Dechuck your shiny new spindle and assemble your tailstock bearing mechanism. You'll need top and bottom nuts, the shoulder washers from the rollerblade wheel and thread adhesive to hold the whole damned thing together. Leave just the pointy bit extending from the top nut, tighten the bottom nut, trim off the excess threaded rod, and press-fit the bearing race into the hole in the tailstock base. **[Figure N7.07]**

The headstock spindle has to grip the stock firmly in some manner to make it part of the drive train and get it spinning. The spindle can be as simple as driving a wood screw vertically into the dead center of one end of the stock, then cutting the head off with a hacksaw. If you want a more traditional headstock assembly, you can grind a shallow point onto a piece of ½" threaded rod, then dremelize a raised X out of it, which you then file sharp so it bites into the wood. As shown, there is a theoretically ideal configuration for this X, the accurate replication of which with a dremel would take Forever + Day. **[Figure N7.08, Figure N7.09, Figure N7.10]**

This kind of spindle is reusable, which is an advantage over the decapitated screw method, but rates a solid 8.7 on the Pain-in-the-Ass-to-Fabricate scale. Either approach works, but I've found that having the surface of the stock in contact with the chuck jaws when the headstock spindle is chucked in place is a real good idea regardless.

Figure N7.07: The exploded spindle . . . **. . . now seen tightened, Loctited and trimmed to fit.**

Figure N7.08: The assembled spindle in position on the tailstock

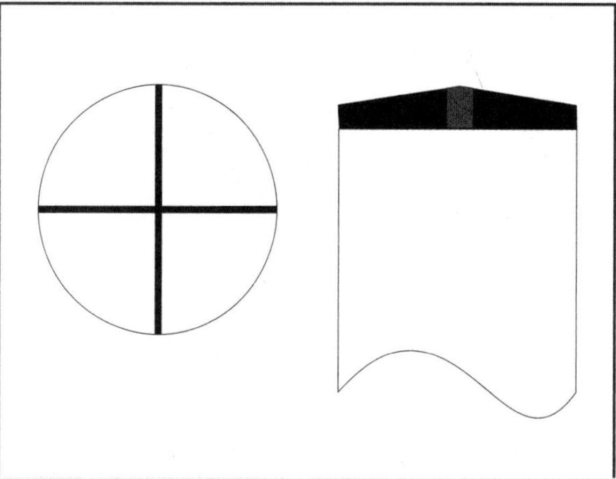

Figure N7.09: The *ideal* headstock spindle tip configuration

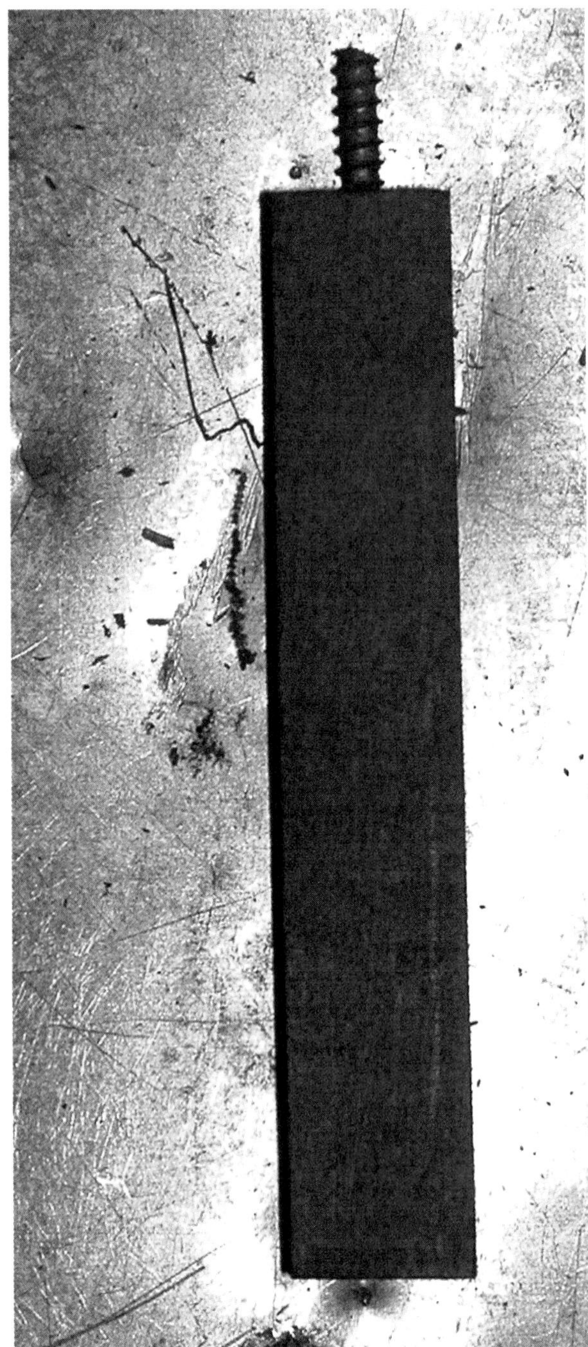

Figure N7.10: **The popular decapitated woodscrew spindle technique**

The tool rest is the last bit of kit to knock together. There are a number of ways to do it and still meet the specifications: vertical, immobile, and capable of coping with not-insubstantial shear force. I got a little fancy with mine, and designed it to straddle the tailstock assembly. This gets the tool rest closer to the work surface (providing vastly more solid tool support), and one clamp mechanism secures both the tool rest and the tailstock assembly to the table. **[Figure N7.11]**

Facing the leading edge of the tool rest with extruded aluminum prevents the shafts of the turning gouges from digging into the surface and harshin' the smooth. Whatever form factor you choose to pursue for your toolrest, it needs to clamp solidly to the press table, but still be easily positionable relative to the stock you're turning. C-clamps will do, but I'm sure you can figure out something slick with a bicycle cam bolt or two. **[Figure N7.12]**

Surprise me.

Turning gouges can be ridiculously expensive. Master wood turners (which I ain't) think nothing of dropping 400 beans on a set of eight Henry Taylors. You can go there if you want, but I'm gonna be jealous. Hacking screwdrivers into gouges lacks the glamour provided by 18-percent tungsten HSS blades and stained and lacquered hardwood handles, but also lacks the wallet-emptying price tag.

Start your gouge collection by buying every honkin' big slot screwdriver you can find at the flea market. Old and disreputable is vastly preferable to new and shiny, just from the enhanced possibility of getting a tool made from proper case hardened steel. It's kinda sad, but they really don't make cheap screwdrivers like they used to.

Complete your gouge collection through patient yet enthusiastic application of grinder, file, and whetstone (in that order) to your newly acquired pile of screwdrivers. Assuming you've been lucky enough to snag properly tempered 'drivers to begin with, don't let the gouge shaping process overheat the metal to the point of breaking the temper. The cool thing about hacking screwdrivers into gouges is that making custom profile tools is almost too easy. You can theoretically repurpose *any* chunk of steel into a gouge of some form, provided it'll hold an edge, and hold its tempering at reasonably high heat. Wood turning is friction-intensive, and the tools can get *damned* hot quickly. It's a bitch getting the initial cutting edge formed on a cold chisel, but they make brutally effective Caveman Deluxe roughing gouges. **[Figure N7.13]**

Somewhat more subtly, I've cut gouges that let me turn multiple copies of a custom-profiled shoulder washer out of UHMD with relative ease. The only potential issue is laying down an accurate 70-degree cutting edge on the metal, a task that can easily turn into a character-building experience when

Figure N7.11: **My tool rest ended up looking like this. It straddles the tailstock assembly for added positioning versatility, and mo' bettah solidity.**

Figure N7.12: **Action!**

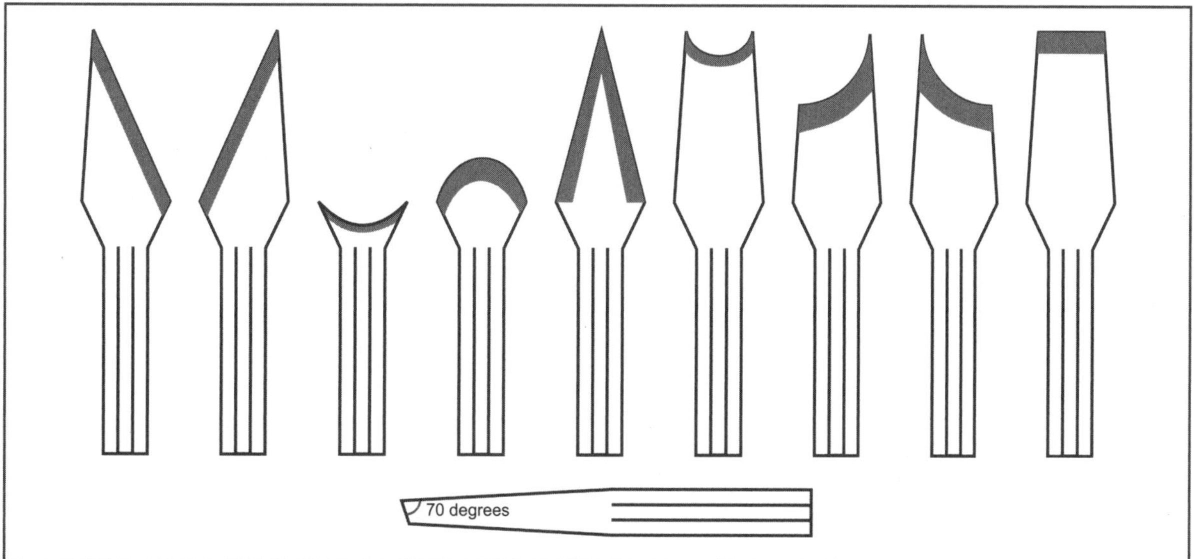

Figure N7.13: **Here are some of the gouge shapes I've used over the years.**

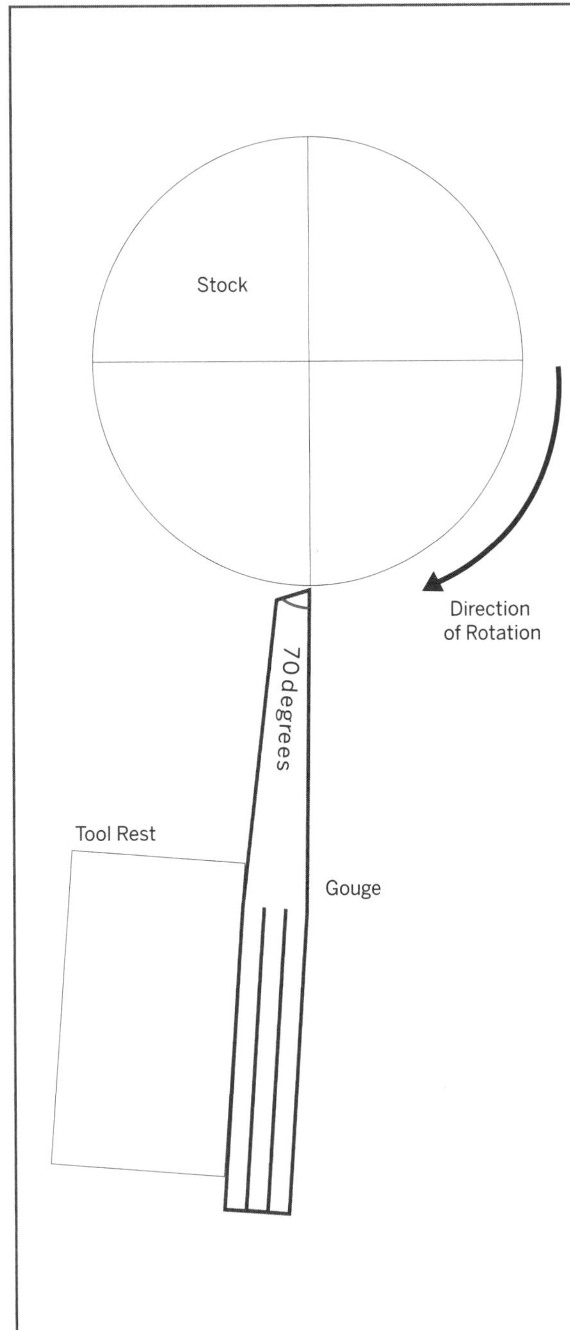

Figure N7.14: **The way of the gouge**

Figure N7.15: **Finding the center of round stock is slightly more problematic geometrically, but dead simple with a quick 'n' dirty center finder jig like this. It's an accurate right-angle trough with a 45-45-90 triangle stuck on one end with double-faced tape. Slam your stock into the trough, scribe along the 45, rotate the stock about 60 degrees, scribe again, repeat, and the intersecting lines are dead center.**

dealing with an overly finicky tool profile. Dremel? Needle files? Bench grinder? Use what's needed, but again, don't let the steel get too hot during the shaping and sharpening processes.

Assemble the components on the drill press, checking the head and tailstock alignment with the appropriate diligence. Prepare your stock by finding the center of each end and marking with a deep punch. Center and firmly seat the stock on the headstock spindle (or drive and decapitate the wood-screw that you're going to use as a spindle).

Once you get comfortable holding the gouge at the proper angle to the stock, woodturning is pretty intuitive. As with so many things, patience and common sense are the keys to success. Safety is a concern: the spinning stock provides enormous opportunity for stuff like clothing, hair, and various household

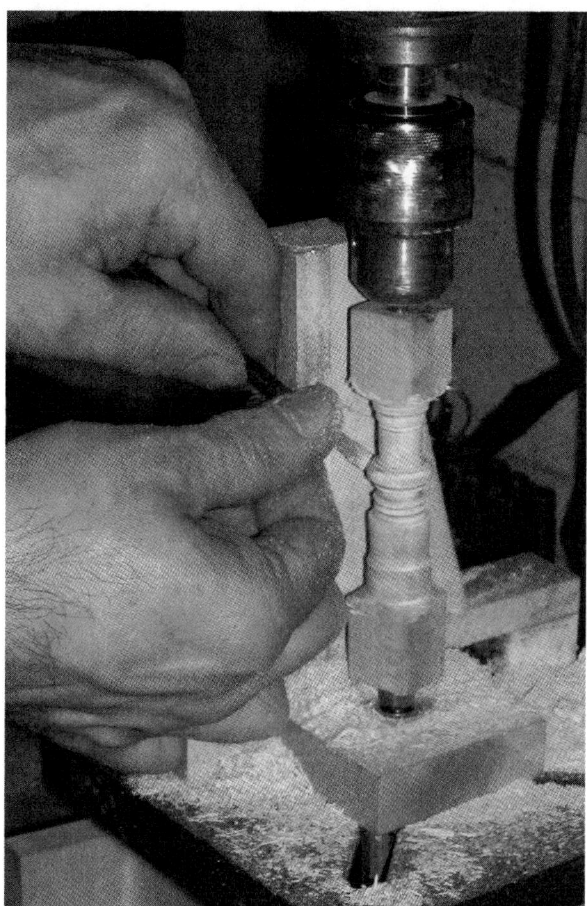

Figure N7.16: **Making something round.**

pets to be snagged and sucked into the whirling wooden vortex of doom. Do please exercise caution. **[Figure N7.14]**

Safely using a lathe starts with ensuring your stock is accurately centered on the head and tailstock spindles. The traditional way is to scribe diagonals across the end faces of your square stock: where they intersect is the center.

The biggest challenge facing a beginning wood turner is roughing square stock down to round. If you're unadventurous, you can avoid the problem altogether by using only round stock to begin with. **[Figure N7.15]**

Lotsa luck finding 2" black walnut dowelling, Bunkie.

The rest of us will start with square stock and use the biggest square-ended gouge we can lay our hands on and a low RPM to slowly remove the not-round bits from the turning stock. Once the stock is rounded, you can increase spindle speed and start getting artistic. (Google up further lathe techniques. There's no end of woodturning enthusiasts in the world, though be forewarned they'll laugh at your bodged together drill press hack. Tough rocks.) You can sand and finish right on the lathe as well, which is very handy. Get the tool rest out of the way first though, okay? **[Figure N7.16]**

The first thing you're gonna notice about turning wood (or turning anything, for that matter) is how quickly your tools go dull. Keep 'em sharp, kids: it's the Maker way.

The next thing you'll notice is how freakin' hot your tools can get if you're not paying attention.

Hot tool = broken temper = will no longer hold an edge = many new cuss words.

So pay attention. Now go make something round.

8 Liquid Len Meets DiscoHead: Ambient Orb Pwnage

The 60s. Between drug-induced memory loss and premature death among experiencers, it's becoming more of a fabled decade than a historically accurate one. People are generally agreed, though, that psychaedelia did in fact occur.

Peace, love, and groovy, man.

Liquid lighting was/is the term coined to describe the flowing ameboid colour fields that result from putting oil, water, and dye in a transparent vessel and shining a focused light through it. If you can figure out a way to induce motion in the vessel, the coloured bits swirl around all trippy-like on the wall and you can pretend you're field-testing alien psychotropic drugs.

Really, it looks better than it sounds.

The 70s. Between drug-induced memory loss and premature death among experiencers, it's becoming more of a fabled decade than a historically accurate one. People are generally agreed though that disco did in fact occur.

Shake your booty, baby.

Despite having been a near-mandatory accoutrement of any self-respecting ballroom since the 20s, mirror balls attained lasting cultural resonance during the Disco Age, when anything even remotely bright and shiny was an essential part of the Discotheque experience.

Stand by for a jarring collision of two kinda fuzzy decades, where inspirational mood lighting means something more than the pathetically understated pastel glow of an ambient orb.

It's not that difficult to fabricate a mirror-tiled sphere; making the cutting jig for the glass cutter is the hardest part. Doing a styrofoam wig stand in mirror tiles is only marginally more difficult, and has a solid 9.8 coolness factor. The sphere? Low 7s at best. Well worth the (minimal) extra effort, and you'll be able to impress friends and neighbors of all ilk with your newly acquired glass-cutting skills.

The liquid light visual is based around the fact that oil and water do not mix. Dye some water and mix it with a clear oil. Shine a focused light through the resulting mélange and project the resulting photochromic fiesta on the wall. It's a party!

The simplest way to do it is in a shallow glass cake pan placed on an overhead projector. You have to stir the mixture by hand to get the oozy flowy liquid effect happening. Where's the fun in that?

A much slicker approach (and the one we'll be pursuing) is to seal the liquid mixture in a circular frame and rotate it slowly in the focal plane of the projector that we're gonna build. We'll cannibalize a swap-meet LED flashlight as the lightsource, use lensing you quite possibly have sitting on your workbench at this very moment, and McGyver together a drive mechanism from a cassette deck, two toy cars and a few rubber bands to rotate the fluid frame. Our close personal friend Mr. Gravity will handle the "makin' stuff swirly" bit.

These are simple mechanisms doing simple things. Despite the overall level of precision needed to make this work smoothly there isn't a single *particularly* challenging aspect to the mechanics of this project.

DiscoHead and Liquid Len were conceived of as a matching pair. During the design phase, unifying the aesthetics and form factors of the enclosures for each piece was an exercise in expanding my vocabulary of cusswords until an epiphanous encounter with white PVC pipe fittings left me whackin' my head with my palm saying "duh . . . of course." Inevitably, the entire concept then took a sharply surrealist turn, encompassing gravity defying optical illusions, melted lead, and simulated ivory.

What You'll Need

There's a lot of shopping to do for these builds. Here's the essentials to start out with; we'll fill in the missing pieces with adaptive repurposing, or, as we say on my Homeworld, "wingin' it."

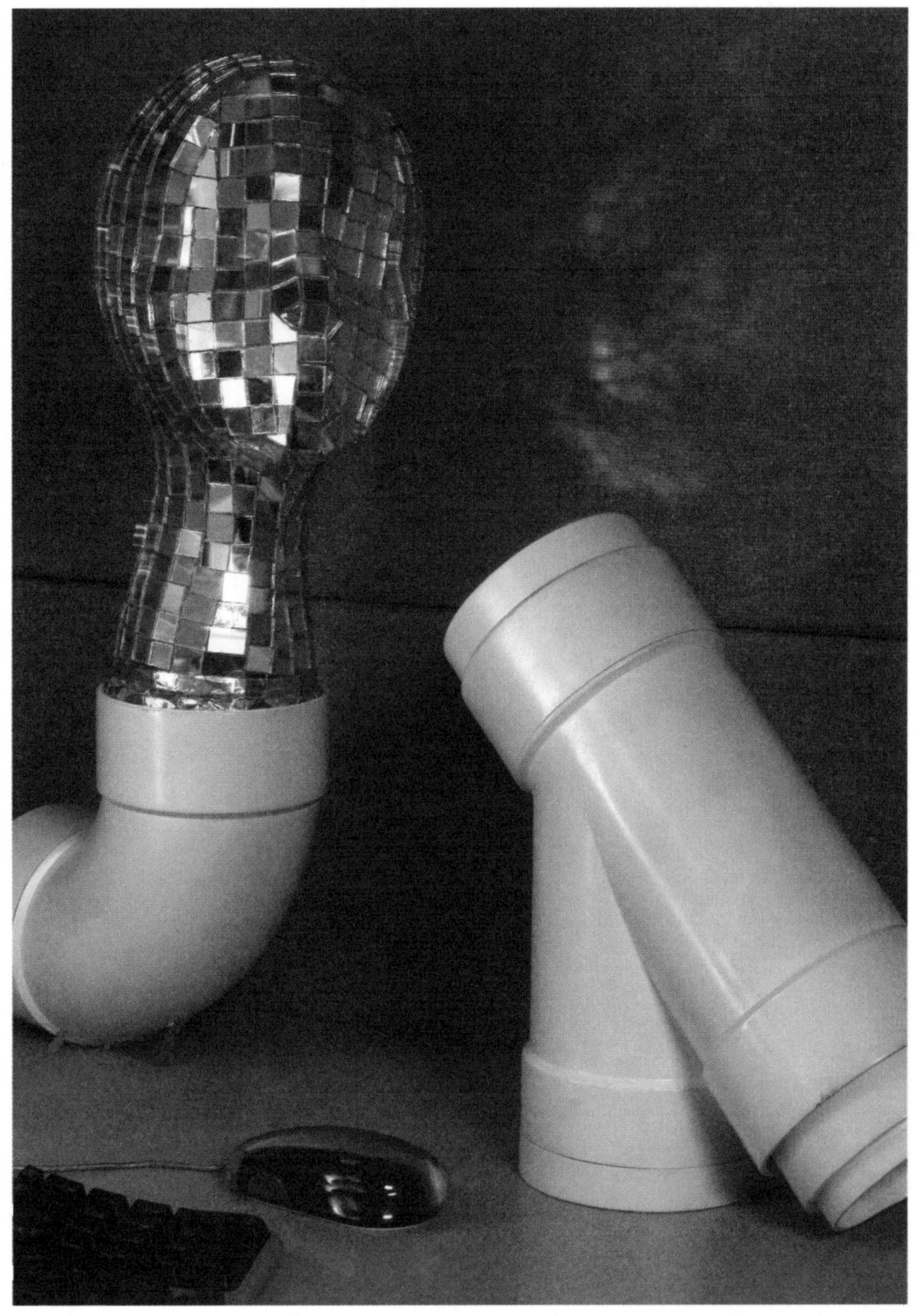

Find the following 4" white PVC pipe fittings:

- A 90-degree elbow (male-to-female)
- A 45-degree Y-joint (male-to-male-to-male, if you can find it, male-to-male-to-female if that's all they have)
- Endcaps (3)
- A 4" to 2" adaptor
- 1 foot of 2" PVC pipe
- A 2" male-to-female PVC pipe fitting.

While you're in the plumbing section, get a few other interesting-looking fittings in various diameters, like male-to-female adaptors, reduction fittings, flushout fittings: raw materials from which you can surgically harvest crucial bits and pieces to make the whole project come together.

We're improvisin' here, people. Work with me.
You also need:

- Single-pole single-throw rotary canopy switches (2)
- A barbecue rotisserie drive motor and about 6" of the accompanying spit
- A small assortment of toy cars and a thrift-shop cassette recorder
- A 2" magnifying glass
- 12" x 12" piece of ¾" medium-density fiberboard (MDF)
- 12" x 12" piece of 3⁄16" plywood
- 12" x 12" piece of ¼" plywood,
- A styrofoam wig stand (they come in various genders and poses . . . be adventurous, but know your limitations)
- 4 pounds of lead
- 6" x 6" 5⁄16" clear acrylic glass such as Plexiglas,
- 12" x 12" 3-mm mirror tiles (2)
- 2 ½" diameter 3-mm glass disks (don't panic: think "dollar-store picture frame", 2 of 'em)
- A 3v DC wall-wart
- A swap-meet two-cell 28-LED flashlight
- AC cords (male-to-bare-ends, 2 of 'em)
- Marrette connectors (a.k.a. wire nuts)
- Shrink-tubing
- Heavy mineral oil
- Food colouring or water-based dye
- A caulking gun–size tube of clear silicon glazing compound
- The uncoated clear plastic discs they put on the top and bottom of spindles of CDRs/DVDRs to make it look like you get more for your money (2)
- Some rubber bands, bits and pieces of wood for your glass cutting jig, a can of PVC pipe cement, and about a pound of modelling clay

Tool-wise, you *need* a glass cutter. They're available priced starting at about 5 bucks for a turret-wheeled traditional style. That's what I use these days, with a jar of light machine oil on the side for cutting fluid. Spend 10 more dollars and get a pencil-grip supercutter with a reservoir handle, which autofeeds cutting fluid into the headpath to make smooth, flakeless scoring a painless experience. If you have the budget, field test a pistol-grip cutter. A lot of first-time glass cutters find them easier to use, and they're definitely less strain on the wrist and fingers.

Glass workers have a couple of different specialty plier styles in their toolbox:

- *Breaking pliers* have the jaws shaped for maximum surface contact on the top jaw, and only tip contact on the bottom jaw. The shape is optimized for snapping scores cleanly without edge crushing.
- *Running pliers* have a bit of a peak in the middle of the bottom jaw, and a straight top jaw. This configuration uses the peak as a fulcrum to provide equal pressure on each side of the score, and takes the stress out of breaking out long straight cuts. Do a bit of research and you'll realize that it's *entirely* possible to modify reg'lar folks' pliers to accomplish the same things as these specialty tools. Breaking pliers are essential, but I'm personally unconvinced of the usefulness of running pliers. Your call.

DiscoHead

The DiscoHead build is straightforward, once you get over the OMYGODIMGONNACUTGLASSWHATIFITCUTSMEBACK thing that occurs to most people when initially faced with a glass cutter and a few sheets of planar silicon oxide. As my beta builders have universally expressed this trepidation, we'll postpone dealing with that issue for now and build the base unit (which will be handy for holding the head while you stick around 350 little bits of mirror onto it later).

As soon as I saw the PVC pipe elbow used in this build, I wanted to make a visual illusion out of it. Overexposure to M. C. Escher? A vaguely remembered flashback to a pharmaceutically inspired hallucination? Beats the hell out of me, but

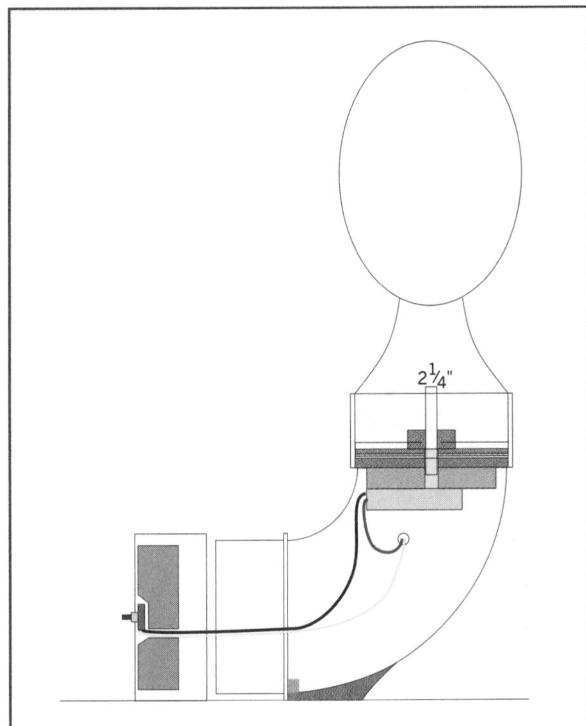

Figure 08.01: So we're building something kinda like this . . .

Figure 08.02: . . . out of these.

before I made it through the checkout at the plumbing supply shop, I had a pretty good idea of how I was going to accomplish it, and took a detour on my way home and picked up a few lead driftnet weights at Capital Salvage.

As it turns out, all it took was 3 ½ pounds of lead hidden in the front pipecap to manipulate the center of gravity to the point where three nearly invisible clear acrylic supports are all that's needed to keep it standing in a display of (apparently) gravity-defying legerdemain. Rather than rely on trial and error to determine this fun-filled fact, I actually did some math.

A small coffee can proved to be the exact diameter I needed as a mould for my lead ingot to fit properly into the endcap. Fortuitously, the same can also served as my melting crucible, peeling away cleanly from the freshly cooled lead when the process was finished. **[Figure 08.03]**

Again with the melting lead warnings: exercise proper caution. Lead melts at stovetop temperatures (327.5 degrees C, 621.5 degrees F), but it's a scandalously toxic substance that accumulates in our body tissues and causes Many Bad Things (see following info). Get a portable hotplate and do the melting outdoors, or under an industrial strength fume hood. Inspect your crucible before each melt, as burning through the bottom of your pot is always a possibility, and generally an unpleasant event. Remember, lead is eutectic, meaning it changes from solid to liquid and back in a temperature range of a fraction of a degree. It may be solid again, but that doesn't mean it's cool again.

Short-term exposure to high levels of lead can cause vomiting, diarrhea, convulsions, coma, or even death. Long-term exposure to lower lead levels can lead to less noticeable but no less serious health issues. Anaemia is common, and damage to the nervous system may cause impaired mental function. Other symptoms are appetite loss, abdominal pain, constipation, fatigue, sleeplessness, irritability, and headache. Continued excessive exposure, as in an industrial setting, can affect the kidneys.

Long-term exposure on a societal level can cause deterioration and ultimate failure of global empires.

Be careful.

Determining the right amount of lead needed to provide proper balance required not only multiplication *and* division, but some foreknowledge of the weight of a completed mirror-tiled head as well. I've been mirroring head forms for years, and have a few still in-house, so I put one on the scale, and came up with a weight of about 2 ½ pounds. Lead weighs 0.41 pounds/cubic inch, and I wanted a pound of extra weight or so onboard to ensure stability when the mass of the motor and turntable assembly was added in. The formula for cylinder volume is $\pi r^2 * H$.

Volume of lead required: 3.5/.41= 8.53 cu"
Radius of the coffee can mould= 1.875"
3.14 x 3.5 x H = 8.53
11.03 x H = 8.53
H = 8.53 / 11.03
H = .78 "

The cutouts in the counterweight for the switch assembly and wiring would (I estimated) remove about 1 cubic inch of lead from the mass, and there would be additional volume loss as the metal cooled down to room temperature and contracted from its molten volume. I rounded the value of H up to 1" to compensate for this volume loss, banged a dent into the side of my mould can at that height and melted down my weights until the molten metal level reached that point. It took about 20 minutes to melt, and 45 minutes until I could comfortably cut away the coffee can from my not-particularly-precious metal ingot.

During that time, I mounted the rotary canopy switch dead center on the PVC endcap and sanded the flashing and mould marks off of both the endcap and the elbow fitting, starting with 150-grit and working down to 600-grit over the entire exterior surface, with a final rubdown with fine steel wool.

Anyway . . .

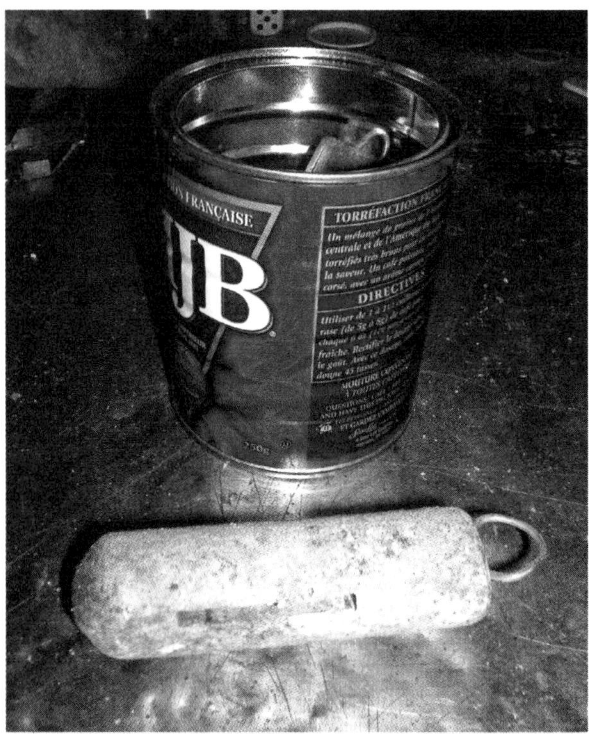

Figure 08.03: **Imagine my unrestrained glee at discovering that a coffee can was** exactly **the right diameter for use as a melting crucible/ingot mould. The grey wurst-lookin' thing? That's a lead driftnet weight.**

Assembling the Base

Once the lead was removed from the mould, I used a large-diameter drillbit and low drill speed to form the switch cavity and wire routing in the lead. Lead is messy to drill. It's ductile enough to form streamers instead of chips when drilled, and the streamers whip around the rotating drillbit like a teeny-weeny dominatrix wielding a single tail. Again, be careful.

Once the counterweight is glued in place, replacing a faulty switch is a problematic endeavour, so — just to be on the safe side — check the switch operation with a continuity tester or multimeter, then finish the endcap assembly by running the switch leads through the hole in the lead weight and using silicon glazing compound to glue the mass into place centered in the endcap. There should be clearance all around for the cap to fit into place on the elbow, so be careful of stray bits of silicon around the edges. [Figure 08.04, Figure 08.05, Figure 08.06]

The cutting list details the shape and placement of the acrylic support struts. Rough-cut them with a coping saw (if you use a power tool, use the lowest speed possible to avoid having the acrylic melt and rebond during the cut), and patiently shape them as illustrated. During the shaping process I used doublefaced tape to occasionally tack the struts into place on the elbow for testing with the endcap in position [Figure 08.07, Figure 08.08]

Remember to form the surfaces that contact the PVC to match both the horizontal and vertical radii. We're gluing these components into place, and full surface contact is essential. Forming the radii isn't difficult, if you attach your abrasive surface to the surface you're forming to and use *that* as your sanding surface. I did my initial shaping with 150-grit,

A Note on Finishing PVC

If you're gonna brave the perils of doing a ***proper*** finish on the PVC fittings, you'll need to be prepared for appalling amounts of gritty white residue from the sanding process.[1] It's messy stuff to work with, but the trick to making PVC pipe fittings look ***not*** like PVC pipe fittings is aggressive surface preparation. Sand out mould flashing and extraneous moulded-in details, then take the entire surface area down to a smooth matte finish with progressively finer sanding grits. Take your time, be thorough, and you'll be rewarded with surfaces that more closely resemble ivory or bleached bone than a product of the injection moulding process. I was honestly startled by how striking the material looks when treated this way. In a matte state, the surface picks up dirt like a magnet, and can be tough to clean; I resolved the issue with a few light coats of clear matte lacquer. If you want a finish that's **not** white, look closely at an acrylic spraypaint like Krylon's Fusion, which is specifically intended to permanently bond to plastic surfaces, reducing or eliminating the threat of chips, flakes, and scratches. Personally, I'm not in love with the "designer colour palette" offered, but some of the metallics look okay.

If you want to regain the high-gloss look you just sanded off in the name of flashing removal, an acrylic floor wax like Future Acrylic is a rightly legendary Makers' way of makin' stuff shiny. Swab on a coat with a lintless rag, hang to dry in a dust-free environment and 20 minutes later, high-gloss goodness you can retouch at need.

1 I did this build during a record breaking heatwave in Vancouver: That old adage that women "glow," men "perspire," and horses "sweat"?

Bullshit. When it's that hot, *everybody* sweats. During the surface prep of the PVC, I ended up looking like I'd been dipped in powdered sugar, with PVC dust clinging to every exposed surface of my body.

I itched for 10 days.

Wear eye protection and a dust mask, and look into those disposable paper coveralls painters use. Learn to breathe through your ears.

Figure 08.04: A switch, a chunk of lead and an end cap: front view

Figure 08.05: A switch, a chunk of lead and an end cap: behind the scenes

then stepped down to finer grades, buffing out the exposed edges of the acrylic to fully transparent with 1500-grit polishing paper and white toothpaste as a final rubbing compound. Your goal is to make the struts as transparent and invisible as possible to enhance the WTF factor of the illusion.

I tried a few different adhesives before settling on cyanoacrylate. The gelled kind was easiest to work with and gives a bond approaching the strength of a solvent-based glue without the nasty fumes and potential for surface damage. Be precise with your component placement, and level out the final footprint thoroughly to give a solid, wobble-free support structure. Buff the cloudiness out of the bottom surfaces, fit the endcap in place, and gaze in awe at your magically balancing handiwork.

The elbow I used had a handy flat spot on one side where the manufacturer's part number had been moulded. When sanded smooth, it was the ideal place for the AC cord. I undersized the hole 1⁄32" and pressure-fitted 6" of cord into the elbow, then used a cable tie around the cord inside to lock it in place. **[Figure 08.09]**

It's *damned* convenient when manufacturers seem to have accommodated repurposing of components by such considerate placement of features. I'm liking this PVC stuff more and more every minute.

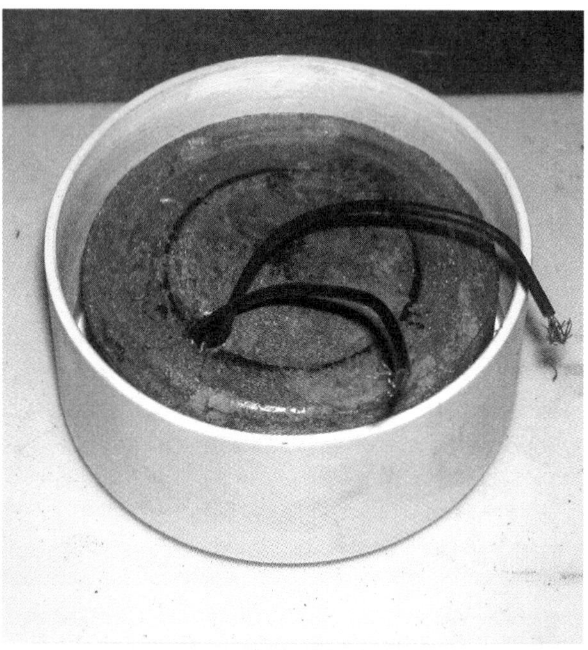

Figure 08.06: **Lead and switch in place on the end cap**

The Motor

The turntable drive mechanism relies on a barbecue rotisserie motor. They're AC-powered, typically 3–5 RPM, and are made to accomodate a 5⁄16" square bar shaft as the rotisserie spit. They're damned handy things for making stuff move, and are quite popular with prop makers and window dressers. (The waving lifelike Santa display in the window of the department store downtown? Powered by Bar-B-Q, as it were.)

Older designs usually come with a removable tin housing around a cast aluminum framework and gear mechanism, with an integrated drive motor, as spec'd by Barney Rubble. These babies are large enough to require a redesign of the mounting system if pressed into use for our purposes, and make a noise similar to a cornered feral kitchen appliance when in use.

Consider them not a first choice.

The drive I used is a fairly modern one, with a fully enclosed mechanism and a barely discernable hum when in motion. $2.50 Cdn at a swap meet, which is a better-than-average price. These things can be found in online auctions for prices ranging from 5 or 6 bucks up to a *highly* optimistic $45 or more. Thrift shops, swap meets, and the "salvaged

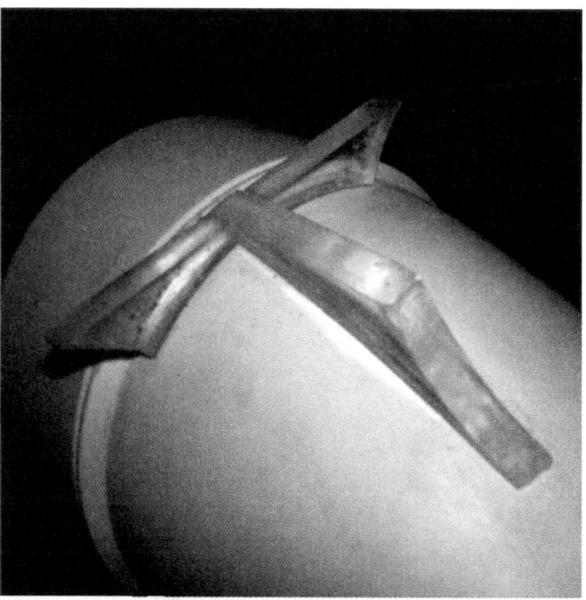

Figure 08.07: **Roger that, control . . . Stealth Support System deployed.**

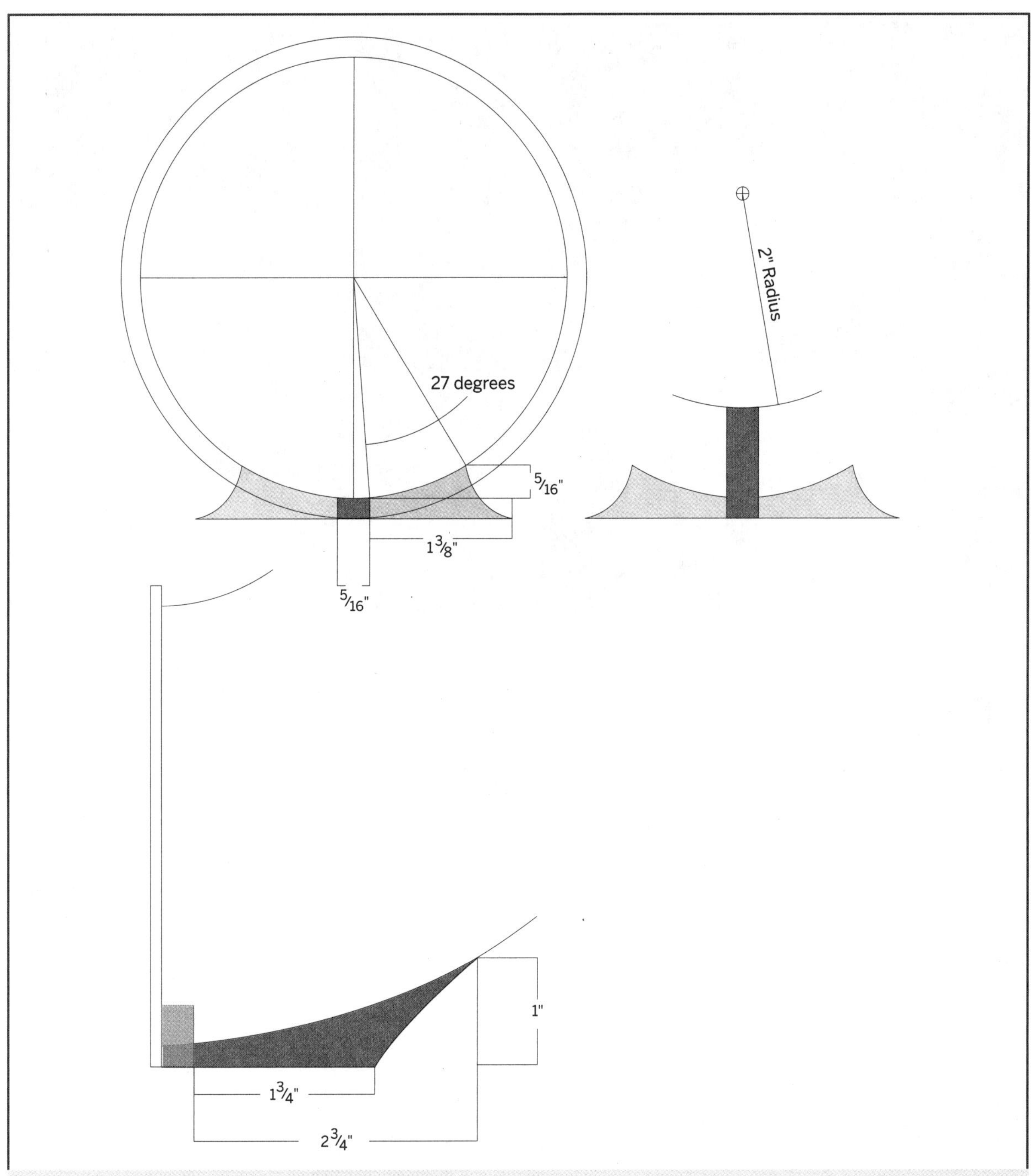

Figure 08.08: **The cunningly contrived Stealth Support System**

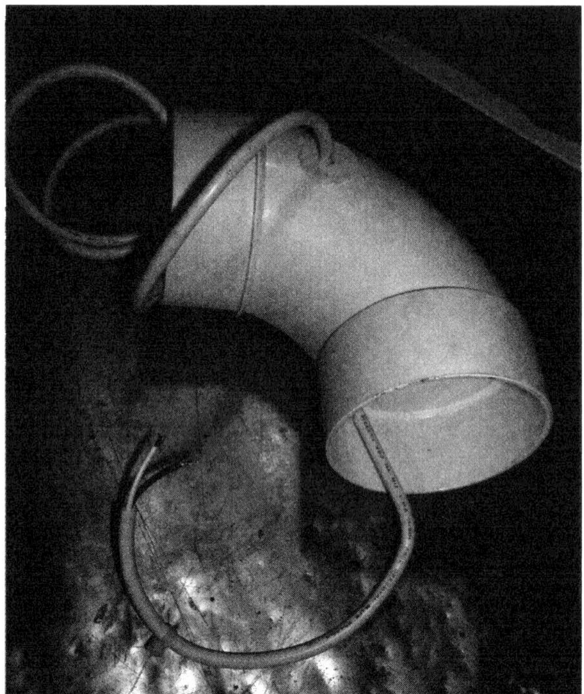

Figure 08.09: **EPS grid interface positioning, facilitated by conveniently placed mould feature**

Figure 08.10: **The humble yet versatile barbecue rotisserie motor. New School/Doesn't Sound Like an Unfortunate Blender Experiment model.**

goods" area of an enlightened scrap yard are superior sources. If you find them in quantity, buy 'em all, and grab any of the square barstock spit shafts you come across as well. You never know when you might need to animate a window display. **[Figure 08.10]**

I'm assuming your support strut fabrication went smoothly and that the top opening of the elbow is reasonably level. We're going to cram a bunch of stuff into that hole to hold the driver motor and the mirrored head.

As is so frequently the case, you need to cut some circles out of wood. Sandwich 4½" square pieces of ¼" and ⅛" plywood with double-faced tape, mark the center, and cut to 4¼" diameter. This stack should fit easily into the top hole of the elbow and rest firmly on the inset lip formed where the elbow constricts to 4" diameter. These are the main plates of the turntable assembly and the mirrored head, respectively. The shaft receiver of the motor is ⅝" diameter, so drill out the center of the ¼"-thick disk to that diameter, and sand the hole about 1/32" larger for clearance. **[Figure 08.11]**

Fitting the motor to the baseplate will take some bodging. In order to drop the drive assembly down to the point where the shaft receiver is flush with the top of the baseplate and the whole lot will actually fit into the elbow, you need to add some spacer battens to the underside of the base. **[Figure 08.12]**

These have to be custom-fitted to match the drive motor mounting configuration, and as there's at least eleventy million different styles of drive motor, you'll have to figure out the exact dimensions you need on your own. It's worth noting that while simple stand-offs *will* work, in the interests of noise suppression, maximizing the amount of material actually in contact with the case of the drive motor is a desirable thing, as it dampens the resonance of the case and helps to acoustically isolate the motor. Size and fit the battens to the drive motor, *then* glue and dowel them into position on the baseplate. **[Figure 08.13]**

Rotiserrie drives are geared for torque and built for endurance; after all, they're expected to have the wellie to spin large pieces of dead pig for hours at a time. That said, the less work they have to do, the quieter they are, so reducing fric-

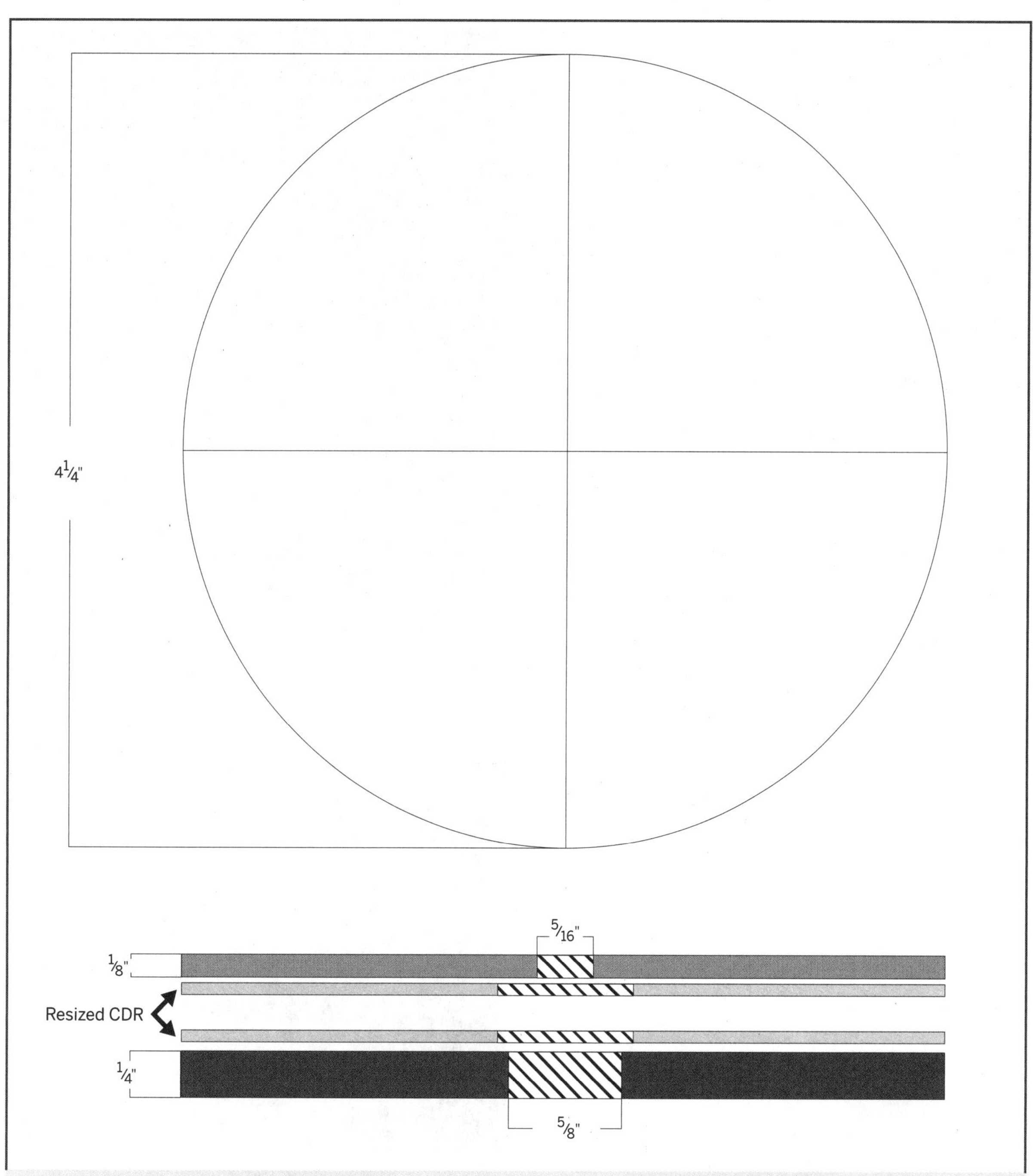

Figure 08.11: The turntable plates: various thicknesses of plywood, plus some CDR blanks

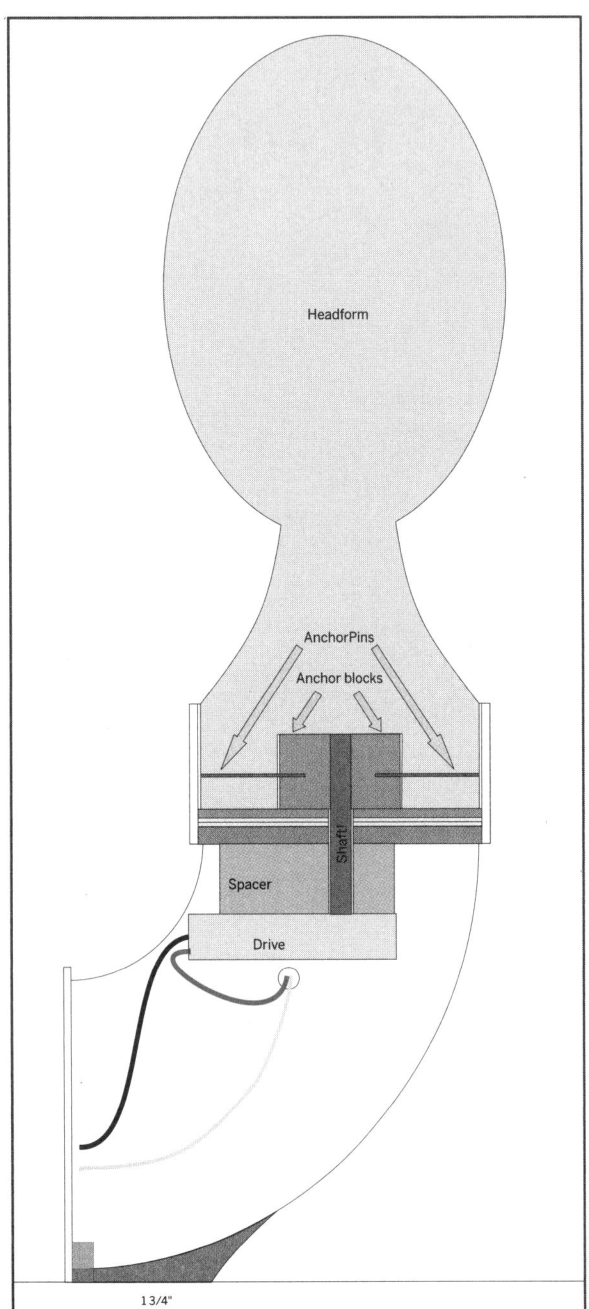

Figure 08.12: The turntable, drive motor, and head interface, in modest detail

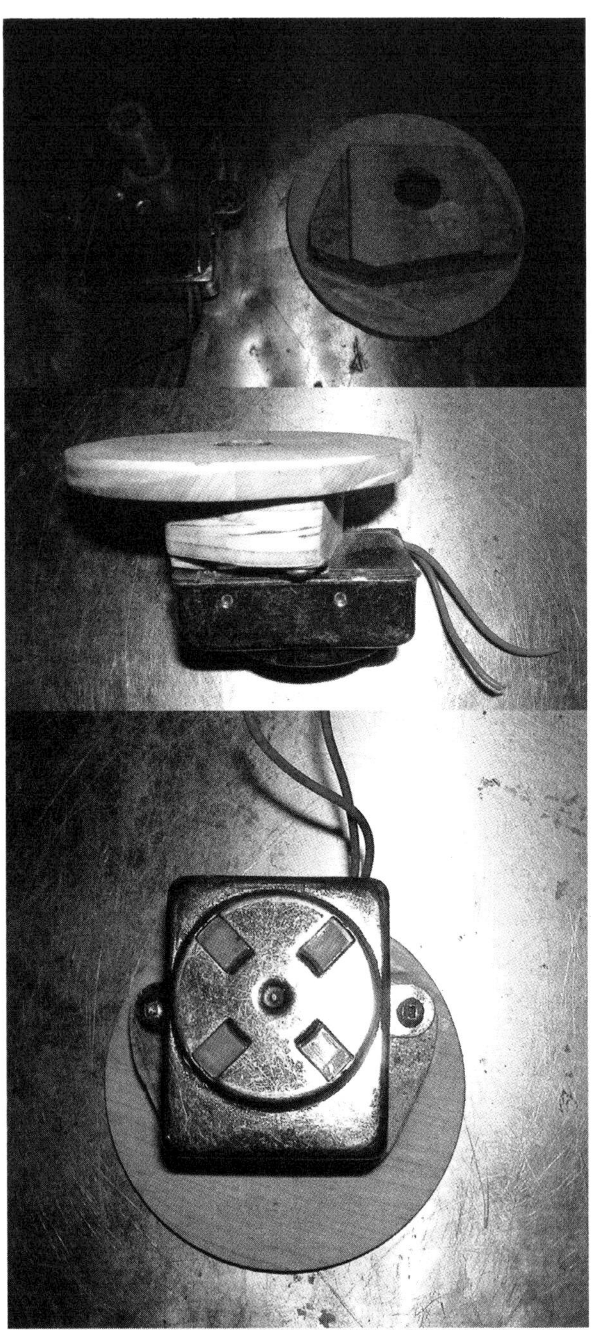

Figure 08.13: Mounting the drive motor onto the turntable baseplate. Your results will undoubtedly vary.

Figure 08.14: **The CDR blank resizing procedure**

Figure 08.15: **Almost looks like I know what I'm doing here, dunnit?**

tion in the drive train is something to work towards. Dig out a couple of the uncoated CDR blanks[1] they pad out spindles with and reduce their diameters to slightly less than the wooden disks you've already made. Dress the edges nice and smooth with 600-grit paper. These slip plates are the closest things to bearings the mechanism is going to have, so neatness counts.**[Figure 08.14]**

Fit the assembled drivemount into place, then slot a 6" length of spit shaft into the receiver. One of your resized CD blanks goes over the shaft and is stuck to the main plate of the turntable with . . . er . . . something sticky. I used a few drops of cyanoacrylate. **[Figure 08.15]**

To form the head base assembly, the foam head form must be trimmed to fit into the top opening of the elbow, while at the same time transitioning in profile from "head" to "drainpipe" in a non-ugly manner. There's not a lot of prior art for this process, so consider yourself a bit of an industrial design pioneer. I used the ⅛" x 4¼" plywood disk as a template, rough-trimmed the foam with a utility knife, then completed the forming and trued up the edge with abrasive-faced block of wood. If you though the sanding detritus from working with PVC pipe was annoying, just wait 'til you start abrading away expanded styrene. **[Figure 08.16, Figure 08.17, Figure 08.18]**

To form the square slot the shaft slots into in the head base (and to provide extra stability and strength to the mounted head), grab a piece of scrap wood and cut four blocks of 1" x ½" x ½". Sand each face with 150-grit. Mount the drive motor in position, put the second resized CD and the head base plate in position, then slot the shaft into the receiver. The four blocks are glued into position on the head baseplate as illustrated, using a square to ensure the shaft remains perpendicular to the baseplate. **[Figure 08.20]**

While the glue cures, carve a correspondingly shaped notch into the base of the foam head. It's okay if it's roomier than needed. Extra surface area for adhesion is a good thing in this case. When you're satisfied with the fit, glue the head base to the foam head with silicon glazing compound, ensuring that the head is accurately centered on the base.

While the silicon cures, wire up the drive mechanism as illustrated. When the silicon has cured, drill and set two lengths of ⅛" brass rod through the edge of the head form and into the wooden blocks that form the drive shaft receiver. This is overkill, but another "better safe than sorry" measure. Reslot the drive shaft into the mechanism, drop in the second slip plate

1 You can try using coated disks that have coastered if you want, but I've never had success in sanding them down to size without having the coating start to flake, lift, and otherwise create friction-enhancing anomalies.

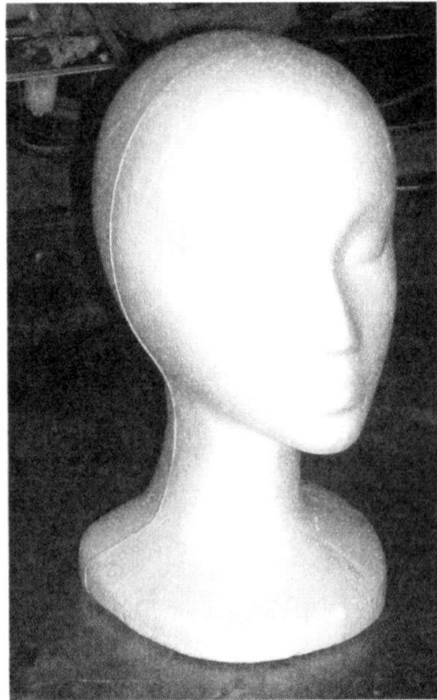

Figure 08.16: **Foam wighead**

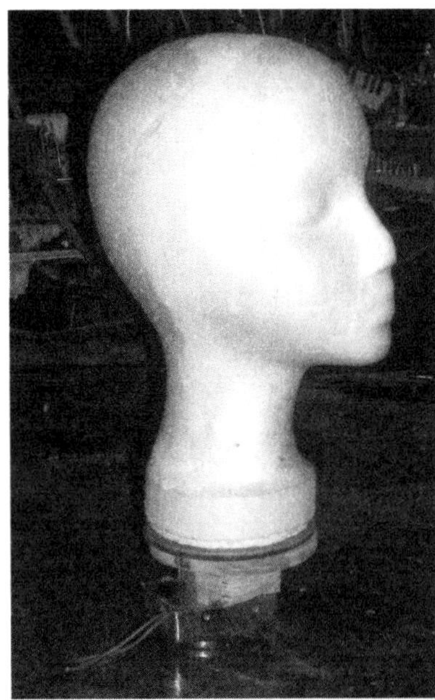

Figure 08.17: **Trimmed to fit**

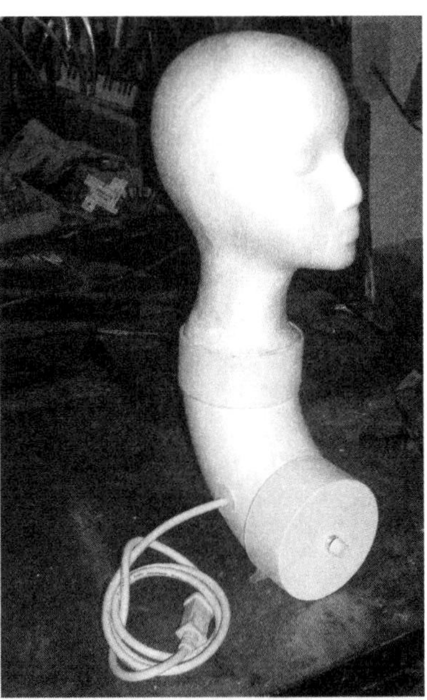

Figure 08.18: **And ready for mirror tiling**

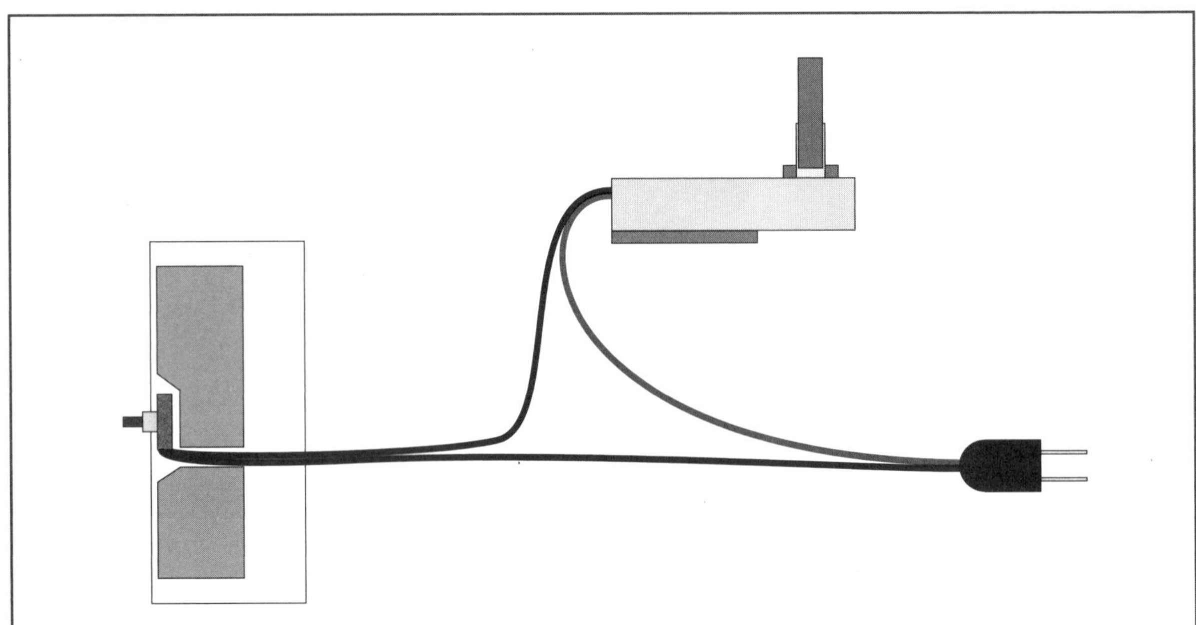

Figure 08.19: **Blah blah blah, blah blah, wiring diagram, yadda yadda, blah blah blah. Ya think it's easy coming up with a fresh and sparklingly witty caption every time a wiring diagram rears its ugly head? Think again.**

Figure 08.20: **Wood blocks form the square slot for the drive shaft *and* reinforce the baseplate–wig head attachment. All this multitasking competence from small bits of scrapwood is damned inspirational.**

(I left this one free-floating rather than attaching it to the head base), line up the square hole in the base of the head with the shaft and slide the head into position onto the turntable. Plug in the drive motor, and turn it on. Thrill to the gravity-defying rotational wonder that you have just fabricated, then enjoy a celebratory cocktail. Tomorrow, you cut glass. **[Figure 08.19]**

Cutting the Mirror Tiles: They Will Not Cut You Back![2]

The mirror tile cutting jig is a dead simple fabrication. What we're building has to hold the sheet of glass firmly at right angles to a straight edge, and the straight edge must provide a broad smooth surface for the side of the glass cutter to traverse. **[Figure 08.21]**

Other than that, the dimensions are yours to decide. You can use medium-density fiberboard (MDF) for most of the build. If you have MDF with plastic laminate on hand, use it for the base, bottom edge guide, and outside edge of the straight edge. Your glass is (should be) 3 mm thick, which is just under ⅛". The underside of the straight edge should *just* clear the surface of the glass, which may require some judicious sanding to get right.

Cutting glass is simple. It's "score and snap." Very little pressure is needed to get the wheel to successfully form the score. Less than five pounds of pressure will do the job. The secret is to apply even pressure, move the cutter smoothly, and keep the wheel going in a straight line. The extended thickness of the straight edge on the jig is there to ensure that you keep the broadside edge of the cutter head properly aligned. **[Figure 08.22, Figure 08.23]**

Cutting fluid is *important*. Some guys swear by motor oil, other folks think power steering fluid is the business. I like a lighter-grade machine oil, like the stuff they use on sewing machines. If you use a dry cutter, the scoring process raises chips and flakes like crazy, which can jam the cutting wheel rotation, cause skipping, or make the score imprecise enough to break away from the line you're cutting. Dipping the cutter head into a beaker of cutting fluid before each score eliminates the chip/flake situation, leaving you free to concentrate on making light, precise scores. Using a reservoired cutter that autofeeds the oil makes it even *easier*.

Breaking out the scores is . . . well . . . a snap. Straight lines, particularly so. There's nothing to worry about. You're not gonna end up lacerated by glistening shards of silica, although I *do* recommend safety glasses to ward off flying bits of extreme pain hitting your peepers. Grab the pane

2 Statement implies no liability or responsibility on behalf of the author in the event of misuse, misadventure, act of deity, or mirror tiles suddenly pulling out a shiv and shanking your sorry ass like a fatted pig. Void in Delaware, North Dakota, Quebec, and/or where otherwise prohibited by law and/or municipal by-law and/or Executive Privilege/ Signing Statement.

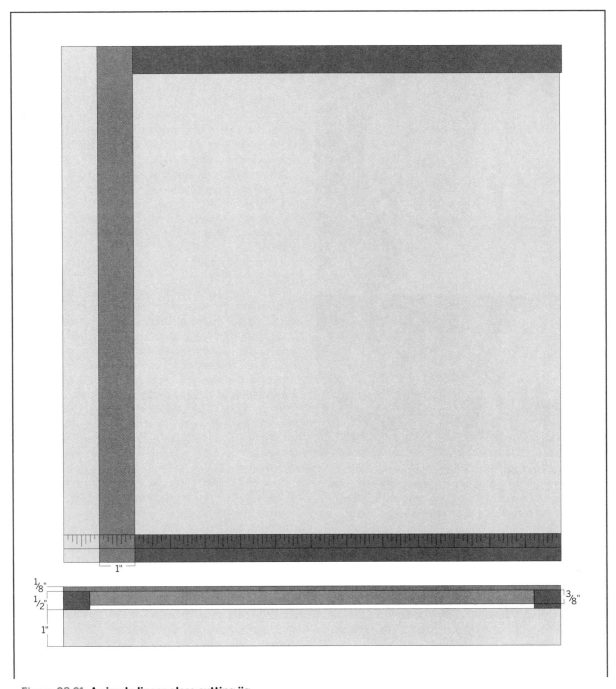

Figure 08.21: A simple linear glass cutting jig

Figure 08.22: **Mirror positioned in jig, ready for enthusiastic application of glass cutter (pictured)**

you've just scored at the edge, thumbs up on either side of the score, with the first knuckles of your index fingers touching on the underside. Twist your wrists as if you're trying to roll the knuckles of your middle fingers into contact, while gently pulling your hands apart. *Click!* There's your break. Practice for a while on some plain glass scrap before starting the mirror cutting; you'll get a feel for the gig in no time. I'm giving you enough information to do the cuts for this project. If the process appeals to you, there's a wealth of information available to expand your knowledge and skillset exponentially.

It's a good idea to keep a soft brush and dustpan on hand when cutting glass to keep the working environment clear of shard/chip/flakes. Besides wreaking havoc with your scoring, shards can foul your jig surface, making the pane hard to line up properly and messing up your meticulously planned right angles.

Score in one continuous motion. Don't "sketch" your way down the line. There's a certain knack to running the cutter

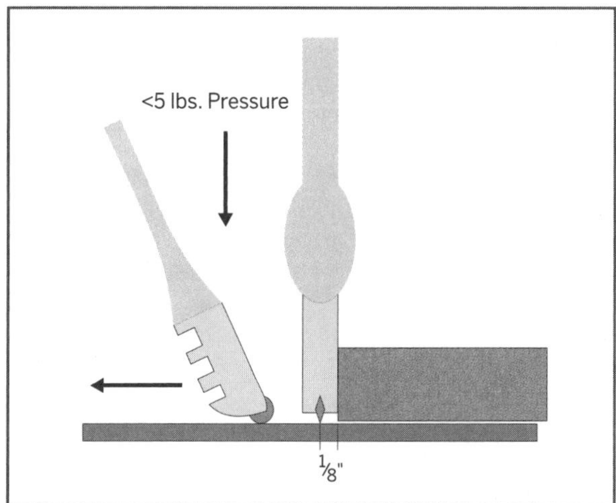

Figure 08.23: **The Way of the Glasscutter**

Figure 08.24: A small dog bowl of mirror tiles

Figure 08.25: The head deflashed and quartered

head off the edge of the pane without chipping; you may want to add a ledge to your jig the same thickness as the glass you're cutting to give the wheel somewhere to go other than down when you hit the edge of the pane.

We're cutting ½" square tiles: use breaking pliers to grab the narrow side of the score if you have to. In a pinch you can use regular blunt-nosed pliers with the jaws padded with a single layer of electrical tape. You don't need to squeeze hard — just enough to keep the jaws closed as you make the break.

Use a whetstone to sand off sharp bits and take the edge off of edges, if you take my meaning. Apply the abrasive *along* the edge: sanding from edge to edge is gonna lift chips from both the facing *and* silvered side of the mirror. This is undesirable.

Warm glass is easier to work with. Not hot: warm. Use a hot-water bottle to warm up the pane every 10 minutes or so. You'll notice the difference.

A fine-point Sharpie is the ideal writing implement for marking glass prior to scoring.

You can mark ruler lines on the scoring side of the jig base, but remember that all measurements must be offset ⅛" (half the thickness of the cutter head) from the straight edge to allow for the position of the wheel in the middle of the head. Score and break one strip at a time. Once your strips are broken out, you can go back and score each strip at ½" intervals, then break out your tiles in one extended snap-happy orgy of breakage. Be precise with your measurement, but not obsessively so. We're tiling an irregularly shaped surface, and you'll find that irregularly sized pieces are essential to making tight fits.

Cut about 1 ½ square feet of mirror into ½" square tiles. You'll need to keep three or four unscored ½" strips on hand to use when cutting the *really* irregular tiles that you'll need to fill in the gaps that square tiles can't cover. **[Figure 08.24]**

When you're finished cutting, wash your tiles gently in warm water, ammonia, and the dishwashing liquid of your choice to remove any traces of cutting fluid. Rinse thoroughly, then pat them dry with massive amounts of paper towelling.

Mirroring the Head

Start the tiling process by sanding the flashing and mould marks off the form with 220-grit paper.

Divide the form into 4 quarters as illustrated, and lay your first lines of tiles down these quadrant lines. **[Figure 08.25, Figure 08.26]**

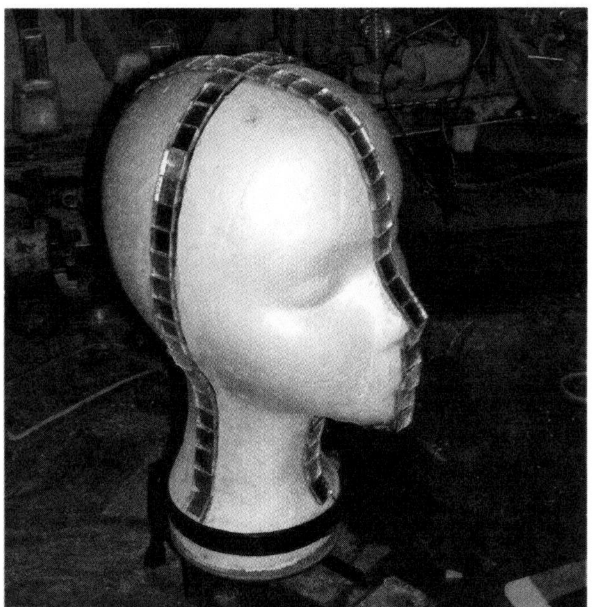

Figure 08.26: **The first lines of tiles laid**

Use a spreader cut from the lid of a resealable food container[3] to spread the glazing compound about ⅛" thick down the line, 6" at a time. [Figure 08.27]

Starting at the top of the head, set the tiles, pressing them firmly into the silicon. Continue the line to the base, taking care that the bottom tile of each row lines up neatly with the bottom tile of adjacent rows to form a smooth mirror termination line You're not going to be able to maintain an orderly "rows and columns" layout through out the process, but the vertical lines should be *fairly* regular.

The silicon sets up enough to lose its tack quite quickly. During a heatwave (such as when I did this build), you have about five minutes working time with exposed compound before it becomes unusable, so avoid the urge to goop up the whole head and get overly ambitious. Try to keep smears and spillage to a minimum to reduce your cleanup time after the job is done.

3 What I'm saying here is that the spreader should be flexible, but still stiff enough to move around a fairly firm gel like glazing compound. The trowels that flooring tilesetters use have shallow notches cut into the blade to leave alternating rows of goop/no goop, which gives excess adhesive somewhere to go other than "out through the seams and smeared all over the place." These guys know their stuff: emulate them.

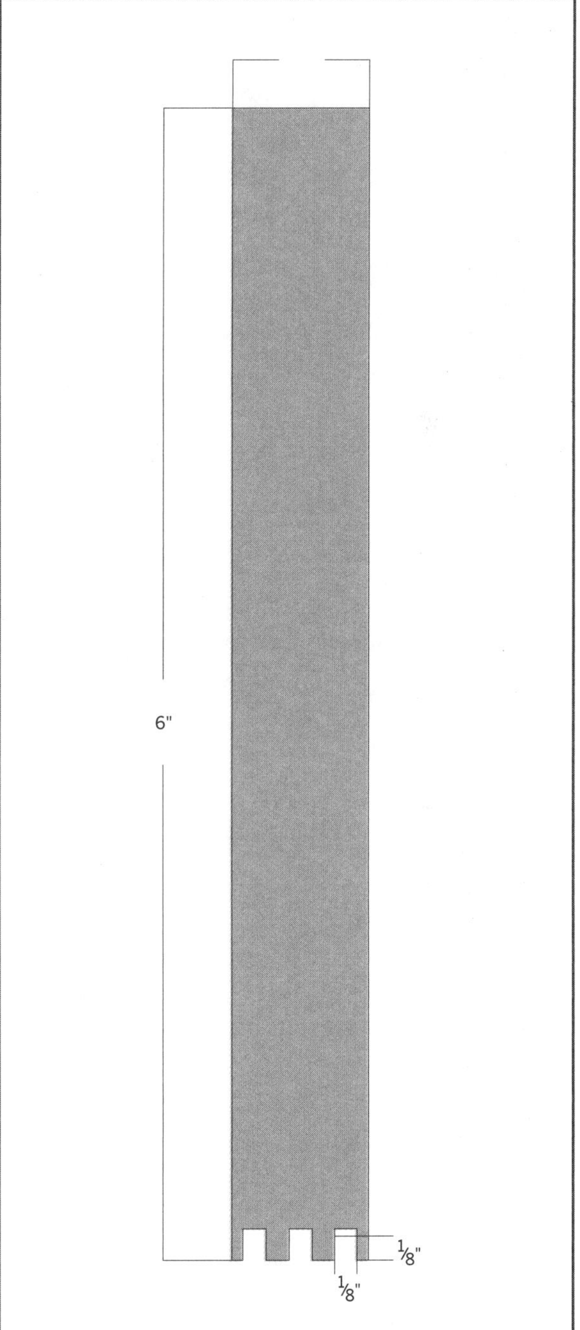

Figure 08.27: **Time well spent: the home-made spreader**

Figure 08.28: **One quadrant at a time. They will** not **all be the same.**

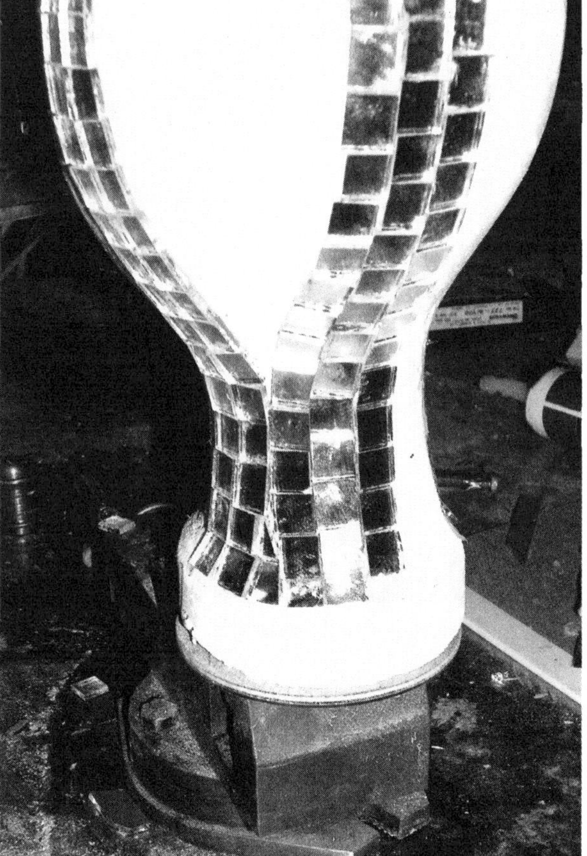

Figure 08.29: **"Honour thy error as a hidden intention":[4] miscut tiles are essential for accurately covering the variable topography of the foam head.**

Your goal is close contact between tiles. You're not looking for evenly spaced grout lines betwen mirror segments, even though they may *want* to occur due to the presence of partially cured silicon flowing out from under the tiles as they're set. Keep a utility knife handy to clean up any overflow traces between tile rows.

Fill in the form one quadrant at a time; you'll find yourself hunting through your supply of tiles looking for the slightly irregularly sized and shaped ones needed to match the contours of the surface. Go back to the cutting jig and score some modestly tapered strips for dealing with the expanding or reducing radii presented by the shape of the form. There's no *magic* tile pattern, although I'm sure the 3D-minded among you could easily fire up your favorite CAD sofware and model a comprehesive tile map and cutting list with relative ease.

I am insanely jealous of those of you who possess these skills. **[Figure 08.28, Figure 08,29]**

This way is more fun. I'd rather have you learn the tricks of the process than me have to teach you, or someone else draw you a map. In this build, I did a slightly different fill-in pattern in each quadrant to illustrate the different methods of dealing with the contours of the form. By the end of the process, you'll

4 Again with the "Oblique Strategies": from the 1975 first edition of same. To me, this succinct paraphrasing of the jazz musician's classic axiom, "If you play it once, it's a mistake . . . if you play it twice, it's on purpose," is Schmidt and Enos's most profound truth.

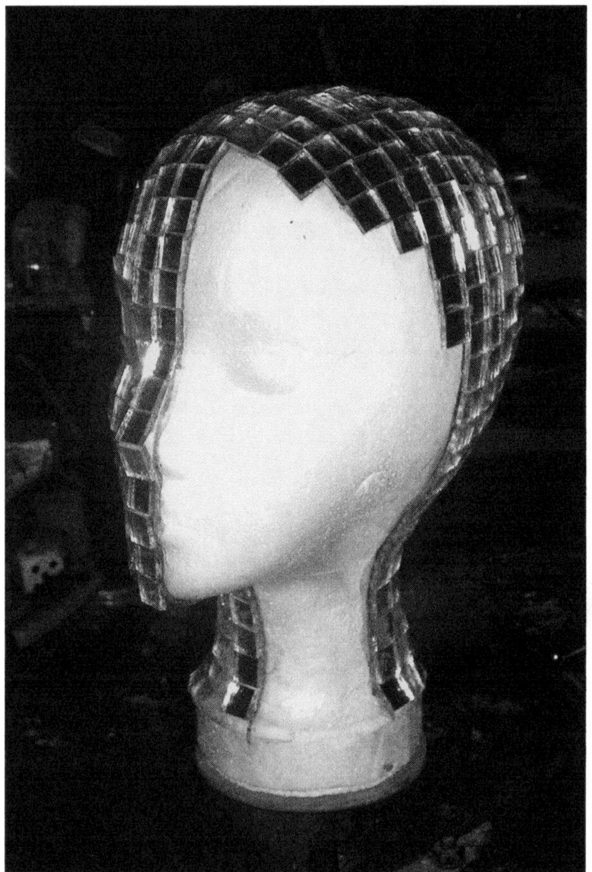

Figure 08.30: As completion approaches, the importance of your prior accuracy becomes increasingly noticeable.

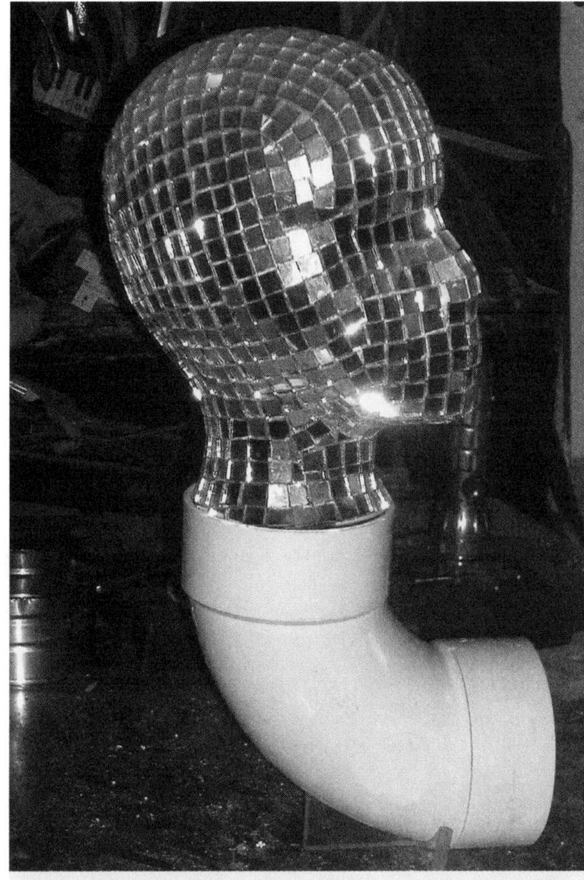

Figure 08.31: As previously noted: coolness factor in the high 9s.

be adept at recognizing impending fill-in patterns and cutting the small tiles needed to execute them. **[Figure 08.30]**

Having a array of shapes, sizes, and angles of reflection on the head results in a pretty chaotic dispersal pattern during use, which is a nice change from the stately, ordered procession of little bright squares ya get from a traditional mirror ball. You can redo sections that you screw up by peeling the silicon from the form and mirror tiles within an hour or so of placement, and troublesome contours can be levelled out a bit with strategically placed larger blobs of glazing compound. Take regular breaks (every 50 tiles or so) to let the freshly glued pieces set up a bit for solidity. Eight hours of steady work finishes the job, but this is a project that's best suited for a weekend. Build the jig and cut the tiles on Friday evening, tile two quadrants each on Saturday and Sunday, and clean the head when you get in from work on Monday.

When it's time to clean up the finished mirror head, the first step is using a utility knife to trim off the inevitable big chunks of goop you missed during the excitement. Surface smears can be handled a few different ways, but I've found that the most efficient method is with a brass wire brush in a dremel. Brass has a Mohs[5] number in the mid 4s, depending

5 The Mohs scale of mineral hardness was devised by mineralogist Frederich Mohs in 1812 . It's a comparative rather than linear scale, based on 10 common minerals ranging from Talc (Mohs number 1) to Diamond (Mohs number 10). It's a useful reference for determining what will happen when two different materials come in contact with each other energetically.

on the alloy, with standard domestic glass and mirror being somewhat harder by comparison with a Mohs between 5 and 6. The glass, being harder than the brass, will resist scratching by the bristles of the brush *within reason* (this means "don't get overzealous"). Low RPMs and light pressure, with the occasional wipedown of methyl hydrate, will do a pretty good job of getting rid of residual silicon.

Avoid using mineral-based solvents, which will dissolve the stryofoam form almost instantaneously. It's a neat effect to see, but mostly counterproductive to the goal of having a completed project that doesn't require a soup spoon to pick up.

When the leftover adhesive has been exorcised, give the mirroring a gentle polish with window cleaner, and dry it with a lint-free cloth.

Now that it's clean, install the head back onto the turntable base, point a spotlight at it (it's gonna have to do . . . we're not building the light projector until tomorrow), pull up the *Saturday Night Fever* soundtrack on your media center, and get down wif your own bad self. **[Figure 08.31]**

Pretty simple, huh?

Now, who's gonna volunteer to mirror tile an entire mannequin?

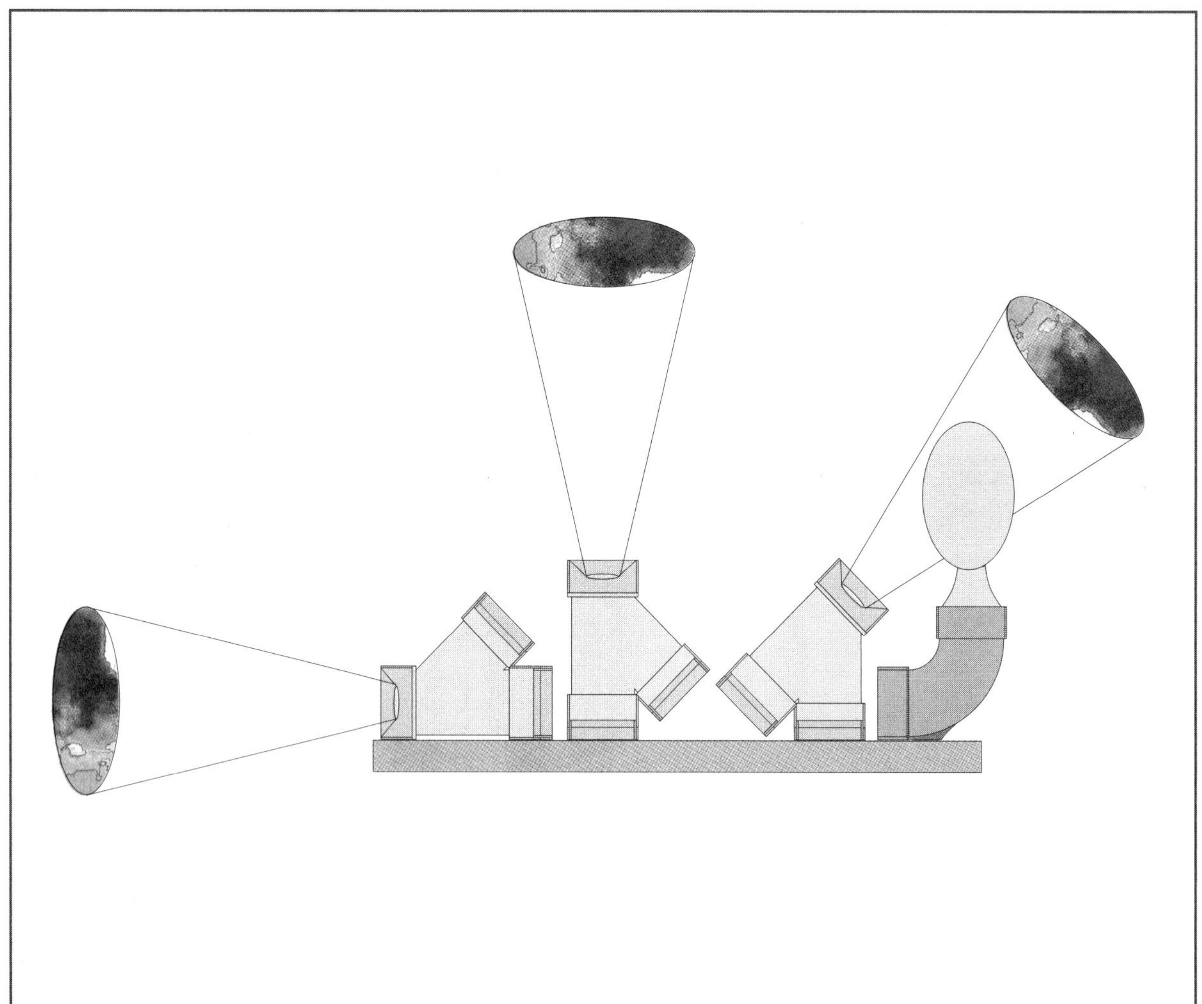

Figure 08.32: 1 PVC Y connector, 0 extra components, 3 useful projection angles

Liquid Len: Plumbing the Depths of Industrial Design

Spend any amount of time doing industrial design and styling, and you learn just how much work is involved in making "simple" work, particularly when you're trying to execute some kinda high-concept unified theme across a number of different pieces. Having committed myself to the whole "white PVC drainpipe" meme doing the DiscoHead, figuring out how to lever the functionality needed by the liquid light projector into the same family of form factors was ponderworthy.

The projector case needed to meet certain performance requirements while still looking like essentially unmodified plumbing components: it had to accomodate a projector mechanism consisting of a power supply, light source, slide holder with low-RPM motor drive (to turn the liquid slide) and lensing, as well as accomodating adjustable focus, user access to a removable liquid-colour slide, and some kind of pan/tilt motion for aiming it in different directions.

After far too much time spent sweating the details of an E-Z-Bild concealable pan/tilt mechanism, I realized that a 4"-diameter 45-degree Y connector could provide a decent range of projection angles. With something closely resembling a plan in mind, I hit the local bigbox home center to forage for fittings. **[Figure 08.32]**

I say again: it's *damned* convenient when manufacturers seem to have accommodated repurposing of components.

Within five minutes of arriving at the formidably broad selection of PVC pipe fittings on display, I had my case design finalized. It was actually kinda disconcerting: I kept thinking to myself, "Huh? That's it? This is supposed to be more difficult."

Cripes, the fittings even *looked* like the purpose-built components they were meant to replace: The 4" to 2" adaptor I grabbed to hold the lens element even had that nicely bevelled bezel effect found on a lot of *real* lens housings. **[Figure 08.33]**

It was a magical moment, the memory of which still brings a small tear of joy to my eye.

The only minor fly in the ointment was the 45 degree Y fitting itself, which I could only find with the placement of the male and female connections in the wrong locations and quantities. Given the range of fittings I had to choose from, I could easily have missed what I was looking for, or it could have been just a matter of them not having room to display all the variations available.

I picked up a few useful looking adaptors, T and Y fittings to add to my ever-growing bucket of miscellaneous pipes 'n' toobs, including 2" and 3" (both ID and OD) fittings for potential use in the optical path, and I was done. **[Figure 08.34]**

Figure 08.33: **The ultimate lens mount tribute act: you'd swear it was a real Nikkor. Except for it being, like, white. And plastic. And 4" in diameter.**

Figure 08.34: **Just in case: a workably varied selection of components**

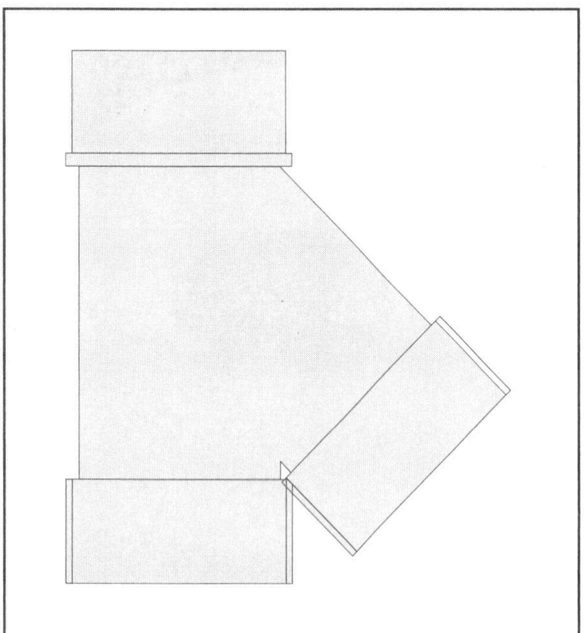

Figure 08.35: **The preoperative fitting**

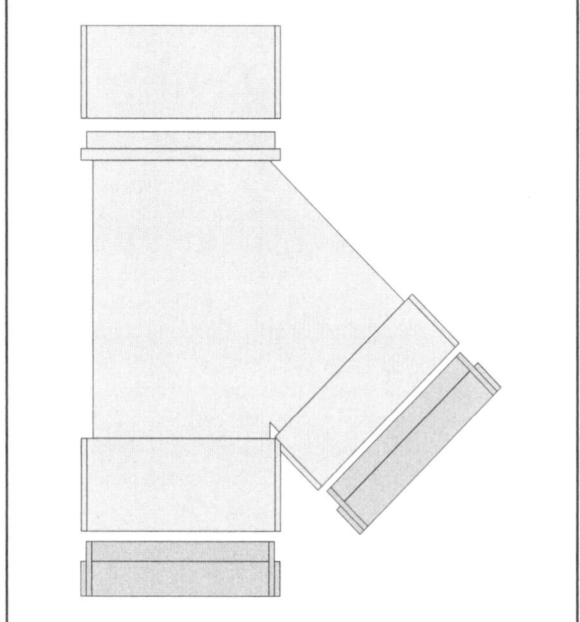

Figure 08.36: **Post-gender reassignment**

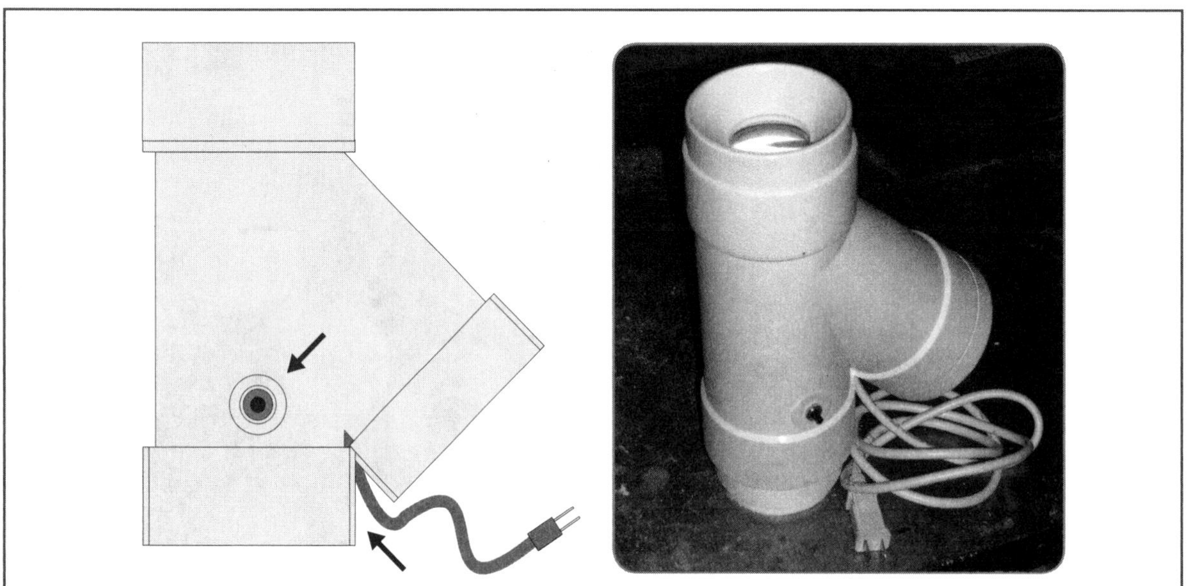

Figure 08.37: **Where the switch and cord go. (Well, duh.)**

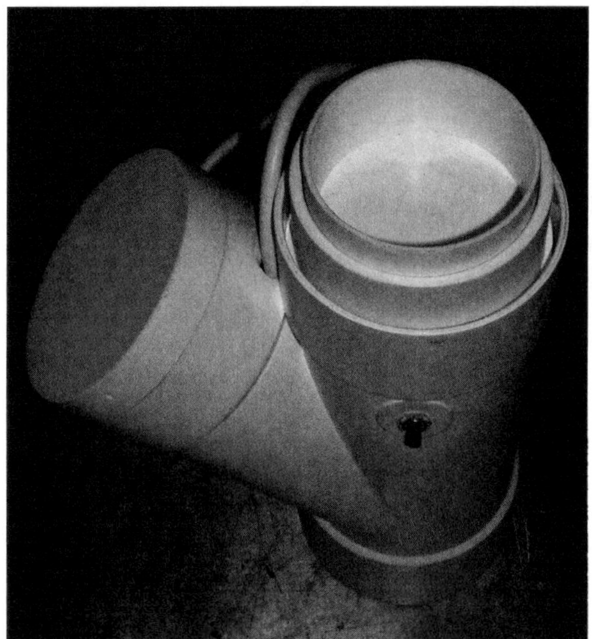

Figure 08.38: **Artsy fartsy nonsense: trying to channel my inner Space Patrol**

Figure 08.39: **A naked wall-wart, supine on the end cap**

Into the Fray

First step is to prep the surface of the PVC components as detailed in the first part of this saga. There's a lot of little nooks and crannies in these parts, so take your time and be thorough. Getting my case and caps to fit together the way I wanted meant doing a sex change on one end (male to female), and performing female-to-male gender reassignment on the two endcaps.

Here's what I started with. The two connections facing downwards are female. Unfortunately, so are the endcaps. Something has to change. **[Figure 08.35]**

The top connection is male; it needs to be female to accept the 4" to 2" adaptor we're using as a lens mount/ focus ring. I used a miter box and hacksaw to remove a female (4 ¼" ID) connection from one of my spare fittings, then cut down the top male conection to ½" in height. I trued up the cut end of the female conection I was preparing to transplant, then cemented it in place with pipe adhesive. The 1½" of male connector I lopped off the top of the Y was cut into two ¾" lengths and cemented into place in the end caps, converting them from female to male. Oish — I'm a regular Stanley Biber.[6] **[Figure 08.36]**

So far, so good.

I cut about ¾" off the angled connection point for purely aesthetic purposes.

The circular flat spot on the body hosts the rotary canopy switch. Both the lighting element and the drive motor run on 3 volts DC. To match the "I have a honkin' thick power cord" aesthetics of DiscoHead, we'll use a concealed wall-wart to convert the power, and run the AC cord as shown out through a slightly undersized hole in the crook of the Y. **[Figure 08.37]**

The 4" to 2" adaptor is your lens housing and focus ring. Ensure that it slides smoothly (but not to the point of being loose) in and out of the top female connection on the Y fitting. Use 320-grit paper to get a good fit, sanding *either* the outer surface of the adaptor or the inner surface of the Y fitting, but not both. When you're satisfied (keep sanding dust *away* from the sliding connection when you're testing it), finish the surface prep on the joint with fine steel wool to match the rest of the components.

6 Also known as the king of sex-change procedures, Dr. Stanley Biber performed more than 5,000 gender reassignments over a 30+-year career. He died in January 2006.

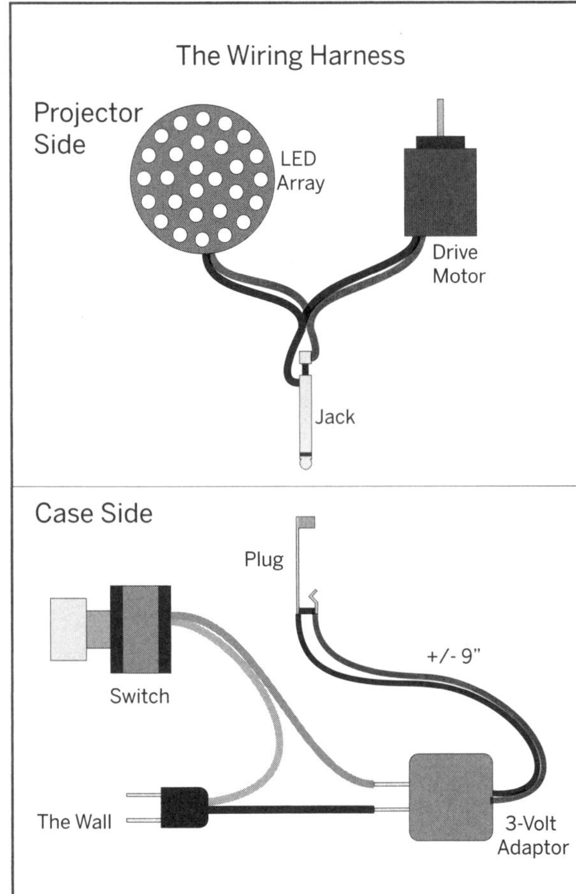

Figure 08.40: Len, meet Jack and the missus: a kludged-together quick-release EPS coupling makes the inevitable dissasemble–tweak mechanism–reassemble cycle a lower-magnitude pain in the ass.

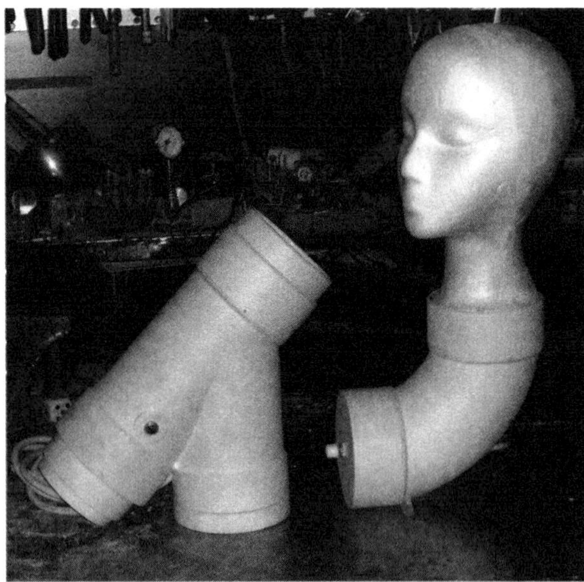

Figure 08.41: Ta-da.

In the material list for this project, I spec'd plain end caps in two locations. The piece I built actually used a 4" to 3" adaptor and an oversized adaptor ring cut from another fitting to form a cap that looked more like the exhaust port from a 50s Space Patrol rocketship. **[Figure 08.38, Figure 08.39]**

Given the location of the AC cord and power switch, mounting the wall-wart transformer on the rear cap (whatever form it may take) is the obvious solution. Carefully extract the transformer from its case and goop the damned thing in place in the center of the end cap with glazing compound. Hardwire the leads of the AC cord to the prongs using the "solder and shrink tube" method detailed in the nano project at the end of this chapter, or directly to the PCB of the wallwart.

To make installation and servicing of the projector mechanism significantly easier, use a jack/plug combination on the DC side of the wiring harness, with a 8" or 9" lead. Once you've wired up the case side of the electrical harness and ensured that Johnny Electron[7] is flowing

[7] In the 80s, I worked at a fairly well-known audio gear manufacturer, initially in the final QC booths, then in Production Engineering and R&D. During that time, I worked with a maniacal designer guy named George Krampera, who introduced me to Johnny Electron. Proudly Moravian, Kramps was *the* proto-Maker. Instrument amplifiers and speaker cabs were his specialty. He earned his wings doing tech support for Iron Curtain–era Czechoslovakian rawk bands, which meant improvising and repurposing just about every conceivable piece of gear and componentry from nonmusical sources. Combine that with a thorough state-provided education in electronics and a weirdly intuitive approach to problem solving, and Kramps was a completely inspirational guy to watch work. Kinda scary though: he thought nothing of swapping components in and out of 300-watt tube amps while the amp was still powered up and under load, armed with only his trusty Weller soldering gun. There'd be sparks flyin' all over the place, but if he ever got shocked, it never showed. He'd just shrug it off and say, "I have a good relation with Johnny Electron."

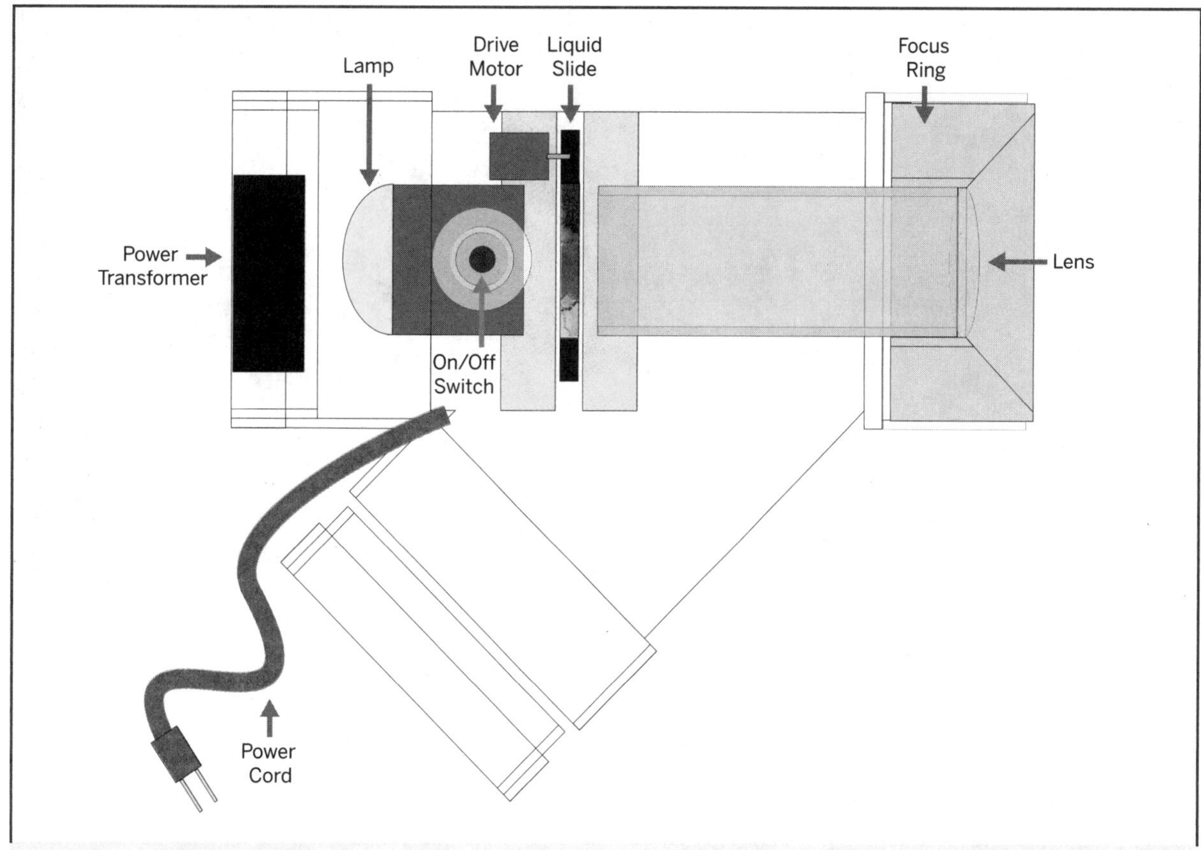

Figure 08.42: How it works.

where he should, the end cap can be glued in place. Use pipe adhesive if your confidence in your componentry and fabrication is high, or a few dabs of glazing compound if there's a chance that you may want to rework something. **[Figure 08.40]**

Ya know, having an industrial design concept start as a spontaneous shopping decision and actually work out the way you planned is a *mightily* satisfying thing to experience. **[Figure 08.41]**

Ever build something consisting of a series of subassemblies that turned out to be *impossible* to assemble when it came time to put it all together? Even with meticulous planning, it still happens once in a while . . . but there you can minimize the chances of that occuring by *paying attention*. The case for this project came together with relative ease. Now we have to consider what's gonna end up being crammed inside, how we're gonna get it there, and how much we'll have to muck about with the innards after they're installed. **[Figure 08.41, Figure 08.42]**

The other end cap can be removable to allow access to the inner workings through the angled ingress. We need this access point to allow swapping liquid slides in and out of the drive mechanism integrated into the optical path. The light source and drive mechanism will be fitted onto a chassis that loads into the case through the top opening, and capped by the lens assembly mounted on the reduction adaptor.

It seems like every project has *one* key component that dictates the dimensions and scale of the rest of the build. In this case, it was the 4" to 2" reduction fitting we're using as the lens housing that set the 2" diameter scale for the optical path.

Figure 08.43: **A quite typical early-60s opaque projector lens assembly, in bakelite**

Optics

The optical path of Liquid Len can become as complicated as you want to make it. I often see pretty good quality opaque projectors from the 60s at swap meets, running in the $5–10 range. They typically have a removable two- or three-element lens assembly housed in black plastic or bakelite. Nice thought, but geez — it'd kack the entire aesthetic conception in one swift motion. **[Figure 08.43]**

Gosh, we can't have that . . . which means removing the lens elements and repackaging them if you want to use that source of optics. The thing to remember in your hunt for lensing is that you're reproducing swirly, blobby, psychaedelic shapoids, not attempting to accurately enlarge an Ansel Adams negative. All you *really* want from the lens is for it to make things bigger, and put them in focus. Any distortions introduced by the optical quality of the lens can kinda be considered bonus visual weirdout factors.

There's a time and a place to get anal about barrel, fisheye, and pincushion distortion. This ain't one of them.

Having established a reassuringly low benchmark for our optical quality, get your motor running, and head out on the highway. You're looking for curvy bits of glass, 2 ⅜" diameter maximum, 2 ¼" minimum.[8] On your way out the door, swing by your workbench and see if you have one of those third-hand soldering assistants lying around. If you do, and can bring yourself to part with the magnifying lens, you can take your coat off and get back to the build; after kludging together an optics test bench and spending about two hours futzing around with a handful of lenses harvested from various projectors, enlargers, and cameras, I glimpsed my third-hand loitering in the vicinity, and had a thought come to me concerning fixed focus lenses. **[Figure 08.44]**

When testing lensing for this project, I had two concerns:

- How big can it make things?
- What's the focal length?

The magnification is a touchy subject: We want a reasonable enlargement factor to occur with a relatively short throw: say, 10 feet. The short throw is essential, because (bright as

8 "Gee, Kaden — where'd that diameter range come from?" Glad you asked, Billy. The reduction fitting allows 4" and 2" ID pipe to be connected. The OD of 2" PVC is 2 ⅜", which is the diameter of the hole on the inner (nonbevelled) side of the reducer, hence the 2 ⅜" max dimension. The minimum dimension *must* be larger than 2" (which is the ID of the pipe); otherwise, the lens would just fall through the big long hole. A minimum diameter of 2¼" effectively provides a ⅛" lip around the lens, ensuring a solid footing for the lens.

Figure 08.44: Gaze in awe at my three-minute optics bench: a plastic cutting board held upright by two 6" clamps serves as a screen; the lighting element, slide holder, and lensing elements are mashed into various-sized blobs of plasticine to hold them in position on a piece of scrap plywood, and a tape measure running alongside the whole mess gives me measurements. Quick 'n' dirty, but good enough to answer the question, "What happens when I shine a light through this?"

they may be) 28 LEDs from a swap-meet flashlight aren't throwing out the kinda lumen count that would let you have a bright image at 50 feet. This is the purpose of the test bench: to show you in real time how the stuff you're dealing with does its job.

Yup, there's actual math available to let you make your calculations without having to resort to anything as primitive as an analog model, but these calculations are dependent on you knowing lots of arcane details about the lens elements you're using, like the curvature of each face of each lens, and the index of refraction of the material the lens is fabricated from. If you have that data readily to hand, get calculatin'. The rest of us will get by with analog modeling of the optical path on a test bench.

Focal length is the *real* concern. Within the confines of the PVC housing, we have a realistic maximum distance of 6" between the liquid slide and the front element of the lensing, in which space we have to get the elements positioned so that the image hitting the projection surface is in focus. Lenses can be made to do a lot of things: here are *some* of the options we face.

Example 1 is fixed magnification lensing. The lens is positioned to provide a focused image on the screen. The image appears inverted, and a fixed percentage larger. Move the screen 20 percent further away from the slide, then move the lens to bring the image back in focus. The resulting projected image is the same size as the before, even though the screen is further away. **[Figure 08.45]**

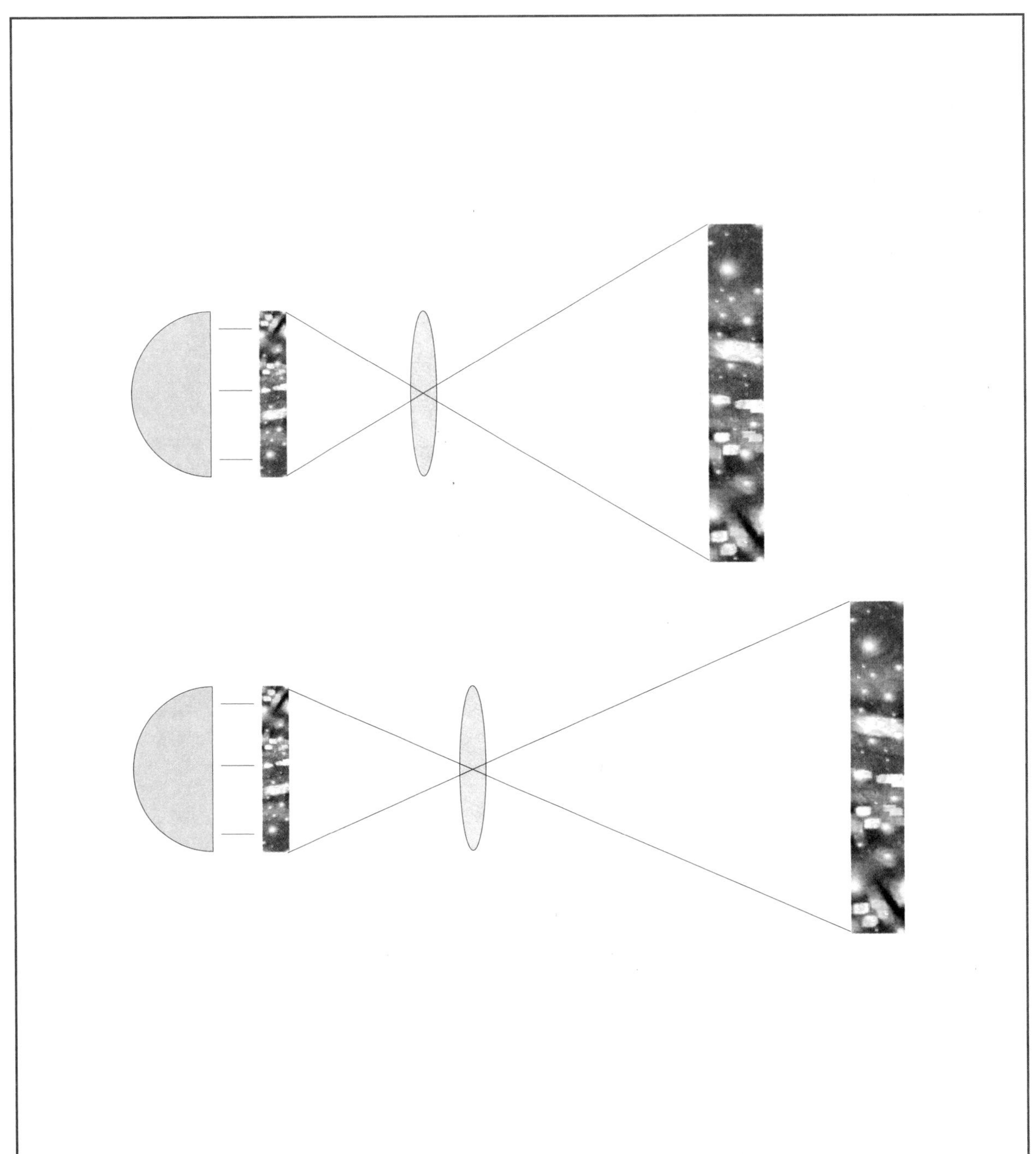

Figure 08.45: **Fixed magnification lensing. No matter where the screen is, once you focus, the image comes out the same size.**

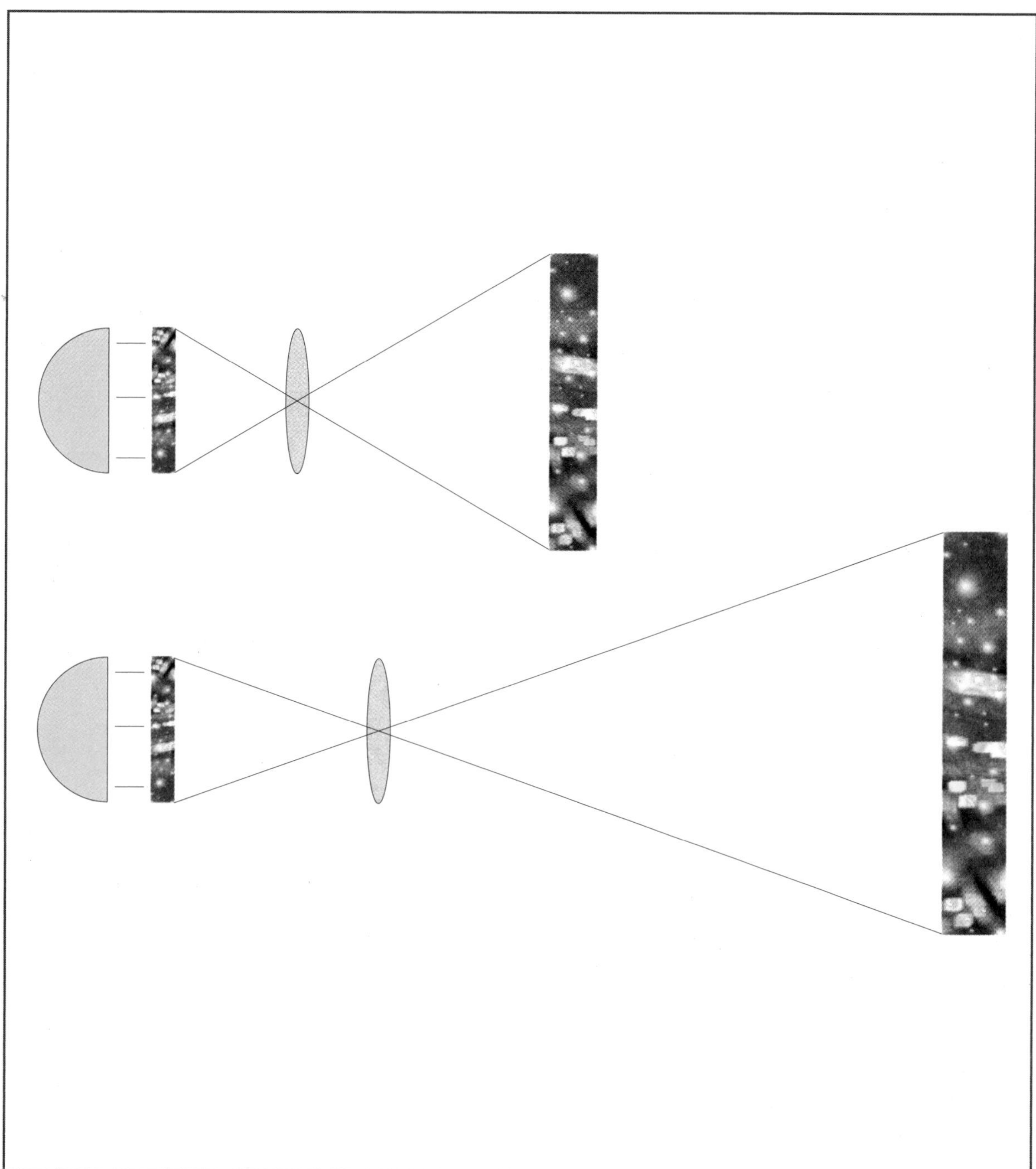

Figure 08.46: **Variable focus/variable magnification. Focus and magnification are adjusted independently. Works, but manual focus is just so 80s.**

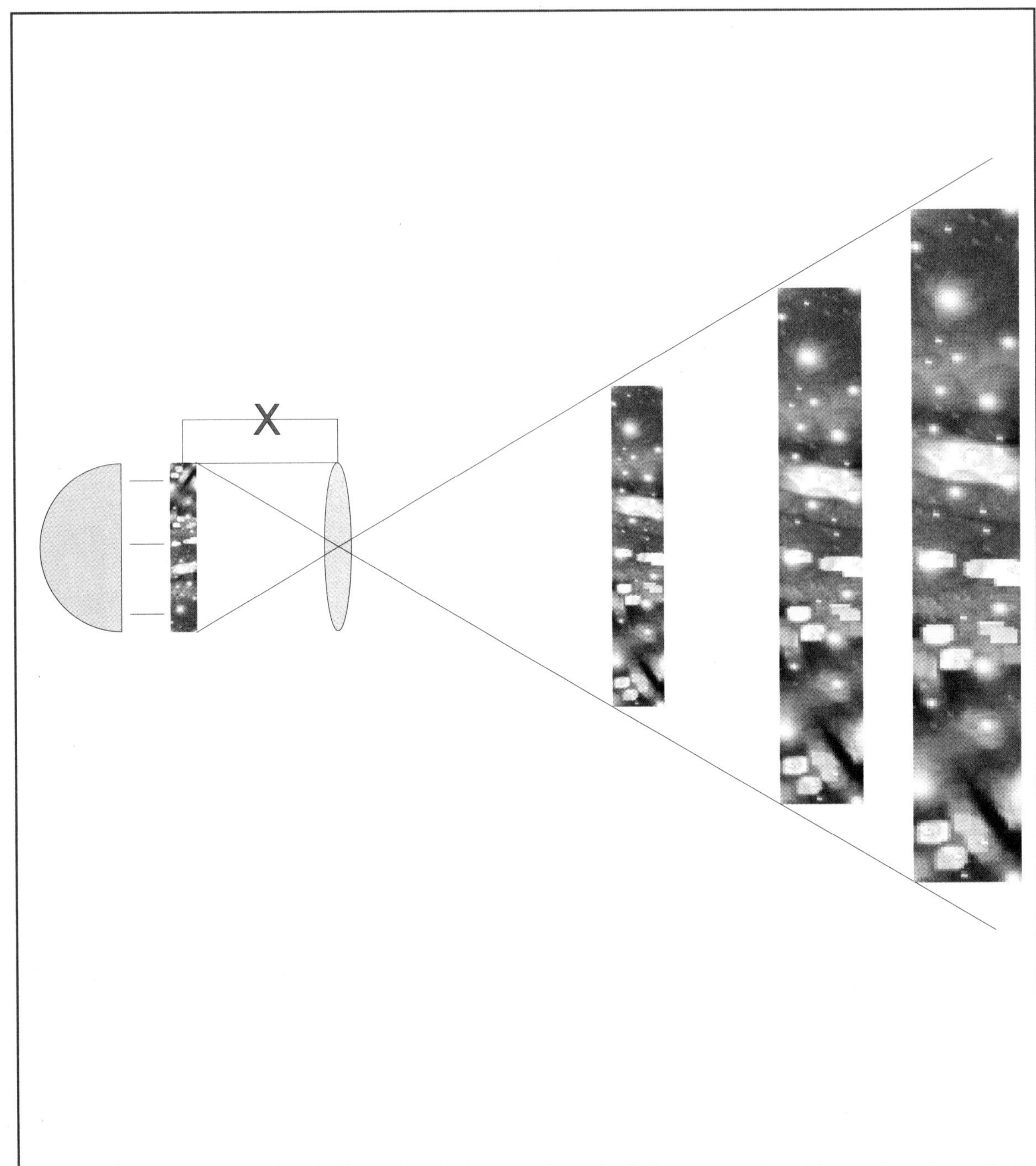

Figure 08.47: **The petite charm of the fixed focus lens**

Figure 08.48: **The thrift-shop flashlight, pre- and post-filleting**

Not even *close* to what we're looking for.

Example 2 is yer bog-standard variable focus/variable magnification optics. The size of the image increases proportionate to the screen distance, but the lensing needs to be repositioned to bring the image into focus at each given distance. **[Figure 08.46]**

Typical, but a pain in the ass. Manual focus is so 80s.

The final example is a fixed focus magnifying lens. Once the lens is positioned the correct distance from the focal plane (that's where the liquid slide is) to get it in focus, the projected image stays in focus, but gets larger when the throw distance is increased. **[Figure 08.47]**

This is what we want.

Believe it or not, the lens from your third-hand thingie delivers the goods, and as an added bonus is 2 ⅜" in diameter. At least the lens from *my* third-hand thingie did: it had a focal length of 6", and delivered a 5'-diameter image at 8 feet, which was just about perfect.

Your results may vary, so go ahead and kludge up an optical test bed to make absolutely sure. We need the test bench to determine a few other measurements needed for the build anyway.

Extract the LED array from the flashlight and solder two leads onto the contact points that formerly completed the circuit with the flashlight's battery terminals. For testing purposes, I use a 9-volt battery terminal and plug that into a variable voltage multi-ended wall-wart with reversable polarity. Remember that LEDs are polarized. The current has to flow in the right direction to light 'em up. **[Figure 08.48]**

I bodged together a reasonably variable lamp mount and slide holder to let me tweeze the distance between the LED array and the focal plane of the liquid slide (if the LEDs are too close to the slide, they may end up coming into focus along with the slide). This depends on the *depth of field* of the lens, which in this case is pretty shallow. Pulling the LEDs back a couple of inches behind the focal plane kept the image bright and the individual LEDs blurred into one continuous light source. The magnifying lens was also fitted into a simulated housing to make it easier to position in the modelling clay. I wedged a piece of brass mesh into the slide slot to give the lens something to focus on (not wanting to be arsed with actually fabricating the liquid slide at that specific moment), and moved the lens assembly around in the light path until the projected image was in focus.

In this case, the distance from the slide to the lens turned out to be just a hair over 5", which I confirmed by cutting an appropriate length of 2" PVC piping, mounting the lens, and

Figure 08.49: **You'll want to use the kind of modelling clay that doesn't air-harden. Like, say, plasticine.**

Figure 08.50: **An exciting test bench action shot, showing the lamp, slideholder, and lens, with an audience of rings, bushings, and adaptors looking on in awe.**

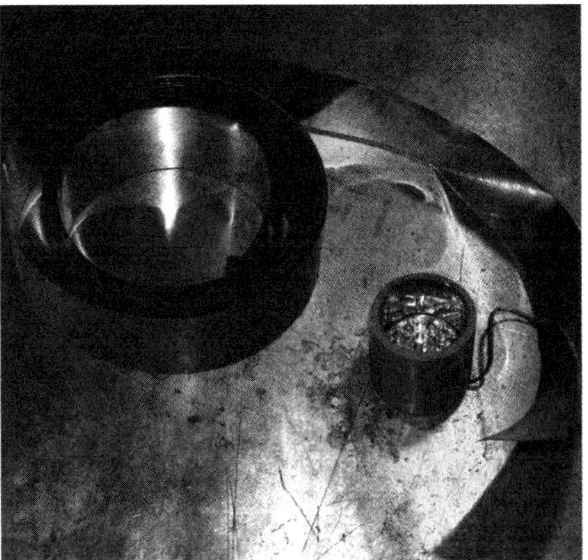

Figure 08.51: **Mo' bettah shiny: albedo enhancement via stainless steel tape.**

Figure 08.52: The lens assembly

assembling a physical simulation of the actual optical path I'd be using.[9]

Notice the presence of multiple flavours of PVC piping (that's the grey and the white stuff) as well as black ABS fittings in my mockup. I've amassed a five-gallon pail full of short lengths of various diameter/thickness/material piping over the years, solely for the purpose of providing sizing rings, bushings and adaptors . . . whenever I bring full lengths of this kinda stuff into the shop, a foot or so of it gets tossed into the bucket immediately to top up the supply. Ninety percent of the time, I can find something in that pail to meet whatever demand the project at hand presents. The other 10 percent of the time I can find something *close*, then sand to fit.

The lamp assembly is 1 ½" of 2" ID PVC pipe with the LED array from the flashlight mounted in one end via a bit of silicon glazing compound left over from the DiscoHead build. The length of the pipe was determined on the optical bench as being the minimum distance needed to ensure the LEDs were outside the focal range of the lensing. Line the inner surface of the pipe with something reflective. I used stainless-steel adhesive tape,[10] but aluminum duct tape is just as good. Increasing the albedo of the pipe wall improves the efficiency of the light transfer and evens out the illumination. **[Figure 08.49, Figure 08.50, Figure 08.51]**

The lens assembly is almost as simple. Getting the magnifying lens to fit neatly into the reduction fitting may involve *slightly* enlarging the 2 ⅜" hole in the reducer. Resist the urge to try resizing the lens itself. Lacking the specialized wet-grinding toolage used for such endeavours, it is an enterprise that can only end badly. When the lens is in place, use a rubber O-ring as a gasket, and a piece of 2" ID ABS piping tacked into place with cyanoacrylate as a lock ring. **[Figure 08.52]**

The white PVC pipe is sized to give the required focal length when the unit is assembled and the lens assembly mated with the chassis. **[Figure 08.53]**

Any focus adjustments needed are made by sliding the reduction fitting in and out. Correspondingly, the rear end of the lens assembly moves in and out of the opening in the chassis into which it fits. I was concerned about the chance of the rear of the lens assembly coming into contact with the liquid slide if the lens is pushed too far back, so I rummaged around and found a short piece of thinwall 2" ID piping, with an OD of about 2 ¼". I used this to add a ferrule to the back

9 Your results may vary. I've since tested half a dozen similar lenses from similar devices and had duplicate results in four out of six instances. Not surprisingly, there *were* some variations, one lens having a focal length of 3", and another having a length just over 5 ½".

10 Apparently used in the auto repair industry; mine came from a thrift shop, two 20' rolls for $4.99. This tape will kick your tape's ass: 2" wide, about 3mil thick. There's no cloth backing or plastic overlay, just metal coated with a sticky-as-hell-to-begin-with-then-cures-up-even-stronger-in-about-two-days acrylic adhesive.

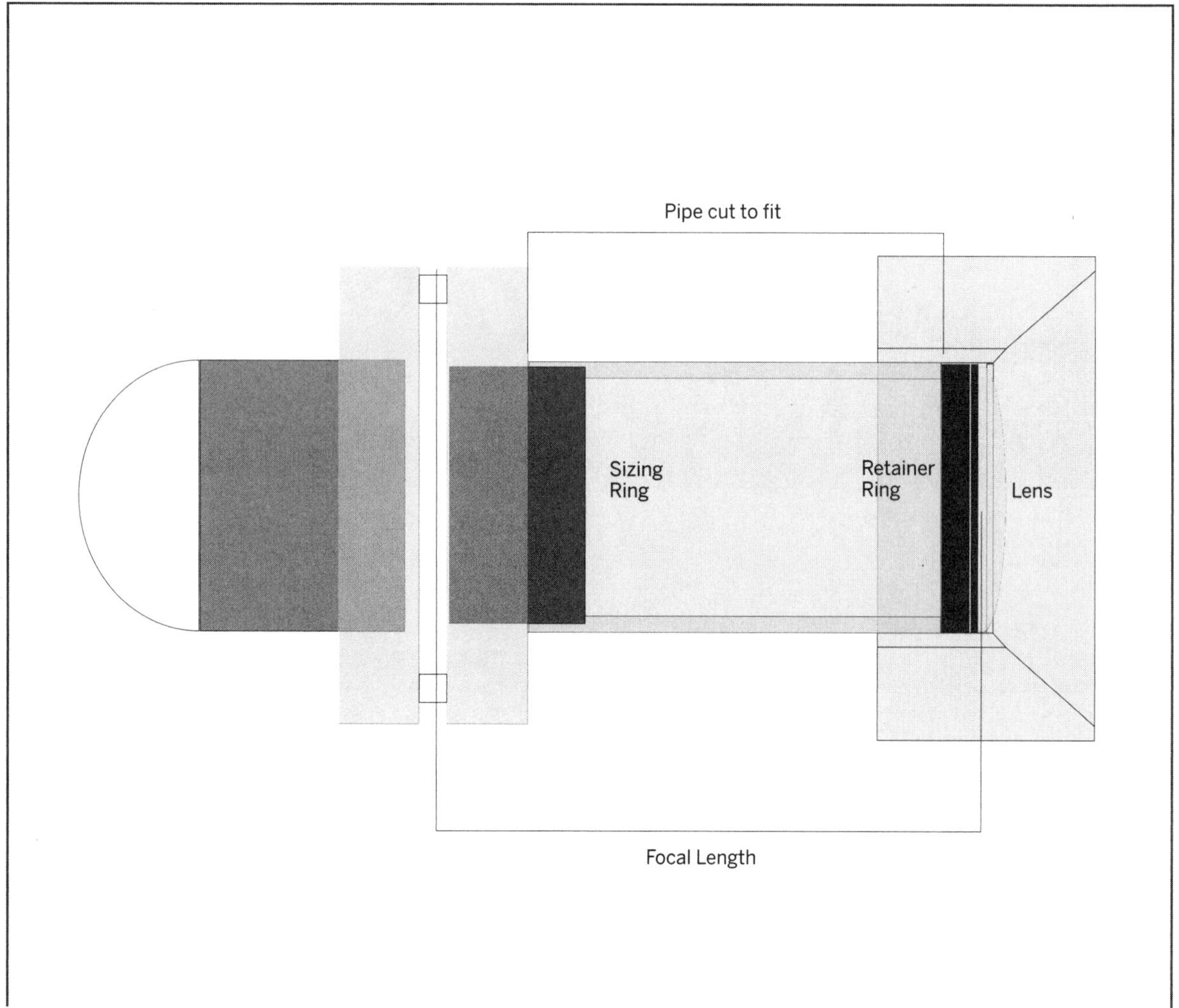

Figure 08.53: **Some critical measurements illustrated**

end of the main section of the lens assembly, which gave me a narrow lip on the pipe that limits the backwards travel of the lens and protects the slide.

Frankly, it's an overcomplicated solution. You can accomplish the same thing by forming a stop lip on the receiver hole of the chassis by drilling most of the receiver hole in the front chassis plate with a 2 3⁄8" hole saw and using a 2" holecutter for the final 1⁄8" or so. **[Figure 08.54]**

The final step in fabricating the lens assembly is lining the inside of the pipe with a nonreflective surface, which helps prevent stray reflections from washing out the colours of the projected image. I used black flocked craft paper held in place with double-faced tape. You could just as easily spray paint the inside of the pipe with flat black enamel, or glue craft felt in place. It's one of those small details that *needs* doing, in whatever fashion. **[Figure 08.55]**

The chassis is the absolute crux of this particular biscuit. It holds the lamp and lensing, and houses the drive mechanism for the liquid slide. You'll need to know the dimensions of your slide before you can proceed with the chassis.

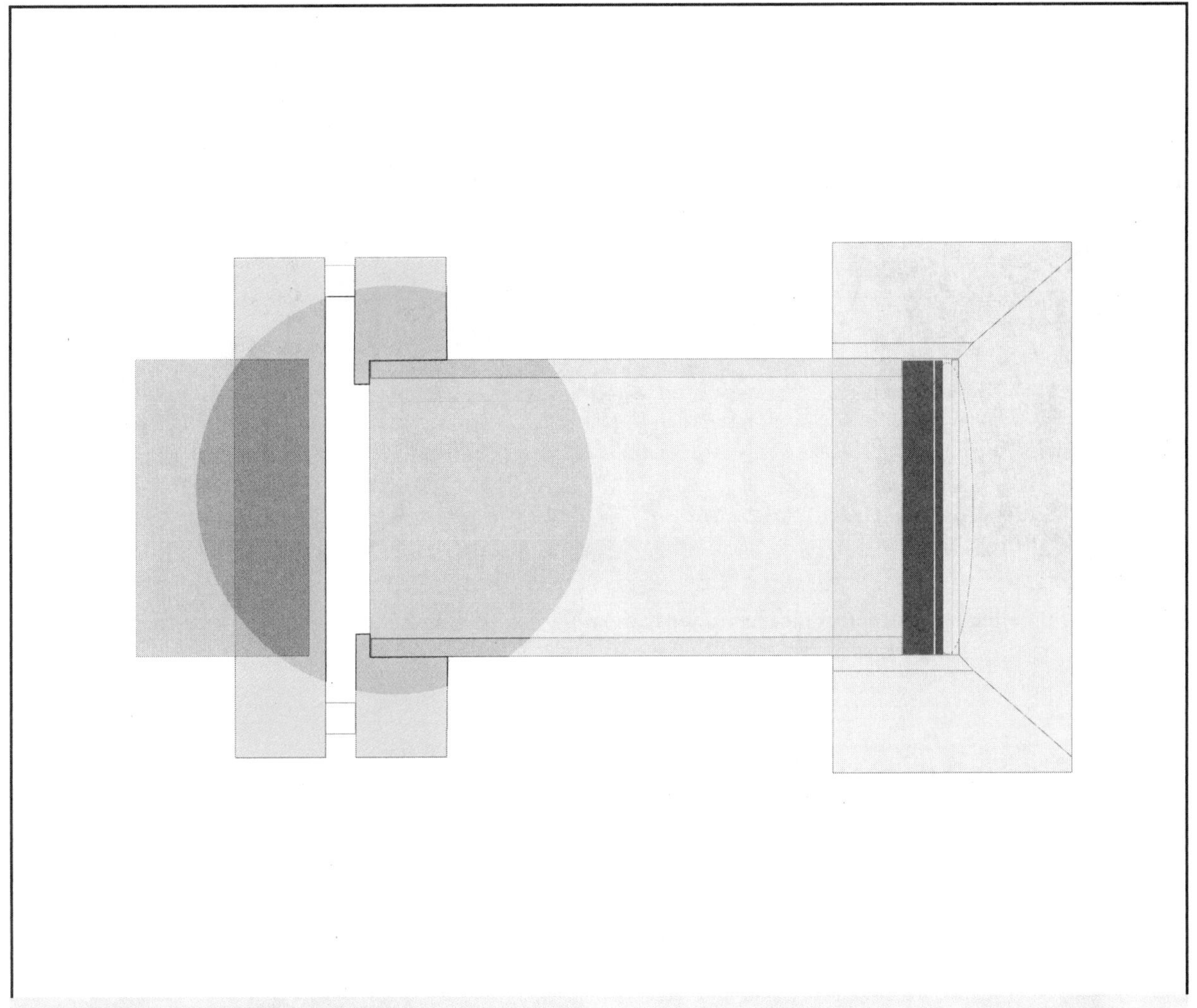

Figure 08.54: Where the lens stop goes

The Liquid Slide

How you chose to construct your liquid slide is entirely up to you. As always, there's a bunch of ways to accomplish the task.

So what's the task?

The liquid slide needs to be round, relatively thin, and have transparent faces. It's gonna contain a relatively thin layer of liquid, which it has to hold without leaking, with the liquid(s) in question being mineral oil and a water-based dye. Use glass discs for the faces: glass is superior to plastic for scratch resistance and optical characteristics. Mineral oil breaks down latex products on contact, so avoid rubber gasket material. To achieve the best oozy blobby shapoidliness, the thinner the layer of liquid contained in the slide, the better. The transparent portions of the slide faces should be not be smaller than 2" in diameter, but the overall diameter of the slide should be kept to a minimum to leave as much room as possible on the chassis for the motor and drive train.

Glass circles in the 2 ¼–2 ½" diameter range aren't uncommon if you look for "components" rather than

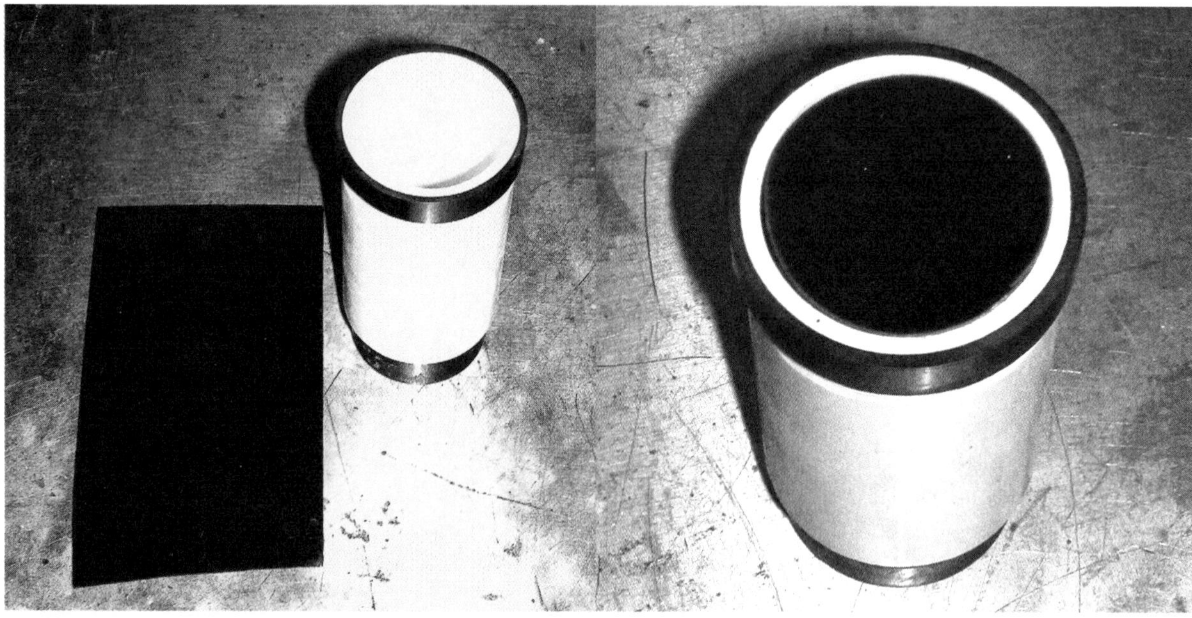

Figure 08.55: **Reflection abatement measures, Lens assembly, implementation of.**

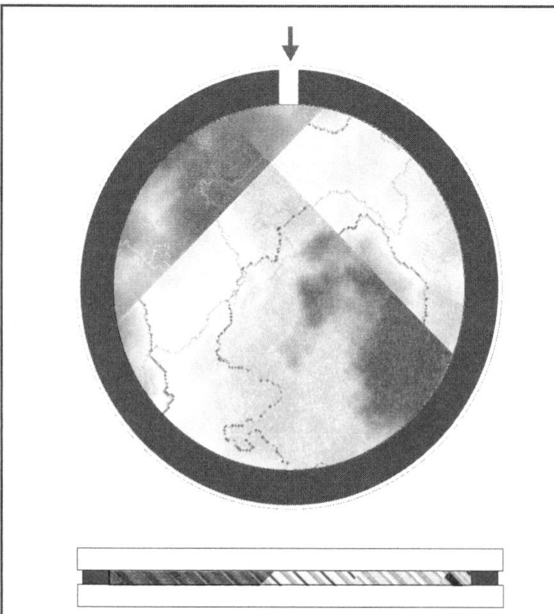

Figure 08.56: **Critical elements of the liquid slide.**

Figure 08.57: **Dollar-store "candles in a can." Do not assume from appearances that they smell like cherries.**

"items." You see them in dollar-store picture frames all the time. The glass is usually about 3 mm thick. Separate two disks with a donut-shaped gasket cut to provide a fill hole, glue the whole mess together, and you have a hollow slide ready to be filled with printer cartridge refilling syringes. Once filled, you can plug the hole with a dab of glazing compound and Bob's yer uncle. I tried a few different gasket materials and found that the plastic lid from a CD jewel case worked well, and was a good thickness. Cut the gasket to a diameter slightly smaller than that of the disks, and use an even coat of gel cyanoacrylate to glue the slide together. Fill the groove in the edge formed by the undersized gasket with glazing compound as a failsafe fluid seal. Your completed liquid slide is gonna be in the neighborhood of ¼" thick. **[Figure 08.56]**

Any good pharmacy[11] will sell you pure, heavy mineral oil. It's thicker than baby oil and is thankfully free of *that smell*, which is guaranteed to trigger catatonia-inducing flashbacks in anyone who has ever changed a diaper. For colour, food colouring is readily available and works like a charm. You may need to cut it 50-50 with water to reduce the density enough for it to pass the right amount of light.

During sourcing for this build I came across some "candles in a can" at a dollar store which featured a glass-windowed aluminum lid on the 2 ½" diameter can. I used one of these lids balanced on top of my lamp assembly as an open-topped test slide to check the colour response from various dilutions of dye. The slide is easy to fill, but a proper bitch to empty, clean and reuse, so it's better to be sure of your dye density *before* syringing it into the actual slide. **[Figure 08.57]**

Use a syringe to fill the slide about 70 percent full of oil, then top it up with a single colour of dye. Plug the fill hole with glazing compound, let it cure, then fill the groove in the edge formed by the undersized gasket with more silicone as a fail-safe fluid seal.

11 Pharmacy, not drugstore. The current trend towards "drugstores" being your one-stop megadeal retail experience gives me hives, and they never seem to stock the stuff you expect a drugstore to carry, like medications, curatives, and bandages.

The prices on patio furniture are usually competitive though. Damned straight, I'm old-fashioned.

Driving the Liquid

The chassis is formed from a pair of 4" disks cut from ¾" MDF. Bond them together temporarily with double-faced tape during the final edge sanding to ensure that they're identical, then carefully fine-tune the size so that they snugly into the case when slid in through the top opening. Leave the disks taped together for the moment.

Use a hole saw to cut the mounting holes for the lamp and lens assemblies through the center point of the disks. If you're planning on implimenting the travel limiting lip on the lens mount (as discussed earlier), now's the time to do it.

The final stage of the build is fabricating the drive mechanism for the liquid slide. I could have taken the ultimate easy way out and sourced a low-RPM gear motor from any number of local and online vendors.

But I didn't.

I could have taken a DIYers easy way out, and tweezed a cassette player drive mechanism to do the job.

But I didn't do that either.

In the name of total bodgeness, and because I'd never actually done this before, I decided that this drive mechanism would be fabricated from scratch, using bits and pieces of thrift-shop toy cars and rubber bands.

Like I said . . . *total* bodgeness.

All-righty then, toy cars and rubber bands it is. Head to the thrift shop and forage for cheap ass toy cars. We need two with ½" diameter wheels and 1⁄16" axles, and one with a motor powered by 2 AA cells.

Here's the concept. The motor from yer typical toy car runs on 3v DC at about 5000 rpm. Ideally, we're looking for the liquid slide to spin at 1 or 2 RPM. This calls for some serious speed decreasin' that can only be achieved with multiple stages of ratio reduction. Here's some math to ponder:

Diameter of toy car motor shaft: 0.0625".
(This is the *motor* diameter.)

Diameter of toy car wheel: 0.5"
(This is the *driven* diameter.)

R (reduction ratio) = *M* (motor)/ *D* (driven)
0.0625 / 0.5 = 0.125

Applying that reduction ratio to 5,000 rpm:
5,000 * 0.125 = 625 RPM

Still a tad fast. Let's drive another (identical) pulley from the 1⁄16" diameter axle shaft of the first one:
625 * 0.125 = 78.125 RPM

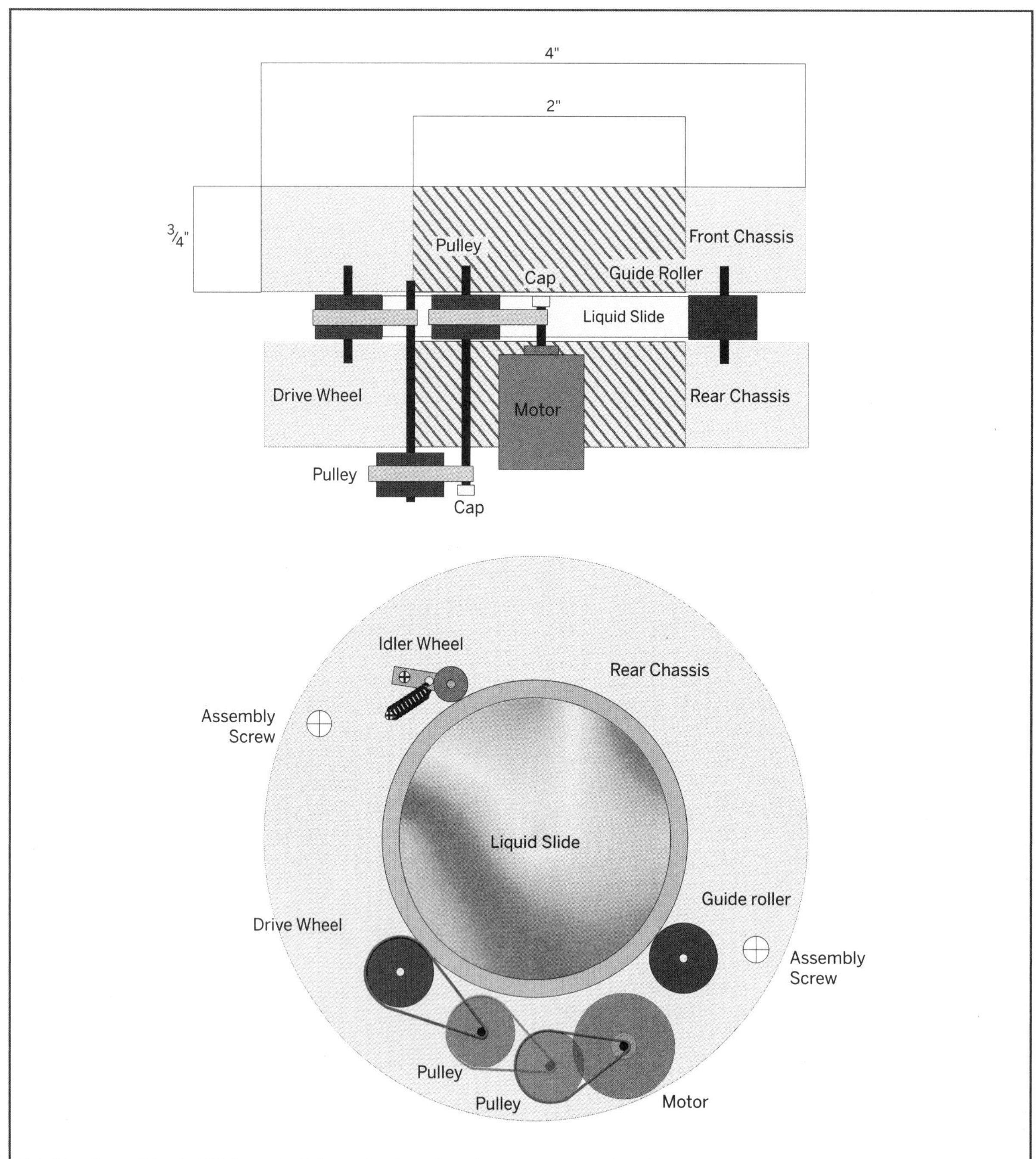

Figure 08.58: Executing the plan in a manner that even a first-timer like me can get it right ended up with the drive train looking like this on the drawing board.

Sheesh . . . one more time:
78.125 * 0.125 = 9.77 RPM

Riiiiight. With this drive train, we have a ½"-diameter wheel spinning at a bit under 10 RPM. Let's do a friction drive on the liquid slide (2 ½" +/– diameter) with that and see what happens.

First, the ratio: 0.5 / 2.5 = 0.2

Apply that ratio to 9.77 RPM: 9.77 * 0.2 = 1.94

Woo (as they say) hoo. Just what we're lookin' for. Isn't it cool when the math turns out just the way you want it? The challenge now is to physically render the mathematics.

It's just like 3DS Max, only real.

Theoretically, there are a *lot* of ways to lay out this drive train. Using components derived solely from toy cars limits the options considerably, and the physical constraints of the chassis and case cramp matters even moreso: the 4" diameter of the chassis *cannot* be compromised if it's gonna slot into the case properly.

The components of the drive train are, for the most part, self-explanatory. The drive wheel, idler wheel, and pinch roller are positioned to hold the liquid slide centered in the optical path, roughly every 120 degrees around the circumference. The pinch roller is the *one* tricky element: it's spring-loaded to apply inward pressure on the slide, holding it snugly against the drive wheel and idler wheel. I pulled my pinch roller assembly intact, complete with spring, from a dumpstered cassette player, but they're common in VCRs and printers too. **[Figure 08.58, Figure 08.59]**

We want the liquid slide to be removable to facilitate colour changes and upgrades. The pinch roller has to be positioned and tensioned to hold the slide in position effectively, but still be able to retract and allow the slide to be easily removed.

The diagram should be fairly self-explanatory. As long as the angular dimensions noted total more than 180 degrees, the idler will hold the slide in place. The range of motion of the idler needs be large enough to allow the diameter of the slide to pass through the gap opened in the drive mechanism when the slide is withdrawn. **[Figure 08.59]**

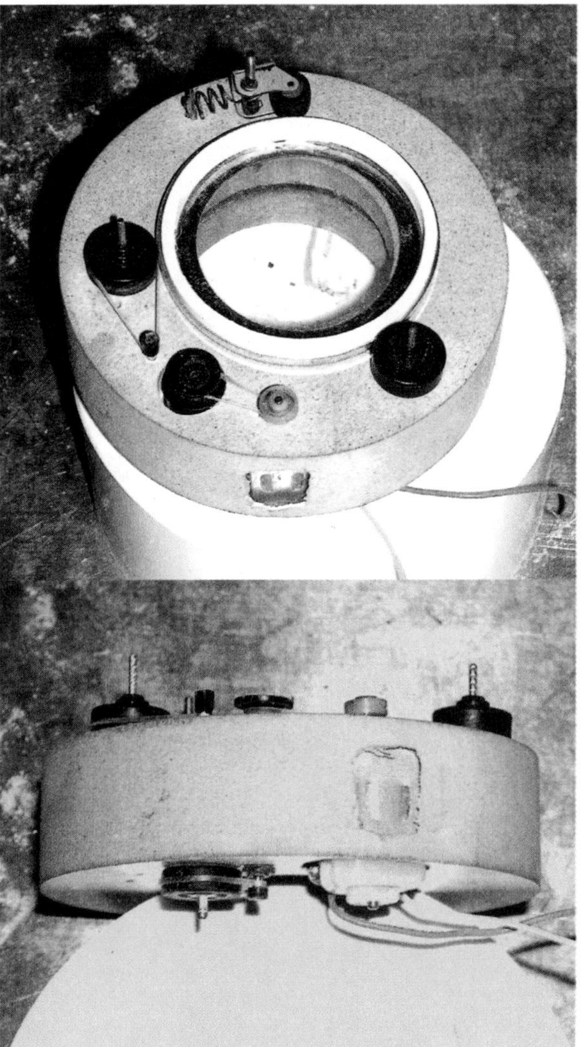

Figure 08.59: And it looked like this, by the time I finished fabrication.

You'll have to do a layout based on the specific components you end up using. Not all toy cars are created equal, nor are their motors. Once you have an accurate drawing of the layout of the drive, mark the position of the axle holes and motor-mounting cavity onto the outer face of the rear chassis element (they're still stuck together with double-faced tape, remember?) and use a 3/64" bit to drill holes straight through the rear chassis component and into the inner face of the front chassis element. The 3/64" holes allow for a tight fit for the axles, and having accurately aligned holes in each chassis element to support both ends of the axles makes the entire assembly gratifyingly stable. The motor cavity gets drilled out with a Forstner bit to a depth of 5/8", with the pilot hole being enlarged to accomodate the motor shaft.

The assembly bolt holes are drilled out to 7/16". You'll need to cut and drill spacers a tad more than ¼" high for the assembly bolts to pass through to hold the chassis plates the correct distance apart when it's assembled (assuming, of

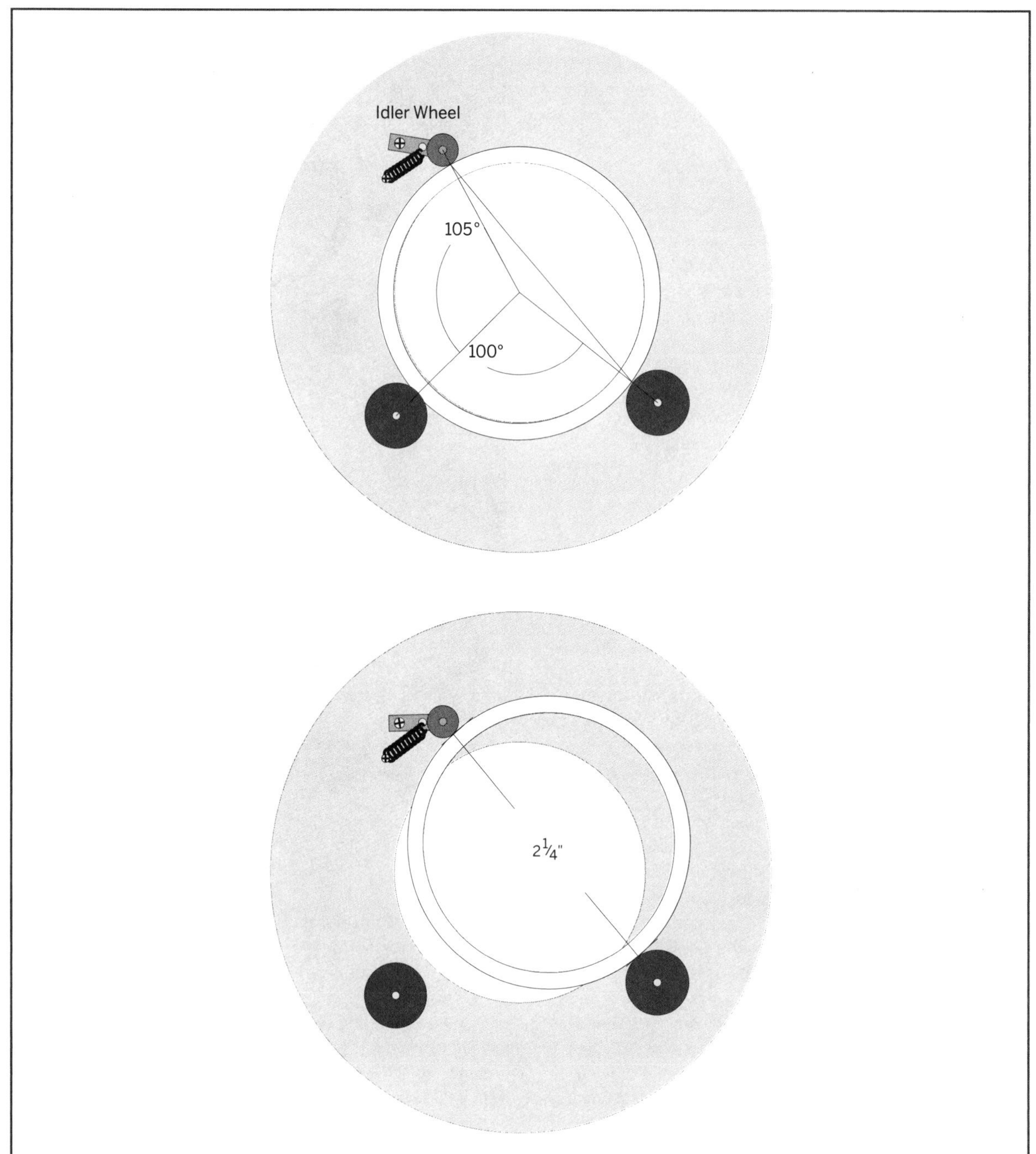

Figure 08.60: The illustrated pinch roller

course, that your slide is slightly less than ¼" thick, as mine was, and the wheels you're using are the fairly typical ½" diameter x ¼" thick).

Drill out to 5/64" the centers of the toy car wheels that you're using as pulleys, so that the wheels spin freely on the axles, then assemble the drive train elements on the rear chassis component, cutting the axles to length as you go. The axles should extend into the front chassis plate at least ¼".

Remember: Measure twice, cut once.

You can add the front chassis plate after you've fine-tuned the drive train. Power up the motor and experiment with rubber bands in different widths and thicknesses as drive belts. I ended up using these kinda silicony bands sold as hair-restraint accessories, but I'm always scoping out new possibilities whenever I come across variations on a rubber-band theme during sourcing. You'll know when you have the right belts, because the drive will run smoothly with minimum noise, and the liquid slide will have a slow, steady rotation. There are lots of plans out there for "workbench power supplies" that are useful as hell for supplying juice to works-in-process. Luddite that I am, I rely on a $5 multivoltage wall-wart and alligator clips.

When the drive is tuned and running smoothly, cap the motor shaft and the exposed axle end on the back face of the chassis to hold the belts in place. Short pieces of a cheap ballpoint pen refill do the job perfectly. Fit the front chassis plate onto the axles, position the spacers, and bolt the chassis together with ¼-20 machine screws. Fit the lamp assembly into the opening in the rear chassis plate and secure it with either a few drops of cyanoacrylate or by setting a length of ⅛" brass rod through the edge of the chassis plate to mount the lamp permanently.

The lens assembly should slide smoothly into the hole in the front chassis plate, leaving you with a completed projector mechanism as illustrated. **[Figure 08.61]**

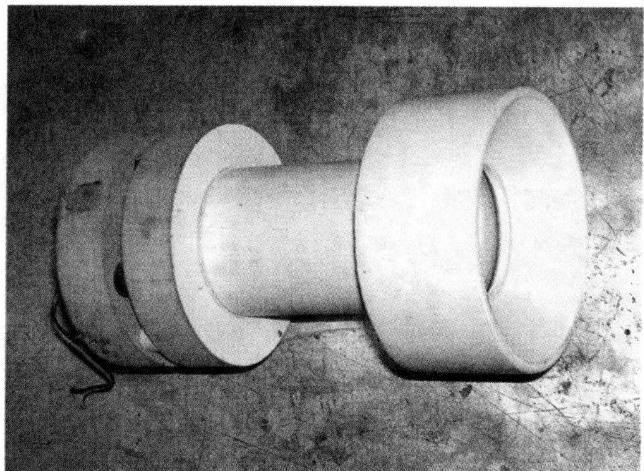

Figure 08.61: **And it looked like this, by the time I finished fabrication.**

Slot your liquid slide into the drive mechanism, jack the two sides of the wiring harness together and slide the projector mechanism into the case, oriented such that the slide removal slot (the bit between the idler wheel and the pinch roller) is accessable from the angled port on the case. It should be a snug press-fit.

Replace the bottom cap on the case and mix up a pitcher of psylocybin daiquiris. You're done.

Dim the lights, introduce Liquid Len to DiscoHead, rummage around on your iPod for that BeeGees/Grateful Dead remix you've been saving for a special occasion, a-a-and . . .

Turn on, tune in, and drop out.

Figure 08.61: **A few details: Mirror fitting, improvised knobs, and the Discohead Rotisserie Spit of Truth.**

‹ Nano-Project › Power-Bar Friendly Wall-Warts

Seems like every week there's a new and exciting take on "the AC adaptor-friendly power strip." This is an issue that has been annoying tech-heads for years; I personally threw my first 9V transformer across the room in frustration in 1980.

I have neither the time nor the money to indulge in extensive market research on every new solution that comes down the pipe. When I wanna plug stuff in, I wanna plug stuff in *now*, dammit.

So I thought about it a bit, and came up with this fairly obvious hack to perform on the 'warts themselves. Stop me if you've heard this one.

For each adaptor you're going to modify, you need a length of regulation-issue AC cord (male to bare ends: length is your call, but make it *at least* 18 inches), about 5 inches of 3/8" shrink tubing, the *will* to void the warranty, and a soldering iron.

Strip half an inch from the bare ends of the AC cord. (I use two-pronged polarized appliance cords reclaimed from stuff I find in dumpsters. The extremely safety-conscious among you may frown at this.)

Slip a 1" length of shrink tube over *both* leads, and 2" lengths over each individual lead. Match up the polarity of the cord with the polarity of the prongs on the adaptor, solder the bare leads to the appropriate prongs, slide the individual shrink tubing lengths over your fresh solders and shrink 'em, then slide the final length of shrink tube over the end of *those* two pieces, and shrink *that*.

Voilà.

Plug it in.

Anywhere.

Figure N8.01: The pieces.

Figure N8.02: The process.

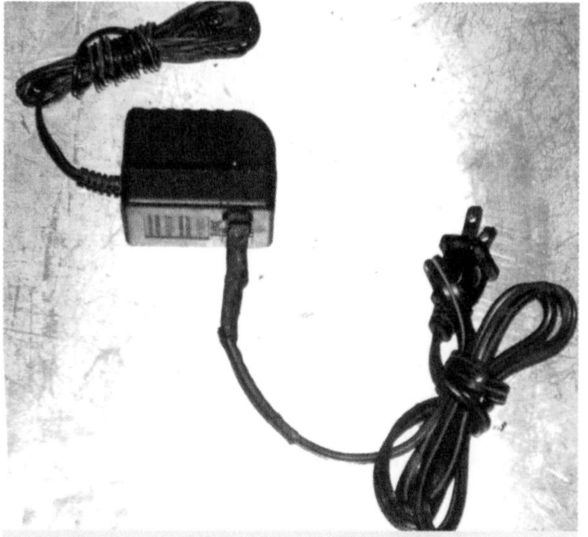

Figure N8.03: The product.

9 The Haze-o-Matic 3000 Fog Machine: The "Fog of War" Comes to the Office

Mood. Atmosphere. Aaahmmbiance. Subtle shifts in the environment that change the feel of a room (or cube) from "warm and inviting" to "cold and clinical" to "Hear me, Prince of Darkness." The fog machine is your absolute go-to mechanism for achieving that crucial combination of fantasy, intrigue, and impending ritual dismemberment so essential in business negotiation today.

They're a lot of fun to build, too. A fogger is an inherently simple mechanism that can become insanely convoluted in the blink of an eye. This is a good thing. Atmosphere is one thing. Atmosphere created by a dangerously complicated-looking apparatus is entirely another. There's a fair bit of foraging for parts involved in this little endeavour, regardless of how you choose to approach the subassemblies, so preplanning is either the best or worst idea ever, depending on how broadly you wanna embrace the great cosmic random. If it was me, I'd wing it completely and design on the bench. Although it is entirely possible to design a sleek and compact fog generator, the coolness factor is noticeably diminished.

What We're Building

We're going old-school here, with a design that vapourizes a glycerin/water mixture to produce fog. Large-scale commercial foggers evaporate dry ice in a hot water bath to achieve the same end without the "low-budget mid-80s Goth club" smell of glycerin-based ambience. You can adapt this design to that technology by enlarging your fog chamber, putting a pot of water on the fog chamber's hot surface, and hand-feeding ice-house dry ice into it during use. The rest of the delivery mechanism remains the same.

It's your decision, but startup time is considerably longer with CO_2-based fog as you wait for the water bath to heat up, and glycerin is generally easier to source quickly than dry ice.

Pinning the mechanism out on the tar pan, you'll find that it works like this. Fog juice (A) drips through valve (B) onto a hot surface (C) in a closed container, which creates hot fog (D). Hot fog rises, which is not the ground-hugging effect you're looking for. Fortunately, there's airflow (E) to blow the hot fog through an internally baffled (F, G, and H, respectively) intercooler full of ice (I, collectively) and out the exhaust. Cold fog (J) hugs the ground like a goff in a cemetery. Robert Smith (K) would approve. **[Figure 09.01]**

Hot in a box? Cold in a box? Liquid delivery? Airflow? Boooyah! This, brothers and sisters, is a subassembly list with *potential*, and a righteous opportunity to field-test your nascent grasp of the Philosophy of Improvisational Fabrication.

Here's what we're gonna do. It'll be fun.

I'll detail the fabrication of the subassemblies *as I executed them for this build.* I'll cover the materials I used, where they came from, and the tech (such as it is) involved in each.

Your challenge is to do them some other way.

Okay. I'll go first. As noted, there are four major subassemblies needed to make a fog machine:

- A fluid delivery system to supply the fog juice
- A hotbox to vapourize the fog juice in
- An intercooler to chill the fog out and get it to hug the ground
- An airflow source to move the fog around

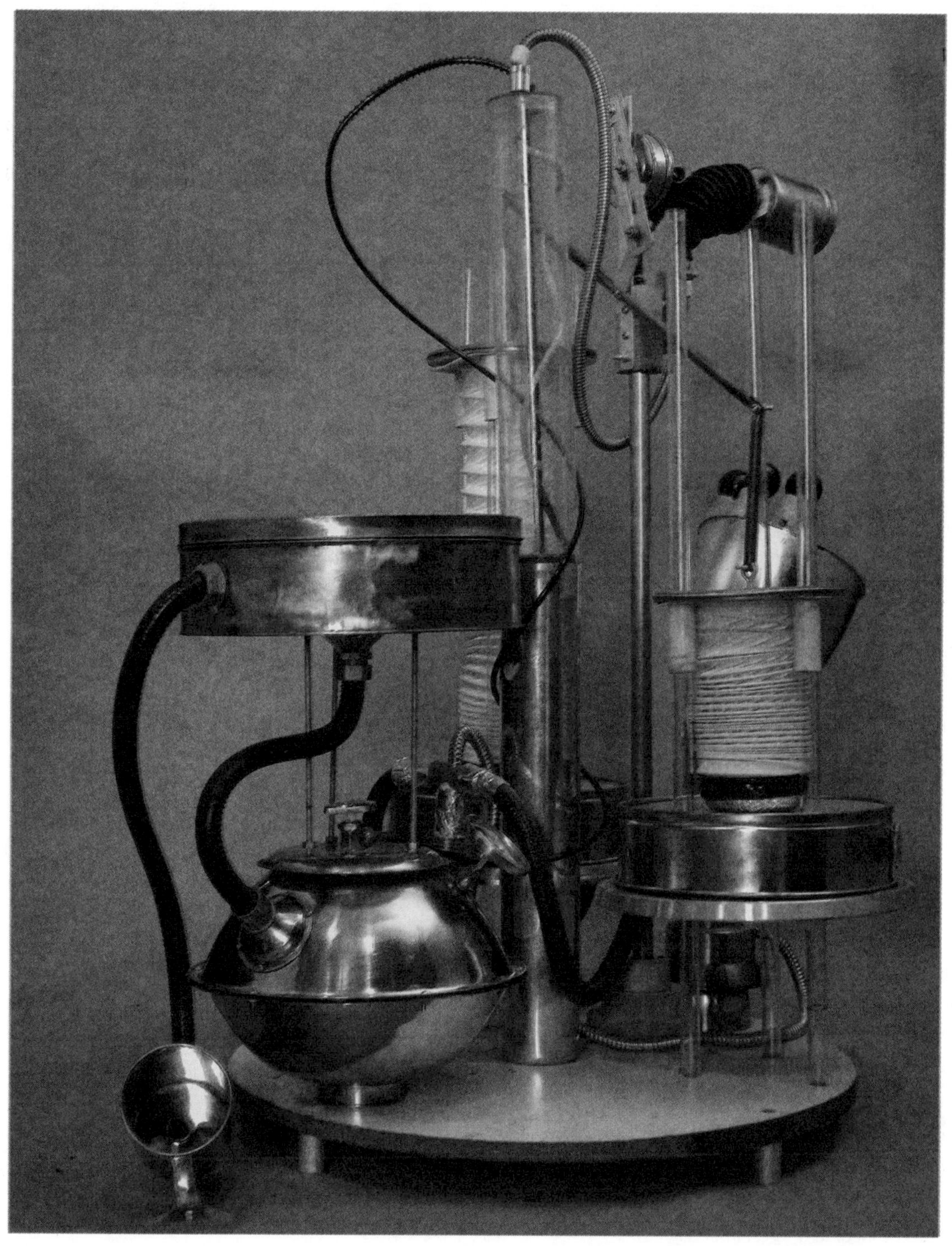

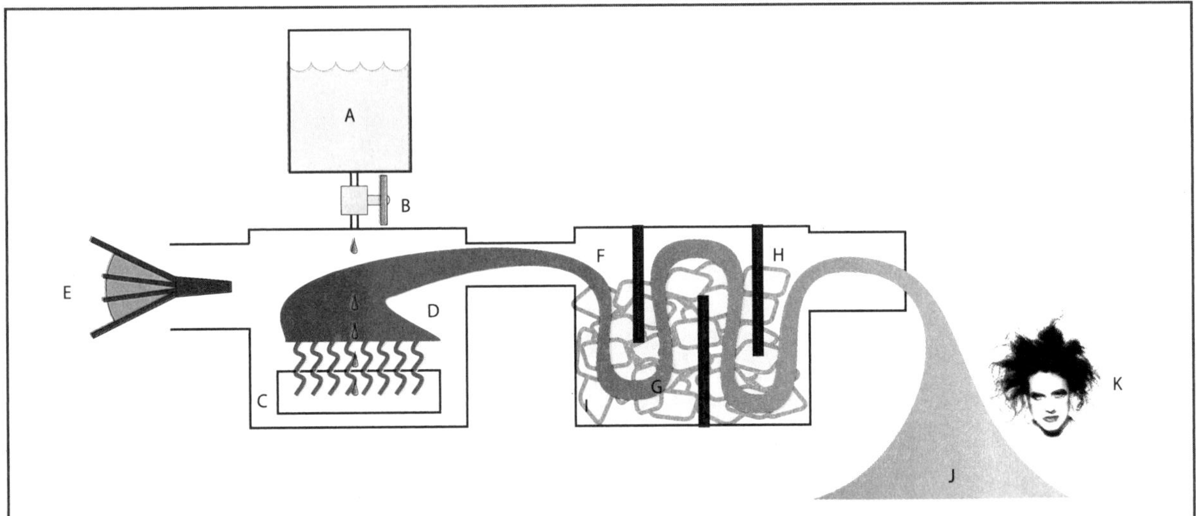

Figure 09.01: **A thumbnail sketch of Fog Machine Theory: Fog juice (A) drips through valve (B) onto a hot surface (C) in a closed container, which creates hot fog (D). Hot fog rises, which is not the ground-hugging effect you're looking for. Fortunately, there's airflow (E) to blow the hot fog through an internally baffled (F, G, and H, respectively) intercooler full of ice (I, collectively) and out the exhaust. Cold fog (J) hugs the ground like a goff in a cemetery. Robert Smith (K) would approve.**

Of the four, only the intercooler is passive, and the rest have performance variables that need to be controlled, which introduces a fifth minor subassembly — the control panel.

Commercially available foggers can be not much bigger than a loaf of marble rye. That doesn't include an intercooler, but it's not a big deal to run the hose into a beer cooler full of ice and let the chilled fog spill out of the gaps in the lid.

Nice industrial design if you're going for a stealth installation, but not an exceptionally entertaining mechanism to watch operate.

Me, I *like* watching machines work. It's inspirational, entertaining, and provides untold added value to the mechanism above and beyond its intended purpose. To that end, I'm gonna make a machine that provides solid entertainment value as well as foggin' the blue blazes out of the room.

The Hotbox

The specifications: sealable, nonflammable container containing a hot surface (fog juice flashes to vapour at anywhere between 200 to about 400 degrees F depending on the recipe — these suckers run hot, no Babylon), with an inlet for the juice, an inlet for airflow, and an outlet for the fog. Plus a hole for the electricity to get in through.

We're lookin' at hotplate in a sealed metal box with four controllable leaks, basically.

So it's off the thrift shop, where, as luck would have it, I snagged two 10" stainless steel mixing bowls, a 7" stainless steel saucer and the cutest little 8" square electric frying pan you've ever laid eyes on, parting with the grand sum of $6.59 Cdn.

I love a bargain, yes I do. **[Figure 09.02]**

The pan fit nicely into one of the bowls when the handle was removed. Unfortunately, making it fit also entailed having to lose the bimetallic thermostat/temperature controller that also served as the AC cord interface. No real biggie; I can always figure out Plan B later. The challenge now was to mount the frying pan into one of the bowls with minimum contact between the pan and the bowl. There's gonna be enough heat buildup just from radiant transfer without adding metal-to-metal conductivity to the equation.

The pan had wonky little Bakelite legs that screwed into 8-32 holes cast into the base of the pan. Two of the legs were broken, so I replaced all four by drilling out wire nut covers and digging up some 1¼" machine screws. I marked the leg positions on the metal saucer and drilled them out to ⅛", as well as finding and drilling out the center of the saucer to ¼". **[Figure 09.03]**

Figure 09.02: **The soon-to-be hotbox**

Figure 09.03: **The saucer attached to the frying pan with the drilled-out wire nut caps serving as thermally nonconductive standoffs**

Figure 09.04: **Forming the base.**

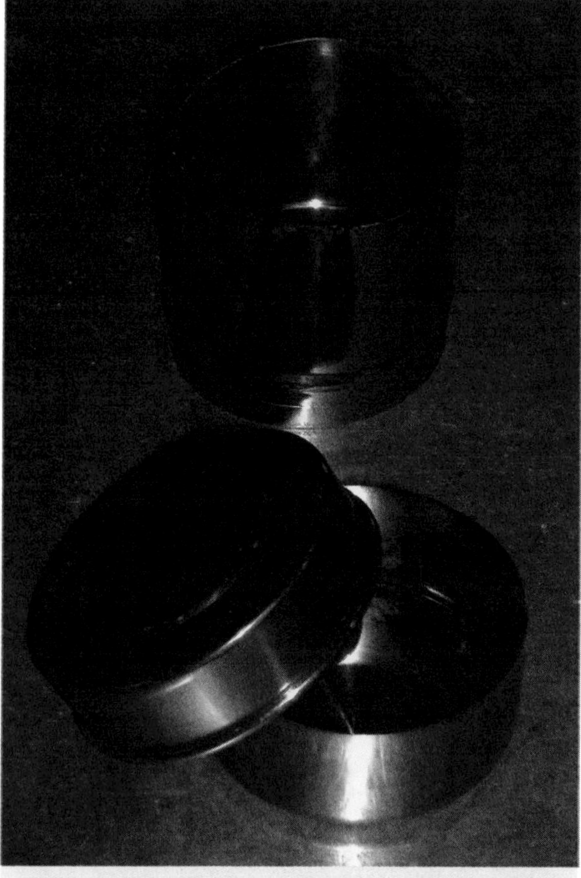
Figure 09.05: **Dollar-store stainless-steel canisters: likely not 316L alloy**

I cut a disk of ¾" plywood the same diameter as the bottom flat part of the bowl, and screwed that to bottom of the saucer, with a chunk of ¼-20 threaded rod running through the center hole. The threaded rod had a nut and lockwasher on the saucer side, with the protruding end passing through a matching hole in the base of the bowl. You can see it on the right in the illustration. **[Figure 09.04]**

I wanted to stand off the base of the bowl from the as-of-yet undetermined base of the fogger, so I hit one of the ubiquitous dollar stores that exist in quantity on seemingly every block of my neighborhood and browsed through the housewares department, where I happened upon a variety of dandy lidded stainless-steel canisters 3" in diameter and about 5" high. **[Figure 09.05]**

Figure 09.06: **It's nonstop gasket mania, courtesy of a dumpstered bicycle inner tube**

I can recognize the work of the Fates when I see it, and they were *clearly* tellin' me that stainless-steel kitchen stuff was the source material of choice for this build.

I grabbed a bunch of the canisters, and whatever else I could see that was round and stainless. I dropped $12, and left with two bags of goodies.

I attached the top of one of the canisters to the bottom of the bowl with ½" 8-32 machine screws and drilled out the center to ¼", giving me a perfectly functional 1" standoff for the bowl, which you can see on the left of **Figure 09.04**.

I spaced out ⅛" holes around the rims of the two bowls, then cut up a dumpstered bicycle inner tube into ½" strips to use as a gasket between the two bowls. The gasket stripping was attached to each bowl with contact cement, and the hole locations punched out with a heated awl. **[Figure 09.06]**

I decided to run the power cord out through the air supply conduit, which eliminated the need for one hole in the hotbox. The frying pan socket array featured a pair of ⅛" x ¾" brass pins for the power, and a 5/16" socket for the thermostat temperature probe. Although my frying pan mounting system worked as intended, holding the pan solidly mid-bowl with only the screws and wire nut standoffs actually making contact with the heat source, there was *maybe* 1/16" clearance between the power supply pins and the wall of the bowl.

In context of "How the hell do I attach the power cord?" this could only be viewed as a limiting factor. **[Figure 09.07]**

Figure 09.07: **Frying pan power cord socket/pin array before . . .**

After a quick pass through eBay to determine that these weensy frying pans were in fact fairly common and easy to replace if I screwed this one up, I hacksawed off the pins to a bit under ½" long, hoping to get enough clearance to be able to use crimps to connect the power leads. The Fates smiled again as the pins were revealed to be:

a) Hollow and
b) As crimpable as actual crimp connectors

I pulled the insulative sleeves off a pair of crimps and slid them onto the power leads along with an inch or so of shrink tubing, stuffed the bare ends of the wire into the hollow pins and made with the crimpin'. The insulation sleeves and shrink tubing fit like they were supposed to, leaving me with conections that are significantly safer than they look in the picture. Just to be sure, I gooped the pins with silicon rubber as well. **[Figure 09.08]**

With the bottom half of the hotbox configured, the upper section was left to house the inlets and outlets. A quick scrap yard run left me $2 poorer and the proud owner of a ½" to ¾" right-angled toilet shutoff valve.

The fog juice inlet needs to be located directly above the heating surface, which meant positioning the valve on the flat "bottom" surface of the upper bowl.

I cut rubber gaskets for the connection from the previously sacrificed inner tube, and resized the ¼" pilot hole I'd

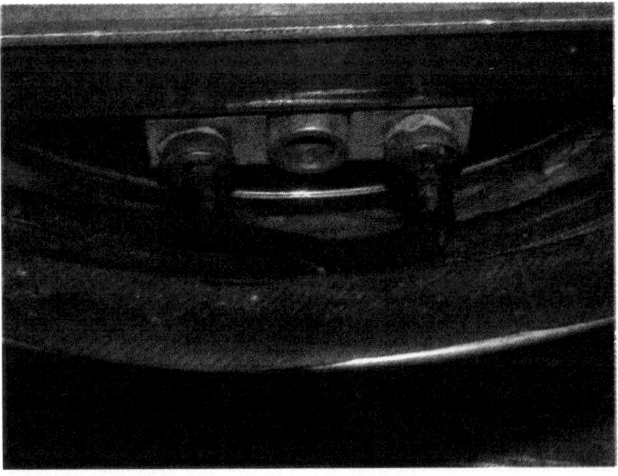

Figure 09.08: **. . . and after my profile reducing modifications.**

Figure 09.09: **Centering the fog juice inlet valve, gasket clearly visible.**

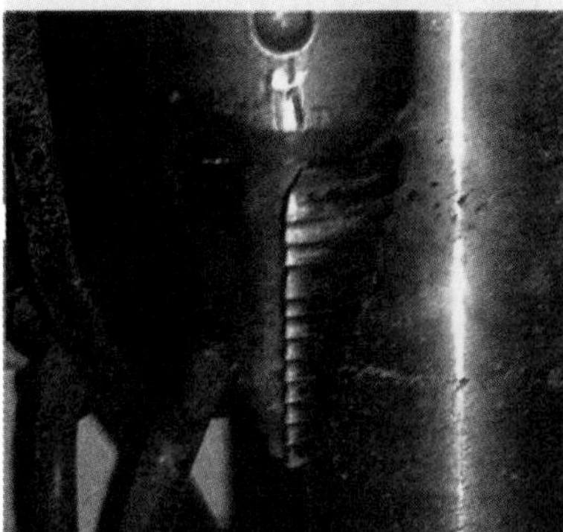
Figure 09.10: **Entirely needful kit: Tapered sheet metal bits are damned handy items for precise hole resizing in thin materials. Stainless is *not* easy to drill. Slow speed, lotsa cutting fluid, and patience will win the battle.**

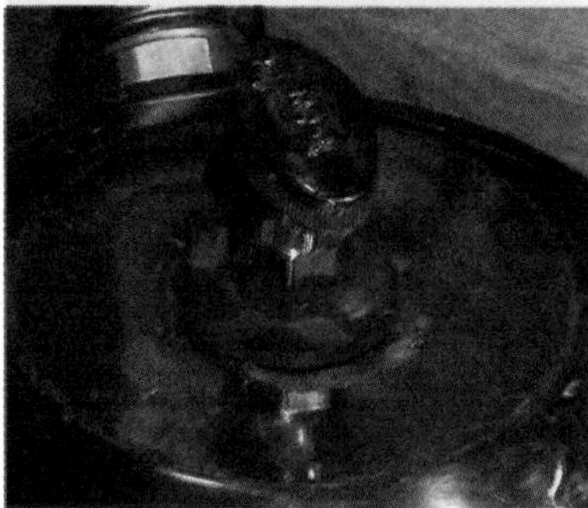
Figure 09.11: **It fits! It fits! (I get excited easily.)**

Figure 09.12: **Sherbet dishes, or flanged fittings in the wild? Context is everything.**

Figure 09.13: **A fine example of *aggressive* repurposing: Dismembered sherbet dish meets electrical conduit union and inner tube rubber, forming a properly gasketted hose attachment point.**

Figure 09.14: **Here's my finished hotbox. Don't worry about the extra fittings visible under the valve on the top. They're part of the assembly structure, which I'll get to later.**

drilled with a tapered sheet-metal bit. [Figure 09.09, Figure 09.10, Figure 09.11]

Among my other dollar store goodies were some of these dandy little sherbet dishes. They're stainless, and diametered at 4" on the top rim, 2 ½" on the bottom. The two sections are spot-welded together with three microscopic tack points. I could separate them with a quick twist, giving me ready-made flanged fittings that could be modified with 1" electrical conduit unions to provide attachment points for the inlet and outlet hoses. [Figure 09.12, Figure 09.13]

Fitted with rubber gaskets, I attached them to the upper bowl with 6-32 bolts and nuts screwed through ⅛" pilot holes after drilling out the face of the bowl to about an inch to complete the ducting. [Figure 09.14]

At this point I had a mostly fully realized and entirely unrealistic aesthetic conception for the device in my head, based on the "kitchen UFO" styling of the hotbox. Getting the rest of the subassemblies to cooperate with my high-concept artistic vision would take patience, finesse, and a large cudgel. [Figure 09.14, Figure 09.15]

The Intercooler

The intercooler warranted some pondering, most particularly from a refrigerant standpoint. As a rule, ice cubes are in short supply in yer typical office environment, and even if they weren't, the issue of disposing of the melted remnants would still be an annoying fact of life. I toyed momentarily with the idea of tweezing one of those cute little desktop fridges into the mechanism, but chucked that idea out the window once I'd confirmed the unrealistic cashflow involved.

So I stuffed the problem into the back of my subconscious to simmer and pressed on.

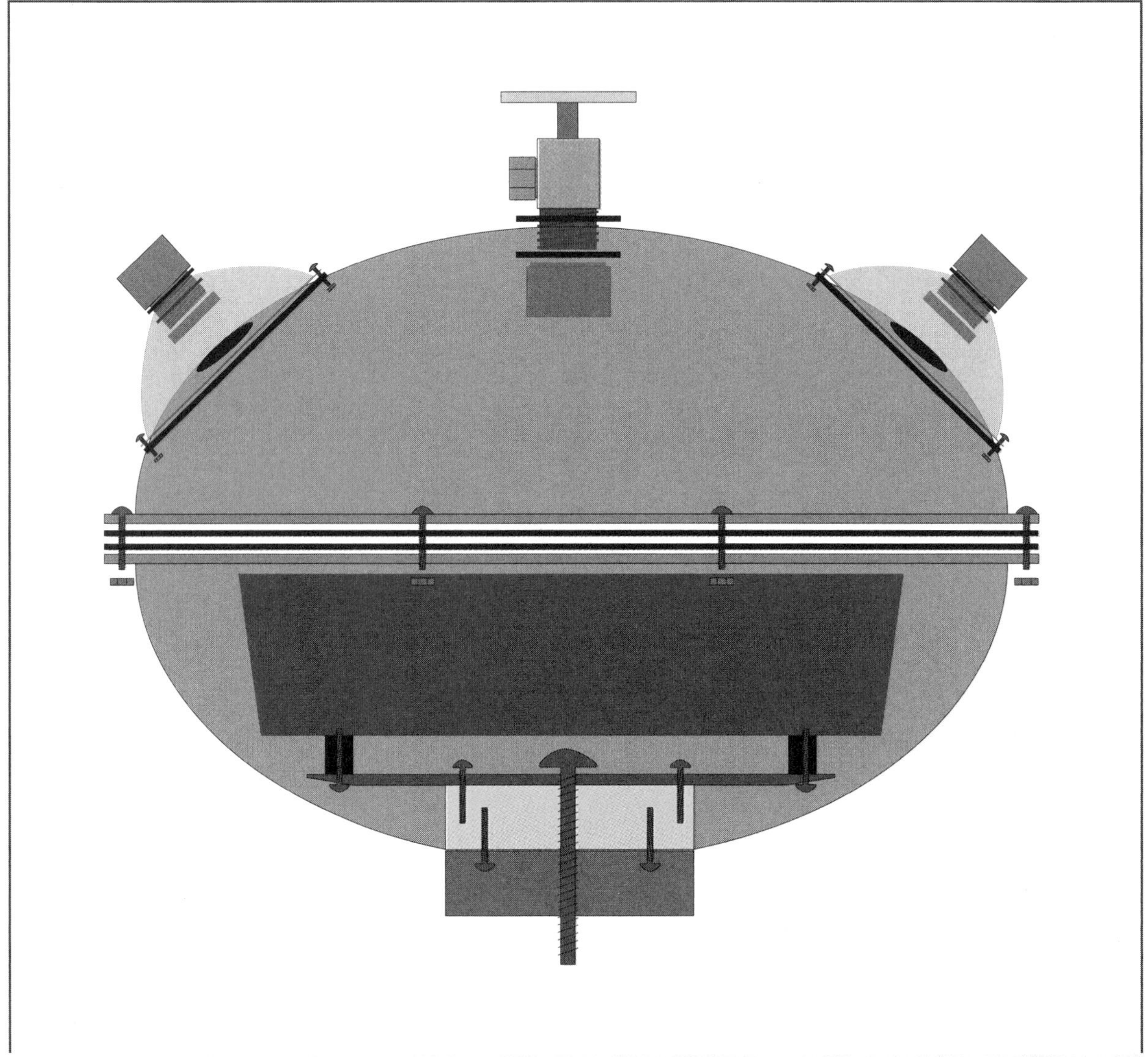

Figure 09.15: **Okay . . . so it's a kitchen UFO: the modestly detailed hotbox. Not shown: the astounding meat thermometer instrumentation hack.**

Regardless of the means of refrigeration, I wanted a top loading fog chiller for convenience sake; I found a likely candidate disguised as a biscuit tin: 15" in diameter, 4½" high, with a press-fit lid — the sort of thing usually associated with overpriced shortbreads, your aunt from Toledo, and the holiday season.

You likely have the same nightmares I do.

Ten minutes with a wire brush and an electric drill stripped the festive paint job from the light-gauge sheel metal, leaving what we might call a contemporary brushed metal finish suitable for any décor. I gave it two coats of clear lacquer to ward off corrosion. [Figure 09.16]

It might have been the lacquer fumes, lack of sleep or some combination of the two, but it was at that point that

Figure 09.16: **It's not your auntie's biscuit tin any more.**

Figure 09.17: **Again with the sherbet dish/conduit union bodge**

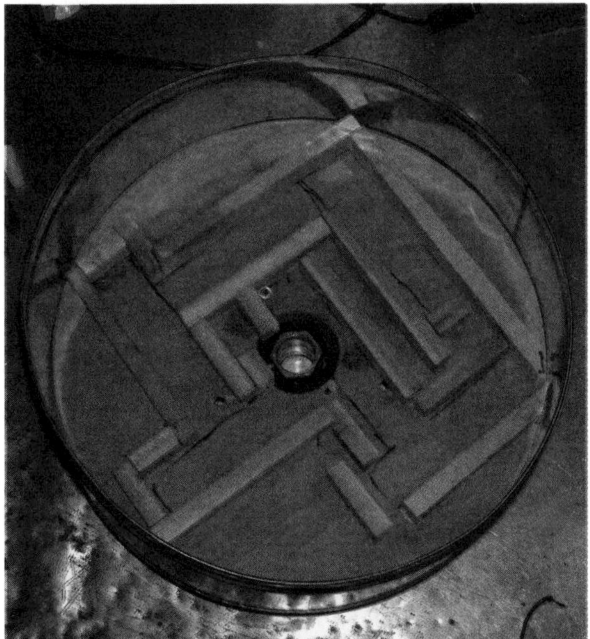

Figure 09.18: **Yup, it's a maze, all right . . . send in Pinky and the Brain.**

picnics, Pac Man, and thermodynamics collided jarringly in my brain and the solution to the ice cube issue fell out of my left earhole, bounced twice on the workbench, and came to a rest leering up at me.

In full accordance with the Laws of Nature©, hot, recently made fog rises. Arranging the subassemblies of the mechanism to take advantage of this effect is a sensible idea; fog is harder to move around than you'd expect, and every bit of bonus motive energy helps.

This means a bottom feed for the intercooler. Simple enough: bung a hole in the center and attach one of the bastard sherbet dish/conduit union combinations used so successfully on the hotbox. [Figure 09.17]

Once in the intercooler, the fog needs to make contact with as much *cold* surface area as possible to increase its density to heavier than air and make it hug the ground in a suitably graveyardish manner.

Substituting reusable picnic basket cold-packs for ice cubes, and positioning them as maze-like baffles within the intercooler results in a residue-free refrigerant system that can be hot-swapped with prefrozen spare components to maintain the temperature differential needed for effective operation.

Wonder of wonders: dollar-store freezer packs are 6" x 4¼". I fitted the intercooler with a 3⁄16" plywood floor, resulting in a

Figure 09.19: **A diagram actually worthy of the term "flowchart."**

Figure 09.20: **Dunno how much longer I'm gona be able to resist using the stereotypical Canadian "hoser" reference.**

snug fit between the freezer packs and the lid of the container, then spent about 20 minutes figuring out a workable maze layout for the baffle system. [Figure 09.18]

Once I had that pattern sussed, I glued scrap-wood battens in position to form slots to hold the freezer packs in position as the maze walls. I crammed six packs into the confines of the intercooler, giving me a quite reasonable 228 square inches of subzero surface area. [Figure 09.19]

The maze ended with a side exit point, which only required a 1" conduit union and an inner-tube rubber gasket to complete.

This is going jolly smoothly, isn't it? [Figure 09.20]

Fluid Delivery

On Saturdays and Sundays, the Vancouver Flea Market operates out of a cavernous building on Terminal Street that originally housed a factory that made wings for Mosquito bombers during the Second World War. It's also about two blocks from a big-box home-improvement center. Guess where I spend a lot of time and money on the weekends?

Anyway, the V.F.M. has about a hundred stalls, hawking everything from piles of miscellaneous junk pulled out of dumpsters a few hours earlier to polished displays of "vintage mid-20th-century memorabilia." That particular phrase immediately makes me feel *old*, because I can remember buying remarkably similar items when they were new, hot and trendworthy.

It's yer typical swap meet, in other words.

There's a certain perverse thrill in finding the same item for sale at both flavours of stalls mentioned earlier, if only to marvel at the price differential.

Case in point: the core component of my fog juice delivery system, the venerable "bubble lamp." Not the classic Nelson hanging globes from the 40s, nor the Mathmos LEDs-in-a-blob-of-silicone numbers currently in vogue, and definitely not the Noma Christmas jobbies with the methylene chloride cylinder and heat exchanger. I'm talking about the ones with an acrylic tube full of water and an aquarium pump pushing bubbles up into it — mid-90s rec room standard equipment and provider of ambience to countless herbally enhanced presentations of Pink Floyd's greatest hits.

You know the ones. They're still available in countless styles and sizes, and currently are balanced on the knife edge between "Whoa...that's hideous" and "OMIGOD! It's so kitschy — I gotta have it."

As it happens, on the particular Sunday of this build, I happened upon identical examples of said bubble lamp at the VFM, one polished, plugged in and glowing proudly, the other shadeless, half empty and half buried in a cardboard box under an assortment of mismatched leather gloves.

"Vintage mid-20th-century memorabilia" price? $50, bulb not included. "Any Item Fifty Cents, 3 for a Dollar" price? Uh... fifty cents. Can't you read the sign?

Half a buck lighter, I headed home and assembled a pneumatically powered fluid delivery system in about 20 minutes (plus the time it took for the silicone goop to cure). [Figure 09.21]

There are a few good reasons for using an air-driven system to deliver fluid. An automotive wiper fluid pump would

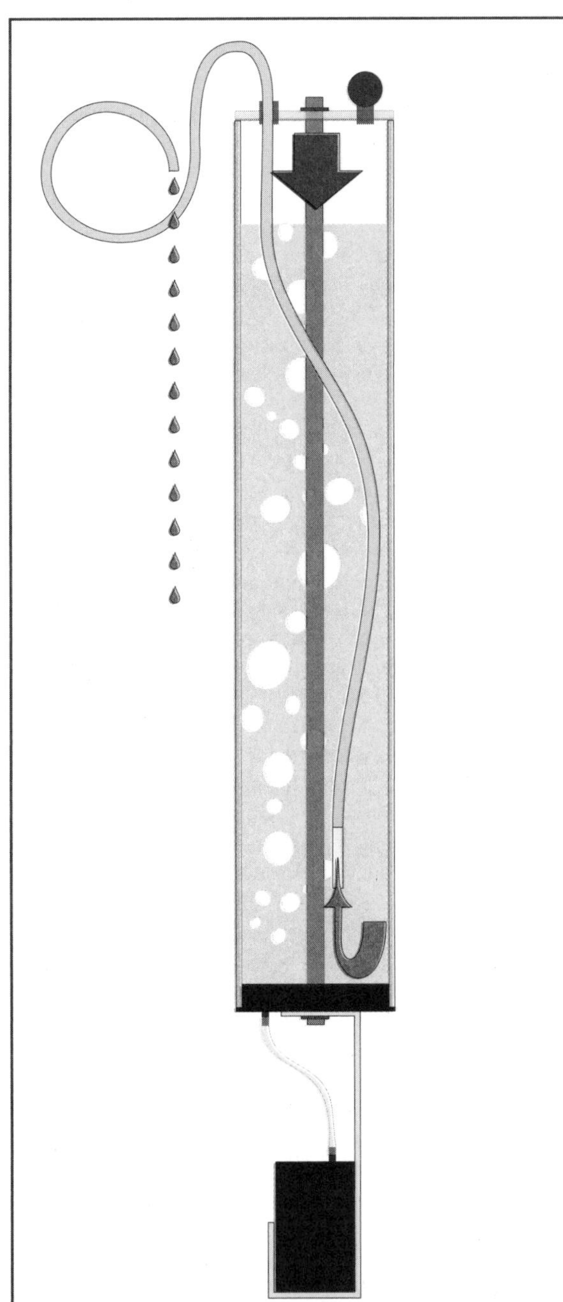

Figure 09.21: **The pneumatic-powered fluid delivery system. Apparently it's popular in certain hydroponic cultivation circles.**

Figure 09.22: **The relevant components of a bubble lamp**

do the job just as efficiently, but the possibility of pump damage associated with tightly attenuating the discharge valve is uncomfortably high. A pneumatically pressurized delivery system effectively eliminates the pump failure issue.

All that's needed is an airtight container with an inlet for pressurized air, and an outlet for displaced fluid. The air pressure builds up at the top of the container, and forces the fluid out through the bottom feeding output tube, up the tube and on to its inevitable vapourization. You don't need a lot of air pressure: 2 or 3 PSI is ample for driving a system with a modest vertical displacement and 3⁄16" output line.

If you happen to use a transparent container, and bubble the air up from the bottom of the tank, then not only do you

Figure 09.23: **From flatbar to compressor mount in three bends and a hole**

Figure 09.24: **Right. Turn the fill hole into the outlet, tap a new fill hole, and kludge together cappage for same, and leave the original hole-in-the-center-for-the-lamprod unchanged.**

get juice-pumpin', you get bubble-makin' too! That, friends and neighbors, is entertainment.[1]

Disassembled and cleaned up a tad, here's what I had: A 3" diameter acrylic tube, 18" long, with removable top and bottom and a piece of lamp rod sized to fit, and a cracked plastic base housing a diaphragm air compressor big enough to warrant rubber suspension shock mounts. [Figure 09.22]

The lamp socket was battered enough to be discardable (quite a feat, considering the crap I find reasons to keep in inventory), but it didn't fit with my plans anyway.

Converting the remnants of the bubble lamp into a pneumatically charged fluid delivery system didn't involve a lot of work. Bending a piece of 1" x ⅛" aluminum flatbar into a C shape to serve as a mount for the compressor was the only time I needed to even pick up a tape measure. The mounting bracket was shaped to cradle the pump, and drilled to fit the lamp rod extending from the bottom of the assembled cylinder. [Figure 09.23]

Two conveniently located screws on the compressor housing were pressed into service to lock the air pump into position, and I added a cable tie for good measure. The compressor mounted upright, with the output line about 2" from the air input of the cylinder. With the output connected to the cylinder, air was routed through a microperforated diffuser molded into the base and up into the cylinder.

Making the cylinder airtight took about five minutes. The bottom fitting was sealed with silicone sealant (including the air hose attachment), and the top (including the lamp rod pass-through) was fitted with a fresh inner-tube rubber gasket and a dab of gasket sealant compound.

The top of the cylinder required a bit of modification: I drilled a ⅜" hole in the acrylic, tapped it to accept lamp rod thread, and threaded in ¾" of lamp rod, adding a cap nut and washer to make an airtight lid. This became my refilling inlet. The existing ½" fill hole on the cylinder top became the outlet tube socket. A short length of thick-walled ½" OD tubing was a snug fit into the hole and served as an airtight fitting for the actual fluid feed line, which was 3⁄16" ID (5⁄16" OD) flexible PVC stuff salvaged from one of those handheld shower attachments. [Figure 09.24]

I ran the outlet tubing right to the bottom of the cylinder, and press fitted an inch or so of brass tubing over the end of the PVC tube to weight it down and ensure that it didn't float to the top of the cylinder and act as an air vent. (Which is what happened the first time I made one of these things. In front of an audience, no less. Oy vey.)

1 Obviously, I have a low threshold of amusement.

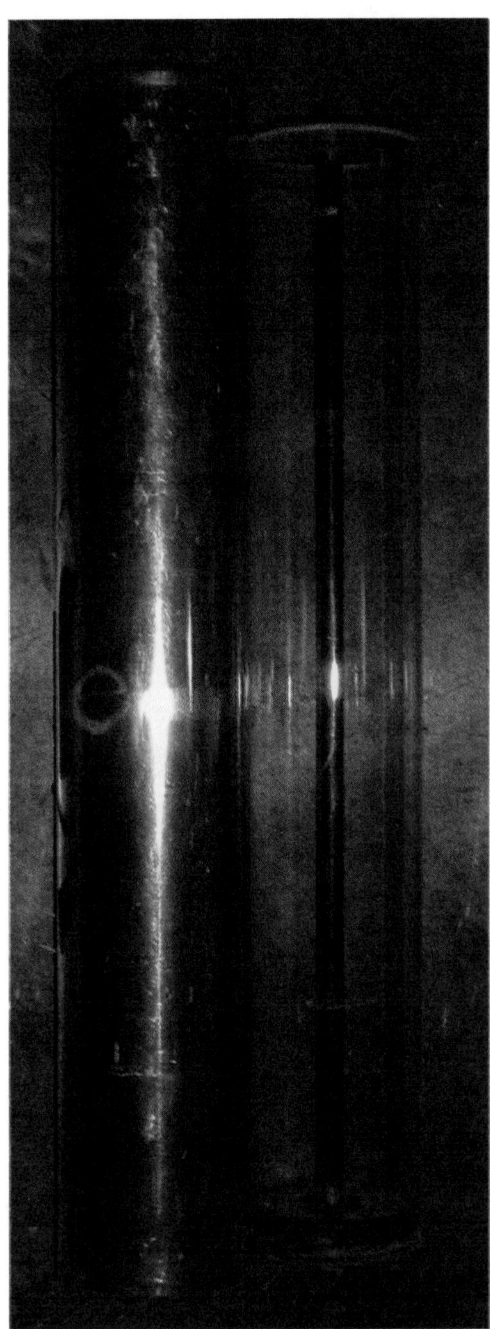

Figure 09.25: **Bubble lamp carcass meets incense canister. Lookit the size of that thing: better make that *Mr.* Incense Canister.**

Figure 09.26: **Solid mounting ensured through judiscious installation of ¼-20 carriage bolts**

A fresh gasket, a new washer on the lamp rod nut then tighten it up, and the fluid delivery system is good to go, aside from the fact that it can't stand upright 'cuz there's this flippin' compressor sticking out from the bottom.

Cunning bugger that I am, I already had that one sorted out.

In keeping with the shiny silver metal theme the Fates had thrust upon me, I dug out a cast-aluminum canister that had (according to the label) once held 500 sticks of atrocious-smelling incense, and just happened to have an ID of 3". The cylinder was originally 22" high, but by the time I cut off the threaded section at the top, I ended up with about 21" of usable length. **[Figure 09.25]**

Musta been *damned* serious incense sticks: the canister walls were 3⁄16" thick.

The air pump fit into the aluminum cylinder with *easily* ⅛" of clearance, followed by the Plexiglas tube, which fit like it was made for it.[2] To facilitate mounting the aluminum

2 Which is quite often the case when you have Inner Diameter matching Outer Diameter.

Well, I was pleased by it anyway.

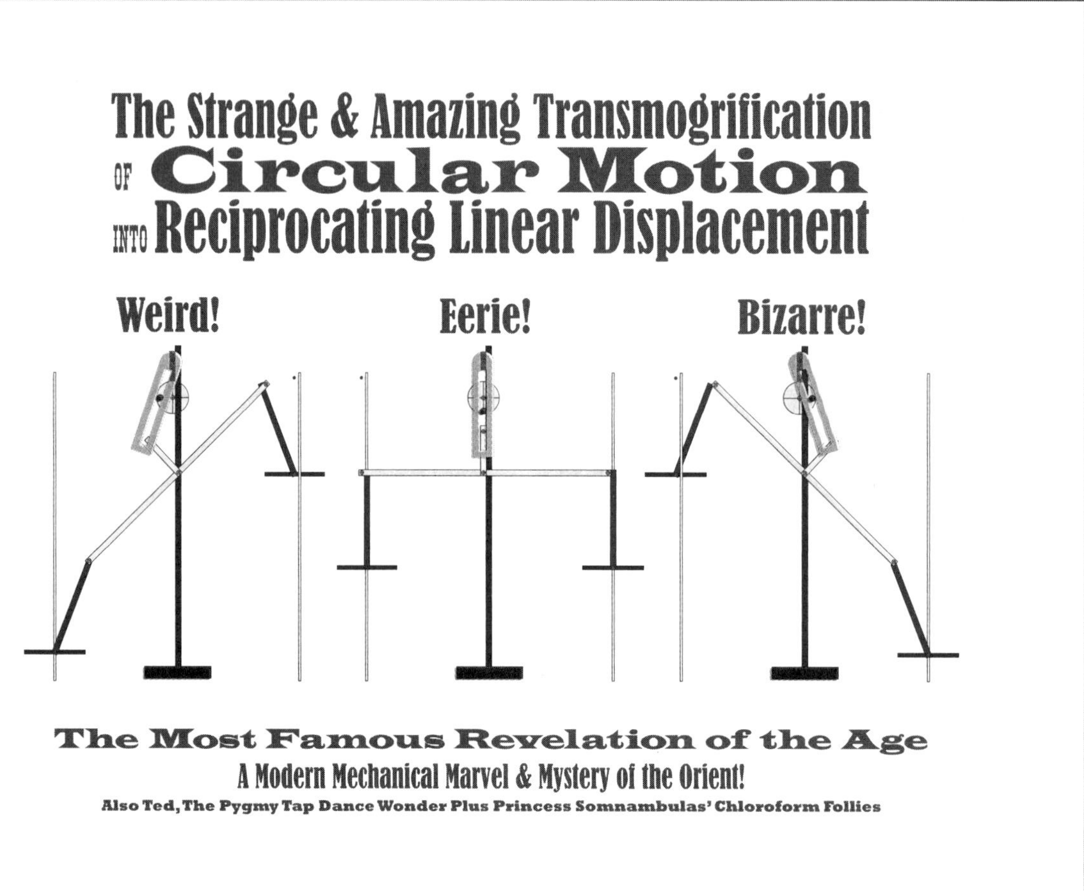

The Strange & Amazing Transmogrification
OF Circular Motion
INTO Reciprocating Linear Displacement
Weird!
Eerie!
Bizarre!
The Most Famous Revelation of the Age
A Modern Mechanical Marvel & Mystery of the Orient!
Also Ted, The Pygmy Tap Dance Wonder Plus Princess Somnambulas' Chloroform Follies

Figure 09.27: **I am unabashedly enthusiastic about the glories of simple, linkage-based mechanisms.**

receiver on the (still undetermined) base, I drilled and tapped three ¼-20 holes, with an additional ¼" hole dead center to run the air pump power cord through.

Worked like a champ, looked like something from Professor Zork's lab. [Figure 09.26]

Thoroughly splendid.

Air Supply[3]

I wanted a pair of reciprocating bellows for the air supply sub-assembly, which meant fabricating a mechanism to convert rotary motion to vertical reciprocation. The drive motor I used was a 6 RPM animatronic gear motor pulled from an animated Christmas lawn ornament, where it had previously seen duty making Vacuum Molded Santa's arm wave cheerily to passing carolers.

The two figures show you the actual motions involved in the mechanism and detail the measurements I used to get the mechanism turning over at a smooth, relentless and mathematically satisfying rate. [Figure 09.27, Figure 09.28]

Having massaged the measurements to an apparently functional point, I prototyped the movement to test the results, using aluminum flatbar and ⅜" square steel box channel "reclaimed" by disassembling one of those articulated arm desk lamps (a common dumpster commodity and excellent source of useful raw material).

3 No, not that insipid band from Australia.

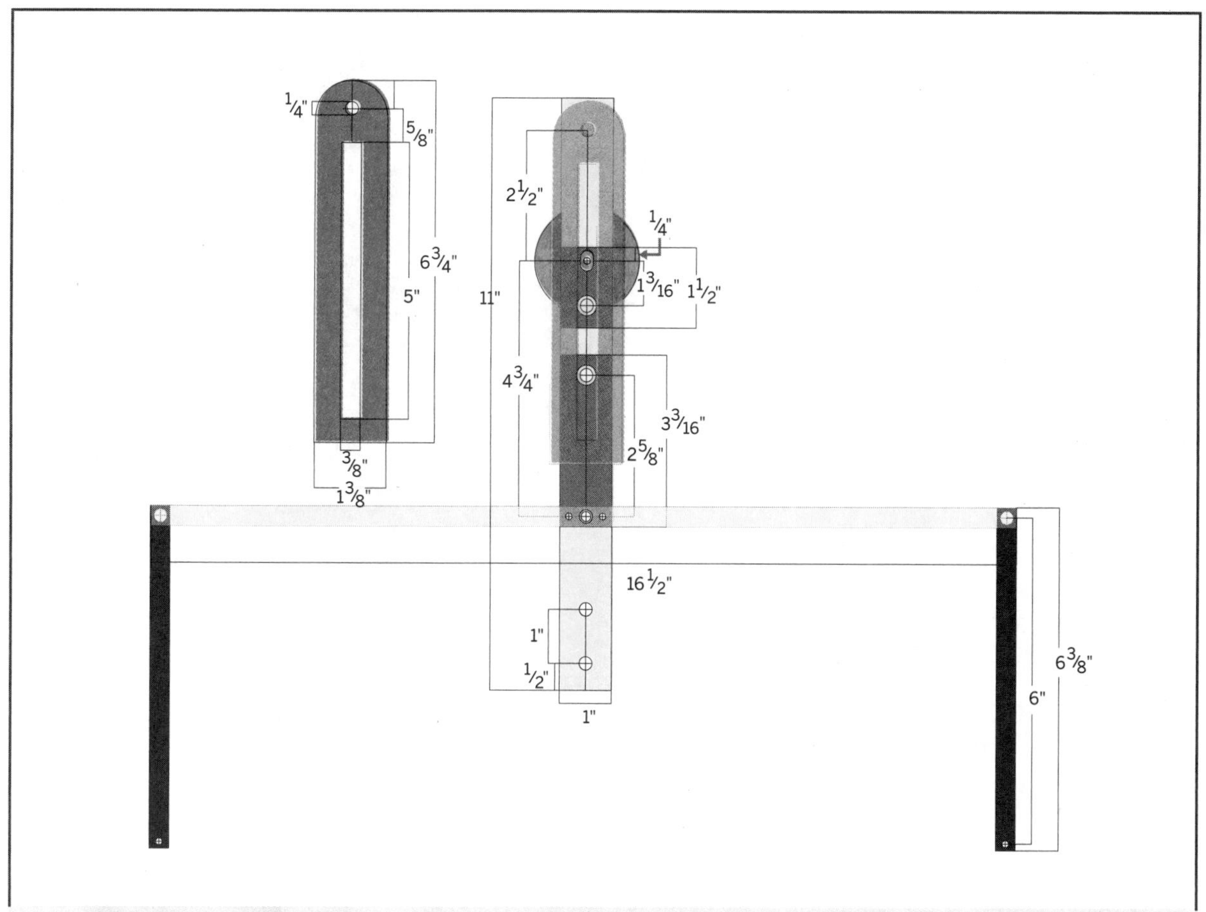

Figure 09.28: Many, many measurements. It's a damned good thing my tape measure charges a flat rate rather than billing me by the digit.

To my absolute amazement, the mechanism worked according to spec with up to 10 ounces of weight hanging from each arm. **[Figure 09.29, Figure 09.30]**

Properly fabricating the movement was just a matter of careful measurement. The hardest part was forming the slot in the slide arm, which was just a matter of drilling tightly spaced holes and filing out the material remaining. **[Figure 09.31]**

The profile view gives a clearer indication of how things go together. I put brass bushing sleeves everywhere I could to reduce friction while maintaining a tight mechanism. None of the bolt or machine screw dimensions are particularly critical, so long as the screw/bushing/hole diameters nest closely. It's actually the bushing *lengths* that are the most critical measurements in getting this mechanism to cycle smoothly. I used 8-32 machine screws for everything except the main rocker arm axle, which called for a ¼-20 carriage bolt. **[Figure 09.32]**

The driveshaft of the gear motor had two flat sides. Forming the proper-shaped hole in the actuator arm was just another case of "two closely spaced holes, then grind away the middle bit." **[Figure 09.33]**

Making the T-shaped lever that actually does the work involved forming a slot in the box channel sized to accept 1" x 3⁄16" flat bar and securing it in position with thread-forming (self-tapping) screws. I drilled out the pivot hole *after* the T was assembled.

I cut out the proper-sized notches and did some creative bending to get the two pieces of box channel to mesh cleanly, but the linkages at the ends of the T arm still needed a bit

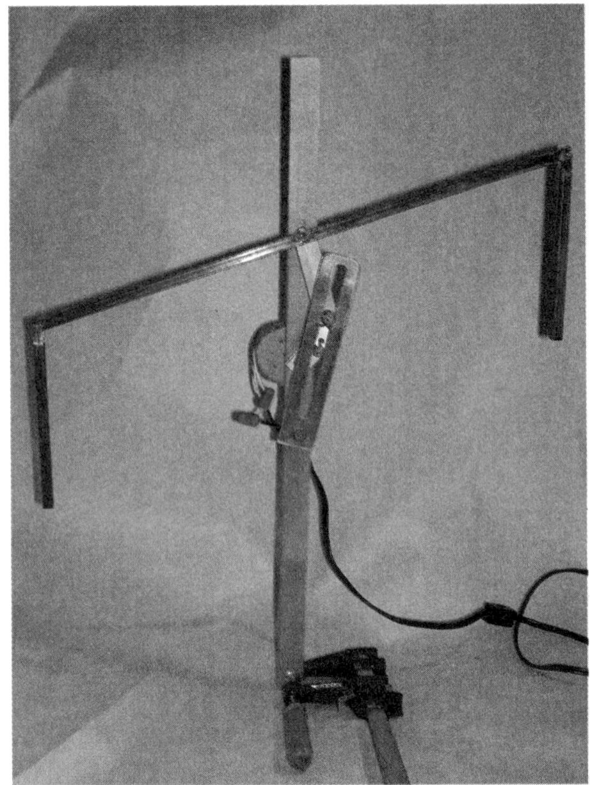

Figure 09.29: **The prototyped mechanism from afar . . .**

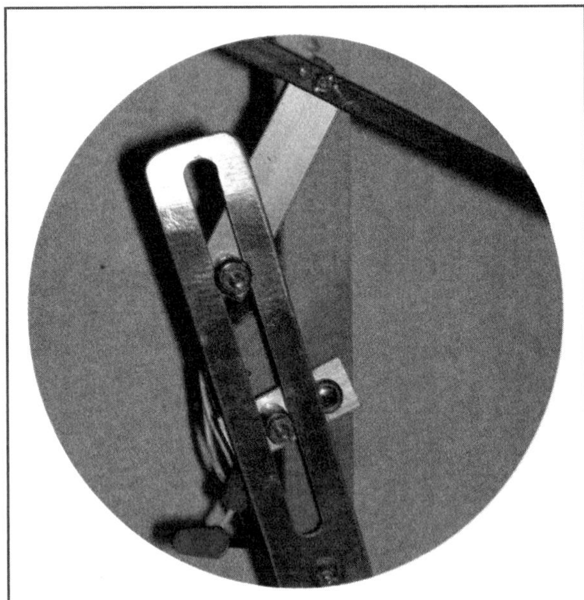

Figure 09.30 **. . . and up close 'n' personal**

of fussing to minimize friction. The fussing involved cutting bushings from brass tubing that were fractionally longer than 3/8", which held them off the box channel while still giving me something to cinch the nuts on the axle bolts down onto. **[Figure 09.34]**

The machine screws anchoring the pins that fit into the slotted arm (on both the rocker and the driveshaft actuator) are threaded into tapped holes. The pins themselves had to fit precisely and move with relatively low friction and as little slack as possible within the slot, which was just a matter of fitting a bushing of the right length into a piece of 3/8" OD brass tubing and dressing the walls of the slot with emery cloth and polishing paper. **[Figure 09.35]**

Once the parts of the mechanism were fabricated, I did the assembly using thread-locking glue on every nut. Havin' things unscrew themselves is just plain unbecoming.

The drive motor needed a proper enclosure/mounting point. One of the dollar-store stainless-steel cannisters cut to length

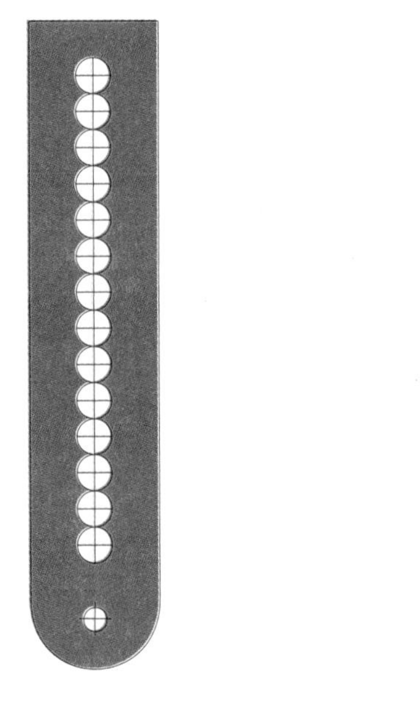

Figure 09.31: **Drill * 14 + file + elbow grease = slot**

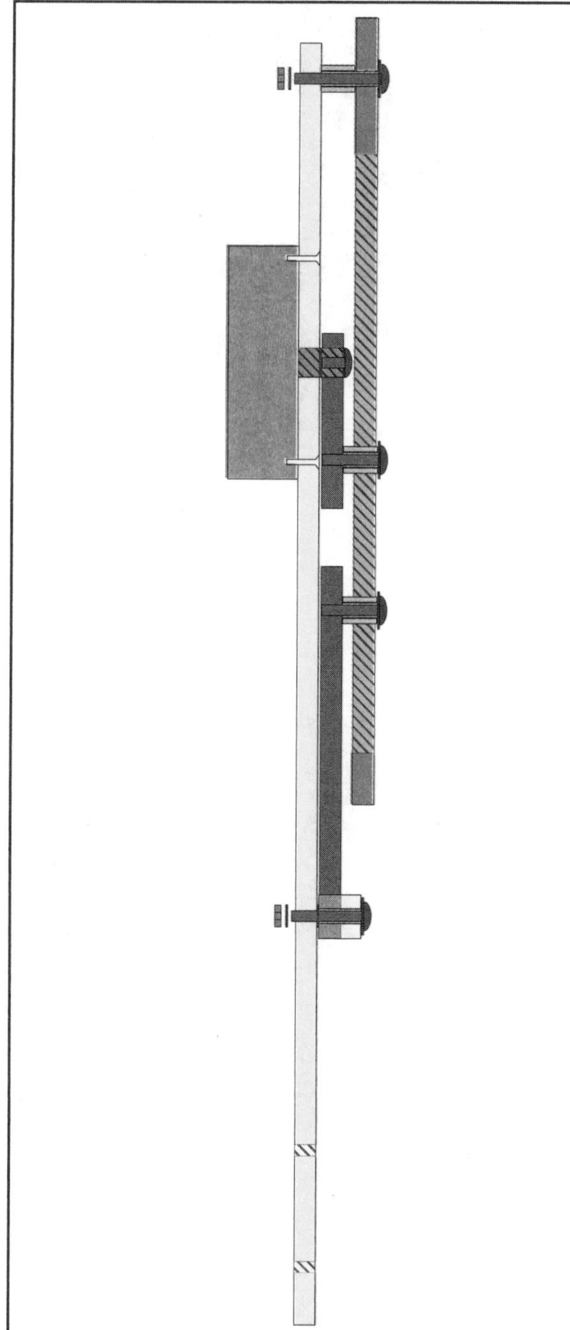

Figure 09.32: **Handsome profile, isn't it? Pay attention to the bushings, spacers, and washers.**

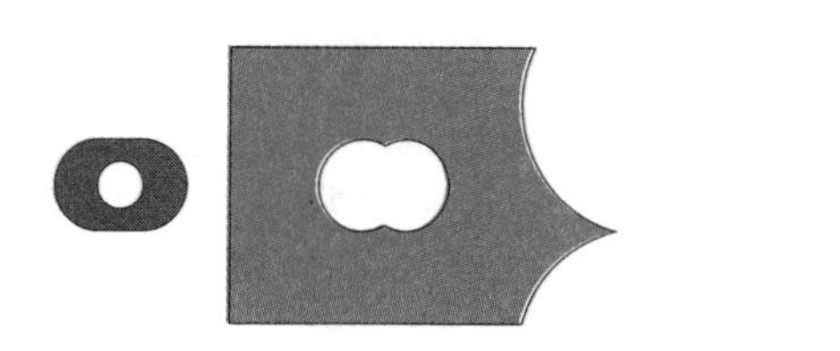

Figure 09.33: **Two closely spaced holes; grind away the middle bit**

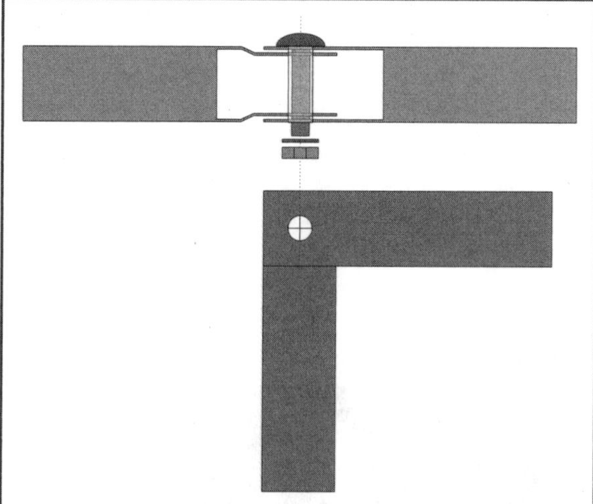

Figure 09.34: **The rather fussy box channel linkage: once again, it's bushings to the rescue.**

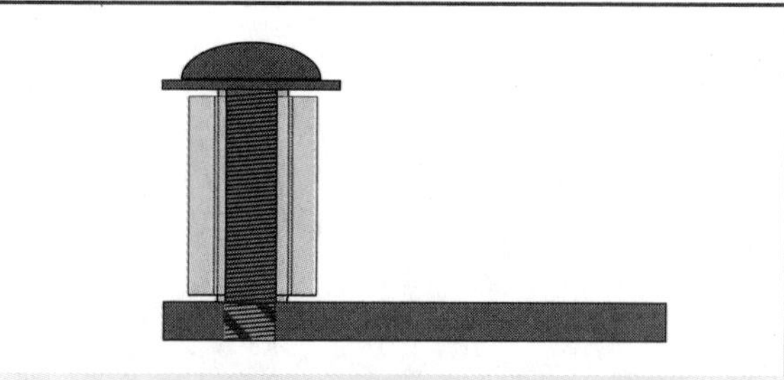

Figure 09.35: **You should have the hang of this whole "nested brass tubing" bushing thing. On the rocker and driveshaft pins (the ones that interface with the slotted arm) a washer with a hole diameter less than the inner bushing diameter and an outer diameter greater than the slot width is added to hold the pin in the slot.**

filled the purpose, once I'd holed out a piece of MDF to cradle the drive and center the shaft accurately and filed away a bit of metal to give the AC leads somewhere to go. I padded the inside of the front face of the case with a layer of craft foam to dampen the motor noise a tad. [Figure 09.36, Figure 09.37]

Just by itself, this is an entirely trippy mechanism to watch operate. This level of trippiness pales in comparison however, to the Antarctically cool scene presented when the bellows are attached to the mechanism and it's actually moving air.

Which means that the sooner the bellows come into existence, the sooner the spectacle unfolds.

Figure 09.36: **The motor housing: repurposed dollar-store canisters, a bit of craft foam, and some MDF**

The Bellows

I made two of the things in the sketch. With a stroke of about 11½", each 4" diameter bellows bladder generates about 1/12 of a cubic foot of air per cycle. At 6 RPM, the twin bellows deliver a single cubic foot of air per minute. This is *paltry* compared to other methods of air movement, but the positive displacement characteristics of the system make every cubic inch count. Vapourized fog juice flashes to a *vastly* increased volume, which is gonna force it through the circuit regardless. The airflow system is just there to help put a wiggle on the process.

And to look relentlessly cool. Which it does.

Figure 09.37: **The inner secrets of the drive motor case.**

Figure 09.38: A matched pair of bellows mechanisms powered by the reciprocating drive mechanism delivers a more-or-less steady flow of air to a valveless manifold that feeds the hotbox.

Figure 09.39: A classic "Piazzolla" by the master himself. Not the bellows motion we want.

Figure 09.40: "There's nothing like a well-rounded parts list." –*K. Harris, 2006*

It's a simple enough mechanism, with the inlet valve, outlet valve, and the bellows themselves being the only moving parts. The top end of the bellows moves up and down on three guide posts, the purpose of which is to control the lateral movement of the bellows and eliminate the possibility of a "Piazzolla."[4] Simple flap valves on the top and bottom of the bellows control the airflow: intake through the top, output through the bottom. The valves operate with flexible membranes, and are formed from a partial laminate of inner-tube rubber and ⅛" craft foam.

When I started the design of the Haze-o-Matic 3000, the only component I was really commited to was the white 4" flexible dryer ducting[5] (pretty much your only off-the-shelf choice to serve as the actual expanding/contracting bladder part of the bellows mechanism). There's a reinforced tinfoil version of the same bellows material available that would have *looked* better alongside the shiny silver metal aesthetic the Fates dropped on this build. Unfortunately, the tinfoil variant can't withstand repeated flexing without developing cracks and leaks, which simply won't do at all.

Them danged Fates . . . waddayagonnado?

Keeping with the trend of "build the subassemblies first, figure out how they all fit together later," I fabricated the bellows as matched self-contained modules to keep my mounting options open.

I pieced together the metalwork from stuff I found in thrift shops, dumpsters and scrap yards like a three-dimensional jigsaw puzzle. Based *purely* on what I could find in matched pairs during an extended 12-hour component foragathon, I ended up with each bellows module consisting of a 12" springform cheesecake pan sitting on a cast aluminum turntable platter, with stainless-steel condiment dishes acting as top and bottom caps for the dryer ducting. Half a 7" Super 8 movie film can fitted with short lengths of 1" ID PVC drainpipe served as the upper sliding chassis. There's nothing like a well-rounded parts list. **[Figure 09.40]**

I was ready to go with galvanized-steel electrical conduit as guideposts, when the transparent acrylic tubing arrived in the shop as if by magic. It's ¾" OD, which made it a perfect fit inside 1" ID PVC drainpipe and added a stylistically consistent accent material to all that damned shiny silver metal. It came courtesy of Kaia "the Sourceress" Howe, who, by means of a non-Euclidean imagination, relentless shopping skills, and prior ownership of just about everything that's ever existed has saved my bacon component-wise more often that I can remember. Everything I know about alternative sourcing, thrift-shop self-defense techniques, and stalking the elusive bargain has been gleaned by peeking over her shoulder.

She still manages to astound me at least once a week.

The (frankly insane) parts list belies the fact that the heart of the build is actually wood. So sue me. **[Figure 09.41]**

4 Bandoneon virtuoso and Tango master Astor Piazzola knows his way around a bellows; such finesse is not to be expected from a mere mechanism. **[Figure 09.39]**

5 Fabricating your bellows bladders from scratch is, of course, entirely possible, but do please take my word for it regarding the inherent pain-in-the-assness of such an endeavour.

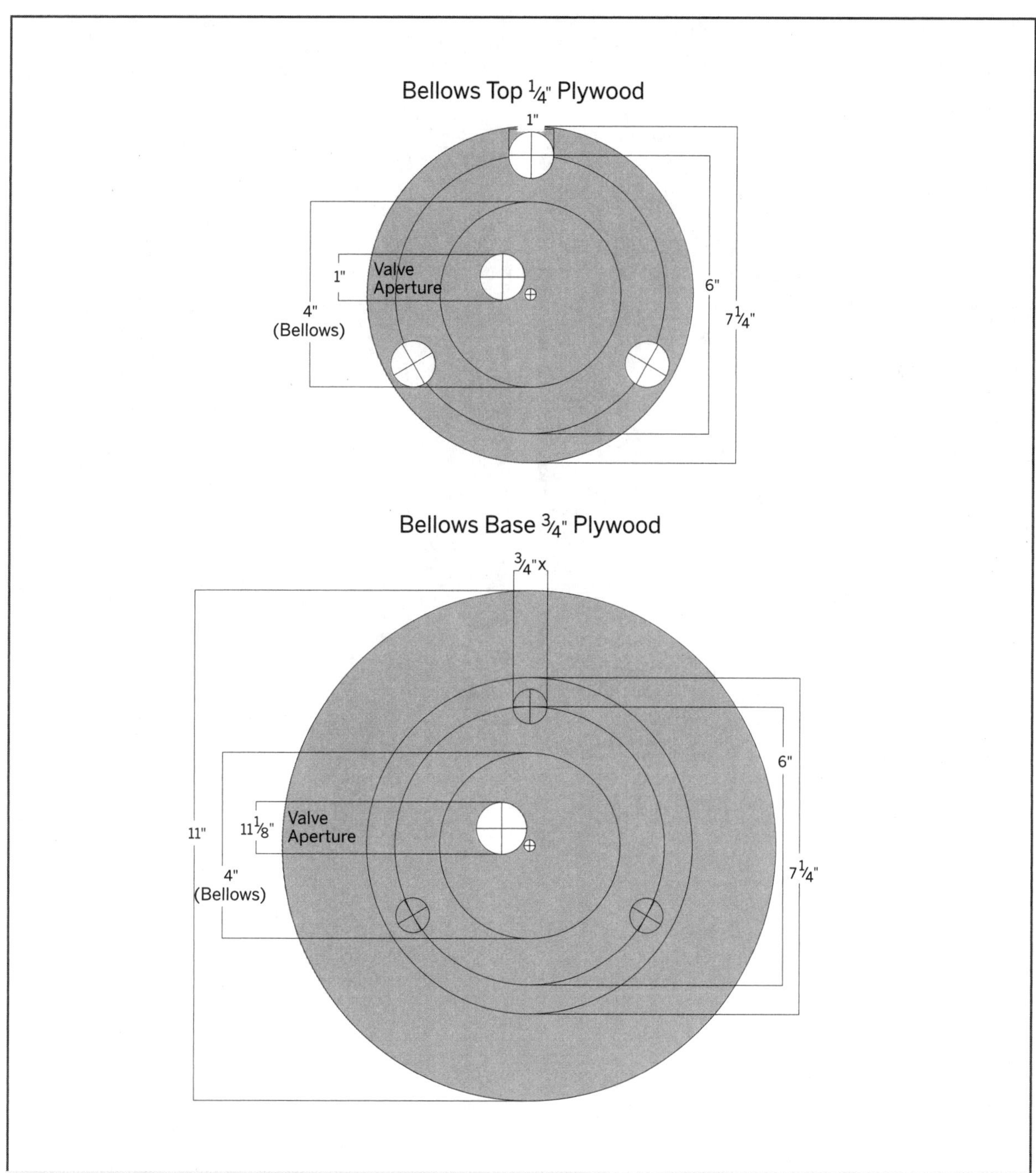

Figure 09.41: **Aaaaaaagghhh — More. Wooden. Circles.**

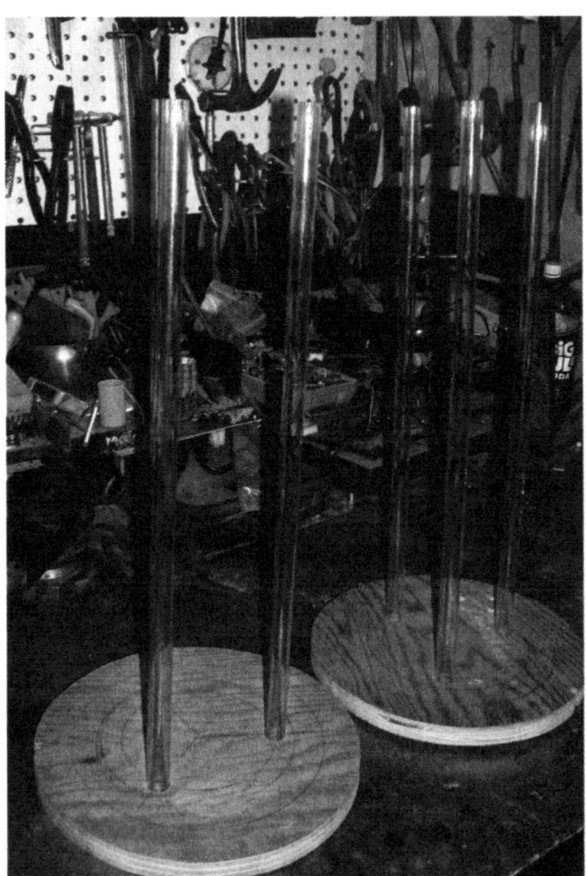

Figure 09.42: **Skeletal Bellows Assembly (not an Icelandic avant-noise ensemble)**

Figure 09.43: **I could make some kinda lame joke here about "upside-down cakes," what with it being a cake pan, and it being upside down and all, but really, what's the point?**

Working from the bottom of the bellows modules up, I laid out the guideposts to give ½" of clearance around the dryer ducting. For the base, I started with a 12" diameter disk of ¾" plywood, and used a ¾" Forstner bit to drill ⅝" deep mounting holes for the guideposts. **[Figure 09.42]**

The disk was sized to fit into the cake pan, which would be mounted upside-down on the turntable platter. **[Figure 09.43]**

The pan's removable bottom panel became the top cladding for the disk once the appropriate holes had been positioned and drilled, with wooden spacers supporting the plywood at the correct height above the platter. The entire subassembly is held together by a single ¼-20 bolt running through the center of the turntable platter, with the sides of the cake pan being removable simply by releasing the springlock and sliding it upwards. As the bellows outlet point is via the underside of the wooden mounting disk, having this kind of easy access is a pretty useful feature.

With the basic framework of the bellows roughed in, I cut and assembled four identical flap valves from craft foam and inner-tube rubber, using cyanoacrylate to bond the two layers together. **[Figure 09.44]**

I'd initially formed the flap with a single cut line, then realized after an initial field test that more material needed to be removed from around the flap to let it seat and unseat without binding. Once I'd made that modification, they worked like a charm. **[Figure 09.45]**

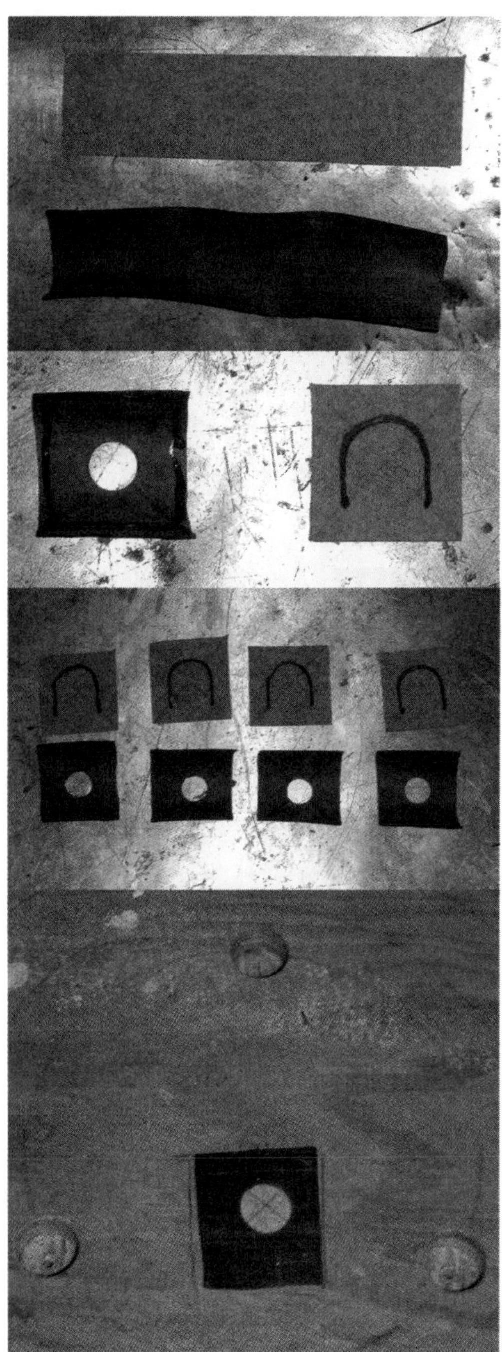

Figure 09.44: **Making flap valves**

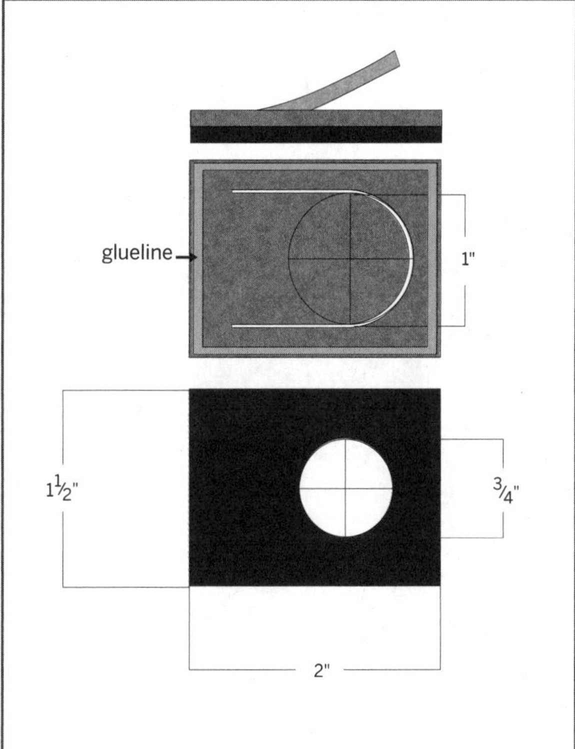

Figure 09.45: **DIY Flap Valves (also not an Icelandic avant-noise ensemble)**

The ports for the valves had to lie within the 4" diameter footprint of the condiment dishes that I used to cap the ends of the ducting, which called for drilling 1¼" holes at each location (to allow room for the flap to open and close) and chiselling out a cavity in the wood deep enough for the valve to lie flush with the surface. Once that was done, I ported the ducting end caps to match the valve location, and lined the cake pan base plate with craft foam to serve as an airseal gasket. Due to the textured surface of the base plate, the end cap got a craft-foam gasket as well, held in position with aerosol contact cement. **[Figure 09.46, Figure 09.47]**

The footprint of the condiment-dish end caps necessitated placing the valve outlets in cramped proximity to the base anchor bolt. To allow me a bit of leeway, when the time came to attach the hoses that would pipe the bellows output to the hotbox, I improvised 90-degree elbows onto the bottom of the wooden base plates out of simple blocks

Figure 09.46: **The outflow passes through a *lot* of surfaces: gasket the bejeezlies out of every single one to minimize leakage.**

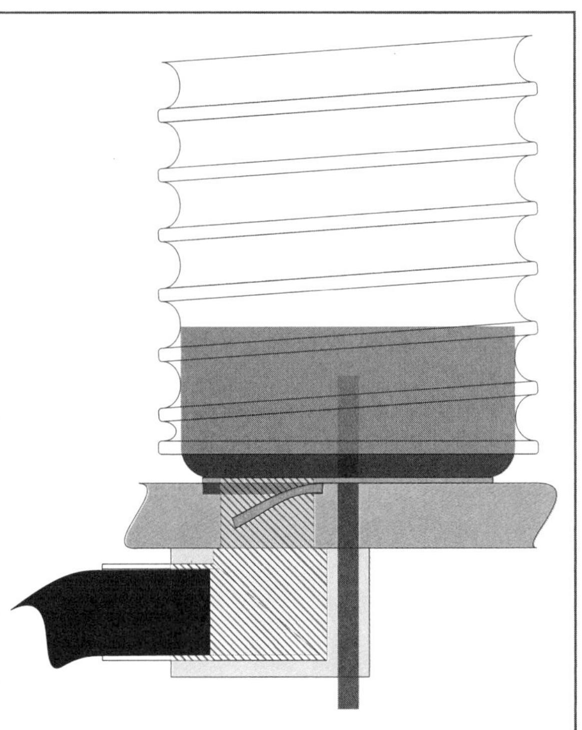

Figure 09.47: **Bellows outflow in detail**

Figure 09.48: **It's just a block of wood wif the proper 'oles in it, innit?**

cut from a 2" x 4" and drilled out. Once the glue was cured, I could finally (or so I thought) assemble the bases of the bellows modules. **[Figure 09.48]**

The top of the bellows — that being the bit that slides up and down, doin' the bellowin', as it were — is essentially the same build as the base of the module, only thinner, and with bigger holes.

Super 8 movie film storage containers are common thrift-shop items these days, forlorn relics of an abandoned technology. I got a stack of 7¼" diameter cans for 5 bucks last year, and have been looking for an excuse to use 'em ever since. They're flat metal cans that separate into two sections, each with a ½"-high rim. To make a bellows slider mechanism, half a canister was fitted with a ¼" plywood insert and holes drilled for the guidepost sliders, which were formed from 2½" lengths of 1" OD PVC pipe. **[Figure 09.49, Figure 09.50]**

To ensure a tight air seal, both sides of the insert were gasketted with craft foam before the flap valve was fitted. The

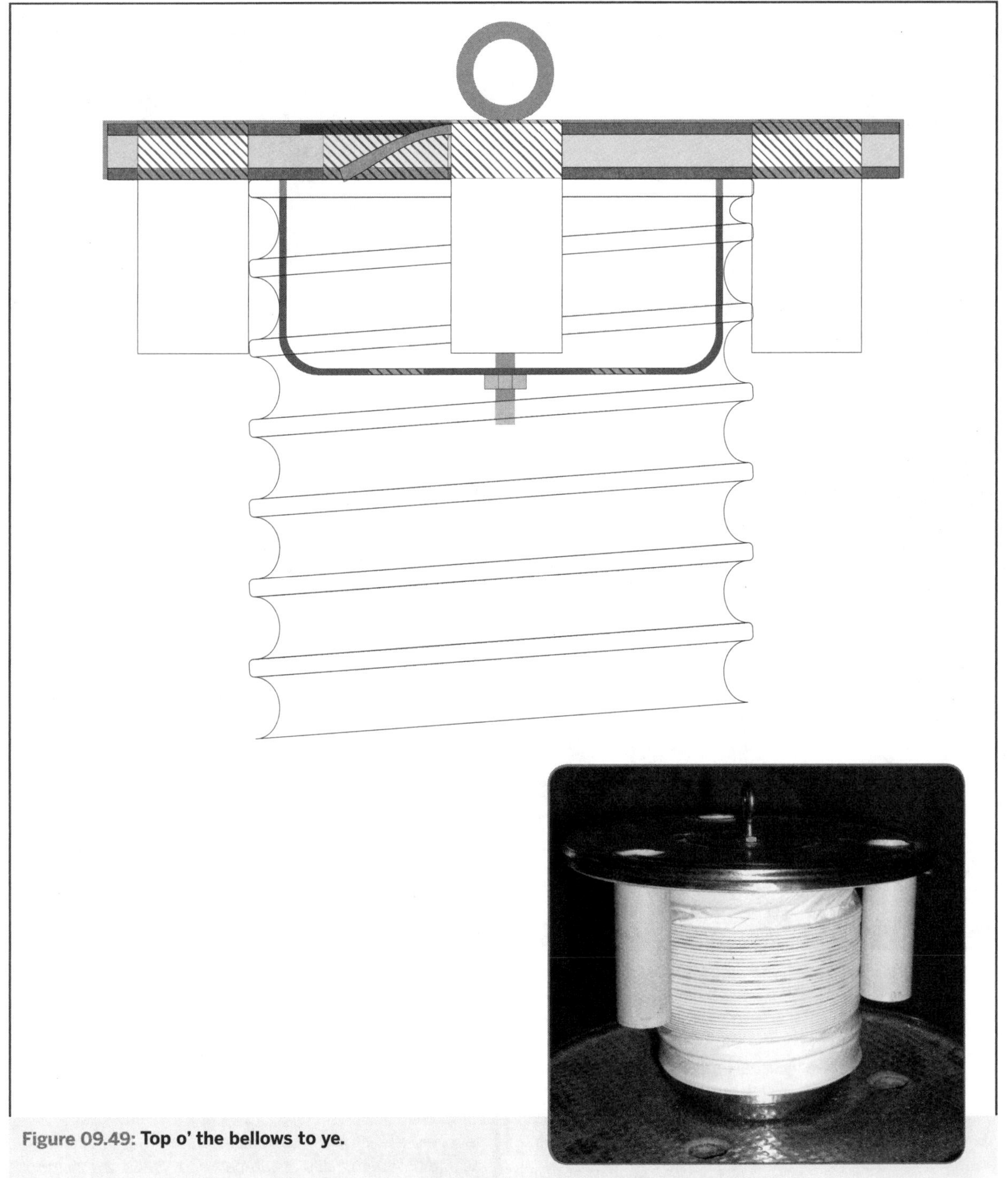

Figure 09.49: **Top o' the bellows to ye.**

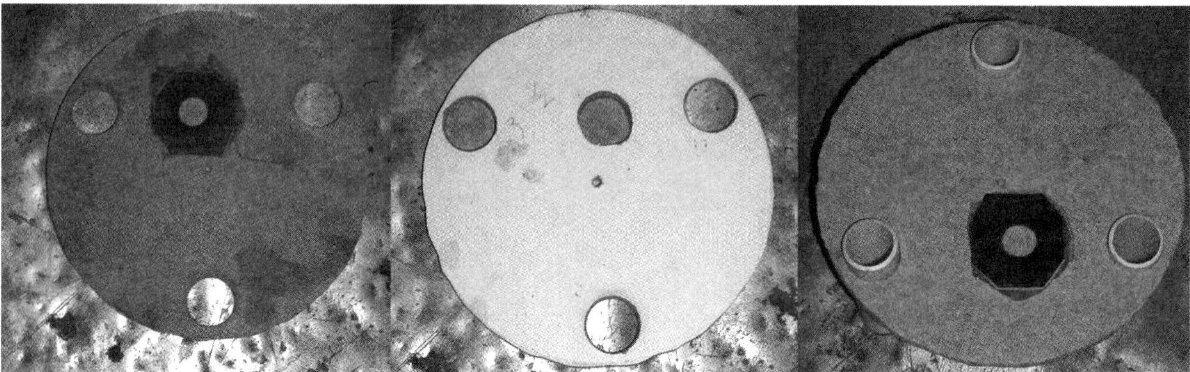

Figure 09.50: **Another round of gasket mania on the inflow valve**

Figure 09.51: **Ready to assemble the top of the bellows**

Figure 09.52: **Fold the dryer ducting over the upper lip of the top end cap, so that it's locked in place by the eyebolt.**

actuator arm of the drive mechanism attaches to a #8 x 2½" eyebolt located in the center of the film can. The extra length of the eyebolt serves as the attachment point for the stainless steel serving dish that acts as the top cap of the bellows. The bottom of the dish needed a few holes drilled in it to provide airflow in to the bellows, and the eyebolt mounts the serving dish with its upper rim firmly in contact with the gasket material on the bottom of the insert. [Figure 09.51, Figure 09.52]

I cut the guideposts to 20"; they press-fitted tightly into the receiver holes in the base plate, and were glued in place one at a time with a dab of two-part epoxy after the alignment was trued up with a square.

Figure 09.53: **The completed bellows assemblies. Final score on attaching the ducting to the bottom end cap? Electrical tape: 2, duct tape: 0.**

The guidepost sliders press fit into the holes in the upper bellows mechanism, then are glued permanently with two-part epoxy. I did the glue-up with the assembled slider mechanism in position on the guideposts at the bottom of their travel, which guaranteed accurate alignment. There's gratifyingly minimal friction between the acrylic and the PVC; the sliders move with unnatural ease.

The bladders themselves were 16" of fully expanded dryer ducting each. The mechanism has a vertical travel of just under a foot, but I wanted a couple of inches of leeway at each end to bugger around with when I made the airseals. I tried a number of methods of attaching the ducting to the end caps, finally arriving at a few wraps of PVC electrical tape as providing the best air seal for the joints. Duct tape, used in this case *for its actual intended purpose*, was not as effective. **[Figure 09.53]**

Strange, but true.

At this stage, I realized that unless I was prepared to drill honkin' big exit holes in the walls of my cake pan bellows modules, the outlet hoses would have to run from my bodged-together connection point on the plywood module base out through the conveniently cast-in holes in the turntable platters.

Which meant that the bellows modules themselves would have to be supported up off the (still undefined) base of the mechanism to provide clearance for the hoses to exit.

Dang.

I couldn't put off finding a base to assemble this damned thing on any longer!

Figure 09.54: **Bellows base stilt receivers**

The Base

Biting the proverbial bullet, I rummaged around in the wood crib for something large and base-like, coming up with a 24"-diameter circle of MDF of dubious provenance. It was battered, and coated with an almost Formica-thick layer of an unidentified white paint, but I was pretty sure I could fit all the subassemblies onto it with a bit of finessing. **[Figure 09.54]**

Activating my artsy-fartsy nonsense super-powers, I decided to perch the bellows modules on acrylic tube stilts positioned to look like extensions of the bellows guideposts. This meant adding a plywood insert to the bottom of the turntable platters drilled to accept the stilt posts, with correspondingly positioned holes drilled into the base. The stilt poles ended up being a shade over 9" high, that being the amount of tubing I had left over from doing the guide posts. **[Figure 09.55, Figure 09.56]**

The modules were positioned and mounted on the assembly base in the context of the drive mechanism geometry, followed by the drive mechanism itself, which needed a bit of finagling to get it mounted at the correct height.

The obvious method would be to set a flanged pipe mount on the base, with the drive mechanism mounted on a chunk of pipe extending to the correct height. Ya think I could find a freakin' pipe mount, retail, scrap yard, or dumpster?

Zilch. Nada. Unobtainium. It's embarrassing to admit. **[Figure 09.57]**

Even the Sourceress was stumped.

Once again, Dang.

Once again, I improvised, this time with a piece of 1" OD steel pipe that was formerly part of a needlessly complicated bookshelf, and a lot of chunks of wood with 1" diameter holes in 'em. The pipe mount was formed by a tiered layer cake kinda stack of MDF disks center drilled to 1", which mounted to the base with glue and dowel pins. The pipe slotted into the hole, and was secured in position with a pair of #8 x 2" machine screws set into the edge of the disks and screwed into holes I drilled and threaded in the pipe.

The drive mount was a glued-up stack of 2½" plywood disks cut with a hole saw, then drilled out to 1". Once the glue was set, I sanded one face of the stack flat to accommodate the flatbar chassis of the drive, which was mounted to the stack with wood screws. A single #8 wingbolt (actually a repurposed eyebolt) locks the assembled drive and mount onto the extension pipe, making it easily removable. **[Figure 09.58]**

In case I needed to easily remove it. Whatever. **[Figure 09.59]**

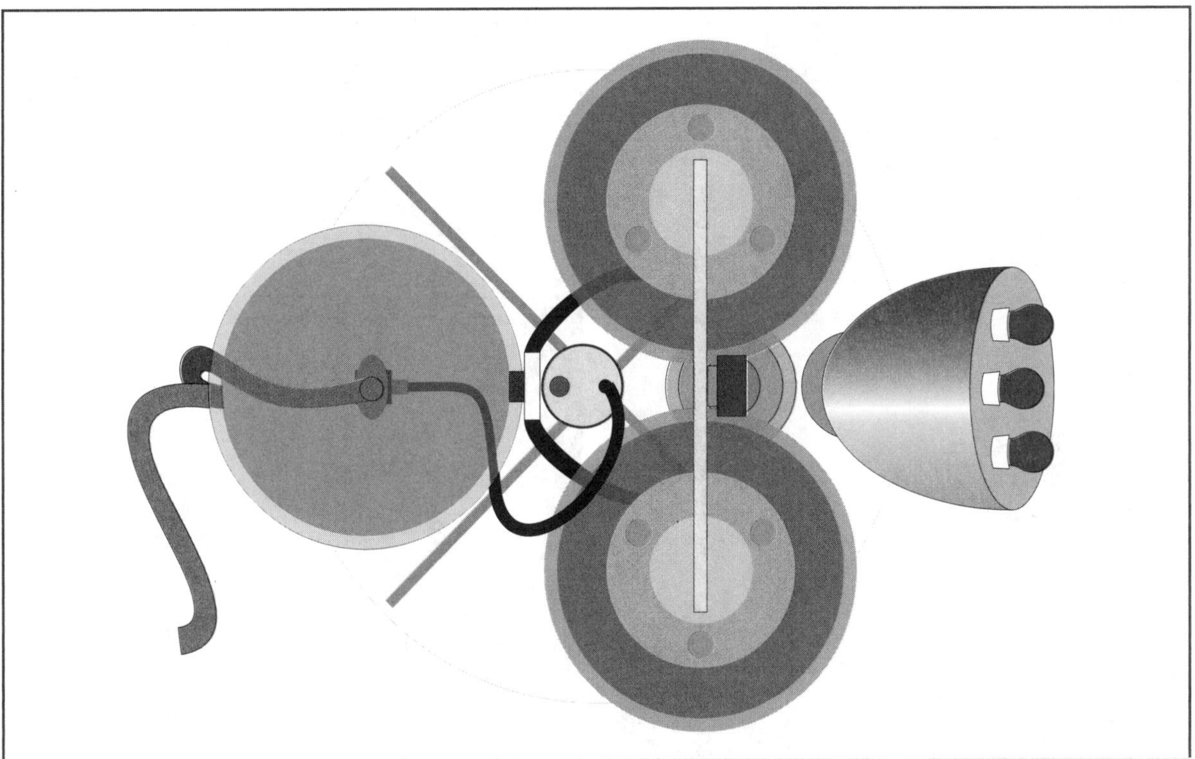

Figure 09.55: **Accordin' to this-here drawing, it's all gonna fit. That bit on the right is the control console, coming real soon.**

Figure 09.56: **The stilt equipped base.**

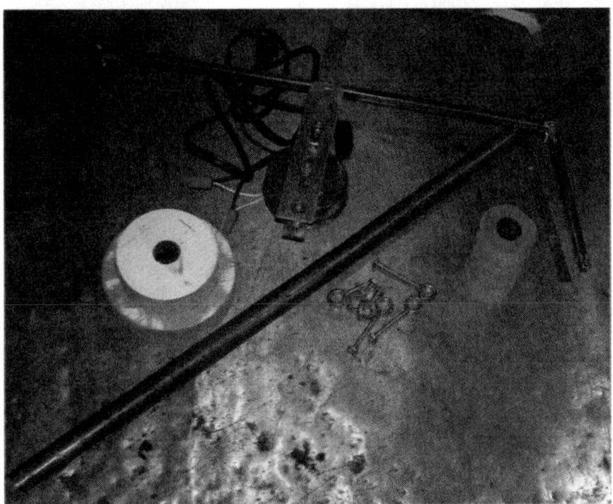

Figure 09.57: **The bellows drive bits 'n pieces queued for installation**

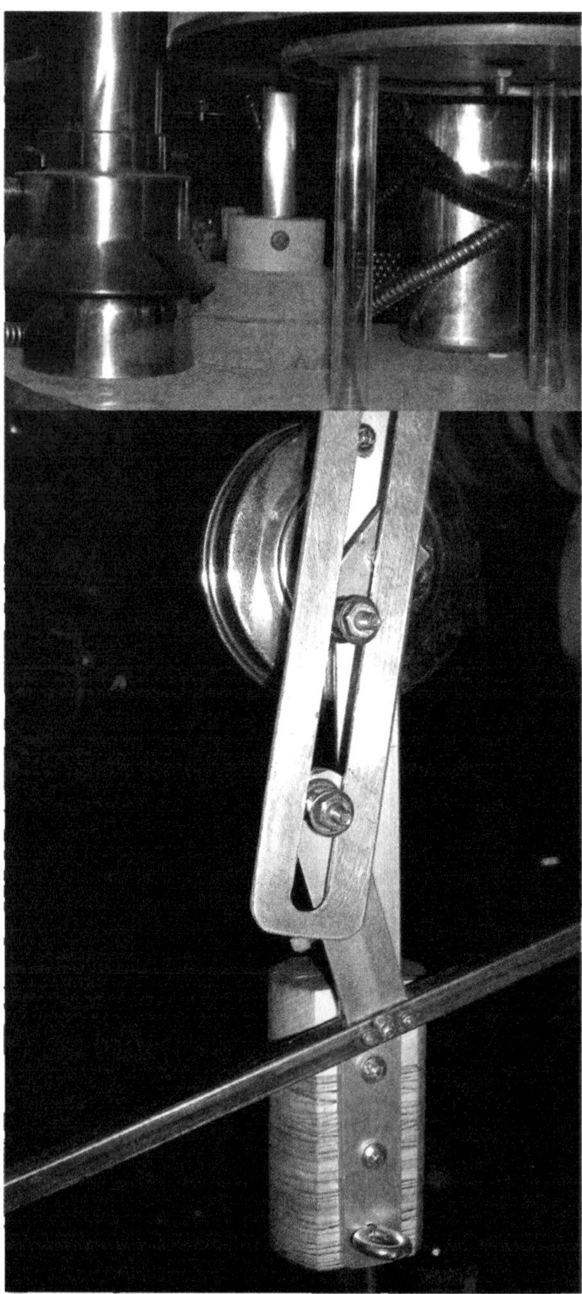

Figure 09.58: Drive mount, with motor assembly mounted on it. The #8 eyebolt at the bottom holds the assembly to the pipe and can be loosened to adjust it up or down.

Figure 09.59: A bit of cable loom and some zip ties take care of the exposed wiring.

There was no need for a bushing on the junction of the drive arm and the top of the bellows. An 8-32 machine screw and nut through the eyebolt completed the connection after I'd sized the slot in the drive linkage to accommodate the full range of movement of the mechanism.

The exposed section of the power cord for the drive motor was concealed with cable loom, and the rest of it threaded down the pipe and out through a ¼" hole in the bottom of the base, from which it will eventually lead to the control panel.

Startlingly, the mechanism worked as spec'd the first time I powered it up, prompting several moments of exuberant fist-pumping self-congratulation. **[Figure 09.60]**

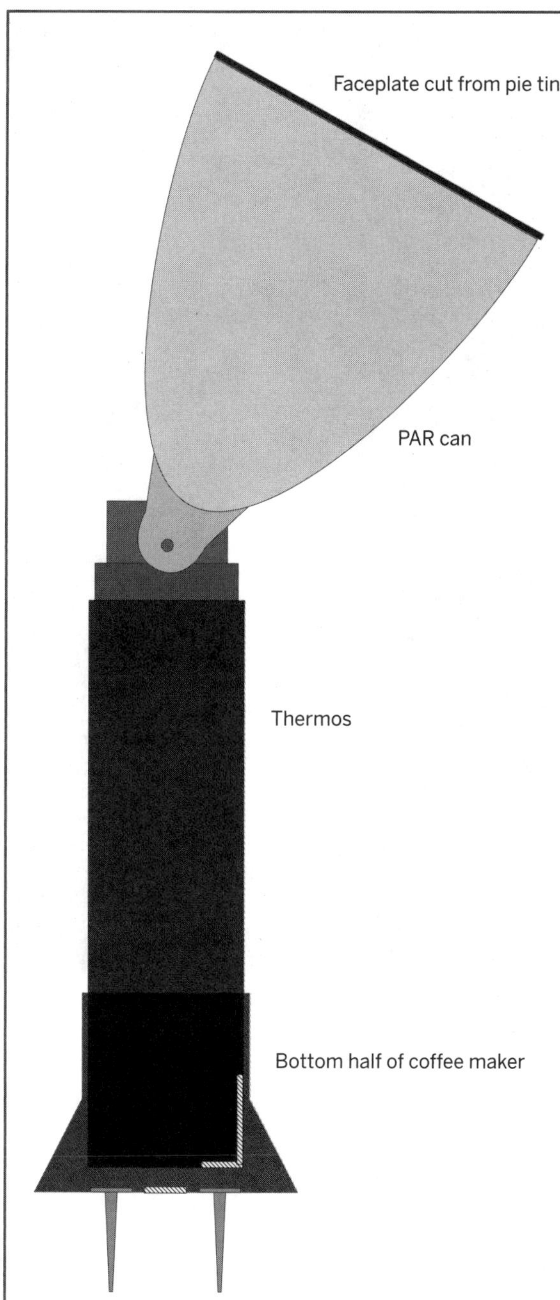

Figure 09.60: The control console assemblage: A very component-specific kludge. Ya couldn't try this one at home even if you wanted to.

Control Console

Ri-i-ight . . . the control console. Almost the last bit of kit to cobble together; fortunately, I had both a plan and a pile of components to build from.

To wit, a miniature coffee pot, a two-cup stainless steel thermos container, an aluminum pie plate and an 8" PAR can.[6] Now, this is one of those component-specific kludged together "bricolages" no one else in their right mind would ever consider attempting. It's also a pretty good illustration of bending mundane components to one's maniacal will, which is why I'm even bothering to detail it.

The throat of the PAR can nested nicely with the top of the thermos container, and only needed to be notched to form "ears" that would let it be angle-adjustable. **[Figure 09.61]**

I cut a template for the notch out of shim stock and used a hacksaw to remove the excess material. **[Figure 09.62, Figure 09.63]**

The pivot axle is a 3" 10-32 bolt. The thumbwheel used to tighten the swivel mechanism was part of the focus mechanism from a derelict slide projector, drilled and tapped to fit.

The coffee maker had a removable bottom section with a top opening that fit the thermos perfectly. I drilled the base of the coffee maker for three mounting screws and a hole for the wiring to enter, and cut a notch out of the bottom of the thermos to pass the wiring. **[Figure 09.64]**

To mount the controls on the face of the control panel, I first needed a face. Enter the pie plate, which cut like paper with tinsnips and gave me an 8"-diameter aluminum faceplate at a cost of . . . not a kipper.

Who bakes pies anymore, anyway?

I laminated the aluminum to a disk of ¼" plywood of fractionally smaller diameter (Yeah yeah, I know: enough with the plywood disks already. Can't help it — it's muh style, maaaan.[7]) and drilled holes for four escutcheon pins around the rim of the can to handle mounting requirements.

6 Oh, that Harris guy and his sordid rock 'n' roll past. "PAR can" is a venerable stage lighting term referring to *Parabolic Aluminum Reflectors*, the staple lamp housing in low-budget Rawk Band lighting rigs. They're parabolic, aluminum, and reflective, in case you haven't already worked that out. None of these factors come into play in this build, other than maybe the shape, which is *totally* 50s sci-fi.

7 Unbelievably obscure reference to Canadian music icon Neil Young: when challenged about his vocal contribution to "Tears Are Not Enough' (the Canadian music industry's 1985 Ethiopian Famine Relief charity song) perhaps being "a little flat," Neil responded to the concerned producer by donning his shades and saying, "It's muh style, maaaan."

Neil did *not* do another take.

Figure 09.61: **The PAR can fits over the thermos body, but to make it tilt, we'll need to cut a slot.**

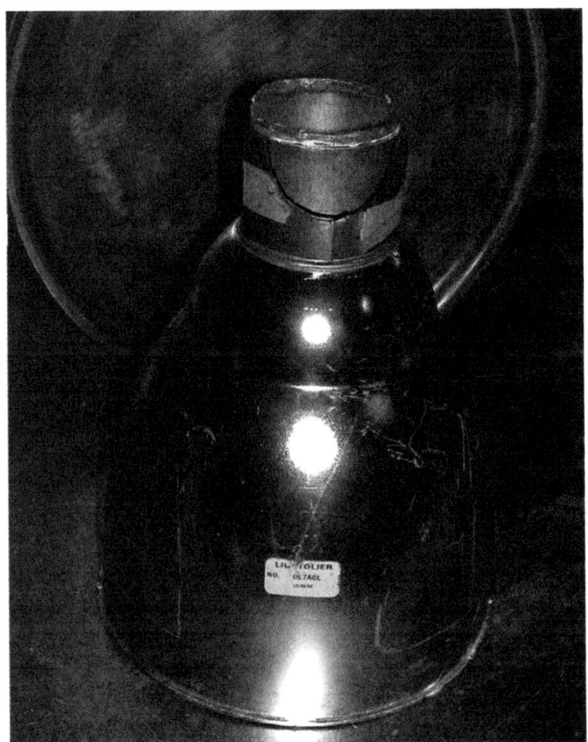

Figure 09.62: **Make a template for cutting the slot. You won't be sorry.**

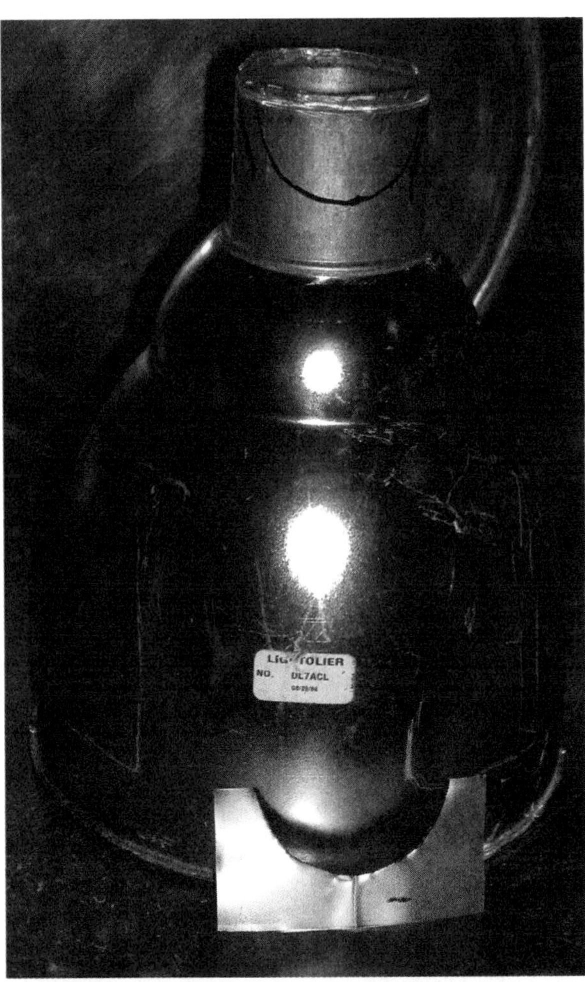

Figure 09.63: **Now trim along the line you made with the template.**

I kept the controls and indicators to a 50s-sci-fi minimum: three switches, a knob, and three incandescent lamps. I used 7.5-watt 1½"-diameter traditional socketed bulbs (commonly sold as "indicator lamps") and honkin' big ceramic sockets. The switches were run-of-the-mill SPST flip jobbies for the power to the air pump, fluid feed, and hotbox, and the knob was attached to a bog-standard dimmer pack, which would control the hotbox temperature. **[Figure 09.65, Figure 09.66]**

The wiring harness is a run-of-the-mill wire nut nightmare; the indicator lamp for the heating coil is in series, post-dimmer, to give a lo-tek visual indicator of knob position:

Mo' brighter = Mo' hotter.

Figure 09.64: **Assembling the control panel housing and stand.**

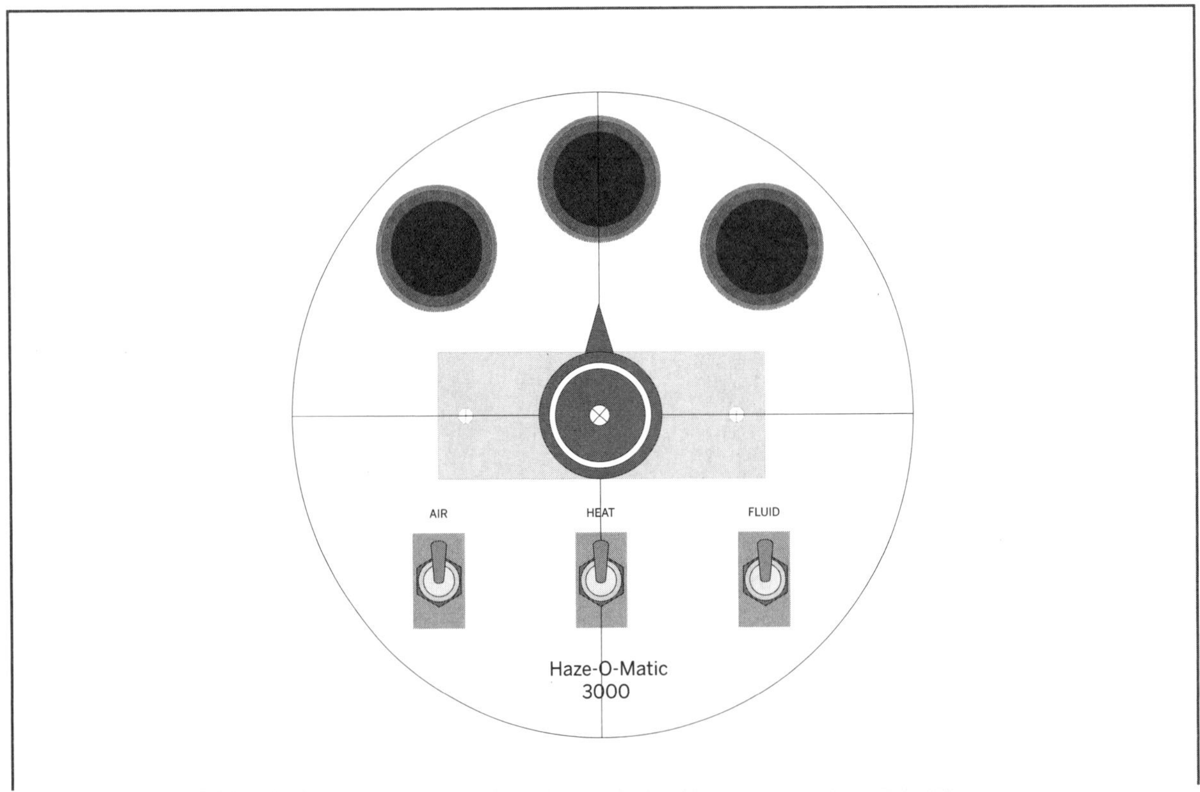

Figure 09.65: **I'll admit it: I love doing physical user interfaces.**

The lamp sockets are screw-mounted, with rubber isolation gaskets to prevent any potential shock hazards. For ease of assembly, I ran the entire control console wiring harness out through the bottom of the coffee pot and through the base of the mechanism, with the actual electrical connections to the subassemblies occurring via wire nut connectors "in the basement." **[Figure 09.69]**

Instrumentation

As mentioned, there's always room for dials, gauges and readouts on a fogger. The digitally inclined among you will doubtless proceed with an Arduino or Make controller board–based solution to monitor and control air flow, hotbox temperature, fog juice level, and feed rate and intercooler in/out temperature gradient. Me, I grabbed a dollar-store meat thermometer and a scrap-yard pressure gauge and bunged them into the mechanism via the ultimately elegant-in-its-simplicity Brute Force method.

Monitoring the hotbox temperature (in particular, the surface temperature of your hot plate) is a good idea; glycerin starts denaturing into nasty 'aldehydes at around 400 degrees C. The operating temperature for a fogger is dependent on the fog juice in use. In the case of a simple water/glycerin blend, the higher the percentage of glycerin, the higher the required operation temperature. Glycerin flashes at 290 degrees C. Consider that to be the top end of your safe operational range, with 100 degrees C as the lower limit.

A cheap-ass dollar-store meat thermometer works via a bimetallic coil that winds/unwinds in relation to temperature due to the differing thermal expansion/contraction factors of the two metals. This means figuring out a way to transfer the heat of the hot plate to the long pointy probe, which would be entering through the side of the hotbox at a 45-degree angle. **[Figure 09.70]**

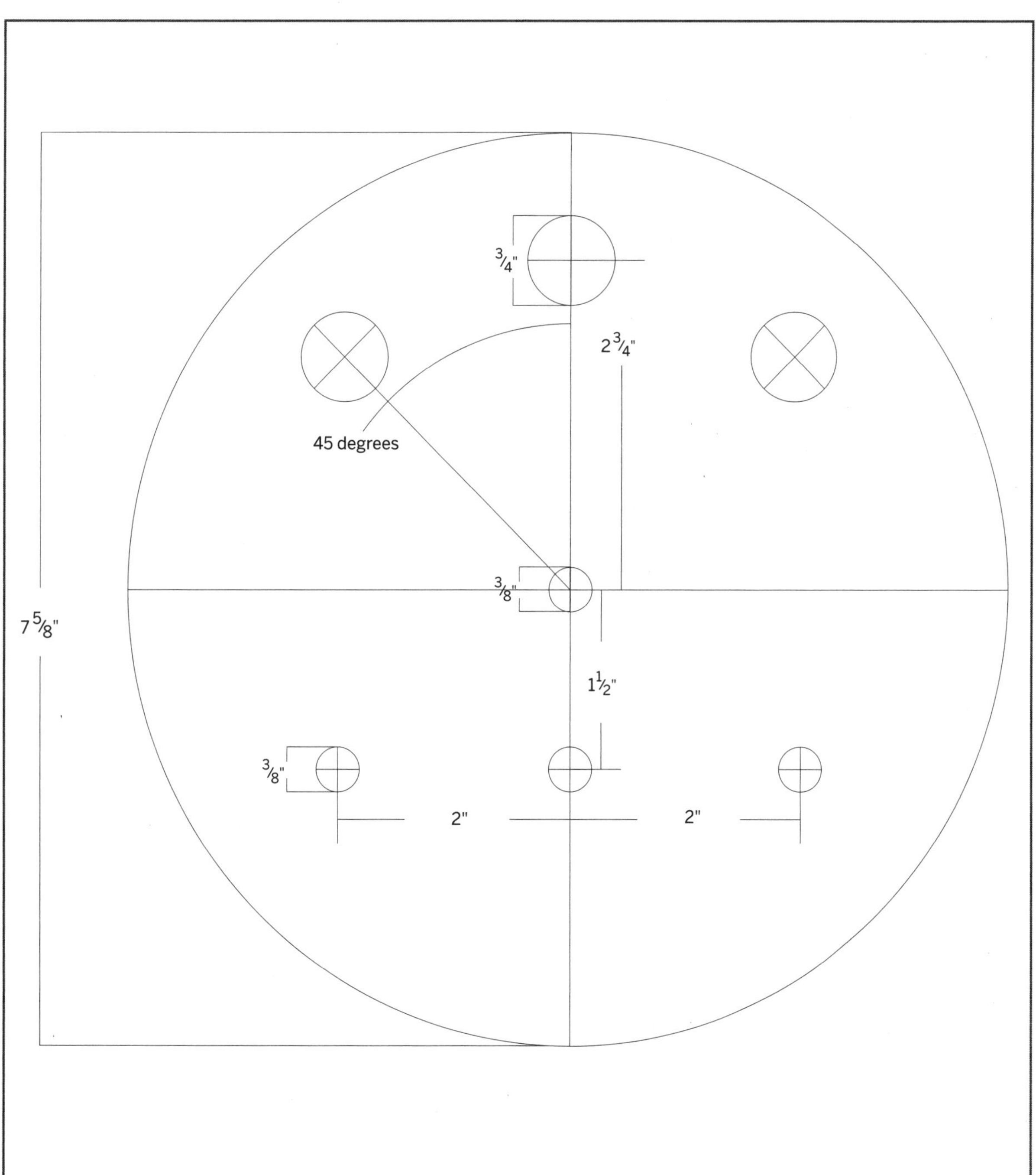

Figure 09.66: Here's the drilling pattern for those of you foolish enough to be following along at home.

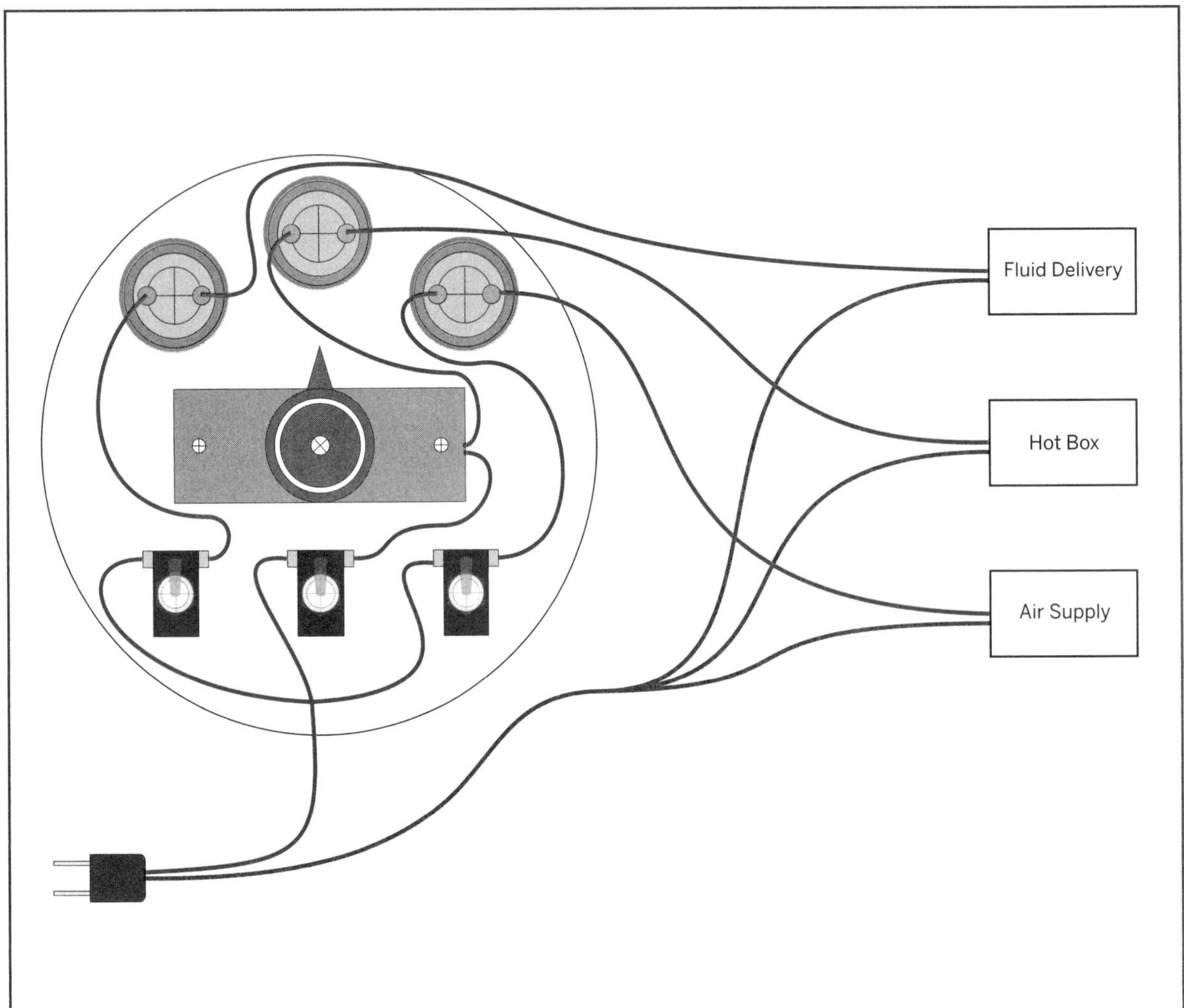

Figure 09.67: **You'll need this map to understand what the hell is going on in the next picture.**

I started by rummaging up a ¾" length of thick-walled brass tubing with an 3⁄16" ID (that bein' the OD of the thermometer probe) and a 1¾" diameter disc of ¼" brass plate. The plate would be the actual heat conductor, with the tubing inset into the plate at the aforementioned 45-degree angle to act as the thermal probe receiver. I dubbed it "The Thermoprobe Heat Transfer Module."

It took two shots to get the angled hole in the plate right: I shoulda sharpened the damned drill bit first.

Duh.

I undersized the hole by 1⁄64", and banged the receiver tube into place with some surprisingly (for me, anyway) precision hammer-work, then drilled a hole for the screw that would mount it tightly onto the surface of the frying pan.

Determining the exact location on the hotbox for the thermometer to pass through was part third-grade geometry, part hardcore eyeballin', and part dumb luck. I wanted the transfer module to lie reasonably close to the center of the frying pan to most accurately reflect the temperature at the spot where the fog juice hit the surface. A few measurements,

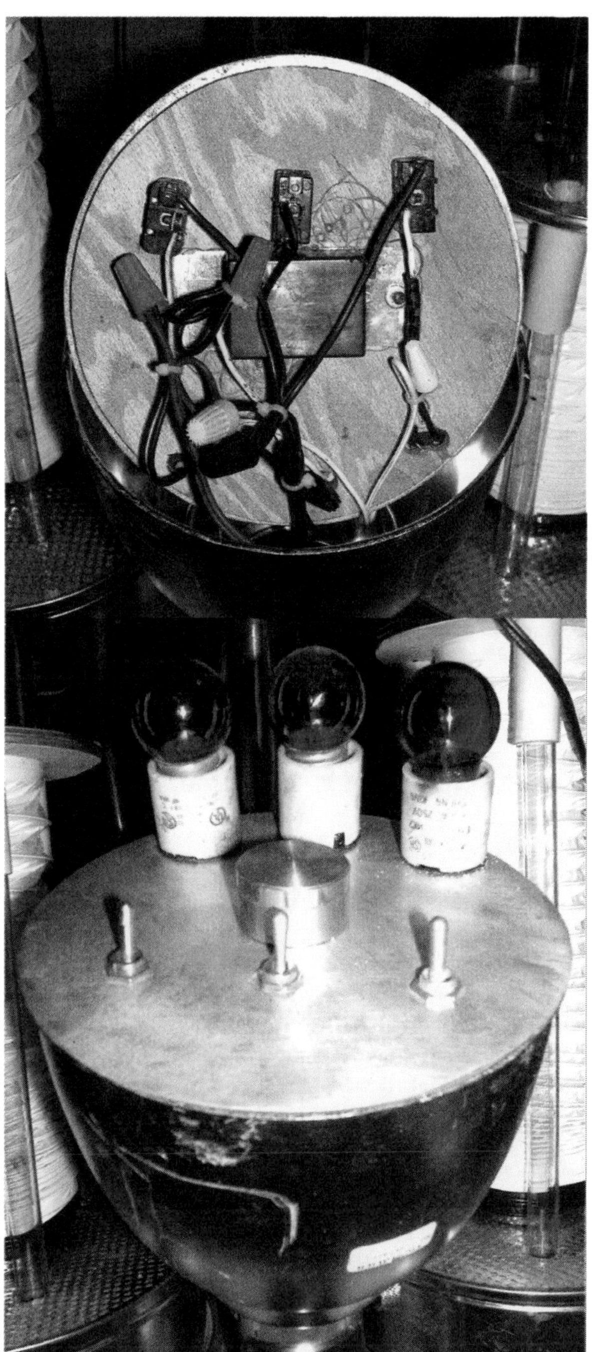

Figure 09.68: **The control console all buttoned up, but as of yet unlabeled**

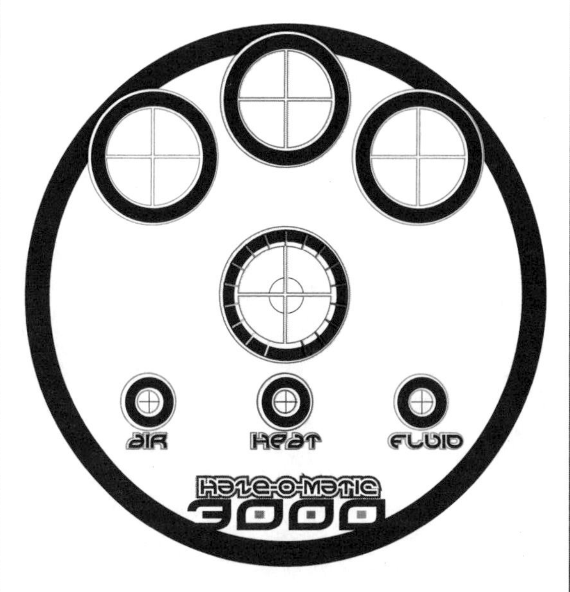

Figure 09.69: **Speaking of labels, here's what I ended up using as a faceplate label: I printed it out on one of those slightly-adhesive-backed inkjet transparency films they market as "window decals," then die-cut the requisite holes using the "sharpened pipe and a big-ass rubber mallet" technique detailed in the Hammerhead build log (Chapter 10).**

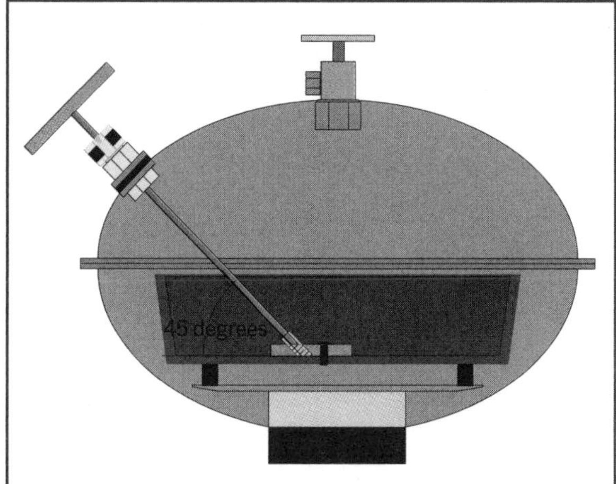

Figure 09.70: **Gawd, what a kludge: the meat thermometer–to-temperature-probe hack.**

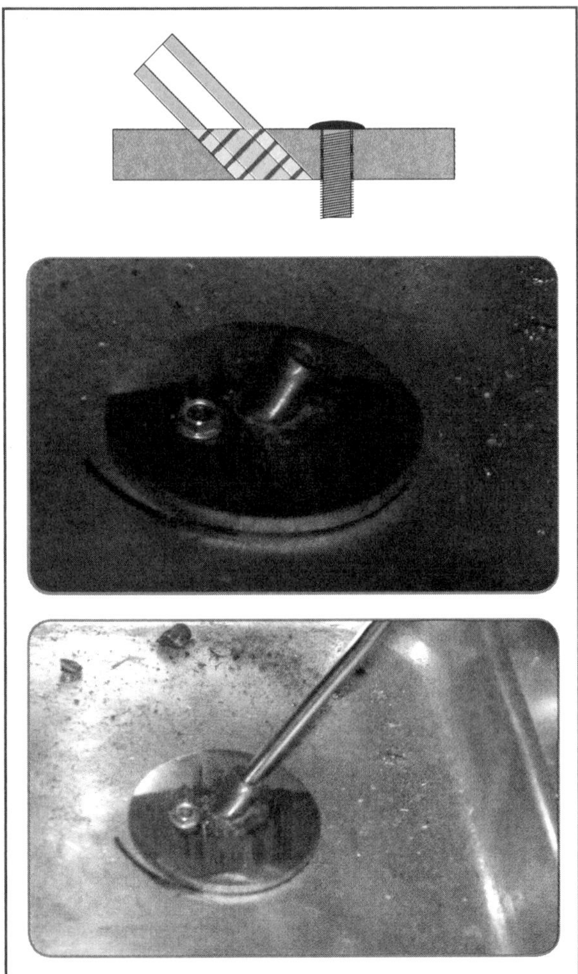

Figure 09.71: **Thermoprobe heat transfer module is GO!**

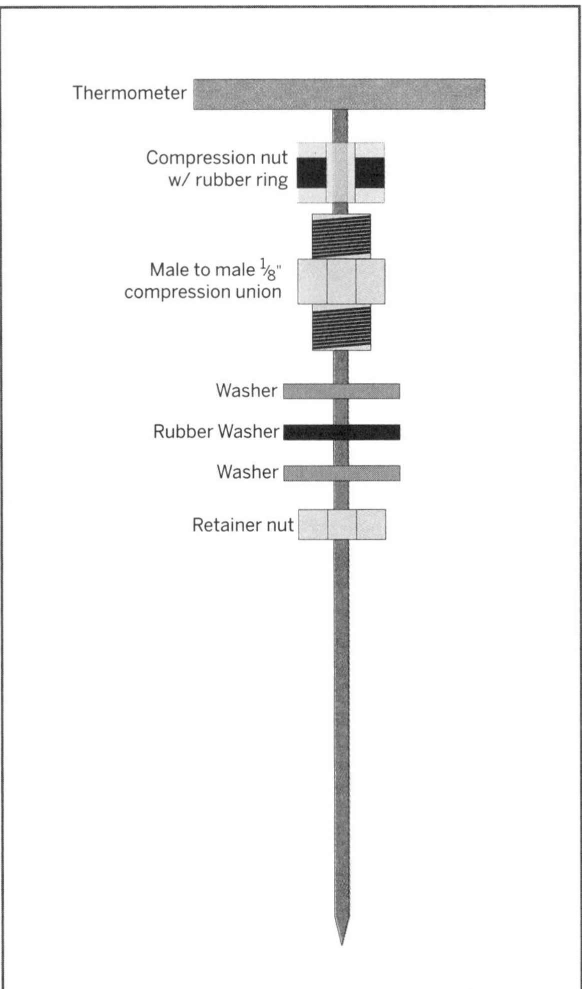

Figure 09.72: **An improvised vapour-sealed thermometer mount. What's not to love about the plumbing supply department?**

a rough drawing and a prayer to the Hole Gods later, I was rewarded with a close approximation of success.

To vapour seal the thermometer pass-thru point, I hit my supply of plumbing components and came up with a ¼" male-to-male compression union. I used a 3⁄16" ID O-ring as the compression washer, and gasketed the attachment point of the fitting with more inner-tube rubber to complete the air seal. These two rubber components inserted enough flex into the system to get me past my *slightly* off geometry after drilling and tapping a mounting screw hole in the bed of the frying pan. **[Figure 09.72]**

During field testing of the thermoprobe, I mapped the operational temperature ranges of the system onto the thermometer gauge, made up a custom gauge plate to simplify the readout, then brute-forced its installation by breaking the sight glass out and gluing it in place with contact adhesive. **[Figure 09.73, Figure 09.74]**

The fluid reservoir pressure gauge is a bit of a luxury, but having already ruptured one supply line, I wanted to keep an eye on any other impending mess. Enter the air pressure gauge. **[Figure 09.75]**

Figure 09.73: **A minimal Penguin–Robert Smith–Death icon-based UI. Quite readable in foggy conditions.**

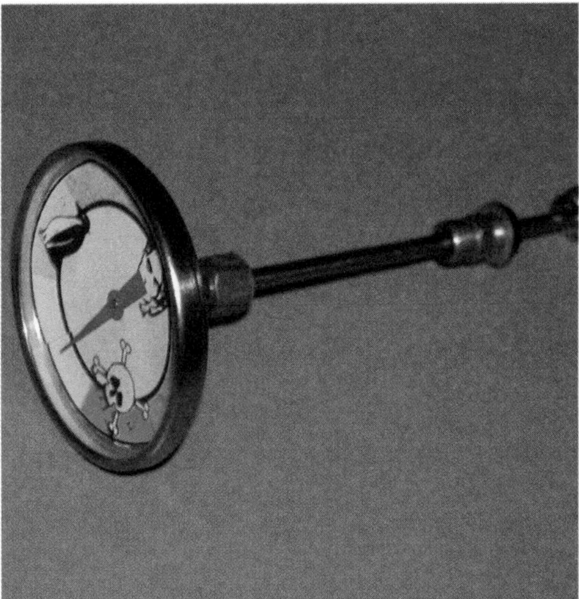

Figure 09.74: **I'll get around to replacing the sightglass someday. No, really. I will. I promise.**

I spent exactly three seconds considering the idea of trying to cram the gauge into the control console before giving myself a quick slap and switching to Plan B.

I spent exactly seven seconds considering the idea of mounting the gauge directly onto the fluid reservoir before giving myself a quick slap and switching to Plan C. I think I might have mixed a cocktail somewhere around then too.

Enter Plan C. **[Figure 09.76]**

Luckily, the pile of extra stuff from my original dollar-store stainless-steel run included a spice canister the exact diameter of the gauge.

Gauge housing? Check.

I had an 8" flexible gooseneck from a desk lamp in one of the parts bins, so I bunged an air line hole and two mounting holes into the base of the canister and bolted it on. The other end of the gooseneck screwed into a hastily bent aluminum flatbar angle bracket, which in turn was screwed onto the drivemotor mount using a couple of ½" lengths of ¼" ID aluminum tubing as stand-offs. **[Figure 09.77]**

Just because.

Nice! Adjustable angle, solid positioning. Ugly as sin though. Again to the parts bins, where, as luck would have it, there happened to be a rubber accordion sleeve for-

Figure 09.75: **0–30 PSI air-pressure gauge. A regular find at scrap yards, these are used in in pneumatic process control systems. They come into 'yards with piles of copper air line that often also have inline pneumatic valves attached. *More* than useful things.**

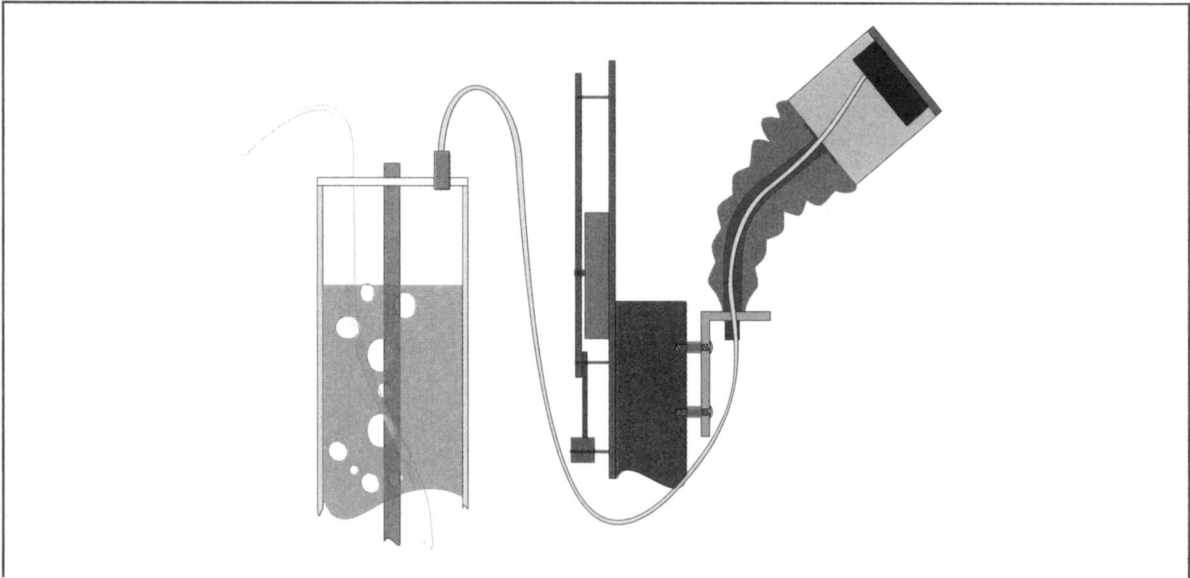

Figure 09.76: **Plan C revealed. Mount the gauge in a spice canister, mount the spice canister on a gooseneck, hide the gooseneck with the rubber accordion from an forklift control lever, and mount the whole shebang on the bellows drive mount with an L bracket.**

merly employed shielding a forklift hydraulic control from the elements. It fit like it was purpose-made. **[Figure 0978, Figure 09.79]**

After a brief struggle convincing the sleeve to cooperate and sit properly, I ran the air line from the gauge, camouflaging its slightly grungy nature with a short length of stainless steel flex held in place at the gooseneck end by a pressure-fitted rubber sleeve.

I added an air line nipple to the reservoir fill cap by drilling it out and soldering in a short length of 3⁄16" brass tube. Once again, ugly as sin, so I plundered Kaia's "Miscellaneous Knobs and Switch Caps" drawer for the tone control knob from a once high-end Fischer preamp. After drilling out an air line–sized hole, it fit precisely over the modified fill cap, effectively shielding innocent eyes from the potentially life-threatening risk of seeing an exposed nipple. **[Figure 09.80, Figure 09.81, Figure 09.82]**

The FCC was undoubtedly pleased.

I looked around in vain for something more to do. Alas, it was not to be.

Figure 09.77: **The mounted L bracket. Also pictured: the artfully-concealed-by-a-bit-of-kitchen-sink-sprayer-attachment-stainless-flex air hose.**

Figure 09.78: **More camouflage: the rubber accordion sleeve at work. Gee, Kaden, how'd ya get it to sit so nice and flush with the base of the ~~spice canister~~ gauge housing?**

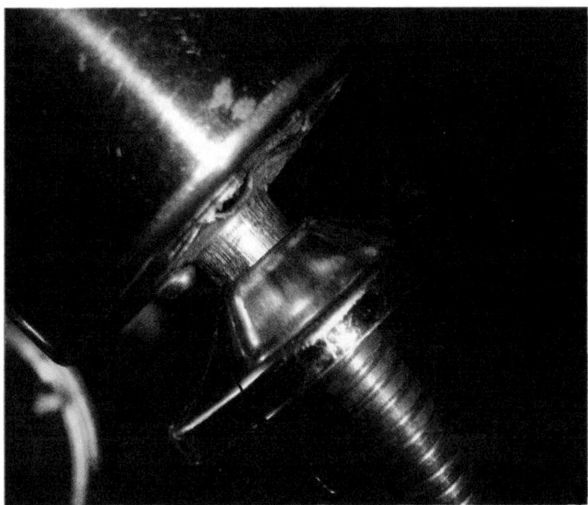

Figure 09.79: **Glad you asked, Billy. With the sleeve peeled back, you can see the hidden thingamabob I pulled off of a dumpstered chandelier. It's exactly the right diameter needed to nest into one of the accordion sleeve folds, where it resolutely holds said sleeve in position.**

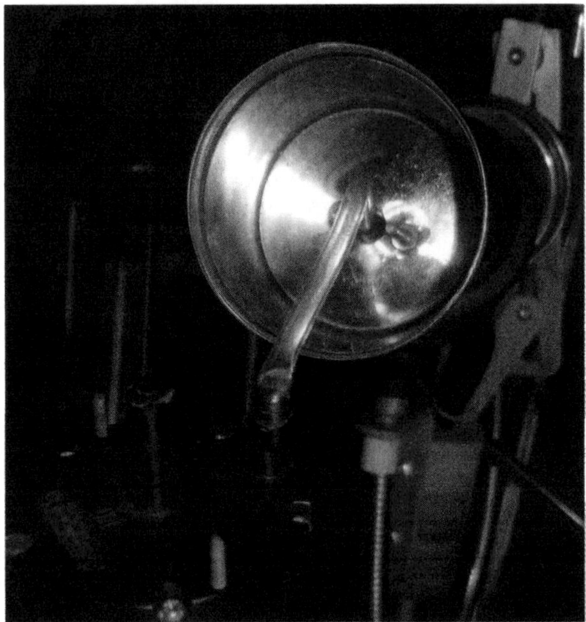

Figure 09.80: **The air line starts here**

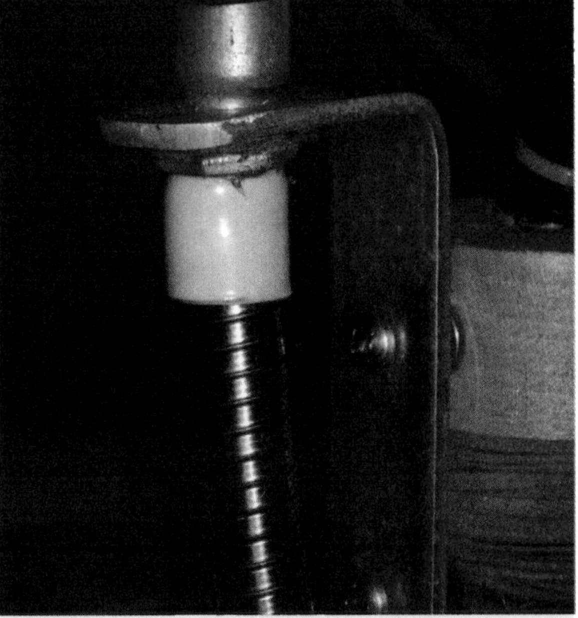

Figure 09.81: **Then leaves the gauge assembly through this chunk of flex and proceeds to ...**

Figure 09.82: . . . the by-now-modified reservoir fill cap. The air line fits onto the brass tubing nipple, with the flex fitting over *that*.

Figure 09.83: A stretched-out spring provides hose kink abatement

Assembly

Having built each subassembly as essentially a freestanding mechanism unto itself, assembling the entire mechanism on the base was essentially just a matter of positioning and screwing the modules into place on the base and running the hoses and power leads.

The fluid feed hose I'd originally spec'd ruptured spectacularly under pressure with the outlet valve closed.

Oops.

I replaced it with a piece of gothishly black aquarium air line with reassuringly thick walls. Unfortunately the new tubing was heavy enough to be prone to kinking under its own weight, a problem which was easily remedied by sleeving the kink-prone area of the tubing with a stretched-out length of coil spring from the Luxo lamp I'd cannibalized for parts at the beginning of this build. **[Figure 09.83]**

I mounted the intercooler above the hotbox, using another 7" stainless steel saucer and three chunks of threaded rod. This was a solution with multiple benefits: it positioned the intercooler to take advantage of the whole "hot fog goes up" thing, it saved valuable real estate on my by-now rapidly crowding assembly base, *and* it made the mechanism as a whole look a little bit more like alien architecture from an early episode of *Dr. Who*. **[Figure 09.84]**

The airflow insertion into the hotbox required an improvised PVC T joint and some keepin'-it-real-style duct tape action to seal the hose connections. The expansion joint pictured is part artsy-fartsy nonsense (oooh, cool . . . shiny! bendy!), part necessity (fluid system in the way, need something that bends). **[Figure 09.85, Figure 09.86]**

The aluminum cable armour coming from the top of the T carries the frying pan AC cord, which snakes around the fog juice tube and connects to the base of the control panel, crimping around a short length of lamp rod threaded into a tapped hole. Because aluminum cable armour is cool. **[Figure 09.87]**

I tested the electrics one circuit at a time, then all at once. Satisfied with the absence of impending shock-based death and destruction, I mixed up a few quarts of fog juice and prepeared for a proper field test.

Figure 09.84: **Stacking the intercooler over the hotbox saved real estate *and* let me make use of the "hot fog goes up" phenomenon.**

The internet has *countless* fog juice recipes, just a Google away; I personally invoke William of Occam and use 4 to 1 distilled water to glycerine. It'll take some effort to fully blend the glycerine with the water. Be persistent. Inconsistent fog juice can frustrate operations.

For the record, the Haze-o-Matic operating manual is simple.

Start with at least a dozen freezer packs, already frozen. More is better, to permit hot swapping at need.

Load a set of freezer packs into the intercooler, then preheat the hotbox at mid range for about three minutes.

Activate the bellows system, followed by the fluid delivery system, with the fluid valve on the hotbox open just a crack.

Adjust the temperature downwards if the resulting fog smells *burnt*. Glycerine can break down into various 'aldehydes at around 400 degrees C, which presents unpleasant health risks.

Once the temperature is stable, increase the juice flow cautiously. The temperature may need to be nudged up a tad if the increased fluid delivery causes the pan to cool down.

Oh, yeah. The Haze-o-Matic 3000.

It turned out like shown. **[Figure 09.88]**

I know you can do better than this, not in terms of raw fog output (anybody could pick up half a dozen $20 foggers at a big-box outlet, put 'em in a box with a common outlet, and call it the Haze-o-Matic 5000XE), but in terms of . . . er . . . the *ambience* created by the mechanism when it's *not* in operation. I expect you to experiment. Don't disappoint me.

I wanna see Goldbergian fog machines of epic complexity. Surreally convoluted mechanisms that spit in the eye of common sense.

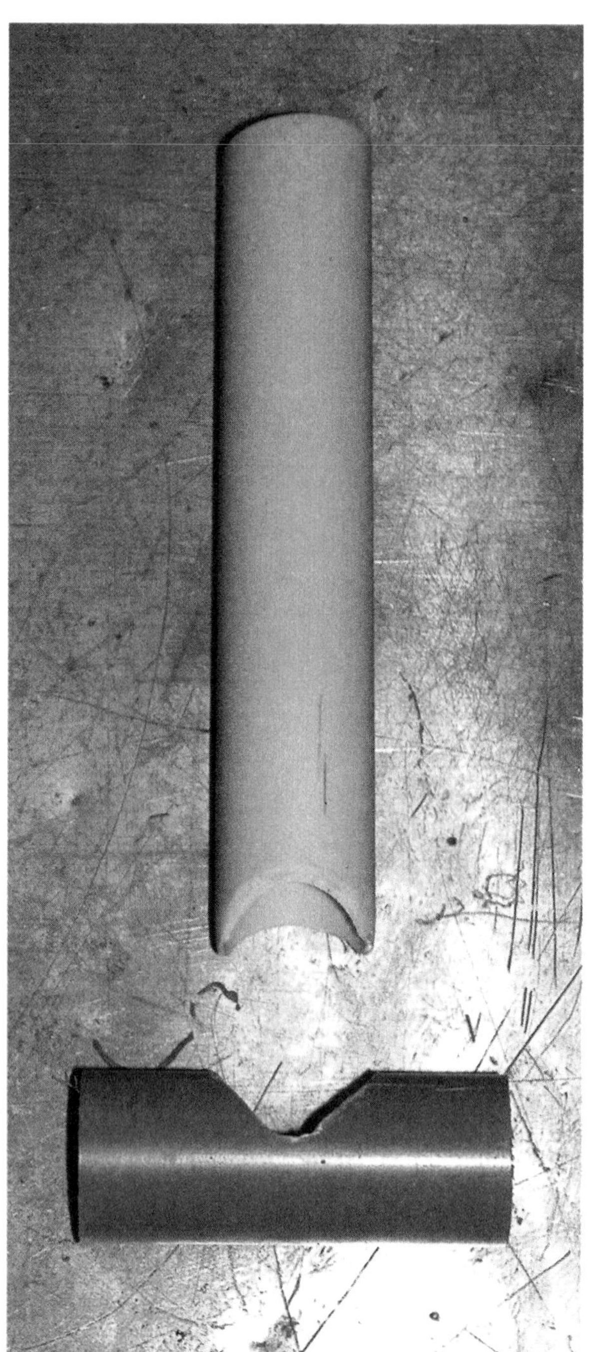

Figure 09.85: **The improvised PVC T joint: the barebones airflow manifold**

Figure 09.86: **A scrap yard expansion joint introduces exciting degrees of both "bendy" and "artsy-fartsy" into airflow routing**

Figure 09.87: **Behold the nonstop industrial stylin' of aluminum cable armour.**

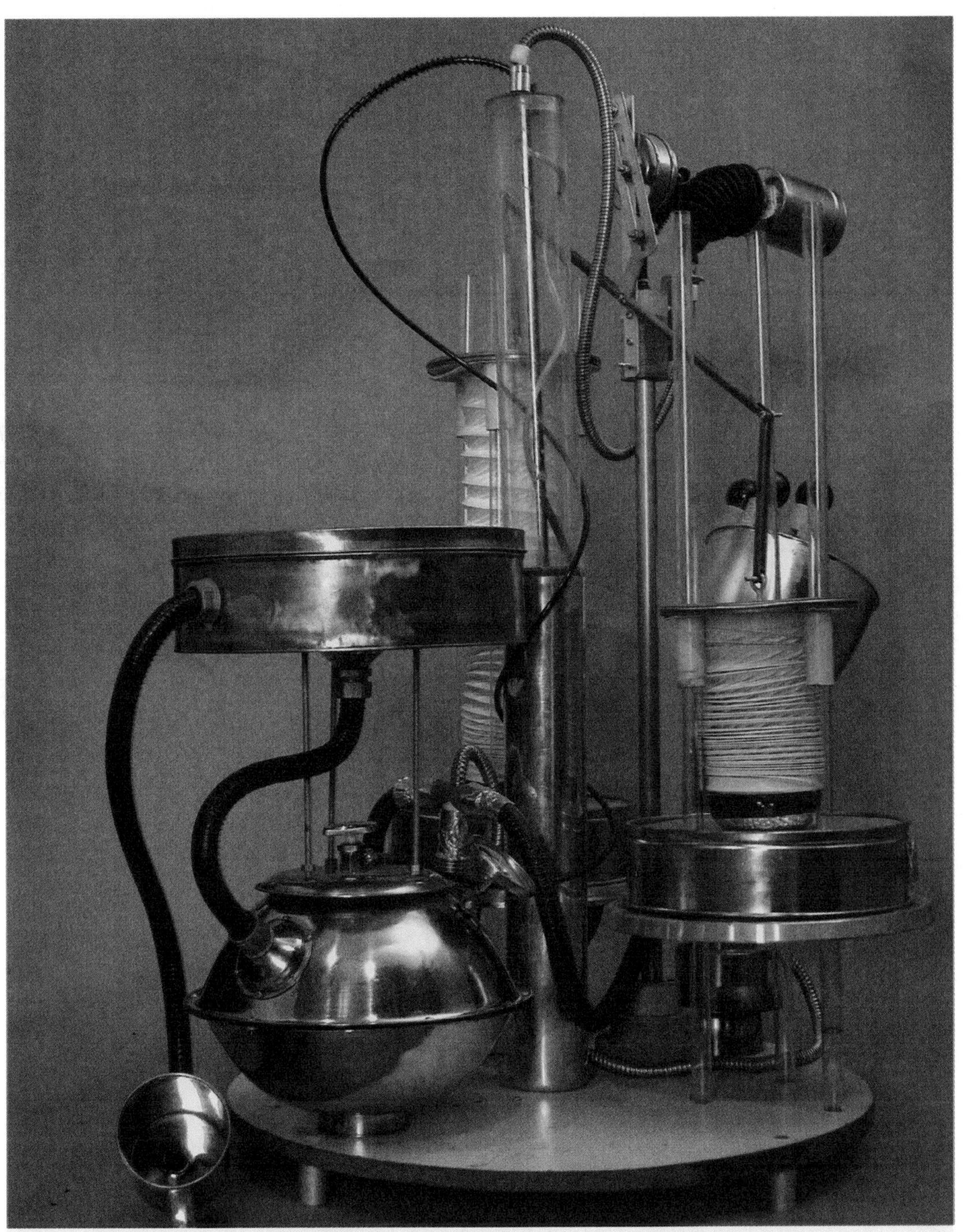

Figure 09.88: **Once again, ta. da. Now go make somethin' better.**

‹ Nano-Project › Stömpe: The Foot-Switched Power-Bar

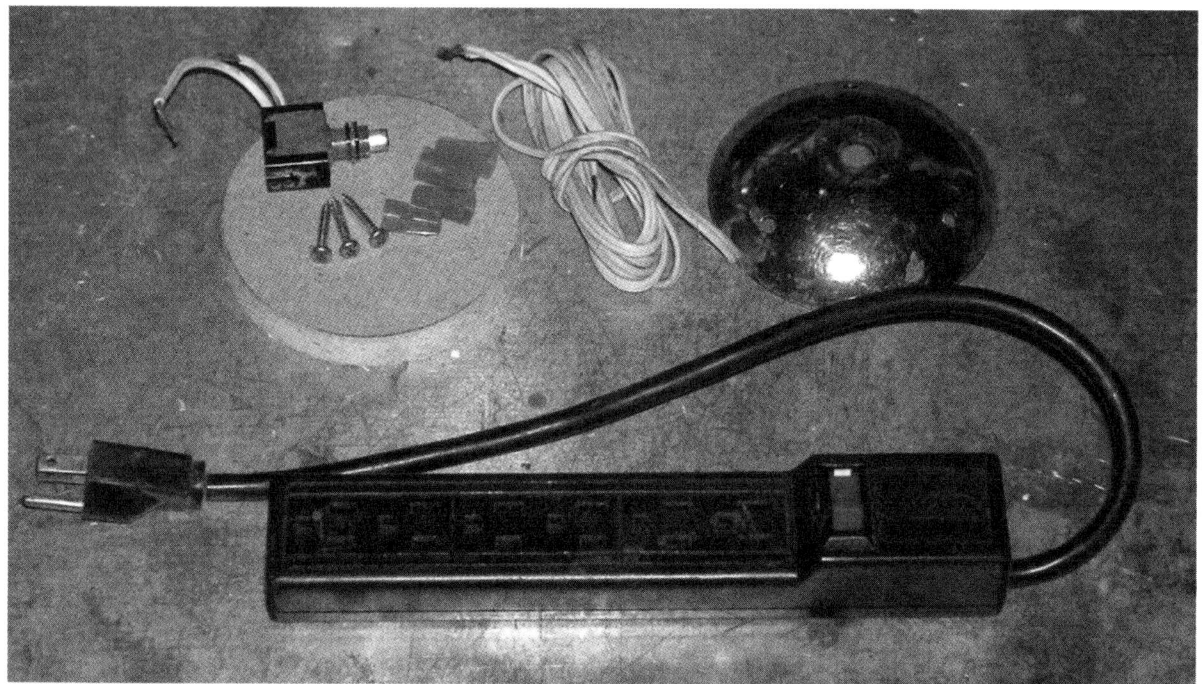

Figure N9.01: **The assorted bits**

Maybe it's my background as a Rawk musician (we, regardless of instrument, are always stompin' on things with our feet — effects pedals, high hats, channel switches, cockroaches — you get the idea), but I think foot-switch actuation oughta be standard equipment on just about everything that has a power switch. The next best alternative is foot-switching the outlet said stuff is plugged into. This approach is actually mo' better than individual foot-switches, since it lets you turn on multiple devices with one stomp. I initially did this hack to let me turn on both my belt/disc sander and its dedicated dust-collection vacuum with a single action.

I just got back from a sourcing trip. Here's what's on the bench: **[Figure N9.01]**

- One Ikea four-socket power-bar (3 clams at the Vancouver Flea Market)
- One generic foot-switch (pulled from the wreckage of an avocado-green Sears/Kenmore vacuum cleaner)
- The ceiling plate from a hideous mid-70s light fixture, which, out of context, is a shiny metal dome kinda thing 4" in diameter.
- About 8' of 16-gauge two-conductor lamp cord. If you're planning on switching exceptionally manly power tools with a total current draw between 10 and 15 amps, you'll wanna use 14-gauge. Except of course if you're planning on a foot-switch extension run in excess of 100 feet, in which case you'd need to use 12-gauge on loads over 10 amps.

The last three components came from North Star Recycling, and cost me the princely sum of one Canadian dollar.

In addition, I'll use some twist-on wire nuts (also called Marrette connectors) three 1¼" #8 wood screws and a circle of ¾" MDF cut to the diameter of the ceiling plate, all from in-house stock.

Start with the stomp box component. A solid wooden base is the most practical approach, if you're repurposing something like that damned ceiling plate.

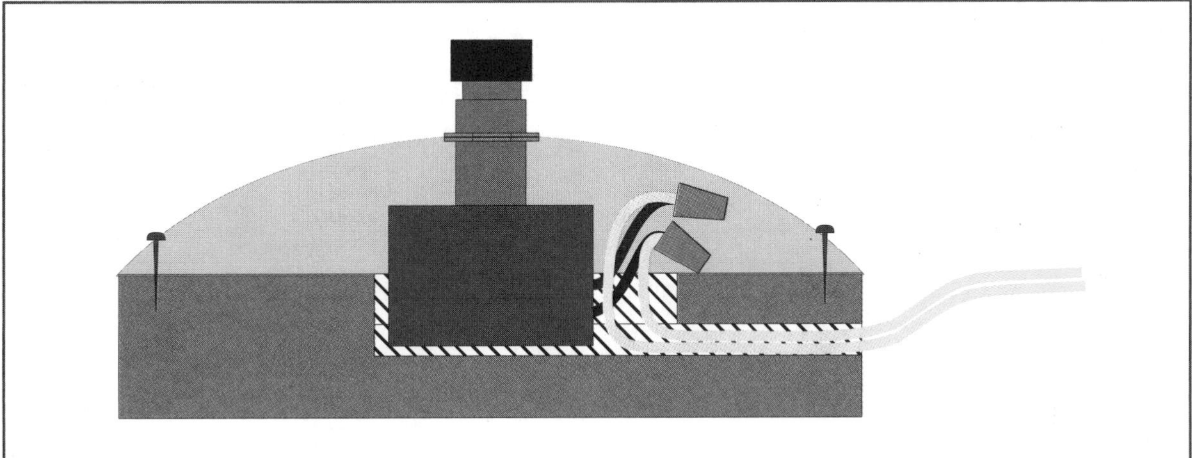

Figure N9.02: **The ever-revealing side view**

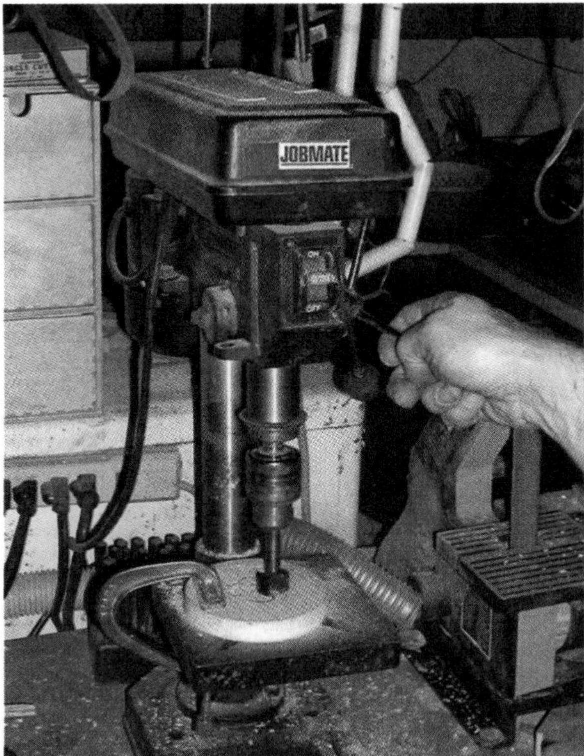

Figure N9.03: **Roughing out the switch cavity via the "buncha close-spaced holes with a Forstner bit" way**

Figure N9.04: **Nothin' pretty, but it accomplishes the task.**

Drill pilot holes for the mounting screws, and use a Forstner bit to rough out a cavity in the middle of the base plate to a depth just over halfway. Flip the base plate on edge and drill from midpoint of the rim along a radius to the center cavity with a ¼" bit.

The vacuum cleaner switch I salvaged had the leads molded into the body rather than screw-equipped terminal posts. I had to use wire nuts to make the connections to the

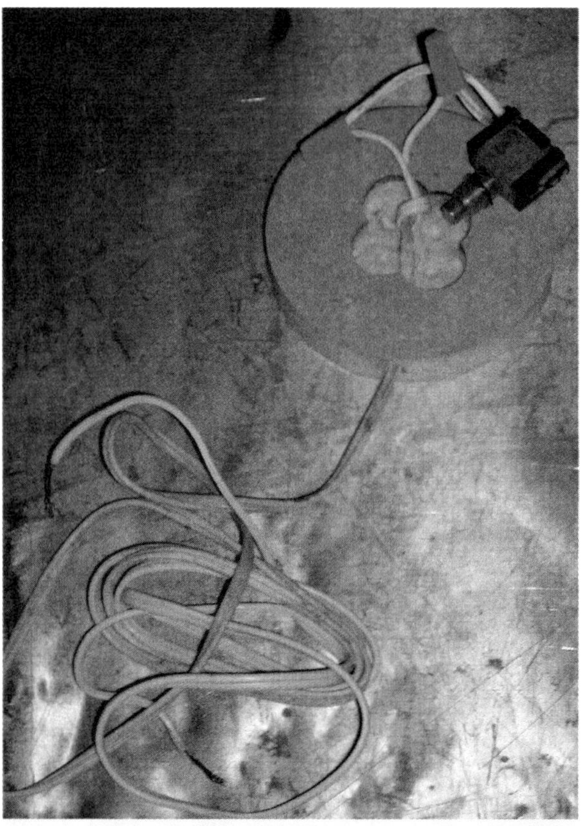

Figure N9.05: **Yes, it's all gonna fit.**

Figure N9.06: **The completed pedal assembly**

Figure N9.07: **IM IN UR POWR BAR, CONNECTING UR LEEDZ**

connecting lead. Tie a knot as a strain relief, and then thread the wire through the ¼" hole you drilled.

Mount the switch in the center hole of whatever you're using with top and bottom nuts, lock washers, and a drop of thread adhesive, and screw it together. I sacrificed a promo mouse pad to skid-proof the bottom of the completed stomp box. Aerosol rubber cement is the ideal adhesive: one coat on the wood, two coats on the mouse pad (with a 5-minute setup after each coat), then stick 'em together. It won't be moving.

Open up the power-bar. **[Figure 09.07]**

In this case, Ingemar and his pals soldered the wiring together. Follow the black wire from the AC cord to the switch, and unsolder it from the terminal. Solder one of the leads from your stomp box to this terminal, and use a wire nut to connect the other lead to the black wire you just unsoldered.

Cut a slot for the pedal cord into the power-bar casing: I used a Dremel, but a medium-coarse needle file will go

Figure N9.08: **Stömpe: not Ingemar's original intention**

through the ABS plastic like butter. Dress the wiring away neatly (you remembered to tie a strain-relief knot, yes?), check the continuity and switch action with a multimeter, and button it up. Plug it in: you're done.

Startle the crap out of visitors by turning on dangerous tools from across the workshop.

10 Hammerhead Live: The Mechanical Drum Machine

This project has resonance with me at countless levels: I've played drums for more years than I care to mention, I've programmed a ton of drum machines, ranging from the legendary Stix ST-305 Programma to the ubiquitous MPC 1000, and my abiding fondness for hammers of all ilks is well-documented. The main appeal, though, is that this is another direct assault against the dreaded office Muzak. Back in the day when I toiled with the faceless masses in "a traditional office environment," the mind-numbing aural ooze that seeped from the ceiling speakers every single second of the freaking day was enough to make me want to poke frisket knives[1] into my ears.

Now, "audience participation Muzak" would have been a different story. An instrument in every cubicle, maybe a barebones guide track pumped through the office PA system, and instantly there's a permanent floating jam session waiting to occur. Instruments come and go as cubizens take five minutes to refresh their psyches, seek out inspiration, or flush spreadsheet cobwebs from their brains. The creative and motivational potential is practically limitless, and we'd finally put a stop to loathsome Mantovanni versions of Steely Dan classics.

It's a win-win scenario from any perspective.

Anyway.

About the name. Ask anyone who's been making music on their PC for any length of time about "Hammerhead." Chances are that if their experience goes further back in time than Reason 2.0, they'll wax eloquent about Bram Bos's legendary percussion sequencer application, which was released in May 1997.

Intuitive, innovative, and *free*, it's where a lotta people got their start making beats, and is still referred to with enthusiastic reverence by folks in the know. I've been using computers in audio production since 1981,[2] and Hammerhead was, for me, the first modern-era music-making application that was actually fun to use. Hammerhead was a similar revelation to a *lot* of people.

It's the inspiration for Hammerhead Live.

Thanks, Bram.

1 Fancy-ass name for a disposable #11 X-Acto blade in a plastic handle, a common-place artifact in a lot of art departments for cutting frisket film. Frisket film is transparent, semi-adhesive, and incredibly useful for complex masking and stencil-making kinda stuff. If you had some, you would likely find 23 OMG!! level uses for it.

2 I still have fond memories of running a Soundchaser system on my old Apple 2. It was a 37 note organ style keyboard connected to Mountain's Digital Audio boards, with 16 voice polyphony, drawable waveforms, and a (gasp) 16 track sequencer. Pre-midi, of course. The Mountain boards were ridiculously noisy and there were no filters, but you could stack up 16 oscillators on one voice. You only had single-note polyphony, but it was a *large* note when you played it.

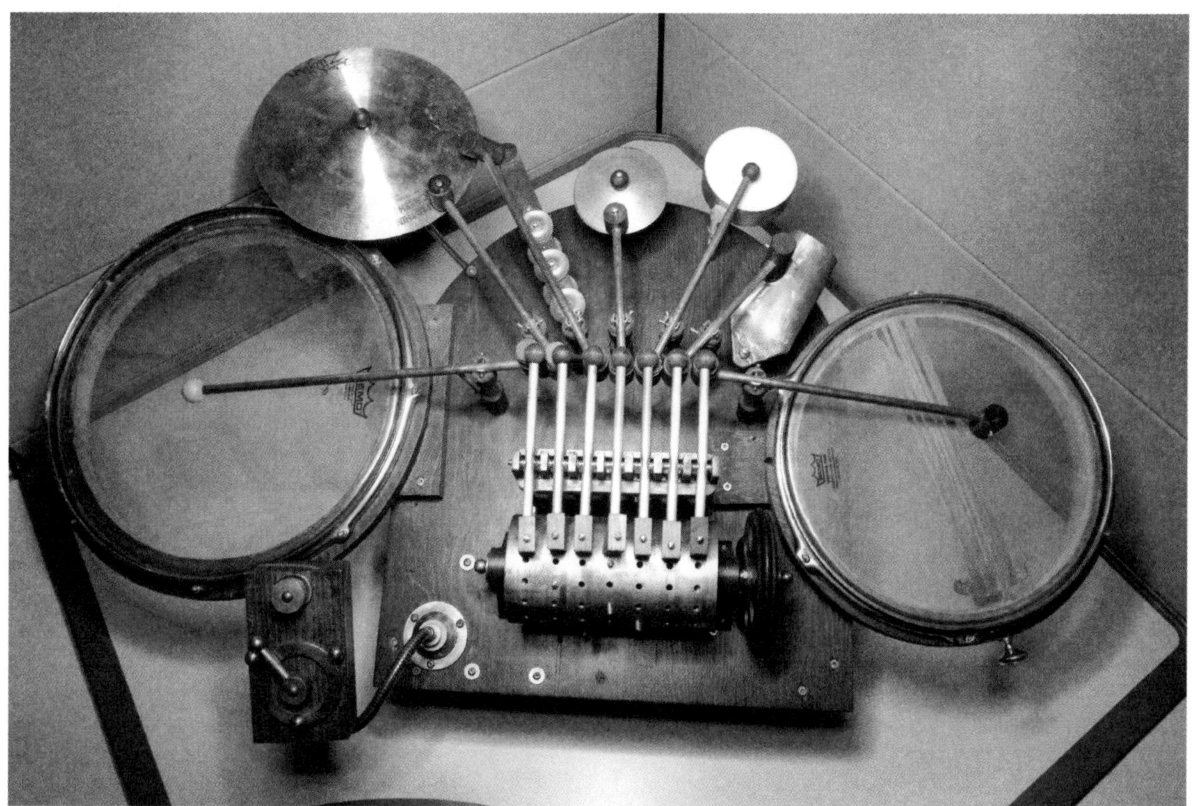

The Mechanism in Question

This, my friends, is a *real* sampling drum machine. Put a sample of what you want to use to make noise under each of the hammers,[3] activate the drive motor, and it's like something out of a Chuck Jones cartoon. Beer cans? Bongos? Biscuit tins? A vintage K Zildjian 12" splash cymbal previously owned and personally autographed by both Vinnie *and* Carmine Appice? A solid gold Kama Sutra coffee pot? Check, check, check, double check, and check: This mechanism plays 'em all. 'Course, to spare your household pots and pans the indignity of once again serving as makeshift Ludwig Super Classics, we'll also bodge together a few almost-real drums, cymbals and percussion instruments to get ya started.

Programmable? Hell yeah: seven dynamic voices, 16th-note resolution, and a tempo range from 1 BPM up to a quite dervish-like 1700 BPM. It's gonna take some dubbing to accurately reproduce "The Amen Break," though.

NOTE: The tempos you can create will depend on your choice of drive motor and gear train. My prototype was powered by a 5,000-RPM sewing machine motor geared to deliver 105 RPM to the pin drum at full revs. Judicious use of springs, which let the hammer position reset quickly enough to actually complete a full motion cycle 16 times per revolution gave the device John Bonham–like dynamics and Pete (the Feet) Sandoval–like speed, but also severely taxed the physical mechanism. My failure to capture on tape the resulting cacophonously catastrophic device failure shames me to this day. My bad.

Versatile? Damn straight, kids. Besides being capable of whacking a noise out of whatever's under the hammers, the

3 Well, not necessarily hammers. Hammerhead Live has interchangeable beaters, so you can bodge whatever you want onto the end of an actuator and have it serve as the "drumstick." But hammers are the first choice, for sure.

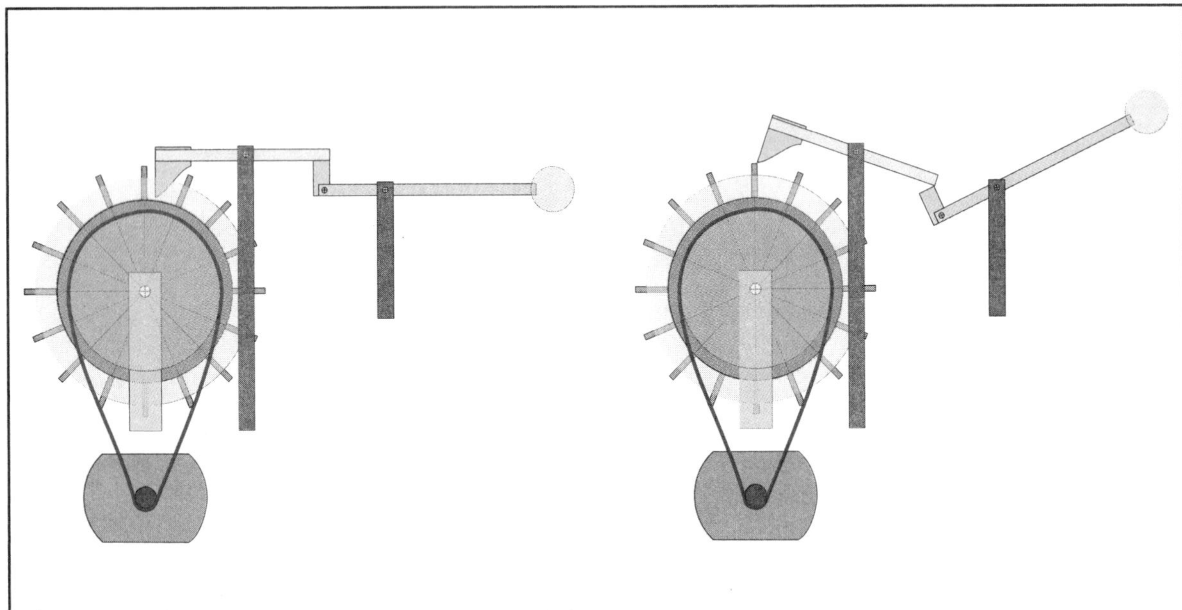

Figure 10.01: **The essence of Hammerhead: the original improved pin-drum-actuated dual-stage floating-transfer lever mechanism. Unfortunately, I can't see T.O.I.P.D.A.D.S.F.T.L.M. catching on as a musical hipster acronym.**

hammers themselves can be equipped with piezo elements[4] to let you drive the trigger inputs of a V-Drum or DTX brain or the CV gate inputs on your Blacet modular.

E-Z to make? More or less. There's some fairly precise hole drillin' involved but we'll be able to jig that up for ease of execution. Everything else is pretty straightforward from a fabrication standpoint. That said, it's a busy mechanism, and there are a lot of parts to make.

From scratch.

What we're building is essentially a music box mechanism that goes "whump whump whump" instead of "plink plink plink." Movable pins protruding from a motorized belt driven rotating drum actuate hammer mechanisms, which then whack a sound out of whatever happens to be under them.

This one is deliberately upscaled to demonstrate the mechanism involved, and because it looks cool. Once you've gotten a handle on the way things go together, I fully expect to see you fabricating 37 hammer versions to retrofit onto the MiniMoog you just scored from the 'Bay.

The idea of a mechanical sequencer banging on the keys of a classic analog synth makes me snicker.

4 The piezo sensor add-on for Hammerhead is a surprise bonus project available as a downloadable PDF file from O'Reilly.

Here's the lever mechanism that's the heart of the machine. As promised, it's a basic music box movement on steroids: Motor rotates pin-studded drum, pins move lever, lever lifts hammer, and when pin is no longer supporting lever, hammer falls. The lever-to-hammer arm interface is contact-only, rather than being a mechanical linkage, so that the motion can turn a corner, as it were, rather than being a strictly linear mechanism. [Figure 10.01]

Why do we need the motion of the mechanism to turn this hypothetical corner?

Because we'll be driving seven of them from the same pin drum, in a configuration like shown. [Figure 10.02]

Zoiks! What the hell have we gotten ourselves into?!!? Yes, kids, it's a big build. Fortunately, pin drum aside, you're building seven of the same mechanism (more or less). With a realistic approach to jigging it's much less formidable than it seems.

This is a metal-intensive device: We're making a mechanism with a lot of moving parts, and it's gotta be able to both give and take a beating.

This is the only time I will use that pun. I thought I'd get it out of the way early.

What You'll Need

Material-wise, you *need* about a foot of 4"-diameter copper pipe.

NOTE: Material substitution is always acceptable, but *please* don't even think about attempting this build with the ubiquitous PVC piping. Ensuring a steady rate of rotation under varying load means harnessing inertial mass to cancel out some of the negative vectors. PVC doesn't attract enough gravity to cut this gig, or sufficient material cohesion to form strong enough threads to hold the event pins in place.

You'll also need:

- 6 feet of ⅜" brass tube
- 3 feet of 5⁄16" brass tube
- A foot or so of 3⁄16"brass rod
- A foot or so of ⅛" brass rod

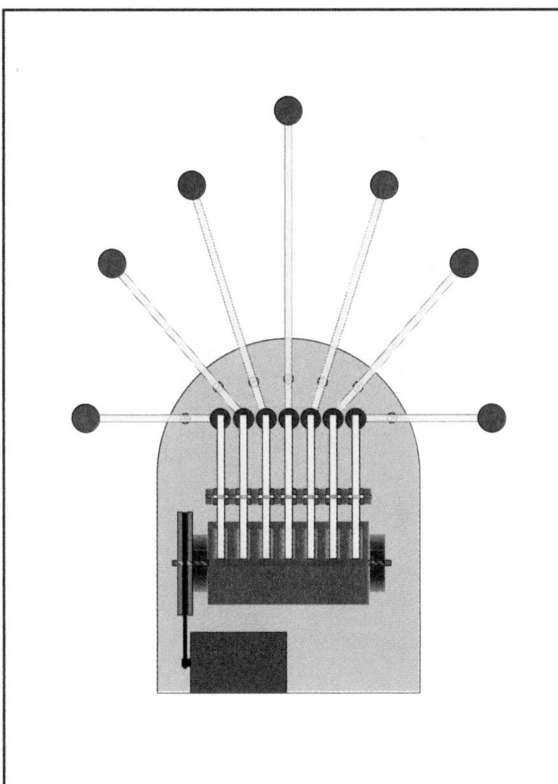

Figure 10.02: Marketing professional: "The flexibility of the lever mechanism will accommodate the most demanding configuration requirements." Musician: "Dood . . . this can do some crazy-ass shit."

- 6 feet of ¼-20 threaded rod
- At least 50 ¼-20 acorn nuts
- One ¼-20 T-nut
- *Lots* of 6-32 and ¼-20 machine screws
- Brass washers to match
- A fistful of 1" and 1¼" #6 wood screws

Wood requirements are more modest:

- 24" x 24" of ¾" plywood
- 18" of ¼" x 6" hardwood
- Three feet of 1" x 4" hardwood
- A foot or two each of ¼" and ⅜" poplar dowel
- Five feet of 1" hardwood dowel. Or a broom handle.
- Oh, and some plywood scrappage for jig building.

The weird stuff you didn't expect?

- A cordless electric drill to cannibalize for parts
- A square foot or so of belt-weight leather
- A mouse pad or two
- 2 rollerblade bearing races
- A sheet of that almost-paper-thin craft foam stuff
- A sheet of craft felt
- A 8"-diameter O ring to use as a drive belt,
- A few dozen ¾" wooden craft balls
- A handful of brass eyelets with a 3⁄16" hole
- A few square feet of ⅛" lead sheeting
- An old bicycle inner tube

That's what I started the project with. I encountered other material requirements along the way and improvised in real time. I *strongly* encourage you to adopt the same "just wingin' it" approach to fabrication.

It builds character nine healthy ways.

Not included in the materials list is what's needed to bung together seven lo-tech "physical 8-bit" percussion instruments. It's your choice as to whether you build these things. The build log and cutting diagram are based around their presence. (See the Preface regarding the cutting diagrams.) If you want to forge in your own direction instrument-wise, don't panic. By the time we reach any crucial stages, you'll understand the mechanism well enough to be able to adapt it to your own nefarious plans.

Clear a lot of space on your bench for the fairly massive mechanism we're making, and prepare to get up close and personal with a big piece of copper pipe.

Figure 10.03: **20 bucks worth of sorely abused 4" ID copper pipe (#2 copper, for those of you practicing your scrap-fu).**

Figure 10.04: **Just about halfway through the arduous task of cutting to length: 2 hours, 3 hacksaw blades, 4 quarts of perspiration, 5 dozen new cuss words. 1 usable pin drum blank.**

Figure 10.05: **Endplugs in place, axle threaded . . . *this* is how it rolls.**

The Pin Drum

The sample pictured is what I started with *after* half an hour with steel wool and kitchen cleanser. It cost me $20 Cdn, which speaks volumes about the current state of the world copper market. **[Figure 10.03]**

Cut the copper pipe to 8½". This will form the pin drum, which will hold the program events for the sequencer.[5]

5 "Program events" . . . yeah, right. What's gonna happen is you'll be drilling and threading 112 holes in the damned thing, into which you'll thread ½" ¼-20 machine screws to trigger the hammers. The further out they extend, the more the hammer travels, and the louder the noise is when the hammer falls.

Cunning, no?

The cuts need to be absolutely square. Lacking a pipe cutter with a 4"+ throat, I armstronged the cuts with a hacksaw and trued up the angles with a file and emery cloth on my dead-flat surface. It took about two freakin' hours. **[Figure 10.04]**

Plug both ends of the pipe with plywood disks. A 4" hole saw is a damned fine investment, giving accurately formed circles with a precise center hole. The center hole is useful for the next step, which is threading 12" of ¼-20 threaded rod through the plugs and pipe to serve as an axle. **[Figure 10.05]**

Make two pillow blocks to mount the pipe axle on. Hardwood is the preferred material. Yes, you'll need two more rollerblade wheel bearing races and bushings. Size the

Size to fit

3/4"

3 3/8"

2 3/4"

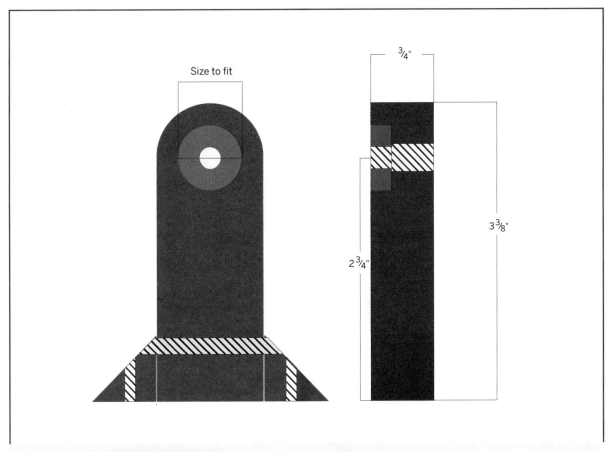

Figure 10.06: The pillow block in detail

bearing holes for a tight press fit around the actual bearing race and zero contact with the bushing: friction is *not* our friend. The only critical dimension is the height. The math of the entire mechanism is based around the pin drum occupying a specific position in space and time, so you can't really mess with the height unless you want to recalculate every other measurement. Other than that, indulge your inner arteest, but build them solid, build them identical, and make 'em removable from the base. **[Figure 10.06, Figure 10.07]**

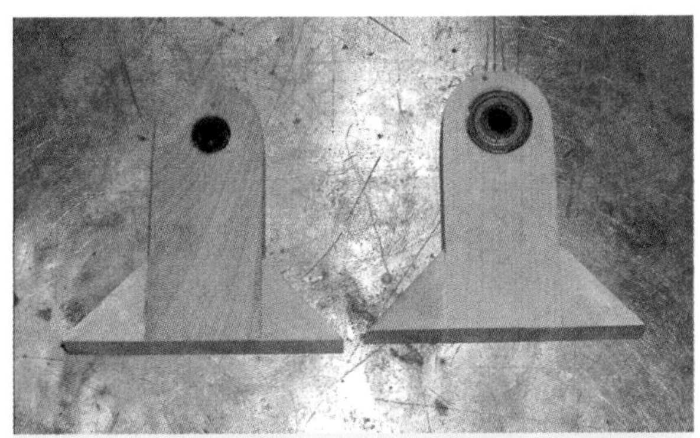

Figure 10.07: The pillow block executed in reasonable-quality maple

The drive pulley is made from a stack of hardwood disks, in this case the cheap, reliable and, er, popular poplar. The outer two disks are 5" in diameter, the inner one is 4¾". Glue them together with the wood grain offset 45 degrees on each disk for strength. **[Figure 10.08, Figure 10.09]**

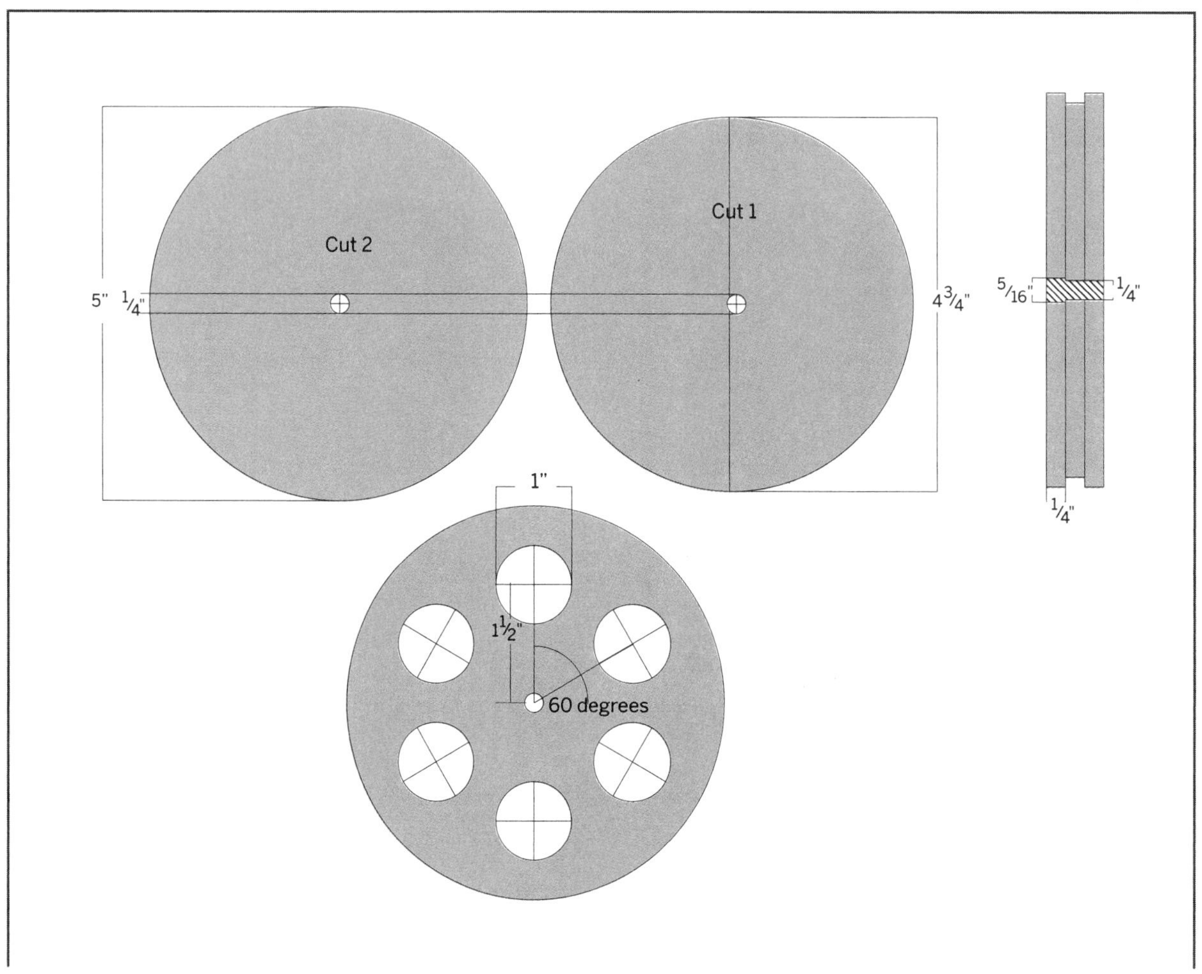

Figure 10.08: **The drive pulley in detail**

In a burst of artsy-fartsy nonsense, I drilled out six 1" holes around the perimeter as illustrated for enhanced steampunk-ishness.[6] Drill the center hole out to 5⁄16" and a depth of ¼" and set a ¼-20 T-nut. **[Figure 10.10]**

Put this lot aside for the moment and point your efforts toward the primary actuators and their support rack. You'll thank me for this brief respite from the pin drum assembly later.

6 C'mon — a mechanical drum machine and you expect it to *not* look steampunk?

Gedouddahere.

The Actuators and Their Rack

The actuator levers are supported by a rack that's dirt simple to make.

Out of hard wood, cut seven ¾" x ¾" x 13⁄16" bottom separator blocks and seven ½" x ¾" x 13⁄16" top separator blocks, then rip yerself some slats and cut eight 6" x ¼" x 3/4" pieces to actually hold the axle. Drill the holes for the one-piece lever axle as located on the cutting diagram by stacking the slats together in a nice neat pile held together with double-faced

Figure 10.09: **Pulley components, in poplar, prior to glue-up. Ya know, try as I might, I just can't for the life of me get enthusiastic about alliteration as a literary device.**

Figure 10.10: **All it takes is six artfully spaced holes to successfully transform the drive pulley from plain to Steampunkalicious. Nothin' short of miraculous, if you ask me.**

tape, then boring the holes en masse with a well-tempered drill press. **[Figure 10.11]**

You'll need to do fairly comprehensive surface preparation for finishing *before* glue-up, or face a ridiculously frustrating bout of sanding, trying to smooth out between the slats after the glue sets up.

Assemble the verticals like a shish-kebab on the 3⁄16" brass rod axle and position the top and bottom separator blocks. True up the angles with a square, make mit der glueundt-klampen and let it cure overnight. In my glue-up (pictured), you can see the scrap wood spacers I used to help position the separator blocks. The width of these spacers is inconsequential, as long as they're 3⅝" long: They're a useful shortcut, but make sure they don't end up glued in to the assembly. **[Figure 10.12, Figure 10.13, Figure 10.14]**

Getting them out is a real pain in the ass. *Cough*.

When the rack is out of the clamps, position and glue the horizontal reinforcement pieces as shown in the cutting diagram. The bottom ones don't necessarily have to have a triangular profile; I just happened to have some scrap wood in that shape in the wood crib. The reason they're there is to widen the mounting footprint of the rack, so it's a good idea to set a few dowels to strengthen the joint.

The top horizontals *must* be parallel to the axle; they're intended as mounting points for any movement dampeners the mechanism might happen to need during tune-up. Dowel them if you want to, but it's not necessary.

Rough out the actuator blocks for the actuator levers from ¾" hardwood stock and drill out the mounting holes to ⅜" and the lock screw holes to 7⁄64". **[Figure 10.15]**

Forstner bits (even criminally dull ones like mine — note the scorching of the wood) can cut nice clean holes into angled surfaces with ease. Use *quality* wood for these components: They're going to see a lot of abuse! I used rock maple heartwood, it being a formidably hard (and consequently stubborn to work with) hardwood. **[Figure 10.16]**

The actuator blocks translate the movement and position of the event pins on the pin drum into vertical motion that we can later use to hit stuff. The portion of the face that makes contact with the moving pins needs to have a ⅜" x 3⁄16" deep guide channel formed in it to ensure consistent interaction with the event pins.

I tried a bunch of different methods of shaping the channel, and ended up roughing in with a dremel, then using 150-grit sandpaper glued to a piece of ⅜" dowel to finesse 'em into shape. A ⅜" spherical shaping bit in a router would have accomplished the same thing in about one quarter of the time and with far less effort required to ensure each channel was of identical depth, if I actually owned said router bit.

Which I don't. C'est la vie.

The actuator blocks will eventually be locked into place on the lever shaft with set screws; tap the pilot holes for these screws with 6-32 threads. Once the mechanism is functioning and fine-tuned, you'll be able to drill positioning holes in the lever shaft to allow variable placement of the actuators, letting you "push" or "pull" the placement of the instrument within the overall groove of the rhythm you've programmed. Take it to the bank, kids: Hammerhead *can* get funky.

The actuator arms are 7" long, cut from ⅜" brass tubing, and drilled through at the 3" point to 13⁄64" to accept the axle. Bung together a quick 'n' dirty jig to get the

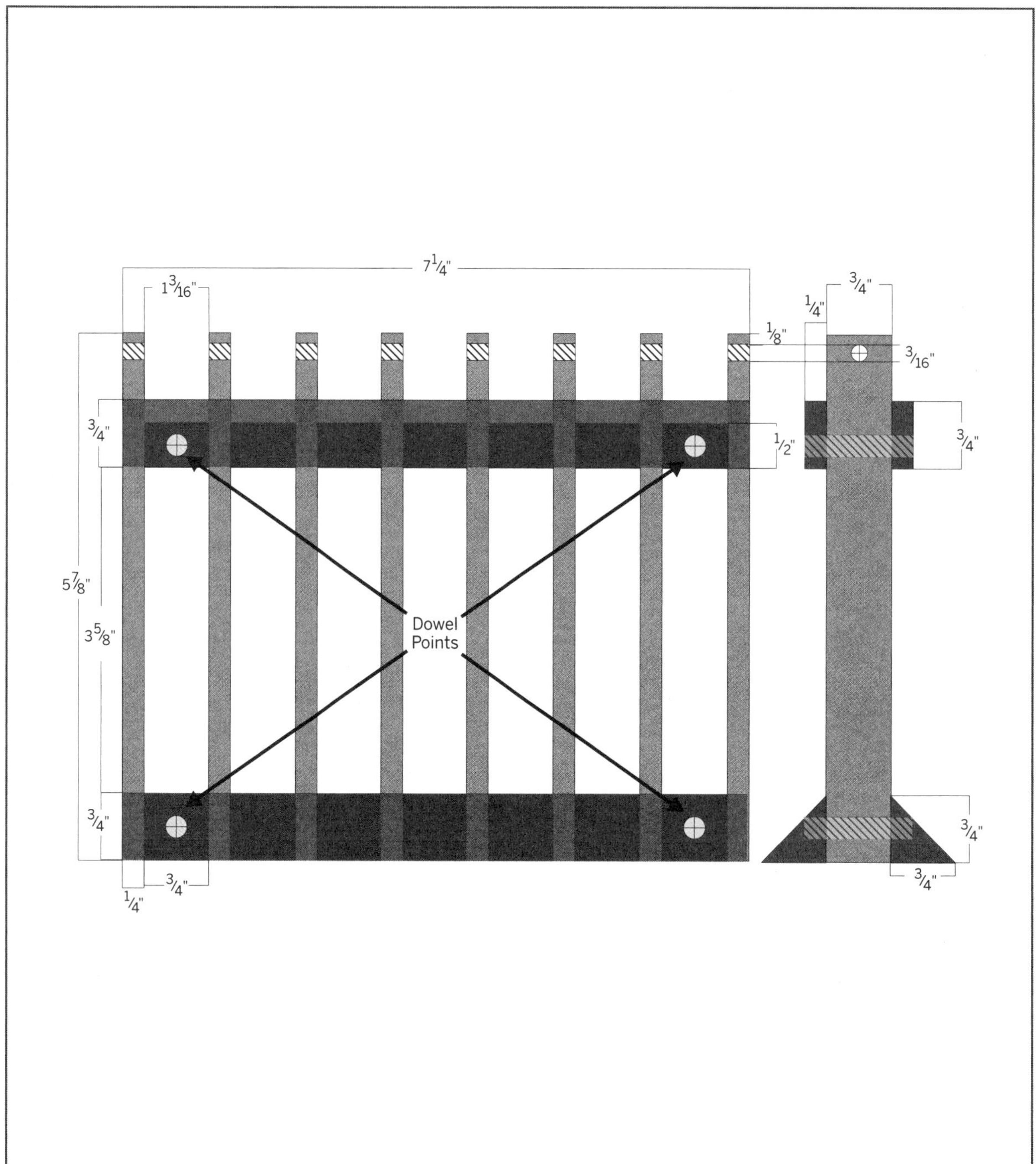

Figure 10.11: **The actuator rack in detail**

Figure 10.12: **Cut and surface-prep your components.**

Figure 10.13: **Position them, using the brass rod axle as an alignment**

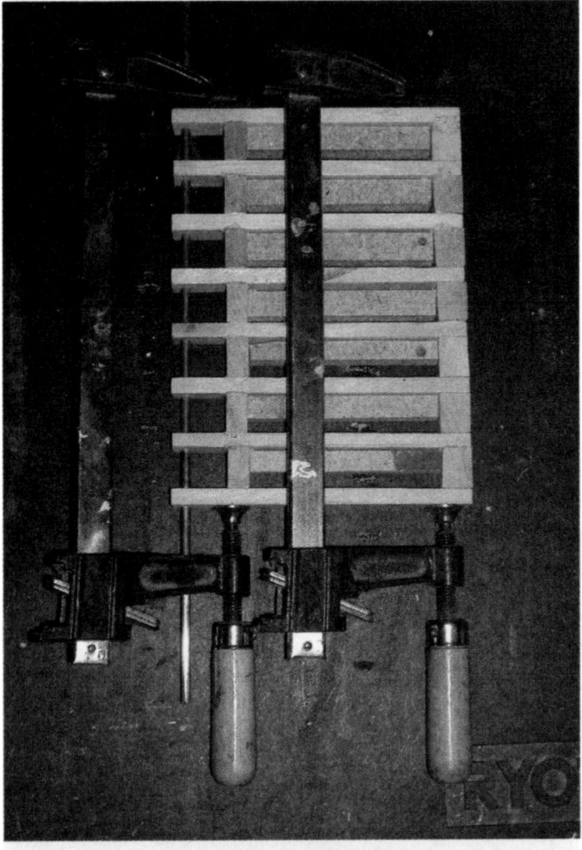

Figure 10.14: **True up your angles, then glue and clamp, using scrapwood as spacers.**

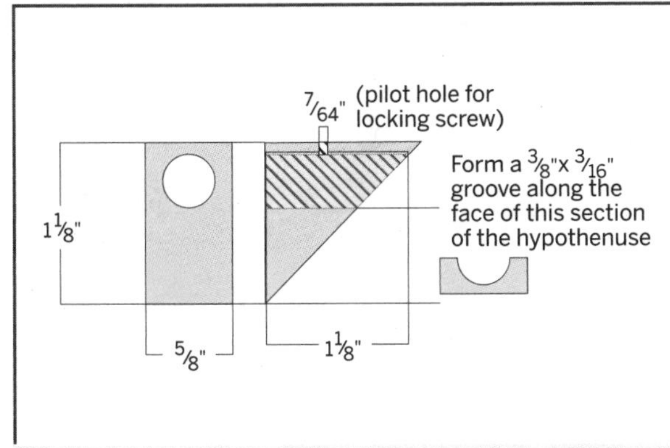

Figure 10.15: **The actuator block. You'll need seven of 'em.**

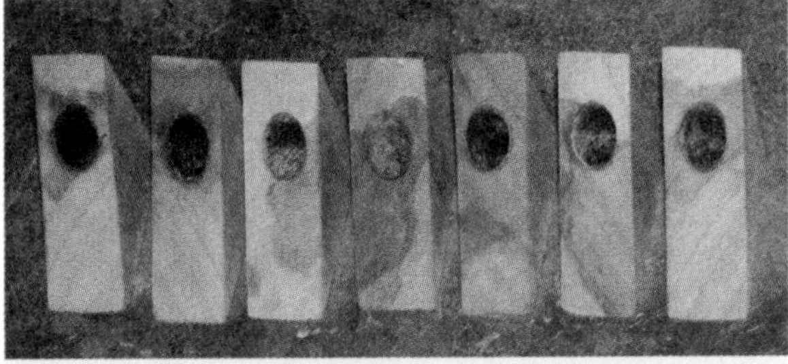

Figure 10.16: **Think the actuator blocks are ugly now? Wait 'til you see 'em after a few hours of usage. At the 2007 San Mateo Maker Faire, I was sweeping up wee piles of sawdust from under the pin drum every hour or two, generated by the abrasion of the event pins on the blocks.**

holes absolutely perpendicular to the tube by drilling a hole the diameter of the tube through a block of hardwood and sinking a guide hole vertically dead center through the diameter. Mark and punch start the hole on the tubing, then slide it into the jig and drill the hole with vastly reduced chance of the bit skating out of position. **[Figure 10.17]**

Install the levers in the rack for a quick test fit, using brass eyelets as spacers to center the levers in their respective slots. Mount the pin drum on the pillow blocks, and line up the actuator rack and drum assembly parallel to each other as shown, with the actuator rack centered in context of the drum. Mark the centers of the actuator block contact points accurately on the pin drum. You may want to adjourn for an invigorating libation and brief period of meditation at this point, since the next step is drilling out the holes in the pin drum, which will be a character-building experience on multiple levels. **[Figure 10.18]**

Figure 10.17: **A quick 'n' dirty jig for making centered holes in the actuator arms**

Figure 10.18: **Temporarily bung together the actuator rack and use it as a template to mark up the pin drum**

Refining the Pin Drum

If you're working from my cutting diagram, there's a template you can print out which will make marking the hole locations an easier task. Me, I couldn't be arsed finding the refill kit for my printer cartridge so I did the markup by hand. I started by drawing a circle and using a protractor to divide it into 22.5 degree arcs, giving me 16 radial segments. **[Figure 10.19, Figure 10.20, Figure 10.21, Figure 10.22, Figure 10.23]**

With the location of all 112 pin holes marked, I carefully punched the drill points, and knocked together a quick drilling jig out of plywood and aluminum angle. **[Figure 10.24]**

The more care you take with drilling the pin drum holes accurately, the better. Hammerhead is never gonna sound like Steve Gadd, but you sure don't want it sounding like that 13 year old down the block who jams Blink 182 songs with his buddies every second Saturday afternoon.

Well, maybe you *do*.

Just don't tell me about it though, okay?

Use a sharp 13⁄64" drill bit and a *lot* of cutting fluid during the drilling process. The copper is gonna heat up something fierce along the way, friction being what it is. Take frequent breaks to admire your handiwork and give the metal a chance to drop a few calories. There'll be burring happening that could impede accurate positioning of the drum as you make your way round 'n' round, down the length of the pipe. Make sure it doesn't get in the way. **[Figure 10.25]**

Copper is softer and more malleable than brass, but it's still going to take its toll on your drill bit. If you have a Drill

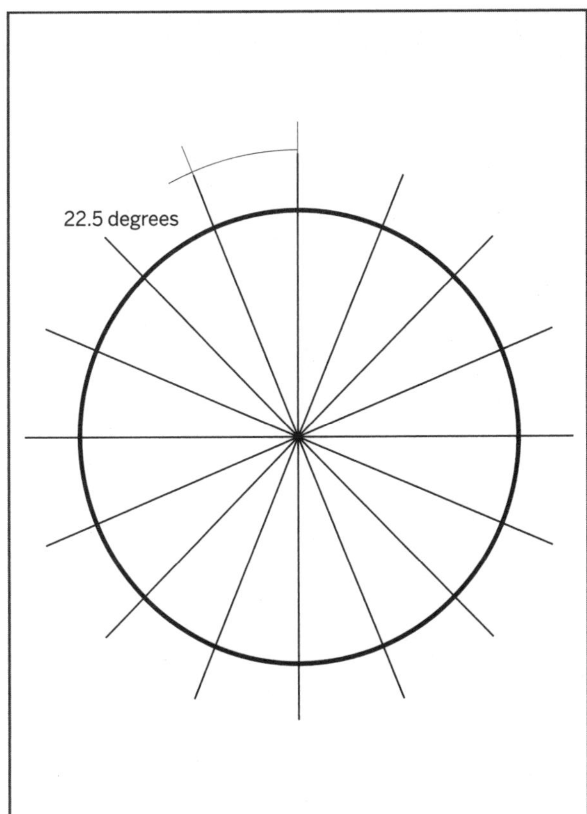

Figure 10.19: **The pin drum hole spacing guide**

Figure 10.20: **I centered the pin drum blank on the circle, and marked the radius points around the base.**

Figure 10.21: **A piece of 1" angle (extruded aluminum in this case) self-aligns on the drum, letting me draw perfectly parallel lines along the length. Oh, Geometry, how do I love thee? Let me count the ways.**

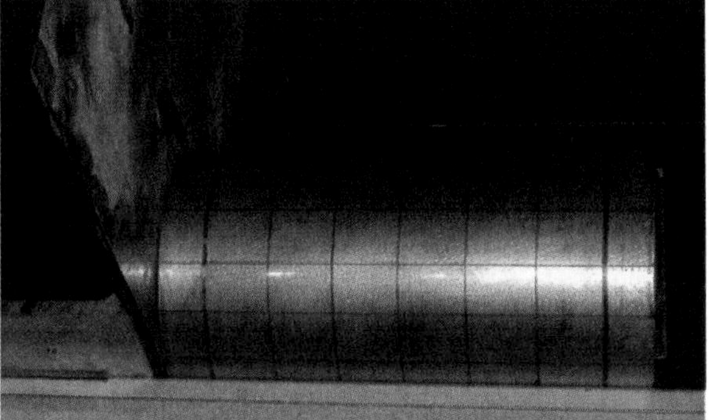

Figure 10.22: **Another piece of aluminum angle clamped onto the fence of the table saw gives me a stable jig for marking the horizontal bands.**

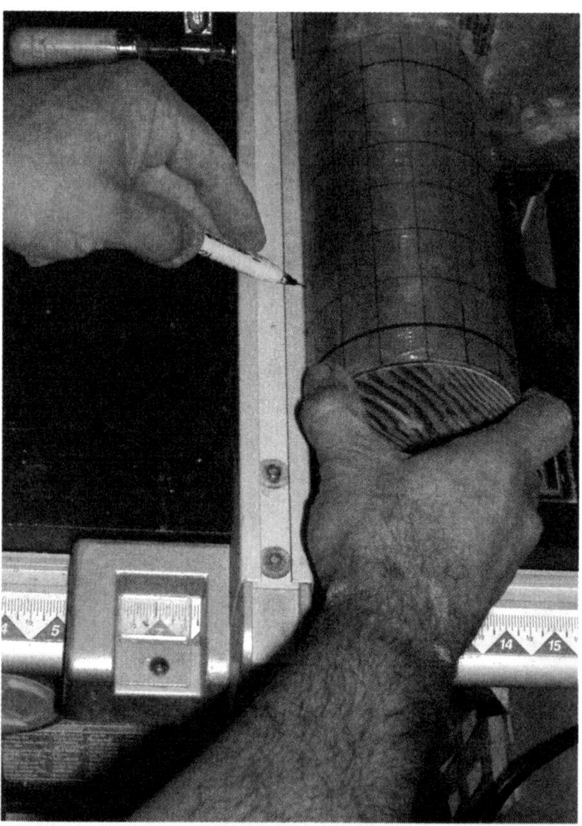

Figure 10.23: **Hold a fine-tipped Sharpie in position, rotate the pin drum smoothly, and Bob's yer uncle.**

Figure 10.24: **T'ain't nothin' fancy: just a tight, solid frame to cradle the pipe and hold it in position. It clamps onto the base of my weensy-ass little drill press and lets me rotate each punch point into position under the bit without losing alignment.**

Doctor, sharpen up at the halfway point of the drillout. If not, switch to a new bit.

To briefly recap: Yes, drill bits get dull. Yes, it makes a difference. No, there isn't an easy way to sharpen them by hand.

Neither are there a great many options available to non-machinists for machine sharpening them accurately.

After about an hour of painstakin' hole-makin', you'll be finished, and relieved the task is behind you.

Now pull out your tap and die set and cut ¼-20 threads into every last one of those holes you just drilled. Take your time and get 'em nice and straight. Tapping a hole in a curved surface is a bit of a challenge.

I'll wait.

Woo freakin' hoo. That didn't take long did it?

Okay. So it *did* take a long time. And your hands hurt from crankin' on that damned tap wrench. And you've got a flake of copper in your shoe and that hurts too.

But you finished the job, you brave little soldier. I'm proud of you.

Now smooth out the surface of the drum with emery cloth and give it a quick rubdown with steel wool. Thread the ¼-20 threaded rod through the drum, centering the length. Lock it in place with a lockwasher and nut at each end, then slide on the pillow blocks. Secure the pillow blocks on the axle with a washer and nut on one end and a washer and the T-nut equipped drive pulley on the other end. Secure the drive pulley with a lockwasher and another nut, and you should have something that closely resembles the illustration. **[Figure 10.26]**

Tack the pillow blocks down on a scrap of plywood and make sure the assembly spins easily; if it does, celebrate with a cocktail and a moment of frenzied air drumming. If it doesn't, find out why, and fix it.

Once again, I'll wait.

Figure 10.25: **The frame in use, drilling out the pin drum.**

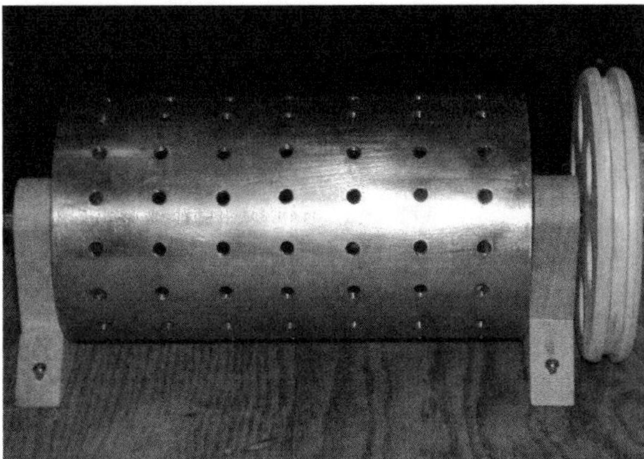

Figure 10.26: **The product of your not inconsiderable labours: A jolly good pin drum. Huzzah!**

With the pin drum assembly essentially completed, the rest of the mechanism gets assembled on the deck around it.

So fabricate the deck.

The Main Deck

Pull out a 2' x 2' slab of ¾" plywood, and shape it into something aesthetically satisfying. Personally, I opted for the ever popular "intersect a circle with a square" approach, with the pin drum centered a few inches in from the square end. This form factor keeps the scale of the levers involved at a reasonable size, but demands a bit of imagination to fit a full complement of percussion instrumentation into the works. This is not a problem, since we're all about imagination, aren't we? **[Figure 10.27]**

AREN'T WE??

That's better.

Anyway, More on that later, during the "cobble together some things that sound like drums" section, and the "how am I gonna get all this stuff to fit" section.

Center the pin-drum-and-pulley assembly on the deck, and tack it in place. There's a lot of stuff to be installed on the underside of the deck, so you'll need to fabricate legs of some sort. As one of the things that'll be living in the basement suite is the drive motor, you'll need to cut a slot in the deck for the drive belt to pass through. The slot pictured was done by cutting out the material between two 1" holes spaced about 3" apart. This measurement was a highly optimistic estimate that proved to be about 30 percent too small to pass the belt without friction. Be smart, kids: make the slot big enough *the first time*. Like, about 4¾" x 1". **[Figure 10.28]**

The legs were cut from a piece of 4" x 4" I found on the ground outside of Terminal City Ironworks.[7] They're glued and screwed in position to provide a wide, stable footprint with maximum available real estate on the underside. At this scale, it's a bit of a stretch to think of Hammerhead as a desktop device.

Maybe it'll fit on the coffee table.

With the deck taking shape, it's best to consider the various bits and pieces that will occupy the basement level *before* we start getting fancy on the top side. I somehow wound up working on both sides of the deck at the same

7 How cool a name is that? Formerly a for-real pouring-hot-metal foundry in Vancouver's seedy Eastside, it's been converted into a location studio for the film and TV industry, hosting productions like *Smallville*, *Blade*, and *Dark Angel* (FWIW, James Cameron has a freakin' enormous entourage, or at least he did when he showed up to oversee the final episode of D.A. Those guys sure know how to disrupt a neighborhood.)

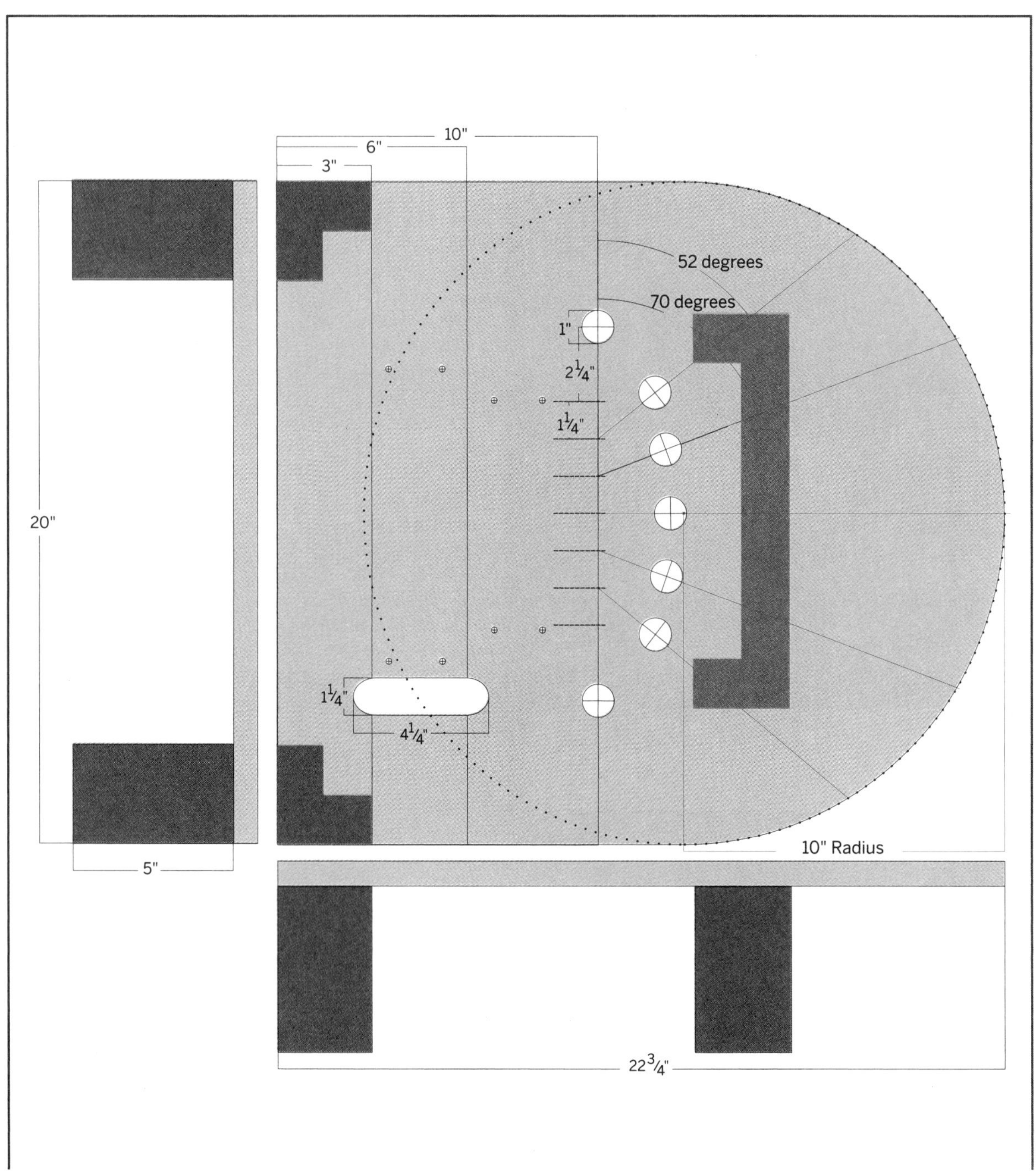

Figure 10.27: **The topography of the Hammerhead deck. Your overall shape may vary. Your mounting positions should not.**

Figure 10.28: **Nicely composed photograph of a drive pulley slot 30 percent too small. Duh**

Figure 10.29: **The naked drill motor. The compact, efficient design offers nary a hint of its propensity for nerve-shredding cacophony.**

time during the project build, which proved to be endlessly inconvenient. I do not recommend trying this at home, unless your workbench is set up like a scaled-down muffler repair shop and equipped with a teeny-weeny hydraulic lift to conveniently hold bulky projects in midair.[8]

The Drive Motor: A Sordid Tale of Electric Drill Abuse

Drivetrain-wise, the only real option is a variable-speed electric drill. They have lotsa torque for those kick drum-intensive heavy-load sequences, and a speed control that can easily be modified to provide accurate, repeatable tempos. I scored an 18-volt rechargable unit on sale for 30 bucks that came with 75 reasonable-quality bits and a dandy firm-sided case with about a dozen pockets that's now serving yeoman's duty as my laptop case. Given those bonus accessories, I didn't mind cannibalizing the drill for parts one little bit.

Once the case is removed, you're left with the trigger-actuated speed controller circuit, the battery clip and the motor/gearbox, each with convenient lengths of wire extending from them.

Put aside the clip and the trigger mechanism for the moment and deal with the motor, which needs a bit of tweaking before use to cinch down the torque adjustment and eliminate any chance of the driveshaft slipping under load. [Figure 10.29]

Before we attempt this, we have to talk about noise. Not *good* noise, like the stuff recorded by Merzbow, Rapoon, or D.V.O.A., but *bad* noise, like the sounds made by dentist's drills, jackhammers, and related power tools. You think an electric drill is irritatingly noisy? Wait 'til you hear one with the casing removed. That "makes you wanna poke your ears out" whine becomes an all-encompassing grating drone capable of driving grown men to tears. In a musical instrument, this trait is generally considered undesirable (except in the capable hands of artists like the aforementioned Merzbow or Rapoon), so we're going to need to implement some stern noise-abatement techniques to deal with the issue.

Despite the claims made by the manufacturers of "acoustic foam" products, the *only* way to successfully suppress noise transmission is by sealing the noise source smack dab in the middle of a whole lot of (acoustic energy–absorbing) mass. To

8 Come to think of it, a hoist-equipped workbench is actually not a bad idea. As it happens, I've had the lift mechanism from a dentist's chair tucked away in the corner for months, waiting for just the right project.

Figure 10.30: **See that yellow thing? It's the forward/ reverse gear shift. We want "forward."**

this end, head to the scrapyard (or local home improvement center, if you're absolutely determined to pay full retail price) and pick up a few square feet of 1/8" sheet lead to use as sheathing. The toxicity of lead is not understated by the popular press; use realistic adult-strength caution when working with it.[9]

Now that we're properly equipped to deal with extraneous noise, the drive train modifications can proceed with impunity.

Modern cordless drills are invariably reversible. The direction of rotation is determined by the position of a yoke-like slider mechanism that changes a gear position inside the gearbox. Hammerhead wants to be driven by a motor rotating in a clockwise direction. Once you've ensured that the gearbox is set to "forward," the gearshift yoke can be safely removed. It should snap out easily. **[Figure 10.30]**

Disassemble the torque controller by removing the chuck from the drill. (There's a left-threaded Phillips head machine screw accessible through the chuck throat that needs to be removed. Once it's out, clamp the short end of an Allen key into the chuck, and give the protruding long end of the key a sharp whack sideways with a hammer to loosen the chuck on its (right-handed) threads.

Screw the chuck off, and remove the screws holding the torque control ring in place. The ring is spring loaded, and is gonna want to fly off as soon as the screws are free, so exercise caution. There's a ring of ball bearings at the bottom of the shaft closest to the motor. The spring presses a plate onto these bearings, forcing them into dimples on the motor side of the shaft. Excess torque forces the bearings up out of the dimples and takes the drive shaft out of gear. This would not be a favourable occurence.

We want to replace the spring with a section of pipe to hold the bearings in place regardless of torque, and sheath the underlying mechanism in lead to dampen the gear noise. **[Figure 10.31]**

The Mastercraft unit I used was spec'd with a 1¼" ID torque spring. Your results may vary. Add a single-layer wrap of lead sheet, which will increase the diameter by ¼", then source a piece of thinwalled steel pipe to fit. Determine the length of pipe required to replace it by measuring from the top of the bearing pressure plate to the top of the extension that holds the spring retention plate. Slide your precisely sized piece of steel pipe over the lead wrap and into the position previously occupied by the torque spring and torque strength adjustor. Position the top plate and replace the screws. The pipe should *firmly* hold the bearing pressure plate in position, allowing no shaft slippage whatsoever. Add another single layer of lead wrapping around the pipe. Use foam-backed double-faced tape to hold it in position. The foam will mechanically isolate the drives' vibration from resonating through the rest of the mechanism. **[Figure 10.32]**

Reinstall the chuck, then set to work on the motormount. You'll need some plywood.

The Motor Mount

The mount is another of those "nested holes" affairs, diameters and depths to be determined by the specifics of your drive mechanism, with allowances for a layer of inner-tube rubber lining the holes as an additional level of vibration isolation. The only other critical dimension is the 3" center-of-hole-to-top-of-mount figure illustrated, which is essential

9 Sheet lead cuts to fit easily with tin snips or household shears, and is readily hand-formable. Avoid contact with the powdery white oxide that may appear on the surface. A coat of aerosol lacquer will go a long way towards controlling its formation and spread. Lead's mass makes attaching it to stuff problematic at times. Foam-backed double-faced tape combined with escutcheon pins where applicable has proven most effective for me.

Figure 10.31: **Swap a chunk of pipe for the adjustable torque control to disable the completely unwanted "slips under high load" feature.**

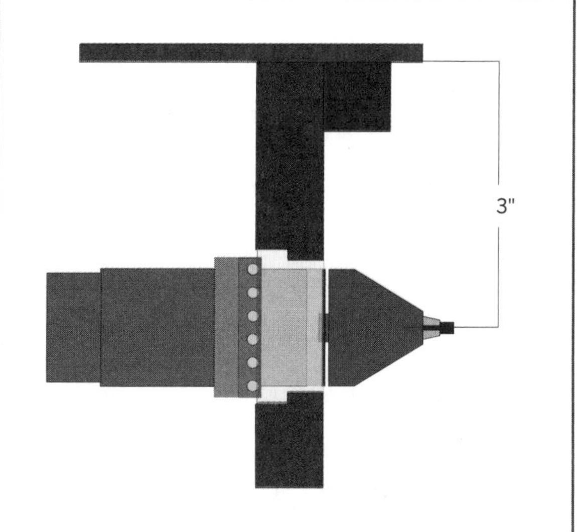

Figure 10.32: **Proper sizing results in a tight press-fit for the drive motor into the rubber-lined mounting hole. There should be no need for additional fasteners to secure the drive. Gotta cut down the parts count somehow!**

for ensuring that the 8" O-ring drive belt fits properly. **[Figure 10.33, Figure 10.34, Figure 10.35]**

With the rubber laminated in place with contact adhesive, the motor should pressfit into place tightly.

Glue and dowel a ¾" x ¾" block to the top edge of the mount to provide a secure mounting platform, then position the mount on the underside of the deck centered in the belt slot using glue and 1¼" #8 wood screws. Your actual drive shaft will be held in the drill chuck, which will make it easy to change drive ratios if need be. **[Figure 10.36]**

Wrap the exposed section of the drive mechanism in a double layer of lead sheet secured with cable ties, then knock together a quick 'n' dirty enclosure to box in the drive mechanism. The enclosure itself doesn't need to be fancy: ¼" plywood will do the job. **[Figure 10.37, Figure 10.38]**

When making your measurements, remember to take into consideration that the enclosure has to be lined with lead sheeting and a layer or two of that craft foam stuff to cut down internal reflection, as well as needing rubber-gasketing to seal off any noise escape routes.

I sized mine to fill the gap between the motor mount and battery housing. It's removable for drive servicing and surfaced with sheet brass shim stock for an extra layer of mass.

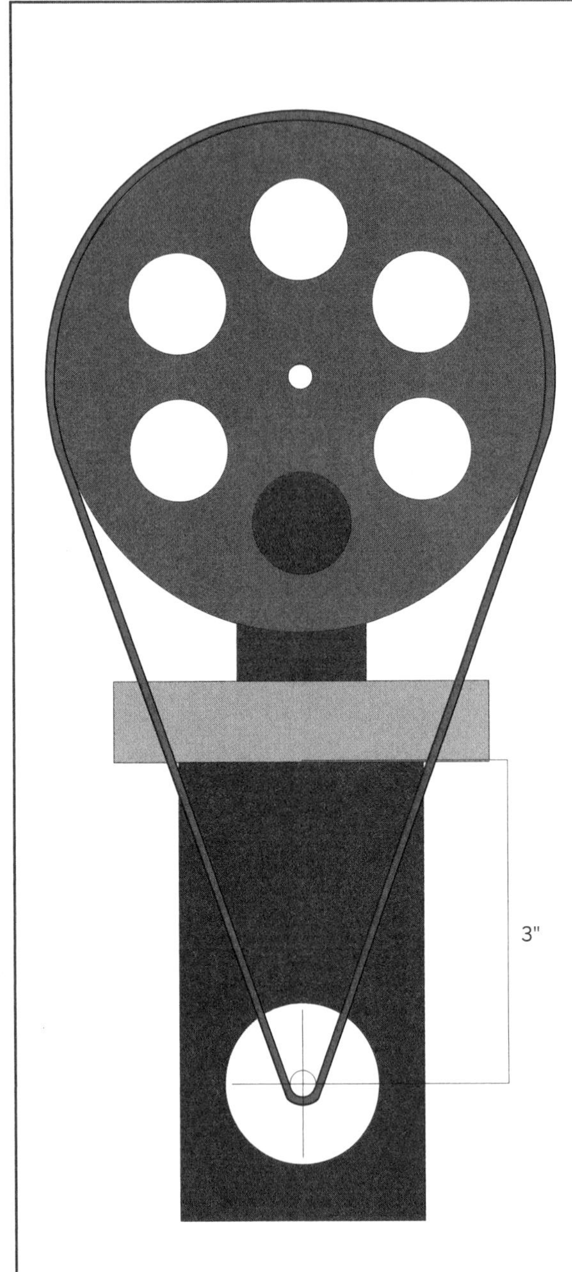

Figure 10.33: **The critical 3" center-of-hole-to-top-of-mount dimension? *Heed it!***

Figure 10.34: **The bit that actually holds the motor**

Figure 10.35: **Seen here glued, screwed, and solidly braced**

Figure 10.36: **The mounted motor.**

Figure 10.37: **More noise abatement: Wrap the exposed section of the drive with a double layer of lead sheet. No, this is not overkill.**

Test your noise reduction and add more insulation and isolation as needed. It took me about a week to get the motor noise down to an acceptable level. I was fully prepared to fill the drive enclosure with lead shot and aerosol foam insulation if need be. **[Figure 10.39]**

Messy? Uh huh, but who cares — as long as it works.

Housing the Battery

Dealing with the battery involved in this mechanism made my brain ache. It's one of those 18-volt multiple-cell jobs in an oversized plastic housing molded to slot onto the bottom of the drill handle and protrude awkwardly in every direction. I hate those damned things, but waddayagonnado?

My first instinct was to rip the actual battery components out of the housing and repackage them in a more compact form factor. This would also entail similarly modifying any spare battery packs I planned on using, as well as having to repackage the charger cradle to accomodate the new form factor. As the "pain in the ass" factor grew, my enthusiasm for this plan waned considerably.

Enter Plan B.

I opted to keep the battery packs and charger "stock" and incorporate a fitted battery compartment into the body of the mechanism.

The battery compartment is a simple side-loading wooden box with mitered joints and the lid held shut with wood screws. Strategically positioned battens hold the battery pack solidly in place. As Plan B was developed *after* the deck legs had been sized and installed, it was purely fortuitous happenstance that there was just enough clearance for the box to fit under the deck in close proximity to the drive motor. The speed controller and power switch get installed in a somewhat more ergonomic location later in the build. To that end, I drilled two ¼" diameter wiring access holes, one leading towards the lefthand side of the deck, the other pointing at the motor. **[Figure 10.40]**

At this point, getting that hulking monstrosity of a battery pack outta my hair was a victory of epic proportions.

Flush with this success, I prepared to wire up the battery clip to the motor lead, and came face to face with the proverbial fly in the ointment. **[Figure 10.41, 10.42]**

It didn't freakin' fit.

By exactly 5⁄32".

Dang. Double dang. Et cetera.

My vocabulary of pejoratives was incapable of accurately expressing my ire.

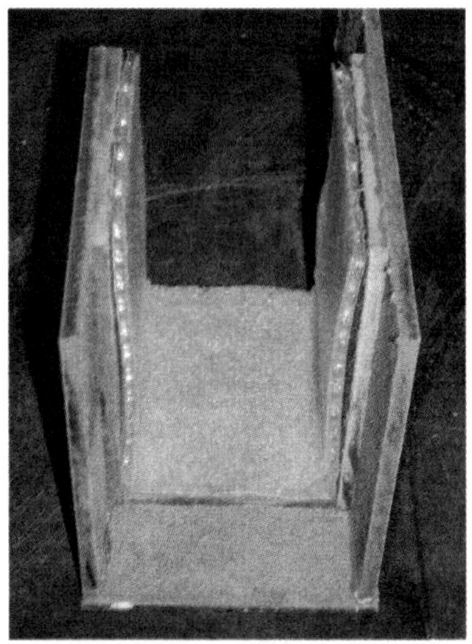

Figure 10.38: The foam-lined motor enclosure. Not yet installed: two layers of lead sheet and another layer of foam. Seriously, the motor is really freakin' noisy.

Figure 10.40: The fitted battery compartment. Or so I thought.

Figure 10.39: See, it's not so bad, once you've sheathed it in brass shim stock.

Figure 10.41: Dang.

Figure 10.42: Double dang.

Measure twice, cut once, kids. Don't be an idiot like Uncle Kaden.

Fortunately, a solution was easy to improvise. I dremelled off the offending solder tabs, sanded away the plastic body of the clip to expose enough bare metal on the clip terminals for a good solder connection, then shrink-tubed the modified battery clip to within an inch of its life. **[Figure 10.43]**

I ended up with about 1⁄64" clearance, and the sense of relief was *palpable*. The cats came out of hiding.

Order was restored to the universe in under 10 minutes, and the build resumed. **[Figure 10.44]**

Cripes, it's getting crowded under the hood. See what I mean about the eternal struggle between form and function? The battery enclosure and noise shield may not be pretty, but they *work*. **[Figure 10.45]**

Figure 10.43: **The cunningly improvised solution: reshaping the battery clip**

Figure 10.44: **HAH! Victory! It fits!**

Figure 10.45: **It's crowded in the basement: battery, motor, and about five pounds of noise abatement, not quite cunningly concealed.**

Figure 10.46: Hot damn! A completed and fully functional drive mechanism.

It is an unavoidable fact of Improvisational Fabrication that on occasion, "crude but effective" is not just the best approach, it's the *only* approach.

Stuff a 3" length of ¼" steel rod into the drill chuck to serve as the pulley, roll on an 8" rubber O-ring, and take it for a spin. If (horror of horrors), through some tragic fabrication error, the belt lacks sufficient tension to grip the drive shaft securely, substitute a larger-diameter drive rod in the drill chuck, with an additional wrap or two of PVC electrical tape to up the coefficient of friction. If the belt proves to be too short to fit, a five-minute soak in hot water will soften the O-ring material enough to let you stretch it to fit. **[Figure 10.46]**

Take a bow — your drive mechanism is done.

All it needs now is something to drive.

Hammers and Pads

With the legs, battery enclosure and motor mount attached, you can now turn the deck over and start laying out and piecing together the rest of the mechanism. Finalize the position of the pillow blocks/pin drum assembly, and set the attachment screws. Partially assemble the actuator rack, with actuators in the first, fourth and seventh positions in the rack, then position the rack so that the tips of the actuator blocks make contact with the pin drum about ⅛" shy of the dead top of the pin drum. **[Figure 10.47]**

As previously noted, the position of the actuator blocks is individually adjustable, so you don't need to be *really* precise; the most important thing is that the rack be absolutely parallel to the pin drum. Mark and drill out 3/32" holes for the rack mounting screws, and attach the rack to the deck with four 1¼" #6 wood screws.

Drill out seven ¾" wooden craft balls halfway through their diameter to ⅜" and pressfit them onto the free end of each actuator arm. They'll be epoxied in place once the completed mechanism is through final tune-up, but for now, a friction fit will serve the purpose. These balls are critical transfer nodes in the device: they do the actual transmission of actuator arm movement to the hammer arms. **[Figure 10.48]**

Heh? Hammer arms? Wuzzah hammer arms??

The hammer arms are the *other* end of the system. Remember when we "turned the corner?" The up and down motion of the actuator blocks gets transferred to the hammer arms, which in turn transfer kinetic energy to the thing that's bein' hit by whacking it with a hammer. Or a block of wood. **[Figure 10.49, Figure 10.50]**

Anything that even remotely resembles a mechanical linkage incorporates a pile of engineering issues in any build, at no extra cost. Eliminating linkages like that removes a lot of potential grief from the build process, and makes this a pretty versatile machine. **[Figure 10.51, Figure 10.52]**

I built the first Hammerhead with the hammer arm positions fixed in place. Modifying the design to let each hammer arm be rotated around the center point of the transfer nodes would take about an hour, and require 3" of ¾" x ¼" brass flatbar, three screws, one washer, and a wingnut per arm. **[Figure 10.53]**

Regardless of how you decide to configure the hammer arm locations, the fabrication process is the same. The only variable factor among the seven required arms is the length of the ⅜" brass tubing that forms the actual lever part of the mechanism. Let's sort out the other components for all seven arms first, then consider length at length as we develop a position on position. In principle the hammer arm is "just another lever"; contextually, it's "just another lever with a bunch of extra stuff attached to it to make it do what we want it to do."

The fulcrum assemblies and transfer nodes are consistent from hammer arm to hammer arm . Fabricating all seven of them en masse, one component at a time, is the most

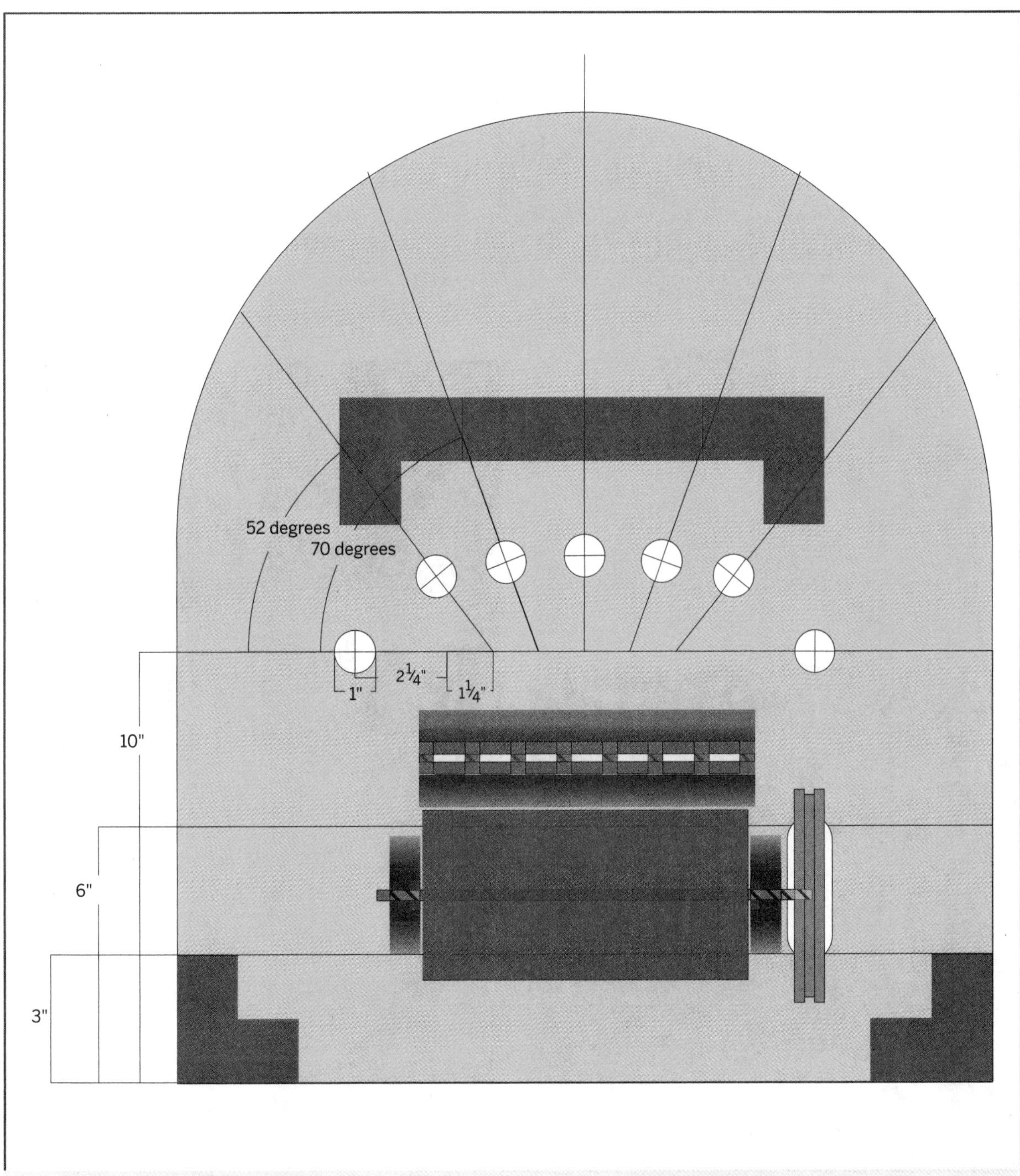

Figure 10.47: Deck topography in higher resolution. The angular measurements shown are from the build model. Your results may vary.

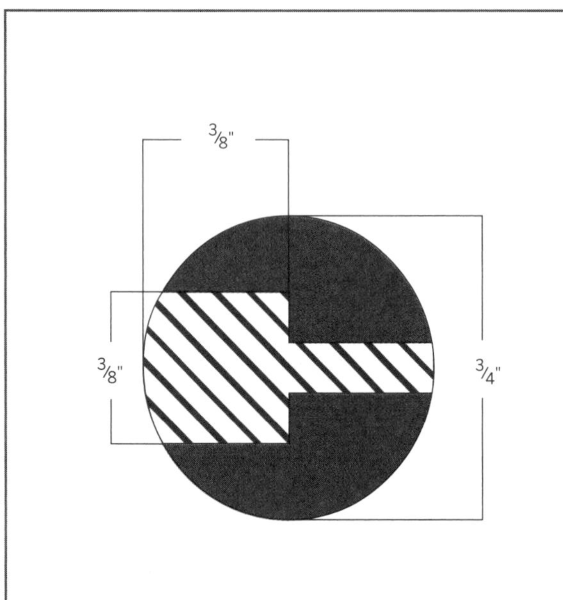

Figure 10.48: **The humble wooden craft ball's amazing transformation into mission-critical componentry: A transfer node is born.**

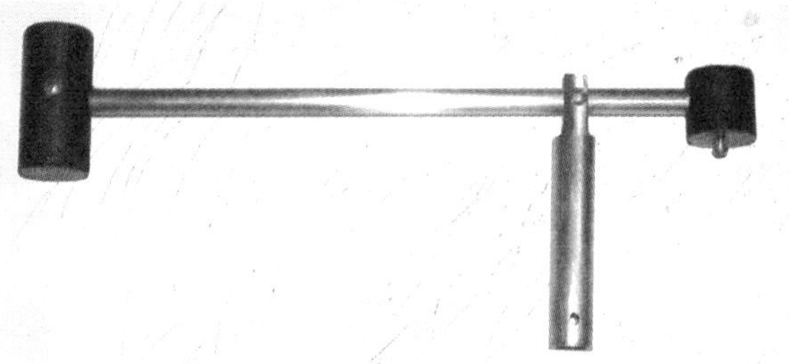

Figure 10.49: **A completed hammer arm. The bit wot does the hammerin'.**

Figure 10.50: **An aerial recon view of actuator arm/ transfer node/hammer arm deployment in the field**

Figure 10.51: **A smiley face SuperBall. The motion is transfered from one lever to the other through contact only, with no fixed mechanical linkage involved.**

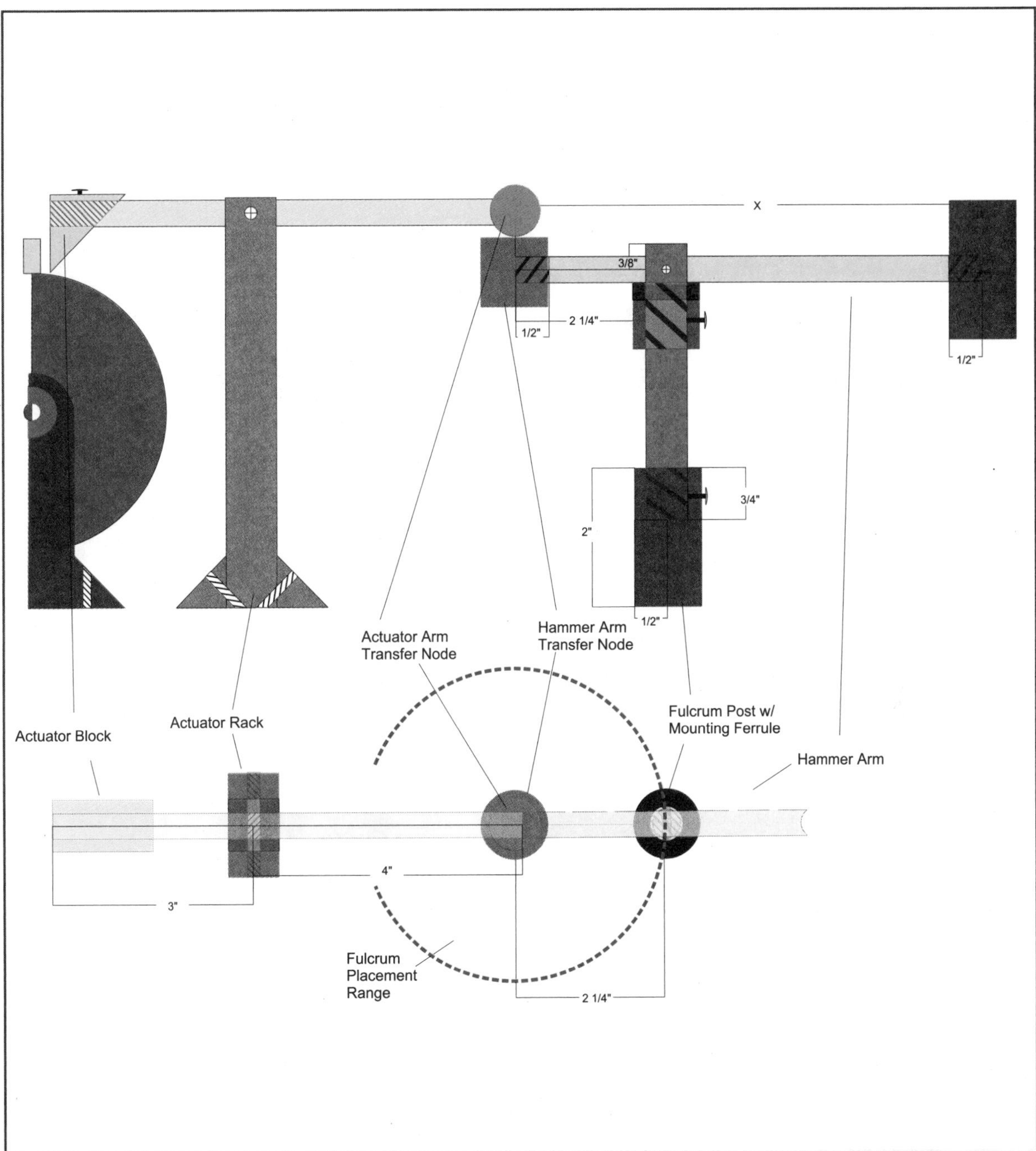

Figure 10.52: **Looking at the mechanism from two angles, the inherent flexibility of a linkageless transmission system becomes apparent: the hammer arm can potentially be positioned anywhere within an arc of about 340 degrees relative to the actuator arm.**

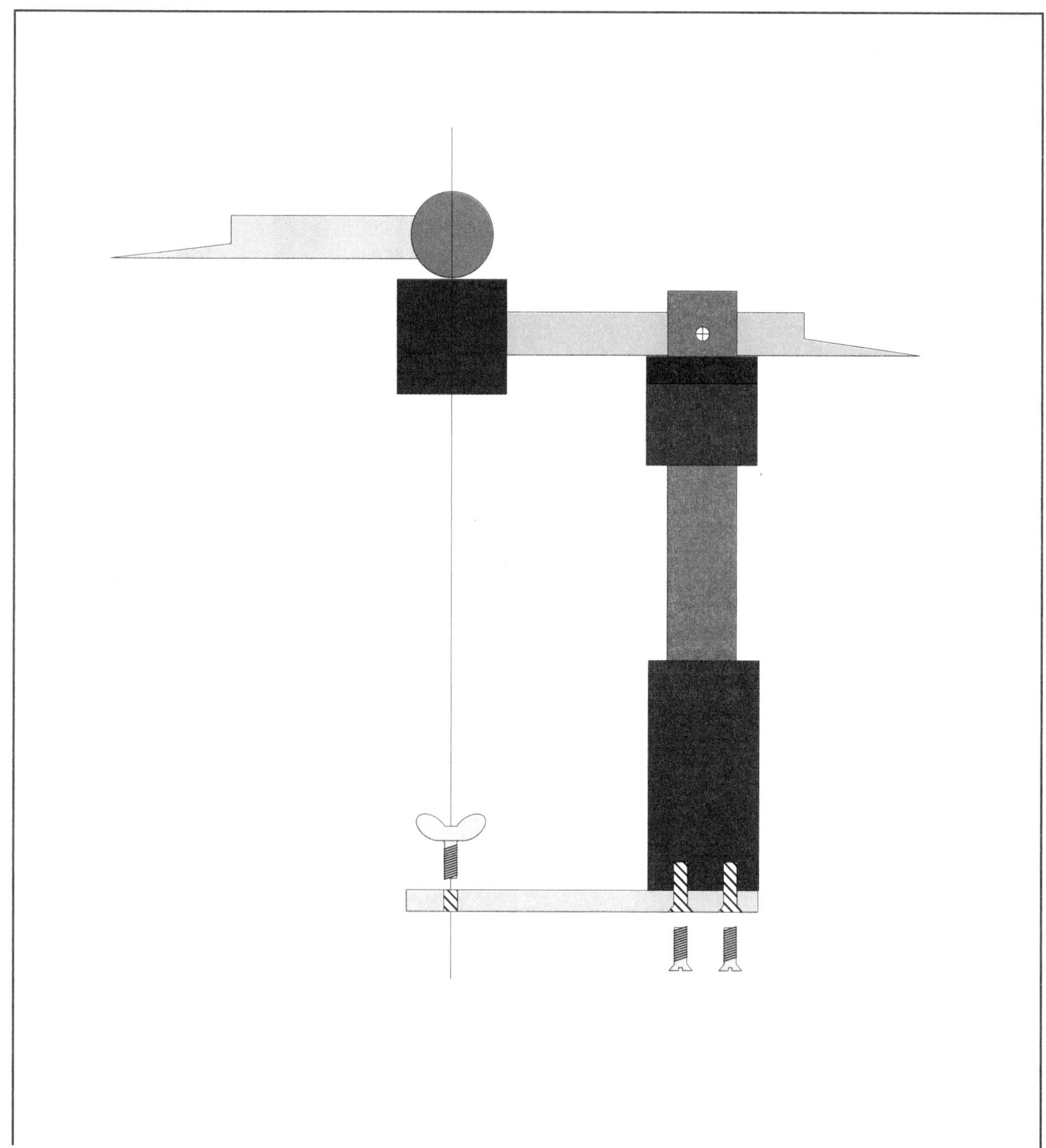

Figure 10.53: **Done right, we can build some adjustability right into the mount of the hammer arm.**

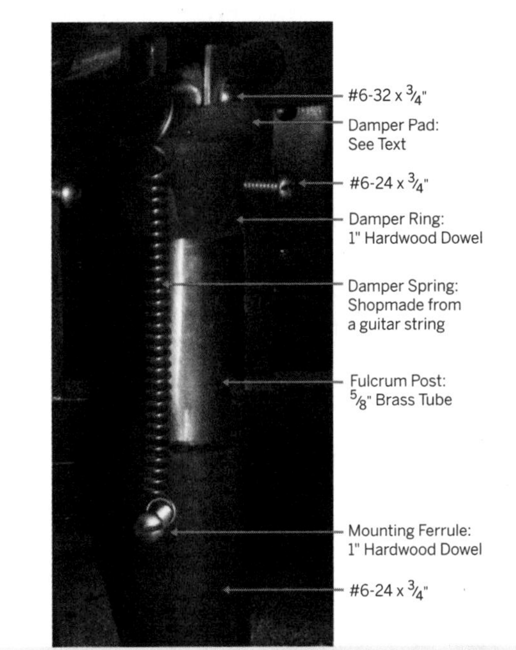

Figure 10.54: **Here's the hammer arm anatomy. With the actual lever out of the way, we're left with an overachieving fulcrum assembly, and a piece of hardwood dowel to serve as the arm-side transfer node.**

Figure 10.55: **The actual "hammer" end that will be doing the percussing is a variable to be dealt with later.**

efficient way to proceed. There are no surprises in the fabrication: it's just cut/drill/cut/drill, ad nauseam. Do your tool setups carefully, jig whatever you can, and proceed patiently. It's a good way to spend a Sunday afternoon. **[Figure 10.54, Figure 10.55, Figure 10.56]**

The fulcrum in question is 4" of 5⁄8" brass tubing notched at the top to cradle the hammer arm, with a 6-32 machine screw serving as the pivot point. The tube is held by the hardwood dowel mounting ferrule, which is the part that actually gets attached to the deck to hold the whole thing in position.

A 6-32 machine screw locks the tube into the ferrule and serves as part of the rebound dampening system, anchoring the bottom end of an expansion spring attached to the hammer arm that helps keep afterstroke arm movement under control. The dampening pad is a sandwich of belt leather and mousepad material held in close proximity to the hammer arm by a piece of drilled-out dowel locked in position with another 6-32 machine screw.

Dampening

The dampening system is an entirely *needful* adjunct to Hammerhead: it suppresses arm bounce (eliminating "false trigger" events from your sequenced rhythms), and holds the at-rest hammer arm in a position that lifts the beater off of the surface of whatever it's whacking, allowing the instrument to resonate fully. Despite the primitive tech involved, it's quite flexible when you take the time to set up the action properly, allowing full control of the range of movement of the hammers and permitting resonance muting and controllable ghost strokes.

The crux of the entire dampening system is the material of the dampening rings. I field-tested dozens of combinations before arriving at the ideal: belt leather and mousepad rubber.[10] Besides the dampening rings, it's also used to surface the contact points of the hammer arm transfer node, cushioning the effects of rebound impact on the actuator blocks.

Laminate the leather and rubber together with contact cement. Roughen the surface of the leather with 50-grit sandpaper before applying two coats of cement with a 10-minute dry time between coats. The rubber needs only one light coat of adhesive. Over-generous application will put too much solvent

10 Okay, so it's not *really* the ideal combination. My field tests actually got better results using a laminate of belt leather and wetsuit neoprene, which is thicker and more resilient than mousepad rubber. Assuming that you likely don't have a scrap wetsuit lying around your shop waiting to be cannibalized for material, I determined that mousepad rubber was an acceptable Plan B material.

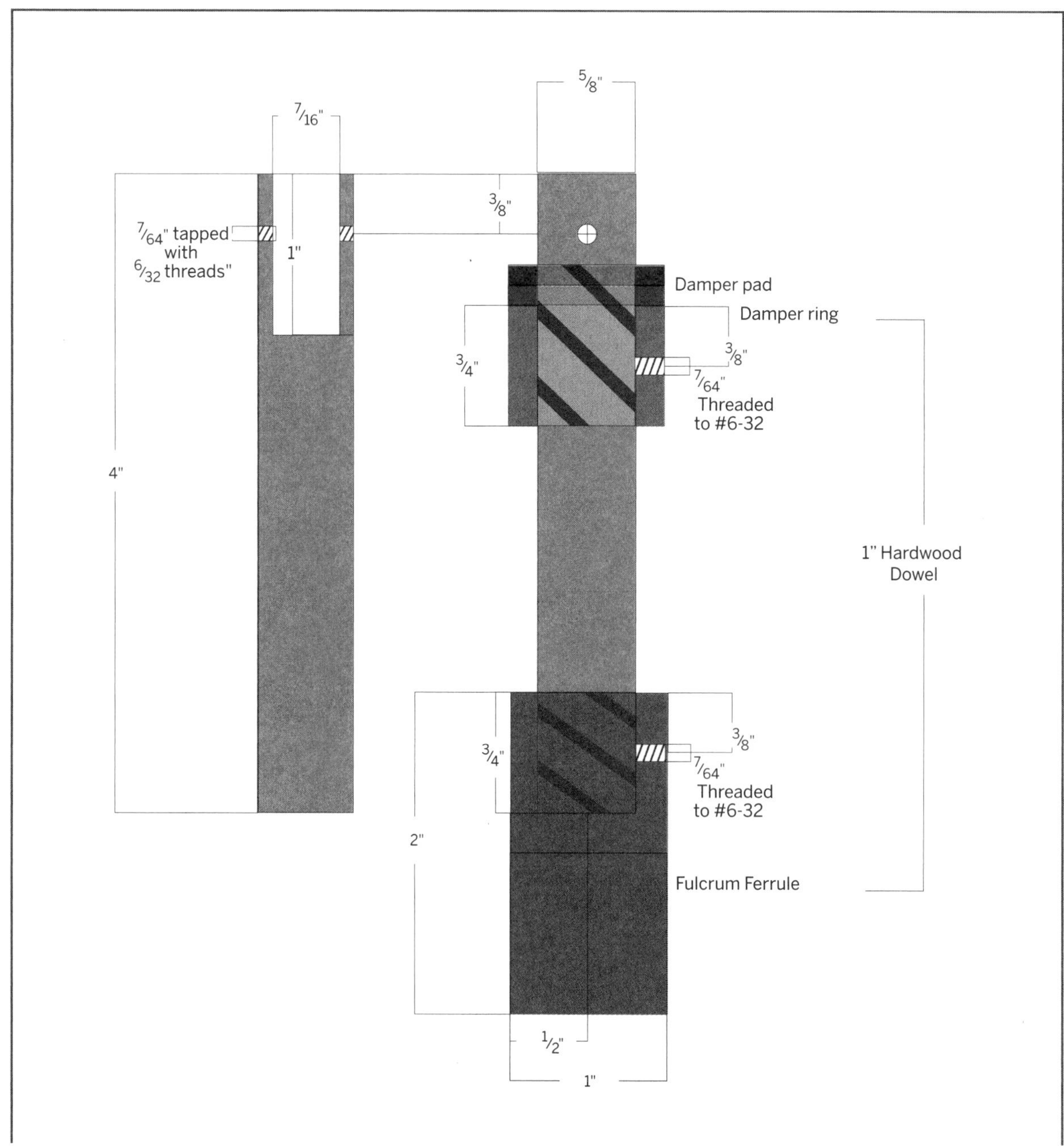

Figure 10.56: **Detailing the hammer arm fulcrum assembly. Ya think it's easy coming up with an endless series of fancy names for tarted up bits of wood and brass? I tell ya, Product Specialists earn their dosh, and that's a fact. Knowing what a chunk of mechanism does is one thing; couching it in terms that John and Jane Public can relate to is a vastly more piquant flavour of Hell.**

Figure 10.57: The dampener laminate in the raw

in contact with the rubber, potentially leading to (literally) material meltdown. When the two surfaces are coated and dry, line 'em up and lay 'em down. Weight down the bond with about 10 pounds of mass (any more will over-compress the rubber, any less results in dodgy bonding) and let it cure at least four hours before attempting to work with the material. **[Figure 10.57]**

Here's a quiz to do while you're waiting for the bond to cure. Cutting the circular pads by hand will:

A. Turn you into the Jack Nicholson character from *The Shining*

B. Consume your entire supply of X-Acto knife blades in the first nine minutes

C. Take about three hours to get right, and even then they won't ***really*** be right

D. All of the above

E. Giraffe

Of course, the correct answer is **D**, "All of the above," unless of course you are a surrealist, in which case I would also have accepted **E**, "Giraffe," **L**, "Pork, or **T**, "A good, sound spanking from a chap named Nigel."

So don't try to cut the pads by hand. You've been warned, and for good reason.

Even the heaviest-duty utility knife will go dull in a flash cutting leather, and mousepad rubber is unfortunately prone to tearing and ragged edges even with a *really* sharp knife. You'll be cutting a *minimum* of fourteen 1" diameter pads, half of them center-punched with a ¼" diameter hole (the node pads), the rest center-punched with a 5/8" diameter hole (the arm pads). Trust me, there's a better way than using a knife. **[Figure 10.58]**

And the better way is?

Die-cutting them. Which is a fancy way of saying "find a steel pipe the right diameter, sharpen the edge of one end into what's essentially a circular knife, and pound the sharpened pipe through the laminate with a rubber mallet like it's a cookie cutter."

NOTE: You'll need a lot of pads. Properly tuning the damping system for different playing circumstances can be pad-intensive. I've had up to three of the damned things stacked together on a given hammer arm for accurate response, depending on the dynamics of the sequence and the mass of the beater attached to the end of the arm in question. Other situations have called for notches to be cut out of the pads to accommodate lightweight beaters in large dynamic sequences. Cut lots of extra arm pads. Using them effectively is part art, part physics, and part voodoo, which by its very nature *demands* sacrifices.

If you have an anvil, lay a piece of ¼" plywood over the top to protect the edge of your die and use it as your striking surface. The leather will take its toll on the cutting edge eventually. For best results, resharpen with a bench grinder or dremel at the first sign of a ragged edge. Punch out the 1"-diameter disks first, then do the center punch-outs with smaller cutting dies. **[Figure 10.59]**

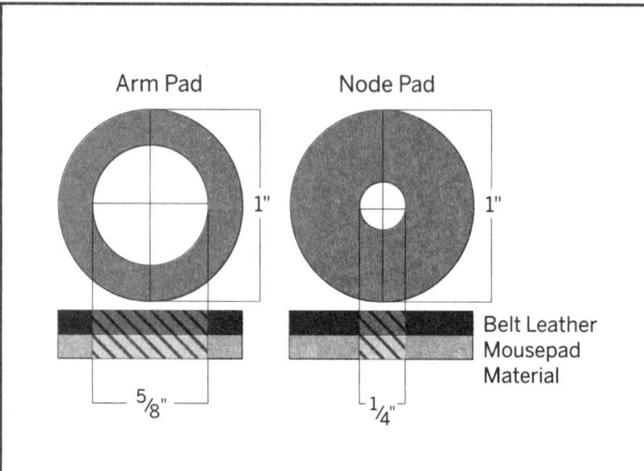

Figure 10.58: **Both flavours of dampening pad. Make a lot of each.**

Figure 10.59: **Anvil, sharp pipe, and mousepad/leather laminate. The hammer's late arriving; it stopped to pick up the beer.**

Figure 10.60: **Less than two minutes work: cutting dies are the bees knees.**

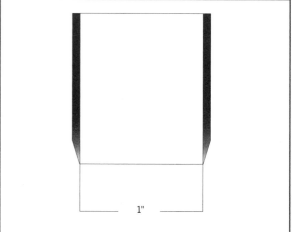

Figure 10.61: **The illustrated cutting die**

Make your dies from the heaviest-gauge steel pipe you can source, and check the ID measurement. You'll be forming your cutting edge from the outside inwards, so it's the *inner* diameter that determines the size of your punch-out. **[Figure 10.60, Figure 10.61]**

Fabricate the transfer nodes per the cutting diagram. The set screw is on the upper face for easy access. The hammer arm will be drilled and tapped to permanently attach the set screw, once the exact position is determined during final set-up of the mechanism. To facilitate access to the set screw, I punched out a 3⁄16" hole in the center of the pads with a leather-worker's turret punch. You'll need to do something similar with yours, either using said turret punch (always a useful tool around the shop), or with a smaller-diameter homemade cutting die.

Attach the dampening pad to the upper face of the transfer node with double-faced tape. Depending on the size of the beater attached to the hammer arm, one or

Figure 10.62: **There currently is no collective noun for a group of damper pad–equipped hammer-arm transfer nodes. Think up a good one and contribute to the evolution of the English language.**

more additional pads may be needed to fine-tune the angle of the arm. The transfer node pads work best when applied with the leather surface up. **[Figure 10.62]**

The arm pads are positioned around the fulcrum post above the wooden dampening ring. Adjusting the position of the ring up and down increases or decreases the effect of the pad(s) on arm movement, and you can add additional pads or portions thereof to get the beater response you want. One pad is mandatory. Slide it onto the fulcrum post, followed by the dampening ring. Use a #6-32 machine screw as the set screw on the dampening ring; the coarser threading will better withstand repeated repositioning. Any pads added subsequently can be slit along a radius and slipped around the fulcrum post while it's still in the ferrule.

The mounting ferrules are pretty much "what you see is what you get." The fulcrum post fits into the ferrule, and the ferrule fits into the receiver hole you drill in the deck. Mount the ferrule to the deck with a #6 x 1¼" woodscrew screwed up from the underside of the deck. The set screw that locks the fulcrum in position *can* be made permanent by drilling and tapping the fulcrum, but I've found it convenient to retain adjustability in the height of the fulcrum. To that end, use a 6-32 machine screw as the set screw. (To adjust the height of the fulcrum in the ferrule, yank out the post and drop 5/8" steel washers down the hole to fit. If need be, you can remove them later with a magnet).

The set screw acts as the bottom anchor for the dampening spring. At present I'm using one spring, on the hammer side of the lever. It is entirely likely that I'll end up adding another set screw on the opposite side of the ferrule to let me use springs on both sides of the lever for additional control of both dampening and strength of stroke. The tension of the spring is varied by sliding the top end up or down the hammer arm. Yes, it's another "crude but effective" moment.

I made the springs in the shop by winding used guitar strings onto a rod, then doing a heat/cool cycle on them with a torch to reset the temper of the wire to the newly wound shape. (I've detailed the intricacies of spring-makin' in Chapter 4: look it up.) With unlimited springage at my disposal, I went the trial-and-error route on length/tension, and discovered that they are variables that are tough to predict. FWIW, my springs averaged 2½" long, and were formed around 8-32 threaded rod. Feel free to substitute rubber bands if you want to forgo the angst of coming up with suitable springs in suitable quantity. You'll achieve the same ends, without the steampunky goodness of coiled bits of wire.

Enjoy "trial and error." It's another of those character-building experiences yer mom told you about.

Right, then: hammer arm length, and the all-important question of positioning the damned things.

Hammers Again

Hammerhead is designed with the hammer arm levers having a common effort length of 2¼". I'm gonna belabour the obvious here and point out that the longer the resistance length, the larger the range of movement. Keep this in mind when sizing your hammer arms: the longer the lever, the longer the stroke. A long hammer arm will end up having a heavier hit than a short one, so be aware of the dynamic range of the noisemaker that each hammer will be hitting when planning your arm lengths. **[Figure 10.63]**

The hammer arm length configuration I've spec'd out in the cutting diagram[11] works with the bodged-together instruments included in the build, even if the real estate requirements of the instruments and their respective dynamic ranges made it a bit of a juggling act. Those of you building to the cutting diagram can proceed with confidence. **[Figure 10.64]**

If your intention is for Hammerhead to serve as a more general-purpose physical sampling percussion sequencer with no dedicated instruments on board, my recommendation is that you opt for a flexible configuration with a wide range of hammer arm lengths of varying effort/resistance ratios at your disposal and a deck sized and shaped accordingly. Maxing

11 1" x 15", 2" x 12", 2" x 10", 2" x 7", each fulcrumed at 2¼".

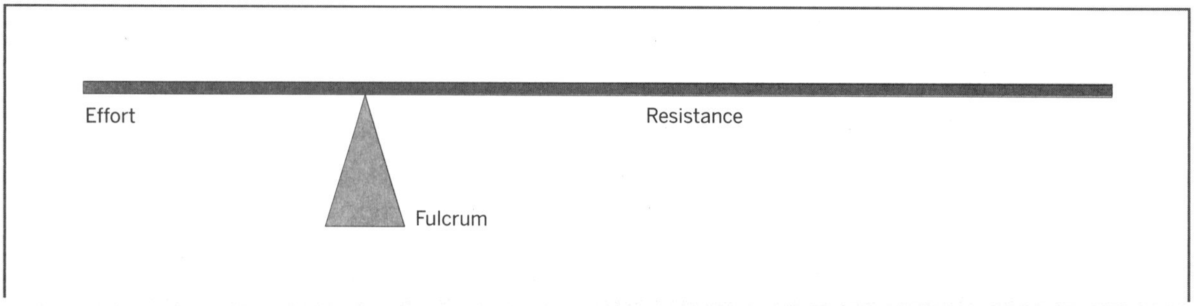

Effort
Resistance
Fulcrum

Figure 10.63: Ladies and gentlemen, please put your hands together repeatedly and enthusiastically for the hardest working mechanism in Making . . . they call it MISTER Primary Mechanism. Welcome, please . . . the Lever.

Figure 10.64: Overhead spycam view of the device in question. Marvel at the positional versatility of the lever assembly.

out the flexibility factor, it wouldn't be an enormous amount of work to fabricate adjustable-length hammer arms. Couple those with the adjustable-position mounting ferrule modification that I outlined earlier and you'd have an emminently adaptable mechanism.

Hammerhead is easily adapted to use just about anything as a beater. If you can drill a 3/8" hole in it, it'll fit on the end of the arm. I've used miniature brass tack hammers, sections of 1" dowel, craft balls, the previously illustrated Smiley Face superballs and honkin' big squishy rubber balls as beaters to great effect. If you're after a more traditional 5A drumstick sound, just chop the tip off a drumstick and sand down the shaft to let it fit into the end of the hammer arm. It can press-fit into place, or be secured with a set screw.

Once you've decided on the lengths you'll be using, fabricating the hammer arms is just a matter of cutting the 3/8" brass tubing to length, and drilling across the radius at the 2 1/4" point with a 1/8" bit.

Assemble all seven hammer arms, and install them on the deck; if you're following my cutting diagram, this entails marking the locations of the mounting ferrules on the deck and drilling a 1" hole 3/8" deep at each location. The ferrules slot into the holes and are screwed in place from the underside. Don't cinch the screws down completely yet. There's *undoubtedly* a spate of angular adjustment forthcoming during tune-up, after which you can lock down everything as tightly as you want.

Control Panel

The control panel for Hammerhead is thankfully a spartan affair: a power switch and a mo' faster knob is all that's needed, a control layout which usually implies minimum fiddly bits, maximum artsy-fartsy nonsense. In the case of this build, only half of the preceding statement was accurate.

The drill speed control is a pulse width modulation circuit, which is needed to maintain motor torque at low revs. It's a transistor, a cute-as-a-button little heat sink, a couple of caps and a couple of resistors, with the trigger itself housing a wussy-assed little molded-into-the-plastic linear pot. I could have just wired a real potentiometer into the circuit, but honestly, what fun is that? Typically, I opted to mount the trigger mechanism itself in a box and fabricate a cam-based actuator to mechanically move the trigger through a musically realistic range of speeds. **[Figure 10.65]**

Yeah, I know: I'm nuts.

But it's a *damned* sweet mechanism.

As Maximum Artsy Fartsy was by this time more-or-less imperative, once the controls were boxed up I added art deco inspired knobs 'n' shit, and mounted the whole damned

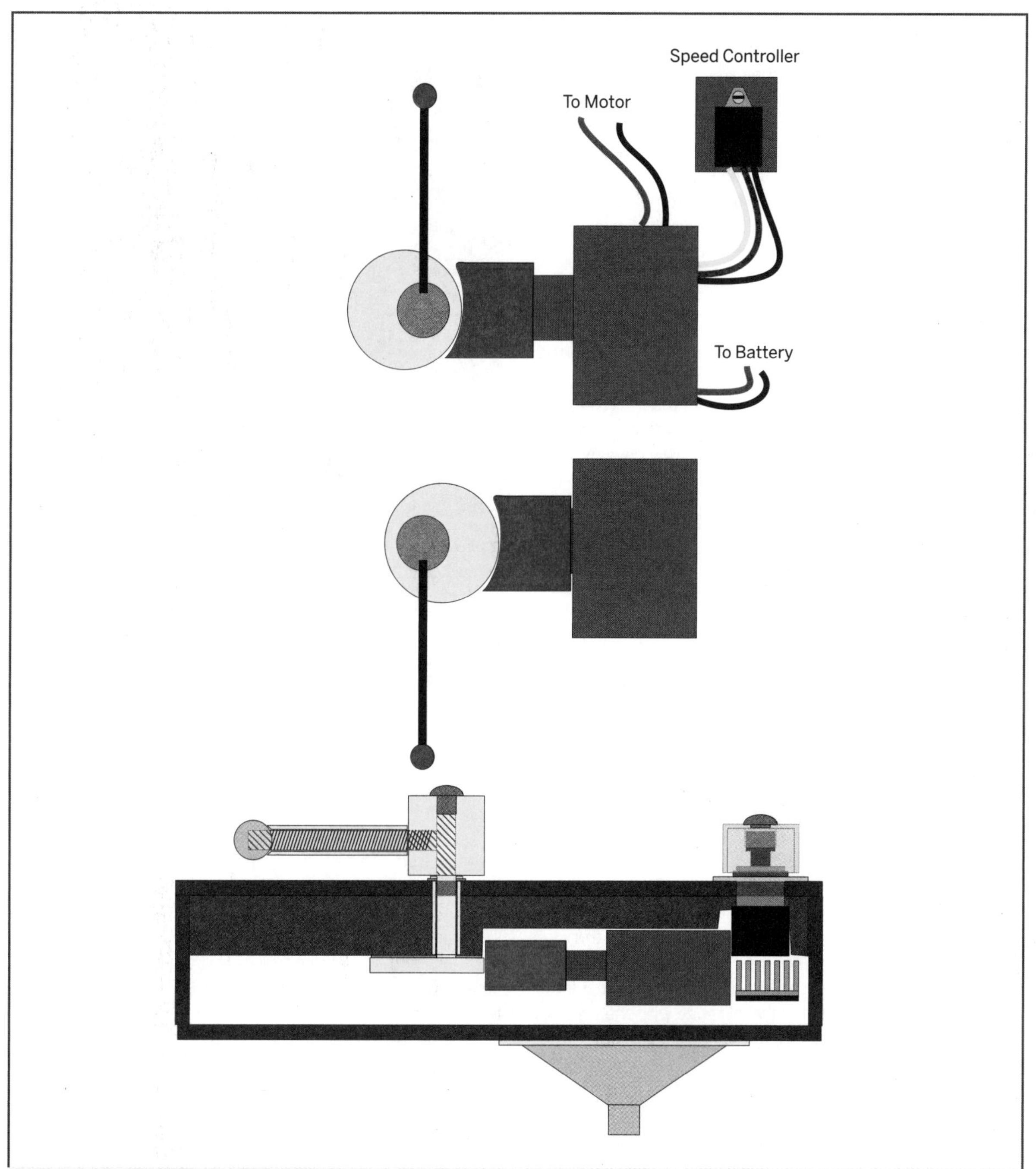

Figure 10.65: **Cripes — I'll put a cam anywhere. Simplicity has never been so complicated. Witness the essential control panel, and its parts.**

control box on a flexible brass gooseneck excavated from a scoop of mystery metal at NorthStar Recycling.

I do not expect you to go to the same lengths in your control panel, but if you do, I want pictures, dammit!

I prototyped the mechanism on a chunk of plywood, looking for an easy way to fabricate it. This breadboard prototype eventually became the actual chassis I ended up using. I used the drillpress, Forstner bits, and a dremel high-speed cutter bit as a quick 'n' dirty router to carve the various cavities out on the surface of the plywood, and roughed out the cam from 3⁄16" brass plate. The trigger on the drill was plastic. Using a metal cam to physically actuate it would have been *dangerously* flaunting the provisions of Moh's Scale (see Chapter 9 on the DiscoHead) and would turn the trigger into a small pile of plastic shavings in no time flat. I used a piece of heavy-duty stainless-steel tape to resurface the face of the trigger where the cam contacts it and ward off the inevitable erosion. I could just as easily have used a bit of brass shim stock attached with double-faced tape to serve the same purpose. **[Figure 10.66]**

Figure 10.66: Cam, trigger, speed control, and stainless-steel tape. From here on it, it gets complicated.

For those of you building along bolt-by-bolt, my apologies: I *did* try to come up with reasonably specific dimensions for the trigger actuator to make it easy for you to duplicate. Once I had a working mechanism for the unit that I was actually gonna use, I borrowed the triggers from a few other drills and tried them out in my prototype chassis. As you'd expect, every single one was differently dimensioned, and none of them was the same as the one I prototyped around. Sadly, if you're going to attempt this mechanism at home, you're on your own for specific numbers.

I can, however, provide you with some practical pointers.

Start with a piece of 3⁄4" plywood *lots* bigger than you plan on using. You can always cut to size after the fact. First, form a cavity that holds the main body of the trigger unit snugly on the three nontrigger sides. It should be half the depth of the body of the trigger. When that's sorted, router or chisel out the path of the trigger itself to the same depth. Half the width of the trigger should be sticking up from the cavity, and you should be able to move the trigger easily through the full travel range with the unit seated firmly in the cavity. **[Figure 10.67, Figure 10.68, Figure 10.69]**

Measure the travel range of the trigger, then rough out the cam.

Start with a metal disk at least 1.5" in diameter and 3⁄16" thick. Find and mark the center, then find and mark a point that's half of the total travel distance of the trigger off center. Drill that point out to 7⁄32", tap the hole for 1⁄4-20 threads, and thread in a length of 1⁄4-20 threaded rod. Now, make the cam wheel/axle connection a bit more permanent: Having the axle unscrew from the cam during use is considered bad form. Fire up your propane torch and lay a dab of solder into the threads on each side of the cam. **[Figure 10.70]**

Congratulations. The eccentric cam you just made, when placed in contact with the trigger and rotated around the off-center axle, will move the trigger through its complete travel range and back every revolution.

Drop the trigger unit into the cavity you made in the first step, then position the cam with the point closest to the axle squarely on the at-rest trigger. Mark the center of the axle position on the plywood chassis and drill the mounting hole out to 1⁄4". Slot the cam assembly into the hole and rotate it, marvelling at your extreme cleverness as the trigger cycles majestically through its range.

Ya ain't out of the woods yet, though. It's one thing to be able to turn rotary motion into linear motion (which is what

Figure 10.67: **The modest exterior of the control box . . .**

Figure 10.68: **. . . and its savagely routered-out inner self.**

we just did), but thats a spring loaded trigger, Bunkie. You need to introduce enough friction into the system to resist the force of the spring that's eager to return the trigger to its off position, but not so much that you can't turn the cam.

Cut a ¾" length of ¼" ID brass tubing, drill out the cam mounting hole in the chassis to the OD of the tubing (betcha it's ⁵⁄₁₆"), and press fit the tubing into the hole, where it'll serve as a bushing for the cam axle. Cut a disk of craft felt the diameter of your cam and punch out an off-center hole to accomodate the axle. Use double-faced tape to stick it to the plywood chassis, positioned to align with the cam when the trigger is at rest.

Voilà: a friction pad.

Slot the cam, and flip over the chassis. Cut a ½"-diameter felt washer with a ¼" hole. If you're smart, you'll be using sharpened tubing as dies to punch out nice neat holes. Slide the felt washer over the axle, followed by a bog-standard ¼" washer and two nuts. Tighten the first nut until enough friction is in the system to fight the drill trigger's spring, then cinch down the second nut to lock it in place.

Bueno.

Man, this is a bitch of a build, innit? One damned thing after another.

Now that the speed controller is functioning, convert your plywood breadboard into an actual control box. You're about to completely change your perspective of the actuator mech-

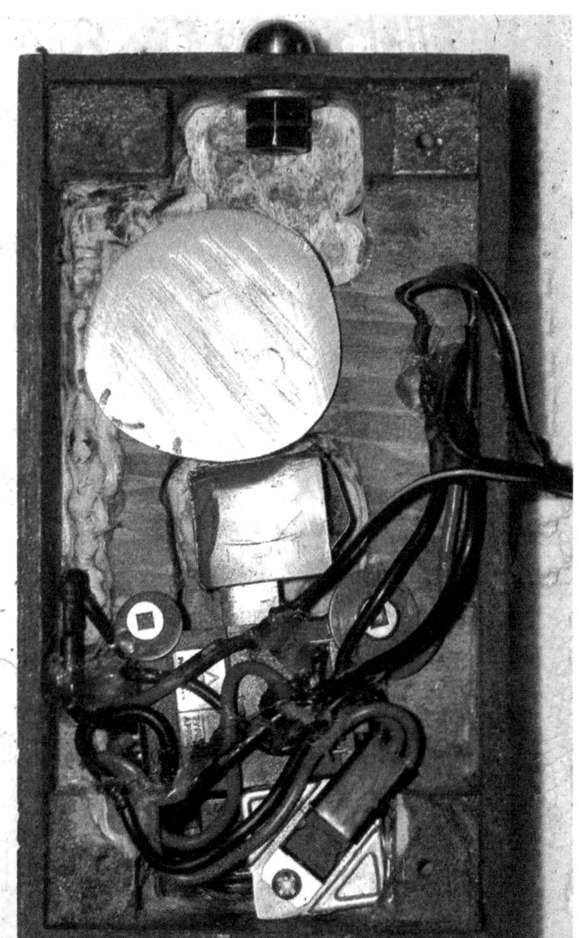

Figure 10.69: **The completed and installed mechanism**

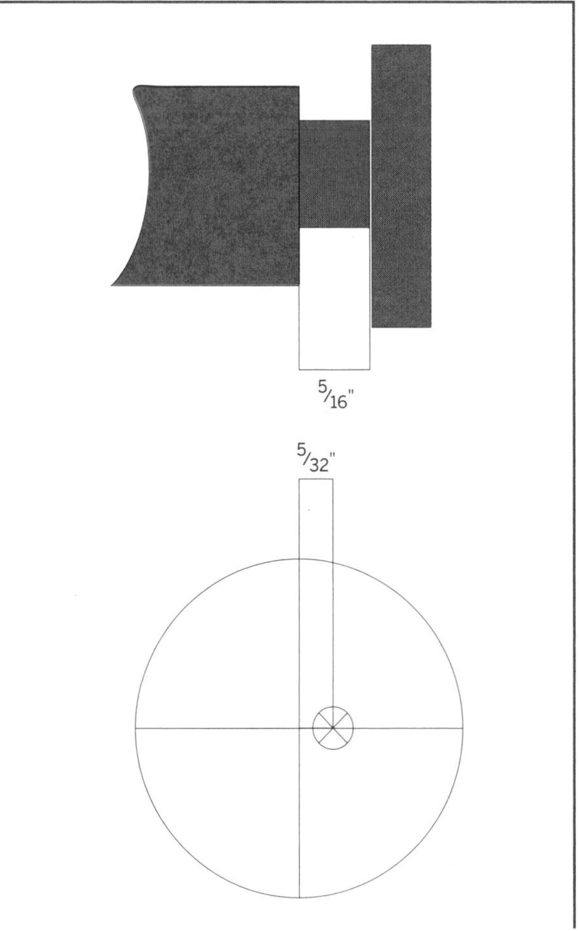

Figure 10.70: **Apply the trigger travel measurement to the cam offset.**

anism you've been working on all afternoon. Up until now, the side with the trigger unit and cam has been "the top." Now it's "the bottom." The face of the plywood chassis with the axle sticking out of the middle is now the top. This is the front panel of your control box.

For the build model, I cut the breadboard to its final size, and added 1¾" bottom, side and end panels to it. Nothing fancy, everything was cut from ¼" plywood, butt jointed, with ¾" x ¾" x 1½" blocks in each corner to strengthen the joints and give me a place to sink the base attachment screws. I skinned the top of the box with 1/8" thick slats salvaged from an wooden orange crate to cover up the ravaged surface of the breadboard plywood, redrilled the axle hole and sanded the bejeezlies out of the whole lot. Once stained and finished, the result had, um, a lot of personality.

Controlling the Controls

Control box? Check. Control mechanism? Check.

Now you need a control interface. Usually, this would call for a knob, but given the friction vector we just bunged into the mechanism, it'll need to be a truly grip-worthy knob, or (back to the whole mechanical advantage thing again) a lever.

I know!

How about a lever *with a knob on it*!

I like that idea. I liked it so much when I first thought of it that I used it.

There's metalwork involved, but it's nothing you can't handle. **[Figure 10.71]**

Remove the nuts and washer(s) you just installed. You're gonna be upgrading.

Start with a 1" piece of 1" brass roundbar. True up the ends and dress the surfaces, find the center and drill it out to 7⁄32". You're drilling a serious hole. Use a slow drill speed, a sharp drill bit, and plenty of cutting fluid.

Take your time.

Source a 1"-diameter washer with a ¼" hole, and cut a 1" diameter felt friction pad. These will go on the axle first to provide a *really* smooth action

Thread the hole you just drilled in your roundbar with ¼-20 threads, and screw the knob blank onto the cam axle, tightening it down onto the felt washer until you've achieved the necessary amount of tension.

Take a minute to consider the range of motion you'll want.

As it stands, your cam cycles the trigger from "full off" to "full on" in 180 degrees of movement. The drill I used in the project maxxed out at 450 rpm, which is on the low side of "typical." With a ¼" drive shaft and a 4¾" main pulley, that reduces to about 72 RPM. At 16 note events per revolution, that works out to an UltraGabbaesque maximum tempo of 1,152 BPM.

Don't even *think* about it.

Hammerhead uses gravity as a return mechanism. It doesn't respond quickly enough to pick up events flying past the actuators at that speed, and if you augment the levers with springs to speed up the response, it will break under load. Let's just say that I know this for a fact. Don't argue.

Realistically, you'll want to use maybe the first half of the trigger travel. The potentiometers on this kinda toolage seem to have a weird curve to 'em: there's lots of "slow" in the first half of the travel, lots of "fast" on the last half, with minimal "medium" in the middle. Finding out how many usable degrees of knob movement you'll be using, and where in the arc they lie is the next step.

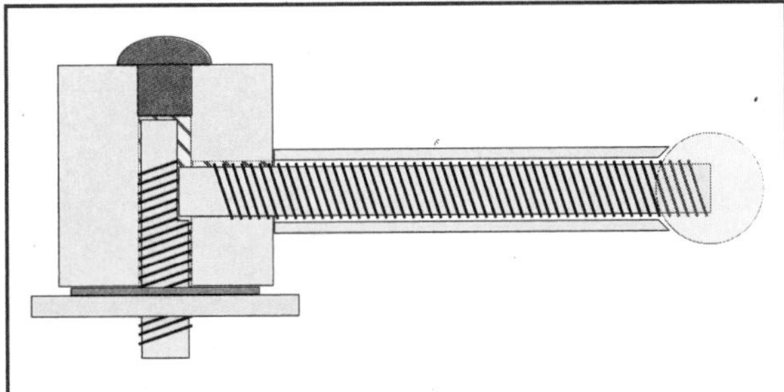

Figure 10.71: A lever with a knob on it. Please, no autographs.

Make sure there's a charge on the batterypack for the drive mechanism, and patch your speed controller mechanism into the circuitry. Don't be fancy. You just want to get the drum turning and get a feel for the curve of the controller, so alligator clips and hookup wire are perfectly acceptable.

Draw a reference line on the panel running from one edge of the panel to the knob. Mark the knob at the reference line.

Reach under the panel and start turning the cam. The lever we're waiting to install also serves to lock the knob in position on the shaft, and until it's in place, any attempt to use the knob to rotate the cam is only going to cinch the knob down tighter on the threads.

This is not what we want to happen. So turn the cam by hand.

There'll be a few degrees of dead zone at the start of the trigger travel. As soon as the shaft begins to move, mark the knob at the reference line.

Keep rotating the cam until the drum is spinning at an obviously excessive rate, then mark the knob again at the reference line. The distance between the first two marks on the knob is the amount of dead zone you need to compensate for. The distance between the last two marks on the knob is the amount of usable rotation available.

Turn the cam back to full rest, and get out the compass and protractor and determine the arc. Once you have the actual number of degrees to work with, center the arc on the faceplate for the leverless knob that's sitting there on the axle waiting for you to finish it. I actually ended up using a little more than 100 degrees of movement by the time I eliminated the dead zone at the start of the trigger travel.

The second mark you made on the cam is where the lever will be located. Mark the position on the knob so that the lever bar will be close to but not in contact with the panel. The axle shaft needs to be filed to a "D" profile perpendicular to the lever position. Carefully mark the axle alignment, then unscrew the knob. **[Figure 10.72]**

Drill the lever mounting hole through to the central mounting hole of the knob to 7⁄32", then tap in ¼-20 threads. File the "D" profile into the axle, then cut a length of ¼-20 threaded rod to 3¼", and a piece of ¼" ID tubing to 2½".

Rummage up an acorn or cap nut to fit onto the threaded rod, then reinstall the knob on the axle. The lever mounting hole should line up with the flat surface of the "D" profile when the knob is properly positioned. Screw the threaded rod into the lever hole until it cinches tight on the axle, locking the knob in position. Slide on the lever tube, and secure it with the cap nut. **[Figure 10.73]**

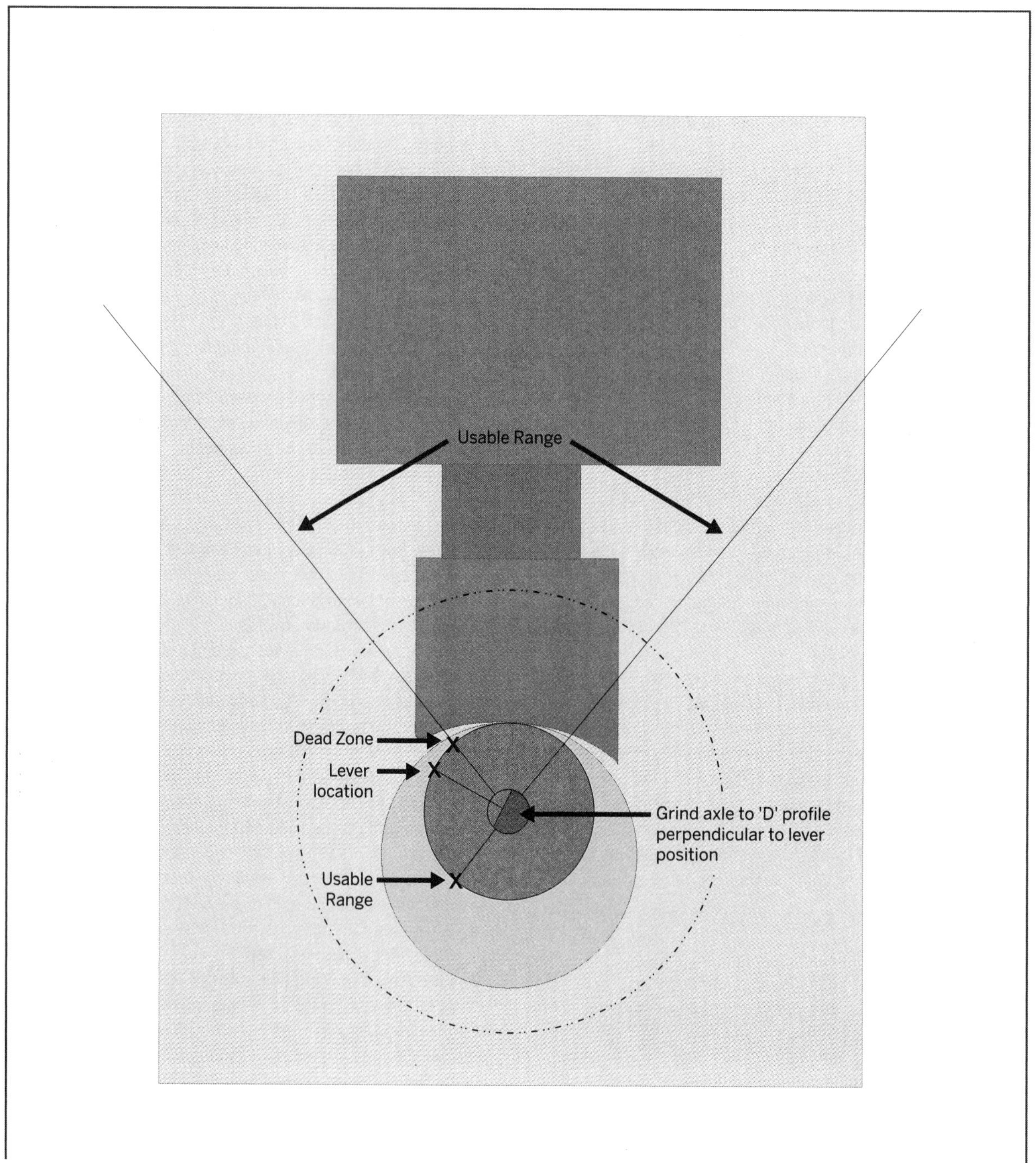

Figure 10.72: Positioning the lever. Don't panic.

Figure 10.73: **A "lever with a knob on it" kit . . .**

Figure 10.74: **. . . seen here fully assembled**

Figure 10.75: **The completed speed control: Maximum Artsy Fartsy**

Hot damn — it's a lever! Grab the handle and savour the smooth, reassuring firmness of the action. **[Figure 10.74]**

I used a copper rivet cut to length to plug the exposed axle hole in the knob, and dug up a ridiculously overscaled 3"-diameter brass washer at North Star to use as a bezel kinda thing around the lever/knob (knever? leob? nah, forget it). This is a prime example of how the aesthetics of piece evolve on the bench, and an equally apt example of the importance of high-quality goat sacrifices to the sourcing gods to ensure rich and bountiful scrapyard harvests.

Your lever will need travel stops to restrict the range of movement: I used threaded balls and threaded rod posts to delineate either end of the travel arc as illustrated, then realized I still had the power switch issue to resolve. **[Figure 10.75]**

Oopsie.

The power switch is a quite nice Switchcraft stompbox number I pulled out of a dumpstered rug sucker. I somehow managed to fit it in at the very top of the front panel, after a false start where I tried it sticking up from one end (which worked, but looked kinda dorky). As I'd committed myself to the whole chunky brass control aesthetic, I had to come up with a cap for the switch that matched the lever/knob thingie.

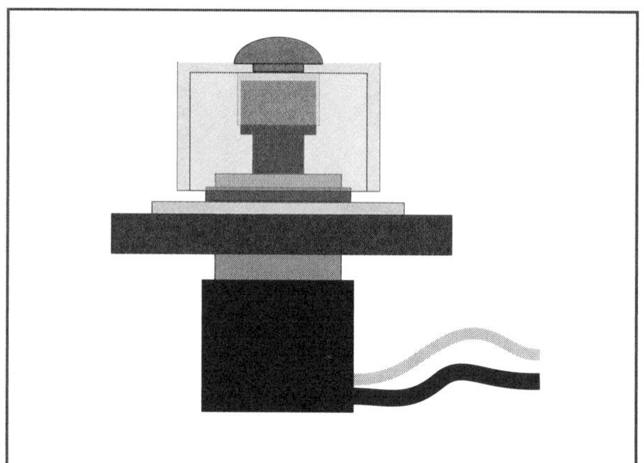

Figure 10.76: **Camouflaging the humble stomp switch**

Figure 10.77: **Inner cup and outer cap, all fluxed up and ready for soldering**

I found a piece of brass tube that press-fitted over the switch pad, did a brute force solder job to mount it in the center of a garden hose cap, then drilled out the center and added the copper rivet detailing. The last step was grinding off the knurling for a smooth side surface, and finding a 1¼" washer to use as a bezel. **[Figure 10.76, Figure 10.77, Figure 10.78]**

Figure 10.78: **The finished power switch: more camouflage. More Maximum Artsy Fartsy.**

Wiring is a no-brainer; you'll need to run a four-conductor lead between the control panel and the battery pack/drive train area. As for the rest of the packaging of the control panel, you're on your own. Get creative. **[Figure 10.79]**

Interfacing the brass gooseneck with the control panel was simpler than anticipated, as it came prethreaded at each end with ⅜-24 threads. It was just a matter of wandering around a scrap yard with calipers and a thread gauge until I found premade components with the right threading. In this case, the bases from run-of-the-mill candle holders filled the roles admirably. All that was needed was to drill mountng screw holes around the edge of each base for mounting hardware. Typically, I couldn't leave well enough alone, and upped the steampunk quotient by adding a few stacked brass washers to each junction to simulate heat sink fins. **[Figure 10.80,Figure 10.81, Figure 10.82]**

Before undertaking the final tuneup of the mechanism, do whatever woodfinishing you feel is necessary. I used a commercial finishing product on this one, primarily because I'd never actually used a Minwax product before. This one is their "Red Mahogany" stain/sealer compound. Brush it on, wipe it off, let it cure overnight, then apply the topcoat of your choice. (In this case, I used that paste wax stuff your mom uses on the hardwood floors. It's pretty rancid smelly glorp, the Minwax, but it works okay.) You'll have to disassemble the mechanism to do the surface prep and finishing. Buff up the metalwork while you're waiting for the finish to cure, and fabricate the fiddly little bits used to get Hammerhead to actually hit stuff.

You'll want a full set of hammers, a set of plus-size hammers, and a set of ball hammers, which are drilled out craft balls. Tap the ³⁄₃₂" holes to accept 6-32 machine screws.

You're well advised to hit the local dollar store and snag a mittful of kid's rubber balls in assorted sizes and densities. When you get home, drill ⅜" x ½" deep mounting holes in them and add them to your stash of potential beaters. **[Figure 10.83]**

The Event Pins

The last thing you need to fabricate is the event pins. They're ¾" long sections of ¼-20 threaded rod with an acorn nut on one end. They screw in to the holes on the pin drum. The actuator blocks ride up them as the drum rotates, then fall back down, initiating the actual stroke of the beater.

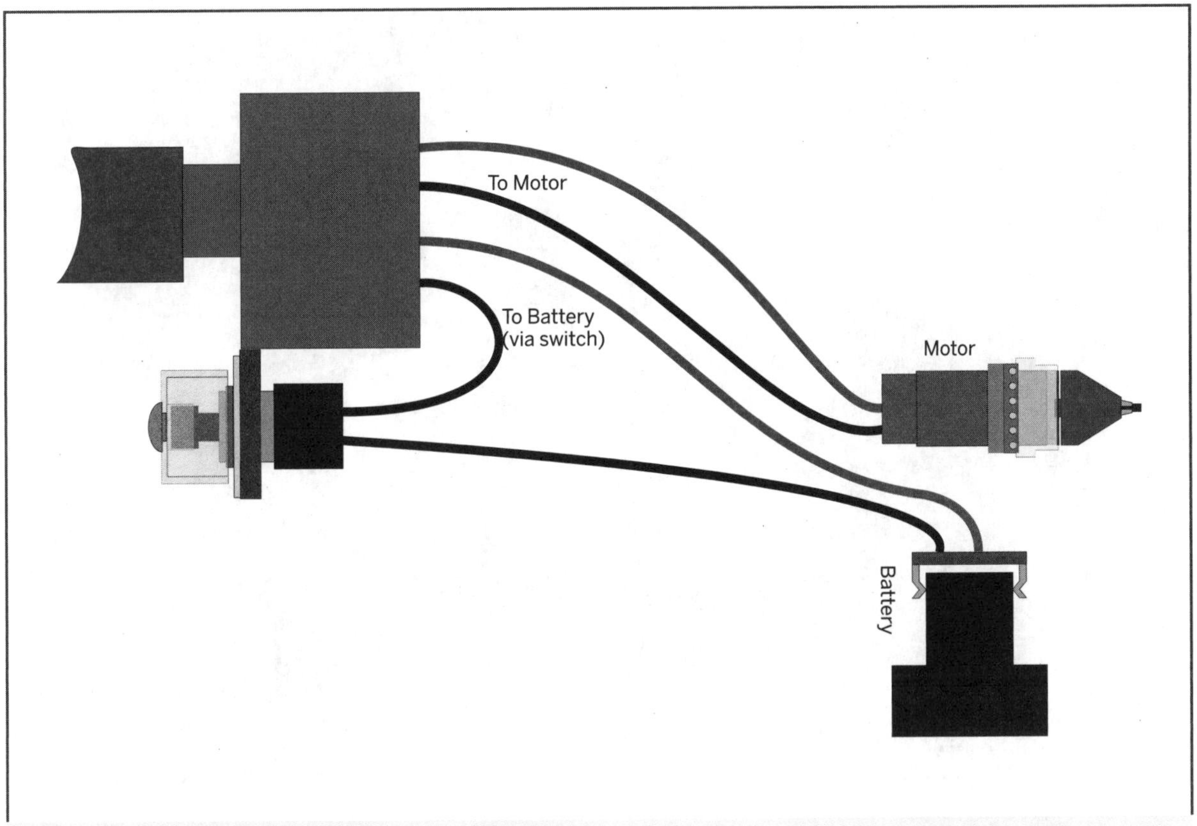

To Motor
To Battery
(via switch)
Motor
Battery

Figure 10.79: **The wiring diagram**

Figure 10.80: **Detail of gooseneck-to-deck interface**

Dynamics are controlled by how far the pins are screwed in: the further in, the shorter the stroke, the quieter the sound.

You'll need a bunch of them. Likely not a full 112, but a bunch. Say 50, just to be on the safe side.

Reassembly should go pretty much by the numbers. Use eyelets as needed to center the actuator arms in their slots in the rack, and scuff up the surface of the hammer arm transfer nodes to ensure a good grip from the tape holding on the dampening pads. Don't attach the pads just yet.

The bearing races can be carefully epoxied into the pillow blocks, and the nuts securing the pin drum axle cinched down and fixed with Loctite. You do ***not*** want the pin drum rotating independently of the axle. Or vice versa.

Secure the pillow blocks on the pin drum axle with a washer and nut on each side, ensuring that the drum spins freely in the bearing races with no pillow block contact. Don't overtighten the nuts, but do apply thread-locking glue to 'em.

Figure 10.81: **A similarly detailed view of the control box–to-gooseneck interface**

Figure 10.82: **And finally, seen here deployed on Hammerhead Live 1.0**

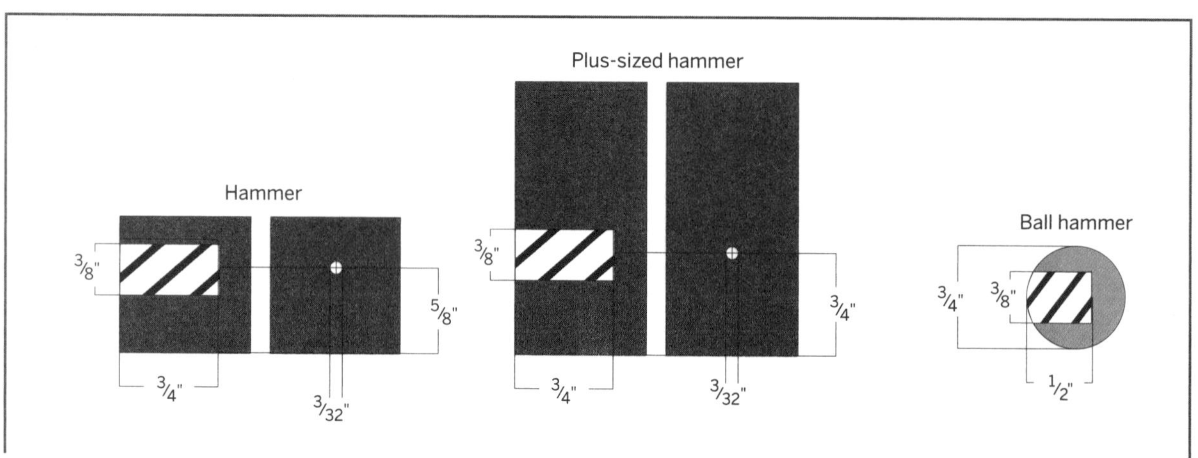

Figure 10.83: **At last. Hammers!**

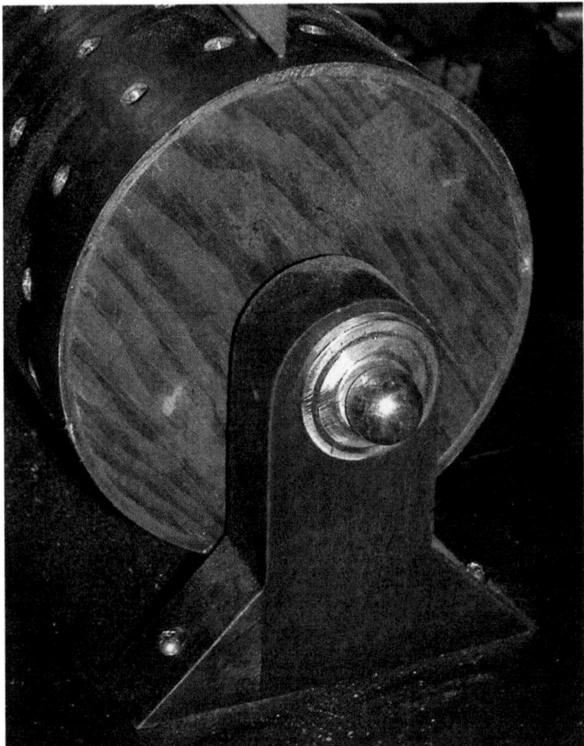
Figure 10.84: **The mounted pin drum**

Figure 10.85: **A good example of a *correctly sized* drive belt slot in use**

Attach the pillow block/pin drum assembly to the deck, position the drivebelt and test the drivetrain. If the belt slips, add a few wraps of PVC electrical tape to the drive shaft. This'll boost the grip of the shaft considerably. **[Figure 10.84, Figure 10.85]**

The actuator arm transfer nodes can be epoxied in place.

Screw a row of event pins into the pin drum. You want a straight line of them, all the same height. Rotate the pindrum to position the trailing edge of the acorn nuts at 12 o'clock, then adjust the actuator block positions to line up exactly touching the pins. Tighten the actuator block locking screws. **[Figure 10.86]**

Assemble the seven hammer arm subassemblies, and mount them on the deck. I'm assuming that you've already determined the general layout of your instruments and associated hammer lengths. It's a close fit to get the transfer nodes lined up and moving and functioning without adjacent nodes making contact. You'll need to spend some time adjusting both the position of the hammer arm nodes on the arms and the exact angle of the arm assemblies relative to the actuator arms. Fine-tune the positioning from the outside arms inward, alternating sides.

When you have a workable set of alignments, tighten the hammer arm transfer node locking screws and apply one dampening pad to the top face of each node. The transfer nodes for each instrument should be in contact with each other and the hammer arms relatively level when the actuator block is at rest, in contact with the pin drum. **[Figure 10.87]**

Change your event pin positions to a staggered row, with each successive pin one hole further back on the drum. Turn on the drive, and watch the hammer arms make successive strokes, as if by magic.

Start out with ball hammers installed on the ends of the hammer arms to serve as beaters. You'll be switching them out as needed during tune-up.

Tuning the Mechanism

You're either gonna love this process, as you learn the Zen of Hammerhead and become one with the device, or hate it, because you never had to go through this when you got your TR-808.

Really, it's not as bad as I'm letting on.

Your goal is to position the dampening pads on the hammer arm fulcrum posts such that a stroke of the hammer arm compresses the pad sufficiently to allow the beater to hit the instrument and then be lifted out of contact with the instrument with minimal bounce. You can add dampening pads to the transfer nodes and the fulcrum, change the position of

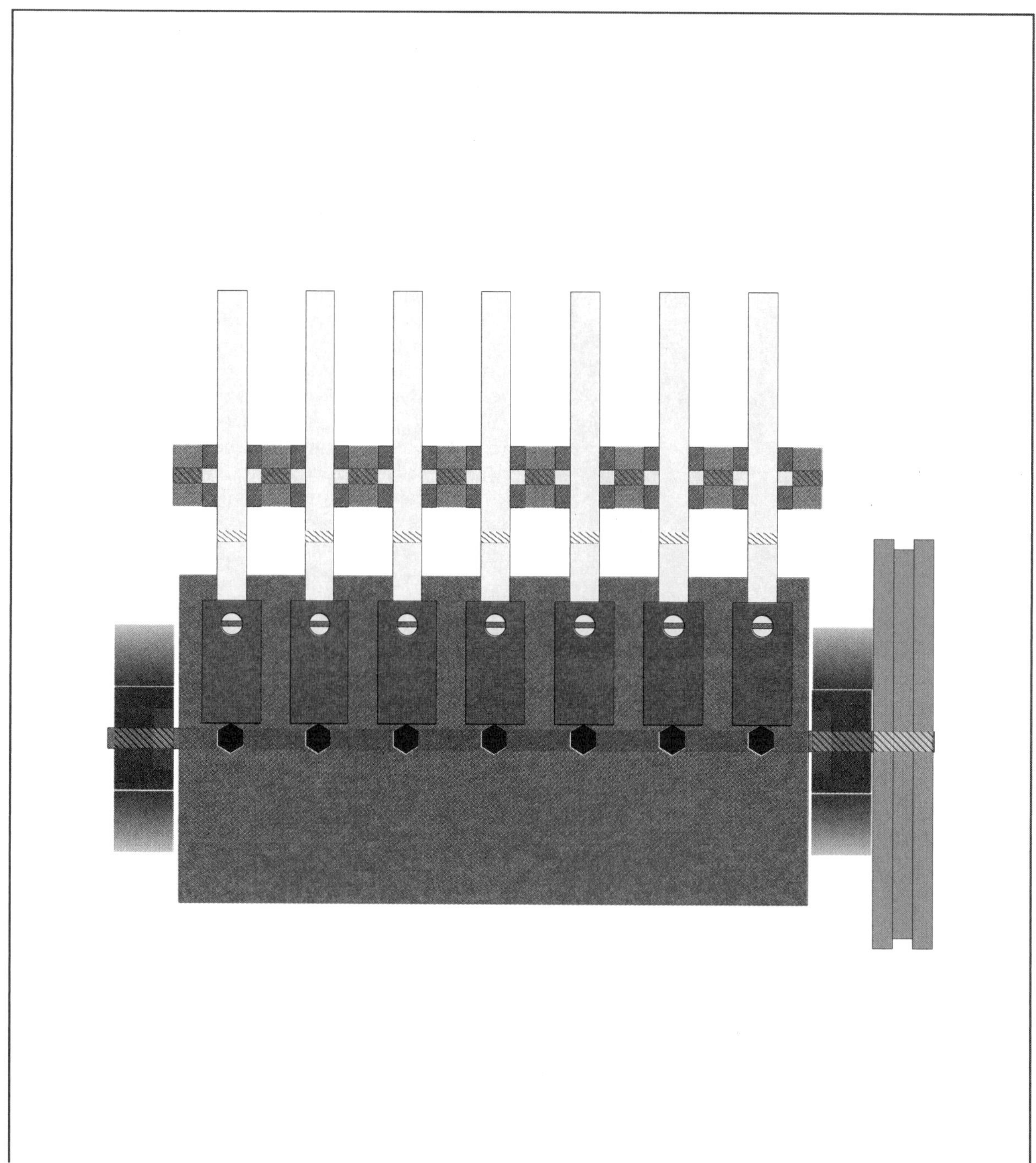

Figure 10.86: **Aligning the actuator blocks with the pin drum: the first of what will soon seem to be endless mechanism adjustments**

Figure 10.87: A workable set of alignments.

the dampening ring, and alter the tension of the spring by sliding it up or down the shaft.

You may need to add dampening only to the hammer side of the hammer arm. Cut away the section of dampening pad that would be under the node side of the arm.

Individual actuator response can be fine-tuned by positioning strips of the laminated dampening material under the actuator arms on either side of the rack. You definitely want the actuator blocks returning to position in contact with the pin drum as quickly and smoothly as possible.

Work on one instrument channel at a time. If you're planning on using a fixed selection of instruments, such as the improvised ones I've detailed, then positioning the instruments is gonna be the most time consuming aspect of the tune-up. You'll have to alter the positioning of each instrument fractionally to find the timbral sweet spot for the hammer to impact before making the mounting job permanent. You may need to tweeze the heights of some of your mounts and maybe add a pad or two to the hammer arm transfer nodes to get the end of the hammer arms within striking distance of the surface of the instruments.

Need a stronger stroke? Add weight to the hammer side of the hammer arms. A friction-fitted movable counterweight added to each hammer arm would be a very useful addition to the device. Add something similar to the block side of each actuator arm and the potential for precision control goes up exponentially.

You can move any instrument forwards or backwards in the pocket of the beat by adjusting the position of the actuator blocks. When you find a relative location for a particular actuator that works rhythmically, make a reference mark on the arm to note the position for future use.

Yup . . . Hammerhead does presets.

If you're using my instrument bodges, here's some hints on positioning and beater selection:

The kick drum is perfectly happy being whumped on just shy of dead center with a soft 1" rubber ball. Use the 1" harder rubber ball for a more techno-sounding kick (although it's gonna be light on the low frequencies).

The snare likes to be hit about 3" off dead center in any direction, and prefers a small, hard beater and a heavy stroke.

The sidestick emulator can be rotated while mounted to change the impact target and the timbre. It seems to work best with a 1" dowel hammer.

The ride cymbal sound depends on what kinda beater cymbal you came up with to make it from. Start with a ball hammer targeting about an inch inside the edge, and go smaller, rather than larger if you want to change beaters.

The hi-hat likes to be whacked with a plus-size dowel hammer right on the edge. Changing the tension on the nut holding the cymbals together changes the timbre a *lot*. Play with that more than anything. Oddly, the 'hat sounds best when the beater *isn't* pulled off after the stroke.

The tambourine also likes the plus-size hammer, and even seems to prefer that the hammer remain in contact with it between strokes.

The cowbell is startlingly flexible. You can rotate it on the mount to target different tones, there's a room full of timbres available, and it never met a beater it didn't like.

Under any circumstance you can feel comfortable calling for more cowbell.[12]

If you've decided to use Hammerhead as a multichannel physical sampler banging beats out of whatever you put under the hammers, be prepared to improvise some method of holding the samples in position during playback. I've had remarkable success using two different approaches.

The first is flexible beanbag kinda things made by pouring a couple of cups of lead birdshot into a sock and tying off the end. The bag moulds to cradle whatever it's holding, and the shot is dense enough to make for solid support.

The second method is nearly as simple, and also involves lead: Cast molten lead into cat-food sized tin cans with a 4" piece of ¼-20 threaded rod sticking up vertically from the center. Add a few nuts and felt washers, and you have movable, solid little stands to mount noisy pieces of metal on.

12 C'mon, you knew I was gonna use that line somewhere, dincha?

I have no doubt that your own improvisational fabrication skills will rise to any additional challenges: You will come to know the way of the Hammerhead, and be inspired to modify it in ways I've never thought of. I fully expect you to keep me apprised of your efforts.

Congratulations — the build's finished. You go make a beat; I'll go make a cocktail. Wasn't that a blast?

The Instrument Bodges

Despite the inherent flexibility of Hammerhead being a physical sampler ("1: Place object under hammer. 2: Allow to be struck"), there are sounds you naturally expect to have available when using a drum machine. Kick drum, snare, hi-hats, and ride cymbal are standard issue, with tambourine, rimshot,[13] and of course cowbell being popular additional voices. We can improvise all these instruments on a dirt-cheap budget. Armed with $25 Cdn and a bus pass, here's what I came up with.

Cowbell

The Cowbell began life as an 8" length of *really* thin-walled 3" copper pipe ($2.50 @ NorthStar Recycling). Scrap yards use big-ass hydraulic shears to cut long chunks of copper and aluminum down to manageable lengths; the picture is what I came home with (after grinding off a bit of solder from one end and marking a few fold lines on the other). Great Caesar's Ghost! The resemblance to a real cowbell is *uncanny!* **[Figure 10.88]**

This is *not* gonna be difficult.

Flatten and fold the closed end of the pipe as illustrated. Copper is satisfyingly malleable. You're looking at about 10 minutes work with a hammer and anvil, perspiration not included. **[Figure 10.89]**

The open-end profile is shaped over the horn of the anvil, which will take maybe 10 minutes of feverish blacksmith emulation. This stage of the process is what determines timbre and voice of the 'bell, so give it frequent *solid* whacks with a drumstick or chunk of dowel to see what it sounds like. Pay attention to what changes the sound, and adjust as needed. **[Figure 10.90, Figure 10.91, Figure 10.92]**

The cowbell mounts on ¼" threaded rod with nuts and lockwashers.

Pipe: $2.50.

Fittings: in-house.

Cash remaining: $22.50.

Case closed.

Figure 10.88: Cowbell egg

13 Sidestick, actually. The technical minds behind modern drum sequencers are apparently *not* drummers and consistently mislabel the sound in question.

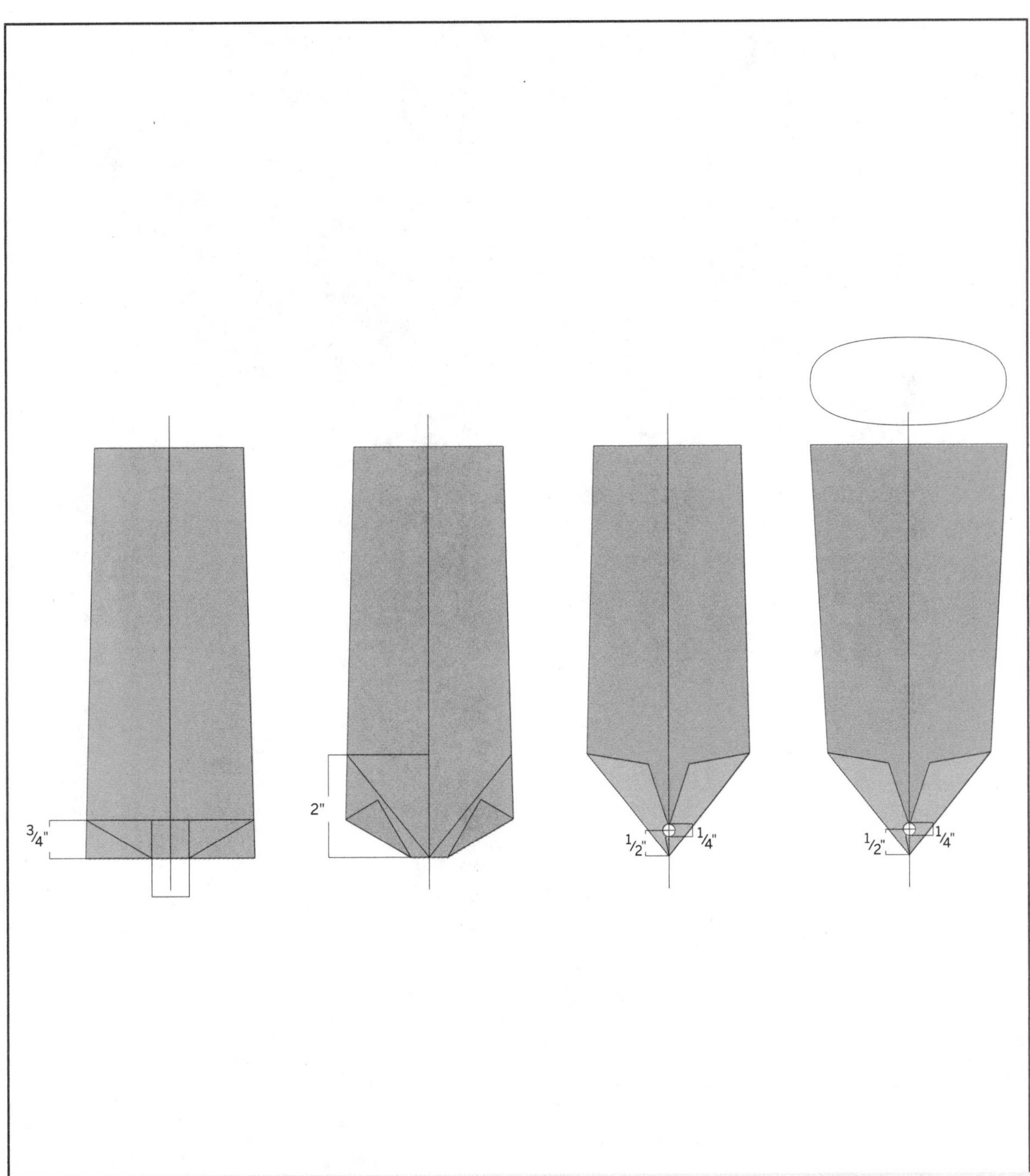

Figure 10.89: **Cowbell shaping, step-by-step**

Figure 10.90: **If this had the letters LP silkscreened on it, it'd sell for about 45 bucks.**

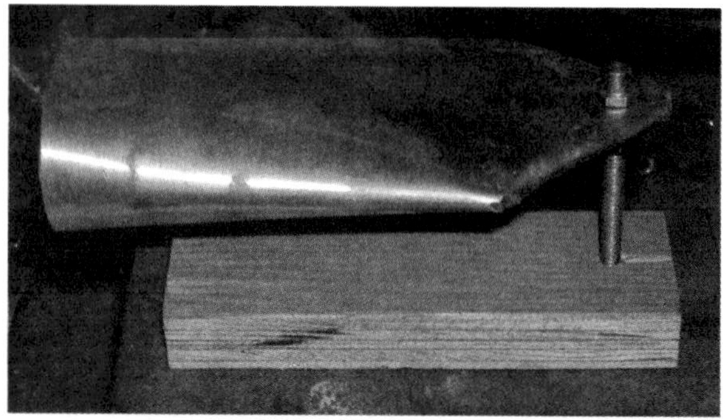

Figure 10.92: **Cowbell: check.**

Figure 10.91: **FINALLY, an opportunity to use the horn of the anvil for its intended purposes!**

Tambourine

The tambourine had to shrink a tad; real estate on Hammerhead is pretty sparse, and accomodating a 10"-diameter empty space with jingles around the perimeter would have been wasteful. I scored a beat-up tambourine in a thrift shop toy department for $1.99 and harvested six pairs of 1½" metal jingles from it. **[Figure 10.93]**

I found a 10" piece of 1" x ¼" maple scrap in the woodbin, spaced out holes 1¼" apart down the length (with the mounting hole 1½" further down, and installed the paired jingles on alternating sides of the slat with 6-32 machine screws sealed in position with cyanoacrylate. **[Figure 10.94]**

It has to be mounted with lateral stability and up 'n' down flexibility (so it'll move when whacked, but not rotate out of position). Easiest way to do that is with the old "dowel-filled-⅜ ID brass-tube" trick, with the rim of the tubing filed to form two hornish projections to dig into the wood of the tambo and reduce lateral motion while providing pivot points for vertical motion. **[Figure 10.95, Figure 10.96, Figure 10.97]**

The height of the mount is determined by the topography of your mechanism. At this stage, the top bit with the horns is the main concern, so cut the overall length of the brass tubing on the long side (say, 5") and trim it to fit during the final assembly of the entire machine.

Tambourine: $2.13 (taxes, doncha know).
Machine screws: $0.97.
Cash remaining: $19.50.
Case closed.

Figure 10.93: **Orphaned tambourine jingles, meet small piece of scrap maple.**

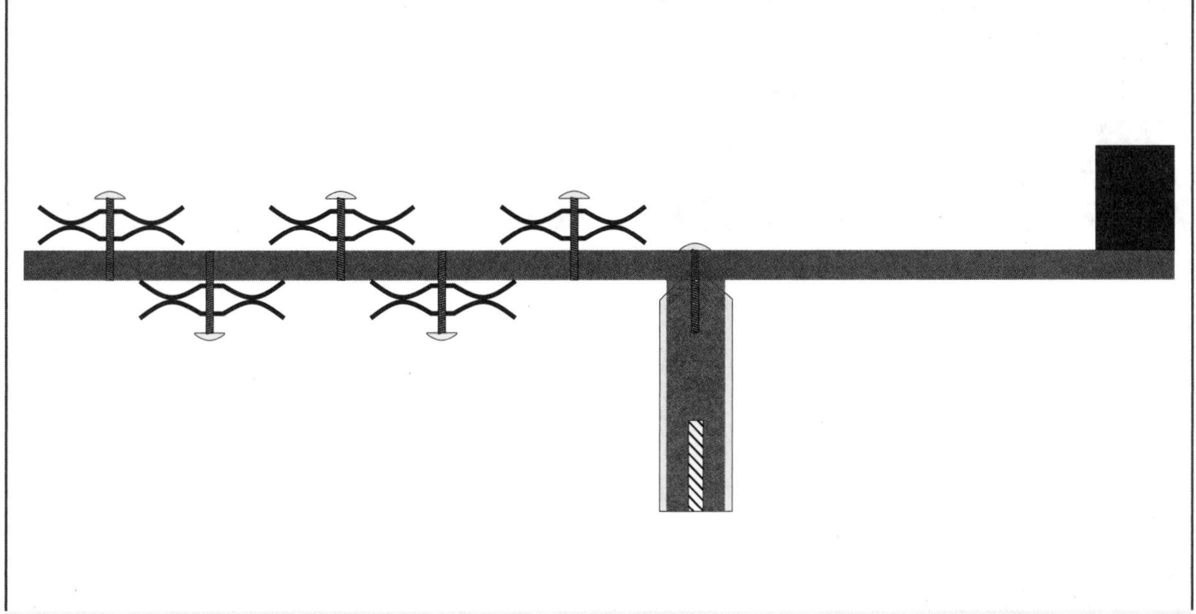

Figure 10.94: **Here's the plan.**

Figure 10.95: **Really, it's a tambourine.**

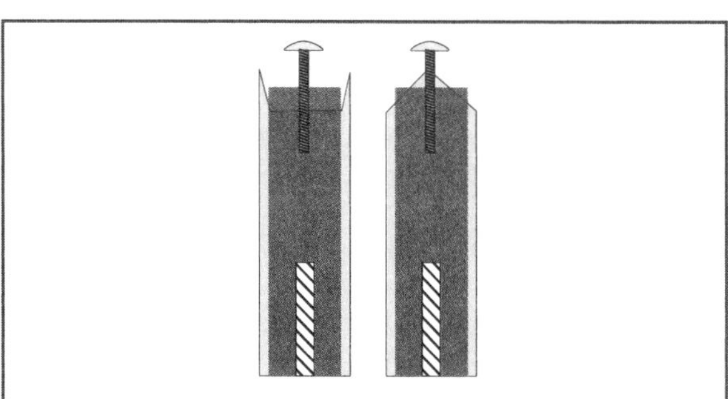

Figure 10.96: **Horn-like projections, illustrated**

Figure 10.97: **Tambourine? Check.**

Figure 10.98: **Nothin' says "sidestick" like tatty copper pipe and unidentified plastic from a fluorescent light fixture.**

Sidestick

The sidestick sound results from using a particular sticking technique on a snare drum. Think "pop ballad," for it's a distinctive kinda-woodblocky-with-more-of-a-click sound. Real drummers can do it by instinct. The tip of the drumstick rests on the drum head, while the butt end is whacked on the opposite side rim. Mechanically replicating the intricacies of the stick motion/palm damping of the drumhead action is, welll, impractical. We can, however, get close to the *sound* with a little fudging. **[Figure 10.98]**

Enter the bit of copper pipe we cut off the pin drum blank. Only one end had been cut at a right angle. The other end was about 15 degrees off perpendicular.

Tough rocks. In the 70s, Slingerland marketed single-headed toms with the shell cut on a similar bias "for added projection." It was good enough for them; it's good enough for me.[14]

14 Full disclosure: I played Slingerland drums for about 15 years. Not as an endorser, but as a full-blown Fan Boi. Thunderous tubs, lousy hardware.

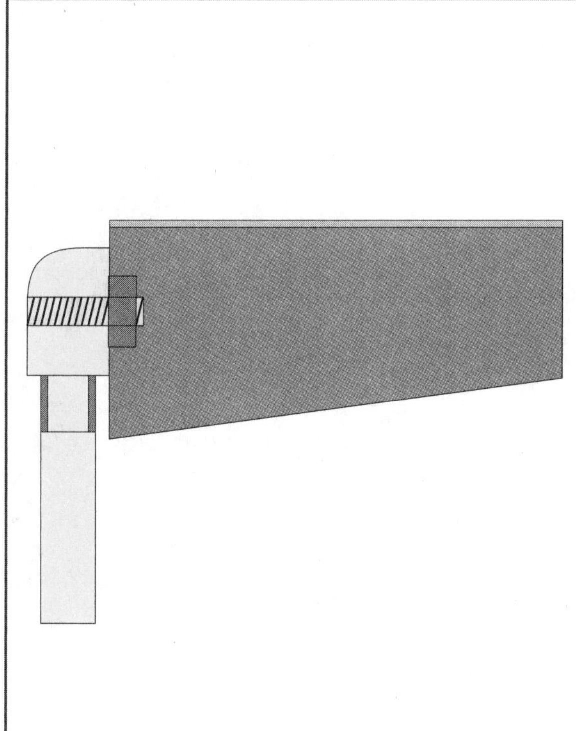

Figure 10.99: **Mounting: pipe fitting to the rescue**

Figure 10.100: **The bits and pieces**

For a head, I rummaged up 5" x 5" of some unidentified plastic formerly in use as a fluorescent lighting diffuser. Rough out a pipe-sized circle from the plastic and roughen the inner surface with steel wool. Grind the edges of the pipe smooth, and glue 'em up with cyanoacrylate. Sand the edge of the plastic flush with the pipe, then drill a 5⁄16" hole in the pipe.

I found a right-angle pipe fitting that fit nicely into a length of 3⁄8" ID brass tubing and soldered them together, then put a 7⁄32" hole through the fitting and tapped the hole for ¼-20 threads. **[Figure 10.99,10.100]**

Bit of threaded rod and some nuts and washers, budda bing, budda bang, budda boom. Knock the little bugger on the head and out comes a fair approximation of a sidestick sound. **[Figure 10.101]**

Total cost: Zero. Zip. Zilch. Naught.

Not a bloody kipper.

Gotta love it.

Cash remaining: $19.50.

Case closed.

Figure 10.101: **Sidestick? Check.**

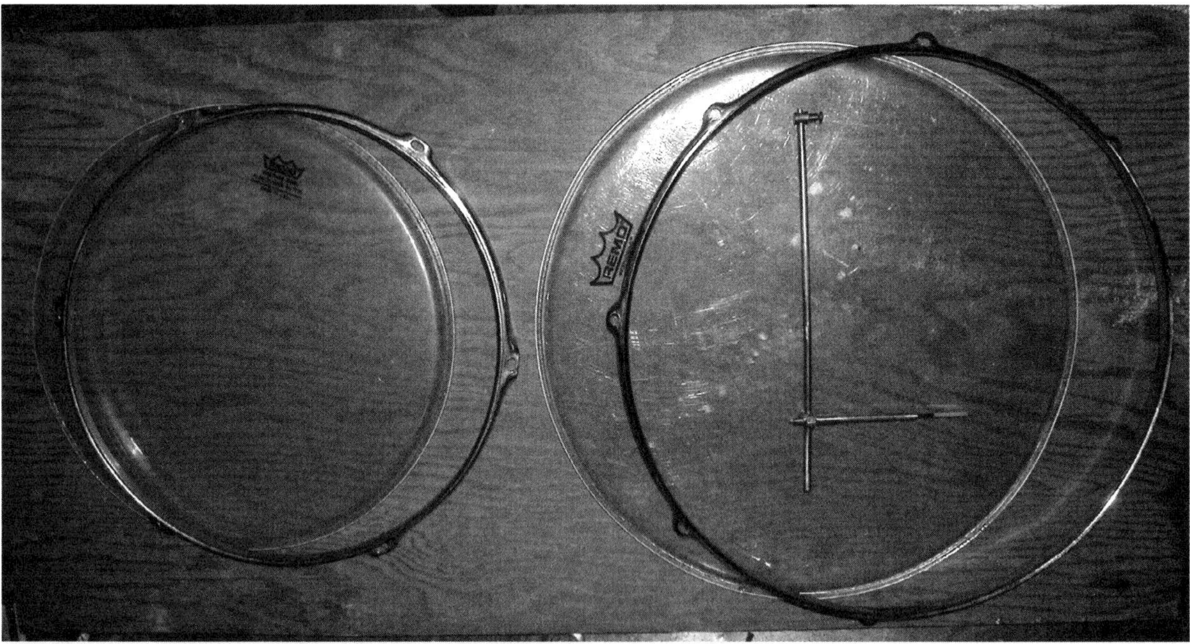

Figure 10.102: **Real drum stuff. Dumpster plywood.**

Kick Drum and Snare

The Kick Drum and Snare are harder to fake. Lower frequencies require a large scale membrane in motion, and the attention grabbing *crack* of a snare is dependent on snare wires slapping against a tight head.

So we're gonna need to make some drums. Working on a budget of . . . lessee . . . $19.50, we're not going to be steam-forming multiple plies of instrument-grade maple into shells, and outfitting said shells with custom-machined brass lugs.

This is not a problem.

We *do* need a few supplies though, so it's down to the local music store and straight back to the rental department. We're looking for hoops and heads. [Figure 10.102]

It is entirely possible to forgo purchasing metal hoops and fabricate what you need out of wood. Thanks in no small way to the efforts of Ray Ayotte, maple hoops have been popular options on high-end drum kits for years, so it's not like there isn't precedence. The fly in the ointment is the material cost of real hardwood dimensioned properly for the purpose. Softwood and plywood won't cut the gig, and we're already using bendy and warp-prone materials for the frames and bearing edges. Having the hoops equally flexible is simply "not on" if we're to have even a remote hope of being able to get the drum head in tune.

This means (barring the sudden appearance of 4' of maple 1" x 12") metal hoops, which come in two flavours: stamped and cast. Triple-flanged stamped hoops are cheap and forgiving. Cast hoops are costly and precise. Guess which type we want?

As for heads, despite the longstanding popularity of stretched animal skins, modern-era synthetic heads are the only rational choice for this project: they're tough, consistent and immune to the effects of humidity. There are countless flavours of drumheads, ranging from extra-thin uncoated single-ply Mylar numbers used as the wire side heads on orchestral snare drums to multi-ply Kevlar weave monstrosities popular with our more heavy-handed brothers and sisters.

We're not gonna be picky. The dimensions we're looking for are 13" for the snare, and 16" or 18" for the bass drum. The hoops can be ugly as sin, as long as they're round and flat. Head-wise, anything reasonably unabused, single-ply and lightweight will work for the snare; the bass drum wants as heavy as possible, preferably two-ply.

Most rental departments have a few boxes of, er, battered drum components that are a trifle overabused to send out on

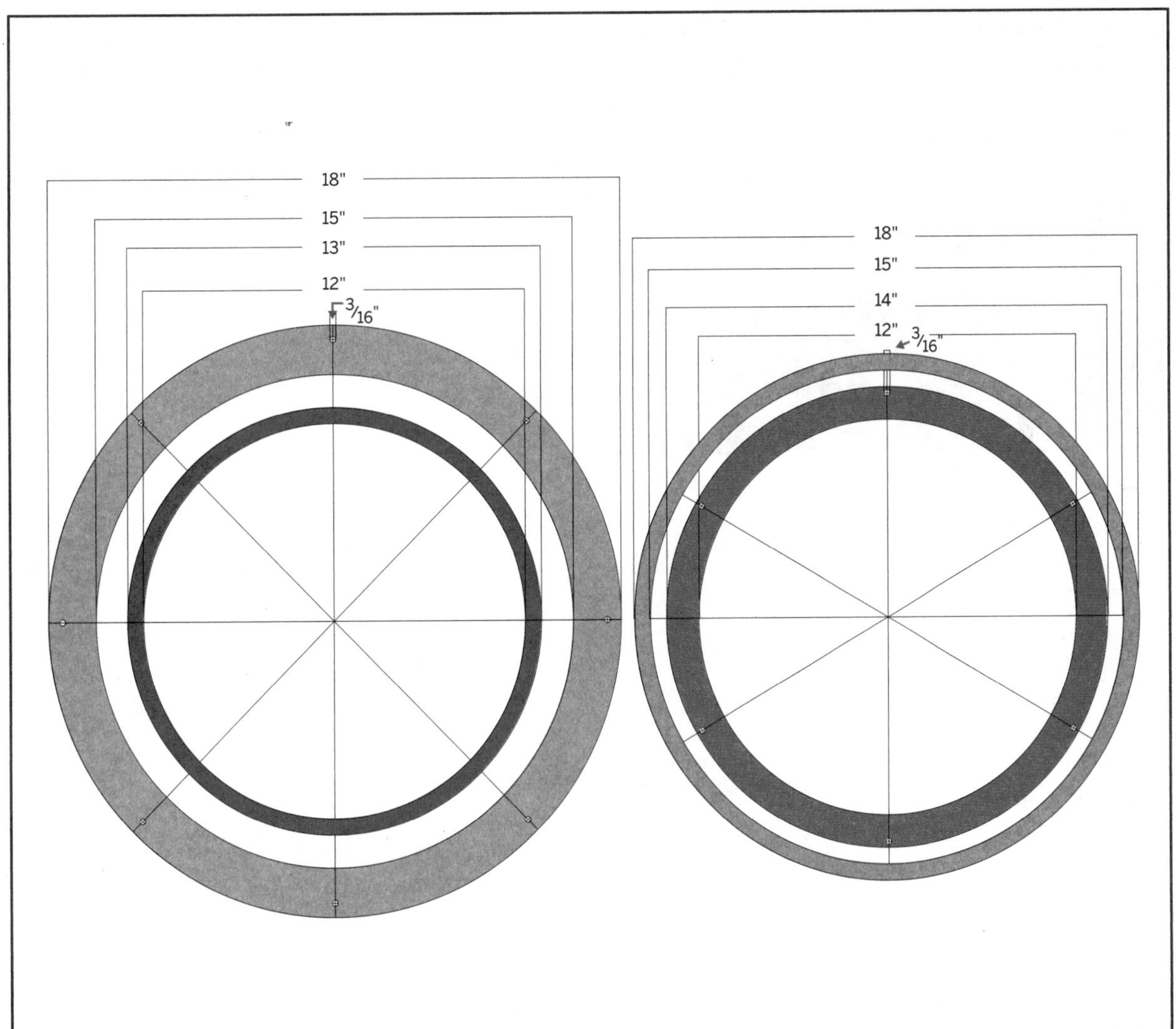

Figure 10.103: **A highly optimized cutting diagram**

stage, but are perfectly suitable for the lo-tek frame drums we're fabricating. Talk to the guys who work there and tell 'em what you're up to. Once they stop laughing, they'll likely help you out a lot.

Those of you lacking a local music shop can consult any of the online auctions and find similar things for similar (or lower) prices. Whatever the source, I walked out of my local with exactly what I needed for $11.30, and pulled a 2' x 4' piece of ¾" plywood out of a dumpster on the way home.

I've learned to cherish moments like that. Most of the time material sourcing is a less-than-expeditious undertaking.

We're gonna forgo such luxuries as shells and lug boxes and fabricate plywood frames for the heads comprised of not much more than a bearing edge for the head to tension over, and screw in points for the rim-tensioning bolts to thread into. **[Figure 10.103, Figure 10.104]**

Judicious planning and careful jigsawing provided frame rings and bearing edges from the dumpstered plywood. The

Figure 10.104: **Making the cuts. Patience, laddie . . . patience.**

upper edge of the bearing rings should be shaped to provide minimum contact with the head. **[Figure 10.105, Figure 10.106]**

NOTE: The mystic voodoo involved in shaping bearing edges on "real" acoustic drums is the stuff of legend among aficionadoes. Personally, I'm content if they're level and relatively even, but there are those who would go to war in defence of the "double 45," "inward 45," "classic," "modern classic," or other such precise variation. Feel free to channel your inner Craviotto and get as in-depth as you want researching the subject.

Face it: we're cutting these things out of plywood with a jigsaw, and fitting them with junked rims and heads. They're not gonna sound like Ayottes. Neither did the original electronic drum sequencers. What we're doing here is the physical equivalent of 8-bit digital audio. This is *good*.

Glue and dowel the rings to the frames, then position the heads and rims and mark the bolt hole locations. The tensioning bolts can be as high or low tech as you want. I was working on a budget, so went low tech, using 8-32 x 1 ¼" machine

The Many Faces of Bearing Edges

Wars have been fought over these shapes

9 out of 10 cloth eared musicians can't tell the difference

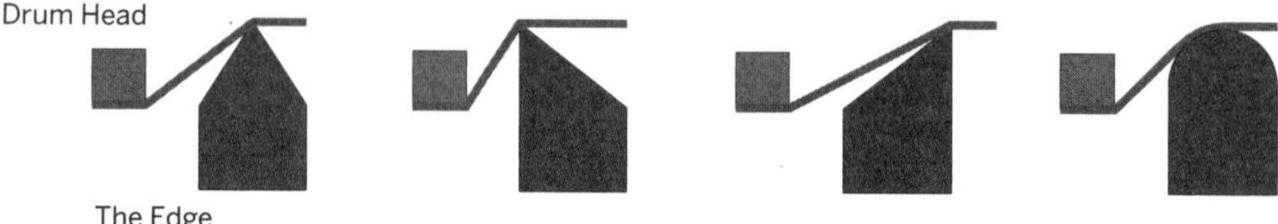

Figure 10.105: **Bearing edges**

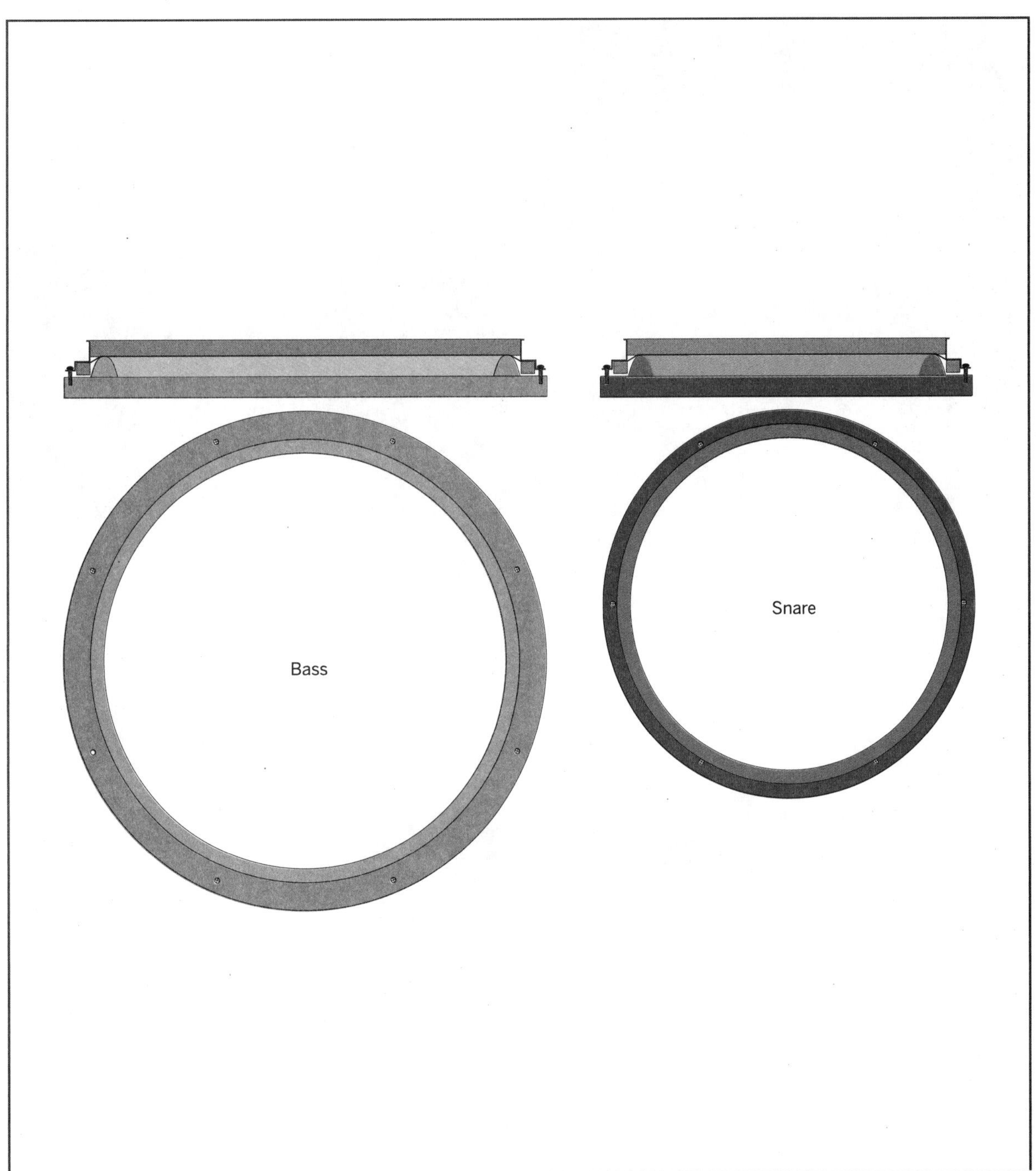

Figure 10.106: **Frame drums are simple. Bearing edges are still a pain in the ass.**

Figure 10.107: **Gluing the rings to the frames. Many, many clamps, please.**

screws straight into the plywood. Had I the budget, I would have gone for proper T-nuts and 10-32 bolts, but this mechanism isn't going to be delivering the constant raw physical assault of a live drummer to stress the tuning, so we're relatively safe. **[Figure 10.107, Figure 10.108]**

Attach a mounting block to the underside of each frame as shown. Dimensions are going to be specific to the placement of the instruments on your project. Glue and dowel into posi-

Figure 10.108: **Great googly moogly! They almost look like drums!**

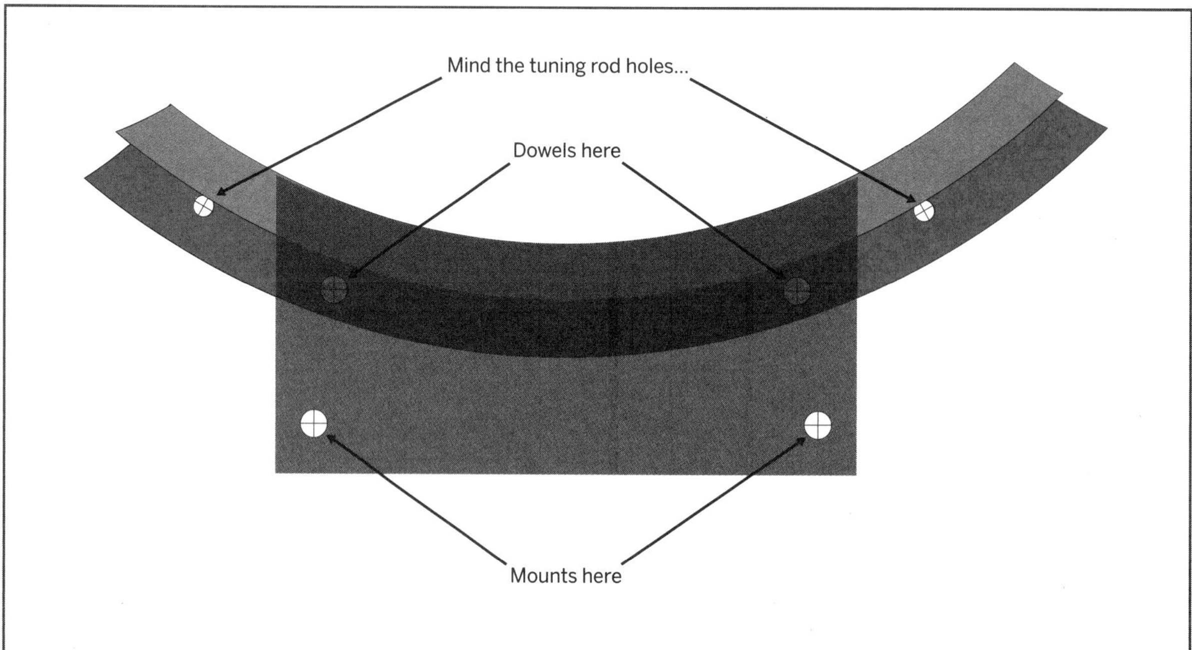

Figure 10.109: **What the hell: plywood drum mounts? Why not?**

Figure 10.110: **Your mount geometry may vary.**

Figure 10.111: **Mine certainly did.**

tion, and drill a pair of mountng holes to accomodate #8 x 1¼" wood screws. **[Figure 10.109,Figure 10.110, Figure 10.111]**

Snares

We need snares. Snares are responsible for the snare drum goin' "crack," rather than "buum." They're multiple strands of (typically) wire stretched across the bottom head of the drum, a feature our instrument is notably lacking. Oh well — c'est la vie.

We'll make ours from wood, rather than from precisely stretched springs, aircraft control cable, or feline entrails. Get out your whittling knife (I'm serious) and shave a handful of thin strips from the edge of a piece of ¼" hardwood. You need strips about 10" long and a uniform 1⁄32" thick. Whittle off longer ones and trim off the thicker and narrower ends. Sort out eight or ten of the most consistent, and glue them evenly spaced across the top of a small block of plywood. **[Figure 10.112]**

Mounting the snare assembly to enable adjustment of the "tension" is kinda finicky. **Figure 10.113** shows the principle involved. A piece of half-round dowel glued onto a short (1½") wooden extension attached to the snare assembly floats on two pins set into the frame of the drum, with a tightenable bolt running through the frame to do the tensioning. Position and install the snare assembly about 1⁄16" below the tightened drum head, then tighten the bolt to bring the slats into contact with the head. Experimentation will teach you the Zen of snare tensioning to get a satisfyingly annoying *qrackkk* out of the instrument. **[Figure 10.114, Figure 10.115]**

Open, unmuffled drums can ring for what seems like hours, and often have irritating overtones scattered around the frequency spectrum. There have been an improbably large number of products brought to market intended to help control these overtones, joining innumerable homebrew methods developed over the years. I think I've been suckered into trying out every single one of them, from duct tape to moongel, tampons to elaborate clip-on-yer-rim Goldbergian contraptions involving felt pads, leaf springs, and oddly shaped bits of cast aluminum. With this level of experience, I can state with absolute certainty that far and away the most effective method is the one which doesn't involve parting with a red cent, doesn't leave sticky crap all over your drumhead, and doesn't require pilfering things from the bathroom cabinet.

Just cut 1" wide rings from an old drum head. The outer diameter is the the diameter of the drum you're muffling, the inner diameter is 2" less than that. Lay it on the top of the head (no adhesive needed) and you're done. Works like magic, removes in a flash, costs (basically) nothing.

These drums *need* rings like this.

Didja notice? The drums are done. Cool.

Total cost? $11.30, plus $1.50 in machine screws.

Cash remaining? $6.70.

Case closed.

Figure 10.112: **I used a piece of cut-off left over from cutting the bearing rings, which gave me the right curve to nest smoothly with the inside face of the snare frame bearing ring. An exceptionally casual wooden snare improvisation, but close enough for Rock + Roll.**

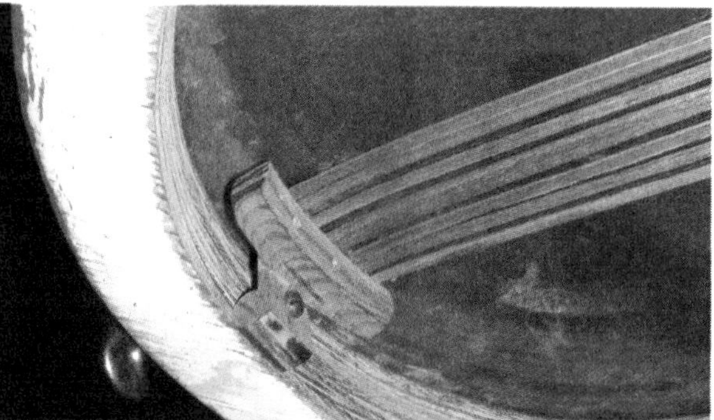

Figure 10.114: **Honestly, I was shocked when this method worked. Thank you, Great Cosmic Random!**

Figure 10.115: **It's a finished snare drum. The bass drum was in the tour bus with three groupies and missed the photoshoot. No matter. Snare drum? Check. Bass Drum? Check.**

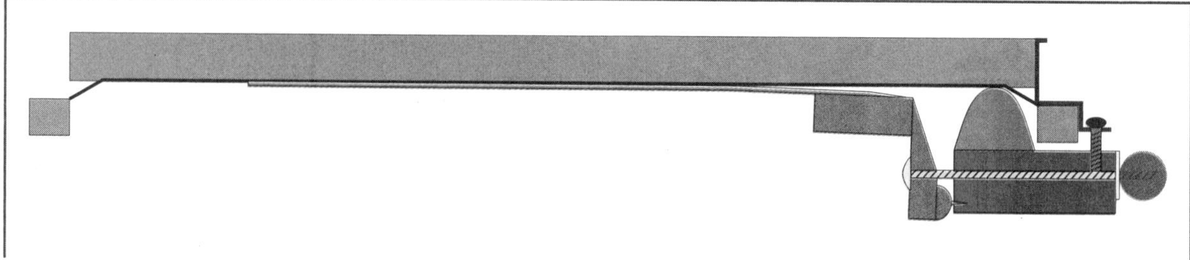

Figure 10.113: **The precariously balanced yet nonetheless effective snare tensioning system**

Cymbals

We're gonna cheat on cymbals, and carve up broken ones to meet our nefarious ends.

Cymbals break far more often than they need too, for a variety of reasons: poor technique on the part of the player, over-enthusiasm during performance, poor selection of cymbal for the genre of music being played. There are a few different ways to attempt to salvage damaged bronzework, but frankly, none of 'em are really effective at restoring a cymbal to its original glory. You can, however, get some useful special effects cymbals out of a little effort.

There are two common types of cymbal breakage: radial cracks inwards from the edge and concentric splits along lathe lines. Pictured are what I harvested from a 14" paper-thin crash with a nasty radial, and 2 little bells from ride cymbals of various weight which had been enthusisatically crashed a trifle too often. All three cymbals came from Northstar Recycling for the princely sum of $5. **[Figure 10.116]**

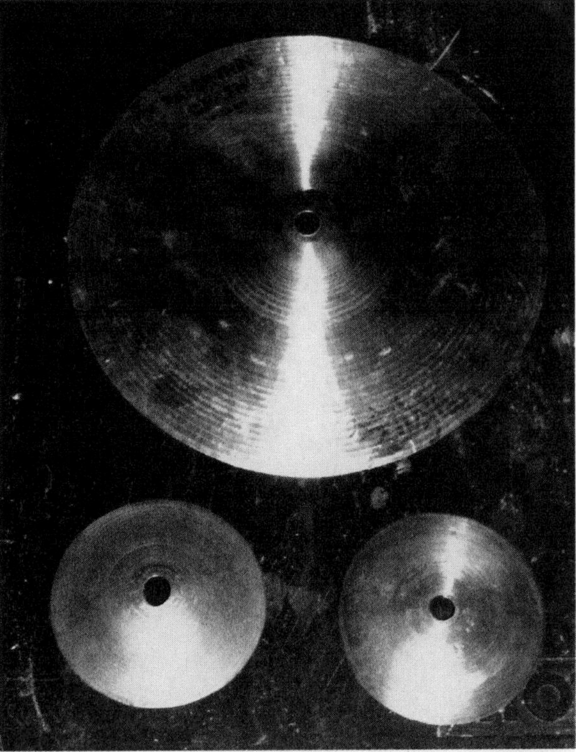

Figure 10.116: **Scrapyard cymbals: Two bells and a splash.**

Harvesting the bells was simple. They were mostly already cracked out, so three minutes with a hacksaw and all that was left was smoothing out the edges on the belt sander. They ended up at about 3½" in diameter. One of the disks was substantialy thicker than the other. As is the case with hi-hats, the thick one goes on the bottom. Despite the high pitched bell-like tone of the individual disks, when placed together, hi-hat-like, they give a nice, crisply metallic "chik" when hit.

Honestly, I was gobsmacked by the tone. I've paid stupid amounts of money for "real" full sized 14" hi-hats that didn't sound as good as these little suckers.

Go figure.

Mounting them in the proper position is done with ⅜" ID brass tubing and ⅜" poplar dowel. Start with a 6" piece of tubing (you can size it to the proper length later) and an 8" piece of dowel. Nest the two together, and secure the dowel from twisting by drilling a hole through the tubing and banging in a short brad. Drop the cymbals over the top of the dowel and cut off the excess dowel flush with the cymbal.[15] Drill down vertically through the exposed top of the dowel, and insert a short length of threaded rod (I used a 1½" length of 8-32 brass) and secure it with two-part epoxy. For a variety of reasons I threaded a ¾" wooden craft ball to act as the retainer nut, and I was done. Lookie, Ma: a teeny weeny hi-hat. **[Figure 10.117, Figure 10.118, Figure 10.119]**

15 When mounting "real' cymbals, felt washers top and bottom are standard to reduce metal on metal contact and eliminate spurious little rattling sounds. To enhance the overall 8-bit grunginess of our instruments we're gonna eschew this convention and embrace the random rattles as "mechanical glitch artifacts."

Forming the ride cymbal out of the paper-thin crash was almost as easy. Due to the insanely thin material, the cymbal is made of, tin snips cut away the cracked section along a lathe line almost like it was, er, paper.

Thicker cymbals are more problematic that way.

Once the snippin' was done, I had a quite reasonable 11" cymbal with a nice 8-bit sound to it. Smoothing out the edges took about 20 minutes, due to the care involved in keeping the metal from overheating. Cymbals are heat-tempered, and excessive heat of friction can bollix the temper and kack up the tonal quality. Slow progress and frequent dips into a bowl of water are the key to machine finishing musical metal. **[Figure 10.120]**

Mounting was just a matter of packing a foot-long length of ⅜" brass tubing with sand (to prevent buckling; I sealed the ends with Plasticine) and bending a graceful 90-degree curve into it. By eye. Via brute force. The mount was made during final assembly of Hammerhead in order to get the size and positioning right. The long end of the tubing mounts into a

Figure 10.117: **The exploded miniature hi hat.**

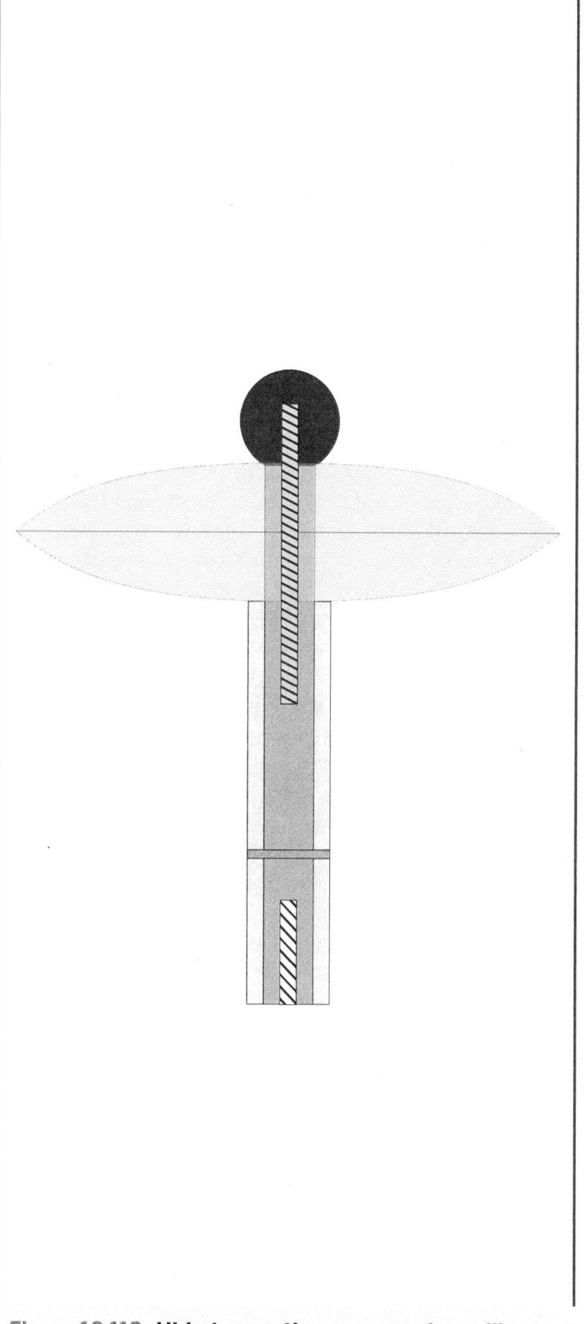

Figure 10.118: **Hi-hat mounting: once again, we'll worry about the height during final assembly. Cut it long, trim it to fit.**

Figure 10.119: **The finished hi-hat. Stubby little bugger, innit?**

Figure 10.120: **Yes, it's a Zildjian.**

hole driled into the edge of the deck, secured with a bolt. The top end gets a short piece of dowel press-fitted and pinned into place, drilled to accept another bit of 8-32 threaded rod. As it happens, the piece of tube I bent up for the mount ended up being fractionally too low when mounted, allowing the cymbal to bang agains the frame of the kick drum. I lengthened the threaded rod by about an inch and bodged on a couple of craft balls to make up the difference and the problem was solved.[16] **[Figure 10.121,Figure 10.122]**

Total cost? $5.00, plus $1.13 for 25 ¾" wooden craft balls.

Cash remaining? $0.57.

Case closed . . . and under budget.

Here's how they all came together. **[Figure 10.123]**

Criminy. Somebody call that Goldberg guy.

Ya know, I like these drums almost as much as I like my other tubs. **[Figure 10.124]**

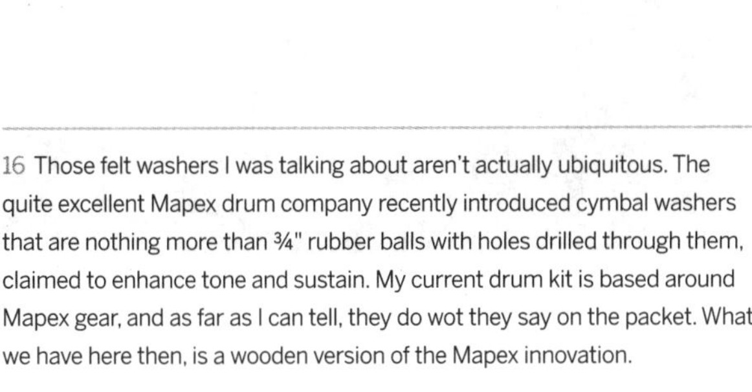

16 Those felt washers I was talking about aren't actually ubiquitous. The quite excellent Mapex drum company recently introduced cymbal washers that are nothing more than ¾" rubber balls with holes drilled through them, claimed to enhance tone and sustain. My current drum kit is based around Mapex gear, and as far as I can tell, they do wot they say on the packet. What we have here then, is a wooden version of the Mapex innovation.

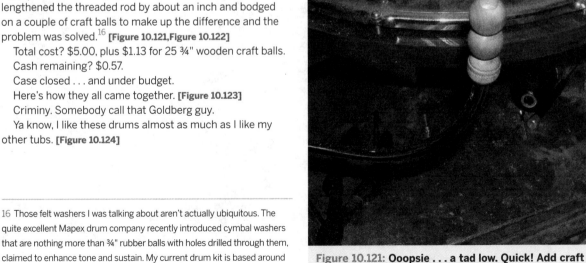

Figure 10.121: **Ooopsie . . . a tad low. Quick! Add craft balls!**

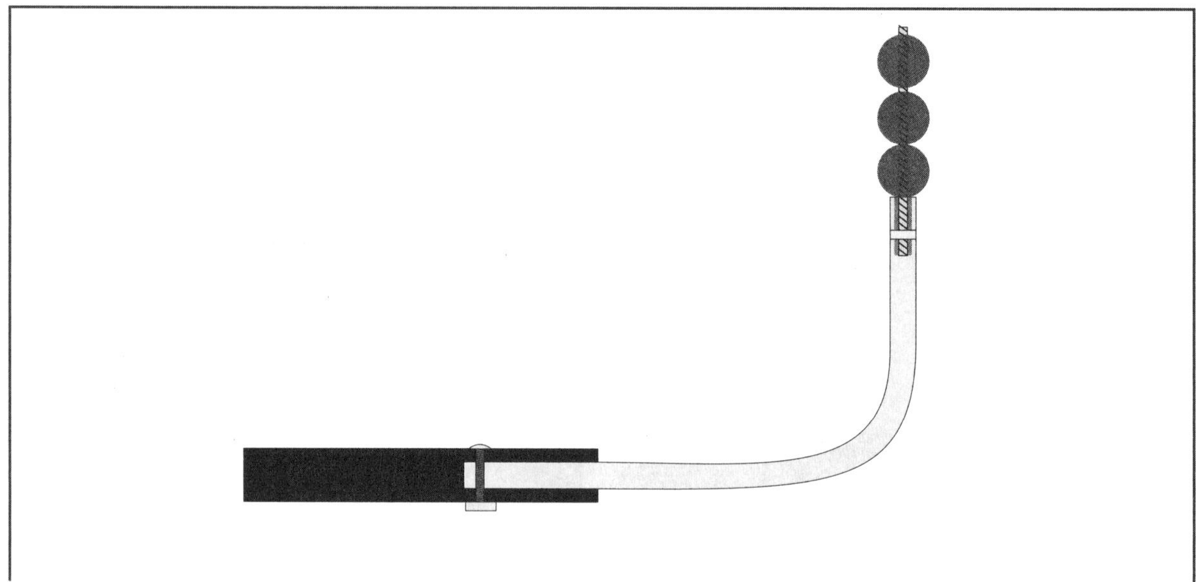

Figure 10.122: **The cymbal mount**

Figure 10.123: **Seen in action. Hi-hat: Check. Ride cymbal: Check.**

Figure 10.124: **My other tubs**

‹ Nano-Project › Scrapers!

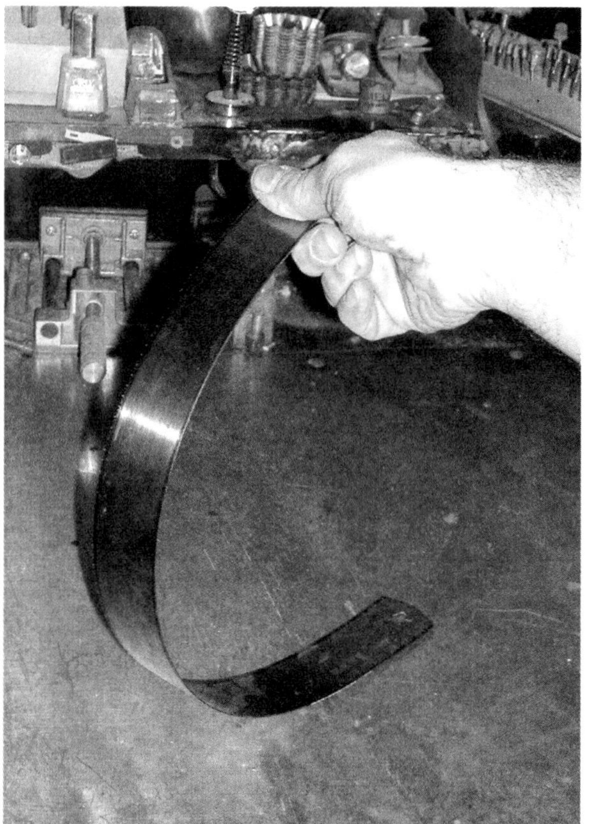

Figure N10.01: **Shown on the right is a cast-off blade from my miter saw. It's 16" x 2", and, as illustrated, really flexible.**

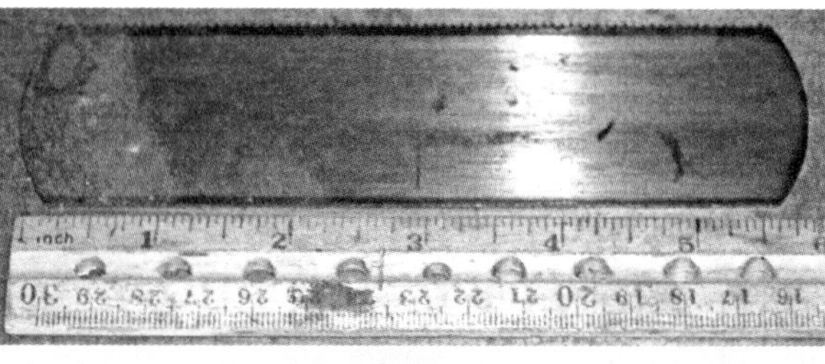

Figure N10.02: **A 6" section of this blade is materially and ergonomically ideal for making a surface scraper.**

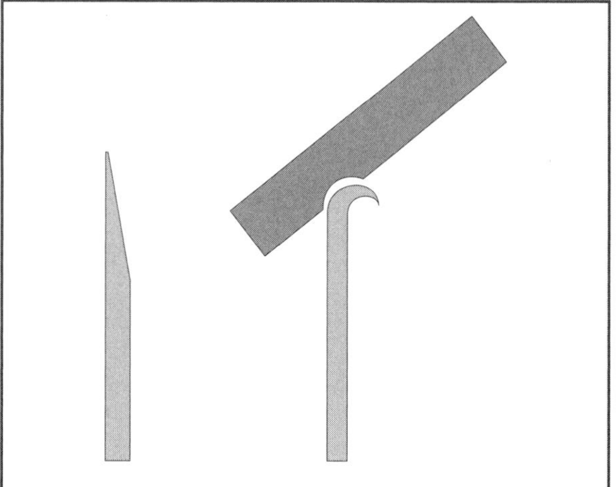

Figure N10.03: **Rolling the hook**

Surface-finishing wood is one of those jobs that can easily eat your brain. The selection of material removal tools available is imposing, and picking the right combination to get good results is a critical matter. Scrapers are cognizant Makers' secret weapons in the battle for smooth wood.

Why they're not standard-issue equipment escapes me. The Fox Mulder in me suspects collusion between an army of mutant mind controllers and the Sandpaper Industry. Trust no one . . .

Anyway, after you've finished making your tinfoil hats, we're gonna recycle a piece of saw blade into a scraper.

The "active ingredient" of a scraper is its rolled-over hooked cutting edge. Once you get comfortable forming the hook, you'll never look back. I learned the process about 20 years ago from a community access cable TV show. It took me about 10 minutes practice to suss out *exactly* the right angle and pressure needed to form the hook. Your learning curve may vary, but here's the basic process. **[Figure N10,01]**

Once you have the metal blank in your sweaty little paws, grind an edge on one long axis. About 30 degrees of angle is a good start. Camber your edge from one side only, as illustrated, using whatever tool you're comfortable with: I used

Figure N10.04: Roll the edge with a piece of tool steel with a shallow groove ground in it.

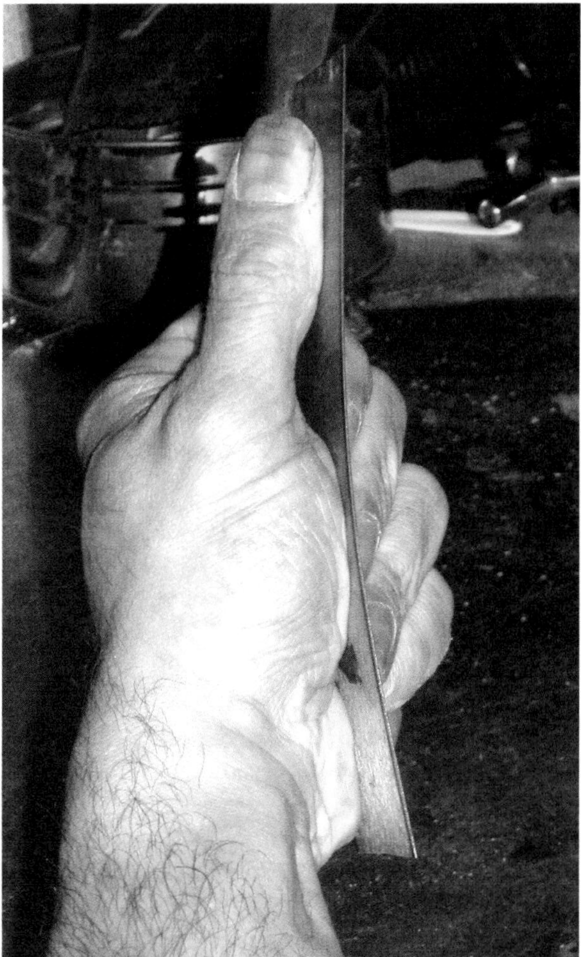

Figure N10.05: If you've done it right, you can feel it with your thumb.

my disk sander, but clamping it in a vise and using a medium-coarse file will accomplish the same thing. Once you've shaped that edge, clean it up and refine it with a whetstone until you can shave a curl off the surface of a fingernail easily. Now comes the fun bit.

Clamp your sharpened blank into a vise, using scrap wood to extend the vise jaws if needed; you want the entire length of the blank firmly supported, with about ¾" exposed at the top. Now grab a handy piece of tool steel (I used a trashed ⅜" drill bit) and grind a shallow semicircular groove in it with a round-profile needle file or some manner of dremelization. You're now ready to roll the hook onto your scraper blank with a *firm* smooth motion, as shown. If you've done it right, you'll be able to feel it with your thumb. That same thumb will also detect any rough spots in your cutting edge. Smooth them out with a few strokes of your whetstone, and you're ready to scrape. **[Figure N10.04, Figure N10.05]**

The key to successful scraping lies in properly harnessing the flex of the blade; it's doable one- or two-handed, as illustrated. There are a surprising number of variables at play here: finger position dictates the shape of the curve, with the thumb(s) providing the tension to the cutting edge. The angle of the blade relative to the surface being scraped controls the *dig* of the hook, and depending on how you rolled your hook, it might take you a few passes to get a comfortable idea of the right stroke.

When you do get the right stroke, you'll create long, regular shavings with little or no effort, and you'll be able to quickly smooth tool marks out of hardwood with comparative ease. This is one of those tools that you need to spend some time with to develop your chops, but once mastered, that will also become your go-to gizmo for surface prep. Keep 'em sharp, and keep 'em handy. **[Figure N10.06, Figure N10.07]**

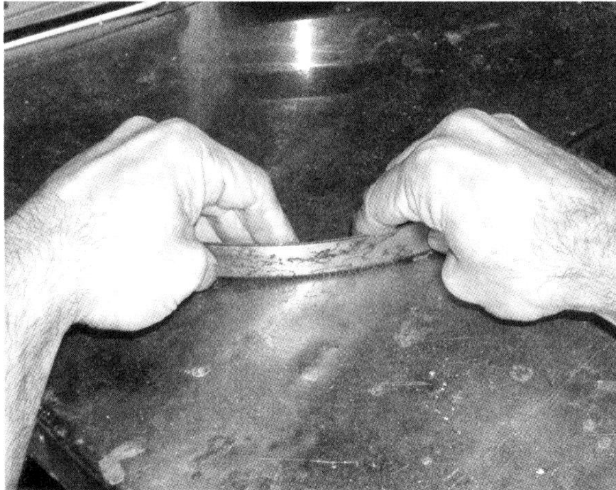

Figure N10.06: **Use two hands or one, but practice a bit to get it right.**

Figure N10.07: **When you're doing it right, you'll make long, regular shavings while getting it smooth.**

11 Homebrew Wood Finishes

Weird Science for Woodworkers[1]

I'm gonna be completely up front with you: this line of study has the potential to be olfactorally challenging. My workshop is in my kitchen, so I have access to the stovetop and range ventilation hood, which keeps the odours (generally) under control. Most of you will likely not be fortunate enough to have a similar arrangement and will be forced outdoors, or at the very least, consigned to the garage with a hotplate. Wherever you find yourself, do ensure that there's Adequate Ventilation™. Your nose, lungs, and other internal organs will thank you later.

Wood finishing is part science, part voodoo, and part compromise. Once you've properly prepared the surface, you've gotta use something to seal the pores, protect the surface, and reduce humidity uptake, but your choice of potential finishes is mind-pummellingly diverse in both aesthetic appeal and degree of difficulty.

Despite the proliferation of Kwiq-N-Ezee wood finish products available at the retail level, I've been cooking up my own finishes for years. It's assembler-language-level woodworking geekiness that appeals to my inner eighteenth-century gentleman inventor. I'm a wax and oil guy. It's the easiest way to get started in brew-yer-own finishes, and there's enough room to explore just within that genre to hold your interest for years. Is this a full and comprehensive tutorial? Hell no. A full and comprehensive tutorial on DIY wood finish chemistry would be about 900 pages. Just covering wax and oil to any degree of depth would be a major tome. This is a thumbnail how-to with enough primary data to get your personal research into the subject pointed in the right direction and hopefully instill in you enough of an interest in the subject that you'll teach yourself more about it.

As with most subjects, think while reading. For best results, a (relatively) dust-free environment is recommended.

1 Kelly LeBrock not included. Oingo Boingo soundtrack sold separately.

Here's your shopping list:

- Beeswax
- Carnauba wax
- Paraffin wax
- "Boiled" linseed oil. (Not actually boiled. In reality, this is yer basic flaxseed oil that's been dosed with metallic driers to reduce the cure time from about two weeks to overnight.)
- Pure tung oil. (Avoid like the plague the deceptive labels announcing a "pure tung oil–based finishing product" or the like. Read the fine-print ingredients if you have to.)

CAUTION: Yet another caution: tung oil is derived from nuts. If you're unfortunate enough to suffer from any form of nut allergy, avoid this substance.

- Turpentine
- Naphtha
- A variety of earth and mineral pigments. (Mine came from Lee Valley Tools, as fine a purveyor of woodworking porn as you will ever encounter. I get all sweaty just thinking about the place.)

- Mason jars in a variety of sizes. (The kind your aunt Tillie used to preserve her homemade cantaloupe/mutton marmalade. You know, glass top and bottom, rubber gasket, screw-on metal rim to hold the whole thing together.)

Sourcing some of this lot in the wilds of middle America would likely have been pretty challenging a few years ago. Luckily, the current global online marketplace makes stocking up for this kind of adventure a matter of a few mouse-clicks and a few days' wait.

And of course, you're gonna need some other stuff:

- Access to the stove. (Or a hotplate, or an electric frying pan.)
- A glass stir rod. (Yeah, it really needs to be glass, although I suppose you could use a piece of stainless-steel rod in a pinch. Avoiding contamination of the stuff you're mixing is a fairly big deal. Glass is good, because it's chemically inert to the ingredients, and looks really cool.)
- A graduated cylinder or big-ass measuring cup. At least 4 cups (or 1 liter, as I am patriotically bound to say).
- Measuring spoons
- A 3-quart saucepan
- Lots of fully surface-prepped wood stock. (Of every species of wood you can lay your mitts on; a mixture that looks ghastly on maple could quite possibly make walnut glow like the cupola of the Taj Mahal.)
- Lint-free rags (lots and lots of lint-free rags). Sacrificing your childhood collection of 'eavy metal band T-shirts would be an ideal solution, and clear out valuable closet space for your current collection of iPod-friendly attire.
- A method of indelibly labeling your jars. (The key word here is *indelible*; the stuff you're putting in the bottles is hard on adhesives and inks, due to it bein' composed of about 50 percent ink and adhesive remover. Spills can make labeling problematic. Sometimes, chemistry is inconvenient.)

The basic principles we're working with? Oil penetrates, wax seals, solvent facilitates blending and penetration. Pigments pigment.

For measurement purposes, we're gonna do everything by volume. None of the measurements are mission-critical, although it's a good idea to remain at least partially aware of the *ratios* involved. My walnut wax recipe happened accidentally, and it took me about three days of unpleasantly cautious measuring and cooking to reverse-engineer the quantities. If I'd been paying attention in the first place . . .

Seems simple enough, dunnit?

Half-fill the sauce pan with water, and set it a simmerin' just short of boiling. You're dealing with extremely flammable ingredients, and doing the double-boiler thing will let you melt and mix stuff without exposing them to hazardous amounts of heat. As it is you're going to be encouraging volatile petrochemical products to vapourise, which is dangerous enough. While the water's heating, let's look at the material specs.

The three waxes you bought each have their own distinctive strengths and weaknesses. Your job is to negotiate a compromise blend of these that does what you want.

Wax	Strengths	Weaknesses
Carnauba	Hard, shiny, smooth	So hard that it's almost crisp; brutal to buff a shine into
Beeswax	Soft, polishes easily, smells nice	Soft, sticky, low melting point
Paraffin	Slippery, shiny	Really, really soft; flaky, oily

There are other waxes, natural and synthetic, commonplace and otherwise, all of which bring their own personalities to the table. Research them, try 'em out, work 'em into your equations.

The oils present a simpler situation. Linseed oil has a richer colour, texture, and scent to it, and (even with the added drying agents) can take its sweet time setting up. Tung oil is lighter all-around, cures harder and more quickly, and generally has less personality. I like linseed oil a lot; I see a lot more depth of grain compared to tung oil, but it comes at the expense of noticeable darkening of the wood. It's one of the factors that you have to be aware of when you're building a finish based on pigmented oil.

Tung oil is lighter in general, and is gonna show your pigments much more cleanly. Once again, there *is* a vast selection of natural and synthetic oils available, again I encourage you to research and field test.

Oil	Strengths	Weaknesses
Linseed oil	Darkens wood naturally	Darkens wood naturally
Tung oil	Less coloured, hard, sets up overnight	Bland, shallow

A solvent has only two salient characteristics: how fast it disappears, and how much it stinks. The range at hand is

"Takes its time and puts the hurt on your nose" to "Almost immediately, and like the Pope's farts." I actually don't mind having to wait a few days for a finish to set up; the impatient amongst you will no doubt disagree. It's your call.

Pigments only seem scary. They're nothing more than oddly coloured dirt and rust, when you look at them closely; the trick is to get them where you want them and make them stay there. They're similar to dyes, but are delivered as a suspension rather than a solution; these are relatively large particles floating around in a carrier liquid, waiting to settle into the pores of the wood you're finishing.

What liquid? A 50-50 blend of oil and solvent is a good start, with the primary challenge during formulation being that of thorough mixing of the pigment into the carrier. Heat the oil in the graduated cylinder (in the double boiler), add an equal amount of solvent, then mix in the pigments, topping up the fluid level with more solvent if you lose too much to evaporation. You can test the colour while the mix is still warm; when you're satisfied, transfer to a clean, dry Mason jar and seal it up. Label the jar appropriately with the ingredients and ratios clearly indicated.

With a good basic palette of pigments at hand (there are about a dozen fairly standard oxides that cover 99 percent of the traditional colours of wood finishes), you'll amaze yourself at the range of colours you can blend together. The thing to remember is that you're laying down a thin, even layer of particles on the surface of the wood. There's not a whole lot of cellular penetration going on, and it's not always easy to maintain a consistent particle density. Be generous with your pigment concentration, and keep it well mixed during application. I've found some disconcerting inconsistencies between pigments from various sources, so I'm hesitant to give specific quantities for specific effects. You're on your own on this one, but following the manufacturers' guidelines is a good (but occasionally unreliable) starting point.

Remember all those pieces of test wood? That's what they're there for, Sparky . . . mix and test, mix and test, mix and test.

Want bright, bold colours? Aniline wood dyes come in a full spectrum of colours, are commonly available at specialty retail outlets, and can transform light-coloured wood into gut-wrenching hues not usually seen in nature. Interesting, not particularly subtle, and not the subject of this discussion. So sue me.

The ingredients on the list will let you colour-match most traditional-looking stains, pigmented oil finishes, waxes, and hybrid oil/wax things like that walnut wax stuff. And of course, you're gonna be improvising like crazy along the way as well. It's the Maker way, innit?

Here's a simple oil/wax hybrid that I use on highly figured woods that gives a nice sense of depth to the grain and buffs up to a warm medium gloss glow. It can be pigmented if you like, but the low oil-to-wax ratio means a higher tendency for the colourant to buff off during polishing.

Pour ¼ cup of boiled linseed oil into your graduated cylinder and put it in the simmering pan of water to heat. Add carnauba wax pieces slowly, stirring as it melts, to get 1 cup of solution. Add about a tablespoon of beeswax, stirring constantly until it's melted. Pour in 3/4 cup of your solvent of choice and continue stirring under heat until the mixture is smooth and homogenous. Pour into a clean, dry Mason jar and seal it tightly. The mixture will solidify as it cools into a firm, slightly creamy paste. To use, just rub a light coat into the wood (with the grain, please), let it set overnight, then buff out with a soft cloth. If you want a higher gloss finish, you can apply a light coat of a suitable wax-only blend after about 48 hours of setup time.

Higher gloss wax blend? This ratio would work on hardwood, but I'd eliminate the beeswax and up the paraffin content on softwood.

Solvent	Carnauba	Beeswax	Paraffin
50%	40%	5%	5%

Walnut Wax?

Solvent	Carnauba	Beeswax	Boiled linseed oil
50%	20%	25%	5%

This stuff is a beautiful finish for walnut. It's tough, with a deep lustrous sheen, and goes on like butter. Use two coats, the first rubbed in by hand until the wood stops drinking the finish, the second an even, light application with a rag, with a 24-hour set time between coats, and a 24-hour set time before buffing.

So go blend a finish, wouldja?

INDEX

H

I

J

K

L

M

N

W

Y

Z